BOTTOM LINE YEAR BOOK

1997

BY THE EDITORS OF

Bottom Line
PERSONAL

Boardroom® Classics publishes the advice of expert authorities in
many fields. The use of a book is not a substitute for legal,
accounting or other professional services. Consult a competent
professional for answers to your specific questions.

Library of Congress Cataloging in Publication Data
Main entry under title:

Bottom Line Yearbook 1997

   1. Life skills—United States.   I. Bottom line personal.
ISBN 0-88723-140-3

Boardroom® Classics is a registered trademark of
Boardroom®, Inc.
55 Railroad Avenue, Greenwich, CT 06830

Printed in the United States of America

Contents

1 • YOUR HEALTH—YOUR WELL-BEING

Roy L. Walford expects to live to 120..1
Illness can be good for you...2
How to make the most of your annual checkup 2
How to protect yourself from your doctor...............................4
Throw away all expired medicines 6
300,000+ over-the-counter drugs…
    Which ones really work? Which ones don't?.......................6
Dangerous drug interactions 8
How to win the chronic-pain wars..10
Win the hospital game, too 11
How to get the best nursing care when
    you're hospitalized...12
How to find the best hospital in the US 13
When not to schedule your doctor appointment 15
Even the best medical labs make mistakes..........................15
How not to overpay for medical care 15
Unqualified care-givers abound 16
Short women, tall women and heart disease 17
Heart disease in women 17
Coronary artery disease kills 250,000
    American women a year...17
Cholesterol-lowering drug and psyllium 17
What you may not know about high blood pressure.............17
What you need to know about high blood pressure..............19
Mostly on a Monday 21
A better way to shrink an enlarged prostate 21
Test for prostate cancer 22
Prostate disease news..22
Melanoma is 5% to 10% deadlier in men than in women 22
How not to get Alzheimer's..22
Alzheimer's disease update 24

Bee sting first aid 24
Five-minute energy boosters 24
Prostate cancer is usually curable 24
How to cut your risk of cancer by 50%...................................24
Treating hypertension..26
Calcium channel blockers and hypertension.........................26
Cholesterol tests vary..27
Don't let bowel trouble ruin your life 27
Rodent danger...28
Avoid covering coughs with your bare hands 28
Treatments for common winter ailments 28
Do you need a pneumonia vaccine? 28
Whooping cough in adults...29
Antacid tablets work better than liquids 29
Snoring…stopping the din just might save your life 29
Dishcloths and sponges are bacteria-ridden..........................31
Bacteria thrive in the cleanest kitchens................................31
Secrets of a better night's sleep 31
Ways to improve your mood...31
All about tinnitus..31
Brush longer 33
Preventing tooth loss 33
All about taking much better care of your
    largest organ…skin..33
Aspartame danger...35
Make your skin look young again without surgery 35
Worst wrinkle generators 37
Flu or food poisoning?..37
Better shaving 37
Beware of pop-up thermometers...37
Jet-engine noise 37
Shoveling snow stresses your heart 38

Easier breathing 38
Tension triggers 38
Fear of heights 38
Bra strap danger 38
What is "drinker's nose"? 38
How women with several roles balance stress 39
Better ice packs 39
The scary truth about blood transfusions…
   and how to protect yourself 39
CPR is a good lesson 41
Secondhand smoke danger 41
Common drugs make driving risky 41
Virtual reality danger 41
Stroke danger 41
Homemade heating pad 42
Ease immunization pain 42
Beauty parlor stroke syndrome 42
Snoring can be dangerous 42
To kick a caffeine habit 42

2 • THE SAVVY TRAVELER

What you should know before taking a cruise 43
What embassies can do for you if you're in a jam 44
Bed-and-breakfasts…what you should know first 45
Read the fine print 45
How to win the frequent-flier game 45
Round-trip to Europe: $100 46
How to get hard-to-get tickets 46
Cheaper travel with split ticketing 47
If your flight is cancelled 47
Empty seat strategy 47
Flying fears grounded 47
Best hotel rates 47
Better hotel stays 48
Tour booking self-defense 48
Mature traveler self-defense 48
Your rights if your flight is overbooked 48
Where to find the best buys in Paris 49
Research and travel 49
Tourists beware 50
Travel comfort 50
Shrewder travel 50

3 • YOUR FAMILY—YOUR HOME

Discipline and much better parenting 51
Parenting made easier…answers to the
   toughest parenting questions 52
Why baby looks like daddy 54
Baby talk 54
Calling your child's doctor 54
When the baby won't eat 55
Questions to ask a baby-sitter 55
Nightmares are not just bad dreams 55
Children and death 55
Imaginary friends are useful for children 55
Teach your child values 55
Encourage your children to express opinions 56
Help kids read better 56
Strategies for getting along better with your teenagers 56
How to know if a puppy will become a happy dog 57
Mature teens 57
How to put on a yard sale that sells 57
Before you paint 58
How tightwad Amy Dacyczyn fixed her own house 58

Home-inspection traps to avoid 59
Tricks and traps in doing business with contractors 60
Home renovation payoffs 61
How to handle annoying neighbors 61
Smart planting 62
Shrubs that attract the prettiest birds 62
Bumper sticker removal 62
Cutting computer cord clutter 62

4 • MONEY SAVVY

Disaster-proof your money 63
How to live fee-free 64
What every woman should know about money 65
Simple way to save $600 a year 67
Where to find cash fast 67
How not to be robbed by your bank 67
Get higher returns on your savings…safely 68
ATM fees on the rise 68
Balancing your checkbook 69
Checking account smarts 69
Big, bad credit card traps 69
All about credit union loans 69
Your home can cost you much less than it does now 69
How to cash in on your home without moving 71
Shop for a mortgage before you shop for a house 73
For a faster sale 73
Save by paying the mortgage faster 74
Adjustable rate mortgage mistakes 74
Home equity loan and credit card trap 74
Choosing the right financial adviser 74
First-time home buyer programs 74
Safety plus liquidity 75
Credit-card errors…how to dispute them and win 75
Common money-management mistakes 76
Barter moves upscale 76
Use less water in the bathroom 76
The shrewd, simple secrets of saving…
   saving…saving 77
How to calculate your net worth 78
If Carol Keeffe could get out of debt…anyone can 78
Emergency funds 79
Beware of reverse mortgages 80
Better money saving 80
Long distance calling plans 80
The Goldbecks' secrets for turning garbage into gold 80
How a reformed spendthrift keeps her spending
   under control…now 81
Safe-deposit box secrets 83
Checking account fraud self-defense 83
Escrow account refunds 83
How not to overspend 84
"Rainy-day" money is a necessity 84
Cheaper checking account opportunities 85
Biggest financial mistakes people make 86
What to do with a financial windfall 86
Fee-based and fee-only planners 86
Key questions to ask before buying a home 86

5 • INSURANCE SAVVY

How to buy the right protection for you 89
How to get your HMO to cover alternative
   medical treatment 91
The big bad bothersome HMO traps…
   how to fight back and win 92

Car insurance trap 93
Hidden cash in health insurance 94
Health insurers' tricks 94
Safer health insurance 94
You may not be as insured as you should be 94
Don't buy too much health insurance 95
Cut auto insurance costs 95
Health insurance and travel 95
How to buy an umbrella insurance policy 95
Life insurance: how much to buy?
    Which kind? What company? 96
Renters insurance is a must 97
Getting your HMO to pay up 97
Car insurance dilemna 97
Lower car insurance premiums 97
First-to-die insurance 98
Buy life insurance now 98
Evaluating life insurance plans 98

6 • TAX SMARTS

Most common mistakes people make
    when doing their tax returns 99
Last-minute tax-saving strategies 101
Tax-free income loopholes 101
Two deductible nondeductible expenses 103
One of today's best tax-saving strategies…
    grantor retained annuity trust 103
How to boost your personal cash flow with tax savings 105
Loopholes in pension plan distributions and IRAs 107
Retirement tax-planning loopholes 108
How to convert taxable income into tax-free income
    for your retirement years 110
Retirement and state tax traps 111
Uncle Sam will pay you to job hunt 111
Strategies for writing off family debt 112
Residence trusts 112
Protecting financial privacy 113
How the IRS finds your assets after you die 113
New traps in dealing with the IRS 113
$63,000 IRS mistake 114
Summer camp has tax benefits 114
Bad debt deducted 114
When music lessons are deductible 114
Disclaimer beats taxes 114
When the IRS becomes aggressive 115
When do you need someone to represent you
    before the IRS? 115
Tax filing must be done through the post office 115
Schedule C tax alert 115
Tax audit alert 116
IRS seizure tactic 117
Tip-off that something is wrong with your tax return 117
Stock gains can trigger higher taxes 117
Think before you sell 117
When to wait before calling the IRS 117
Proving that you are not a responsible person 118
Asking the IRS to remove a late filing penalty 118
Unpaid liability problem 118
When you don't report all your income 118
Installment sale payment taxation rules 119
Easily overlooked deductions 119
Early distributions 120
Sure IRS audit red flag 120
Tax-preparer loopholes 120
Independent contractors 121
New rights for taxpayers 122

IRS loses too… 122
Valuable tax-saving compensation ideas for 1997 123
A very helpful tax quiz 126
How to establish legal residency 126

7 • SMART BUSINESS MOVES

The limited liability company 127
When failure breeds success 129
Growth leaders 130
Home businesses that you can start for under $1,000 ...130
How to ace any job interview 131
When to say "no" to a job offer 132
Who's a better boss—a man or a woman? 133
What good managers have 133
How to be an effective boss in the new workplace 133
How to make it in the singles market 134
Nerd power 135
Reading body language 135
What phone companies really charge for a call 136
How to cut costs without cutting the company's throat 136
How to cut the company's utility bills 137
How to sell when you're out of stock 138
There are ways to cut legal costs—they're not difficult ...138
Smarter pricing strategy 140
Smarter bill paying 140
How to set up better retirement plans for
    company executives 140
Travel costs will rise 141
Bonus to new owner is deductible 142
Telemarketer's obligation 142
Create your company's own world wide web site 142
Weekend entrepreneuring 144
Don't be fooled by people who always appear busy 145
Computers for sales forces…the time has come 145
Workplace violence is still growing—avoidance strategies ...146
Job-finding secrets…demand is there 148
Good news about 401(k) plans 150
Where the jobs are 150
Smarter job hunting 150
Career changing: planning strategies 150
Customer credit problems—early warning signs 151
Injury and the pregnant worker 152
New horizons 152

8 • THE WINNING EDGE

The new age of people skills and
    the service revolution 153
Better thinking 154
No more blues 154
Cure negative self-talk 154
Create your own learning plan 154
Eight ways to master stress and improve your health ...155
How to keep worry, fear and anxiety under control 157
Verbal abuse…self-defense 159
Learn to say no 160
A new form of intelligence more powerful than IQ 160
Time for a change? How to change 162
Six ways to winning friends and influencing people 163
How to make new friends 165
How to read faces…yes…faces 166
What your body is saying when you are silent 168
How to ask for what you want 168
Improve your mood 170
Mini-meditation 170

Stress is normal 170
How your emotions affect your health—
    proven ways to stay well 170
The smart way to handle negative emotions 172
Best way to control anger 173
Best ways of handling lies 173
Smarter marital argument resolution..............................174
Some people can make us sick 174
Think your way out of boredom and sleepiness 175
Etiquette mistakes that even polite people make 175

9 • INVESTMENT SAVVY

Economists look ahead, one year, five years, 10 years 177
How Anne Scheiber turned just $5,000 into $22,000,000 179
Sheldon Jacobs reveals his secrets of
    winning personal investing 181
Frugal investing made easy 182
The stock market can do great things for you
    on only $50 a month 183
Top stock-portfolio newsletters......................................185
Bear-proofing your portfolio 185
Beware of hidden risk 186
Costly investment mistake 186
Diversification is a good thing..186
Do not ride a stock down 186
Hot…hot…high tech 187
If the stock market makes you nervous…there are
    attractive alternatives for you 188
Is it time for smaller stocks? 189
Protective options versus stop-loss orders............................189
Mutual fund investing's seven deadly sins 190
How to put together the right mutual fund
    portfolio for you 191
Peter Lynch's powerful rules for mutual fund investors.........191
Answers your big questions about mutual funds 192
Mutual fund trap 193
No-load stocks can be bargains.......................................193
Best performance figures...193
What's in a name? 194
A family investment club 194

10 • RETIREMENT PLANNING

New definitions of retirement...195
How to make the most of IRAs..196
401(k) double check..197
Secrets of a secure retirement from Ted Benna—
    inventor of the 401(k) 198
Lump sum or monthly annuity distribution…
    which one is better? 199
Retirement investment strategy formula 200
Your IRA may be your biggest asset…
    here's how to make the most of it 200
Don't have too much money in your IRA 202
Review your 401(k)...203
Better investments for retirees 203
To retire comfortably by the age of 65….............................203
Preretirement Social Security double check.......................203
Smarter 401(k) investing...203
Examine your 401(k) plan 204
Planning ahead—you and your 401(k)...............................204
Retirement savings mistake 204
Best places to retire overseas 204
The common mistakes retirees make
    when they relocate...206

11 • ENJOYING YOUR LEISURE

Secrets of flea marketing 207
What casinos don't want you to know...............................208
Las Vegas winner 210
How to become a game show contestant…
    how to win…too 210
Shrewder lottery playing 212
How to bluff like a poker pro..213
Recording your family's life story 214
Funtastic children's museums in the US............................214
A wonderful zoo 215
You and your ancestors..215
Tip guidelines 217
How to get better restaurant service in any restaurant 217
How to relax on vacation 218
Main source of boredom 218
Better pumpkin carving 218
Finding hard-to-find videotapes 218
Smarter video renting 218

12 • ESTATE PLANNING

Biggest estate-planning mistakes and
    how to do everything right.................................219
How the rich keep their assets 221
Write a last love letter to file with your will 223
Ten most frequently asked questions about living trusts 223
Estate planning and second marriages..............................224
Will signing smarts 226
Estate planning strategy...226

13 • VERY, VERY PERSONAL

Answers to the most common questions about sex 227
How to have great sex every time.....................................228
Never criticize in bed..230
Fragrance that heightens male sexual response 230
Unnecessary surgery...230
Hysterectomy alternative 231
Missed pap smear tests 231
Kegel exercises beat incontinence in women......................231
Control premenstrual depression 231
Natural strategies for avoiding troublesome
    breast cysts 231
Infertility and women 232
All men can be dads..233
Unexplained infertility..233
Women and conception 233
Stress and low-birth weight babies 233
Half of the weight women gain during pregnancy
    is due to bodily changes 233
Women's role in impotence 234
Treat impotence promptly..234
Size of the average penis 234
Half of the people under 40 have cohabitated 234
Baldness remedy alert...234
Baldness cure coming?...235
Better personal ads 235
Sexual fantasies and gender 235
Burnout…how to prevent it 235

14 • NUTRITION, FITNESS AND EXERCISE

Why diets fail 237
Strategies for lifelong health 239

Foods that can change your mood 241
How food allergies affect behavior 241
Soybeans are very, very good for your health…
    how to make them a wonderful part of your diet 241
Thin women live longer 243
Reduce risk of stroke 243
Proven new nutritional plan for beating arthritis 244
Fasting can be very good for your health…
    how to do it right 245
People often mistake thirst for hunger 246
Underactive thyroid and obesity 247
Weight gain causes food problems 247
No more overeating during the holidays 247
Beauty queen tells how she took off 185 pounds…
    and kept them off 247
How to reduce food intake and lose weight
    without feeling deprived 249
How to resist the foods you love 250
All about olestra 251
Cholesterol, nutrition, weight and more 251
Ten secrets of successful weight loss 252
Ten more ways to lose 10 pounds 254
Dieter's diary 254
Watch what you eat 254
Low-fat cooking basics 255
What tomatoes can do for you 255
Healthier ways to cook hamburgers 255
Creamy dishes without cream 255
Nonfat pancakes 255
Less gas from gassy foods 256
Red meat/breast cancer connection 256
Drink your milk 256
Drinking milk puts out chili pepper fires 256
Milk: another view 256
Vitamin D is important 256
Vitamin C and your teeth 257
Don't discount beta-carotene 257
Sparkling waters may be sugary 257
Does caffeine really boost thinking ability? 257
Kids and fiber 257
Food's fiber content 258
Cereals listing whole grains first are best 258
Beware of trendy fish preparations 258
E. coli strikes vegetarians 258
Food and flatulence 258
Large fish danger 258
How to shrink a potbelly: seven strategies that work…
    two that don't 259
Physical fitness does keep us alive longer 260
Health clubs can be unhealthy 260
Not all motorized exercise machines work 260
The path to excellent health 261
Relieving cramps while exercising 262
Exercise cuts risk of diverticulitis 262
Exercise and arthritis 263
Exercise helps to cure insomnia 263
Teens don't exercise enough 263
Exercise improves hearing 263
Exercise vs. breast cancer 263
Microwave cooking is declining 263
Beware…the "healthy" diet can actually be bad for you 264
The Japanese secrets of diet…longevity and good health 265
Better eating on the road 266
Safe, lasting weight loss…breakthrough drug
    regimen makes it possible 267

Inexpensive ways to shape up 268
Cook with wine 268
Safer exercising for beginners 268

15 • VERY, VERY SMART EDUCATION

Educational TV 269
How to handle a child's bad report card 269
How to do well on standardized tests 270
Investing for education 272
College financial aid 272
Better buys in college education 273
Great games for kids 273
What to do when your child hates school 273

16 • CONSUMER SAVVY

Return mail free 275
What to buy…when 275
Be wary of extended warranties 276
Upgrading your computer 276
Correct credit report mistakes as soon as possible 276
How to protect yourself from your very own credit 276
Best ways to slash credit card costs 278
Frequent-flier programs more enticing 279
It pays to haggle 280
How to hire the best home contractor for you 280
Shop around for medication 282
Credit cards are being revoked 282
Credit card warning 282
Better auction buying 282
Cheap long-distance telephone calls via the internet 283
Save thousands of dollars on airfare 283
Buy the right toys 283
How to cut your family's medical bills…fast 284
Examine hospital bills closely before paying 285
Save on towing charges 285
Unshrink wool sweaters 286
Less expensive ways to enjoy life much more 286
Cut home heating bills by 10% 287
Wintertime money savers 287
Before buying your first computer 288
Tipping tips 289
Refunds on late mail delivery 289
Laptop computer survival 289
Easier software shopping 289
Winterize air conditioners 289
Co-op buying savvy 290
Better house hunting with kids 290
Better home buying 290
Better lemon buying 290

17 • YOUR CAR

Air-bag recall 291
And…here's how to make your car run cheaper and longer 291
Beware of cellular phones in your car 291
Safer stopping on icy roads 291
Before your lease ends…what to do 293
Car shopping 293
Keep automatic transmissions cool 294
For bargains on cars 294
New car savings 294
How to buy a used car 294
Car rental savvy 295
Get the best car-leasing deal 296
Almost-new cars at used-car prices 296

Odometer tampering is rampant 296
Drivers beware..296
Car accident smarts 296
The new car leasing traps can be avoided............................297
How to complain about the car you just bought 298
Smarter car buying strategy 298
Auto-repair rip-off 298

18 • SELF-DEFENSE

Choosing a PIN 299
A password that is easy to remember is easy to break 299
ATM trap 299
New bank scam..300
Credit card safety 300
Hotel safety 300
Business opportunity scams 300
Garbage can fraud ring 300
Watch for thieves in ladies' room 301
Home repair frauds...self-defense 301
Long-distance telephone service scam................................301
Microwave danger 301
Be wary of unsolicited callers..301
Prescription drug self-defense 302
What the new food labels really mean 302
Airplane pillows can spread disease 302
Car seat safety 302
Wraparound sunglasses...302
Nose piercing is dangerous 303
Gym equipment may be dangerous.....................................303
Common hospital billing errors 303
Self-service gasoline danger 304
Gas-burning appliance danger 304
Lethal gas leaks 304
New ATM scam 304
Little known allergen exposed 304
Protect your garden 305
New help for acrophobia 305
Know exactly what is in your wallet 305
Is your tap water safe? 305
How burglars think...and what you can do to
    protect your home 307

19 • TECHNOLOGY 1997

What you need to know about the internet..........................309
Internet marketing 311
Foolproof PC security essentials...311
E-mail is easy to send directly 312
Computer servicing warning 312
Computers and your eyes..312
New computer hazard 312

20 • NATURAL HEALING BASICS

The relaxation response 313
How to enhance your body's natural ability to heal.............315
Beat stress and depression the natural way 317
Melatonin...miracle or madness? 319
All about melatonin 319
Antioxidants and fewer health problems 321
The natural supplement that fights heart disease 322
Magnets...stop pain...ease arthritis...
    help heal broken bones and more 323
Deepak Chopra's secrets of having
    boundless energy..324
Just relaxing aids health..325
All about herbal remedies 325
This Chinese herb kills germs cold 327
Green tea helps prevent cancer 327
Herbal remedies that kill 328
Which mineral supplements should you take? 328
Lessons from our prehistoric past:
    why we get sick...how not to get sick 329
Asthma relief 331
Amazing flower remedy heals...and heals
    and heals 331
Using aromatherapy to stay super-healthy 332
Warming the heart 333
The cure-all oil 333
Ginkgo biloba: memory booster 333
Fatty acid fights strokes 334
Why take ginseng? 334
Calcium is not expensive 334
The health/success connection 334

1

Your Health—
Your Well-Being

Roy L. Walford
Expects to Live to 120

From Bulgarian yogurt to goat testicle implants, countless life-extension programs have been promoted. But only *caloric restriction* has been validated by scientific evidence.

More than 50 studies have shown that animals fed a calorie-restricted diet live 30% to 50% longer than animals allowed unrestricted eating. Calorie-restricted rats live about 55 months, compared with about 38 months for rats fed a "normal" diet.

No life-extension studies have been performed on humans. But my experience with Biosphere 2, the research habitat where I served as resident physician, supports the animal data.

Biosphere 2 was a self-contained habitat built under a massive dome in the Arizona desert. I lived there with seven colleagues from September 26, 1991, to September 26, 1993.

Since we could eat only what we could grow inside the dome, we often had to get by with less than we had been accustomed to.

Most of us consumed 1,800 to 2,200 calories a day. The average adult eats 2,400 to 3,000 calories a day.

Biomarkers and aging:

During our time in the Biosphere, all team members experienced significant improvements in various "biomarkers" for aging.

Blood pressure, cholesterol levels, fasting blood sugar levels and white blood cell counts all declined. Meanwhile, our general health, disease resistance and overall vitality improved.

Blood samples taken during our stint in Biosphere indicated that insulin levels also declined. The hormonal changes were exactly like those seen in calorie-restricted animals.

How caloric restriction works:

Studies suggest that caloric restriction retards the aging process by…

…boosting the body's ability to repair damage to its own genetic material (DNA).

1

…keeping the immune system "younger" for a longer time.

…increasing the body's production of antioxidants. These natural compounds help control levels of "corrosive" body molecules known as *free radicals*.

How to cut back on calories:

If you are interested in extending the quality and quantity of your life, discuss caloric restriction with your doctor. Caloric restriction is not recommended for children, adolescents or pregnant women.

How many calories should you eat? It's hard to give one number that is appropriate for everyone. However, I suggest you start your antiaging plan by eating 1,800 calories a day.

On such a diet, weight loss is inevitable. But don't lose weight too fast. *Best:* In your first year on a calorie-restricted diet, lose no more than 25% of your weight.

If you lose weight more quickly than that, or your weight fails to stabilize after several months, increase your calorie intake. In animal studies, too-rapid weight loss shortened life spans.

Most helpful strategies:

•**Focus on foods with maximum nutritional value**—vegetables, fruits, grains and fish. You can eat as much of them as you want without exceeding your caloric guidelines.

•**Avoid sugar and alcohol.** They represent empty calories. You can, however, occasionally eat cookies, ice cream or other treats—so you don't feel deprived.

•**Eat less fat.** Try to get no more than 20% of your daily calories from fat.

•**Exercise.** While regular activity will not extend your life span, it will extend your *health span*. That's the period during which you remain active and healthy.

Ideal: Moderate exercise most days of the week, alternating between aerobic and muscle-building activities.

Source: Roy L. Walford, MD, professor of pathology at the University of California, Los Angeles, School of Medicine. He is the author of *The Anti-Aging Plan*. Four Walls Eight Windows.

Illness Can Be Good for You

Some disease symptoms show that the body's natural defenses are working properly. Fever is a defense against infection. Nausea and vomiting remove potentially fatal toxins from the body. Coughing also removes toxins. Disease and health are more closely related than most people realize. The human body repairs damage by having cells divide—but the same mechanism gone awry can lead to cancer.

Source: Randolph M. Nesse, MD, professor of psychiatry, University of Michigan Medical School, Ann Arbor, and author of *Why We Get Sick: The New Science of Darwinian Medicine*. Times Books.

How to Make the Most of Your Annual Checkup

The end of the year is the time when most people see their doctors for an annual physical exam.

Many people have these exams at that time because the visits cost them next to nothing by November and December.

Reasons: They've either met their health plans' deductibles…or their HMOs allow them to have a free physical before year-end.

While studies have shown that annual checkups aren't really necessary if you feel fine, you can make the visit more valuable by asking your doctor six questions…

For which health problems am I most at risk?

One of the most important aspects of the annual exam—and one of the most neglected —is preventive medicine. If you know the ailments that are likely to affect you, you can take steps now to prevent them.

New evidence suggests that anyone at risk for heart attack should also take 0.4 mg of folic acid daily, the amount contained in most multivitamins…or eat several portions of green, leafy vegetables each day.

Reason: Folic acid lowers high levels of the chemical homocysteine, which has been implicated as a potential cause of heart disease.

What your doctor recommends will depend on your age, gender, habits, medical conditions and family history.

Strategy: Before going to your doctor's office, research what medical conditions run in your family and confirm the cause of death of all close relatives, including aunts, uncles and grandparents. You can get this information from family members, doctors or medical records for deceased relatives. Hospitals generally keep charts for several years after someone has died.

Important: In order for the doctor to personalize your preventive medical care, you must also be forthcoming about your lifestyle. Tell the doctor about anything that may be relevant to your medical care.

How am I doing compared with last year?

Doctors today are extremely busy and aren't always as patient as they should be. It's not unusual for them to race through your checkup.

Strategy: Slow your doctor down by asking him/her to compare this year's data with last year's and explain all the differences.

Example: If you have a history of high blood pressure, review the numbers with your doctor. Blood pressure readings above 140/90 are considered high. Remember, though, that blood pressure readings are variable and just being in a doctor's office can be enough to raise a person's pressure by 20 points.

Any decision to start or change therapy should be based on multiple readings, preferably some done outside of the doctor's office as well—such as with a home blood pressure device.

Also helpful: If you've read anything new about your medical conditions, mail copies of the articles to your doctor about one week before your appointment, along with a letter politely asking him to review them. At the very least, bring the articles with you. It's hard for a doctor to comment intelligently on something he may not have seen.

Can I cut down—or eliminate—any of the medications I'm taking?

Many people take medicines they don't need —or no longer need. Since almost all drugs have side effects, it's generally best to take only those that are necessary. Your annual checkup is a good opportunity to review what you're taking.

Strategy: Make a list or bring in all of your prescription and over-the-counter medications. Your doctor may not be aware of the drugs other doctors have prescribed…or you may still be taking a drug that was prescribed a long time ago.

Only if the doctor knows everything you're taking can he eliminate dangerous redundancies, spot potential interactions between drugs and make sure you're taking each drug correctly.

Are there other doctors I should be seeing?

Many doctors in HMOs and other managed-care plans limit referrals to specialists because such visits are expensive and plans often deduct some of the cost directly from the doctor's pay. In other cases, referrals are limited because they may not be considered critical.

But in some cases, such visits are necessary. *Examples…*

•**Diabetics** should get annual referrals to eye doctors (ophthalmologists).

•**People who have histories of skin cancer** may need to have regular follow-ups with a dermatologist.

•**People whose asthma has not responded well to therapy** may need to see an allergist—since most asthma is now believed to be triggered by allergies.

In general, if you have symptoms that the doctor can't figure out—or there are conditions that haven't improved despite therapy—this may be the time to push for a consultation with a specialist or for a second opinion.

What screening tests should I have?

Screening tests can pick up cancers early or detect internal imbalances that could result in problems. Different medical organizations have different recommendations about which screening tests you should have and how often. In patients with no known risk factors or family histories, most agree on the value of…

•**Blood pressure readings** every other year.

•**Cholesterol tests** every five years.

•**Colon cancer tests** after age 50—tests for hidden blood in stool should be done annually

...an internal exam with a sigmoidoscope every five years.

- **Pap smears** for women every one to three years.
- **Breast exams** by a doctor for women every year starting at age 40.
- **Annual mammograms** starting at 50.
Also possibly of value...
- **Vision**, hearing, urine analysis and thyroid function tests after age 65.
- **Testicular exams** every three years by a doctor for men under age 40 and rectal exams annually after age 40.
- **Prostate-Specific Antigen** (PSA) testing for prostate cancer. Although the American Cancer Society recommends PSA testing yearly after age 50, most other professional groups are withholding judgment. It is not proven that PSA testing saves lives, and there is the possibility that by causing unnecessary surgery, it may do more harm than good. If test results are a surprise, you may want to redo the test.

Based on your personal risk, your doctor may recommend additional tests.

Examples: Women who have family histories of breast cancer may want to start being screened earlier...fair-skinned individuals may need regular exams for skin cancer.

Questionable tests: There are tests that are generally considered to be outdated because their results aren't very useful. *They include...*
- **Yearly cardiograms**—also known as EKGs. This test isn't helpful for most people because it is not a good predictor of who will get heart disease. However, it is probably reasonable to have one cardiogram at age 35 or 40 as a basis for comparison if problems develop later on.
- **Chest X rays**—even for people who have been smoking for years. These tests have little value because they don't detect lung cancer in time to improve the cure rate. But they do add billions to our medical bills and expose people to unnecessary radiation.
- **Routine stress tests.** These tests have also fallen from favor—except for people at very high risk for heart attacks.

Important: Many tests not recommended for routine screening are still useful in evaluating people with symptoms.

Do I have all of my immunizations?

We often neglect the importance of immunizations for our own well-being.

More than 60,000 American adults die annually of vaccine-preventable diseases such as pneumonia, tetanus, hepatitis B and influenza.

Example: Anyone with a chronic illness or over age 65 should consider getting a flu shot. Annual flu shots not only protect you against influenza—but lower the death rate from all causes by 28%.

Reason: Many people who die of such things as heart attacks or strokes were weakened by influenza. By getting flu shots, you also protect your older or chronically ill friends and family members from catching the disease from you.

Source: Timothy McCall, MD, internist practicing in the Boston area. He is author of *Examining Your Doctor: A Patient's Guide to Avoiding Harmful Medical Care.* Birch Lane Press.

How to Protect Yourself From Your Doctor

Our health care system has become so complex and depersonalized that the chances of your doctor making a mistake are increasing.

That doesn't mean your doctor is incompetent—but rather that he/she is human and often overextended by the demands made by insurance companies, organized health plans, the government and patients.

Medical errors can take the form of overtesting or undertesting...misdiagnosing...prescribing medications incorrectly...overlooking subtle signs of disease...withholding important information...advocating unnecessary procedures...failing to recommend needed ones.

The way to avoid medical errors is to be assertive with your physician and assume the ultimate responsibility for your health care.

Error: Your doctor doesn't warn you about possible drug interactions with newly prescribed medication.

Example: You come down with bronchitis, and your doctor prescribes the antibiotic erythromycin to treat it even though you are also taking the antihistamine Seldane to manage your allergies. This is a potentially dangerous combination of drugs that can cause irregular heart rhythms.

The doctor is aware of the dangers that this combination of drugs can trigger. This error occurs because he is focused on treating your infection. It doesn't register that you're also taking the antihistamine...or he may not even know you are taking Seldane because he wasn't the doctor who prescribed it for you.

Solution: Help your physician focus on important concerns, such as drug interactions, by bringing with you a list of the medications you are currently taking. Say, *Doctor, with my allergies, my diseases and current medications— will the medication you're prescribing create any problems?*

Error: Your doctor isn't up to date on cholesterol treatment guidelines.

Example: Three separate blood tests indicate your total cholesterol level is within acceptable ranges and show your HDL level— the "good" cholesterol—is low at 25 milligrams per deciliter. Yet your doctor doesn't prescribe any treatment.

While your doctor realizes that keeping your total cholesterol level under 200 milligrams per deciliter is important to reduce your risk of heart disease, he may not be aware that experts have recently deemed the HDL level to be important as well.

Solution: Ask your doctor to go over your total cholesterol...HDL ("good" cholesterol)... and LDL ("bad" cholesterol) numbers and discuss the significance of each. Your HDL should be more than 35...and your LDL should be less than 130. If any of these numbers are abnormal, particularly if you have other heart disease risk factors, insist that your doctor prescribe lifestyle and/or drug treatments. If he won't comply and doesn't provide a good reason, find a new doctor.

Error: Your doctor fails to talk with you about early cancer detection. With only limited time for each patient, most physicians focus on treating what is ailing the patient that day. Preventive exams, therefore, may be forgotten.

Solution: Schedule a visit with your doctor to talk about your cancer risks and to set up a schedule of screening tests and exams you should have based on your family and personal history. Then be vigilant about making sure those scheduled exams and tests are performed.

Error: Your doctor fails to rehearse you for a heart attack. Again, doctors are busy treating illness and it may not occur to them to schedule preventive medicine appointments.

Solution: Since heart disease is the number-one killer of men and women—you should schedule an educational appointment around age 50. Make it at age 40 if you have risk factors for heart disease, such as diabetes, high blood pressure, obesity or family history. The goal is to go through a heart attack drill with your doctor. Points to discuss...

•**The symptoms of a heart attack.**

•**What to do if you experience symptoms.** These steps include having someone drive you to an emergency room within one-half hour of onset—before severe damage to your heart muscle occurs or your heart rhythm becomes irrevocably abnormal.

Error: Your doctor is quick to prescribe medications.

Example: You seem to have an upper-respiratory virus—and you ask your doctor for an antibiotic. He gives you one. Months later, when you have a raging bacterial infection, you find you are resistant to several antibiotics, making it dangerously difficult to resolve your current infection.

This mistake occurs because doctors feel pressured by patients to offer cures, and they may give in to the demand for antibiotics in order to keep patients in their practice. But there's no way to tell for sure whether upper-respiratory symptoms are being caused by a virus, which must simply run its course...or by bacteria, which can be eradicated by antibiotics.

Solution: If you have a routine upper-respiratory infection that is not too severe, let your symptoms run for four days before taking a prescription drug. In many cases, viral illnesses will start to dissipate by then. If they don't, ask your doctor for an antibiotic. Of course, let your doctor know promptly if your symptoms worsen.

5

Error: You are diagnosed with cancer, but your doctor treats your condition without referring you to an oncologist—a cancer specialist. The physician or surgeon who diagnoses your cancer may feel he can adequately treat it, but he may not be up to date about the latest therapies.

Example: A urologist diagnoses you with prostate cancer and surgically excises the malignant tissue. After the operation, you find out that you're impotent—and that you could have been treated with radiation instead, which might have controlled the cancer and retained your sexual potency.

Solution: Always request a referral to an oncologist whenever you're told you have cancer. See the cancer specialist early on for a confirmation of your diagnosis and to explore all your treatment options. Your primary care physician can work with the oncologist to determine and provide your treatment.

Error: You have several vague symptoms—fatigue, difficulty concentrating, depression, constipation, weight gain—but your doctor fails to test your thyroid function. Because symptoms of thyroid disorders mimic those of many other diseases, including psychiatric disorders, and may affect many organs of the body, your doctor may not suspect the thyroid. Yet thyroid disease is very common in both men and women, particularly as they age.

Solution: If you haven't been feeling well for some time and have lots of symptoms that are hard to pin down, insist that your doctor order a thyroid function blood test. Also ask about a thyroid screening if you've been diagnosed with another disorder and the treatment doesn't seem to be working.

Error: Your doctor diagnoses stomach pain over the phone.

Example: You call your doctor because you have abdominal pain and queasiness, and he says it's probably just a stomach flu and you should wait it out. But it worsens overnight and you are rushed to the hospital with a burst appendix.

The reason this oversight occurs is that the doctor may be trying to save you a trip to his office...or he may not have time to see you.

But he simply can't diagnose abdominal pain over the phone with any degree of certainty.

Solution: If you develop stomach discomfort that is different from anything you've experienced before—especially if you have a fever, nausea, vomiting or pain that is localized to a specific site in your abdomen—insist on seeing your doctor or go to the emergency room. You're facing a potential emergency, and you have to be persistent to get your point across.

Source: Richard Podell, MD, clinical professor of family medicine, University of Medicine and Dentistry of New Jersey–Robert Wood Johnson Medical School in New Providence, NJ. He is author of *When Your Doctor Doesn't Know Best.* Simon & Schuster.

Throw Away All Expired Medicines

Some medicines, like codeine, become more potent with age, while others lose effectiveness. Taking out-of-date medicine is an ineffective way to try to save money.

To make medicines last as long as possible: Do not store them in the bathroom. Bathroom moisture and germs can cause medicines to deteriorate prematurely.

Source: Timothy McCall, MD, an internist practicing in the Boston area. He is author of *Examining Your Doctor, A Patient's Guide to Avoiding Harmful Medical Care.* Birch Lane Press.

300,000+ Over-the-Counter Drugs...Which Ones Really Work? Which Ones Don't!

There are more than 300,000 different over-the-counter (OTC) medications on the market today. Some of these drugs are highly effective. Others are not.

How can you find the best drug for what ails you? Here are 15 common ailments and the most effective OTC medication for each.*

*OTC medications are meant for use by individuals who are generally healthy. If you have a severe or chronic health problem, it's always best to seek medical care from a doctor.

•**Arthritis.** Ibuprofen usually works better than aspirin or acetaminophen.

•**Athlete's foot.** Products that contain clotrimazole (Lotrimin AF) or miconazole (Micatin) are equally effective.

•**Backache.** Stick to ibuprofen, aspirin or acetaminophen. No other over-the-counter medication or even prescription medication works better.

"Backache pills" are ineffective. Worse, they contain an ingredient whose safety has not been fully established.

•**Colds.** In adults, ibuprofen is best for relieving muscle aches and/or sore throat pain and fever.

To relieve cough, take a drug containing dextromethorphan. To relieve congestion, take a drug containing pseudoephedrine.

Sudafed Cough and Ambenyl-D Decongestant Cough Formula contain both of these medications.

These preparations also contain guaifenesin which is a highly effective over-the-counter expectorant.

For children: Products that combine acetaminophen, pseudoephedrine and dextromethorphan are best. *Examples:* Bayer Select Head & Chest Cold…DayCare…Tylenol Cold Non-Drowsy.

•**Nasal congestion.** In addition to being highly effective, oxymetazoline nasal spray causes fewer side effects than nasal spray containing xylometazoline or phenylephrine. *Example:* Afrin 12 Hour.

Caution: Oxymetazoline can be irritating if used more than twice a day.

•**Constipation.** In general, it's best to stick to a slow-acting preparation—something that contains methylcellulose, psyllium or polycarbophil. *Examples:* Disoplex…Fiberall…FiberCon…Naturacil. These "bulking agents" provide relief within a day or two. They are less likely than fast-acting agents to be habit-forming or to cause cramps, stomach pain, diarrhea or other side effects.

If you need immediate relief, use a preparation that combines a stool softener like docusate or mineral oil with phenolphthalein, a laxative that stimulates bowel movements.

Examples: Colax…Doxidan…Ex-Lax Extra Gentle…Phillips' LaxCaps…Agoral.

For fastest relief (one to three hours), take a product that contains magnesium, castor oil or sodium phosphate. *Examples:* Haley's M-O… milk of magnesia…Alphamul…Citro-Nesia.

•**Fever.** Ibuprofen works best, although acetaminophen is better for infants as well as for adults whose stomachs are sensitive to ibuprofen.

Danger: Aspirin can lead to a potentially fatal brain disease called Reye's syndrome when taken by children or young adults with influenza or another viral illness. *Also:* Excessive use of aspirin can cause stomach upset—even ulcers.

•**Heartburn and indigestion.** Use a "concentrated liquid" product that contains magnesium hydroxide and aluminum hydroxide. *Examples:* Almacone II…Gelusil II…Maalox TC…Mylanta II…Simaal 2 Gel.

Avoid antacids with calcium. They stimulate production of stomach acid, causing pain and possibly making ulcers worse.

•**Hemorrhoids.** Use a product that contains an anesthetic, such as benzocaine, dibucaine, pramoxine, diperodon…or tetracaine with zinc oxide, petrolatum or cocoa butter. These are available in ointments or suppositories. *Ointments:* Anusol…Nupercainal. *Suppository:* Medicone Hemorrhoidal.

•**Insomnia.** The most effective products are those that contain the antihistamine diphenhydramine. *Examples:* Compoz…Sleep-Eze 3…Sleepinal…Sominex 2.

If you're suffering from insomnia and pain, take ibuprofen in addition to one of these diphenhydramine products.

•**Nausea.** Although millions of people rely on Dramamine, its active ingredient, dimenhydrinate, is not as effective as meclizine, the active ingredient in Bonine.

Cyclizine (Marezine) is slightly less effective than meclizine. Unlike meclizine, however, its drowsiness effect can be offset with coffee or other sources of caffeine.

•**Poison ivy.** Hydrocortisone creams are best, but they can thin the skin and leave you more vulnerable to infection if used longer than a few weeks. *Examples:* Anusol HC-1…

Bactine…Cortaid…Dermtex HC…Hytone…Lanacort…Rhulicort…Preparation HC.

• **Premenstrual syndrome.** For pain, use ibuprofen. For bloating, take a product that contains pamabrom. *Example:* Odrinil.

Caution: To avoid insomnia, heart palpitations and anxiety, do not take any painkiller that contains caffeine if you already get a lot of caffeine from coffee, tea or colas.

• **Sore throat pain.** Cepacol, Vicks Sore Throat Lozenges and other products that contain benzocaine are effective. However, they can lead to allergic reactions.

When relieving sore throat pain, it is better to stick to lozenges that contain the anesthetic dyclonine. *Example:* Sucrets.

• **Sunburn.** Ibuprofen is best for relieving sunburn pain. You might also try cold-water compresses and a product that contains benzocaine. *Examples:* Aerocain…Americaine…Burntame…Lanacane…Solarcaine.

To reduce redness, try something that contains hydrocortisone. *Examples:* Anusol HC-1 …Bactine…Cortaid…Dermtex HC…Hytone …Lanacort…Rhulicort. Use sparingly to avoid side effects.

Remember—no drug cures sunburned skin. Serious burns should be treated by a doctor.

Source: David O. Thueson, PhD, vice president of discovery for Cosmederm Technologies, a research and development firm based in La Jolla, CA. He is the author of *Thueson's Guide to Over-the-Counter Drugs.* New Harbinger Publications.

Dangerous Drug Interactions

Every year, thousands of people combine drugs they are taking with other medications and foods that produce negative reactions. In most cases, they weren't aware there would be a problem, since the medications and foods seemed harmless.

Here are just some of the most common hazardous drug interactions—and what you can do to protect yourself and your family from harm.

Drug/food interaction:

No doubt your pharmacist has cautioned you to avoid taking certain antibiotics with dairy products. This combination can reduce the effectiveness of the medications.

But many pharmacists and doctors are unaware of some unusual drug/food interactions. *Foods that could cause problems with some medications:*

• **Grapefruit and grapefruit juice** contain compounds that can interact powerfully with medications—and cause devastating side effects. Examples…

• **Blood pressure medications**, such as Procardia and Adalat (*nifedipine*) and Plendil (*felodipine*), are dangerous when combined with grapefruit, resulting in higher blood levels of blood pressure medications. Symptoms may include facial flushing, nausea, dizziness, confusion, palpitations or irregular heartbeat.

• **Seldane or Seldane-D:** Just one glass of grapefruit juice or half a grapefruit may trigger a dangerous rise in Seldane levels in the blood, which could lead to an irregular heart rhythm and cardiac arrest.

• **Green, leafy vegetables** such as broccoli, Brussels sprouts and cabbage reduce the effectiveness of the blood thinner Coumadin (*warfarin*), a commonly prescribed blood thinner that prevents blood clots. These foods are rich in vitamin K, which helps the blood to clot. Coumadin, meanwhile, works by counteracting vitamin K's clotting action.

Consuming a small amount of vitamin K–rich foods daily probably won't pose a problem. But if you usually skip these vegetables and then overindulge, at a Chinese restaurant, for example, you reduce the drug's effectiveness and put yourself at risk for a blood clot or stroke.

• **Oatmeal and other high-fiber foods** may interfere with the absorption of Lanoxin (*digoxin*), a drug prescribed to control an irregular heart rhythm, which can lead to blood clots and stroke. Take Lanoxin two or three hours before or after eating high-fiber foods.

• **Salt substitutes** are used by people with high blood pressure. But they contain high amounts of potassium. If consumed with potassium-sparing diuretics such as Aldactone (*spironolactone*)—which are prescribed for high blood pressure or congestive heart failure—they can cause potassium levels to soar, increasing the risk of cardiac arrest.

•**Licorice and Lanoxin**—or a diuretic like Lasix (*furosemide*)—can lead to low levels of potassium, causing irregular heart rhythms and cardiac arrest. One piece of licorice probably won't hurt—but regular handfuls of licorice could be deadly.

Prescription drug interaction:

•**Antibiotics vs. blood thinners.** Antibiotics like Flagyl and Protostat (*metronidazole*) can cause problems when taken with the blood thinner Coumadin. The antibiotics prevent the body from purging Coumadin, and if Coumadin levels get too high, life-threatening bleeding could occur.

If you are taking both metronidazole and Coumadin, you must be monitored carefully by your physician and have frequent blood tests.

•**Antibiotics vs. antihistamines.** Macrolide antibiotics such as clarithromycin, erythromycin and azithromycin can boost blood levels of the antihistamines Seldane and Hismanal (*astemizole*) to dangerous—and potentially lethal—levels.

RX/OTC drug interaction:

Don't assume over-the-counter (OTC) medications are risk-free. Teamed with certain prescription drugs, some can cause complications. *Examples…*

•**Pain relievers.** Aspirin…Advil and Nuprin (*ibuprofen*)…Aleve (*naproxen*)…and Orudis KT (*ketoprofen*) can reduce the effectiveness of beta blockers, such as Inderal (*propranolol*) and Lopressor (*metoprolol*), which are prescribed to treat high blood pressure.

If this happens, blood pressure can rise, increasing the risk of heart attack and stroke. If you are taking a beta blocker, check with your doctor before adding a pain reliever. If your doctor prescribes a beta blocker and aspirin, he/she should monitor your blood pressure.

•**Antacids can inhibit the absorption** of the heart and blood pressure medications Capoten (*captopril*) and Tenormin (*atenolol*), as well as Lanoxin.

And the activated charcoal added to counteract gas may reduce the effectiveness of a number of drugs, including tricyclic antidepressants such as Elavil (*amitriptyline*) and the diabetes medications Diabinese (*chlorpropamide*) and Tolinase (*tolazamide*).

•**Allergy and cough/cold remedies** that contain pseudoephedrine, ephedrine, phenylpropanolamine or phenylephrine should not be combined with a monoamine oxidase inhibitor antidepressant like Nardil (*phenelzine*) or Parnate (*tranylcypromine*). Your blood pressure could soar, leading to a hypertensive crisis and stroke.

Guarding against interactions:

•**Make your doctors aware** of the prescription and OTC drugs you are taking and have your doctors check for interaction potential. Ask them to consult drug reference books and/or computer reference programs before you leave the office.

•**Have all prescriptions filled** at a single pharmacy, preferably one that keeps computerized data on all your medications and can zero in on possible interactions. Tell your pharmacist about OTC drugs you are taking.

•**Make a list of key questions to ask.** When a new drug is prescribed, don't assume doctors and pharmacists are aware of every drug interaction—or if they are, that they will remember to alert you. List the following questions and give copies to your doctor and pharmacist to fill out independently. If one contradicts the other, speak with both to get the correct answer.

•**What is the medication's name?**

•**What is the dose?**

•**What time(s) should I take it?**

•**Should I take it with food?** After eating? Before eating? How long?

•**Should I avoid any foods?**

•**Are there vitamins or supplements I should avoid?** Increase?

•**Are there any precautions or warnings** I should know about?

•**Are there any contraindications** that would make this drug inappropriate?

•**What other prescription medicines should I avoid?**

•**Are there any OTC remedies** I should avoid?

• **What side effects are common** with my medicine?

• **Are there any side effects** that are so serious you would want to know about them immediately?

If your doctor or pharmacist tells you that a drug won't interact adversely with another medication or food, don't assume that no interactions exist. Though rare, life-threatening interactions can go undetected by drug companies, the medical establishment and the Food and Drug Administration for months or even years after a drug hits the market.

So...if you experience any strange symptoms that cannot be easily explained, ask your doctor to contact the drug's manufacturer and file a report with the FDA.

Source: Joseph Graedon, one of the country's foremost experts on drug interactions. He has served as a consultant to the Federal Trade Commission on nonprescription drug advertising and as a member of the advisory board of the University of California (San Francisco) Drug Studies Unit. He is author, with Teresa Graedon, PhD, of many books on health topics, including *The People's Guide to Deadly Drug Interactions*, St. Martin's Press, and *The People's Pharmacy: Completely New and Revised*

How to Win the Chronic-Pain Wars

If you suffer from headaches, back pain, neck pain or joint pain that persists for more than six to eight weeks, you may be experiencing chronic pain.

The good news is that now you can do more than just put up with it.

Origins of chronic pain:

The body requires about six weeks to heal following major injuries—broken bones, surgical incisions, etc. The pain associated with those injuries, however, can be felt long after the body has healed.

The acute or short-term pain that immediately follows an injury is directly related to how much damage the body has sustained. But pain that persists longer than might be expected following such conditions is chronic pain—and it is *not* related to the amount of damage that was sustained.

For years, chronic pain has been thought of as a disease itself and, therefore, the favored approach was managing the pain rather than looking for a cause of the pain.

Causes of chronic pain:

Muscles are the major cause of chronic pain. They produce pain in four ways.

Emotional stress is the chief culprit that makes us tense our muscles without even being aware of it. Not surprisingly, all the day-to-day stress we experience affects the body. You tense your muscles, and you feel pain. And that pain may travel to different parts of the body.

Most chronic pain should not be seen as evidence of disease. It may, however, serve as your barometer of tension. The other causes for muscle pain are weaknesses and stiffness, spasm and trigger points.

How to reduce chronic pain:

• **Tune in to what your body is telling you.** If you are experiencing persistent pain, you have a problem and should get help. Unfortunately, many doctors may not be able to help with your back or neck pains.

Reason: Although about 80% of the human body is made of muscle, most doctors are not taught a "hands-on" approach to examining muscles or evaluating the possible effects of muscle tension, weakness or spasm. As a result, muscle-related pain may not be recognized by your doctor or managed appropriately.

If previous pain-management strategies have not worked for you, look for a doctor who has expertise in muscle-related pain. Screen potential doctors to see if they incorporate evaluation and treatment of muscles in their pain-management regimens.

• **Stop thinking of the pain as a disease.** It will be more difficult to get rid of your pain if you make it the focus of a lot of worry and concern.

Try to carry on with as many normal daily activities as you can. Don't be afraid of movement, even if it's a little uncomfortable. Movement is necessary for chronic pain sufferers because muscle inactivity worsens the pain.

• **Begin a moderate exercise program.** This does not mean taking strenuous aerobics classes...or jogging five miles a day. In fact, both types of exercise should be avoided.

Better: Start a walking or swimming program, beginning with a modest distance and gradually increasing your goal as you feel more comfortable. Work with your doctor to develop the appropriate regimen for you. Work up to 30 to 40 minutes of exercise, three or four times a week.

Always remember that a proper exercise program starts with relaxation techniques such as meditation...then limbering and stretching prior to the initial exercise...followed by a cool-down period, which ends with relaxation again.

In addition to helping you stretch and strengthen, the process will help your mind release tension and stress, the major causes of chronic muscle-related pain.

If your pain is associated with danger signs —fever, chills, night sweats, headaches and malaise—it could indicate an underlying disease or potentially serious problem. You should consult your doctor.

Source: Norman Marcus, MD, diplomat of the American Board of Pain Medicine...president of the International Foundation for Pain Relief...and medical director of the New York Pain Treatment Program at Lenox Hill Hospital. *Pain Hotline:* 800-474-1276. Dr. Marcus is author of *Freedom from Pain.* Simon & Schuster.

Win the Hospital Game, Too

No one can control when hospitalization for an ailment or operation will be necessary. But if a hospital stay is necessary, there are steps you can take to minimize the risk of injury and infection—and maximize your comfort and care.
Before you go:

•**Be sure you need the treatment.** All procedures—and hospital stays—involve risk. Get a second opinion from another specialist before having any procedure. If the second doctor disagrees with the first doctor, get a third...or fourth opinion. The goal is to get a consensus.

Example: If your first doctor urges you to have a bypass, but two or three other cardiac specialists feel your condition can be treated effectively with medication and diet, you

would probably be wise to accept the recommendation of the majority.

•**Ask your surgeon how many such procedures he/she performs each year.** An adequate number depends on the procedure.

Example: If you need a bypass, look for a surgeon who has done 100 bypass operations within the last year.

•**Ask the doctor what his surgical success rate is.** Ask him how that compares with national figures for the same procedure. And confirm this with the medical director of the hospital.

•**Make sure the hospital your doctor chooses is the best one for your condition.** Different types of hospitals do different types of procedures well.

In general, local community hospitals are fine for uncomplicated procedures such as gallbladder removals, births, hysterectomies, etc. But for a more serious procedure—such as open-heart surgery or a transplant—you're better off at a hospital that is affiliated with a major university *and* that has top specialists with extensive experience in the type of medical care you require.

•**Have all your preoperative tests done as an outpatient prior to admission**—preferably several days in advance. You don't want to be admitted to the hospital only to discover that a blood test or an X ray indicates your surgery should be postponed. This unnecessarily prolongs your hospital stay, which would also increase your costs.

•**Meet with your anesthesiologist or nurse-anesthetist *before* you are admitted.** Give him a list of all the prescription and over-the-counter drugs you are taking. Tell him about any medical conditions you may have.
In the hospital:

•**Cut needless hospital costs by bringing everything you require**—including tissues, hand and body lotions, vitamins and medications for chronic conditions. Make sure these items do not appear on your bill.

If possible, have a friend or relative visit you each day for companionship and to speak up for you if you are not able to. Studies show that patients who ask the most questions—or who have family members who ask questions

—get better care and have better outcomes than those who don't.

•**Understand that you can say *no* to anything.** One of your most important rights as a patient is your right to refuse services and treatment you don't want or understand.

Example: If you are getting a good night's rest without taking a sleeping pill, you can refuse the sedatives that are routinely administered to patients.

•**Question all tests.** Patients are sometimes given routine tests that are unnecessary, such as X rays or blood tests—or tests that are meant for other patients.

Key: Ask your doctor to tell you about every test in advance. If you were not advised of a test, ask the person who was sent to administer it whether your doctor ordered it...why the test is being done...and what the risks are.

•**Reduce your risk of medication mishaps.** Ask your doctor to show you the drugs he is prescribing for you while you're in the hospital. Note the shapes, colors and sizes.

If a nurse tries to give you an unfamiliar pill or liquid, refuse to take it until your doctor has been contacted and has identified and approved the medication.

Also ask your doctor what each pill is for and how often it should be administered. Keep a list so you don't forget.

•**Curb your risk of infection** by politely asking everyone who touches you—doctors, nurses, technicians—to wash their hands in the sink in your room. Unwashed hands are the leading cause of infections in hospitals, since doctors and nurses commonly move from room to room carrying germs.

If you must receive fluids intravenously, ask that the IV bag be mixed by the pharmacy staff—not by a nurse or technician. IV bags that are opened by nurses or technicians have higher risks of being contaminated with microorganisms circulating in the hospital.

•**Insist that your bathroom be cleaned and disinfected on a daily basis**, especially if you share a room.
Negotiate your rights:

•**Ask the staff to rearrange their schedules to fit your needs.** If your doctor wants blood taken every eight hours, ask the technicians to draw your blood at 11 pm, when you are just going to sleep, and again at 7 am, when you wake up, rather than at 8 pm and 4 am.

If the housekeeping staff routinely cleans your room at 2 am—this is not uncommon—ask that they come back between 7 am and 9 pm.

•**If you don't want to be disturbed** by interns and medical students marching into your room during their rounds, tell the nurse or a patient representative (a hospital employee who acts as an arbitrator between you and the hospital) to note your wishes on your chart.

•**If your medication does not sufficiently control discomfort**, ask a nurse to call your physician and get approval to increase your medication.

Also helpful: Ask about less expensive, alternative methods of pain control that may be available at the hospital. These include acupuncture, relaxation techniques and biofeedback.

Source: Charles Inlander, president of People's Medical Society, the largest nonprofit consumer health advocacy group in the US, 462 Walnut St., Allentown, PA 18102. Mr. Inlander is author of numerous books, including *Take This Book to the Hospital with You: A Consumer Guide to Surviving Your Hospital Stay.* People's Medical Society.

How to Get the Best Nursing Care when You're Hospitalized

People devote lots of time to choosing a doctor. But when it comes to a hospital stay, your nurse is at least as important as your physician.

Doctors tend to make only short, infrequent visits to the bedside. Nurses are on hand 24 hours a day—not only to administer drugs and monitor your vital signs, but also to calm your anxieties and be your confidante.

To get the most from a hospital's nursing staff...

•**Insist on having a registered nurse care for you.** Before checking in to the hospital, call ahead to find out about the nursing staff on your ward. Ask whether you'll be cared for by a registered nurse.

You may be told that there is an RN on your floor—but he/she might be there in a supervisory capacity only. A floor RN is generally responsible for overseeing several patients...and will probably be stationed down the hall from your room. He lacks the time to be reponsive to the needs of any single patient.

If you're told you can't be assured of an RN and that you'll have to foot the bill for a private-duty RN, write a letter of protest to the hospital administrator. If the administrator declines to comply with your wishes, find another hospital.

Be leery of any "nurse" not wearing a name tag. Recently, administrators in a hospital where I worked instructed the nurses not to wear their name tags. That way, patients could not tell whether they were being cared for by an RN, a licensed practical nurse (LPN) or a nurse's aide.

In many cities, cost-conscious hospitals have been replacing highly paid RNs with nurse's aides...and patients are unaware that aides caring for them may have been bagging groceries at Safeway a month earlier. Not surprisingly, hospital mortality rates are going up in these cities.

• **Make sure your nurse is working within his/her specialty.** Like doctors, nurses are often specialists. If you're in the hospital for, say, heart surgery, you don't want a nurse who specializes in pediatrics.

Problem: To meet changing staffing requirements, hospitals sometimes transfer nurses from their regular ward to another ward. "Float" nurses sometimes lack the experience necessary to provide good patient care.

Example: I'm trained as a coronary care nurse. That's been my specialty for the past 17 years. Once I was floated to an organ transplant unit, where I was asked to give a patient an anti-rejection drug. I declined. I simply didn't know enough about the drug or transplant patients to feel comfortable doing that.

• **Avail yourself of all that your RN has to offer.** Nurses can do more than monitor vital signs and administer necessary medications. In many states, they can administer drugs and initiate certain procedures—without a doctor's specific instructions.

Your nurse is also there to educate you. Before I give a patient a new drug, I always ask, *Do you have any idea what I'm giving you?* If not, I tell him the name of the drug, explain the dosage, etc.

Your nurse is also trained to act as your confidante and advocate. If you're afraid to discuss your condition with your family or your doctor, your nurse can act as the go-between.

• **Treat your nurse with respect.** Nurses are skilled professionals. They work alongside doctors, not under them. Unfortunately, some patients treat nurses like unthinking bubbleheads. But if you suddenly take a turn for the worse at three in the morning, it's your nurse who'll be there to take care of you—not your doctor.

• **Don't put up with a bad nurse.** If your nurse is nasty or inattentive, ask the charge nurse to find you another RN.

Source: Echo Heron, RN, a critical care nurse in coronary and emergency medicine. She is the author of *Intensive Care: The Story of a Nurse* and *Condition Critical: The Story of a Nurse Continues.* Fawcett Columbine.

How to Find the Best Hospitals in the US

When it comes to your health—and your life—there's no point in taking the slightest risk or settling for less than the very best hospitals, best doctors, best equipment, best systems.

That's true even if it's only for your peace of mind in an era where horror stories abound.

Example: A nurse who hastened older patients' trip to the grave.

Though you can reduce the odds of a mistake by choosing your hospital carefully, even good institutions aren't completely free of accidents.
Options:

Choosing a great hospital, as opposed to just a good one, is much easier than you probably believe. Most people have misconceptions about just how wide the choice is...

Myth: Your doctor must be affiliated with a hospital for you to be admitted.

Reality: While most people want to stay with their own doctors, if a particular hospital is important to you, you can go with its doctors. Contact the hospital of your choice. As long as it performs the procedure you need, its own doctors will examine you and treat you according to the results of the examination.

Moreover, since most insurance policies today require a second opinion, they nearly always pay for the second exam as well as whatever portion of the medical procedure is covered by your policy.

Myth: The best hospitals have such a long waiting list that it's difficult to get in.

Reality: Nearly all top hospitals in the country want you to be their patient. In most cases, that's how they make the money that allows them to provide excellent service.

Myth: Top hospitals charge top prices.

Reality: Many of the best are among the least expensive.

Example: The Mayo Clinic in upstate Minnesota is one of the world's best medical institutions. It is also modestly priced at $434 a day for a semiprivate room. That compares with more than $1,000 a day at the University of California Medical Center in San Francisco.

Some hospitals will lower their rates if you can demonstrate a financial need. While smaller regional hospitals can often provide excellent service, it's usually wise to choose one of the relatively new type of medical centers modeled after the Mayo Clinic system. *The advantages:*

A broad array of the latest procedures and equipment.

Treatment by a team of doctors who pool their expertise before deciding which procedure, if any, you'll need.

Exception: For people with conditions that require highly specialized treatment, it may be best to choose a hospital that concentrates specifically on that ailment.

Narrowing the choice:

In addition to asking your doctor's advice, research your ailment thoroughly before deciding which hospital is best for you. *Research steps...*

•**Contact the national organization** that serves people with the ailment, such as the American Heart Association or the Epilepsy Foundation of America. If you aren't sure of the proper group, ask your doctor or call the American Medical Association. 312-464-5000. Associations can give you the names of hospitals that treat your condition, including those that are experimenting with new procedures.

Local chapters of associations can often steer you to nearby members who have been patients. It can often pay to contact these people and ask about their experience in the hospital that you're considering.

•**Read the latest literature** about your medical condition. Associations can usually recommend books and articles, which can also be located through computerized services now available at most public libraries.

Through reading medical literature, you can often determine which hospitals have the most advanced and successful treatments. Also, literature usually mentions doctors you can contact for recommendations.

Before making a final decision on a hospital, talk with people on its administration and medical staffs...

Ask about—the quality of its nursing staff. It's usually a good indicator of the hospital's all-around quality. Ask whether the nursing staff has won any awards. The answer can be surprisingly revealing since the staffs at second-string institutions rarely win awards.

Ask about—the job turnover in the nursing staff, and be wary of a hospital that loses more than 15% to 20% of its nurses a year. And in most excellent hospitals, about half the nursing staff have earned a bachelor's degree.

Ask about—the hospital's quality-assurance program. This is a computerized program that monitors patient care so that doctors know on an hour-by-hour basis the treatment each patient receives. Eliminate any institution that doesn't have a quality-assurance program. The best programs provide highly detailed data, not just general information about a patient's condition, location and treatment. Also, look for a program that's administered by doctors instead of nonmedical personnel.

Be cautious about an institution that hesitates in answering your questions. The best hospitals are usually forthcoming.

Former patients, however, are usually reliable information sources on how well the nursing staff communicated with them. That's important because one of the first tipoffs of a second-rate institution is the failure of nurses to communicate.

Even among the country's very best hospitals, several stand out above the others...

•**Cleveland Clinic.** The hospital is best known for its excellence in heart surgery and treatment. Other top-rated specialties include organ transplants, epilepsy, gastroenterology, gynecology, laryngology and pulmonary diseases. A semiprivate room costs $675. The staff includes nearly 600 physicians, 715 residents and 1,273 nurses.

9500 Euclid Ave., Cleveland 44195. 216-444-2200.

•**Johns Hopkins.** Surveys of doctors have given Johns Hopkins top ratings in more specialties than any other hospital. These include allergies, cardiology, dermatology, neurosurgery, pediatrics, psychiatry and rheumatology. It has 955 residents and 1,654 physicians. A semiprivate room costs from $560 to $654. Johns Hopkins has 1,479 nurses.

600 N. Wolfe St., Baltimore 21287. 410-955-5000.

•**Mayo Clinic.** Mayo is top-rated in many specialties, including cancer, cardiology, geriatrics, rehabilitation and urology. The hospital charges $434 for a semiprivate room. It has 1,647 physicians, 1,311 residents and 3,267 registered nurses.

200 First St. SW, Rochester, MN 55905. 507-284-2511.

•**University of Pennsylvania Hospital.** The University of Pennsylvania Hospital has earned a worldwide reputation in several fields, including early treatment of breast cancer. Other specialties include dental medicine, infectious diseases, radiation therapy, kidney treatment and general surgery. Registered nurses number 1,313. There are 650 physicians on staff as well as 1,006 residents. The price of a semiprivate room is $939.

3400 Spruce St., Philadelphia 19104. 215-662-4000.

Source: John W. Wright, who conducted a nationwide survey of over 200 doctors and 150 hospitals, and is co-author of *The Best Hospitals in America, a Guide to the 88 Top-Rated Hospitals in the US and Canada.* Visible Ink Press.

When Not to Schedule Your Doctor Appointment

If you're facing a subtle or potentially serious ailment, you need the doctor's undivided attention. Avoid scheduling your appointments for just before noon or at the end of the day. At those times, your doctor may be distracted by thoughts of getting a bite to eat...or going home.

Source: O.T. Bonnett, MD, a family practitioner in private practice in Raton, New Mexico. He is author of *Confessions of a Healer: The Truth From an Unconventional Family Doctor.* MacMurray & Beck.

Even the Best Medical Labs Make Mistakes

And they can be dangerous—even deadly. The biggest errors occur on routine tests—especially Pap smears and PSA tests (for prostate cancer). If a test comes back negative and you still think something could be wrong—*get retested.* Ask your doctor to send the test to a different lab...or to send it to the same lab but under a different name. *Never* use the doctor's *in-office* lab—their error rates are much higher than commercial lab rates. *Also:* Always make sure the lab your doctor uses is certified by the College of American Pathologists. If you don't trust the lab your doctor uses, ask him/her to use a properly accredited one.

Source: Charles Inlander, president, People's Medical Society, 462 Walnut St., Allentown, PA 18102.

How Not to Overpay For Medical Care

•**Ask your doctor for a discount.** Patients often assume that doctors' fees are set in stone. In fact, many physicians will give a 5% to 15% discount—if you pay the bill directly.

Direct payment eliminates the paperwork hassle that arises when your doctor must interact with your insurer. But you'll never know if your doctor is willing to give a discount if you don't ask. If you submit the bill to your insurance company, make sure it reflects the discounted fee.

For extra leverage: Ask your insurance company what fee is considered "usual and customary" in your part of the country. If your doctor's fees are out of line, point this out to him/her. He may be even more willing to give you a discount.

• **Avoid unnecessary office visits.** If your doctor schedules a follow-up visit only to discuss test results, "see how you're doing," etc., ask if you can phone him instead.

• **Ask that routine exams** be performed by the doctor's assistant. Physicians often perform routine exams, tests and even minor surgical procedures that can be handled just as well—and much less expensively—by a nurse practitioner or a physician's assistant.

If your doctor doesn't have a qualified assistant, consider finding one who does. If you prefer being treated only by the doctor, don't settle for his assistant.

• **Count your pills.** Some medications cost several dollars—per pill. To stretch your prescription dollar, count pills in the bottle as soon as you get home from the drugstore.

If even one pill is missing, call the pharmacist and ask that the extra pill be sent over. If you have a chronic condition, buy prescription drugs in bulk from a mail-order pharmacy.

Caution: Not all insurance prescription plans cover mail-order purchases.

• **Ask your doctor for free samples** of prescription drugs.

• **Avoid hospitalization for minor tests** and surgical procedures. Many matters that used to require a day or more in the hospital can now be taken care of on an outpatient basis...or even in the doctor's office.

Caution: Procedures involving general anesthesia should be done only in the hospital. Complications that sometimes arise when the patient is unconscious can be very difficult to treat outside a hospital.

If hospitalization is required, ask your doctor if blood tests, bacterial cultures, EKGs, etc., can be performed—before your admission—

at a freestanding diagnostic lab. Such labs will routinely charge 40% less than hospitals.

• **Avoid buying toiletries from the hospital.** It is not unusual for hospitals to charge $5 for a toothbrush and similarly exorbitant amounts for water pitchers, drinking glasses, etc. Tell your nurse that you have arranged for a friend or family member to bring you these items. If the nurse objects, ask your doctor to intervene.

• **Scrutinize hospital bills.** Though hospital billing departments don't try to rip patients off, mistakes are common, and they usually favor the hospital.

Typical mistakes: Patients are billed for lab tests that were scheduled but never performed...for medications that were ordered but never dispensed...for tests or procedures that had to be redone because of a hospital staffer's error. Hospitals have even been known to charge parents of baby daughters for circumcisions.

Ask the hospital's billing department to explain any charges you don't understand. If the hospital fails to clear up any problems with your bill, seek help from your state or local consumer affairs department.

Helpful resource: An Austin, Texas-based firm called MedReview (800-397-5359) will double-check your bill. *Fee:* $50 for $1 to $2,500 of hospital charges...$75 for $2,500 to $7,000 of charges...$100 for $7,000 to $10,000 of charges.

Source: Marti Ann Schwartz, author of *Listen To Me, Doctor: Taking Charge Of Your Own Health Care.* Mac-Murray & Beck.

Unqualified Care-Givers Abound

Medical treatment of patients by unqualified health care workers is common. It is especially widespread in hospitals...but it even happens in doctors' offices.

Self-defense questions: What training have you had to perform this procedure? Are you certified in this field? How many times have you done this procedure? How frequently do you do it? Are you a nurse—or a nurse's aide? If you are not satisfied with the answers you hear, ask that someone who is qualified care for you.

Remember: Even noninvasive procedures have risks.

Source: Charles Inlander is president of People's Medical Society, 462 Walnut St., Allentown, PA 18102.

Short Women, Tall Women and Heart Disease

Short women face a greater risk of heart attack than tall women. Recent data from the 35-year-old Framingham Heart Study reveal that the shortest 25% of women had a 72% higher risk than the tallest 25%. No increased risk of heart attack was found in short men, contrary to previous reports.

Source: Daniel Levy, MD, medical director, Framingham Heart Study, Framingham, MA.

Heart Disease in Women

Heart disease kills one out of every two women. Ten times more women die of cardiovascular disease than die of breast cancer. While women are, on average, 10 years older than men when heart disease strikes, it still kills as many women as men.

Source: Liz Applegate, PhD, professor of nutrition, University of California, Davis, writing in *Runner's World,* 33 E. Minor St., Emmaus, PA 18098.

Coronary Artery Disease Kills 250,000 American Women a Year

It accounts for more deaths than cancer, lung disease, AIDS and accidents *combined.*

Source: Hugh C. Smith, MD, professor of medicine, Mayo Graduate School of Medicine, Rochester, Minnesota.

Cholesterol-Lowering Drug and Psyllium

Cholesterol-lowering drug *colestipol* (Colestid) can be used more economically and more effectively when mixed with the natural fiber supplement psyllium. Patients who took half (2.5 g) their usual dosage of colestipol, plus 2.5 g of psyllium, had greater declines in the all-important cholesterol-to-HDL ratio than when they took colestipol alone. Fewer side effects were reported with the mixture, too. Consult your doctor first.

Source: J. David Spence, MD, director, Stroke Prevention and Atherosclerosis Research Centre, Robarts Research Institute, London, Ontario, Canada.

What You May Not Know About High Blood Pressure

More than a third of all Americans have high blood pressure. Yet many people are unaware that high blood pressure—also known as hypertension—can be treated and prevented if caught early enough.

Even people with mild hypertension ignore the problem or fail to spot it quickly through medical checkups.

Danger: By the time hypertension causes medical complications, the heart may have already been damaged.

Here's what you may or may not know about high blood pressure and what you can do to control it…

•**What's normal—and what's not.** Most people have their blood pressure taken when they go in for a checkup every few years. But if your blood pressure rises above 140/90, more frequent readings may be needed.

Less severe high blood pressure or Stage I—from 140/90 to 160/100—can often be managed with lifestyle changes. When blood pressure is consistently higher, medication is usually necessary.

If your blood pressure is normal, it should be checked every two or three years throughout your adult life.

•Being tense or nervous will not give you high blood pressure. The term hypertension refers to elevated pressure in the arteries, not to someone's personality. Many calm, cool-headed people have hypertension…many anxious, jittery people have perfectly normal blood pressures.

Nervousness may cause a short-term rise in blood pressure because of the adrenaline response. But there's no evidence that a nervous personality or even a stress-filled life causes hypertension.

•Blood pressure is variable. Your blood pressure does not remain constant. It can fluctuate by as much as 20 to 30 points a day.

Your blood pressure is at its highest during the early morning hours—just before and as you awaken—and when extra blood is needed, such as when you are exercising.

It is at its lowest during sleep and restful times, dropping to the lowest point from about 1 a.m. to 4 a.m.

•Blood pressure can change with the weather. Generally, your blood pressure drops during hot weather or when you're perspiring a lot. Warm weather causes blood vessels to dilate—and that lowers blood pressure.

In cold weather, blood pressure readings may be raised because blood vessels constrict. Unless weather conditions are extreme, the change isn't enough to be medically significant.

•Excessive alcohol consumption can increase risk. Moderate to heavy drinking—three to five drinks daily—can raise blood pressure over the long term.

Reason: Though large amounts of alcohol may dilate blood vessels, which can lower blood pressure, drinking also increases the heart rate, which raises blood pressure and cancels the dilation effect. Alcohol can also affect certain hormone systems that regulate blood pressure.

Cutting back on alcohol can bring levels to within normal range in some individuals. One or two drinks daily generally do not affect blood pressure, and some researchers have found that small quantities of alcohol can protect against cardiovascular disease.

Treatment:

•Exercise is good—but not all kinds. For some people, mild, repetitive exercise over time helps reduce blood pressure slightly. For others, it reduces levels significantly. It's not necessary to take up jogging or join an exercise club unless you need or prefer a structured plan. Walking or other leisure activities are satisfactory.

Warning: Vigorous isometric (pushing) exercises, like weight lifting (free weights or weight machines), should be avoided by anyone with high blood pressure or heart disease. The tightened muscles constrict blood vessels and can raise blood pressure. Avoid inversion bars and "antigravity boots," from which you hang upside down and do sit-ups. This increases blood pressure levels.

•Losing weight is the most effective non-drug method to reduce high blood pressure. Excess weight increases the volume of blood in the body, constricting blood vessels and putting extra demands on the heart, which elevates blood pressure. In some cases, losing as little as 10 pounds can return blood pressure levels to normal. If you plan to lose a significant amount of weight (more than 30 pounds), ask your doctor to monitor cardiovascular effects.

•Sex will not dramatically affect hypertension. Though sex can raise blood pressure temporarily—particularly with a new or unfamiliar partner—just minutes after the peak at orgasm, it will drop back to levels equivalent to or lower than before.

•Good nutrition can help keep levels in line. Lowering sodium intake helps some people with high blood pressure—about 20% or 30% of all cases. Others are hardly affected at all. Because most of us have too much salt in our diets, it's a good idea to cut back—regardless of your blood pressure readings.

Best way: Be aware of salt in cooking and on the table, as well as hidden sources of sodium. Many processed foods that don't taste salty—soft drinks, ice cream, breakfast cereals—are high in sodium.

Other dietary factors: Both potassium—found in fresh fruits and vegetables, unprocessed meats and fish—and calcium are thought to have protective effects. The minimum daily intake of potassium is 2,000 mg, but 4,000 mg is optimal.

Adequate calcium—800 mg to 1,000 mg a day for adults—rather than high doses is best. Your daily sodium intake should be about half that of potassium.

Source: Marvin Moser, MD, clinical professor of medicine at Yale University School of Medicine, New Haven, CT. He is author of *Lower Your Blood Pressure and Live Longer*, Berkley, and *Week by Week to a Strong Heart*. Avon.

What You Need to Know About High Blood Pressure

High blood pressure is the most overlooked health problem in the US. Only 14 million of the estimated 70 million Americans who have it are getting adequate treatment.

The rest may *feel* fine, but they're at increased risk for stroke, heart attack, kidney failure and other ailments.

To find out more about detecting and treating this "silent killer," we spoke with prominent cardiologist Dr. Vincent Friedewald…

•*When is blood pressure considered high?* Any pressure above 120/80 is high. We used to think that only the second (diastolic) number mattered. Now we know that the first (systolic) reading is important, too.

Hypertension is ranked in stages. *Stage 1:* Systolic 140 to 159, diastolic 90 to 99. *Stage 2:* Systolic 160 to 179, diastolic 100 to 109. *Stage 3:* Systolic 180 to 209, diastolic 110 to 119. *Stage 4:* 210/120 or higher.

•*My blood pressure is only slightly elevated. Is that cause for concern?* Even Stage 1 hypertension can cause serious health problems. I believe that everyone should try to maintain a pressure of 120/80 or lower.

•*What causes high blood pressure?* We don't know the full story. However, blood pressure is a reflection of how hard your heart is pumping…and of the size of your arterioles, special blood vessels that act as gatekeepers between the arteries and the capillaries, the tiniest blood vessels.

Arterioles dilate or narrow according to nerve signals from the brain, which bases its "decisions" on feedback from nerve endings near the heart. These nerve endings constantly monitor your blood pressure.

This feedback loop boosts your pressure when you exercise or undergo psychological stress and lowers it when you're asleep or relaxed.

In hypertension, blood pressure is *consistently* higher than it should be—whether you are stressed or relaxed.

Ninety percent of people with high blood pressure have *primary* (essential) hypertension. This condition seems to be largely hereditary, although excess weight, lack of exercise, high salt intake, alcohol consumption and age can also play a role.

•*What about the other 10% of cases?* They're the result of other ailments—typically kidney disease, thyroid or adrenal gland problems or sleep apnea. Once the underlying disease is diagnosed, blood pressure can usually be controlled.

•*How do I know if I have high blood pressure?* The only way to know is to have a doctor measure it…or buy and use your own blood-pressure monitor. *Cost:* From $25 to $30. Ask your doctor to make sure it's properly calibrated.

A single high reading—especially a diastolic reading above 90 or a systolic reading above 140—may be cause for concern. However, it does not necessarily mean you have hypertension.

A single measurement may not be representative of your blood pressure throughout the day. And about one in five people who visit the doctor exhibit high blood pressure *simply because they're nervous.*

Your doctor must be careful to distinguish real hypertension from this "white-coat" variety. Aggressive treatment of white-coat hypertension can be dangerous.

To tell if your blood pressure is *consistently* high, you must take several readings—preferably over a period of days or weeks.

If you are diagnosed with hypertension, your doctor should follow up with a thorough physical exam. This exam should include an electrocardiogram, a urinalysis and it should also include blood tests for…

- **Glucose**
- **Creatinine**
- **Potassium**
- **Calcium**
- **Blood lipids**
- **Uric acid**
- **Complete blood count**

•*What can I do to lower my blood pressure?* If it's just a bit high, you can probably nudge it down into the safe range by making a few lifestyle changes…

•**Lose weight.** Overweight people who reduce their body weight by 5% to 10% often experience a significant drop in blood pressure.

•**Cut back on alcohol.** Alcohol in any form raises blood pressure. Have no more than one ounce a day—the amount in two beers, a glass of wine or a jigger of whiskey.

•**Exercise more.** Get 30 to 60 minutes every day of moderate activity—walking, jogging, bicycling, etc. Becoming fit can lower your blood pressure by six to seven points.

•**Quit smoking.**

•**Reduce sodium intake.** Some people are salt-sensitive, others aren't. My advice is to stop using a salt shaker…and to avoid processed foods, which account for two-thirds of daily salt intake.

•*Is there any special diet that can help?* In addition to restricting your salt intake, try to eat calcium and potassium-rich foods (especially fruits, grains and vegetables). These minerals promote excretion of sodium.

Being a vegetarian also seems to lower blood pressure. Vegetarians not only eat more fruits and veggies than their meat-eating peers, but are also thinner.

Some people swear by magnesium supplements, fish oil, garlic and other purported pressure-lowering remedies. But there's no hard evidence that these products have any beneficial effect.

•*Does caffeine have any effect on blood pressure?* Yes. Two cups of coffee can boost pressure by 15 points, for up to two hours. But since the effect is transient, I don't normally recommend limiting coffee intake for my hypertensive patients.

•*When is it appropriate to treat hypertension with drugs?* If you're more than a few points above normal, your doctor will probably prescribe antihypertensive medication in *addition* to lifestyle changes.

There is now a wide variety of effective antihypertensives…

•**Diuretics remove sodium and water from the bloodstream**, shrinking blood volume and dilating arteries. Diuretics are especially effective in African-American and elderly individuals…and in individuals whose blood pressure is salt-sensitive.

Diuretics can deplete potassium levels, so any patient taking them should have his/her potassium levels carefully monitored.

•**Beta-blockers** reduce the force of each heartbeat and block the release of hormones that boost blood pressure.

Beta-blockers can cause fatigue, insomnia and sexual problems. They should be avoided by those with asthma or heart failure.

•**A.C.E. inhibitors** slow key chemical interactions in the bloodstream that lead to hypertension. Relatively free of side effects, they can cause coughing and—rarely—swelling of the face and limbs.

•**Calcium-channel blockers** have been in the news recently because one short-acting form of nifedipine (Procardia, Adalat) has been linked to heart attack. Although not all doctors are convinced this study is valid, most now use sustained-release formulations.

Can hypertension be cured? Once you have essential hypertension, the condition never goes away. You'll have to monitor your blood pressure on a regular basis for the rest of your life. However, with a combination of lifestyle changes and well-tailored medication, most people can bring their pressure down to safe levels.

Source: Vincent Friedewald, MD, clinical assistant professor of medicine at Baylor College of Medicine in Houston, and a visiting professor at the University of Notre Dame in Notre Dame, IN. He is the author of *Ask the Doctor: Hypertension.* Andrews and McMeel.

Mostly on a Monday

More strokes occur on Mondays than any other day of the week. *Most common time:* Between 8 am and noon. Working men—but not working women or retired men or women —are more likely to have a Monday stroke. *Least likely day for a stroke:* Sunday.

Source: Study of a 40-year collection of data from more than 5,000 men and women, ages 30 to 62 at the time the study started, led by Margaret Kelly-Hayes, EdD, RN, associate clinical professor of neurology, Boston University School of Medicine, published in *Stroke.*

A Better Way to Shrink An Enlarged Prostate

Once they turn 50, many men notice that they have a weaker or forked stream of urine, dribbling after urination or more frequent urination.

A man experiencing these symptoms is likely to be suffering from enlargement of the prostate, the walnut-sized gland surrounding the urethra. Prostate enlargement—also known as *benign prostatic hypertrophy* (BPH)—can kink the urethra, causing any or all of the above symptoms.

Because these symptoms can also be evidence of prostate cancer, it's smart to have your doctor give you a digital rectal exam—just to make sure. In fact, since some cases of prostate cancer cause no symptoms, it's a good idea for every man over 50 to have an annual prostate exam.

One popular but largely ineffective conventional treatment for BPH is the prescription medication *finasteride* (Proscar). This drug blocks the conversion of testosterone to a more potent form called dihydrotestosterone. After six months or so, finasteride does decrease the size of the prostate. But symptoms usually persist. In addition, though finasteride is reasonably safe, it causes impotence in a small percentage of users.

In a recent study, the drug *terazosin* (Hytrin), which seems to relax the muscle layer in the urethra, was far more effective than finas-

teride. But terazosin often causes low blood pressure. That can lead to dizziness, lightheadedness and heart palpitations.

Doctors commonly treat BPH using a surgical procedure called *transurethral resection of the prostate* (TURP). Unfortunately, TURP can cause incontinence and/or impotence. Just recently, the FDA approved microwave therapy as a treatment for BPH. This therapy has been shown to increase urine flow. It's probably much safer than surgery.

Fortunately, several alternative therapies can control symptoms of BPH without causing side effects. I often prescribe the herb saw palmetto (*Serenoa repens*). Unlike finasteride and terazosin, saw palmetto has no adverse effects. In fact, many herbalists consider it a potent aphrodisiac! The usual dose for the extract is two 80-mg capsules twice a day...or a dropperful of saw palmetto tincture twice a day. (These are available at health-food stores.) Two or three months of treatment may be necessary before you see an effect.

Nutritional supplements can also help control BPH. Zinc (45 to 60 mg a day) is particularly important. However, zinc can deplete copper levels. If you take zinc for more than a month, 1 to 2 mg of copper should also be taken daily, preferably not at the same time as the zinc.

I also recommend vitamin B-6 (50 to 100 mg a day) to my patients with BPH. It's best to take a B-complex vitamin containing this dose.

Essential fatty acids may also be helpful, so consider adding flaxseed (linseed) oil, sunflower oil or soy oil to your diet. A teaspoon a day is all you need. In fact, simply making salad dressing with one of these tasty oils is more than sufficient.

Another source of essential fatty acids is evening primrose oil. Two 500-mg capsules a day is adequate.

Although it's okay to combine any or all of these therapies, I prefer using the saw palmetto alone for eight weeks. That may be all that's needed. If symptoms persist, I would add the nutritional supplements.

Source: Adriane Fugh-Berman, MD, a Washington, DC-based medical researcher who specializes in women's health and alternative medicine. She is the author of *Alternative Medicine: What Works.* Odonion Press.

Test for Prostate Cancer

The usual test for prostate cancer isn't always reliable. In a recent study, the prostate-specific antigen (PSA) blood test gave 65% false positive and 20% false negative results. In other words, almost two-thirds of those who tested positive for cancer turned out to be cancer-free (following a biopsy). One-fifth of those who tested negative actually had cancer. *Coming:* New "free PSA" test yields fewer false positives, eliminating up to 76% of unnecessary biopsies.

Source: William J. Catalona, MD, chief, division of urology, Washington University School of Medicine, St. Louis.

Prostate Disease News

Men suffering from enlarged prostate should not rush to change medication based on the recently publicized study claiming one treatment (Hytrin) is superior to another (Proscar).

Reality: The two drugs work differently. Hytrin relaxes the muscle surrounding the prostate, reducing discomfort. Proscar shrinks the prostate but does not affect muscle tone and may not relieve the voiding discomfort immediately. Both drugs are well-tolerated, and most sufferers would benefit from either one or a combination of the two. *Note:* After age 50, most men have enlarged prostates.

Source: Steven Berman, MD, is assistant professor of urology, Beth Israel Medical Center, and a urologist in private practice in New York.

Melanoma is 5% to 10% Deadlier in Men Than in Women

Possible explanation: In women, melanoma tends to develop on the arms or legs, where it's easier to recognize. In men, melanomas tend to develop on the trunk, which is more often covered. *Also:* Women are quicker to see a doc-

tor when they notice a suspicious lesion. Men often wait until the lesion is larger or even ulcerated—and harder to treat. Hormonal differences between the sexes may also play a role.

Source: Perry Robins, MD, associate professor of dermatology, New York University Medical Center, New York City, and president, Skin Cancer Foundation, 245 Fifth Ave., New York 10016.

How Not to Get Alzheimer's

Alzheimer's disease—the most common cause of progressive deterioration of mental function—now afflicts four million Americans.

The latest on this devastating illness…

•*What causes Alzheimer's?* There are several theories. Two of the most widely circulated ones, however, have been largely debunked…

•**Aluminum.** Though high levels of aluminum are often found in the brains of Alzheimer's patients, there is no evidence that this metal causes the disease. It is safe to use aluminum pans and to drink from aluminum cans.

•**Zinc.** As with aluminum, there is insufficient evidence to indicate that an excess of dietary zinc causes Alzheimer's. But one recent study *did* find a link between zinc and the clumping of proteins in the brain, a condition associated with Alzheimer's.

In light of this study, I think it's prudent to stick to federal guidelines for daily zinc consumption—15 mg for men and 12 mg for women.

•*If aluminum and zinc aren't the problem, what is?* Heredity may be to blame. Researchers have identified several different genes for Alzheimer's, including three that cause the form that strikes before age 65.

Researchers have also found a gene that produces a protein called *APOE4*. A study published recently in *The Lancet* suggests that if you inherit a copy of this gene from one parent, you have a 35% chance of developing Alzheimer's by age 90.

•*Is heredity the sole cause of Alzheimer's?* No. Recent studies suggest that some cases of Alzheimer's are associated with…

• **Head trauma.** A history of head injury doubles the chance that you'll get Alzheimer's. Thus it's vitally important to use seat belts, purchase a car with airbags and wear a helmet when riding a motorcycle (or—better—avoid motorcycles entirely). It's also a good idea to avoid boxing and other sports that can lead to head trauma.

• **Head circumference.** Researchers found recently that people who get Alzheimer's tend to have smaller heads than those who don't. If this provocative finding is confirmed, doctors may someday be able to assess a patient's risk by measuring his/her head circumference and other risk factors.

• **Education.** Alzheimer's patients tend to have less formal education than those without the disease. Formal education may delay the onset of the disease by four to five years.

• *How is Alzheimer's diagnosed?* No single test can diagnose Alzheimer's with absolute certainty. Doctors make a probable diagnosis on the basis of physical, psychological and neurological exams.

First, we perform lab tests to rule out other possible causes of dementia. The list of dementia-causing ailments includes stroke, thyroid disease, liver and kidney disease, vitamin deficiency, depression and long-term use of tranquilizers, antiulcer agents, antihypertensives and heart medications.

If you must take one or more of these drugs, make sure your doctor has prescribed the lowest effective dose.

Next, we observe the patient for signs that the dementia is progressing slowly. Rapidly progressing dementia usually suggests a problem other than Alzheimer's.

Finally, we look for memory loss *plus* impairment in one or more areas of mental functioning, such as language, visual perception and the performance of everyday tasks. Alzheimer's involves a *combination* of deficits.

• *How can I assess my risk of developing Alzheimer's?* Two experimental tests that have been in the news recently are the…

• **Eyedrop test.** The patient's eyes are dilated with eyedrops. In individuals with Alzheimer's (or a predisposition to Alzheimer's), the drops cause the pupils to dilate significantly wider than in people who face little risk of the disease.

Problem: Not everyone with Alzheimer's has dilated pupils after getting the drops…and many people without Alzheimer's do.

• **APOE4 test.** Using this blood test, doctors can determine if you have inherited one or more copies of the Alzheimer's gene.

I'm not recommending this test for my patients—even those with symptoms or a family history of Alzheimer's. All it can tell you is that if you inherit two copies of the gene, you're 2.5 times more likely to get Alzheimer's than someone who has not inherited this gene.

The real question, of course, is why anyone would want to know his risk of Alzheimer's—since there remains no effective means of preventing the disease.

• *What can I do to lower my risk?* Alzheimer's risk appears to be lower among people who take aspirin, ibuprofen or another non-steroidal anti-inflammatory drug on a regular basis.

For postmenopausal women, estrogen-replacement therapy (ERT) seems to reduce the risk of the disease by almost half—or at least delay its onset.

• *I read that mental activity helps prevent Alzheimer's. Is that true?* We don't know that for sure, but I encourage my friends, family and patients to stay mentally—and physically—active, just in case.

Reading, doing crossword puzzles or engaging in other mentally demanding activities stimulates your brain cells. This may enhance connections between the cells, slowing the rate of age-associated memory loss.

• *What about "smart foods" and "smart drugs?"* Some people have started taking so-called cognition-enhancers— drugs and nutrients such as deprenyl, DHEA, ginkgo biloba and acetyl-l-carnitine. Unfortunately, there is no substantial evidence that these agents prevent Alzheimer's.

• *What's the best treatment for Alzheimer's disease?* At present, the only treatment is the prescription drug tacrine (Cognex).

Tacrine is by no means a cure. But tests have shown that it improves learning and recall in

20% to 40% of patients with mild to moderate disease.

Unfortunately, tacrine becomes less effective after six months of use. The drug may also cause liver toxicity, so its use must be closely monitored.

Source: Peter V. Rabins, MD, MPH, professor of psychiatry at Johns Hopkins University School of Medicine, Baltimore. He is coauthor of *The 36-Hour Day* (Warner Books), a guide for Alzheimer's caregivers. Contact the Alzheimer's Association (800-272-3900) for more information. If you're caring for an Alzheimer's patient who is taking tacrine, the Alzheimer's FamilyCare line (800-600-1600) is a helpful resource.

Alzheimer's Disease Update

Separate studies have shown that use of nonsteroidal anti-inflammatory drugs and estrogen supplements seems to delay the onset of Alzheimer's symptoms. *Also:* Those who have higher levels of education and intellectually demanding jobs develop symptoms much later in life. *Smart for everyone:* Keep your mind sharp. Use it in new ways—solve puzzles, learn a foreign language, etc.—in order to increase the number of connections in the brain. These exercises can help you maintain brain function if you ever develop Alzheimer's disease.

Source: Zaven Khachaturian, PhD, director, Office of Alzheimer's Disease Research, National Institutes of Health, Bethesda, MD.

Bee Sting First Aid

Remove the stinger if it is visible by scraping gently with a butter knife or credit card. Do not squeeze the area and pull with tweezers or fingers—that can release more venom.

After removing the stinger, wash the area with soap and water and apply a cold pack to reduce pain and swelling.

Though rare, serious allergic reactions to bee stings occur within minutes. If the person who has been stung collapses, develops hives or swollen lips or eyes or has trouble breathing, call 911 immediately.

Source: Recommendations from the American Academy of Allergy, Asthma and Immunology, 611 E. Wells, Milwaukee 53202.

Five-Minute Energy Boosters

Call a friend on the phone to chat. Do a yoga stretch. Look at the sky. Look at family pictures. Pet a cat or dog. Browse through travel magazines. Visualize being at the beach or in the mountains. Wash your face. Plan an after-work treat. Sing. Watch tropical fish.

Source: Marcia Yudkin, PhD, editor, *The Creative Glow*, Box 1310, Boston 02117.

Prostate Cancer Is Usually Curable

Prostate cancer is usually curable. About 90% of men who are diagnosed with prostate cancer before it has spread beyond the prostate gland—and who are then treated surgically—can expect to live at least another 15 years.

Source: American Institute for Cancer Research, Washington, DC.

How to Cut Your Risk of Cancer by 50%

If you think cancer rates have fallen in recent years, think again. Between 1973 and 1991, US cancer incidence rose 19% in men and 12% in women.

Cancer strikes roughly two of every five Americans—and kills more than 500,000 Americans a year. These numbers are especially tragic, because most cases of cancer are avoidable.

We all know how important it is to avoid smoking...wear sunscreen...and drink moder-

ately, if at all. But these are just three of many anti-cancer strategies. *Other vital precautions...*
Eat much less fat:

A high-fat diet has been linked to cancer of the colon, breast, prostate, ovary, uterus and skin. But casual attempts to limit your fat intake aren't enough.

To really reduce your risk, bring your fat intake to no more than 20% of total calories (instead of the 35% to 40% that's typical of most Americans).

Get into the habit of choosing low-fat or nonfat salad dressings, sauces and spreads. Give up high-fat dishes. If you must eat chips, cookies, etc., look for nonfat versions.
Eat more fiber:

Dietary fiber—the component of fruits, vegetables and grains that passes undigested through the body—helps prevent colorectal and other gastrointestinal tract cancers.

Other studies suggest that fiber may lower the risk of breast cancer as well.

Aim for 25 grams of fiber a day. Start each day with a breakfast cereal that has eight to nine grams of fiber per serving. *Other fiber-rich foods:* Whole-grain bread (4 g a slice)...pear (4 g) ...mango (3.7 g)...black beans (15 g a cup).
Eat more fruits & vegetables:

Individuals who eat five to nine servings of plant foods a day have half the cancer risk of those who eat few fruits and vegetables. (One serving equals one-half cup of cooked vegetables, or a medium-sized apple, orange or banana.)

In addition to being full of fiber, fruits and vegetables contain potent anti-cancer compounds. The best-known of these compounds are vitamins C and E and beta-carotene. These antioxidants protect the body against free radicals, unstable molecules that turn normal cells cancerous.

Fruits and vegetables also contain a family of anti-cancer compounds called phytochemicals. Chief among these are sulforaphane (found in broccoli, cabbage and other cruciferous vegetables) and allyl sulfides (found in garlic and onion).

Important: Vitamin supplements do not contain these vital cancer fighters.

Avoid pesticide residues:

Although pesticides pose a lesser threat than cigarette smoke and other carcinogens, they are believed to be responsible for 20,000 cases of cancer a year.

Self-defense: Carefully wash all fruits and vegetables with warm, soapy water. Buy organic produce whenever possible.
Be physically active:

There's growing evidence that exercise helps prevent cancer. A recent Harvard study showed that physically active individuals have only 30% to 80% the usual risk of colorectal cancer.

Incorporate physical activity in all aspects of your life. Take stairs instead of elevators... walk to the supermarket...bike to work.

It's also good to participate in formal exercise, such as jogging, biking, etc. *Ideal:* Thirty minutes at a time, four times a week.
Stay slim:

A recent *New England Journal of Medicine study* confirms what doctors had long suspected—that even moderate weight gain increases the risk of endometrial cancer and breast cancer...and possibly colon cancer.

Self-defense: Eat healthfully and get regular exercise...and consult a dietician or weight-control specialist if you find yourself getting fat.
Practice safe sex:

While cancer isn't transmitted sexually, some sexually transmitted diseases are associated with an increased risk of cancer.

To avoid nasty germs, limit your number of sex partners. Always use a latex condom unless you are certain that both you and your partner are disease-free and monogamous.
Reduce psychological stress:

While there is no direct evidence that stress causes cancer, it's prudent to include stress-reduction techniques as part of your cancer-prevention program.

Excessive stress impairs immune function, thereby permitting cancer cells to survive...and leads people to adopt unsafe health practices.

One of the easiest and most powerful stress-reduction techniques is creative visualization.

What to do: Sit comfortably in a quiet, dimly lit room. Close your eyes. Take three deep breaths. Tense and release your muscles from head to toe. Envision yourself in a mountain meadow, a lush valley or another soothing landscape. Don't just see yourself there. Try to conjure up sounds, odors, etc.

Have regular screening tests:

Successful treatment for cancer depends on early diagnosis…and the best way to catch cancer in its earliest stages is via regular screening exams. Here are the most important ones…

•**Breast cancer.** Women should perform a self-examination of their breasts once every month and have a doctor-performed exam at least once a year. *Over 50:* Have a yearly mammogram.

•**Cervical cancer.** Women should have an annual Pap smear and pelvic exam.

•**Testicular cancer.** Men should check their testicles monthly. A doctor can show you how.

•**Prostate cancer.** Men over 50 should have a digital rectal exam (DRE) and a prostate specific antigen (PSA) test annually.

•**Skin cancer.** Men and women over 40 should have an annual full-body skin examination, performed by a doctor.

•**Colorectal cancer.** Men and women over 50 should have an annual DRE and an annual blood-in-stool test, with a sigmoidoscopy (examination of the lower bowel) every three years.

Know your family tree:

An individual's susceptibility to many forms of cancer appears to be at least partially hereditary.

You cannot change your genes, but if cancer runs in your family, you can design a personal prevention program that involves more intensive screening.

If your father developed colon cancer at 47, for example, you might get your first sigmoidoscopy in your late 30s.

Helpful: Chart your family tree, including grandparents, parents, aunts, uncles and first cousins. Indicate which relatives developed cancer, and at what age. Discuss this chart with your doctor, and work out a screening schedule that's right for you.

The question of asprin:

Recently, a large, well-designed study found that a single aspirin taken every other day reduces the incidence of colorectal cancer by 50%. If colon cancer runs in your family, ask your doctor whether aspirin therapy makes sense for you.

Source: Moshe Shike, MD, director of clinical nutrition at Memorial Sloan-Kettering Cancer Center, and professor of medicine at Cornell University Medical Center, both in New York City. He is coauthor of *Cancer Free: The Comprehensive Cancer Prevention Program.* Simon & Schuster.

Treating Hypertension

Hypertension for people older than age 65 remains a treatable problem. People older than 65 whose hypertension was treated with drugs had 33% fewer strokes and 25% fewer fatal heart attacks than those who were not treated.

Important: Price-shopping for medication. In one city, prices for a 30-day supply of one commonly prescribed antihypertensive ranged from $10 to $68.

Source: Henry Sacks, MD, PhD, director of the clinical trials unit, Mount Sinai School of Medicine, New York. Compilation of results from studies of more than 15,000 people aged 60 or older, conducted by researchers at Mount Sinai School of Medicine, Harvard School of Public Health and the New England Medical Center.

Calcium Channel Blockers And Hypertension

Inexpensive diuretics are often just as effective at controlling high blood pressure as calcium channel blockers and other newer, more costly—and dangerous—antihypertensive drugs. Yet doctors are prescribing the new drugs more and more often. In 1982, 59% of all antihypertensive drugs prescribed were diuretics. That proportion fell to 33% in 1988. Diuretics cost as little as $5 a year. New antihypertensives can cost up to $1,400 a year.

Source: Mark Monane, MD, associate physician in gerontology, Brigham and Women's Hospital, Boston.

Cholesterol Tests Vary

Cholesterol tests can vary from day to day by as much as 16%. Factors affecting results include illness and pregnancy.

Helpful: Have your doctor perform two or more tests before you make any major lifestyle changes.

Important: Cholesterol testing should include a de-termination of your HDL ratio—the ratio of total cholesterol to HDL ("good") cholesterol. A healthy ratio is *under four*. This measure is a much better predictor of heart disease risk than overall cholesterol readings.

Source: Glen Griffin, MD, former primary care physician who now writes and lectures on following a low-fat diet and coauthor of *Good Fat, Bad Fat: How to Lower Your Cholesterol and Beat the Odds of a Heart Attack.* Fisher Books.

Don't Let Bowel Trouble Ruin Your Life

If you're experiencing abdominal pain, constipation, diarrhea, flatulence, nausea and/or loss of appetite, you may have irritable bowel syndrome (IBS).

IBS—also known as nervous indigestion and spastic colon—is a vague label for a very common ailment. While not dangerous, IBS can cause considerable discomfort—and disrupt your lifestyle. Some IBS sufferers are so afraid of venturing too far from a bathroom that they spend almost all of their time at home.

IBS symptoms are similar to those of other disorders (including a serious condition known as Crohn's disease). Don't make the mistake of self-treating the problem. Have your symptoms checked by a doctor. He/she should take a thorough medical history…and may want to check your stool for parasites or use a flexible viewing scope called a sigmoidoscope to examine your large intestine.

Many cases of IBS seem to benefit from the addition of fiber to the diet. Ask your doctor about taking daily doses of the herb psyllium. Powdered psyllium, sold under the brand names Metamucil, Fiberall, etc., is a "bulking" agent. It absorbs water from the intestine, promoting larger stools and helping bowel function return to normal. The easiest way to take psyllium is to stir a dose into a cold beverage. Drink it quickly—or you'll have a glass full of unappetizing slime.

Caution: Too much psyllium can cause intestinal gas, bloating or even diarrhea. Start with a half-teaspoon a day, then work up to one or two teaspoons. If symptoms worsen, lower the dose.

Another effective remedy for IBS is peppermint. An anti-spasmodic, peppermint relaxes the intestinal muscle, helping to relieve cramps. It is available in drugstores and health-food stores.

Peppermint tea works well. *Even more effective:* Peppermint oil capsules—especially enteric-coated ones. They dissolve in the intestine where the problem occurs, rather than in the stomach.

Consider taking one to three peppermint capsules three times a day, between meals. If a burning sensation occurs while defecating, lower the dose or try another intestine-soothing herb, such as chamomile, lemon balm or ginger.

A tea or infusion (tea that has been steeped for about 30 minutes) made from any of these herbs can be very effective. A teacupful three times a day, before meals, should do the trick.

Some IBS sufferers get relief simply by steering clear of certain "trigger" foods, such as wheat and milk. To identify the culprits, avoid any suspect food that you normally eat for three full weeks. Then eat a lot of that food in one day. See if your symptoms get worse.

Don't ignore the psychological aspects of IBS. Many cases seem to go hand in hand with anxiety and/or depression, so stress-reduction techniques may prove helpful. Try meditation, relaxation training, yoga, massage or any other drug-free activity that you find relaxing. Exercise is an excellent stress-reducer.

If symptoms persist, your doctor may prescribe an antispasmodic drug called Bentyl and/or the antidiarrhea drug Lomotil. But these drugs are appropriate only if all the nondrug remedies have failed. Given my experience treating IBS, I think that's unlikely.

Source: Adriane Fugh-Berman, MD, Washington, DC-based medical researcher who specializes in both women's health and alternative medicine. Her articles have appeared in *The New England Journal of Medicine, The Lancet* and other leading medical journals.

Rodent Danger

Hantavirus, which causes the respiratory illness that claimed several lives, is thought to spread via inhalation of tiny particles of rodent droppings.

Self-defense: If you see signs of rodent infestation in storage rooms, cabins, etc., don't vacuum or sweep the floor. That can stir up feces-laden dust. *Better:* Don work gloves and a filter mask, then sprinkle or spray the floor with a mixture of bleach and water. Sweep the mess into a plastic bag, then dispose.

Source: Bruno Chomel, DVM, PhD, assistant professor of population health and reproduction, School of Veterinary Medicine, University of California, Davis.

Avoid Covering Coughs With Your Bare Hands

Germs and viruses cling to bare skin…so muffling coughs or sneezes with your hand makes it more likely that you will pass your germs along to others. *Better:* Sneeze into your elbow…or use a tissue to cover up—then throw it away immediately and wash your hands. In addition, when you feel a cough or sneeze coming on, turn your head away or look down before you sneeze.

Source: Charles Inlander, president, People's Medical Society, Allentown, Pennsylvania and author of *77 Ways to Beat Colds and Flu.* Walker & Co.

Treatments for Common Winter Ailments

Spending more time indoors with others during the winter raises your risk of coming down with an illness. For anything worse than a cold or mild bronchitis, see your doctor.

Problem	Symptoms	Treatments
Bronchitis	Heavy cough, low-grade fever.	Antibiotics are useless for viral variety, but of marginal benefit for bacterial. If cough is dry, suppressants such as dextromethorphan or codeine (by prescription) are useful.
Cold	Low-grade fever, mild muscle aches, runny nose, sore throat, cough.	Rest, lots of noncaffeinated beverages, pain relievers, such as acetaminophen. Avoid multisymptom cold remedies. Vitamin C may reduce symptoms. Antibiotics are useless.
Ear infections	Fever and constant ear pain—often worse on one side.	Antibiotics such as amoxicillin or trimethoprim/sulfa (sold as Bactrim or Septra), pain relievers, decongestants.
Influenza	Similar to common cold. With fever greater than 101° F, headaches, severe muscle aches, chills.	Rest, fluids, pain relievers. If caught in the first two days, prescription drugs such as amantadine can help. Regular antibiotics are useless.
Sinus infections	Constant pain in the face, eyes or upper teeth, fever and/or thick nasal discharge.	Same as ear infections.
Strep throat	Severe sore throat with white spots on tonsils, fever and swollen glands in front of neck.	Penicillin, if not allergic. Need to take for 10 days even if feeling better. Pain relievers, salt-water gargles, throat lozenges or hard candy are helpful.

Source: Timothy McCall, MD, an internist practicing in the Boston area. He is author of *Examining Your Doctor: A Patient's Guide to Avoiding Harmful Medical Care.* Birch Lane Press.

Do You Need a Pneumonia Vaccine?

The pneumonia vaccine is often as important as the flu vaccine. Unlike the flu vaccine, which must be given annually, the pneumonia vaccine is usually given only once.

Important: Anyone over age 65—or younger people with conditions such as diabetes, cancer, or kidney, heart or lung disease —should be vaccinated.

Urgent: Increasing resistance of pneumococcal bacteria to penicillin and other antibiotics makes this vaccine even more important.

Source: Timothy McCall, MD, internist practicing in the Boston area. He is author of *Examining Your Doctor: A Patient's Guide to Avoiding Harmful Medical Care.* Birch Lane Press.

Whooping Cough in Adults

Adults can get whooping cough—usually thought of as a childhood disease. Symptoms in adults mimic those of bronchitis or a cold, but the distinctive severe coughing fits with whooping sounds are usually not present. Currently available vaccines do not help adults. Childhood vaccines wear off by the time you reach your teenage years, and adults do not tolerate boosters well so they are not given.

Self-defense: See your doctor for any cough that lasts more than one week. Whooping cough is not usually dangerous to adults, but it can last for months and can often be highly contagious.

Source: Seth Wright, MD, director of research, department of emergency medicine, Vanderbilt University, Nashville.

Antacid Tablets Work Better than Liquids

Antacid *tablets* work better than antacid *liquids.* Researchers compared Tums E-X and Mylanta Double Strength tablets with the liquid antacids Mylanta II and Extra Strength Maalox. *Result:* The tablets were more effective at controlling heartburn and acid reflux. *Theory:* When chewed, tablets mix with saliva to create a protective film that adheres to the esophagus longer than swallowed liquids do. *Also:* Chew-

ing promotes production of saliva, which contains natural acid-fighting substances.

Source: Malcolm Robinson, MD, clinical professor of medicine, University of Oklahoma, Oklahoma City. His study of 65 heartburn sufferers was published in *Gastroenterology,* American Gastroenterology Association, 7910 Woodmont Ave., 7th Floor, Bethesda, MD 20814.

Snoring... Stopping the Din Just Might Save Your Life

The nightly din of snorers can drive spouses to distraction—not to mention separate sleeping quarters. That can cause relationship problems. Especially loud snoring can repeatedly wake the snorer himself, causing chronic daytime sleepiness.

Even scarier, snoring is sometimes symptomatic of *sleep apnea,* a condition linked to stroke and heart attack.

Why you snore:

During sleep, all your muscles relax deeply, including those surrounding the airway at the back of the throat.

In snorers, the airway partially collapses, becoming so narrow that it vibrates with each breath.

True to the stereotype, men are more likely to snore than women. Older men are more prone to snoring than younger men.

Obesity tends to promote snoring, too, particularly when excess weight in the neck compresses the airway.

Remedies that *don't* work:

Over the years, the problem of snoring has spawned a host of solutions, both high and low tech. Most are of dubious value.

Most recently, snorers have worn a Breathe Right nasal dilator while sleeping. This bandage-like device widens the nostrils and seems to reduce snoring—but only temporarily.

Another approach is to wear pajamas with a tennis ball sewn into the back—to keep the sleeper from lying on his back. While this strategy appears to work in the short term, its long-term effectiveness is unknown.

Some snorers have tried special pillows that change the position of the neck to keep the head extended. While it stands to reason that extending the neck would widen the airway (and thus reduce snoring), no studies have shown this to work, either.

A recent addition to the anti-snore arsenal is an electronic wrist alarm. Whenever it detects snoring, it gently vibrates to signal the snorer to change position.

If this gadget really works—it hasn't yet been proven—the cure could be worse than the disease. It would interrupt sleep that's already disturbed.

Remedies that do work:

Two approaches *have* been shown safe and effective in reducing snoring. Because of their relatively high cost, they're generally used only when the problem becomes intolerable.

•**Intraoral device.** This molded plastic and metal mouthpiece, placed in the mouth over the lower teeth, pulls the jaw forward to enlarge the airway during sleep. It must be custom-fitted by a dentist. Cost: $600 to $800.

•**Surgery.** In a procedure known as *uvulopalatopharyngoplasty* (UPP), the surgeon removes excess soft tissue from the back of the throat. This procedure brings substantial relief from snoring in nine out of 10 cases.

Originally, this procedure was done with a scalpel, under general anesthetic in a hospital operating room. In the last few years, doctors have begun to use a laser.

Advantage: Laser uvuloplasty requires neither general anesthesia nor hospitalization. *Cost:* $2,000 to $2,500.

Downside: Postsurgical pain can be considerable, and the removal of soft tissue may give your voice a slightly nasal sound.

When snoring is serious:

In some sleepers, the airway collapses altogether, stopping normal respiration. Most people with this condition, known as sleep apnea, exhibit a distinctive pattern—loud, habitual snoring, followed by a brief period of silence. Deprived of oxygen, the sleeper awakens and, with a gasp and a snort, resumes breathing. Typically, he falls back to sleep within a few seconds.

In severe cases, this cycle recurs up to 80 times an hour.

The consequences of untreated sleep apnea can be serious indeed. Sleep is severely disturbed, night after night. This can leave you feeling drowsy during the day. Daytime drowsiness hampers your ability to concentrate. It also raises your risk of having an automobile accident up to sevenfold.

And because the cycle of suffocation causes enormous surges in blood pressure, people with apnea have an increased risk for stroke and heart attack.

Key risk factor: Obesity. A snorer whose neck size is 17 or larger has a one in three chance of having sleep apnea.

Getting help for apena:

If you snore loudly—particularly if your bed partner notices the "gasping" pattern—see a sleep specialist. He/she may recommend that you be evaluated in a sleep laboratory, where your sleep pattern and blood oxygen level can be monitored.

In some cases, sleep apnea can be controlled by losing weight. If weight loss doesn't help, ask your doctor about *continuous positive airway pressure* (CPAP).

Patients being treated with CPAP wear a face mask that's hooked up to a small air compressor. The mask feeds a constant stream of pressurized air through your nose, helping to keep the airway open.

About 60% of people can use the device comfortably for relief of symptoms. *Cost:* About $1,200.

When CPAP fails, surgery to enlarge the airway may be necessary. This involves repositioning the jaw or the hyoid bone (located in the neck below the tongue).

Source: Allan I. Pack, MD, professor of medicine and director of the Center for Sleep and Respiratory Neurobiology at the University of Pennsylvania, Philadelphia. He is also the medical director of the National Sleep Foundation, 1367 Connecticut Ave. NW, Suite 200, Washington, DC 20036.

Dishcloths and Sponges Are Bacteria-Ridden

Dishcloths and kitchen sponges are often infected with *salmonella, staphylococcus* and other disease-causing germs.

Self-defense: Replace rags and sponges with paper towels. Or use a germ-resistant sponge such as O-Cel-O brand and wash it in hot water after each use. And be sure to wash your hands with an antibacterial soap after handling uncooked meat.

Good news: Adopting these simple strategies could prevent 90% of all food-borne illness.

Source: Charles Gerba, PhD, professor of microbiology, University of Arizona, Tucson.

Bacteria Thrive in the Cleanest Kitchens

Self-defense: Clean cutting boards thoroughly after each use with hot soapy water…sanitize sponges by running them through the washing machine frequently—and replace them every few weeks…wash manual can openers after each use…wipe counters and appliances often with a sanitizing solution of one quart water and one teaspoon chlorine bleach.

Source: Bessie Berry, acting director of the Meat and Poultry Hotline, US Department of Agriculture, Washington, DC.

Secrets of a Better Night's Sleep

Things to avoid before going to bed…
• **Alcohol.** Its sleep-inducing effect is short-lived, and it can make you wake in the early morning hours.
• **Spicy foods.** They can cause stomach upset.
• **Excessive liquids.** They can cause a need

to urinate that can wake you during the night.
• **Anger.** Going to bed mad can interfere with a good night's sleep.
• **Anxiety.** Plan the next day before going to bed so thoughts don't keep you awake.
• **Smoking.** Nicotine dependence is linked to depression, which results in insomnia and other sleep disorders.

Helpful: Smells of lavender, spiced apples and the seashore lower stress levels and can help many people sleep.

Source: Peter Tanzer, MD, clinical assistant professor of medicine, University of Pittsburgh School of Medicine. He is author of *The Doctor's Guide for Sleep Without Pills.* Tresco Publishers.

Ways to Improve Your Mood

Exercising is the best way to improve your mood. *Other ways to cheer yourself up:* Listen to music, read, talk to friends or do chores.

Source: Robert Thayer, PhD, professor of psychology, California State University, Long Beach.

All About Tinnitus

Tinnitus…ringing in the ears…takes various forms. Sometimes continuous and sometimes intermittent, it can sound like hissing…humming…buzzing…or even a roar that makes sufferers feel as if they have an ocean sloshing around in their heads.

Between 20% and 30% of the population—40 to 70 million Americans—experiences tinnitus at one time or another. It's especially common in persons over age 50.

The precise cause of tinnitus is often hard to pinpoint. Many cases seem to involve the gradual deterioration of the cilia, tiny hair-like structures in the inner ear that turn sound waves into nerve impulses.

As your sensitivity to external noises declines, the cilia become sensitive to internally generated sounds—such as those produced by the circulatory system or jaw muscles.

Caution: While tinnitus is usually benign, it can be a manifestation of a serious medical problem. See a doctor to rule out leaky heart valves…high blood pressure…narrowed arteries in the neck…aneurysms…and other causes.

Your doctor will want to know when your tinnitus started…how long each episode lasts …how often you suffer from it…whether it's in one ear or both…and whether the ringing pulses in time with your heartbeat. A pulsing tinnitus may be related to a circulatory disorder.

Your doctor should also ask about…

•**Allergies.** Some cases of tinnitus are caused by breathing obstructions or blockages in your ear canal.

•**Family history.** If any family member suffered from deafness or another hearing disorder, odds are you will, too.

•**Exposure to loud noises.** Working in a noisy environment without ear protection can cause deafness and tinnitus.

•**Medications.** Many drugs can trigger tinnitus, including aminoglycosides, used to treat infections…loop diuretics, for congestive heart failure…cisplatin, a chemotherapy agent…nonsteroidal anti-inflammatory drugs (NSAIDs) …tricyclic antidepressants…quinine, used for cramps…antimalaria agents…and even plain, old aspirin.

Other triggers:

Your doctor should examine your ears, nose and throat carefully. Tinnitus can be caused by impacted earwax, fluid in the ear, infections or a hole in the eardrum.

He/she should check you for a clicking in the jaw…and use a stethoscope to see if a blockage or narrowing is causing a "hum" in your circulatory system—or if you have a leaky heart valve. In the latter case, you'll probably need to have an echocardiogram.

If earwax is the culprit, your doctor can remove it…or you can extract it yourself using an over-the-counter wax-removal kit. Do not insert a cotton swab in your ear. It can push the wax in deeper.

Hearing tests should also be conducted by an audiologist. In most cases, these tests show that tinnitus is linked to hearing loss. Depending upon your medical history and the findings of these tests, you may need to undergo magnetic resonance imaging (MRI) to check for evidence of brain tumor, aneurysm or stroke damage.

Lab tests:

Several lab tests can be helpful in pinpointing the problem…

•**Blood count.** Some cases of tinnitus are caused by anemia or infections.

•**Cholesterol level.** High levels suggest that you may have blocked arteries.

•**Thyroid function test.** An overactive or underactive thyroid can cause ringing in the ears.

•**Sedimentation rate.** An elevated value may reflect inflammation or infection, either of which might cause tinnitus.

Preventing tinnitus:

The best way to prevent tinnitus is to avoid loud noise—especially amplified music at concerts or from powerful stereo systems.

If you're frequently exposed to loud noises at work or at home, buy a pair of ear muffs like those used at shooting ranges. Wear them religiously.

Rule: Any sound loud enough to cause pain is loud enough to cause tinnitus and/or deafness.

The role of emotions:

Tinnitus is sometimes linked to chronic anxiety and/or depression—although it's unclear whether these emotional states cause the condition or merely accompany it.

Recent research shows that relaxation techniques like meditation and yoga are helpful in preventing tinnitus. For those already bothered by ringing in the ears, transcendental meditation and biofeedback sometimes help.

In biofeedback, patients use special equipment to monitor their pulse rate and blood pressure—then use breathing and muscle relaxation techniques to control these functions. This is done under the guidance of a licensed psychotherapist or psychologist. For maximum benefit, you'll probably need six to 10 sessions over the course of eight weeks.

Hearing aids and masking devices:

Some tinnitus sufferers get significant relief from hearing aids and masking devices that produce "white" noise (the sound of static).

Occasionally, people get relief simply by tuning a radio between stations.

Sound maskers are tuned by an audiologist to produce noise that is identical to the ringing in your ears. Playing a tuned masker at low volume helps make tinnitus less annoying.

If your doctor or audiologist recommends a hearing aid, get one—and use it. *Reason:* Since tinnitus often accompanies progressive deafness, boosting the volume of voices and background sounds may help cover up a ringing in the ears. Used in combination with a sound masker, a hearing aid can also help tinnitus sufferers sleep.

If your doctor cannot pinpoint the cause of your tinnitus, ask him about antidepressants. Taken in the doses used to treat depression, these medications sometimes cause tinnitus. However, when taken in minuscule amounts, they often relieve the problem.

Often helpful: The benzodiazepines alprazolam and oxazepam...the anticonvulsant carbmazepine...and the tricyclic nortriptyline.

Source: Jerry O. Ciocon, MD, chief of the geriatrics section at the Cleveland Clinic in Fort Lauderdale, FL.

Brush Longer

Three to four minutes of brushing are needed to get teeth really clean. The average person brushes for less than one minute. *Helpful:* Listen to the radio or stereo while you brush. Most popular songs last three to four minutes.

Source: Academy of General Dentistry, 211 E. Chicago Ave., Ste. 1200, Chicago 60611. Send for the Academy's free pamphlet *Brush Up on Your Dental Facts for Adults and Seniors.*

Preventing Tooth Loss

Tooth loss caused by advanced gum disease can now be prevented. *Secret:* A gel containing amelogenin, a naturally occurring protein derived from pigs. Applied to the surgically exposed and cleaned surfaces of a patient's tooth roots, the gel speeds regeneration of the periodontal ligament, which attaches teeth to the jawbone. In a recent study, those who received the gel regained an average of 66% of the lost ligament within 16 months. The gel's manufacturer has applied for permission to sell it in the US.

Source: Ingvar Magnusson, DDS, professor of oral biology, University of Florida, Gainesville.

All About Taking Much Better Care of Your Largest Organ...Skin

Prominent Dermatologist Dr. Joseph P. Bark answers the most common questions about skin care...

Why is my skin always so dry? Dry, flaky skin is usually the result of too-frequent bathing. Each time you take a bath or shower, you wash away natural oils that keep skin moist and supple. As we age, our skin tends to dry out even more.

Try bathing less frequently, and use sponge baths most of the time.

Except for a few mild antibacterial soaps like Lever 2000, deodorant soaps are too drying.

Better: Superfatted soaps like Dove, Basis, Neutrogena and Camay. They clean the skin without washing away protective oils.

If you like bath oil, apply it directly to your skin after your bath. Putting oil in the tub reduces its effectiveness—and makes your bathtub dangerously slippery.

Moisturizers: Inexpensive products like Lubriderm, Aveeno or Vaseline Intensive Care work just as well as high-priced "cosmetic" moisturizers.

What can I do about wrinkles? Stay out of the sun! About 80% of wrinkling stems from exposure to ultraviolet (UV) light...and sunlight plays a key role in most of the hundreds of thousands of skin cancers diagnosed in this country each year.

If you plan to be out in the sun for even a short while, wear sunscreen. Don't stop at SPF

15. Buy the highest-rated sunscreen you can find. I regularly use SPFs of 30 to 50.

Don't be stingy when you are applying sunscreen, either. It takes one full ounce of sunscreen to cover an adult who is wearing a bathing suit.

Men: Use sunscreen instead of aftershave.

Sunlight isn't the only cause of wrinkles. As time goes by, gravity causes skin to sag...and many people get expression lines and "sleep creases" on their faces as well.

The prescription drug tretinoin (Retin-A)—a vitamin A derivative originally developed for acne—can be used to flatten fine lines around the eyes, mouth, etc.

Bonus: Tretinoin reverses pre-malignant skin lesions before they turn into cancer. However, it has no effect on deep wrinkles or badly sun-damaged skin.

I advise most of my patients to apply two to three pea-sized dollops (about one gram) of tretinoin each night at bedtime.

What about surgery for wrinkles? Injections of collagen (the fibrous protein that gives skin its structure) are quite effective for many types of wrinkles. I prefer the Zyderm brand of collagen—because it most closely resembles human collagen. Touch-up injections may be necessary every six to eight months.

Minor wrinkles can also be removed by a procedure called dermabrasion, which involves "sanding off" the top two layers of skin with a rotating wire brush. Or, a doctor can perform a chemical peel, in which acid is used to accomplish the same thing.

The most effective means of eliminating wrinkles is cosmetic surgery. It works well against creases caused by sun or facial expressions, though it has a limited effect against deeper, gravity-induced wrinkles.

I'm all for cosmetic surgery, as long as the patient has realistic expectations.

What causes acne? Acne has little to do with how often you wash your face or what you eat. Nor is it a consequence of oily skin. Acne occurs when cells lining the "exit canals" of the skin's oil glands clump together, blocking the flow of oil to the surface of the skin.

Result: Oil backs up. This inflames the gland and surrounding skin. It also promotes growth of bacteria, which further inflame the skin.

What causes oil gland cells to become sticky? A genetic predisposition to high levels of testosterone and other androgens. These are the so-called "male" hormones, although they're found in both men and women.

Acne can also be triggered by heavy perspiration, psychological stress and by cosmetics—especially cold cream. It can clog oil glands and cause pimples even if you're not acne-prone.

Is effective treatment for acne available? Absolutely! Even severe cases usually clear up after a few months of antibiotic therapy. Taken orally or applied in creams, antibiotics kill bacteria in the oil glands and break the cycle of inflammation. Treatment usually takes at least five months.

For cystic acne (in which the oil glands have ruptured, causing scarring), results can often be obtained with the prescription drug isotretinoin (Accutane). Taken orally once or twice a day, this synthetic vitamin A derivative dries out the exit canals and reduces the activity of oil glands.

Isotretinoin works well for the worst 5% of acne cases, clearing them up permanently in about 20 weeks. It is not especially effective against mild acne.

Because of the risk of side effects, isotretinoin use must be supervised by your doctor. Side effects include dryness and chapping, aching muscles, elevated cholesterol...and birth defects, when taken accidentally by pregnant women.

Total cost: $1,800, including lab tests and monthly follow-up visits to the doctor.

If you or someone you love has acne, do not make the mistake of letting it go untreated. Without treatment, most cases worsen...causing embarrassment and permanent scarring.

How can I get rid of dandruff? Shampoo every day with Neutrogena T-SAL or another tar shampoo. These products work better than "medicated" dandruff shampoos.

Caution: Tar can give an orangish tint to gray or white hair. If you've gone gray, stick to a medicated shampoo.

If dandruff persists, you may be suffering from seborrheic dermatitis, a yeast infection of the scalp. You can't "catch" yeast from a comb —we all have it already. In some people, the yeast simply flares up from time to time.

Seborrheic dermatitis can be controlled with a prescription anti-fungal product called keto-conazole (Nizoral). It's available in shampoo or cream form.

What's the best remedy for oily skin? Try drying the oily patches with an alcohol-based astringent like Sebanil. Use antibacterial soap like Dial or Zest.

Are warts contagious? Yes. Warts are caused by skin viruses that spread easily. Someone with a wart on his/her hand can pass it along simply by shaking hands with someone else, especially if the other person has an abrasion or nick.

You can also cause warts to spread to other regions of your own body—by picking or scratching your skin.

Because of the risk of contagion, warts need prompt, aggressive treatment.

Over-the-counter wart remedies generally are not strong enough to remove warts. *My treatment of choice:* Cryosurgery. In this procedure, the doctor sprays liquid nitrogen on the wart, causing it to freeze and then gradually peel away. This may have to be done several times. *Cost:* $40 to $60 per wart.

How can I get rid of age spots? Over-the-counter bleaches don't really work—they're just not strong enough. What does work: Cryosurgery. Just as with warts, the age spots freeze and peel off in a week or two.

How dangerous are tanning salons? They're an absolute menace. I often say that if a group of scientists got together to invent the most effective way to destroy human skin, the tanning bed is what they would devise.

Light from a tanning bed is up to 1,000 times more damaging than natural sunlight—because the light source is so much closer. And recent evidence suggests that exposure to UV light also destroys vital immune cells, making people more vulnerable to infections and possibly to cancer.

My skin is constantly itching. What does that mean? A chronic itch should be checked out carefully by a dermatologist. It could be a symptom of contact dermatitis, an allergic reaction to something in your environment…a side effect of medication…or even a sign of liver, kidney or other systemic problems.

Itching may also be a symptom of eczema, a condition that produces patches of dry skin. Eczema can be treated with hydrocortisone cream, and by following the advice for dry skin.

Parents: Instead of telling a child not to scratch (almost impossible), give him/her a tube of medicated cream. Tell him to rub it gently into the affected area whenever it itches.

Source: Joseph P. Bark, MD, a dermatologist in private practice and a staff physician at St. Joseph Hospital, in Lexington, Kentucky. He is the author of *Your Skin: An Owner's Guide.* Prentice Hall.

Aspartame Danger

Aspartame can cause hives. In a recent study, 50 of 75 individuals who suspected an aspartame (NutraSweet) link experienced relief from hives after avoiding the artificial sweetener for two weeks. Hives returned in all 22 who chose to try aspartame again.

Source: Anthony Kulczycki, Jr., MD, associate professor of medicine, Washington University School of Medicine, St. Louis. His study was published in the *Journal of Allergy and Clinical Immunology,* 11830 Westline Industrial Dr., St. Louis 63146.

Make Your Skin Look Young Again Without Surgery

Just a few years ago, a face-lift was the only way to deal with skin that was wrinkled, sun-damaged, sagging or scarred. No longer.

While surgery is still required for serious problems, there are numerous safe, inexpensive nonsurgical techniques for rejuvenating your skin. *Here's a look at your options…*
Sunscreen and moisturizers:

Sunscreens don't just *prevent* skin damage. They also help fade *existing* fine wrinkles.

Moisturizers keep skin soft and supple and *temporarily* improve its appearance. But they

neither prevent nor reverse wrinkles. In fact, wearing moisturizer without sunscreen can raise your skin's vulnerability to sun damage.
Alpha hydroxy acids:

Glycolic, lactic, citric and other *alpha hydroxy acids* (AHAs) are found in a growing number of cosmetics. Excellent moisturizers, they also seem to minimize wrinkling, sun damage and acne—if used on a daily basis.

Even more effective: Prescription AHA products, which contain higher concentrations of the acid. They're available from your dermatologist.
Vitamin A derivatives:

Tretinoin (Retin-A) is a potent drug originally developed as a treatment for acne. In recent years, doctors have begun prescribing this vitamin A derivative to fade fine lines around the eyes...and to get rid of stretch marks and liver spots. It's surprisingly effective when used on a regular basis, although it can take a year or more for the effects to become apparent.

Tretinoin makes the skin appear smoother by thickening its outermost layer and "compacting" the layer of dead skin cells.

Caution: Tretinoin can cause redness and dryness...and can raise your susceptibility to sunburn. Because of the possible risk of birth defects, it's inappropriate for pregnant women.

Another formulation of tretinoin, Renova, is the first drug developed specifically for wrinkle removal. It reduces fine facial lines, brown spots and surface roughness just as effectively as ordinary tretinoin—and it's less likely to irritate the skin.
Chemical peels:

Chemical peels involve the application of concentrated AHAs (40% to 70% acid vs. 0.5% to 10% acid for over-the-counter AHA products). Peels are administered in a doctor's office.

A series of light *glycolic acid* peels helps remove damaged skin and improves the appearance of crow's feet and minor acne scars. The peel may cause stinging, as well as slight pinkness for a day.

Deeper peels, using *trichloracetic acid* (TCA) or *phenol,* are needed to obliterate wrinkles around the mouth, eyes and forehead, to correct irregular pigmentation and to eliminate liver spots.

The effects of a peel last for several years. However, peels may cause considerable pain, as well as persistent redness, skin tightness and scarring. Phenol peels are inappropriate for people with heart or kidney disease...or with dark skin.

Warning: Recovery from a TCA or phenol peel isn't pretty. Crust-like scabs that appear immediately after the peel can take up to two weeks to heal. During this period, it's essential to avoid the sun.
Dermabrasion:

This procedure involves use of a rotating wire brush to "sand" off the upper two layers of skin, smoothing its appearance. Results last for several years.

Dermabrasion is good for removing acne scars, pockmarks and small wrinkles around the lips. For severe blemishes, two procedures, six to 12 months apart, may be necessary.

Caution: Dermabrasion can cause infection, scarring, variations in skin tone and extreme sun sensitivity. As with peels, the skin crusts over. Full recovery can take several months.

Also as with peels, dermabrasion works best for people with light complexions.
Laser peel:

In this procedure—a new alternative to dermabrasion and chemical peels—the doctor uses a laser to "shear off" the epidermis. Laser peels are less likely than chemical peels to cause scarring and overlightening. They are also more precise.

Although crusting and redness still occur with a laser peel, recovery is usually faster. Laser peels are particularly effective against wrinkles around the eyes, age spots, scars and facial discoloration.
Collagen injections:

Doctors can inject you with a natural protein called collagen to plump up facial skin and help fill in severe (cystic) acne scars and deep wrinkles.

Effects are immediate and last for four to eight months, until the collagen is resorbed. Then a new round of injections must be administered.

Infection and sun sensitivity at the injection site can occur following the injections. And allergies to collagen can cause excessive firmness and purple discoloration. This can last up to six weeks.

To make sure you're not allergic: Have two collagen allergy tests prior to receiving the injections. Do *not* have the injections if you have rheumatoid arthritis, Graves' disease, lupus or another autoimmune disorder.

Instead of collagen, some doctors have begun injecting fat "harvested" from elsewhere in the body (buttocks, back, etc.). Because the injected material is part of the body, there's no danger of allergic reaction. Unfortunately, it's not clear just how long fat injections last.

Source: Joseph P. Bark, MD, a dermatologist in private practice and a staff physician at St. Joseph Hospital in Lexington, KY. He is the author of *Your Skin: An Owner's Guide*. Prentice Hall.

Worst Wrinkle Generators

Frowning and squinting. Reduce frowning by becoming aware of the tension that goes with it. When you feel the tension, try to relax your forehead muscles by gently massaging them with your fingers. Squinting is usually caused by sensitivity to bright light.

Self-defense: Buy sunglasses that filter ultraviolet A and B light, and wear them in all seasons.

Source: *The Essence of Beauty* by Adrianna Scheibner, MD, dermatologist in private practice, Beverly Hills. A&A Publishers.

Flu or Food Poisoning?

Many 24-hour illnesses with flu-like symptoms are actually mild cases of food poisoning.

Self-defense: Cook chicken and meats until they are no longer pink and the juices run clear. Defrost them in the refrigerator or under cool water rather than letting foods sit out on the counter…use a clean cutting board…heat leftovers thoroughly.

Source: Bessie Berry, director, Meat and Poultry Hotline, US Department of Agriculture, Washington, DC.

Better Shaving

In the morning wait 20 minutes after waking to shave. Skin is slightly puffy in the morning and hair follicles aren't yet fully raised. *After exercise:* Take a three-minute cool-water shower to tighten pores before shaving—since exercise opens pores, which can make skin extra sensitive.

In areas with hard water: Change your razor blade more frequently—every two or three shaves instead of every five or six. Mineral deposits in the water will quickly dull the blade.

To prevent irritation: Use a water-based moisturizer or shaving cream. Oil-based moisturizers and creams are more likely to irritate skin.

Source: Fred Wexler, director of research, Schick's Silk Effects and Personal Touch razors, quoted in *Weight Watchers Magazine*, 360 Lexington Ave., New York 10017.

Beware of Pop-Up Thermometers

Pop-up thermometers come in many brands of turkey and some brands of chicken and sometimes pop up before the poultry is properly cooked. That could mean serving a turkey or chicken containing harmful bacteria that have not been killed in cooking. *Possible result:* Nausea, vomiting and diarrhea, and even more serious problems for seniors and the very young. *Self-defense:* Use a meat thermometer to confirm the "doneness" of the poultry.

Source: Bessie Berry, director, Meat and Poultry Hotline, US Department of Agriculture, Washington, DC.

Jet-Engine Noise

Jet-engine noise can harm hearing, especially if you're sitting in economy class. Many people whose ears feel stuffy after a flight think pressure problems are the cause. But cabin noise alone can cause the problem. Any temporary hearing loss usually corrects itself quickly. To avoid it in the first place, sit in front of the engines and wear ear plugs.

Source: *Travel Fitness* by Rebecca Johnson, San Francisco attorney and frequent traveler. Human Kinetics Publishers.

Shoveling Snow Stresses Your Heart

Shoveling snow stresses the heart more than an all-out run. After two minutes of shoveling wet snow, heart rates of nine out of 10 men soared far above the zone recommended for aerobic exercise (70% to 85% of maximum heart rate). After 10 minutes of shoveling, heart rates reached 97% of maximum...and blood pressure was higher than when the men ran to the point of exhaustion.

Source: Barry Franklin, PhD, director of cardiac rehabilitation, William Beaumont Hospital, Royal Oak, MI.

Easier Breathing

People with breathing disorders feel better if they move to a lower elevation. The lower the elevation, the more oxygen is in the air and the easier oxygen is transferred to blood. Some people who live at high elevations will benefit from moving to sea level.

Source: Norman H. Edelman, MD, consultant for scientific affairs, American Lung Association, 1740 Broadway, New York 10019.

Tension Triggers

Tension can be set off by authoritarians who make you feel meek and childlike...anger that makes you feel out of control...other people's anger that frightens you...loud people...being teased...speaking in public...fear of appearing foolish...fear of making mistakes...a lull in a conversation during which you tend to babble ...insecurity around strangers. *Self-defense:*

Visualize the worst scenario in one of these moments, and imagine yourself overcoming the adversity. Knowing you can deal with the worst will give you the confidence to succeed.

Source: *Hit the Ground Running: Communicate Your Way to Business Success* by Cynthia Kreuger, communications consultant in Wheaton, IL. Brighton Publications.

Fear of Heights

Fear of heights may be overcome by using computerized virtual-reality simulations. By exposing patients to a virtual-reality computer program that produces a perception of height, researchers have found that fearful reactions to real-life experiences of heights were substantially reduced.

Source: Research by Kaiser Permanente, Oakland, CA, cited in *The Futurist*, 7910 Woodmont Ave., Bethesda, MD 20814.

Bra Strap Danger

Narrow, too-tight bra straps that dig into your shoulders can cause pressure on the cervical nerves in your spine, causing headaches.

Source: Phala Helm, MD, professor of physical medicine and rehabilitation, University of Texas Southwestern Medical Center, Dallas.

What is "Drinker's Nose?"

That's redness and bumpiness of the nasal skin. In most cases, the condition is caused not by drinking but by *rosacea*, an allergic reaction to the tiny mites that live in our oil glands. Rosacea often clears up upon application of the mite-killing drug MetroGel. Tetracycline can also help.

Source: Joseph P. Bark, MD, a dermatologist in private practice and a staff physician at St. Joseph Hospital, in Lexington, Kentucky. He is the author of *Your Skin: An Owner's Guide*. Prentice Hall.

How Women with Several Roles Balance Stress

Women who balance several roles—wife, mother and career woman—can have less stress than women who concentrate on only one. *Reason:* If you have a problem in one area of your life, you can feel satisfied from the others. *Helpful:* Reduce stress by keeping expectations realistic, setting attainable goals and prioritizing responsibilities.

Source: Myrna Ruskin, president of Myrna Ruskin Associates, a stress-management firm, 35 Sutton Pl., New York 10022 and author of the audiotape program *How to Get Married Without Feeling Harried*, available from the author.

Better Ice Packs

If ice cubes aren't available, use a bag of frozen peas. It will hug body contours, easing pain and helping to heal. *Important:* Wrap the bag in a cloth to prevent ice burn...apply for 10 minutes at a time.

Source: Peter Bruno, MD, internist for the New York Knicks basketball team.

The Scary Truth about Blood Transfusions...and How to Protect Yourself

Although the nation's blood supply is safer today than ever before, many people remain fearful of catching AIDS or another disease from a transfusion.

The blood supply is now remarkably safe, especially when compared with 10 years ago. Risk of catching a serious infection is roughly one in 5,000. There are several explanations for this increased level of safety...

Widespreed screening:

In the early 1980s, donated blood was screened only for hepatitis B and syphilis. Not until 1985 was testing for the AIDS virus (HIV) implemented on a nationwide basis.

Most blood banks did not launch efforts to screen for AIDS prior to the availability of a specific test, arguing that the risk of catching AIDS from a transfusion was tiny and the cost high. In fact, up to 2% of the units of blood transfused in some cities in the early 1980s harbored HIV. Thousands were needlessly infected, including Arthur Ashe and Ryan White.

Today, the Food and Drug Administration keeps close watch over blood banks. It doesn't hesitate to close down those that don't follow regulations.

More accurate HIV testing:

Until recently, blood banks tested only for the presence of *antibodies* to HIV (not the virus itself). *Problem:* It can take a while *after* infection for antibodies to form. There is a window of time when a person's blood is infectious even though the virus isn't detectable via conventional antibody testing.

To offset this problem, more sensitive antibody tests have been developed.

Result: The window has shrunk from 24 weeks to about four weeks. In addition, the FDA is expected to license a test for HIV itself. This new test, which will be mandated for use by all blood banks, should shrink the window even further.

And prospective blood donors are thoroughly questioned about possible risk factors for AIDS (homosexuality, intravenous drug abuse, etc.) before they are allowed to donate blood.

Bottom line: Roughly one in 400,000 transfusions now results in transmission of HIV. The new test should reduce the incidence to one in 700,000.

Fewer transfusions are given:

A generation ago, doctors recommended transfusions even in cases that weren't life-threatening—to help people feel less tired after surgery, for example.

Today, doctors order transfusions only to save lives—not to make patients feel better.

Beyong aids screening:

Blood banks now screen donated blood for the two strains of HIV, syphilis, hepatitis B and C, plus two other potentially deadly pathogens...

- **Human T-lymphotropic virus** (HTLV-1 and HTLV-2). Close relatives of HIV, these viruses cause cancer and other illnesses.

- **Cytomegalovirus** (CMV). It can cause a life-threatening infection in premature infants, chemotherapy patients, AIDS patients, transplant recipients taking immunosuppressant drugs and other individuals with poor immunity.

Diseases for which we are not yet testing, but which may be cause for concern, include...

- **Hepatitis G.** This newly discovered strain of hepatitis is less virulent than other strains—but more persistent. A screening test for hepatitis G is probably at least a year away.

- **Chagas.** This one-celled organism (protozoan) causes chronic infection, which can lead to heart failure.

As more people enter the US from areas where Chagas is endemic (chiefly Central and South America) the incidence of the disease in the US will increase. Even so, the number of cases spread by transfusion will probably remain low. Tests for Chagas are being evaluated by the FDA.

How to avoid bad blood:

What can individuals do to protect themselves from tainted blood? First, it's important to remember that *blood transfusions save lives* ...and that people have died because they *refused* transfusions. Having said that, there are ways to minimize your risk...

- **Pre-deposit your own blood.** Autologous donation—banking your own blood—is the single most significant precaution you can take. Barring human error in the handling of your blood (extremely unlikely), your risk of contracting a transfusion-related illness is essentially zero.

- **Recycle your blood.** Many operating rooms are now equipped with "cell-saving" devices that collect blood draining from the surgical incision and reintroduce it into the body.

Called *intraoperative autologous transfusion* (IAT), this technique is often effective in emergency surgery—so it's definitely worth asking for. It cannot be used for intestinal surgery,

tumor removal or any other operation in which blood could be contaminated with bacteria or cancer cells.

- **Know your options.** In California, surgeons are now required to inform patients of their transfusion options. This is *not* the case in all states.

If your surgeon doesn't explain your options, ask him to do so. Alternatives should be discussed at least six weeks before surgery.

If significant blood loss is expected, a *series* of autologous donations may be required over several weeks. Blood cells can be stored for up to 42 days, frozen plasma for up to one year.

The surgeon isn't necessarily to blame if you should need a transfusion. However, you're likely to lose *less* blood under the hands of a good surgeon. Ask how many times he/she has done this procedure.

Some hospitals can provide plasma or platelets taken from one person. "Single donor" blood is generally less likely than "pooled" blood to carry disease. However, this isn't always practical. Given today's careful screening practices, the increase in safety is marginal at best.

Some patients scheduled for surgery ask friends and relatives to donate blood. The assumption is that blood from someone you know is safer than blood from anonymous donors.

In fact, friends and relatives are likely to be first-time donors (whereas the community supply consists mostly of blood from repeat donors), so their blood hasn't been subjected to repeated testing. Ironically, it may be less safe.

- **Ask about blood-boosting drugs.** Over the last decade, researchers have identified hormone-like substances that spur production of red blood cells, white blood cells or platelets. In many cases, these factors can be synthesized using recombinant DNA technology—and used as drugs.

Erythropoietin (EPO), one of the first of these to become commercially available, helps the body make more red cells. It's helpful for some patients with kidney failure and other chronic conditions that used to require repeated transfusions.

However, since the body takes up to a few weeks to manufacture blood cells in response to the EPO, its value in surgery is limited.

Source: Edgar G. Engleman, MD, professor of pathology and medicine at Stanford University Medical School and director of the University's Blood Center, both in Palo Alto, California. In 1983, under Dr. Engleman's direction, Stanford's blood center was the first in the world to test donated blood for the AIDS virus.

CPR Is a Good Lesson

Teaching cardiopulmonary resuscitation (CPR) to family members of heart patients makes the patients feel better. Physicians have long felt that if heart patients know that their relatives are learning CPR the heart patients will become anxious and depressed about the thought of a fatal heart attack. But real research found it was just the opposite.

Source: Kathleen Dracup, RN, DNS, holds the Hassenplug Chair of Nursing, University of California, Los Angeles.

Secondhand Smoke Danger

Secondhand cigarette smoke hurts pets, too. Dogs exposed to cigarette smoke are 1.5 times as likely to develop lung cancer as those that live in smoke-free homes. Dogs with short to medium-length noses were at greatest risk of lung cancer, while long-nosed dogs were more likely to develop nasal cancer. The study gives greater credence to warnings about secondhand smoke, since dogs are unlikely to be exposed to other occupational hazards and usually live primarily in a single environment. And while this study only included dogs, other indoor pets—such as cats and birds—may be at even greater risk, since they live the majority of their lives indoors.

Source: John S. Reif, DVM, MSc, professor of epidemiology, Colorado State University, Fort Collins.

Common Drugs Make Driving Risky

Cold and allergy medicines, blood pressure medications, tranquilizers, sedatives, amphetamines and some antidepressants can cause vision impairment.

Self-defense: Any time you notice a vision change while you're taking a medication, talk to your doctor. If possible, don't drive until he/she says it is all right.

Source: Arol Augsburger, OD, dean, school of optometry, University of Alabama at Birmingham.

Virtual Reality Danger

"Cybersickness" affects up to 30% of people who use virtual reality (VR) gear, like that found in shopping malls, video arcades and flight simulators. *Symptoms:* Cold sweats, nausea, vomiting, eye strain and disorientation. These symptoms have persisted for up to 12 hours in helicopter pilots trained in a simulator.

Source: Robert Kennedy, PhD, vice president, Essex Corp., a Columbia, Maryland-based consulting firm that specializes in human-machine interactions. His remarks were reported in *TechnologyReview*, MIT, W59, 201 Vassar St., Cambridge, MA 02139.

Stroke Danger

Women with osteoporosis are more likely to suffer stroke than women with healthy bones, although no one knows why. The association between stroke and osteoporosis was just as strong as that between stroke and high blood pressure, the best-known risk factor for stroke.

Source: Warren Browner, MD, associate professor of medicine and of epidemiology and biostatistics, University of California, San Francisco. His study associating low bone density and risk of stroke in 4,024 elderly women was published in *Stroke*, Box 843543, Dallas 75284.

Homemade Heating Pad

Fill a tube sock with uncooked rice, knot the top, then microwave on high for three minutes. This creates a pad that will mold easily around any painful joint and hold its heat for about one hour—without risk of burns.

Source: Allison Scheetz, MD, instructor of medicine, and David Mathis, MD, assistant professor of medicine, Mercer University School of Medicine, Macon, GA.

Ease Immunization Pain

Ease the pain your child experiences from immunizations with an active distraction, such as blowing bubbles or reciting the ABCs. This is more effective at taking a child's mind off the pain than a passive distraction like listening to music or watching a video.

Source: Gina French, MD, fellow in behavioral and developmental pediatrics, Ohio State University College of Medicine, and leader of a study of almost 150 children, ages four to seven, who were getting shots.

Beauty Parlor Stroke Syndrome

Beauty parlor stroke syndrome is caused by tilting one's head back over a shampoo sink in a beauty parlor. The neck-straining position squeezes vertebral arteries and limits blood flow to the brain. Frequency and danger level of the syndrome are unknown.

Self-defense: Anyone at strong cardiovascular risk who extends the neck beyond a comfortable position for long periods—including people getting extensive dental work or undergoing manipulation—should not move the neck forward or back more than 15 degrees. Stop any time movement is uncomfortable.

Source: Bruce Yaffe, MD, internist and gastroenterologist in private practice, 121 E. 84 St., New York 10028.

Snoring Can Be Dangerous

It can be a sign of obstructive sleep apnea, a condition in which breathing periodically stops during sleep, causing the blood's level of oxygen drop. In less-serious cases, mild to moderate snoring may be associated with high blood pressure, sleep interruption, excessive daytime sleepiness and personality changes. *Bottom line:* 45% of normal adults snore occasionally—but 25% snore all the time and should see a doctor specializing in sleep disorders.

Source: Michael J. Papsidero, MD, otolaryngologist and associate director, Mount Sinai Nasal-Sinus Center, Cleveland.

To Kick a Caffeine Habit

Jot down how many cups of coffee or other caffeinated beverages you drink daily...immediately cut consumption...continue to taper off by mixing your brew with more milk and less coffee each day...keep your mug filled with a caffeine-free beverage (decaffeinated coffee, herbal tea, fruit juice, water). Don't expect immediate results. It can take up to three weeks before you feel comfortable without caffeine.

Source: Connie Diekman, RD, American Dietetic Association, 216 W. Jackson Blvd., Chicago 60606.

2

The Savvy Traveler

What You Should Know Before Taking a Cruise

• **Virtually all cruise fares are termed "all-inclusive prices."** This means they cover accommodations, meals and entertainment, transfers and use of facilities.

Not included: Liquor, personalized spa or beauty treatments and some shore excursions.

• **The only real "wild card" in the price of a cruise** is whether it includes airfare to and from the ship's port of departure and return. Many prices do. However, if you don't want or need it, make sure you receive an "allowance" that translates into a price cut.

• **Almost all ships have doctors**, although the level of treatment varies from ship to ship. The *Queen Elizabeth*, for example, has its own operating room. Many ships, particularly older ships, are limited in the type of service they can provide.

• **Cruise lines have improved their facilities to accommodate disabled individuals**, providing such things as larger rooms and bathrooms. Nonetheless, older ships—those five to 10 years old or older—tend to be less accessible. These ships may not provide elevator access to all floors.

Problems:

• **Not all ships are well-equipped to handle children.** Yet some offer wonderful programs designed for kids of all ages. Beyond programs and events, these ships also tend to have baby-sitting services, children's dining rooms, special kids' newspapers and, of course, several playrooms.

• **The destination of your cruise determines how far in advance you need to book.** Cruises to the Mediterranean, Europe, Bermuda, Asia, Alaska and Canada have limited seasons, which means space fills up fast. These cruises should be booked six months in advance. Caribbean cruises are generally more available. Bookings need to be made no more than 30 to 60 days in advance.

• **Rarely is crime a problem while on ship.** However, passengers always have the option of placing valuables in a safe. Unfortunately, crime can surface at ports of call.

•**Cancellation policies are available through travel agents at relatively low fees.** They guarantee refunds should you need to cancel your trip. Most passengers can probably skip them unless they're involved in businesses where schedules change rapidly.

•**Unlike airlines, which require advance notice for special menus**, cruise ships can accommodate virtually any dietary need on demand.

Source: Marylyn Springer, an authority on passenger ships. Ms. Springer writes about the cruise industry for newspapers and magazines, and authored seven editions of *Frommer's Guide to Cruises*. Macmillan Publishing Co.

What Embassies Can Do for You If You Are in a Jam

When Americans face legal or medical trouble abroad, they often call the US embassy for help. But in some cases, there is little the embassy can—or will—do for you.

The embassy will...

•**Replace a lost or stolen passport.** *Cost:* $65. A consul can issue you a replacement, often within 24 hours. If you believe your passport has been stolen, first report the theft to the local police and get a police declaration.

•**Help find medical assistance.** If you get sick, you can contact a consul for a list of local doctors, dentists and medical specialists, along with other medical information. If you are injured or become seriously ill, a consul will help you find medical assistance and, at your request, inform your family or friends.

•**Help get funds.** Should you lose all your money and other financial resources, a consul can help you contact your family, bank or employer to arrange for someone to send you funds. In some cases, these funds can be wired to you through the Department of State.

•**Help in an emergency.** Your family may need to reach you in an emergency or because they're worried about you. They should call the State Department's Overseas Citizens Services (202-647-5225). The State Department will relay a message to the consul in the country in which you are traveling. The consul will try to locate you, pass on messages and report back to your family.

•**Help if you're involved in a dispute** that could lead to legal or police action. A consul can provide a list of local attorneys.

Additional helpful resource: International Legal Defense Counsel (ILDC), which has helped release many detained and arrested Americans (215-977-9982...*fax:* 215-564-2859).

•**Help if you are detained by local authorities.** A consulate representative will visit you, notify friends, provide a list of attorneys or get relief if you are held under inhumane or unhealthy conditions.

•**Help find missing Americans during civil unrest or a natural disaster.** Travelers in troubled areas should register at the embassy when they arrive so they can be located during an emergency.

•**Help you do business.** Depending on the embassy, assistance might include a library of local and US trade publications, a file of Americans doing business in the country or a file of complaints against local businesses.

The embassy will not...

•**Act as a travel agent,** bank, lawyer, investigator or law enforcement officer.

•**Find you employment**...get you a residence or a driving permit...act as an interpreter...search for missing luggage...or settle disputes with hotel managers.

Last-ditch help:

You should expect professionalism from a consulate officer dealing with distressed travelers. If you are jailed or in another type of trouble, however, and the embassy is not being helpful, have your employer or a family member in the US contact your congressional representative, who can usually notify State Department or embassy offices so that your plight will gain attention.

Warning: This approach should be undertaken with care. Political pressure is resented by embassy officers, and they are in a position to be of instrumental assistance. Moreover,

Congress has done few favors for the State Department lately.

Source: Peter Savage, an ex-foreign service officer and now a security professional. He is a consultant to the Parvus Co., an international security firm, and author of *The Safe Travel Book.* Lexington.

Bed-and-Breakfasts... What You Should Know First

Bed-and-breakfast questions to ask to avoid unpleasant surprises: Have the owner and manager had any hospitality training? What type of breakfast is served? Can it be served in the room? Are meals served family style to all guests—or is there a restaurant? How big are the rooms? Do they have private bathrooms? How old is the plumbing? What exactly does the view look like? Is anyone on duty late at night? Can the temperature of the rooms be individually controlled?

Source: *Smart Money Magazine*, 1790 Broadway, New York 10019.

Read the Fine Print

Read the fine print in travel ads to find out what is *not* included in the low prices shown in big type. Airlines and travel agents constantly look for ways to advertise prices that seem low and leave out airport departure taxes, custom levies, passenger facility charges, per-day fees on car rentals and other costs. Charges omitted from the advertised price are supposed to be listed in small type somewhere in the ad—but some ads fail to list all charges. *Self-defense:* Before booking, ask what the total price will be.

Source: Nancy Dunnan, New York–based financial writer and author of *Your First Financial Steps.* HarperCollins.

How to Win the Frequent-Flier Game

If you want to fly anywhere in the US free, most airlines require that you have at least 25,000 frequent-flier miles. While it sounds as if you have to do a lot of flying to hit the magic number, there are many ways to reach that goal.

Winning ways:

•**If you fly only occasionally**, stick with one airline. Your miles will add up faster if you use one airline rather than many different airlines.

Working against you: In many cases, earned miles expire at the end of the third calendar year after you've earned them. Your airline's plan-mileage statement will remind you when your miles are due to expire.

Self-defense: If you fly a few times a year, use Continental, since miles don't have an expiration date. *Next-best deal:* Delta Air Lines —miles don't expire if you fly at least once every three years.

•**Take advantage of your plan's partners.** It's possible to accumulate miles without ever flying. Airlines have formed alliances with other companies—hotel chains, car-rental agencies, long-distance phone carriers, restaurants, florists, credit card issuers, etc.

Strategy: Call your frequent-flier program's service center for a list of its partners. It may be worth your while to favor these hotels, car-rental agencies and other companies to get the extra miles.

Don't forget about long-distance phone companies. All the major ones have tie-ins with specific airlines—AT&T (Delta, United and USAir) ...MCI (American, Continental, Northwest and Southwest)...Sprint (Alaska Air, America West and TWA).

How they work: You get a total of five miles for every $1 spent on residential long-distance calls. You must first call your long-distance carrier and sign up.

Credit cards are also a great opportunity to earn points. You can find out the details of an airline's program by contacting its frequent-flier service center.

Strategy: It's possible to pay bills, such as your insurance or mortgage, with a mile-building credit card. This strategy is only good if you don't run a balance. You certainly don't want to pay additional credit card interest on your mortgage or anything else just to get miles.

•**Do what you can to achieve elite-level status.** If you actually can fly 25,000 miles during a calendar year on a single plan, most airlines will reward you with elite-level status for the next year. This means you'll earn more miles for the same flights—often 25% to 50% more. You'll also qualify for free upgrades from coach to first class, without using earned miles. Sticking with one airline will make it easier to reach elite-level status.

If you have 24,500 miles near the end of a year, it could be worth buying a ticket just to reach the 25,000 mark and elite-level status.

Example: Continental has a *three-tier* elite-level system. If you fly 50,000 miles in a year, you'll reach its Gold Level and receive unlimited seat upgrades for one year, so long as first-class seats are available on the flight of your choice.

Miles from hotel stays or car rentals don't apply toward elite-level status.

•**Read your frequent-flier newsletters.** You don't want to miss out on opportunities to earn miles. Airlines often make special offers and alterations to their frequent-flier programs.

Example: I recently purchased a ticket from Denver to London on an American Airlines flight that stopped in Dallas. Then American announced in its newsletter that for a limited period, it would award bonus miles for flights from New York to London. So I switched my routing so that I flew from Denver to New York to London. I earned 25,000 bonus miles —plus mileage from Denver to London. There was no fee for switching because of my particular ticket. Travelers should call their airlines first to check about fees for changing tickets.

•**Plan ahead to redeem your miles.** If you try to use your frequent-flier miles on the spur of the moment, you could run into trouble. Some airlines charge service fees of $50 to $100 if you give them less than three or four weeks' notice when using miles toward a free ticket.

Worse: Ordering too late to obtain seats to your destination at all.

Strategy: If possible, reserve your ticket six to eight months in advance. Airlines set a certain number of seats aside for frequent-flier tickets—typically about 7% of the plane. If those seats are taken when you reserve, you won't be able to use your miles for that flight.

By reserving this far in advance, you're likely to beat other frequent fliers, even for seats on flights to popular destinations.

Source: Randy Petersen, editor of *InsideFlyer,* which publishes news and information about all of the major frequent-flier programs, 4715-C Town Center Dr., Colorado Springs 80916. He is author of *The Official Frequent Flyer's Guidebook.* Airpress.

Round-Trip to Europe: $100

Air couriers get super discounts in return for not checking bags on overseas flights. Couriers take important documents, machine parts, etc., to overseas destinations. They usually can take only carry-on luggage for themselves. In return, an air courier pays as little as $100 to $150 for a round-trip ticket to Europe from New York…and $100 to $250 for a round-trip ticket to the Orient from California. Couriers must travel on courier companies' timetables.

Source: William Bates, president, International Association of Air Travel Couriers, 8 S. J St., Lake Worth, FL 33460.

How to Get Hard-to-Get Tickets

Airline tickets on "sold-out" flights to popular US destinations are often available—if your travel agent knows where to look. Many airlines have sophisticated computer-reservation systems that find empty seats for passengers continuing on to foreign destinations. Once you reserve such a route, you can cancel the foreign portion and retain the domestic flight. Ask your travel agent to check their availability.

Source: Tom Parsons, editor of *Best Fares Discount Travel.*

Cheaper Travel with Split Ticketing

When buying airline tickets for foreign travel, check to see if splitting the ticket—buying the return ticket in the destination country—is cheaper because of favorable exchange rates. Travel agents have no trouble making such arrangements. *Example:* Ticket-splitting for a trip to Nairobi from Los Angeles would save a traveler $1,190.

Further savings: Instead of picking up the return ticket in the US, have the travel agent arrange to have it picked up when you arrive at your destination.

Source: Melanie Jenkins, editor, *Travel Expense Management Newsletter*, Box 1442, Wall Township, NJ 07719.

If Your Flight Is Cancelled

If your flight is canceled, do not wait at the gate with everyone else. Go to a pay phone, call your travel agent or the airline's 800 number, and rebook. Find out if your ticket will be accepted by another airline that has a flight leaving earlier than the next one offered by your airline. Consider flying to a different city—near the one you want to reach—if you can conveniently get to your destination anyway.

Helpful when flights are delayed: If all planes are delayed three hours, and your ticket is for a 4 p.m. flight, try to rebook for the delayed 1 p.m. flight.

Source: Herbert Teison, editor, *Travel Smart*, 40 Beechdale Rd., Dobbs Ferry, NY 10522.

Empty Seat Strategy

Increase the chances of having an empty airline seat next to yours. Ask for an aisle seat in the center section of wide-bodied planes (middle seats are generally the last to go). If you are traveling with a companion, book aisle and window seats in a three-seat row—there's a good chance the middle seat won't be assigned

…if you're a frequent flyer, ask about being assigned to a preferred section where middle seats are the last to go.

Source: *Consumer Reports Travel Letter*, 101 Truman Ave., Yonkers, NY 10703.

Flying Fears Grounded

Expect to feel nervous and accept these feelings as perfectly normal—for you…Take deep, calming breaths to help reduce your anxiety…move around as much as possible before and during the flight. Stretching, wiggling and bending will help you take your mind off your fearful thoughts.

Source: *The Experts' Book of Practical Secrets from the People Who Know*, edited by Edward Claflin. Rodale Press.

Best Hotel Rates

Don't try to obtain a discount hotel rate…

…after bringing your heavy luggage into the lobby. It's obvious you aren't going anywhere else.

…after 9 p.m.—night clerks rarely have authority to give discounts.

…by calling the hotel chain's 800 number. The agent there reads off a computer screen and doesn't have authority to negotiate with you.

To get a bargain rate:

• Call the hotel's front desk directly.

• Book your room well in advance, so the hotel agent knows you have time to shop around.

• Mention any affiliation that may entitle you to a discount—such as to a professional group, travel group, AAA, AARP, etc.

• Don't accept the first rate offered to you—many hotels often have a "fall back" rate that they will quote if, and only if, a customer is reluctant to accept the standard rate.

Source: Herbert J. Teison, editor, *Travel Smart*, 40 Beechdale Rd., Dobbs Ferry, NY 10522.

Better Hotel Stays

What hotel managers do when they are hotel guests:

• **Look out the window** for noisy highways or loading docks.

• **Check immediately** to see if the television works.

• **When ordering room service**, specify enough milk for cereal.

• **Avoid rooms close to the elevator**, ice machine and conference rooms.

• **Check to see if the alarm clock was set by a previous guest.**

• **Ask for an upgrade.**

• **Ask about a frequent-guest program.**

Source: Coopers & Lybrand, LLP, management consultants, 1301 Avenue of the Americas, New York 10019.

Tour Booking Self-Defense

To protect your deposit when signing up for a tour, make sure the tour company belongs to the National Tour Association or US Tour Operators Association. Both have consumer-protection plans. Pay with a credit card if possible—but if you must use cash, get a receipt.

Source: Gene Malott, editor, *The Mature Traveler*, Box 50400, Reno, NV 89513.

Mature Traveler Self-Defense

People with heart conditions should consult their doctor about the need for supplemental oxygen before traveling by plane. *Also…*

• **People with pacemakers** should carry information about their unit.

• **Pack a health kit containing adhesive tape,** anitbacterial soap and diarrhea medicine.

• **Take along bottled water on day trips in hot climates.**

Source: Bradley A. Connor, MD, founder and medical director of Travel Health Services, 50 E. 69 St., New York 10021.

Your Rights if Your Flight Is Overbooked

Even though airlines have the right to bump you from a flight, they'll do so only as a last resort…and you can reduce your chances of ever having this happen to near zero.

• **Avoid traveling during the Thanksgiving and Christmas holidays.** Most bumpings take place during those periods.

• **Fly airlines with low bumping rates.** American and United Airlines are lowest. Southwest is highest.

• **Secure an advanced boarding pass and seat assignment when you buy your ticket.** This puts you in a better position than ticket holders without seat assignments.

• **Arrive early at the boarding gate and check in.** Late arrivers are at the top of the list to be bumped.

When to get bumped:

If you're not in a hurry and your flight is overbooked, you can *volunteer* to be bumped, usually in exchange for a free ticket or monetary voucher good for up to a year and a seat on the next flight to your destination.

You receive a *denied boarding compensation* coupon to use next time you fly. When you do fly, the airline often will try to upgrade you to first class as a compensation for your having been bumped (even though it was voluntary). Delta is particularly generous with upgrades.

Caution: Before you volunteer to be bumped, ask when the airline will get you on another flight. If there's a long wait until that flight, ask if the airline will provide free meals, faxes and phone calls, as well as any ground transportation you might need.

If the airline needs several people to volunteer to be bumped and gets only some of them, they may offer cash—usually starting around $200—in addition to a free ticket. Then, if they still don't get enough volunteers, they may raise their offer as high as $500.

Source: Charles Leocha, author of *Travel Rights*. World Leisure Corp.

Where to Find the Best Buys in Paris

With the dollar improving against the French franc—and greater airfare discounts to Europe —more Americans are traveling to Paris. *Here are wonderful hidden values I found during my recent trip to Paris...*

Apparel:

•**C. Mendès** is an outlet that has Yves St. Laurent and Christian La Croix designs for women from last year's collections. The fabrics and tailoring are exquisite. Prices are 50% below department store or specialty shop prices.
65 rue Montmartre, 2nd floor. Phone (from the US): 011-33-1-4236-8332.

•**Dépôt Grandes Marques** has men's designer clothing, including Guy Laroche, Cerrutti, Carven and Ungaro.
15 rue de la Banque, 3rd floor. 011-33-1-4296-9904.

•**Dépôt-vente de Passy** discounts the clothes of all the major men's and women's designers, from Armani to Valentino.

Example: A gorgeous Montana jacket was a steal at $300.*
14 rue de la Tour. 011-33-1-4520-9521.

•**Maxi Librati** houses a women's coordinated collection of a Paris-based designer for good prices.

Examples: On sale: Blouses for $100... jackets, $280...and skirts, $120.
32 rue Ave. Marceau. 011-33-1-4723-8433.

Cosmetics:

•**Le Bon Marché** is an old-fashioned department store that stocks, among many other things, a wide selection of French-made cosmetics and treatments not available in the US.

*Prices are based on five francs to the dollar.

Examples: Bourjois, a brand made by Chanel ...Leclor...Onagrine...and Phas.
At the intersection of rue du Bac and rue de Sèvres. 011-33-1-4439-8000.

Hotels:

•**Hôtel Ferrandi** is secreted behind a row of 19th-century town houses on a quiet Left Bank street. This three-star hotel has 42 rooms, each with a marble bathroom.

Double-room occupancy (per couple): $92 a night...and $196 for a deluxe suite with canopied bed.
92 rue du Cherche-Midi. 011-33-1-4222-9740.

•**Les Rives de Notre-Dame.** Centrally located along the Seine and facing Île de la Cité and Notre-Dame, this four-star hotel has nine sound-proofed rooms, all decorated in sunny colors and province-inspired furnishings with exquisite baths.

Double-room occupancy (per couple): $200 to $330 per night.
15 Quai Saint Michel. 011-33-1-4354-8116.

Restaurants:

•**Les Bookinistes** is a modern bistro with a warm neighborhood ambiance. A dinner with appetizer, entrée and wine comes to $30 per person.
53 Quai des Grands Augustins. 011-33-1-4325-4594.

•**Pile ou Face** offers fabulous food with an emphasis on farm-fresh ingredients. Book well in advance for lunch—a sensational buy at $50 per person for a four-course meal.
52 bis rue Notre-Dame des Victoires. 011-33-1-4233-6433.

Source: Susan Dresner, president of Ways & Means, a wardrobe and management consulting firm in New York specializing in money-saving shopping strategies. She travels extensively and is author of *Shopping on the Inside Track.* Peregrine Smith.

Research and Travel

EarthCorps volunteers spend one to two weeks helping scientists on projects designed to protect threatened habitats, save endangered species and preserve cultural heritages. The research expeditions take place in 21 states of the United States and 54 countries. Participants make tax deductible contributions (about $1,600 for two weeks and as low as $600 for one week) that support research and cover food and lodging. Transportation is extra.

Source: Earthwatch, Box 403ZA, Watertown, MA 02272.

Tourists Beware

Criminal "cabbies" in Mexico cruise the streets looking for tourists, pick them up, then rob them.

Self-defense: Do not hail a cab on the street. Use hotel cars found in front of most hotels… or cabs operating from taxi stands.

Source: Tom Parsons, publisher, *Best Fares Discount Travel Magazine,* 1301 S. Bowen St., Arlington, TX 76003.

Travel Comfort

Use airplane pillows for your back instead of your head. Stuff a pillow into the small of your back before buckling your seat belt, and just leave it there for the entire flight. The pillow will help prevent back pain.

Also helpful: Try to get an aisle seat so you have a few extra inches to do shoulder shrugs, neck rolls and other exercises—then do them every hour. Get up and walk around the plane periodically—this works especially well on the big planes with double aisles used on overseas flights. Men should take wallets out of their back pockets to avoid putting extended pressure on the sciatic nerve.

Source: Gene Malott, editor, *The Mature Traveler,* Box 50400, Reno, NV 89513.

Shrewder Travel

Beware of travel guidebooks. They often contain incorrect or out-of-date information.

Examples: Wrong addresses and hours of operation…recommendations for hotels and restaurants that have long since gone out of business…inaccurate museum guides.

Problem: Long publishing lead times make complete accuracy impossible…many books are updated only every two, three or even four years.

Self-defense: Use more than one book when traveling…make sure you have an up-to-date map—available from the local tourist office… always call ahead to confirm addresses, hours of operation and other information.

Source: Elaine Petrocelli, owner of Book Passage, a travel bookstore in Corte Madera, CA.

3

Your Family— Your Home

Discipline and Much Better Parenting

Disciplining children is hard for most parents. Almost all worry whether they have gone too far—or not far enough—when using punishment to correct a child's behavior.

For the past 25 years, I have been helping parents develop more effective ways to discipline their children.

Here are my strategies:

•**Punish only when necessary.** Any punishment loses its effectiveness with overuse. As a result, punishment works best when it is infrequent. Nonetheless, punishment for infractions must be consistent. For example, if a child hits a sibling, the punishment must be the same each time to uphold that law in your house.

•**Avoid harsh punishments.** A harsh punishment often stops misbehavior in its tracks, but it doesn't necessarily teach the child the proper lesson. Harsh punishments cause children's behavior to worsen. Severe punishments cause hostility and resentment.

Example: Your child disregards your order not to ride his/her bike outside a three-block radius of the house. It's a mistake to punish him by taking the bike away for a week. *Reason:* The child forgets about what he did wrong and thinks instead about how to cope with the punishment. His focus changes from *I shouldn't disregard my parents' safety rules* to *I hate riding that stupid bike anyway.*

Better: Take away the use of the bike for the rest of the day. The child easily associates his misbehavior with the loss of the bike and vows to do better.

•**Identify the problem and the punishment.** Children need to know exactly what is expected of them.

Example: Tell your child that all homework must be completed before he may watch TV. Be equally clear about the consequences of breaking that rule...*If you watch TV before your homework is done, tomorrow you won't* *watch TV at all.* Ask the child to repeat this back to you.

Important: Avoid saying everything as a threat.

Better: A straightforward, adult conversation.

The child has a better chance of remembering the rule and correcting his behavior. The child can't say he didn't hear or understand you.

• **Follow through with any punishment.** If you threaten to punish a child for misbehavior, you must be ready to impose that punishment.

Example: You tell your child that he can go with you to a basketball game if he finishes all his homework. If his homework is not done, you calmly tell the child that he is unable to go.

You can't let your child talk you out of the punishment. If you do, he learns how to avoid punishments, not how to improve his behavior.

• **Ignore some bad behavior.** This surprising piece of advice works in certain situations.

Example: A child is swearing and being reprimanded for it constantly. Since even negative attention is better than none, the child continues the behavior.

Better: In cases like this one, where bad behavior is used simply to get your attention, you may want to make a deliberate attempt to ignore the behavior. Although it may get worse at first, the child will soon learn his annoying behavior is not getting your attention and he will drop it.

Exception: Repetitive misbehavior may be a cry for more positive attention. In this case, parents must ask themselves, *Am I too critical?* and *Have I balanced positive and negative attention?* In addition, parents should always give positive attention to desirable behavior.

• **When correcting a child**, always make eye contact. Reprimands are more effective when you are sure a child is listening. Move closer to the child, and raise your voice slightly. Get him to look at you before you speak.

The expression on your face should be neutral, not smiling or bug-eyed with anger. Holding that eye contact for a moment after speaking is a very powerful technique.

• **Use punishments that fit the crime.** For running up phone bills—take away the telephone. For being disrespectful of property—have him use his allowance to pay off damages.

Other rewards and privileges that can be removed as punishments: Staying overnight with a friend…attending a party…going to a special event…using the family car…playing video games.

• **Use a time-out when no particular punishment fits the crime.** As with any punishment, reserve sending a child to his room for serious infractions so that it does not become ineffective through overuse. Time-out has a dual purpose—it is a negative consequence—and the isolation allows the child time to pull himself together.

Rule of thumb: Have a young child sit in a chair for about one minute per year of age. Older children can be sent to their rooms.

• **Use rewards instead of punishments.** There are times when a reward for good behavior is more effective than a punishment for bad behavior.

Example: To help your four-year-old learn to sleep in his own bed at night, you offer a 25-cent reward to get the new behavior started. For the next few days following successful nights, you hand over a shiny new quarter. Once the child is sleeping in his own bed, phase out the payment. Discuss this with your child in advance so he knows the reward is short-lived.

Source: James Windell, MA, LLP, a psychotherapist in private practice specializing in family problems and a clinical psychologist with a juvenile court psychological clinic in Michigan. He is the author of *Eight Weeks to a Well-Behaved Child*, Macmillan, and *Discipline: A Sourcebook of 50 Failsafe Techniques for Parents*. Macmillan.

Parenting Made Easier…Answers to the Toughest Parenting Questions

Parents of elementary school children often come to me with questions about how to discipline their kids.

Here are some of the most commonly asked questions and my advice on how to be an authoritative—not an authoritarian—parent…

• How can bedtime be made less stressful? Children love to stay up as late as possible for a variety of reasons.

Some of them equate staying up with being grown-up. Others believe that by going to bed, they will miss out on something particularly exciting.

In many households, the result is tension, causing anger to be directed at children. This often leads to an argument between spouses.

Solution: Set up a nightly schedule—and enforce it. Allow some calm one-on-one time. This is not a good time for wrestling. Instead, make reading a regular part of the bedtime ritual, and choose children's books you enjoy.

Make a distinction between going to bed and going to sleep. Tell the child, *You can go to sleep anytime you want, but you must be in bed by 8:30.*

Once in bed, your child can be left with a choice of options—such as listening to the radio or reading a book. But the kitchen is closed, and after 8:30 is "grown-up time."

• Is spanking acceptable in some situations? It's OK to feel like spanking your child —but I always advise against acting out your anger by hitting.

When parents hit, they are teaching children that this response is acceptable when you're angry. Children learn by watching and emulating your behavior.

Besides, hitting does not help children change their negative behavior in the long run. It also doesn't allow children to reflect on their behavior. Hitting hurts—and when children are hurt, they feel like hitting back.

Better: If you are angry enough to hit, give yourself a time-out. Count to 10 and, if necessary, leave the room immediately.

I wholeheartedly approve of using consequences that fit the crime.

Example: If the child watched two hours of TV when he/she was only to have watched one, ban TV the next night.

• How can I get my kids to eat what I serve? You can't—so stop worrying about it. It is also a mistake to equate finishing everything on your plate with good behavior. If you try to force your child to eat, he will soon see food as a way to control you. In the long run, you and your child may be left with more than just nutrition problems.

Solution: Focus on eating meals together… and exchanging ideas rather than talking about the food. Eating should be about hunger, not about pleasing or upsetting parents.

• How can I get my kids to turn off the TV when I ask them to? TV is like dessert. You don't give children chocolate three times a day just because they think it tastes good.

You have to be in charge of the television, not your children. Expecting them to limit TV themselves because it is not good for them is like asking them to show restraint in a toy store.

Solutions: Give children some choices over what they watch but not how much. You set the time limits. They can mark in the television guide on Sundays the shows they want to watch, but you have final approval over content. Try to make other types of entertainment more exciting or appealing.

• Is there a way to stop fights between siblings? Expecting children not to fight is unrealistic. Cries of *It's not fair…Give it back! …and Get out of my room!* will likely ring throughout your house until the children leave for college.

Trap: Getting involved in their fights by taking sides and trying to settle them. The child who has been blamed will then start a new fight to even the score—if not with his sibling, then with you.

Do not intervene unless it's absolutely necessary—such as when the fight becomes too physical or mean-spirited. Instead, encourage the children to work it out between themselves—and learn important problem-solving skills at the same time.

Example: When one child complains that a sibling stole a toy, say, *If you two can't work it out yourselves in the next five minutes, I'll have to take the toy away from both of you.*

Never ask, *Who started it?* Each child will simply point to the other.

• How can I get my children to listen when I speak to them? If you want them to listen more—talk less. Keep it short and impersonal. Don't give speeches.

Examples: Say, *The screen door is still open. It needs to be closed...*or, *We always wear our seat belts in the car.*

Important: Leave some power to children. Avoid daily skirmishes about less important matters such as clothing choices, and concentrate on more important rules like those about under age drinking, safety, etc.

•**When my spouse and I disagree about child rearing**, how can we find a middle ground? The reality is that you and your spouse will probably disagree. Since each of you were brought up by different parents, it is likely that you will react very differently to your child's behavior.

Once you accept this reality, try not to contradict each other in front of the children. If you do, you are just giving them the opportunity to divide and conquer.

Example: Your spouse discovers that your son has forgotten to feed the dog again. He cancels the boy's sleepover with a friend on Friday night—but you think this punishment is too harsh considering the crime.

Solution: Say nothing in front of the child, but discuss it with your spouse later. You might say, *I know we don't always agree, but I think you handed out a very heavy punishment for a fairly light crime.*

If your spouse decides to go along with your approach, he/she can do so without the child knowing that he was overruled. At the very least, you will be working it out together in private.

Important: If children are aware that you and your spouse are divided on a certain issue —and they often seem to know this even before they speak to you about it—do not let them use it to their advantage.

Avoid saying in front of your children, *Dad was wrong.* Instead, say, *Dad and I don't feel the same way about this.* The goal here is to become an authoritative parent—neither permissive nor authoritarian.

Source: Nancy Samalin, founder and director of Parent Guidance Workshops, 180 Riverside Dr., New York 10024. She is the author of *Love and Anger: The Parental Dilemma.* Penguin.

Why Baby Looks Like Dad

Infants tend to resemble their fathers more than their mothers. But older children do not necessarily resemble either parent. The early resemblance to fathers may have an evolutionary reason—fathers may have unconsciously noted the resemblance and been more willing to care for children who looked like them.

Source: Study of 122 people by Nicholas Christenfeld, PhD, social psychologist, University of California at San Diego.

Baby Talk

To convey disapproval of a baby's behavior, be sure to match words and tone of voice with facial expression.

Trap: The slightest smile at "cute" misbehavior in a baby will make any verbal reprimand meaningless.

Source: *Baby Tactics: Parenting Tips that Really Work!* by parenting adviser Barbara Albers Hill. Avery Publishing Group.

Calling Your Child's Doctor

When calling your child's doctor, have the following information on hand—child's weight ...medications he/she is taking...any allergies to those medications...temperature...what exactly is worrying you...any treatments you've tried so far...changes in your child's sleeping, eating, toilet or drinking habits.

Also: Inform the doctor about any recent injuries, illnesses, infections or exposure to others who are or were sick.

Source: James A. Taylor, MD, director of the Pediatric Center, University of Washington, Seattle.

When the Baby Won't Eat

Try again tomorrow. *Reason:* It's natural for a baby to reject unfamiliar tastes. But most babies will eventually learn to like most foods. In a recent study, when babies were offered pureed peas or green beans for 10 consecutive days, they ate twice as much on the tenth day as they had on the first.

Source: Study by researchers at the University of Illinois, Urbana-Champaign.

Questions to Ask A Baby-Sitter

Does he/she have children—and who cares for them...what were the ages and sexes of children she has worked with...would she be able to stay late if a last-minute problem came up...does she know first aid and infant CPR...what would she do if your child got hurt or became ill...how would she handle a baby who cried continuously for an hour. *Also:* Get several references—and check them.

Source: Ellen Galinsky, Families and Work Institute, 330 Seventh Ave., New York 10001.

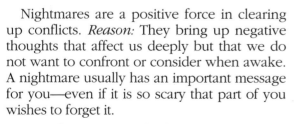

Nightmares Are Not Just Bad Dreams

Nightmares are a positive force in clearing up conflicts. *Reason:* They bring up negative thoughts that affect us deeply but that we do not want to confront or consider when awake. A nightmare usually has an important message for you—even if it is so scary that part of you wishes to forget it.

Source: *The Dream Sourcebook: A Guide to the Theory and Interpretation of Dreams* by Phyllis Koch-Sheras, PhD, clinical psychologist, Charlottesville, VA. Lowell House.

Children and Death

Tell children about death in age-appropriate ways. Do not make up stories—children will sense that they are false or will be frightened by them. *Example:* Saying that a dead person has gone peacefully to sleep and will not wake up again may not reassure a child—it may make him/her fearful of going to bed. *Better:* Take the child to a quiet place, and explain that the person has died. Ask the child if he knows what that means. Take your cue from his response to know how far to go in explaining what happened—and when to stop.

Source: *The Caregiver's Manual: A Guide to Helping the Elderly and Infirm* by Gene Williams, a journalist in Queen Creek, Arizona, who was prompted to write the book by the lingering illness and death of his mother. Citadel Press.

Imaginary Friends Are Useful for Children

They help kids entertain themselves and develop their imaginations. Imaginary playmates usually befriend children between the ages of two-and-a-half and six. Boys and girls are equally likely to have them. Only children —and ones at least five years older or younger than the closest sibling—are more likely to have imaginary friends.

Helpful: Give your child space and privacy with the friend. Never belittle him/her for talking to someone invisible. Play along—within reason. Keep your distance—children want to control these friends themselves.

Source: Charles Schaefer, PhD, psychologist and professor, Fairleigh Dickinson University, Hackensack, NJ.

Teach Your Child Values

Be responsive to his/her requests when they come with words like *please* and *thank you* ... hug him or pat his shoulder when you see him being nice to someone...ask before taking or using something that belongs to him…tell the truth—and admit it if you are caught in a lie… help him think of ways to be nice to other people.

Source: Ann LaForge, contributing editor, *Child,* 110 Fifth Ave., New York 10011.

Encourage Your Children To Express Opinions

Ask your children for their opinions at least once a day. This shows that you value their feelings, ideas and opinions.

Helpful: Offer age-appropriate choices, such as what to wear, when to eat, and how—and whether—to clean their bedroom…ask them to recommend something to do on weekends or at night…talk politics—local, national or family—at the dinner table, and listen to everyone's opinion…encourage your child's independence by cultivating your own tolerance, even if that means accepting his/her choice of clothing, hairstyle or jewelry without criticism.

Source: *Super Kids in 30 Minutes a Day* by Karen U. Kwiatkowski, MS, MA, an Air Force officer and mother of four. Robert D. Reed Publishers.

Help Kids Read Better

When asking kids about something they've just read, ask them questions that require thinking skills, not just recitation of specific facts and details.

Examples: Why did you like/dislike a character?…how is the character the same as or different from you?

Also: Before finishing the story, ask them to predict the ending. And use every opportunity to illustrate how reading is used in the "real world."

Source: Richard Robinson, PhD, professor of education, College of Education, University of Missouri-Columbia and author of *Twenty-Five Ways to Help Your Child Become a Successful Reader.* Language Arts Consultants.

Strategies for Getting Along Better With Your Teenagers

When teens are difficult, most parents respond by tightening the reins. But while laying down strict rules may make you feel in charge, getting tough generally produces a negative long-term result.

Better: Instead of trying to change your teen, work on changing those parts of your personality that will allow teens to behave more responsibly.

What to change about you:

•**Let your teens find solutions to their own problems.** To get used to taking a hands-off approach to your teen's everyday problems, such as lost belongings, forgotten lunches and sibling squabbles, make a list of the following questions…

•**Whose problem is this?**

•**Who should be the one thinking of a solution?**

•**Who has the power to make the solution succeed?**

Write either your name or your child's name next to each item. If your name is not on your list, the solution should not be up to you either.

Forcing teens to face consequences tells them that they are responsible for themselves. Letting a teenager think through problems for himself teaches him how to make decisions, how to recognize what can and can't be done and how to weigh the options.

•**Don't make judgmental remarks.** Without realizing it, many parents express opinions, worries and judgments every time they speak to their teens.

Better: Your advice need not always be so quick and forthcoming. Teens deserve the right to make their own decisions, within reason, of course, and, if necessary, their own mistakes.

•**Be a better listener.** When your teen speaks, simply repeat what has been said and wait. It can take some time for the real problem or worry to come to the surface of your child's lips.

Example: Your daughter tells you she hates the sweater she's wearing and wonders aloud if she should change. Instead of rushing in with comments and suggestions and questions, just listen to her worries. You may find out that it is her weight—and not the sweater —that is the real problem.

She may also surprise you by happily making her own decision about whether to change or to accept her figure as is.

Teens often don't want an opinion or an answer—just a listener.

•**Create stress-free short encounters.** Practice acceptance and encouragement by getting together with your teen for five- to 10-minute periods—without using the time as a chance to criticize behavior.

Example: Ignore the backpack on the floor or the forgotten chore. Instead, say to your teen, I have some fresh strawberries for you. As you eat together, be careful not to flinch, frown, criticize or complain.

Rule of thumb:

A teen needs times when he simply feels valued and encouraged and accepted. If all encounters are about your dissatisfaction with his behavior, he will become discouraged.

Research shows that children who face long periods of discouragement tend to get in trouble.

Work on your relationship with your teen rather than focusing narrowly on the behavior. If the relationship is good, the behavior can— and probably will—fall into place.

Source: Louise Felton Tracy, MS, a middle-school counselor in Los Gatos, California, mother of six children and author of *Grounded for Life?! Stop Blowing Your Fuse and Start Communicating with Your Teenager.* Parenting Press.

How to Know if a Puppy Will Become a Happy Dog

Test a puppy's personality before buying it. *Hold it so its feet are a few inches off the floor.* A normal puppy will struggle a bit, then settle down...a dominant one will keep struggling ...a submissive one will dangle passively. *Hold the puppy on its back on your lap and comfort*

it. A normal puppy will struggle a little, then settle...a dominant one will keep fighting...a submissive one will quickly give in or may panic. *Put the puppy on the floor and toss it a small object.* It should chase and play with it— not grab the object and take it away ...or appear to be frightened of it.

Source: *Choosing a Dog: A Guide to Picking the Perfect Breed* by Nancy Baer, head trainer and general manager, Academy of Canine Behavior, Bothell, WA. Berkley Books.

Mature Teens

Teens are getting better and better compared with teenagers 25 years ago. Only 10% of high-achieving teens tried marijuana in 1994, compared with 27% in 1972...91% of sexually active teens now use contraceptives, compared with 52% two decades ago...and 68% say they have a happy family life, up from 59%.

Source: Survey by *Who's Who Among American High School Students.* Educational Communications.

How to Put on a Yard Sale that Sells

•**Don't decide today to have a yard sale tomorrow.** Planning is the key to a successful yard sale. *Helpful:* If you regularly hold a yard sale, set aside a closet or out-of-the-way corner in which to store items you want to sell. Price items as you put them away so you'll be well-organized when the time comes to hold the sale.

•**Hold your sale over at least a two-day period** to give as many people as possible the chance to shop your goods. *Even better:* A three-day sale, with the first day on a Friday, when you get fewer, but more serious, shoppers.

•**Be objective when deciding what to sell.** Don't be sentimental with items that once meant something, but that you no longer use or need. Let somebody else develop an emotional attachment to your junk.

•**Know what sells**…wooden chairs and tables…lamps…wicker baskets…patio furniture…lawn and garden tools…overcoats…appliances—especially in their original boxes. *Be aware:* Old toys, dolls and other items might be collectibles—so don't give them away. *Also:* Campy is chic, so don't be afraid to put out your old bowling shirts, celebrity mementos, lava lamp, club pins, ties and hats, etc. *Important:* Don't try to pawn off stained or broken goods—you'll only drive away potential customers.

•**Price items reasonably.** *Helpful:* Shop similar items in antique and thrift stores—and then price your goods 25% to 50% lower.

Source: Dean King, author of *The Penny Pincher's Almanac, Handbook for Modern Frugality: Hundreds of Simple Ways to Spend Less and Get More.* Fireside.

Before You Paint…

Professionally mixed paint colors vary from can to can. *To avoid color inconsistencies:* When using more than one can of the same color paint, pour all the cans into a large bucket…stir well…then pour the paint back into the individual cans for easy use. The technique, called "boxing," assures consistent color throughout the job.

Source: Jack Luts, retired painting contractor, 30 Green Ave., Madison, NJ 07940.

How Tightwad Amy Dacyczyn Fixed Her Own House

Six years ago my husband Jim and I bought a house in Maine that needed quite a bit of fixing up. To save money, we decided to do a lot of the work ourselves. We're not done yet, but we're very happy with the results so far.

We're not exactly gifted craftspeople. My greatest skill is attention to detail. Jim is competent with tools, but he's not a pro. He calls himself a "wood butcher." We know that when you fix up an old house, you eventually own a home that is worth more than you could afford if you bought it today.

Here's what we've learned from our adventure—and what can be applied to any type of remodeling project…

Why a fixer-upper?

While economic necessity was a big reason we bought a house that needed work, getting a great deal was important, too. If you have the vision to see what a house can become after some work, buying one that's not perfect can be very smart.

Example: Our 1890 farmhouse was recently appraised. We were told it is now worth the purchase price, the labor and materials that have gone into it and as much as $50,000 more.

Lessons: Look at houses that need cosmetic work, not interior demolition. Avoid any place that has undergone extensive modern renovation in the past 50 years. It's something for which you pay extra but have to rip out completely if you want to restore the home to its original country feel.

Time-saver: Tour only those houses you might really buy. We went into only 10% of the 176 houses with "for sale" signs that we drove by.

How to attack:

•**Take your time.** Conversations with family and friends convinced us that the biggest renovation mistakes are due to two factors…

•**Rushing a decision**—there's less time pressure than you think.

•**Veering away from your personal taste in design.**

Example: I like white walls. On a whim, I stained the wooden walls in my home office. Eventually, I repainted them white.

•**Write a master plan.** Writing down everything you want to do to your home helps you set priorities and establish a reasonable schedule.

A plan also helps you spend your money wisely. It forces you to ask, *If I do project A, will project C look good next to it?*

•**Handle the eyesores and discomfort zones first.** Jim and I attacked the grimy, filthy kitchen first. We removed the dreadful wallpaper, patched the plaster and painted the walls white. We fixed a small hole in the ceiling with a piece of Sheetrock we found on the property. We put a piece of plywood down as a new bottom for the woeful sink cabinet.

Our kitchen "island" was created by using a large, freestanding antique counter we found in the woodshed. We refinished the top, painted it and hauled it into the kitchen.

All of this renovation took only a few hundred dollars—and yet it made the house livable.

•**Start with small tasks rather than major ones.** This will help you feel good quickly about the property you just bought.

We fixed up the kitchen as best we could but stopped work before it was done in the "country living" style we wanted. Eventually, we bought a beautiful $350 antique cupboard and other accessories to complete the look. I also bought an antique wood-burning stove. Instead of paying $800 for a restored one at an antique shop, I bought one through a newspaper ad for $350.

•**Hold off on desirable but less necessary tasks.** They can wait. Only after we took care of the kitchen and put in a small furnace to heat part of the house that was unheated did we go to work on the rest of the house. We took eight utility trailer loads to the dump.

We then landscaped the property by cutting the grass and weeds for the first time in probably decades. This cost no money, but the aesthetic result was remarkable.

•**When you see water damage**, act quickly. If you wait, the problem will be much worse—and more costly to fix.

Example: A foundation sill in the back of the carriage house was beginning to rot. We handled this immediately.

•**Don't assume you can't do something.** I refinished many old doors that were unsightly because ancient coats of varnish had become dark and dried. I used an ordinary paint scraper, then relied on denatured alcohol and steel wool to smooth off the remainder. How did I learn what to use? I was visiting someone who was refinishing woodwork— and I asked.

•**Do one room or project at a time.** This eases confusion, makes the home livable and allows you to feel a sense of accomplishment. Small triumphs—even just repainting a windowsill—give you the momentum to see the work through to completion.

Besides, no one wants to live in a place where almost everything looks unfinished.

•**Keep details consistent.** Don't mix old and modern styles. You can buy used items from shops that salvage materials from old houses or you can buy old-looking—but actually new—pieces from renovation supply places.

Browse through *Country Living, Old House Journal* and other publications to find sources in your area.

•**Hire outside help only when necessary.** Here are some compelling reasons…

•**There are health risks.** We hired professionals to replace our asbestos roof when it sprang a leak.

Important: If someone else is doing the dangerous work, relocate your family during the project. Or have the work done before you move in.

•**You lack the skills.** Although we probably could have made kitchen cabinets ourselves, they would never have looked as good as we wanted them to. The result we wanted required real craftsmanship.

•**You're up to your eyeballs handling the rest of your life.** Jim and I had four young kids when we began work on the house. A year later, we had twins. So we hired some carpenters for work we could have handled ourselves—if we had the time or the energy.

Source: Amy Dacyczyn, editor of *The Tightwad Gazette*, RR1, Box 3570, Leeds, ME 04263. Her latest book is *The Tightwad Gazette II.* Villard Books.

Home-Inspection Traps

Home inspectors can find possible problems in electrical, plumbing, heating and cooling systems, as well as with the roof, chimney, gutters and other outside areas.

What they often miss: Defects concealed under carpeting, inside walls or in other inaccessible areas.

Caution: Be wary of using an inspector recommended by a seller's real estate agent. He/she may be reluctant to say anything that could kill the deal. Find an inspector through referrals from your lawyer, friends or relatives. Urge him to find defects.

Source: David Schechner, partner, Schechner & Targan, 80 Main St., West Orange, NJ 07052.

Tricks and Traps in Doing Business With Contractors

The number of people fixing up, remodeling or building their homes is rising, attracting shifty contractors and builders hoping to make a fast buck.

The Better Business Bureau reports that home remodeling is number two—after retail stores—on its list of industries that generate the most consumer complaints.

Some bad contractors are outright thieves, while others take shortcuts at the home owner's expense in order to move on to the next job quickly.

To better protect yourself, here are the biggest traps now being set by inept or tricky home contractors and builders and how to defend yourself...

Trap: Contractors who substitute materials. A good plan for remodeling or building calls for specific parts or materials.

Reality: Even with good plans that outline the materials you want, some contractors may substitute cheaper ones. Sometimes the substitutions could produce a dangerous situation. One contractor installed plastic plumbing instead of copper pipes. That winter, the pipes began to leak and eventually burst.

Self-defense: When you first negotiate a contract, be sure the contractor is aware that you want receipts for all the materials he/she uses. Then, be sure to review them.

Trap: Painting shortcuts. If painting is being done, watch the preparation. That's when most rip-offs occur.

Painter's opportunity: A painter saves 40% of the labor needed to paint a house if he doesn't prime the surface. This may result in water damage and rot in a few years.

Sometimes, painters will lure you in with a low bid that doesn't reflect the cost of "extras," such as stripping window frames or plastering ceilings. Then they'll hit you with the full estimate after they and their crews have taken over your house and draped everything.

Self-defense: At the outset, insist that the painter specify in the contract precisely what will be included in the job. Then compare those tasks with the ones that other painters include in their bids.

If you are having the outside of your house painted—after the preparation has been completed but before the paint is applied—climb up the ladder and do a spot check to make sure the whole surface has been scraped, sanded, patched and primed. Nail holes should be filled, seams should be caulked, and there should be no flaking paint. In particular, look under the eaves and near gutters.

Trap: Roofing and drainage shortcuts. To save money, many bad contractors install shingles without first properly preparing the roof. Bad builders may neglect to set up a drainage system to pipe water away from the house.

Danger: Damage to the roof...or drainage next to the foundation. The latter may trigger basement leaks, which can cost you a huge amount of money to fix later.

Self-defense: When you talk to your contractor about the roofing work, make him explain what he will be doing to prepare the surface for the shingles. Ask about the quality of the flashing—the thin metal strips that seal around the shingles to prevent leaking into the roof. You should request high-quality flashing, which is made of either copper or aluminum.

Important: Think about the way precipitation hits your house. Does snow sit on the roof...or do driving rains from the south hit the windows? In snowy areas, an ice and water shield that extends halfway up the roof from the eaves might prevent ice damage. In places hit by driving rain, windows should have flashing all around the frame, not just at the top.

Before you buy a newly built house, make sure that someone has attached a drainpipe to the gutter so that water will travel at least 10 to 15 feet away from the house after it comes down from the roof.

Trap: Inflating the bid. Many contractors and tradespeople will inflate their bids when they are dealing with someone who lives in an upscale part of town. The theory is that you can afford to pay more, so you should.

Self-defense: For minor repairs, call the plumber or electrician and ask for an idea of costs before you give your address. If you don't like the bid, consider hiring a contractor from a neighboring community where prices aren't so high.

Example: When we remodeled our kitchen, the same cabinets were 20% less expensive from Denver dealers than from dealers in Boulder. That saved us $1,200.

Trap: Taking the money without doing the work. Some bad contractors are actually scamsters. They'll take your money for materials they haven't bought—or for work they haven't yet done—and then go on to another job.

Others will keep working only until you have paid them in full and then quit—leaving dozens of minor or major tasks undone. *Self-defense...*

•**Never pay a contractor completely for work that has not been done.** Always hold back enough money—we recommend 20%—to ensure that he will keep coming back until it's completely finished. Also, only pay for materials once they are delivered to your site. Pay for labor as it is completed—not in advance.

•**Leave a margin for error.** Make sure you never pay more money than the value of work that has been completed. Many contractors will move to the next job before finishing yours unless a significant amount of money is at stake. At the least, you should withhold enough to hire someone else to finish the job.

•**Always insist on an escrow account** when you make a deposit on a home you're having built. Otherwise the builder might use the cash for other purposes. Nearly all new-home builders require a substantial deposit—5% to 15% before beginning work. Make sure

the money is put in escrow and disbursed at closing only after construction is complete.

Source: Alan and Denise Fields, coauthors of five books on how consumers can save money, including *Your New House: The Alert Consumer's Guide to Buying and Building a Quality Home.* Windsor Peak Press.

Home Renovation Payoffs

Have a contractor add a second bathroom, and you'll recoup 98% of the project cost when you sell your house. Build a deck, and you'll get back only 72% of the outlay. *Other examples:* Renovate a kitchen, 95%...add a master bedroom and bath, 91%...add a family room, 88%...build a two-story addition, 84%... remodel a bathroom, 82%...renovate the exterior, 75%. *Note:* The payoff is greater on do-it-yourself projects, provided the job is well done.

Source: *Tips & Traps When Selling a Home* by Robert Irwin, a retired real estate broker in Rancho Palos Verdes, CA. McGraw-Hill.

How to Handle Annoying Neighbors

The secret of confronting obnoxious neighbors and getting them to change their behavior is knowing how and *when* to present your argument.

Solutions:

There's an old expression, *No one hears his own dog bark.* When you first confront a neighbor, assume he/she means well. A good opener is *I'm sorry to bring this up, but...*that makes it easier for the neighbor to apologize by saying, *Gee, I'm sorry it bothered you.*

If you start with threats, your neighbor may become defiant...and possibly belligerent. Once relationships between neighbors turn nasty, they are extremely difficult to untangle and the problems frequently become worse.

Solution: Pleasantly but firmly make your point and explain how the situation is affecting you. When they stop their annoying behavior, send a thank-you card.

If your plea is ignored:

•**Document several additional occurrences of the problem.** Write down the hour the noise occurred and how long it lasted.

•**Mail a copy of the detailed log** to the offending neighbor with a letter politely explaining the problem.

•**If the problem persists**, draft another letter, repeating when the noise occurred. Have other affected neighbors sign it, and send it to the offending party.

•**If your pleas are still ignored**, call the police the next time the noise occurs.

•**If the neighbor ignores police warnings**, you can sue in small-claims court for financial damages by converting the effect of what your neighbor is doing to you into monetary value.

Source: Cora Jordan, an Oxford, Mississippi, attorney and mediator specializing in neighbor disputes. She is author of *Neighbor Law: Fences, Trees, Boundaries & Noise*. Nolo Press.

Smart Planting

Planting trees around your house can save up to 25% on home energy bills. They block the wind in winter, and keep the house shaded in summer. Next to good insulation, energy-conscious landscaping is the best way to cut cooling and heating costs.

Source: Marc Schiler, associate professor of architecture, University of Southern California, and coauthor of *Energy-Efficient and Environmental Landscaping*. Appropriate Solutions Press.

Shrubs That Attract the Prettiest Birds

Highbush Blueberry provides sweet, flavorful berries for more than 100 species of birds, including Eastern bluebirds, black-capped chickadees, robins, orioles, tufted titmice, flickers, towhees and kingbirds.

In addition, small birds—such as sparrows and common yellowthroats—will probably nest among the bushes and brambles. This shrub's glossy oval leaves turn brilliant red in fall, and lovely white or pinkish bell-shaped flowers appear in late spring and at the onset of summer.

Planting: This shrub favors moist, well-drained, acidic soil and full sun. Hardiness varies widely, so buy locally for best results.

Source: Peter Loewer, who has written more than 22 books on gardening, including *The National Wildlife Federation's Guide to Gardening for Wildlife: How to Create a Beautiful Backyard Habitat for Birds, Butterflies and Other Wildlife*. Rodale Press.

Bumper Sticker Removal

Carefully pull up a corner and force gentle warmth under it with a blow-dryer. While blowing warm air, peel off as much of the sticker as possible. When the surface cools, use a cloth saturated with a solvent like mineral spirits or De-Solv-It to remove and dissolve the glue. Test the solvent first in an inconspicuous area to make sure it doesn't damage the paint. Keep a clean cloth saturated while rubbing back and forth—a dry cloth could scratch. After removing the glue, rinse off the solvent and polish the area.

Source: Don Aslett, founder, The Cleaning Center, a retail and mail-order company specializing in cleaning supplies.

Cutting Computer Cord Clutter

Replace overlong cords with shorter ones (of the right type, of course)…reel up any cord slack and twist-tie it into a neat, compact coil…consolidate power cords into one neat group by using a power strip that doubles as a surge supressor…improve the appearance of cords that run parallel by taping or tying them together.

Source: Don Aslett, founder, The Cleaning Center, a retail and mail-order company specializing in cleaning supplies.

4

Money Savvy

Disaster-Proof Your Money

How to protect your savings from life's biggest dangers…

Life is filled with unexpected challenges to your financial well-being—from injury and illness to fires and other accidents. *Steps to take to defend your assets…*

•**Disability insurance.** We all know that every family member who brings home a paycheck needs life insurance. If that person dies and isn't insured, it could leave a family financially devastated.

However, until you reach your late 60s, you are far more likely to be disabled—and unable to work—than to die.

Example: If you are between ages 35 and 55, you have a greater than 50% chance of suffering a disabling accident or illness that lasts longer than three months.

If you don't have disability insurance—and the family relies on your income—you must buy it.

The right amount: Calculate how much it costs you to live now…and how much less you could get by on in a pinch. If you'd need at least 60% of your current income, buy enough disability coverage to pay at least 60% of your current income each year to age 65.

Important: If you can afford it, pay extra to buy coverage that is adjusted periodically to keep up with inflation.

And—only buy coverage that pays off if you can't work at the job *you were trained to do.* Some policies only pay off if you are so badly disabled you can't work at any job.

•**Life insurance.** Couples with young children generally buy life insurance only to protect against the premature death of the breadwinner. They seldom buy life insurance for a spouse who stays home or works part-time caring for the children.

Trap: If the child-rearing spouse dies at a young age, someone else must be hired to raise the children until they can fend for themselves. Years of hiring child-care help can be very expensive.

Buy 10- to 15-year level-term insurance to cover the child-rearing spouse until the children are grown. The premium can't be raised during the 10- to 15-year term. Neither can the insurance be canceled if the person gets sick.

Limits: Buy enough insurance to pay child-care costs until the youngest child is 16. You shouldn't need protection after that...and you can drop the policy at that time.

•**Scams and fraud.** More and more people are losing money to scams today than ever before.

Beware of investments that are supposed to make you rich...of offers of interest rates on savings deposits far higher than any legitimate bank is currently paying. Beware of anyone who offers help for a fee—whether it be to find a job or restore your credit rating.

Never buy an investment over the phone—or by mail—unless you have initiated the contact and/or unless you have dealt with the party before.

Never send money to an organization or institution of which you have never heard...no matter how impressive its name sounds. When in doubt, ask a lawyer or accountant for advice.

And never forget the oldest advice of all—*If it sounds too good to be true...it almost certainly is.*

•**Health insurance.** Health maintenance organizations (HMOs) can provide a high level of health care for less than you'd pay for care in the open market.

Warning: Many HMOs turn out to be great deals for people who are well...but lousy deals for people who are sick.

Be leery of an HMO that makes you sign an agreement that you agree to accept arbitration in all disputes. If you were to sign such an agreement, you could be blocked from suing—even in cases of major malpractice.

Important: Learn the HMO's policy on referrals to specialists before you sign up. Doctors at some HMOs are penalized financially if they refer you to a specialist. Therefore, the only way to get the specialist's help is by paying for it yourself.

Choose an HMO where doctors are free to refer you to a doctor outside of the HMO's network when it is necessary to do so.

•**Homeowners' insurance.** Few people realize how many gaps there are in even the best homeowners' insurance policies.

Examples: You need extra-cost supplemental insurance to recover the full value of jewelry, furs or other valuables lost to fire or theft...you'll have to pay extra to recover the cost of replacing lost or damaged items—rather than being reimbursed at their current depreciated value.

Important: You not only must buy special coverage for flood and for earthquake damage, but complete coverage requires two policies—one for the dwelling...the other for the contents.

Go through all policies with your insurance agent to learn exactly where you need extra protection.

Whatever coverage you have, you will only get fully reimbursed if you can document that you owned all the items you claim were lost or damaged.

Save all receipts and canceled checks that prove ownership—and value. Go through your home with a camera or camcorder, photographing everything. That will prove to the insurance company you lost all that you claim you did.

Important: Purchase a single "umbrella" policy that will cover you against liability claims for whatever reason.

Cost: Basic umbrella policies provide $1 million in coverage. Adding an umbrella policy to your basic homeowners' and auto policies should add no more than 10% to your total insurance bill.

Source: Kenneth Stern, CFP, president of Asset Planning Solutions, Inc., tax, retirement and estate planning specialists, 17055 Via Del Campo, Suite. 101, San Diego 92127. He is author of *Safeguard Your Hard-Earned Savings.* Career Press.

How to Live Fee Free

It's easy to save $1,000 or more by reducing or eliminating annual financial fees...

•**Banking.** Many banks charge monthly check-writing or ATM fees that add up to as much as $150 to $200 a year on checking accounts. But the competition among banks looking for deposits is so strong that you can find fees as low as $50 a year if you shop around.

Don't make the mistake of passing up a no-fee checking account just because it requires a minimum balance. It often makes sense to take money out of some investments and deposit it in the bank to meet the no-fee minimum.

Potential annual savings: $160 or so if you transfer $1,000 from a money fund yielding 4% to the bank, thus eliminating $200 in fees on your checking account.

•**Brokers.** If you're an active investor and you make your own investment decisions, consider a discount broker. It can drastically reduce your commissions.

But discounters aren't all the same. Traditional discounters such as Charles Schwab (800-435-4000) and Fidelity (800-544-8888) offer some services such as free investment research. They will also save you as much as 40% on commissions. Deep-discount brokers such as Wall Street Discount (800-221-4034) and Arnold Securities (800-328-4076) take a more bare-bones approach but offer even bigger commission cuts.

Potential annual savings: It depends on how many trades you make each year. The greater the number, the greater the savings.

•**Credit cards.** If you run a balance of $1,000 a year, a low-rate card could cut your interest costs in half.

If you pay off your balance every month, choose a card that doesn't carry an annual fee.

Potential annual savings: $35 to $100 for a no-fee card…or $72 in interest charges if you run a balance of $1,200 and switch from a 19% card to a 13% card.

•**Mutual funds.** Many mutual funds sold by brokers carry sales charges—or "loads"—of 2% to 5%, which are used to compensate the people who sell them to investors.

Better: Choose no-load funds, such as those sold by Vanguard, T. Rowe Price and Fidelity. On a $1,000 investment, you would save as much as $50.

Also avoid high annual fees that some funds charge. *Ideal:* Choose stock funds with annual fees of less than 1.25% and bond funds with annual fees of less than 1%.

Potential savings: Roughly $150 on an investment of $10,000…annually.

Source: Jonathan Pond, president of Financial Planning Information Inc., in Watertown, MA. He is the host of *"Finding Financial Freedom with Jonathan Pond,"* a PBS special feature.

What Every Woman Should Know About Money

Any married woman today is likely to fall victim to one of what I call The Three Ds—*Death, Divorce* or other *Disasters. Consider these stunning statistics…*

•**One-half of all marriages** will end in divorce.

•**Nearly 80% of married women** will become widows and remain widows for an average of 15 years.

•**If the husband is 40 or younger** he is three times more likely to be disabled than to die, and after age 55 the chances are he will be disabled for a year or more.

Yet few wives know much about family finances beyond routine, day-to-day matters. Even many high-powered career women tend to abdicate a role in investment decisions and forward planning. But if a woman heard about a vaccine for a disease that was bound to strike one out of two people, she would probably dash to the doctor to get it.

No woman should be ignorant about money—how it is spent, where it is kept, how it is invested, how it is owned. Ignorance will leave a woman vulnerable while she is married—and in trouble when she is no longer married.

The more a woman knows the better off she is.

It is vital to know the law in one's own state as it applies to marriage. Women should know their rights and what will happen to them in case of divorce or death.

Community-property states. There are some variations, but basically each spouse owns half of all the property amassed during the marriage, no matter who earns the money or what name is on the title.

Exceptions: Inherited property and gifts.

Debts are also community property. If a husband borrows money that he then blows at a casino in Las Vegas, half the debt is the wife's.

Common-law states. A spouse doesn't automatically own half the property. Joint ownership has to be specified when it's acquired. Otherwise, ownership rests with the title holder. He has the right to sell or mortgage the property, even if it is the family home. If a spouse dies without property in her name, she has nothing to leave for the support of, say, an aged, dependent parent.

In the case of divorce or death, however, the assets a couple acquired during the marriage then become *marital property* to be divided. The split is rarely 50/50.

Knowing a wife has some legal rights to her husband's money, as he does to hers, can and should spur her to take an active role in family finances.

The bottom line:

Six things women usually don't know about their husband's money, but should…

- **How much he spends.**
- **How much he has.**
- **How much he owes.**
- **How much insurance he has and what kind.**
- **How the assets** (savings accounts, property, stock, etc.) are held.
- **How he is leaving it** (the will).

One way a wife can begin learning about her husband's money, and her own, is to think of the family as a small company. Make up the same kind of corporate reports that a business would. Start with a look at what the family has. Make a list of all its assets. *Include:*

- **Personal property** (items like the house, furniture, car, etc.).
- **Financial assets** (stocks, bonds, savings accounts, etc.).
- **Real estate**, business partnerships and hidden assets, such as stock options, pension funds, insurance (cash and benefit value).

Indicate how each asset is owned.

Then look at what the family owes—its liabilities. *Include:*

- **Outstanding taxes.**
- **Mortgages.**
- **Loans** (business, personal, car, home equity).
- **Credit card debt**, installment debt, margin debt on brokerage accounts.

The family's net worth is the difference between assets and liabilities.

The other important *corporate report* is a cash-flow statement—how much money is coming in, how much is going out.

Make a list of total income, from salary and bonuses to dividends and interest.

Then track expenditures—every item right down to newspapers and magazines. The two should be equal. If outgo is larger, obviously the family is spending too much.

Having a firm grasp of the facts and figures enables a woman to know how she would manage on her own if something happened to her husband or the marriage. If she doesn't know now, she'll really have problems later on.

Even more important, not knowing about the family money can leave a woman in a marriage in which she does not play an equal role in making decisions. It can leave her feeling dependent and vulnerable. Knowing about the assets, helping to keep the records and taking part in decision making are all part of the economic partnership that modern marriage is supposed to be.

The will:

If a couple makes financial decisions together, they will probably discuss wills. The husband's will shouldn't come as a surprise to the wife.

Some couples think that if one spouse dies without a will (intestate) the surviving spouse will inherit everything. *Not true*—except for jointly held assets, state law dictates how the money is disbursed. *Examples:*

- **In Oklahoma**, a surviving spouse receives one-half the estate. Children get the other half. If there are no children but a parent or sibling survives the husband, the widow would get all the marital property plus a one-third interest in the remaining estate.

•**In California**, a community-property state, each spouse already owns half the marital property. The surviving spouse would inherit half of her husband's community property and a portion—from one-third to one-half, depending on surviving children, parents or siblings—of his separate property.

Talk to your husband:

It is hard to admit vulnerability—especially in money matters. Whether based on a tradition of dependence or the reality of lower wages, a lot of women—even those with substantial earning power—fear they will wind up destitute.

Women have taken care of home, husband, children and parents. It is time they started taking care of their finances.

The keys are knowledge and participation.

Source: Shelby White, a financial writer who has written and lectured extensively on the subject of women and money. She is the author of *What Every Woman Should Know About Her Husband's Money*. Random House.

Simple Way to Save $600 a Year

Save all your loose change in a can or jar. As the container fills, deposit the money in the bank. Saving a dollar a day plus all your pocket change should give you savings of $50 a month—or a total of $600 a year. *Strategy:* Let your buying habits help you. *Example:* If you buy a newspaper every morning for 35 cents, make it a habit to pay with a dollar—and save the 65 cents in change.

Source: Barbara O'Neill, CFP, author of *Saving on a Shoestring: How to Cut Expenses, Reduce Debt, Stash More Cash*. Dearborn Financial.

Where to Find Cash Fast

Don't pull out your high-interest-rate credit card when you need a large sum of cash quickly. *There are much smarter sources to tap first…*

•**Negotiate a home-equity line of credit.** You win two ways with a home-equity loan—rates are low and the interest you pay on it is tax-deductible. Take the time to shop around for the best deal. Competition is forcing banks to lower their borrowing costs.

Caution: You can lose your home if you are not careful about repaying the loan.

•**Cash in your certificates of deposit.** The only penalty you pay is forfeiting three or six months' worth of interest.

Caution: People who hold long-term, high-yielding CDs from years ago probably would want to look for some other source of cash.

•**Borrow from parents and friends.** If you are borrowing less than $10,000, the money can be treated as a gift and will not be taxed. If, however, you want the money to be treated as a loan, you must work out a payback schedule and pay a reasonable rate of interest.

Caution: Borrowing from parents, friends or relatives can strain your relationship.

•**Borrow from your 401(k) plan.** In general, you can borrow from 401(k) plans to pay college tuition or medical costs or make the down payment on a house. The money must be repaid in five years. Check with your 401(k) plan administrator at work because rules vary.

•**Obtain a margin loan** through your stockbroker. They usually carry very low interest rates because your stocks and bonds are used as collateral. *Drawback:* The IRS does not allow you to deduct the interest payments.

•**Borrow from your IRA.** You can withdraw money from your IRA once a year, as long as you put the money back into a new IRA account at the end of 60 days.

Source: Lewis J. Altfest, L. J. Altfest & Co., 140 William St., New York 10038. He is author of *Lew Altfest Answers Almost All Your Questions About Money*. McGraw-Hill.

How Not to Be Robbed By Your Bank

Bank fees are on the rise. Here are my favorite ways to reduce or avoid them.

•**Automated teller machines (ATMs).** The average cost for making a withdrawal at your own bank is now up to $1. But this fee can rise to around $2 when you take out cash from an ATM that is not owned by your bank.

Self-defense: Stick to your bank's ATM... and find a bank that charges for ATM use only if your account balance falls below a specific amount.

You can also cut down on ATM fees by using the machines less frequently. Plan a weekly budget, and use the ATM only once each week to withdraw enough cash.

• **Minimum-balance fees.** An increasing number of banks now charge a fee if your balance dips below the minimum requirement for even a single day. Other banks still base the fee on your average daily balance over the course of a month.

In both cases, such fees can be avoided.

Self-defense: Look elsewhere for a better deal. Small banks, credit unions and savings and loans tend to have much lower balance requirements and substantially lower fees. Before giving up on your current bank, however, ask if it has a different type of account—one with fewer "bells and whistles"—that would be more cost-efficient for you.

• **Nuisance fees.** Believe it or not, some banks now charge customers $3 just for calling to find out their balances.

Self-defense: If you already have an account at such a bank, threaten to take your business elsewhere unless those charges are rescinded.

Call the bank manager and begin by saying politely that you have been a good customer for a long time. If you don't get any satisfaction from the manager, speak to the bank's vice president of operations.

Warning: This approach probably won't succeed if your account is at a large money-center bank. Generally, the smaller the bank, the more flexible it will be.

If you must switch, don't sign up for a new account without reviewing the institution's full fee schedule. Ask the bank for a copy.

• **Safe-deposit boxes.** When banks send out renewal forms for safe-deposit boxes, some ask you to pay for insurance on the box's contents. It's optional, and, in most cases, it is best to decline the coverage.

Reason I: Such insurance shouldn't be required to protect your valuables. The bank's vault is supposed to do that.

Reason II: The insurance may be virtually useless. If the boxes are looted by robbers, the claims adjuster won't necessarily believe that the items you say you stored were actually in the box.

Better: Insure the contents of the box in a rider to your homeowner's policy.

• **Inactivity/activity fees.** Some banks now have penalties for depositors with idle accounts. Conversely, some tack on extra fees for customers who make "too many" withdrawals and/or deposits.

Strategy: Ask your bank about its activity-fee policy. If it doesn't make sense, write a letter to the president or bank manager politely threatening to withdraw your money.

Source: Edward Mrkvicka, Jr., president of Reliance Enterprises, Inc., a national financial consulting firm based in Marengo, IL. He is a former CEO of an Illinois bank and author of *The Bank Book: How to Revoke Your Bank's "License to Steal."* HarperPerennial.

Get Higher Returns On Your Savings...Safely

Put your excess savings into higher-paying six-month or one-year CDs or in money market funds. If interest rates are going down, buy CDs...if they are going up, buy money market funds. Consider out-of-state banks, which may pay higher rates.

Important: Don't be afraid to cash in a CD —even if you're hit with an early withdrawal penalty—if you can buy another CD at a rate that is high enough to more than make up the expense.

Source: Alexandra Armstrong, CFP, chairman, Armstrong, Welch & McIntyre, Inc., a financial planning firm, 1155 Connecticut Ave. NW, Suite. 250, Washington, DC 20036.

ATM Fees on the Rise

Almost all banks charge customers who use machines owned by other banks. Now many of those other banks are charging customers *access fees* as well. *Result:* The average cost of withdrawing money from an ATM anywhere other than your own bank is expected to rise to about $2 or more. *Self-defense:* Use a bank teller…or use your own bank's machine. If you must regularly take out funds elsewhere, withdraw larger amounts less often. Fees are not determined by the amount withdrawn. The average ATM user withdraws only $55. At an ATM with a $2 fee, the withdrawal cost is a very high 3.63%.

Source: Edward Mrkvicka, Jr., president, Reliance Enterprises, a banking consulting firm, Marengo, IL.

Balancing Your Checkbook

When you can't balance your checkbook—and you know you've added correctly—you've probably transposed a number.

Example: $235 for $253. *How to tell:* Subtract the difference between your balance and what the bank says you have. If the resulting number is divisible by nine—18…27…36, etc.—there's been a transposition. Go back, and carefully compare each of your entries against the numbers in the bank statement.

Source: Eric Gelb, CPA, assistant vice president/corporate finance for a major US bank and author of *Checkbook Management: A Guide to Saving Money.* Career Advancement Center, Inc.

Checking Account Smarts

Avoid a bank checking account that charges a monthly fee when your account drops below a certain limit for one day. *Better:* An account for which monthly fees are determined by the average daily balance.

Source: Mary Hunt, publisher, *Cheapskate Monthly*, Box 2135, Paramount, CA 90723.

Big, Bad Credit Card Traps

Beware of complicated interest-calculation methods that can wipe out the benefits of a credit card's grace period. With the two-cycle billing method, you'll need at least two back-to-back, no-balance months to avoid interest charges.

Also: Grace periods themselves are being shortened—some banks give only 20 days, down from 25 to 30.

Self-defense: When switching cards, avoid both traps.

Source: Gerri Detweiler, financial writer and credit card and debt-control consultant in Woodbridge, VA. She is author of *The Ultimate Credit Handbook.* Plume.

All about Credit Union Loans

Credit union rates are generally better than bank and savings-and-loan rates. Credit unions usually charge less for new-car and personal loans…and pay more on certificates of deposit and money market accounts.

Reason: Credit unions are exempt from federal income tax, their workers are often volunteers, and their office space may be subsidized by the sponsoring business or association. Credit unions are membership associations—you must be eligible to join.

More information: Credit Union National Association, 800-358-5710.

Source: Gail Liberman, editor, *Bank Rate Monitor*, and author of *Improving Your Credit and Reducing Your Debt.* John Wiley & Sons.

Your Home Can Cost You Much Less Than It Does Now

Owning a home is a major part of the American Dream—and a very expensive part. But it doesn't have to be that way. Most Americans needlessly pay too much on their real estate taxes, insurance and escrow/impound accounts.

Here are steps you can take to lower your cost of home ownership by $200 to $2,000 each year—or even more...

• **Reduce your property taxes.** The National Taxpayers Union estimates that 60% of home owners are overassessed and pay more in property taxes than they should.

Reasons: Property values have declined in many states. In addition, individual assessment mistakes made by local tax authorities are common.

Every property owner can appeal to the local assessor, yet fewer than 2% ever do because they fear that once the assessor investigates, the assessed value will be increased rather than lowered.

The facts: You don't need a lawyer to appeal. What you need are facts about comparable sales in your neighborhood showing that homes similar in size to yours were sold for less than the comparable assessed value. *Note:* Assessed value and market price are seldom identical.

Check property tax records at the town, city or county clerk's office—the records can be in any of the three offices. Or ask that relevant information be mailed or faxed to you.

Even if property values have not declined, it's worth checking assessor records. Many homes have their features misrecorded. Make sure the number of rooms, total square footage and the size of the lot are accurately recorded.

Many localities offer special reductions for senior citizens. They should contact the tax assessor's office to ascertain whether they are receiving the appropriate assessment reductions due them.

To avoid a higher reassessment, check your home's listing in the local tax rolls to be certain your home has no amenities that the assessor has mistakenly listed for your property.

• **Accelerate mortgage payments.** Paying more than the minimum on your mortgage each month offers guaranteed long-term savings by putting the power of interest compounding to work for you instead of for your lender. *How to do it right...*

• **Pay half your monthly mortgage every two weeks.** By using this strategy, you will make 26 payments—the equivalent of 13 months rather than 12. Most lenders won't let you do this every two weeks, but they will let you pay more each month.

More is less: Approximate by dividing your monthly payment—excluding taxes—by 12 and adding the resulting sum to each mortgage payment. *Result:* You'll make the equivalent of 13 payments per year and pay off a 30-year mortgage in between 18 and 22 years.

• **Prepay a set amount per month.** Prepaying just $25 a month on a 30-year, 8% fixed-rate mortgage will save you $23,337 over the life of the loan. Prepay $100 a month and you'll save $62,456 in interest—and own your home "free and clear" almost 10 years ahead of schedule.

• **Reduce insurance costs.** There are several strategies you can use to significantly reduce your insurance costs...

• **If you bought your homeowners' policy through your mortgage lender**, your premiums are probably too high. Get a competitive bid from an outside insurer.

• **Raise your deductible from $250 to $500**, and you will save 10% or more on annual premiums.

• **If the value of your home is now sharply lower than when you bought it**, consider reducing the *replacement cost coverage* portion of the policy, which protects property replacement.

• **Eliminate Private Mortgage Insurance (PMI).** PMI protects the bank in case you default. It is required when the starting equity in your home is less than 20%—or if you have blemishes on your credit report. The cost of PMI is $250 to $560 or more annually for every $100,000 borrowed on a mortgage.

Trap: Many home owners are paying costly PMI fees unnecessarily. *This is most likely if...*

...you live in an area where property values have recently risen.

...you have never calculated when you will be able to stop paying PMI.

...you prepay regularly on your mortgage.

Unfortunately, lenders don't tell you when you're eligible to discontinue PMI.

Self-defense: Calculate your equity by figuring out your mortgage balance. Get this from your lender. Then subtract that number from today's value of your home, based on recent sales of similar homes in your neighborhood—or ask a realtor to give you an estimate. If the answer (your equity) exceeds 20% of the present-day value, you should no longer have to pay PMI. When this is so, contact the lender in writing. Demand to have PMI eliminated. This is your right.

Note: In an area where housing prices are very soft, lenders may raise the equity threshold to 25%.

• **Get refunds and reduced payments from your escrow/impound account.** This is a separate account held by the mortgage lender that you pay into each month for the property taxes and hazard insurance the lender pays for you. It is called an "impound account" in California and the West. *Federal say that lenders…*

• **Cannot require more than two months' payments as a cushion.** Some now require cushions of four months or more, which is illegal.

• **Must send you a statement early in the year** projecting how much escrow payments could increase. A year-end statement will compare projected and actual payments.

• **Must consider money already in the account when calculating** the monthly payment for the coming year—resulting in lower payments for most home owners.

Strategy: Find out how much is in your escrow account by checking your monthly statement or calling your lender. If the lowest balance during the year is more than twice your monthly payment—principal, interest, taxes and insurance—complain to the lender.

• **Make sure you're receiving legally mandated interest.** Millions of consumers don't receive interest on their escrow accounts, though they should.

Important: Financial institutions in California, Connecticut, Iowa, Maine, Maryland, Massachusetts, Minnesota, New Hampshire, New York, Oregon, Rhode Island, Utah, Vermont and Wisconsin are now required to make interest payments. The rates range from 1.6% to 5.25%, and payments are usually made annually.

On an average balance of $2,000, 5% interest comes to $100 a year—*for the life of the mortgage.* That could mean as much as $3,000 in your pocket.

Strategy: If your home is in one of the 14 states and you're not getting interest, complain to your lender or contact the American Homeowners Association.

Source: Richard Roll, president and executive director of the American Homeowners Association (AHA), an independent organization in Washington, DC, that helps educate consumers about better ways to buy and own homes. For AHA's *Tax Reduction Kit* or its *Escrow Refund Guide,* call 800-470-2242, or write to AHA Member Services, 2121 Precinct Line Rd., Suite. 3000, Hurst, TX 76054.

How to Cash in on Your Home Without Moving

Your personal wealth may in large part consist of the equity you've built up in a home that you've owned for a number of years.

Now, or in the future you may want to cash in on this wealth while keeping your home. *Here are ways to do it…*

Refinancing:

You may be able to replace your current mortgage loan with a new loan carrying a lower interest rate—increasing your free cash every month.

Rule of thumb: The cost of refinancing probably is worthwhile if it enables you to reduce your interest rate by two percentage points or more…or to switch to a type of mortgage (from adjustable to fixed rate, or vice versa) that is better suited to your current circumstances.

If the new loan is larger than the old loan, it may provide a substantial payment of cash up front.

Interest paid on a refinancing is usually considered tax-deductible mortgage interest, provided total borrowing against the home does not increase by more than $100,000.

Requirements: Lenders treat refinancings like original mortgages, so you must have good credit and sufficient income to make repayments to obtain the loan.

If you are simply replacing an old loan, you may be able to refinance up to 90% of your home's value. But if you will receive cash through the refinancing, borrowing probably will be limited to 75% of the home's value.

Refinancings of *second* homes receive harsher terms. Usually only 70% of the home's value may be refinanced, and "cashing out"—taking out your equity in cash—is rarely allowed.

Age is *not* a consideration with a refinancing. You can't be denied a 30-year loan even if you are 97 years old, provided you meet the lender's credit requirements.

On a refinance, as with original mortgages, borrowers can expect to pay fairly expensive fees—for appraisals, credit reports, mortgage insurance, escrow and recording fees, title insurance, mortgage points and the like. However, many of these may be financed along with the loan.

Finding a loan: Today's lending market is very competitive, with many different lenders offering comparable products. So it's best to seek out a capable and considerate loan officer at a reputable institution to deal with, rather than pick a lender by looking at the terms of advertised loans.

Home equity borrowing:

A home equity loan is a second mortgage taken against your home. Interest on up to $100,000 of such financing is usually tax deductible as mortgage interest no matter how the money is spent—a tax break that has made this a very popular form of borrowing.

An equity loan may also take the form of a line of credit that is secured by your home and enables you to borrow funds only as they are needed—such as when college tuition bills become due. As with a first mortgage or refinancing, you must have good credit and demonstrate your ability to repay.

Limits: Home equity borrowing and the balance of a first mortgage combined usually cannot exceed 70% to 85% of your home's value. Your repayment ability will be evaluated on the basis of the combined first-mortgage and equity-loan payments you will owe each month, relative to your income.

Disadvantages: Equity loans often carry higher interest rates and have shorter repay-ment periods—typically 10 or 15 years—than first mortgages. So you'll make a larger repayment for every dollar borrowed. *And:*

•**Equity loans carry the same kinds of fees as first mortgages**, although these fees will be smaller if a smaller amount is borrowed.

•**With an equity line of credit** you may incur a substantial "document preparation fee" every time you borrow funds.

Caution: Many equity loans call for a balloon payment after a period of years. At that point the entire balance of the loan will be due and payable at once.

Don't take out such a loan unless you are sure you will have the funds to repay it.

Strategy: An equity loan typically is a better deal than refinancing when you wish to borrow against only a portion of your home's value and when a refinancing wouldn't significantly lower the interest rate from that on your existing mortgage loan.

Reverse mortgages:

Even if you lack the credit rating or income to qualify for a conventional loan, but have paid off or almost paid off the mortgage loan on your home, you may still be able to extract cash from it through a reverse mortgage. Here, the lender pays *you* money each month in a lump sum or in payments as you need them. The lender doesn't care about your credit rating because the loan will be paid off with funds raised from the sale of your home at the end of the loan term—typically, when you move from the home—or die. (The loan may be repaid with other funds if they are available.)

If proceeds from the sale of the house exceed the loan amount, the balance is paid to you—or your estate.

Generally, the older you are, the larger the monthly payment you can receive through a reverse mortgage, since the value of the loan is paid to you over your life expectancy, which is shorter for those who are older.

However, the details of payment schedules and other terms can vary greatly, and should be considered—and negotiated—carefully.

Advantages: A reverse mortgage provides ready cash...and you don't have to make any repayments during the loan term...the payments you receive are tax free, since borrowed amounts are not taxable income…you don't need good credit to get a loan.

Major disadvantage: Your home must eventually be sold if other funds aren't available to pay off the loan.

There are three types of reverse mortgages:

•**FHA-insured loans.** Government insurance protects the lender of the loan against loss should the home's value drop to an amount insufficient to repay the loan.

•**Lender-insured loans.** The lender obtains insurance against loss through the private market.

Insurance premiums for both of these insured loans are added to the cost of the loan and paid by the borrower.

•**Uninsured loans.** The lender assumes the risk of loss on the loan.

Fees and closing costs for all types of reverse mortgages are similar to those on a conventional "forward" mortgage, but usually may be paid with borrowed funds.

Pros and cons of various reverse mortgages:

•**FHA-insured reverse mortgages** are the most common and readily available. They are now offered in 43 states. But FHA loans cannot exceed the FHA's 203b amount, which varies by region. So if your home is worth much more, you won't be able to tap the difference with an FHA-insured loan.

•**Privately insured reverse mortgages** are similar in many ways to FHA loans, one important difference being that larger loans are available in the private sector.

•**Uninsured loans cost the least in fees** and expenses and can provide the largest amount of cash. But because of the risk to the lender, they usually have a set term—such as 10 years—after which you must sell the house. *Don't consider such a loan unless you are sure you'll then be willing to move.*

You can find lenders who make FHA-insured loans by calling your local office of the Department of Housing and Urban Development (HUD) in the government listings in the phone book, or the *Fannie Mae information line:* 800-732-6643.

Look for non-FHA loans that may be available in your area by inquiring with local realtors and mortgage banks.

Critical: Remember that in the end you could stand to lose your home through a reverse mortgage. Examine loan terms scrupulously before committing.

Source: H.L. Kibbey, host of the radio talk show "House Calls" and author of *The Growing Older Guide to Real Estate*, Box 1885, Lake Oswego, OR 97035.

Shop for a Mortgage Before You Shop for a House

Knowing how much financing you can get focuses your search.

Helpful: Talk with at least three lenders. Have one run your credit reports so you can correct errors. Ask the lender how it views negative items in your record—and prepare explanations. If you qualify, lenders issue a "hand-holding letter" stating the maximum loan amount.

Strategy: If you plan to spend less than the amount for which you qualify, have the letter state the lower amount—so sellers don't know you could spend more. Having a hand-holding letter makes you more attractive to a seller who has comparable bids from different buyers.

Source: Peter Miller, real estate broker in Silver Spring, MD, and author of several books, including *Buy Your First Home Now.* HarperPerennial.

For a Faster Sale

Commissions are negotiable when selling real estate—though the standard is 6%.

For a faster sale: Offer bonuses to agents who sell quickly or at your price. Offering a trip, TV set or old car or boat that you no longer want will make your property stand out. You can also offer a higher commission for a faster sale—but tangible items may be more likely to attract agents' attention.

Source: *Tips and Traps When Negotiating Real Estate* by Robert Irwin, real estate broker and consultant, Los Angeles. McGraw-Hill.

Save by Paying The Mortgage Faster

Your biggest lifetime expense isn't buying your home, *it's paying the mortgage.* But every $1 extra you can *prepay* goes directly to reduce your principal...and small monthly prepayments could cut 10 years off the term of your mortgage and cut interest payments by one-third. Three ways to set up a prepayment plan for your mortgage...

•**Do it yourself.** Budget enough each month to pay your monthly bill plus one-twelfth of a monthly payment. By the end of the year, you'll have made a 13th payment.

•**Have the bank do it**. Many mortgages can be converted from monthly to twice-monthly or every two weeks. That accelerates both the payments and your saving. There's no margin for error, though. Missed payments put your house at risk.

•**Have someone else do it.** Authorize a bonded, FDIC-insured third party to debit your bank account every two weeks for the mortgage money and to make 13 mortgage payments per year.

Important: Mark all extra payments as "prepayment to principal." Make sure the lender credits your mortgage account. Keep accurate records that document your prepayments.

Source: Richard Roll, president and executive director of the American Homeowners Association, an independent organization that educates consumers about home ownership, Washington, DC.

Adjustable Rate Mortgage Mistakes

Between 38% and 46% of all adjustable-rate mortgages are adjusted incorrectly—usually in ways that favor the lender. *Other common mistakes made by banks and other mortgage-holders:* Improperly credited monthly payments ...principal prepayments incorrectly credited to escrow accounts.

Source: American Homeowners Foundation, a nonprofit organization in Arlington, VA, which audits ARMs and splits any refunds with the homeowner.

Home Equity Loan and Credit Card Trap

Deductible credit card interest is being pushed by banks offering cards tied to home-equity loans. The cards are linked to home-equity lines of credit, on which interest is tax-deductible. Therefore, interest on items that you charge with the cards is also tax-deductible. *Beware:* Someone who falls behind on payments could lose his/her home. No credit card purchase is worth that risk.

Source: Ruth Susswein, executive director, Bankcard Holders of America, 524 Branch Dr., Salem, VA 24153.

Choosing the Right Financial Adviser

Before hiring a financial adviser, carefully read Part II of the Securities and Exchange Commission Form ADV—which must be given to clients. It explains services, fees, investments and the adviser's educational background.

Also request Part I of the form, which details legal history. Check the adviser's track record and consistency of performance.

Source: John Markese, president, American Association of Individual Investors, 625 N. Michigan Ave., Chicago 60611.

First-Time Home Buyer Programs

Special first-time-buyer programs may be available to those who have owned homes before. A first-time home buyer is usually defined as someone who has not held title to property for at least three years. Ask lenders in your state how they define a first-time buyer—and what special programs are available. Typical incentives include special, low down payments and lower-than-market mortgage interest rates.

Source: *Your Money and Your Home: A Step-by-Step Guide to Financing or Refinancing Your Home* by Sidney Lenz, executive vice president, Countrywide Funding Corporation in Pasadena, CA. Griffin Publishing.

Safety Plus Liquidity

Earn higher interest—while still having access to your money—by "laddering" your CDs. *How it works:* Invest your money in equal amounts (say, $1,000 each) by buying CDs with maturities of one, two, three, four and five years. After one year, when the first CD matures, reinvest the money (including all interest) into a new five-year CD. You can risk putting away money for that long because in another year your next CD will mature. *Benefit:* Within a few years all your money will be earning higher, five-year interest rates without your having to tie up all your cash for five years at a time.

Source: Jane Bryant Quinn is author of *Making the Most of Your Money: Smart Ways to Create Wealth and Plan Your Finances in the '90s.* Simon & Schuster.

Credit Card Errors... How to Dispute Them And Win

Here are the most common credit card problems and how to straighten them out...

• **There's a problem with the merchandise purchased with the card.**

Solution: The Fair Credit Billing Act (FCBA) gives you the legal right to withhold payment on a credit card charge if the merchandise you purchased was different from what you ordered...or it was delivered on the wrong day... or it was delivered in the wrong quantity.

Under the FCBA, you can also refuse to pay a credit card charge for merchandise you did not accept.

Example: A new refrigerator was delivered to your home, but it was the wrong color so you refused to accept delivery and the delivery people left with the refrigerator.

How to dispute the charge: Once you notice the charge on your statement, write a letter to your credit card issuer at the address listed on your statement for billing errors and inquiries.

Don't include the letter with your payment for other items on your bill. And don't procrastinate. Under the FCBA you only have 60 days* to protest the charge. In your letter include your name, address, account number, the specific charge you're disputing and why.

Send your letter certified mail, return receipt requested. After the credit card company receives your letter, it has no more than 90 days to prove the charge is valid—or it must remove it from your bill.

Telephone trap: Don't just call the customer service number to complain. Telephone complaints aren't covered under the law, so you lose the clout the law gives you when you write.

The FCBA does not cover questionable charges when...

• **You have changed your mind about a purchase.**

• **The merchant has a clearly posted "no refunds" policy.**

• **You are disputing the "quality" of merchandise or services you bought.**

Helpful: If you're buying something valuable, such as gems, artwork or antiques, always get the seller to write on the sales slip all promises about quality and authenticity.

• You want to dispute a charge because of the poor quality of goods or services. These types of disputes are common.

Solution: You can dispute a credit card purchase if the quality of the goods or services was unsatisfactory as long as:

• **The amount of the charge was $50 or more.**

• **The purchase was made in your home state**—or within 100 miles of your billing address.

• **You have made an effort in good faith to resolve the problem directly with the merchant.**

There's no time limit for disputing charges because of quality. But there is one big catch—you can only dispute the amount of the charge you haven't paid off. If you've already paid the bill in full, you're out of luck.

*The 60-day period usually starts from the postmark date of the bill on which the charge appeared.

Write it out. Although quality disputes don't have to be in writing, I strongly suggest you do so anyway. Again, send your letter return receipt requested. You can continue to withhold payment on the charge until the matter is resolved.

•**There's a charge on your bill you don't recognize.**

Solution: You have the right to ask your credit card company to provide documentary proof of the charge.

If the issuer produces "proof," such as a sales slip, but you did not make the charge or authorize someone else to make the charge, the most you can be responsible for is the first $50 of the unauthorized charge—and that's only if your card was actually used in the transaction.

Example: If someone stole your credit card number and used it without the plastic card, you are not responsible for any of the unauthorized charges.

If the issuer balks at taking the unauthorized charge off your account, tell the issuer you want to sign a "fraud affidavit" certifying you didn't make the charge. That should indicate you are serious about not paying.

Credit background: Keep all records relating to any type of credit problem—or credit report problem—for seven years. That's the length of time negative information can be reported on your account.

If your account is transferred to another financial institution, for example, you could find the same problem popping up again. Keep your records to quickly clear up misunderstandings about past accounts.

Source: Gerri Detweiler, consumer credit consultant in Woodbridge, Virginia, and head of public policy for the National Council of Individual Investors. She is author of *The Ultimate Credit Handbook*. Plume.

Common Money-Management Mistake

Mistake: Withholding too much in taxes from your paycheck. That is like giving the IRS

an interest-free loan. Ask someone in your company's benefits department to help you calculate the correct amount, or consult your tax preparer. *Another smart strategy:* Pay off your credit card debts, which cost about 15% in interest and are not tax-deductible.

Source: Stuart Kessler, CPA, Goldstein Golub Kessler, 1185 Avenue of the Americas, New York 10036.

Barter Moves Upscale

Travel barter is increasing by almost 20% a year, as companies looking to slash airfare and hotel costs sign up with trade exchange companies. *Examples:* A drafting supply company saved $18,000 by bartering surplus pens, markers and other supplies for 354 rooms for a sales meeting. A veterinarian pays for his Caribbean resort vacation by earning barter credits at an animal hospital that participates in his barter club. *Helpful:* The International Reciprocal Trade Association (IRTA) will soon offer a new on-line referral service to reputable trade exchange companies.

Source: Paul Suplizio, CEO, International Reciprocal Trade Association, Alexandria, Virginia, quoted in *Crain's New York Business*, 220 E. 42 St., New York 10017.

Use Less Water in The Bathroom

By putting a brick or weighted jug in the toilet tank to reduce the amount of water used with each flush. The amount of water saved will depend on the amount displaced by the object in the tank. *Also:* Turn off water while shaving or brushing teeth—this saves two gallons of water each time.

Source: Earth Systems Consultants, Fremont, CA.

The Shrewd, Simple Secrets of Saving... Saving...Saving

There are only two ways to boost your savings—by increasing your income or cutting back on spending. In my experience, I have found that it is far easier to trim your expenses than to take on another job or more work to increase earnings.

Here's how to save more—and why finding the money is probably easier than you think...

•**Draw up a budget.** No matter how much you make, it's important to know where your money goes.

Strategy: Calculate your monthly net income. Then list your monthly expenses—including rent, bills, payments for loans, etc. This will tell you how much you can spend on hobbies, luxuries and other nonessential expenses.

Important: Saving should be part of your budget. Otherwise, it's easy to use up your money without putting anything aside for retirement, college or a rainy day.

•**Don't spend unexpected money that falls into your lap**—whether it's a tax refund, a gift from your parents, a bonus or lottery winnings. Instead, save it, and put it into the investment of your choice. While this may seem a tough line to take if you are someone who views such unexpected money as an invitation to indulge in a shopping spree, this approach is realistic. It represents "found" money that hasn't been earmarked for a specific purpose.

•**Divert any spending shortfall into savings.** Say you budgeted $2,000 for a vacation but spend only $1,500. Instead of using the leftover $500 for clothes, put it into savings. Or, say you save $20 a week by using a food club for your groceries instead of going to the supermarket. Save it, don't spend it.

•**Make the most of retirement savings plans at work.** They have a *triple*-barreled advantage. Not only are the earnings generated within a 401(k) free from state and federal tax until you withdraw the funds, but many employers match the money you contribute.

Failing to participate—at least up to the extent of your employer's match—is like leaving money on the table. Furthermore, by opting to defer part of your current pay and put it instead into a 401(k) plan, you lower your current taxable income.

•**Set up and contribute to an IRA.** The current limit is $2,000 a year—but a married couple with an unemployed spouse can contribute up to $2,250, splitting the contribution as they choose, as long as neither contribution exceeds $2,000.

•**Establish an automatic investment plan with the mutual fund of your choice.** The mutual fund deducts a preset amount—at least $50 a month—from your checking account. The virtue of this approach is that what you don't see, you don't spend.

Finding money to save:

If your budget is so strained that you don't think you can spare a penny for savings, here are some hints to free up some cash...

•**Have your paycheck directly deposited into your checking account.** This way, you won't be tempted to take a few dollars off the top when you cash it.

•**Limit your use of automated teller machines**. If you're the type who spends whatever is in your wallet, these machines can ruin the best intentions. Set a weekly cash budget, and take out what you need for the week on Sunday.

•**Curb your impulse buying.** Only go shopping with a list—and stick with it. Steer clear of spending temptations, such as sales or odd-job wholesale stores, where everything sells for less than a dollar and you can spend a small fortune on nonessentials in minutes.

•**Change your lunchtime eating habits.** Instead of buying sandwiches at the deli, brown-bag it. Instead of buying soft drinks from a vending machine or at a deli, buy a six-pack at the supermarket and stash it in the office fridge. By doing this you'll cut your daily lunch bill in half.

Traps to avoid:

No matter what approach to saving you take, beware of these mistakes...

Mistake: Keeping your savings in a low-rate passbook account. Sometimes these accounts pay as little as 1% to 2% interest.

Better: Put your savings into a money-market mutual fund, which generally pays several percentage points higher. Or—better still—put your savings into a no-load short-term bond fund, which usually pays several points above CDs and money market funds.

Mistake: Dipping into savings to pay recurring expenses. Savings should be used for major long-term investments, such as a house or your children's college education. This money should not be used for items such as car repairs or vacations—expenses that should be built into your budget.

Mistake: Stashing long-term savings in an account that compounds interest only annually. The difference between paying interest daily vs. yearly can be significant over time, especially when large sums of money are involved.

Example: If you invest $10,000 in a bank certificate of deposit paying 8%, you will earn $800 in interest with annual compounding… $816 with semiannual compounding…$824 with quarterly compounding…$830 with monthly compounding…and $833 with daily compounding.

Source: Avery Neumark, an attorney and accountant who is director of employee benefits and executive compensation for the CPA firm of Rosen, Seymour, Shapss, Martin & Co., 757 Third Ave., New York 10017. He is a commissioner of the New York State Insurance Fund, which writes workers' compensation policies for business.

How to Calculate Your Net Worth

List all your assets at their actual or estimated fair-market value. Then list all your liabilities—all the money you owe, including credit card debt and mortgages. Your net worth is your total assets minus your total liabilities.

Check your net worth every January to monitor your progress.

Added benefits: Because it lists your assets and liabilities, a net-worth statement can serve as a prepared financial statement when you apply for a loan…and it is a good measure of your available emergency money.

Source: Barbara O'Neill, CFP, New Jersey, and author of *Saving on a Shoestring: How to Cut Expenses, Reduce Debt, Stash More Cash.* Dearborn Financial.

If Carol Keeffe Could Get Out of Debt… Anyone Can

When I was young and single, I spent all of my money. When I was married with two incomes, no children and a monthly rent payment of only $95—my husband and I spent all of our money.

No matter how much money there was, there was never enough.

By the early 1980s we had two kids. I quit work and my husband was earning $20,000 a year as a teacher. We also had $7,000 in debt.
Our first mistake:

In the beginning, we tried the conventional approach to paying off our debts. Every month, I'd pay as much as I could toward our seven different outstanding credit card bills. But this approach was a total failure. It didn't leave us enough money to live on. We were four people living on one modest income. We could have used a good chunk of that credit card payment for food and household expenses.

As a result, a few weeks into every month, we had to use credit cards to buy things like toothpaste, soap and gas for the car. By the start of the next month, instead of our credit card bill going down, it was higher than the month before.
Our solution:

Finally, I discovered a plan that worked for us. The approach freed us emotionally, so we were no longer held hostage to the ridiculous concept that joy and fulfillment are only possible if you have no bills. I recognized that unpaid bills are like dirty dishes—no one likes them, everybody has them and there will always be dirty dishes if you eat. But dirty dishes and bills don't have to rule your life.

Here's how we got out of debt…

• **Don't worry if you can't pay large sums toward your balances.** The conventional wisdom is that you should pay more than the minimum required, so you can eventually extinguish your credit debt.

I began by paying only the minimum. That's because it's the only way I could start to reduce our debts and still have enough money to live on. After years of paying more than the minimum, running out of money mid-month and winding up deeper in debt the following month, I decided there had to be a better way.

Example: Instead of pulling a whopping $100 out of our small checking account and sending it to our card issuer, I'd pay the suggested $22 minimum. That left us with $78 to spend on things like car repairs, laundry soap and groceries. I reveled in the freedom and the feeling of control that came with having cash.

Important: Make sure that the bank that has issued your credit card requires a minimum payment that is large enough so that it pays off some of the principal, as well as the accrued interest, on your balance. Otherwise, you'll never, ever succeed in getting out of debt. Also, make sure that the interest rate you're paying on your outstanding balance is not too high. In today's low-interest-rate environment, you should consider switching banks if you're paying much more than 6.9%.

One suggestion: Consumers Edge Gold MasterCard, The Bank of New York, Box 6998, Newark, Delaware 19725, fixed 5.9% above the prime lending rate, no annual fee. 800-942-1977.

• **Stop using your credit cards.** The only way to wipe the slate clean if you're paying the minimum due on your credit card bills is to not run up a higher balance the next month.

But not using credit is more easily said than done. If you have become dependent on your credit cards just to get by like I had, it may take a few months of minimum payments and socking cash away before you can make it through the month without charging.

Strategy: My new approach worked because my goal was to *enjoy life with the money we already had*—not to be prisoners of our bills. By making the choice to put less toward the bills and *more* for our independence, I felt in control. Feelings of empowerment replaced the helpless feeling of relying on our credit card to get us through the month.

• **When you completely pay off a credit card's balance**, reward yourself by setting up a special savings fund for a special purpose. I'll never forget how excited I was when I paid off my first credit card balance under this new system. It was a $300 department store bill that had required a fairly steep minimum payment of $60 a month.

When it was paid off, it was like getting a $60 raise. There were all sorts of things I could do with that newfound money. I decided to put $10 a month into a family-camping account…$20 a month into an account for future car repairs…and to leave $30 a month in my checking account for other purchases.

If you follow this approach, you are emotionally free—and financially free—to make real choices about what to do with your money. It's no longer just work and bills…and bills and work.

Source: Carol Keeffe, who leads workshops on money, time and family management, Box 1965, Lynnwood, WA 98046. She is author of *How to Get What You Want in Life with the Money You Already Have*. Little Brown & Co.

Emergency Funds

If you must withdraw money from a 401(k) retirement savings plan before age 59½, do so early in the year—so other interest-earning accounts can help offset the 10% tax penalty charged by the IRS on early 401(k) withdrawals.

If your withdrawal is for buying your first house, time the purchase so that you close early in the year during which you take the withdrawal.

The mortgage interest and real estate tax deductions can also help offset the taxes you will have to pay on the 401(k) withdrawal.

General rule: Withdrawing early from a 401(k) account should be a last resort for funds.

Source: Ted Benna, inventor of the 401(k) and president of The 401(k) Association in Langhorne, PA.

Beware of Reverse Mortgages

The truth about reverse mortgages. Despite recent promotion of reverse mortgages by banks, mortgage bankers and others, reverse mortgages are not generally a good idea for older home owners. They're offered mainly to older people with premium properties and low or no mortgages.

How they work: The lender contracts to send you monthly checks for a specified period (five, 10, 15 years). Sometimes the term is open- ended. The total of these payments plus interest (which can be hefty, including interest on interest), can include a share of the home's appreciated market value over the life of the deal and is repaid when the loan period expires…or you die…or when you move out and the house is sold.

Problem: You've worked all your life to pay off a mortgage that probably cost you $3 for every dollar that you borrowed—and now you may be doing that again, giving the lender back $3 of the equity you have built up in your house for every dollar that he/she lends you to live on. If the deal ends while you are still alive, you (or a surviving spouse) may have to sell your home to meet this large debt and then find someplace else to live, without benefit of those nice monthly checks.

Better alternative for most people: Sell your home to your kids and continue to live there while they enjoy tax advantages and the benefit of any appreciation, or sell it to others, keeping all of the profits for yourself, and rent a condo. Either option will probably be much better for you financially.

Helpful: Most states offer tax relief, low-cost loans and other forms of support to help older home owners stay in their houses.

Beware: Commercial lenders aren't being altruistic. Reverse mortgages offer lenders, at worst, a good return on their investment and, at best, a possible gold mine, at your (and your heirs') expense.

Source: Edward Mrkvicka, Jr., president of Reliance Enterprises, Inc., 1206 Alsace Way, Lafayette, CO 80026.

Better Money Saving

Break down your financial goals into manageable parts. *Example:* Instead of worrying about how long it will take to save $500 and then giving up in frustration, concentrate on saving $10 a week for a year.

Source: Bill Staton, CFA, is president of The Financial Training Group, which holds personal finance seminars nationwide. He is author of *How to Become a Multimillionaire on Just $50 a Month.* To order: 300 East Blvd., B-4, Charlotte, NC 28203.

Long Distance Calling Plans

All telephone users should join one of the many long-distance calling plans offered by AT&T, MCI, Sprint and other carriers. *Reason:* Without a plan, you're paying the telephone equivalent of list price for your calls. While calling rates vary by the distance of the call and the day and time it is placed, they're invariably higher than the equivalent calling plan rate. *Also:* Long-distance rates are rising fast—they're up 17% in the past two years.

Source: Neil Sachnoff, president, TeleCom Clinic, a tele-communications research, consulting and publishing com-pany, Edison, NJ.

The Goldbecks' Secrets For Turning Garbage Into Gold

The next time you're ready to toss something into the trash, ask yourself, Can this item be repaired or transformed into something different?

With a little creativity you can turn garbage into gold. Some of our favorite moneysavers…

•**Children's clothing.** With today's smaller families, a traditional hand-me-down approach may not work. The key is to use what you have available to you.

Example: Colorful adult clothing can be turned into garments for newborns or young children. For instance, the sleeves of an old sweatshirt can be made into baby pants.

You can extend the life of infant wear that has snap-fastened crotches by using snap-in false bottoms that add three or four inches in length. These extenders are available from One Step Ahead (800-950-5120)…and The Right Start Catalog (800-548-8531).

•**Used tires.** Today, between two and three billion tires lie exposed in North American landfills and scrap yards—a number that is increasing by 150 million to 200 million each year. That's one reason to reuse tires. Another is that they are waterproof and resistant to wear and tear.

It's easy to create a tire swing for your children by attaching a heavy-duty metal chain or rope to a used tire. If you don't want to make the swing yourself, consider ordering one from P'lovers (800-565-2998).

Doormats can be made from many reused materials, but the most popular source is rubber tire strips. Simply attach the strips with heavy-gauge wire. These durable doormats can be left outside for years. Dirt shakes right out and mud washes off easily with a hose.

Used tires can also be converted into durable outdoor planters.

•**Wood and paper.** Wood reclaimed from shipping pallets and fence posts is particularly suitable for plant containers.

Biodegradable pots for seedlings can be made from newspaper strips aided by a wooden form. The pots can go directly in the ground, diminishing transplant shock. You can also order planters made from reclaimed wood from Bronx 2000's Big City Forest (718-299-1183)…Hoka-Hai Enterprises (215-843-5237).

•**Used calendars.** Don't throw out your 1995 calendars come January. They probably feature beautiful works of art or photography, and you can use the pages in arts and crafts projects and for gift wrap.

With a kit, you can turn old calendar pages into envelopes, unique gift bags and decorative lunch sacks. You can order these kits from Anthony's Originals (508-655-8937).

•**Rugs.** Incorporate remnants of decorative rugs that are too small to use as floor coverings

into pillowcases for floor pillows. Most seamstresses can handle this task.

•**Trophies.** Instead of spending $10 to $100 on a new trophy, buy a used one at a flea market or pawnshop for about $5. An engraver can create a new nameplate to place on it.

Source: Nikki and David Goldbeck, leading experts on preserving the environment. They are known for the many books they have written together over the past 20 years, including *Choose to Reuse*. Ceres Press.

How a Reformed Spendthrift Keeps Her Spending Under Control…Now

The best way to keep spending under control is to stay away from places that tempt you to buy what they sell. What I do to keep my spending in check…

Don't shop in pretty places:

I rarely go into malls, but recently I had no choice but to venture into one. We were leaving on a trip, and I had to buy shirts for my husband.

When I arrived at the mall, I parked close to the men's department so I wouldn't have to walk through much of the store. I made a bee-line for the shirts, racing past a handbag display as fast as I could and not stopping for even a minute to look at them.

I use these strategies all the time. When I have to make a purchase, I pick my shopping centers and malls very carefully. Basically, I shop in the least-attractive stores…those I don't enjoy very much.

I also avoid supermarkets as much as I can. When I have to go into one—every three or four weeks to stock up—I go with my husband, who is not a compulsive shopper.

The Price Club is an ideal place for me to shop. The one closest to us is not air-conditioned. The lights are dim. It's certainly not pretty. I buy in bulk, and I pay cash. I don't bring a checkbook or credit cards, which means I have to do some advance planning to have the right amount of cash with me. It's embarrassing to run out of money at the checkout counter.

My rule is to pay cash as often as I possibly can. This forces me to control impulse purchases. I always have to think ahead as to how much cash to carry with me—and at that point I am much more likely to be in control. Therefore, I am not being influenced by what I see.

Here is what I ask myself before I buy anything that costs more than $20:

- **Do I really need it?**
- **If the answer is yes**, can I afford to pay for it with cash?
- **If I can,** do I already own something that would serve just as well? This question alone saves me plenty of money.
- **If I don't have anything that will do the job**, do I know for a fact that I have found the best value? Have I really checked around enough to know?

If the prospective purchase passes all of these checkpoints, I still wait at least 24 hours before making the purchase.

The result is that I often wind up not buying the item—and not regretting it either—simply because it would be too much trouble to go back the next day to get it.

Find the fun in saving:

The funny thing about saving money is that eventually you begin to find gratification in it and start putting money aside for investments. That new, delayed gratification takes away some of the hunger for instant gratification.

I still work at it. I want my temperament—which is compulsive and out to impress everybody—to work for me as a saver the way it worked for me as a spender. I used to feel that spending money was the only way to feel significant.

I've made great progress. Now, we eat out at restaurants far less often than we used to…and when we do eat out, we often share dishes. I find splitting food is less wasteful than asking for doggie bags and taking home leftovers—where they would spoil in the refrigerator.

Since my husband and I both travel for our jobs, we try to combine vacations with business travel as often as we can. That cuts the after-tax cost of our trips. And—we always plan how much cash to take with us. We restrict our use of credit cards to an absolute minimum.

Beat the catalog temptation:

I did a lot of personal reflection to figure out precisely where I got the most excited about spending.

The answer is when I bought from catalogs. I discovered that my greatest pleasure came from the looking and ordering. The process of looking through the catalogs and dreaming that I could have anything I wanted was more satisfactory than receiving the goods.

Now, when catalogs arrive at my home, I look through them and carefully select all the things I think I need. I fill out the order form …add the sales and delivery charges…and total the bill. I write the amount on the outside of the envelope—and put the order and the envelope in my desk drawer for seven days. Usually, when I take them out of the drawer a week later, I look over the order and throw it out. I've already had my thrill.

Enjoy it without owning it:

My other great discovery was that I don't have to own things to enjoy them. I used to go to Nordstrom and admire the beautiful china, crystal and silverware…or go to shops where the sheets were $400 each. I would feel that I needed these things.

The reality was that I did not need them. I do need to enjoy them, though.

Strategy: I go into those stores without my handbag—as if I were going to a museum to admire beautiful things. I continue to enjoy them—without spending money to buy them, store them, clean and polish them and buy insurance to protect them. Admire, not acquire.

Take the big-purchase test:

I have even given up owning my own car. Fortunately, my husband and I work near each other, so we drive to work together. If I absolutely need a car for a few days for a business trip, I rent one. We've found we can manage quite well with only one car—and it's a sacrifice I find myself willing to make while we build up our savings. There are so many better ways to use $10,000—in cash or invested—than sinking it into a car.

Strategy: When struggling with the decision of whether to spend or to save money, try this…

•**Pretend your monthly payments** on your home or car are $500 higher.

•**Every month**, put that $500 into the bank, a mutual fund or some other savings. Never miss a "payment."

•**After six months**, evaluate how you feel about having to make that $500-per-month "payment." If it was a struggle, was the sacrifice worth what you might buy with the money? Did some unexpected expense come up that made it very difficult—maybe even impossible—to put away that $500? Think about what the implications would be if you missed a mortgage or car-lease payment.

After taking this test, you will be in a better position to make the decision as to whether or not you should commit yourself to that big expense.

Share spending secrets:

A lot of excessive spending is done secretly. Mine was.

Fortunately, big spenders often marry people who want to save. But the spenders too often wind up in charge of the finances—and cover up their out-of-control spending. To stay in control…

•**The spouse who is more inclined to save** should be put in charge of the bank account and checkbook.

•**Confess your spending weakness to those close to you**—even to your friends and neighbors. Tell them that you are making every effort to get control of your spending problem. Once you are open about it, you will find that other people's knowledge of the problem will help you help yourself.

Source: Mary Hunt, a reformed spendthrift and publisher of *Cheapskate Monthly*, Box 2135, Paramount, CA 90723. She is author of *The Cheapskate Monthly Money Makeover*. St. Martin's Paperbacks.

Safe-Deposit Box Secrets

Joint rental of a safe-deposit box is better than renting one individually—if the co-renters have a stable, trusting relationship.

An individual who rents a box alone may have trouble retrieving its contents if he/she cannot get to the bank. This problem is solvable by giving a friend or relative a key and power of attorney.

Caution: If an individual box owner dies, the box is sealed by law to anyone except his court-appointed personal representative. However, if a joint renter dies and the bank is not notified, it is legal for the co-renter to remove the contents and place them in another box rented in his own name.

Source: Theodore Hughes is an estate attorney in Okemos, MI, and author of *Own It and Keep It*. Facts on File.

Checking Account Fraud Self-Defense

Never give your account number—or the numbers printed along the bottom of your checks—to anybody, including anyone claiming to work for your bank. Give account numbers only to businesses you know are reputable. Report lost or stolen checks immediately. Properly store or destroy canceled checks and keep new ones in a secure place.

Source: Cindy Fuller, associate director, American Bankers Association, 1120 Connecticut Ave. NW, Washington, DC 20036.

Escrow Account Refunds

Escrow account refunds are due for millions of mortgage holders whose lenders require the escrow accounts for real estate taxes and homeowner's insurance. New federal escrow rules will reduce the required monthly payments for many. *Meaning:* Many people have overpaid for years and are entitled to money back.

Self-defense: Have your escrow account privately audited to determine if a refund is due. If it is, contact the lender, give the results of the audit and ask for the money back immediately.

Source: Richard Roll, president, American Homeowners Association, Washington, DC. *Do-It-Yourself Escrow Refund Guide* is available by calling 800-470-2242.

How Not to Overspend

During any holiday season most people spend more than they should on parties and gifts for others and for themselves.

Here's why we overspend—and how to limit your postholiday debt.

The urge to splurge:

We are a nation of overspenders. *The big reasons for such excess...*

• **Seduction by hard-to-resist advertising.** Everyone is influenced to spend money by the promises of enhanced status and improved self-image on TV and in print advertising. Although it is natural to respond to these enticements, spending is likely a problem if it is causing you to spend all you have or even to go into debt.

• **Sense of entitlement.** Credit cards enable us to buy what we want and not deal with the consequences until later. We may say to ourselves, I deserve this, whether we can afford the item or not.

• **Need to combat emptiness.** In our high-speed culture, we spend money, whether we have it or not, to counteract feelings of loneliness or depression—or even as an outlet for feelings of elation.

• **Fear of looking cheap.** When buying gifts for others or throwing holiday parties, many people overspend on food and accessories because they don't want others to think they are stingy. Once you confront these self-defeating behaviors, you'll be on the road to recovery.

How to avoid overspending:

• **Get an overview of your money.** Write down how much you earn each day after taxes ...and list all of the money you owe, including credit card debt, car loans, etc.

By calculating your earnings and listing your debt, you are becoming more aware of how long it takes to earn what you're thinking of spending—and how hard it is to pay off what you still owe. Consider taking the list of debts along when you shop.

• **Keep a spending diary**. Before a shopping trip, write down your feelings about what you're considering buying. During and after your trip, the more honestly you record your thoughts and feelings, the better you'll understand what tempts you to overspend—and how you can stop it.

• **Avoid your "points of temptation."** Many overspenders tend to be more tempted in certain predictable places, such as malls. Others begin by planning to shop for friends but end up buying many items for themselves.

Solution: Consider alternative environments. Here are my favorite strategies...

• **Before you go shopping**, make a list of what you intend to buy and set a limit on how much you will spend.

• **Consider taking a friend who is not an overspender**...or call a trusted, frugal friend before and after the trip to hold yourself to your spending plan.

• **Identify a long-term spending goal you really want to achieve**, such as money for a trip to the Caribbean. As an incentive to stay within your limits, take along a photo that reminds you of this goal when you go shopping.

• **Do what it takes to slow the spending process.** It will give you more time to think about what you're doing.

Example: Don't buy anything impulsively —even if it is on sale. Walk out of the store and think about the purchase for at least a half-hour. If you still want that item—and can afford it—then you can go back and buy it in a less emotional state. You may even decide on a more practical choice that would leave you some money to spare—or decide you don't need the item at all.

Source: Olivia Mellan, a therapist in private practice who specializes in money psychology, 2607 Connecticut Ave. NW, Washington, DC 20008. She is author of *Overcoming Overspending* and *Money Harmony*. Walker & Co.

 # "Rainy-Day" Money Is a Necessity

How much you need depends on your age, health and job outlook. The traditional advice is to have three to six months' worth of living expenses in cash. But that may be too much if you can easily borrow against assets with a home-equity line of credit or brokerage margin account…or if you have cash-value life insurance. It may also be too much cash for two-income households, unless you are spending both incomes, since it is unlikely both earners would lose their jobs at the same time.

Do keep more cash on hand if: Your work is seasonal…you own a business…you have one income and your job may be at risk… or you are facing disability or severe illness.

Source: Alexandra Armstrong, chairman, Armstrong Welch & MacIntyre, Inc., financial advisers, Washington, DC.

Cheaper Checking Account Opportunities

Service charges are rising at financial institutions, especially at large banks—where they've risen as much as 400% over the last 10 years.

Checking accounts have become particularly expensive.

If you have a checking account at a big bank, there's a cheaper alternative. Making some phone calls to comparison shop can save you $100—or more—year after year. *Great alternatives…*

•**Credit unions.** Credit unions charge much lower service fees on their share-draft (checking) accounts. They also have much lower balance requirements—sometimes as low as $250—and they charge less for checks.

Other benefits: Lower charges on overdrafts and higher interest rates on NOW accounts.

More than 60 million Americans belong to credit unions—many more are eligible to join. To find out which credit unions might accept you as a member, call 800-358-5710.

•**Savings and loans.** S&Ls may not offer quite as good a deal as credit unions, but they're usually much cheaper than large banks. The huge banks really don't care about keeping you as a customer. But a small, local S&L (or very small bank) does and may even

custom design an account for your needs—if you ask.

Negotiate: Most people think it's impossible to negotiate with a financial institution. It's not. If you can, use your past history as a good bank customer to leverage. When possible, link your request for special consideration to a pending transaction. Say, I'm about to deposit $3,000. I assume that entitles me to free checking.

Note: The smaller the institution, the easier it will be to negotiate because your business is needed.

Example: To avoid an overdraft fee, ask the S&L or bank to alert you whenever you're about to be overdrawn. Also, ask that you be allowed to make a same-day deposit to square the account.

Strategy: Keep asking until you find a sympathetic bank officer. If that doesn't work, speak to the vice president of operations.

•**A different account at a large bank.** Some big banks offer cheaper accounts for senior citizens, students and the disabled, but they usually don't advertise them. You have to ask to get the deal. Credit unions and S&Ls may also offer special accounts. Often, there are also special deals for people who write very few checks each month.

Example: Paying 10 or 15 cents per check if you write no more than five checks per month.

•**Stockbrokers' cash-management accounts.** You get free checking for your annual fee of $100 or $125. Some deep-discount brokers may charge lower fees. If you're paying high monthly fees now, this could be a good deal.

Of course, it's only sensible if you find the convenience of the account's other features to be a major benefit. Otherwise, you can pay lower overall fees somewhere else.

•**Money-market funds**—and mutual funds. These are great alternatives for people who write only a few large checks each month. In most cases, there is a limit of five checks per month, with a minimum of $250 per check.

•**Checks from private companies.** You can save about 50% by ordering checks directly from private companies. These checks meet all national standards. Call Checks in the Mail

(800-733-4443) or Current (800-533-3973) for information.

Source: Edward F. Mrkvicka, Jr., president of Reliance Enterprises Inc., a national financial consulting firm in Marengo, Illinois. A former CEO of an Illinois bank, he is author of *The Bank Book: How to Revoke Your Bank's "License to Steal"—and Save Up to $100,000.* Harper-Perennial.

Biggest Financial Mistakes People Make

Paying too much interest on a high credit card balance...not raising the deductible on homeowner's and auto insurance policies to at least $500...neglecting to write a will...not putting as much money as possible into a tax-deferred retirement savings account.

Source: Alexandra Armstrong, CFP, chairman, Armstrong, Welch & McIntyre Inc., a financial planning firm in Washington, DC.

What to Do with a Financial Windfall

Pay down debt before making investments. Start by eliminating your most expensive debts. Get rid of credit card debt first—you could be paying 20% interest on it. Then eliminate car loans (usually around 10% interest), student loans (8% to 10%), home-equity lines of credit (variable rates) and life insurance loans (about 7.5%). If the windfall is large enough, consider paying off your home mortgage and then invest anything you have left.

Source: Keith Gumbinger, vice president, HSH Associates, a Butler, NJ, firm that collects interest-rate data.

Fee-Based and Fee-Only Planners

Fee-based financial planners are not the same as fee-only planners. Fee-only planners take a flat fee or percentage of your assets and may then have less incentive than commission-based planners to sell you additional products. But fee-based planners take up-front fees and commissions on trades.

Self-defense: Get in writing exactly how a planner will be compensated before you sign an agreement. When in doubt, choose a fee-only planner.

Source: Harold Evensky, investment adviser, Coral Gables, FL.

Key Questions to Ask Before Buying a Home

If you haven't shopped for a home or purchased one in the past five years, consider yourself a first-time home buyer. That's how much the real estate market has changed in this short a period of time.

Big difference:

Today's home sellers have become more sophisticated about finding ways to get the most money for their homes.

The period also has seen the emergence of brokers who represent buyers instead of sellers...on-line brokerage services...new types of mortgages...and changing rules governing the information that brokers and sellers must disclose to you.

Some of these changes are great for buyers—but you need to know how to take advantage of them. *Start by asking yourself these questions...*

• ***What do I need in a home...and what do I want?*** Start by deciding what you want—and what you really can't do without. Otherwise, you are likely to buy a house that satisfies some of your wishes, but not all of your requirements.

Self-defense: Sit down with your spouse and make a list of the things you want in a house. That list might include being in a certain school district, proximity to work or family, a certain size or type of house, amenities such as a pool, a great kitchen or a place for your antique billiard table, and so on. Then refine that list down to the things that you absolutely cannot live without.

Keep both lists handy when you're looking at homes to make sure your priorities are straight.

•*How much can I afford to pay?* Most people overestimate the amount they can afford. The rule of thumb that brokers often cite says that with 8% mortgage rates you can pay two and a half to three times your gross income. By that measure, a person with a gross income of $110,000 could buy a home for $275,000 to $330,000. But the rule doesn't take into account other debt or major financial obligations such as paying children's college tuitions.

Helpful: As a starting point, use the more conservative guidelines that lenders usually rely on. They generally figure that borrowers can spend 36% of their gross income on debt —including mortgage, car loan, credit cards and the rest—and as much as 28% just on a mortgage.

Beware: In recent years, some lenders have stretched those guidelines to let home buyers borrow more. But avoid going beyond the traditional limits, even if your lender says it's alright.

•*What kind of mortgage is best for me?* Mortgages used to come in two varieties— fixed 15-year and fixed 30-year loans. Now you can choose between fixed-rate and variable-rate loans with widely different terms. Some fixed-rate loans even convert to variable-rate loans after a certain period, which can be as long as 10 years.

Before you choose a loan, decide how long you are likely to live in the house.

If you are planning to stay more than five years, a fixed-rate mortgage may make more sense.

Warning: Avoid gimmicky loans that increase your cost by large amounts over time.

Example: Negative-equity loans have a fixed payment, but if interest rates rise, the lender tacks on extra payments at the end. In effect, you end up paying interest on interest—a terrible idea.

•*Should I use a buyer's broker?* Traditionally, the broker works for the seller. But during the past seven years, buyer's brokers have emerged as a mainstream choice for home buyers. A buyer's broker will look after your interests—offering you information about the property and the neighborhood that a seller's broker might not provide.

Some home buyers worry about having to pay a commission if they hire a buyer's broker. But 99% of the time, the seller will agree to pay the commission, which will be split between the buyer's and the seller's brokers.

•*How do I negotiate successfully?* Many first-time home buyers give up the opportunity to save thousands of dollars because they don't know how to negotiate properly. The key to a successful negotiation is to have information on your side.

For starters, you need to figure out approximately how much a particular house is worth in the current market.

You also must figure out what the list price on various homes really means. Home sellers typically build in some negotiating room, but that will change in different markets.

Helpful: Start out by going to see every house on the market that is in your price range. Carry a camera and take pictures. Have your broker give you information about comparable homes that have sold in the market in recent months…and note the difference between their list prices and sales prices.

Also, ask a broker to tell you the average number of days that homes in the area have been listed on the market—and whether that average is climbing or shrinking. If it's climbing, then the market is slowing down and you may be in a stronger position to bargain.

Source: Ilyce Glink, nationally syndicated real estate columnist based in Chicago, and author of *One Hundred Questions Every First-Time Home Buyer Should Ask.* Times Books.

5

Insurance Savvy

How to Buy the Right Protection for You

If you are among the 25 million Americans who do not receive health coverage at work, it is still possible to find a great health insurance policy.

There are even options for people who are dissatisfied with the coverage they receive from their employers.

Here are the most important questions people are asking me now...

• *What are the least-expensive health-coverage options available?* For individuals and their families, there are actually just two—Health Maintenance Organizations (HMOs) and Preferred Provider Organizations (PPOs).

•**HMO plans are usually the most affordable** for individuals or families, and they provide medical care through networks of physicians.

Benefits: Unlike traditional health insurers, if you sign up for an HMO, you won't have to fill out forms after each doctor's visit. You also won't have to worry about meeting a deductible requirement. You probably will pay $5 to $10 per doctor visit.

How HMO coverage works: When you are ill, you first consult your primary care physician, who is also known as the gatekeeper. He/she will then refer you to a specialist—if necessary.

Exception: Most plans permit women to visit a gynecologist without a gatekeeper referral.

If you choose an out-of-network doctor or hospital, you are generally not covered. You also must first obtain permission from your primary care physician to see an in-network specialist. Out-of-network specialists are not covered at all.

•**PPO plans are slightly more expensive than HMOs.** They too provide medical care through a network of doctors.

Big difference: There are no gatekeepers... you can consult a specialist without first getting a referral from your primary care physician. Your copayment—or fee—for each doctor's visit is comparable to HMO rates. Remember, out-of-network doctors and hospitals are not covered.

•***How do monthly costs of HMOs and PPOs compare?*** A family of four with HMO coverage in any major US city could expect to pay about $500 per month. For PPO coverage, that would be $525 per month.

•***What if you don't like the idea of network care?*** Many insurance carriers have stopped selling traditional or indemnity plans to individuals. Insurers that still sell them usually make it tough to qualify because of strict underwriting standards. If you are opposed to network care, see if you can apply for indemnity coverage through an organization to which you belong.

Drawback: While you have complete freedom to use the doctor of your choice, such plans are very expensive. A family of four that chooses a plan with a $200 deductible and a reimbursement rate starting at 80% of the first $5,000—and 100% of all expenditures above that—would pay about $850 monthly.

•***Can you combine the flexibility of an indemnity plan with the cost savings of an HMO or a PPO?*** Yes, with a Point-of-Service (POS) plan. It allows you to decide whether to consult a network doctor or out-of-network doctor any time you need medical care.

Members' costs vary: When you stay within the network, the charge is $5 to $15 per visit. If you choose to go out of the network for care, your costs will be higher, since insurers will reimburse only 70% to 80% of the cost of a doctor's visit once you meet the plan deductible.

Monthly cost comparison: POS plans cost more than HMOs or PPOs, but less than traditional indemnity plans.

Example: A family of four in a major city would pay about $600 per month for an HMO/POS plan and about $630 per month for a PPO/POS plan.

Drawback: In today's insurance market, individuals and their families cannot purchase POS coverage. It's only sold to businesses, which offer it to employees.

Helpful: If you're self-employed—or own the company—you can apply for POS health-care coverage as a business, rather than as an individual.

How to find a great HMO or PPO:

Because there are many different types of plans and consumer options keep changing rapidly, it makes sense to consult a licensed insurance agent who works with a range of insurers and can help you compare your choices.

Selection priorities: While low cost is important, it should not be your top consideration. *More important:* Evaluate the quality of the insurer and its network by contacting present and former policyholders, the Better Business Bureau and your state department of insurance.

Over time, you'll tend to use doctors in the network more and more, so it pays to shop for a plan whose network physicians are conveniently located—and who are well qualified—to meet your family's needs. Networks are growing rapidly as more doctors join them. While your physician may not be a member now, that may change in the near future.

If you don't love the choices your agent has suggested or are concerned that they're too costly, sign up for the best plan that's available now. Then, in three to four months, ask your insurance agent to survey the marketplace to see if better products have become available.

Health care policies are changing so rapidly these days that it is possible something better will come along soon.

When employees need more insurance:

In some cases, people who already receive health care coverage from their employers need additional protection. To decide whether you need more coverage, ask yourself—does my policy only provide hospitalization coverage? If so, it makes sense to buy an HMO or a PPO plan to cover other medical costs. Choose a plan with the best physicians, but don't worry about its hospitalization feature since you're already covered.

Important: If your decision to seek additional coverage is due to your unhappiness with the doctors who belong to your plan's network, don't despair. A growing number of states, such as New Jersey, have passed "any willing provider" laws. These laws require

HMO and PPO networks to accept any willing physician who meets their licensing, training and other standards.

That means your physician choices may soon improve within your existing plan. So it makes sense to wait, rather than spend money for supplementary coverage.

Coverage for retirees:

Retirees often ask whether it makes sense to supplement Medicare coverage with an HMO or PPO plan. The answer is no. That's because Medicare will cover most of the cost of your basic medical and hospital services. What you need is a different kind of supplementary insurance policy known as Medigap, which pays retirees for any expenses that Medicare fails to reimburse.

Trend to watch: The federal government has started working with some HMO insurers to provide in-network medical care to retirees. *How it works:* If retirees sign up and commit themselves to only visiting network physicians, they won't need to purchase Medigap coverage. Instead, they will pay only $10 per doctor's visit and Medicare will reimburse other expenses. If this option is available to you, it's worth considering.

Source: Sam Beller, CLU, ChFC, president of Diversified Programs, Inc., an insurance sales organization, and Diversified Advisory Services, Inc., a financial services organization, 450 Seventh Ave., Suite. 500, New York 10123. He is author of *The Great Insurance Secret.* Diversified Programs.

How to Get Your HMO To Cover Alternative Medical Treatment

All HMOs rely on primary care doctors to provide or approve most care for their members. They also tend to cover only "medically necessary" and "nonexperimental" treatments.

Therefore, HMOs may not be willing to reimburse members for alternative medical treatments such as acupuncture, biofeedback, massage therapy and chiropractic care.

But such treatments are growing in popularity. More than one third of all Americans have already tried at least one of them.

Here's how to get your HMO to pay for alternative approaches...

• **Find out if the HMO must pay for the treatment in your state**, and under what circumstances. Some states now require that health insurers pay for certain treatments—especially chiropractic care. Your state's insurance department can fill you in.

• **Convince your primary care physician** to recommend an alternative treatment. Explain how it will likely succeed in treating your medical problem. Some HMOs will pay for alternative treatments—if you get a referral from your HMO doctor. Call the HMO to find out its policy.

• **Ask alternative treatment providers** if they know of HMOs that cover their care. Ask if they will allow referrals for alternative treatments. There may be limits—for example, chiropractic treatment for lower back pain may be covered, while the use of alternative therapies for chronic illness may not be.

• **Ask your employer to add alternative therapies to your benefits.** Some HMOs offer riders that expand coverage to include nontraditional therapies. It will cost your employer more, so you will probably see somewhat higher premiums as a result. The larger the number of your fellow employees who want such a benefit, the more likely it is your request will be granted.

• **If treatment is denied coverage**, use tax-sheltered money. Many employers offer flexible spending accounts, which permit you to set aside pretax dollars to pay for uncovered medical expenses.

Acupuncture and chiropractic care qualify, since the IRS has ruled that both are tax-deductible medical expenses. The IRS hasn't ruled on other treatments, so check with your employer. Also find out if you need a medical doctor's referral before getting your treatment.

Be careful when you set aside money in a flexible spending account. If you don't use all the money that is set aside by the end of the year, you forfeit the remaining amount.

Source: Alan Raymond, vice president of public affairs for Harvard Pilgrim Heath Care, an HMO in Brookline, MA, and author of *The HMO Health-Care Companion: A Consumer's Guide to Managed-Care Networks* . Harper-Perennial.

The Big Bad Bothersome HMO Traps...How to Fight Back and Win

As an attorney who represents consumers who are trying to force health insurance companies to pay their claims, I have recently noticed several disturbing trends.

In an effort to keep costs down, a growing number of managed-care providers and HMOs are denying or limiting payment in a number of situations.

Here's what is most worrying—and how to fight back...

Worrisome trends:

•**Increase of bonus incentives.** A growing number of HMOs and managed-care systems provide doctors, administrators and claims adjusters with financial incentives to deny or cut back coverage to customers.

Insurance companies seldom disclose these financial arrangements to customers, except when disputes turn into lawsuits.

•**Hidden arbitration clauses in plan documents.** Most people don't realize it, but when they sign up for coverage through some plans, they abandon their constitutional rights to a jury trial in the event of a health care policy dispute or fraudulent business practice.

Instead, they have agreed to file an arbitration suit, which is typically decided by administrative panels with strong ties to the medical community. In many states, these panels cannot award consumers more than the cost of contested medical services.

The impact on you:

•**Insurers may discourage doctors from referring patients to specialists.** I've encountered this problem often in cases when consumers require treatments that are expensive or somewhat new or unusual.

Typical problem areas: High-risk pregnancies...cancers...multiple sclerosis...and other serious diseases.

Some HMOs and managed-care systems deny full reimbursement to primary care physicians who refer patients to specialists, no matter how severe the patients' illnesses.

That means primary care physicians lose money when they recommend specialists, leading to an ethical conflict that their patients only learn about if they sue the health care provider.

Solution: The best thing you can do under these circumstances is complain. Start by making an argument in writing to your primary care physician about why you believe you need a specialist's care. The next step is to complain to your HMO's board of directors. If the board isn't sympathetic, consider consulting a specialist and filing your claim, and hope for the best. Your health always comes first.

•**Insurers may discourage doctors from recommending acute rehabilitation care.** Based upon my experience, this problem typically occurs among patients over age 65 following a serious stroke...a serious injury that results in paraplegia or quadriplegia...or hip surgery.

Although the problem is widespread, it's most pronounced when Medicare patients receive their care from HMOs.

Solution: Don't succumb to the marketing pitches you hear from HMOs. There's absolutely no reason to assign your Medicare coverage to an HMO—you'll only wind up limiting your freedom of medical choice.

•**Insurers may refuse to pay for certain emergency treatments.** This usually happens when an HMO patient has a medical emergency while traveling and must be treated at a hospital that doesn't belong to the HMO. It's also common in states where people often work more than one hour from their homes and must seek treatment at nonmember hospitals.

Trap: Providers often deny claims on the grounds that the patient should have been treated at his/her own hospital or could have been transferred to a member hospital.

Solution: Always request a letter from the emergency room facility documenting that you experienced a medical emergency and were unable to be transferred to another facility without endangering your health.

When insurers won't pay claims:

At both HMOs and traditional insurers, more and more medical claims are being challenged by insurers on the grounds of being "not medically necessary."

In these cases, it's the insurance plan doctor's judgment against any other physician's judgment. Regardless of what your doctor tells you, the decision may be influenced by bonus incentives.

Some HMOs and insurers are even disallowing claims as unnecessary—after they have been recommended by physicians and preapproved.

Example: I've seen cases in which a woman stayed in the hospital for five days after a cesarean section—under doctor's orders. Then the HMO or insurance company refused to pay for more than two days' bills, despite the fact that the patient could not have discharged herself early from the hospital.

If your HMO or insurance company tries one of these ploys to deny you or a family member medical coverage, here's what you can do...

•**Start by following the insurer's complaint procedure.** Most health care policies require you to report your grievance to a specified person or department.

Don't forget to put your complaint in writing and include all relevant documentation. Retain a copy for your records, then send the complaint by registered mail.

•**If this fails, turn to state regulators.** If your complaint is with an insurer—even one with a managed-care policy—complain to your state insurance department. Be sure to include a copy of your original complaint, plus all of the relevant correspondence.

If your complaint is with an HMO, turn to your state department of corporations. You may want to report cases of severe bad faith or fraudulent behavior to your state attorney general and/or local Better Business Bureau.

•**Make as much noise as possible.** Since state regulatory oversight in these areas is often weak, you may improve your chances by also reporting your problem to the local consumer hotlines and consumer affairs reporters at television stations and newspapers.

•**Seek legal redress if necessary.** If the sum in dispute is small, you may be wiser to sue in small-claims court. Check your state limits to see if this solution will work for you. Otherwise, you may want to consult an attorney.

Important: If a lawsuit seems likely, you are better off hiring a contingency fee attorney so that you'll only be charged if you win your case.

If your policy includes an arbitration clause, you'll still be better off with a contingency lawyer—but finding one to represent you may be difficult since the financial payoff is limited.

Strategy: Interview several contingency fee attorneys who specialize in HMO lawsuits. The initial consultation should be free.

Also find out whether your state permits arbitration awards larger than your contested medical claims. That should increase your chances of finding a lawyer to represent you.

•**Protect your interests before signing up for coverage** and long before potential problems can arise. *Steps to take...*

•**Question potential insurers or HMOs** about arbitration clauses and hidden financial incentives for denied claims. If any exist, don't sign up.

•**Check with state agencies and consumer groups** to see if your HMO or insurer has a record of complaints. If so, that's another reason to avoid signing up.

•**If you've got no choice** because your employer offers only one type of coverage, I advise you to:

•Put your objections in writing.

•Save a copy for your records.

•Send your letter to your plan representative by registered mail as proof that the insurer or HMO has been informed of your objections. Also give a copy to your employer's plan administrator.

This may help protect your legal interests in the event that you ever face a policy dispute.

Source: William Shernoff, founding partner of Shernoff, Bidart & Darras, a Claremont, CA, law firm that specializes in consumer claims against insurance companies. Mr. Shernoff is author of *How to Make Insurance Companies Pay Your Claims.* Hastings House. His firm answers questions about health insurance coverage and insurer disputes.

Car Insurance Trap

Insurers in most states are not required to disclose their underwriting guidelines. *Result:*

Applicants don't know why they're rejected…policyholders don't know what's required to stay insured. Many unwittingly lose coverage. If you've been treated unfairly, contact your state insurance commissioner. If coverage was suspended, ask that the commissioner have the company reinstate your policy until the dispute is resolved.

Car insurance strategy: Take the highest deductible you can afford—and don't file small claims. View insurance as protection against only major damage or loss.

Source: Robert Hunter, head of the insurance group, Consumer Federation of America, 1424 16 St. NW, Washington, DC 20036.

Hidden Cash in Health Insurance

If you and your spouse both receive family medical coverage through your employers, you should take advantage of each other's plans. *Reason:* Most insurance plans pay 80% of routine medical bills—but many partners forget they can file with their spouse's plan for whatever wasn't initially paid by their own insurer. *Big plus:* Many plans allow you to go back three years to file a spouse's unsubmitted claims. *Helpful:* Set up three folders—one for each spouse's medical claims and a third for those claims that are to be filed with the other spouse's plan.

Source: Alexandra Armstrong, chairman, Armstrong Welch & MacIntyre Inc., financial advisers, 1155 Connecticut Ave. NW, Suite 250, Washington, DC 20036.

Health Insurers Tricks

Some health insurers trick members into paying more of their hospital bills than they should.

How it works: Though your insurer is supposed to pay 80%, some get discounts from hospitals—without passing on the savings to you.

Self-defense: Pay the bill. Ask your insurer what it paid. If your share is more than 20%, it is likely that your insurer owes you money.

Source: Robert Hunter, head of the insurance group at the Consumer Federation of America, 1424 16 St. NW, Washington, DC 20036.

Safer Health Insurance

State-approved health insurance policies are likely to be safer for you than those that are unapproved—especially if your state has a guaranty fund to protect you if the insurance company experiences any financial problems. Before buying a policy, make sure it is approved by your state's insurance regulators. *Caution:* Approval does not guarantee a good policy. Many shoddy policies are state-approved, either because they meet absolute minimum requirements or simply because the state insurance department is understaffed.

Source: *Money for Nothing, Tips for Free! Quick Advice on Saving, Making and Investing Money* by Les Abromovitz, financial writer, Pittsburgh. Great Quotations Publishing.

You May Not Be as Insured as You Should Be

Your homeowner's insurance may not protect your kids at college. Coverage varies from company to company. Most insurers will accept claims for up to 10% of the value of the family's homeowner policy under off-premises coverage. But many companies exclude students living in off-campus housing, saying an off-campus apartment is a separate home requiring renter's insurance. Whatever your company's policy, consider buying extra insurance for expensive items like jewelry and computers.

Source: Robert Hunter, head of the insurance group at the Consumer Federation of America, 1424 16 St. NW, Washington, DC 20036.

Don't Buy Too Much Health Insurance

Many Medicare recipients buy more health insurance than is actually necessary, paying for policies that duplicate coverage they already have. Don't buy more than one Medigap policy. If you are covered by an employer's plan, you probably do not need any Medigap policy at all.

Source: William M. Shernoff, founding partner, Shernoff, Bidart & Darras, a Claremont, CA, law firm that specializes in consumer claims against insurance companies.

Cut Auto Insurance Costs

Shop around: Rates can vary as much as 100%, depending on the coverage desired.

Don't overbuy collision and comprehensive coverage: The average driver files a collision, fire or theft claim only once every 10 years or so.

Use bigger deductibles: An increase of $50 in the deductible can reduce comprehensive coverage cost by up to 30%, collision by 10% to 20%.

Eliminate duplicate coverage. Don't buy medical payments coverage if the family already has adequate medical insurance through job-related benefits.

Take advantage of discounts that insurance companies offer for low mileage, driver education courses, and geographic location. *Most common saver:* Insuring a second car on same policy as first vehicle.

Source: *Money.*

Health Insurance And Travel

Check coverage with your health insurer before leaving home. If you travel out of the country—or even out of state—you may pay more for any needed medical treatment because you are not using a preferred provider. Some HMOs make no provision for out-of-area treatment—you must pay everything out of your own pocket.

Self-defense: Find out the rules before you go. If you travel regularly to one particular location, ask for a list of preferred providers there.

Source: *Money for Nothing, Tips for Free! Quick Advice on Saving, Making and Investing Money*, by Les Abromovitz, financial writer, Pittsburgh. Great Quotations Publishing.

How to Buy an Umbrella Insurance Policy

Anyone who owns a home or significant assets needs an umbrella insurance policy.

An umbrella policy protects your family's assets in the unlikely—but possible—event of your being sued for damages in a lawsuit. It also covers you against suits filed as a result of accidents beyond those that occur in your home or car, as well as legal fees to defend against such a suit.

What a policy costs:

Most umbrella policies are inexpensive. For $150 to $300 a year, you can buy up to $1 million in coverage.

Cost-saving strategy: If you don't want to increase your total insurance costs by adding umbrella coverage, increase the deductibles on your auto and homeowner's policies.

Shopping strategies:

When shopping for a policy, ask your insurer for a comprehensive breakdown of what is—and what is not—covered.

Important: Don't leave risky gaps between your umbrella policy and your auto and homeowner's policies.

Reason: Most umbrella policies are structured to provide $1 million of coverage—after your first $300,000 in liability losses, which are covered by your auto and homeowner's policies.

Self-defense: Check your existing policies, and eliminate any gaps. If necessary, raise your auto or homeowner's deductibles to balance out the added cost of higher liability protection. Shopping for a policy:

Start by contacting the insurers who have sold your family its policies. If their rates are reasonable and their coverage levels comprehensive, you'll reduce complications by keeping your coverage under the same roof. Ask your insurer if you can qualify for a discount by adding an umbrella policy to your coverage. Special needs:

•**Operating a home-based business.** You may need a separate, commercially oriented umbrella policy to protect you against related liability risks. A total of $1 million dollars' worth of protection may not be sufficient. Ask your insurance agent for recommendations.

•**Owning more than one home.** If you own primary and vacation residences, a good policy should cover both. But it pays to investigate, particularly if one or more properties provide significant rental income.

•**Serving on a nonprofit board.** Some umbrella policies include Directors and Officers (D&O) liability protection, but others do not. If you are asked to serve on a board, ask if the board is covered by the nonprofit's insurance. If it is not, check your own coverage before joining the board of your child's nursery school, your co-op building or any other nonprofit.

Note: As a rule, for-profit companies buy D&O coverage for their boards.

Source: Robert Hunter, head of the insurance group at the Consumer Federation of America (CFA), a consumer advocate organization, 1424 16 St. NW, Suite. 604, Washington, DC 20036. He is author of *Buyer's Guide to Insurance*, available from CFA.

Life Insurance: How Much To Buy? Which Kind? What Company?

Most people are unsure whether they have enough—or too much—life insurance. Here's a five-step plan to help you know for sure...

Step 1: **Add up your current assets.** Figure out how much money your family would have if you died today. Include retirement funds and other savings, Social Security benefits and your spouse's earnings.

Step 2: **Calculate your family's future needs.** Your family will need income to cover living expenses, which you can assume will grow with inflation. Their needs also might include providing for children's educations, mortgage payments, funds for special needs such as a car or home improvements and bequests.

Step 3: **Calculate the gap between your family's projected needs and the value of your assets.** This will tell you how much insurance coverage you need.

Important: Your calculation must take into account the likely impact of inflation on your survivors' living expenses. Ask a broker, accountant or other financial professional to calculate the present value of your family's future needs...and your current assets, including the present value of future Social Security and other income. The difference between those numbers equals the amount of life insurance you should buy.

For most people, term insurance will be more appropriate than a cash-value policy because it's more affordable and easier to understand.

Step 4: **Shop widely for a policy that suits your needs.** Don't just call your friendly neighborhood insurance agent who, for example, coaches your son's Little League team.

Take advantage of phone services that provide price comparisons and that compare other features, such as an insurance policy's guarantee period and the insurer's financial-strength ratings.

Example: Quotesmith (800-431-1147) compares prices of 150 term-life policies sold by brokers. It sends the price comparisons via first-class mail the following business day. This service is free.

Helpful: Don't overlook low-load term-life insurance policies, which generally have competitive prices and are convertible to low-load cash-value policies. Call The Wholesale Insurance Network (800-808-5810), which provides free quotes on low-load policies from several insurers. Be prepared to answer a wide variety of personal and health questions.

***Step 5:* Update your calculations every few years.** People often neglect to account for the ways in which their families' financial needs change over time.

Example: If you earn more money as you move up the career ladder, your family's standard of living will improve and you will probably want to protect it.

Likewise, as you have more children, your projected costs and financial responsibilities will increase sharply, and you should buy more insurance.

Source: Glenn Daily, a fee-only insurance consultant, 234 E. 84 St., New York 10028. He is author of *Life Insurance Sense and Nonsense.*

Renters Insurance Is a Must

Renters insurance protects your personal possessions in case of damage. It also covers your liability for damages that you, family members and pets inflict on other people in your rented apartment.

Renters insurance is also important because the landlord's insurance will not likely cover the contents of your apartment.

Types of renters insurance: Replacement value, which will cover the full cost to replace a destroyed item…actual cash value, a less-costly policy that repays only the actual cost of a lost item minus depreciation.

Caution: Valuable items, such as heirloom jewelry and antiques may need separate, additional coverage.

Source: Jayna Neagle, Insurance Information Institute, 110 William St., New York 10038.

Getting Your HMO To Pay Up

When your Medicare HMO denies a benefit, challenge the decision. Your HMO must pass your appeal to the Health Care Financing Administration's contractor for independent review. If you have any questions, your HMO must also provide specific instructions on how to appeal.

Good news: Medicare HMO decisions are frequently overturned in full or in part on appeal.

Source: Charles Inlander, president, People's Medical Society, 462 Walnut St., Allentown, PA 18102.

Car Insurance Dilemma

If you report an accident, your rates may go up or your policy may be canceled. If you don't report it and seek coverage—if you are sued, for example—your insurer may not protect you.

Safest: Report any accident that involves another person—even if it seems to be his/her fault. If others are not involved, you can consider paying the claim yourself.

Source: Robert Hunter, head of the insurance group at the Consumer Federation of America, 1424 16 St. NW, Washington, DC 20036.

Lower Car Insurance Premiums

Lower car insurance premiums are easier to find as carriers face fewer losses and make lower payments to policyholders. Some insurers are even forgiving accidents and giving rebates to customers.

Important: See if your insurer offers an accident-forgiveness program or other discounts …shop around for rates… and never drop an insurer until you have been approved by another.

Source: Mary Griffin, insurance counsel at Consumers Union, a nonprofit consumer advocacy group in Washington, DC, and publisher of *Consumer Reports.*

First-to-Die Insurance

First-to-die life insurance insures two lives—but pays off when the first person dies. It can let a surviving spouse maintain his/her standard of living, even if the medical costs of the partner's final illness drain the couple's savings. *Cost:* For a husband and wife ages 55 and 53 respectively, it will cost about $5,000 annually for $250,000 of coverage. After 10 years, earnings on the accumulated cash value should be more than the annual premium.

Source: Henry Weil, editor, *Retire with Money*, Time & Life Bldg., Rockefeller Center, New York 10020.

Buy Life Insurance Now

Buy term life insurance *now*—before rates increase. *Background:* A new model regulation approved by the National Association of Insurance Commissioners will force many insurance companies to meet higher reserve requirements—the cash insurers must put aside to cover payouts. *Result:* Level-premium term policies, in which premiums stay the same for more than five years, may cost up to 15% more.

Source: Glenn Daily, a fee-only insurance consultant, 234 E. 84 St., New York 10028. He is author of *Life Insurance Sense and Nonsense.*

Evaluating Life Insurance Plans

Get a minimum of three life insurance quotes before deciding which policy to buy. First, get a quote from an independent agent. Then call the Wholesale Insurance Network (800-808-5810). Finally, get a quote from a quote service, which obtains information from you by phone and then searches for the lowest rates for which you qualify. There is no charge for the service. *Some quote services:* MasterQuote, 800-337-5433…Life Rates of America, 800-457-2837…TermQuote, 800-444-8376…Quotesmith, 800-431-1147.

Source: Glenn Daily, a fee-only insurance consultant, 234 E. 84 St., New York 10028. He is author of *Life Insurance Sense and Nonsense.*

6

Tax Smarts

Most Common Mistakes People Make When Doing Their Tax Returns

If you are planning to prepare your own tax return this year, beware of these common filing errors that can needlessly cost you valuable tax dollars in April.

Before you begin:

The most basic filing mistake is not getting an early start on preparing your return. An early start assures ample time to find tax-saving strategies...pull together any extra information you need...and obtain all forms and statements that must be filed with your return. *What you'll need...*

• **Information returns.** These include W-2 forms from employers and 1099s from banks, brokers and others that have paid you income this year. Forms should be mailed to you by January 31.

• **Past years' returns.** Use these as a guide to help you with this year's filing. *Reasons:*

• **Deductions found on old returns** will remind you to take the same deductions this year.

• **Old returns may include carryover items** that you have forgotten about, such as capital losses in excess of $3,000 incurred in a past year.

• **If you discover new deductions this year** that you could have claimed in past years but didn't, you'll be able to file amended tax returns for the past years to get tax refunds. Use IRS Form 1040X, *Amended US Individual Tax Return.*

Deadline: The refund deadline on old returns is three years after their filing. So, if you filed on April 15 three years ago, you'll have to discover the potential refund before that date this year—another reason to prepare your return early.

If you don't have copies of your past years' returns, you can get them from the IRS by filing IRS Form 4506, *Request for Copy or Transcript of Tax Form.*

•**Comprehensive records.** Don't rely on your checkbook register to be the sole source of your deductible expenses. Go over all your canceled checks, credit-card receipts, bills and investment records. You may come across deductible items you weren't aware of. *Examples:*

•**Gambling losses** (lottery and raffle tickets, etc.) are deductible if you *had* gambling winnings and you itemize on Schedule A.

•**Taxi fares incurred** on behalf of a charity or to receive medical treatment.

•**Stocks, bonds or loans** that have become worthless in the past year.

•**IRS forms.** Quickly go over your planned filing strategies and carefully read the instructions on your tax return to be sure you have all the IRS forms and schedules you need. To get a missing tax form, call the IRS (800-829-3676) and ask for it. Do it early to avoid having to delay your filing while waiting for the form. Filling out forms:

When you are finally ready to sit down and fill out your tax return forms, avoid these all-too-common mistakes…

•**State taxes.** Remember that the amount of state tax you can deduct on your federal return is the amount you actually paid during calendar 1996—which could exceed the amount shown on your 1996 state return. *Special situations…*

•**A payment made toward your 1995 state taxes** is deductible on your 1996 federal return if made in 1996.

•**A payment of state taxes for 1996** that accompanies a state return filed on April 15, 1997, is not deductible on your 1996 federal return. It will be deductible on the 1997 return.

•**An overpayment of 1995 state taxes** that you elected to apply to your 1996 state tax bill is a deductible payment for 1996. Be careful. It's easy to overlook it if you total up your state tax payments by looking only at your W-2 and your checkbook.

•**1099s.** Do not attach 1099 forms to your tax return—the IRS gets its own copies.

And do not just add up the 1099s and then report their total. List the amount reported on each 1099 separately on your return.

Reason: IRS computers look to match the amounts reported on 1099s with the numbers on your return. If the figures don't match, your return may be flagged for extra examination.

•**Charity.** A canceled check is no longer adequate proof of a charitable deduction for a gift of $250 or more claimed on your tax return.

To deduct such a gift, you must have received an acknowledgment letter from the charity describing the gift—and you must obtain the letter before you file your return.

•**Dependency exemptions.** Claim every exemption that you are entitled to take.

•**If you are one of several people who support an individual**—such as children supporting an aged parent—and no one among you provides more than half the individual's support, you may still be able to claim a dependency exemption by filing IRS Form 2120, Multiple Support Declaration. You can then assign the exemption to one of those who is providing at least 10% of the support.

•**When divorced parents have children**, it makes sense for the parent in the highest tax bracket to claim the exemptions for the children to maximize tax savings.

Exemptions can be shifted from the custodial parent to the noncustodial parent. To do so, file IRS Form 8332, *Release of Claim to Exemption for Child of Divorced or Separated Parents.* Before you file:

Beware of these errors before sending your return to the IRS…

•**Social Security numbers.** The IRS processes your tax return and subsequent actions concerning it—refunds, correspondence, etc.—by Social Security number. So be sure the numbers you report are correct—transposed digits can cause problems. *Also…*

•**Joint filers** should always report their Social Security numbers in the same order. The IRS processes returns by the first number reported, so switching the order of numbers on returns or correspondence can cause confusion.

•**Have Social Security numbers for all children.** *Exception:* If a child was born in November or December of 1996, you can write 11/96 or 12/96 in the place for the number.

•**Check math and forms.** If the math on your return is incorrect, its processing and any refund owed to you will be delayed. The form will also draw unwanted extra attention from the IRS.

If any required tax forms or schedules are missing, similar problems will result.

Also, be sure you properly sign your return. It's not valid without a signature.

•**Addressing forms.** Use preprinted mailing labels supplied by the IRS whenever possible. The bar codes on them speed processing. If you address your return by hand, be sure to legibly fill in the correct IRS address and your correct Social Security number.

Source: Julian Block, a tax attorney in Larchmont, NY, and a former special agent for the IRS. He is author of *Julian Block's Tax Avoidance Secrets.* Boardroom Classics.

Last-Minute Tax-Saving Strategies

With Congress and the president seriously considering cutting taxes, it may pay to postpone some of your income until January.

If you can put off receiving some wages and capital gains until next year, you will hold down your 1996 taxes. In addition, by deferring some expenses into 1997, you may receive a tax benefit next year that you would have lost had you paid the expenses this year. *Steps to consider before year-end...*
Wages and capital gains:

•**If allowable**, ask that year-end bonuses be paid after January 1. Any 1997 tax cut will likely be retroactive to the first of the year. Be sure the check will be dated after January 1.

•**If you run a part-time business**, ask that money you are owed be paid early next year instead of now.

•**If you are looking for a place to temporarily park $10,000 or more**, consider investing it in a 90-day Treasury bill. You will earn about 5.5%, and federal taxes will be due in 1997, when the Treasury bill matures.
Expenses:

To be able to itemize deductions, married couples filing jointly must have at least $6,550

in deductible expenses...single filers must have $3,900.

Strategy: If you will not exceed this amount this year, put off December expenses until January, so they can be used to push you over the limit next year. *Deductible expenses to consider postponing...*

•**A December real-estate tax bill.** If possible, use the grace period to delay payment until January 1.

•**Nonreimbursed medical expenses.**

•**Charitable contributions, such as clothing.**

•**Nonreimbursed job-related expenses**, such as uniforms. *Important:* These are subject to limitation based on Adjusted Gross Income.

Source: Laurence I. Foster, a tax partner with the personal financial planning practice of KPMG Peat Marwick LLP, 345 Park Ave., NY 10154.

Tax-Free Income Loopholes

Not all the money you receive is taxable income, even though the IRS might like you to think it is. *The types of tax-free income...*
Tax-free windfalls:

•**Gifts and inheritances.** You do not pay income tax on money or property you receive as a gift—or inheritance. Any gift tax owed is the responsibility of the person who gave the gift. In the case of an inheritance, federal estate tax is paid by the decedent's estate, not by the beneficiaries.

If you inherit property that has increased in value, such as the family home, you receive it at its stepped-up estate value. This allows you to avoid tax on the gain.

And when you sell the property, you use its stepped-up value, rather than the original cost, to calculate your taxable gain...another big benefit.

•**Life insurance proceeds.** The beneficiary receives the proceeds of life insurance policies free of tax. But the decedent's estate may be liable for estate tax on the proceeds.

•**Borrowed money**—this includes borrowing up to $50,000 from your company pension plan—is tax-free. *Reason:* Borrowing is not treated as a taxable transaction.

Trap: If a debt you owe is canceled, the amount of debt forgiven might be taxable income to you.

• **Gain on the sale of your home.** If you or your spouse is 55 years of age or older, the first $125,000 of gain from the sale of your house is tax-free. To qualify for the $125,000 exclusion, however, you must never have used this tax break before and you must have owned and lived in the home for at least three years out of the past five.

Tax deferral: If you buy a new home within two years before or after you sell the old one, no tax is generally owed on the gain, provided that the new home costs at least as much as the amount you got for the old one.

• **Scholarships and fellowship grants** are tax-free provided you are a degree candidate and the money is used strictly for tuition, fees, books, supplies, and required equipment. (Grants for room and board are taxable.)

• **Employee awards of tangible personal property** (not cash) for length of service or safety achievements...up to $400 per employee or $1,600 if the employer has a qualified plan...are tax-free. (Awards for suggestions to an employer are generally taxable.)

• **Property settlements between spouses** in a divorce are not taxable to the recipient. However, the recipient takes over the tax cost (basis) in the property and will be taxed on any gain when the property is sold.

• **Child support and alimony.** Child-support payments are tax free to the recipient. Alimony is generally taxable, but it can be tax free if the parties agree.

• **Damages received in a lawsuit** due to personal injury or sickness and certain kinds of discrimination are tax-free.

• **Rollovers.** No tax is payable on a lump-sum payout from a company pension plan directly transferred into an IRA within 60 days. More tax-free income:

• **Fourteen days' rental income.** You can rent out both your house and vacation home for up to 14 days and not pay tax on the income. The money does not have to be reported on your tax return.

• **Municipal bond interest.** Generally, the interest is exempt from federal income tax and sometimes from state and local tax as well.

Problems: Interest from certain "private activity" municipal bonds is subject to the Alternative Minimum Tax (AMT). Also, municipal bond interest is taken into account in figuring your income level to determine whether any of your Social Security benefits are taxable.

• **Return-of-capital dividends.** Some companies pay dividends that are considered a return of your investment in the company. These are wholly or partially tax-free. However, your tax cost in the stock has to be reduced by the amount of untaxed dividends.

• **Life insurance policy dividends** are generally considered a partial return of the premiums you paid and are not taxable. You don't have to pay tax on these dividends until they exceed the accumulated premiums paid for the policy.

• **Annuity payments.** The part of an annuity payment that represents the return of your investment in the annuity contract is not taxed. Pension and IRA distributions that represent non-tax-deductible contributions are also not taxed.

• **Education savings bonds.** Interest on US Series EE savings bonds issued after December 31, 1989 is tax-free to many taxpayers if the bonds are later redeemed to pay for education expenses.

Limits: This exclusion is not available for married taxpayers with income in excess of $93,450 and single or head of household filers with income greater than $57,300.

• **Children's wages.** Dependent children can earn up to $3,500 in 1995—tax-free.

• **Children's investment income.** Dependent children can receive up to $650 of investment income tax-free.

Also tax-free:

• **Workers' compensation.**

• **Social Security payments** if your income is less than $32,000 if married filing jointly...or $25,000 if filing single.

• **Federal income tax refunds** are not taxable. (However, any interest the IRS pays on a late refund is taxable.)

• **State income tax refunds**, provided you did not itemize deductions on your federal tax return for the previous year. If, however, you itemized your deductions for the year, your state refund is taxable. State refunds are not taxable if you were subject to the AMT the previous year and got no tax benefit for your state tax payments.

• **Disability payments** from accident or health insurance policies paid for by the taxpayer are generally not taxable. But they're usually taxable if your employer paid the premiums.

• **Foreign-earned income.** The first $70,000 of salary earned in another country is excluded from US tax if you were a resident of that country for the entire tax year. *Also excluded from US tax:* Some of your housing expenses.

• **Fringe benefits**—certain ones from your employer—are tax-free.

Examples: Health and accident insurance, pension plans, up to $50,000 of life insurance coverage, up to $5,000 of death benefits, child- and dependent-care expenses, legal services under group plans, supper money, employee discounts, transit passes not exceeding $60 per month.

• **Reimbursed medical expenses** not claimed as itemized deductions.

• **Reimbursed travel and entertainment expenses** that you adequately account for to your employer do not have to be reported on your tax return (unless the reimbursement is included on your W-2).

• **Amounts received for insurance reimbursement** up to the amount of your original cost for the property that was lost or damaged.

Source: Edward Mendlowitz, partner, Mendlowitz Weitsen, CPAs, 646 Highway 18, E. Brunswick, NJ 08816.

purchases and late-paid taxes. But interest on home-equity loans of up to $100,000 is fully deductible.

Loophole: Take out a home-equity loan on your first or second home and use the proceeds to pay off personal debt. Your interest payments will then be deductible. You will have converted nondeductible personal interest payments into deductible mortgage interest.

• **Deduct medical expenses of dependents.** Even though you may not be able to claim a personal exemption for your contribution to the support of relatives because they had a gross income of $2,500 or more, you can still deduct any medical expenses that you pay on their behalf. *Key:* You must provide more than one half of the relative's support.

Loophole: Instead of giving your relative cash to pay medical bills, pay the bills yourself. This may give you a deduction.

Whoever is claiming a dependency exemption for a parent under a multiple support agreement (Form 2120) with other relatives should also pay the dependent's medical expenses. *Reason:* In determining qualification for the exemption, the payment of medical expenses is treated as part of the dependent's support. The payment is also deductible as a medical expense.

Impact: You get a double tax benefit for the same payment…a dependency exemption and a tax deduction.

Another way to get a double benefit is to make a charitable contribution on your parents' behalf. The payment is included in calculating support. You get a charitable deduction.

Source: Edward Mendlowitz, partner, Mendlowitz Weitsen, CPAs, 646 Highway 18, E. Brunswick, NJ 08816

Two Deductible Nondeductible Expenses

• **Take interest deductions.** Interest on personal debt is not deductible. This includes interest on car loans, college loans, credit cards, revolving charge accounts, installment

One of Today's Best Tax-Saving Strategies… Grantor Retained Annuity Trust

As part of a complete tax program, Grantor Retained Annuity Trusts (GRATs) can be a very effective way to transfer future growth of rap-idly appreciating property—at little or no tax cost.

How GRATs work: A person puts property into a trust for the benefit of his/her heirs but retains an annuity for himself—a stream of income for a number of years.

Taking back an annuity for yourself reduces the taxable part of the transfer. If the annuity you keep is big enough or runs long enough, you can eliminate essentially *all* of the gift tax that would otherwise be due on the transfer of property to the trust.

Example: You transfer $1 million into a GRAT and reserve a $245,200 annual annuity for yourself for five years. Because the value of the property put into the trust is equal to the value of the annuity (plus an interest factor), there is practically no taxable gift (computed at 7.2%, the December 1995 rate).

However, let's say the property is worth $5 million after five years. *Result:* You have transferred $5 million to your heirs without incurring any additional gift tax at all.

Because the GRAT's success is tied to future appreciation in the property, it works best with assets that are volatile or quickly appreciating.

Examples: Biotechnology stocks or companies that do business related to the Internet.

Strategy: Each security that you put into a GRAT should be held in a separate trust. That way, the stocks that perform well won't be used to make up an annuity shortfall from stocks that don't perform so well.

Example: You fund a GRAT with two stocks, each worth $1 million, and you reserve an annuity of $490,400 a year for five years.

At the end of two years, one stock is worth $3 million and the other is only worth $250,000. The shortfall will have to be made up by the better-performing stock. This will bring back to you some of the appreciation that would have otherwise gone to your beneficiaries.

Drawback: For gift tax purposes, the annuity is measured at the time of the transfer. However, a generation-skipping transfer tax kicks in after the annuity has run, so GRATs are not usually used for transfers to grandchildren, only to children.

Example: You transfer $1 million into a GRAT for your grandchildren and reserve an annuity of $245,200 a year for five years. No gift tax is due. But if the value of the shares remaining in the GRAT grows to $5 million after five years, the generation-skipping tax will be figured on that $5 million amount when your interest ends, not on the initial gift reduced by the annuity.

A GRAT will not reduce your present estate taxes, but will remove future growth.

Reason: You receive an annuity equal to the value of the property you gave up. Therefore it should be used in conjunction with other estate planning techniques.

Advantage: A GRAT will work even if the property put into trust does not generate cash, because a GRAT can pay an annuity in kind. The market value of the shares is measured on an ongoing basis.

Example: You put 25,000 shares worth $10 a share into a GRAT and reserve an annuity equal to $61,300 for five years. If the stock didn't move at first, at the end of Year One, you would receive 6,130 shares as an annuity payment. If the share price rises to $50 in Year Two, you would receive only 1,226 shares.

What should you do with the stock that you get back? Create a new GRAT if the company is still rapidly growing. Yes, that will create a lot of paperwork. But the resulting savings will be worth the hassle and cost because you can transfer a lot of property without paying taxes.

Strategy: Annuities are generally thought of as level payments over time. But GRAT annuities can rise by as much as 20% a year from the preceding year.

Example: If you receive a $50,000 annuity in the first year, you can take as much as $60,000 in the second year.

There is no limit as to how far annuity payments can fall. *Caution:* Once payments decrease, they can rise only 20% a year.

And the full annuity payments must be outlined from the start in the trust instrument and cannot be changed.

Example: If you expect your stock's price to rise in two or three years, you may wish to create a six-year GRAT. Use level payments in

Year One through Year Three, then increase the payments over the next three years.

Drawback: If you die during the trust term, the property will be included in your estate and you will have lost the intended tax advantage.

In addition to stocks, consider funding a GRAT with vacant real estate that is ripe for development. To make the annuity payment, each year a small piece would get deeded back to you.

You can also fund a GRAT with shares of a closely held business or an S corporation. *Caution:* Any trust or shareholder must be an eligible S corporation shareholder.

Annuity payments must last at least two years. There is no limit on how many years annuity payments can last, but the longer the annuity, the more risk you assume of dying during the term. Anyway, the value of the later payments will not be very large.

Strategy: It makes more sense to use a series of short GRATs than one long GRAT because GRATs are usually funded with volatile assets. You don't want good years supporting poor years.

Source: David S. Rhine, CPA, director of family wealth planning and tax partner, BDO Seidman, LLP, 330 Madison Ave., New York 10017.

How to Boost Your Personal Cash Flow With Tax Savings

Smart tax planning can increase the amount of cash in your pocket. Here are ways to cut your tax bill and increase your after-tax income without incurring any cash expenditures…
Salary and job expenses:

An increased expense account may be better for you than an increase in salary.

Reason: Salary income is fully taxable, but reimbursements received from an employer for business expenses that you incur are tax-free.

Key: Almost every employee incurs some unreimbursed job-related expenses.

Examples: Subscriptions to business periodicals…driving for work…meals and entertainment costs…dry-cleaning costs incurred on business trips…books on work-related subjects…education and training…office decorations…special work clothes…stationery used for work, etc.

But while unreimbursed business expenses are deductible, the deduction is likely to be restricted. *Reasons…*

•**You can only deduct** job-related expenses if you itemize deductions.

•**Employee business expenses** are included with miscellaneous expenses—the total of which is deductible only to the extent that it exceeds 2% of your Adjusted Gross Income (AGI). So if, for example, your AGI is $50,000, you get no deduction for your first $1,000 of expenses.

•**Some items are subject to further deduction limits.** *Example:* Meals and entertainment are only 50% deductible.

All of this makes it unlikely that you'll get a full deduction for all of the expenses that you incur for work.

However, none of these limits apply to expense reimbursements you receive from your employer—you receive them all 100% tax-free. Thus, by taking an increased expense account instead of a raise in salary, you may come out ahead tax-wise. And your employer may come out ahead, too, since it doesn't owe employment taxes on reimbursement payments—making it easier to negotiate such a deal. Similarly, it can pay to take some of your compensation in the form of fringe benefits rather than as salary, even if the benefits are fully taxable.

Examples: A surplus computer…vacation use of a company-owned house or boat…use of a company vehicle.

By splitting tax and economic savings, you may both come out ahead, compared with taking a raise in salary.

Caution: Make sure that your expense reimbursement arrangement is an accountable plan—in which you must provide evidence of your expenses to your employer. Otherwise, the payments to you will be included in your taxable income.

Interest:

By carefully planning your "debt portfolio," you may increase your interest deduction at no cash cost.

Key: Interest on consumer borrowing is no longer deductible. But interest (subject to some limitations) can be deducted on home loans, business borrowing and investment borrowing.

Example: You are planning to buy a $20,000 car—and make a $20,000 investment in the coming year. Instead of financing the car with a loan and making the investment with cash, consider doing the reverse. That is, buy the car with cash and borrow to finance the investment. Because investment interest is deductible, you may generate a deduction that you would not have had otherwise.

Similarly, if you own a business or have a sideline business, you can borrow to make business purchases and use the cash saved for consumer items.

Or you can take a $100,000 home-equity loan and use it to pay off consumer debt replacing nondeductible interest with deductible interest. Interest on a home-equity loan is deductible, regardless of how you use the proceeds.

Note: To get a deduction for investment or business interest, the borrowed money must be used for an investment or business purpose. If you borrow against an investment or business asset and use the loan proceeds to pay off consumer debt, you will not get an interest deduction.

Investments:

Don't forget to deduct every expense related to managing your investments. *Deductible:*

•**Phone calls to your stockbroker** or mutual fund.

•**Subscriptions** to any investment newsletters and periodicals.

•**Books on investment topics.**

•**Trips to your broker's office.**

•**The reasonable cost of attending an annual meeting** of a company in which you have invested.

•**Legal fees** related to receiving investment income.

•**Safe-deposit box to hold investment items**—stock certificates, jewelry, etc.

Legal fees:

Many legal expenses create deductions that are frequently overlooked.

Example: The cost of drafting a will is a nondeductible personal expense. But the cost of estate tax planning in the course of drafting a will is deductible. Thus, by obtaining an itemized bill from your lawyer that breaks out fees related to estate tax planning, you can obtain a deduction that you wouldn't have had otherwise.

Legal fees incurred to receive taxable income also are deductible. So if you hire a lawyer to collect overdue alimony, interest on a debt or dividends on an investment, you can deduct his/her bill.

In addition, you can deduct fees paid to a lawyer handling divorce negotiations that are attributable to efforts to receive or minimize alimony. Again, get a separate itemized bill that breaks out alimony-related expenses.

Retirement plans:

Many 401(k) and Keogh plans let account owners borrow against their accounts, in amounts up to 50% of the account assets. So a 401(k) or Keogh plan may offer valuable tax deductions, tax-deferred investment returns and cash. When you borrow from your retirement account, you borrow from yourself. You don't have to get the approval of any bank loan officer, so the account can be a source of tax-free cash to pay for college, a down payment on a home loan or similar expenditures, usually at a lower rate than you would pay at a bank.

You will owe interest on the loan, but you pay it to yourself and it is not deductible. The loan account receives it on a tax-deferred basis—making your interest payments an attractive investment. The plan's terms may limit the amount and frequency of loans and the purposes for which they may be used. So check with your plan's trustee for more details.

Depreciation:

This is a no-cash-cost deduction that can shelter income from tax.

Caution: If your expenses exceed your income, the net loss may not be deductible. Losses from rental property are passive and only deductible against passive income, such as rental income.

Self-employed individuals can invest in depreciable business assets to shelter business income from tax.

Example: A doctor may own his office building and diagnostic equipment.

Charity:

Instead of giving cash to charity, give long-term appreciated assets.

Reason: You get a deduction for the property's appreciated value without having to pay tax on the gain. If you give cash, you'll face capital gains tax on the property.

Also, get paid for cleaning out your closets by donating clothes to charity. Be sure you get an itemized receipt.

Home office:

If you work at home, a home-office deduction enables you to deduct a portion of previously nondeductible expenses—such as utilities, insurance and maintenance—plus depreciation. Otherwise, nondeductible expenses can't generate or increase a loss from your business.

Caution: A home-office deduction is a red-flag audit item. Be sure you qualify by using part of your home exclusively for business and as the principal place where you conduct your business.

Wage withholding:

After applying tax-saving ideas, convert them into cash flow by filing a new W-4 form with your employer to reduce the taxes withheld from your salary. Remember that you are entitled to claim as many withholding allowances as you qualify for, so long as the amount of tax withheld from your salary accurately balances your final tax bill for the year.

Source: Laurence I. Foster, tax partner in the personal financial planning practice at KPMG Peat Marwick LLP, 345 Park Ave., New York 10154.

Loopholes in Pension Plan Distributions and IRAs

Taking an IRA or pension distribution is fraught with tax traps. There are loopholes here, too. It's important to know what your options are.

Basics:

IRA and pension plans have the same distribution rules. Amounts distributed are taxed to the recipient. Voluntary after-tax contributions are not taxed at the time of distribution. Only the interest on such contributions is taxed.

Trap: The return of voluntary and nonvoluntary contributions is allocated proportionately to each amount distributed. If your account is mixed between voluntary and nonvoluntary contributions (that is, amounts you contributed and amounts your employer contributed), you can't dictate that a distribution be taken wholly out of nontaxable, nondeductible contributions.

Trap: Undistributed amounts left in your IRA or pension plan at the time of your death are subject to both estate tax and income tax, and possible excise tax depending on the size of the account.

Minimum distributions:

Minimum distribution rules in the tax law require you to start taking money out of your retirement accounts by April 1 of the year following the year you turn 70½. (That's right, it's April 1, not April 15.) After that you must take a minimum amount out each year.

Trap: If you wait until April 1 after you turn 70½ to take out your first distribution, you must also take a second distribution for the second year by December 31.

Caution: The penalty for taking out too little or taking the money too late is 50% of the amount that should have been withdrawn but wasn't.

Early distributions:

If you take money out of your account before the date you turn 59½ you might be subject to a 10% early withdrawal penalty.

Loophole: You can avoid the penalty either by taking the money out as an annuity in annual installments based on your life expectancy *or* by using the money for medical expenses.

Excess accumulations:

There is an excise tax equal to 15% of annual distributions from all retirement plans in excess of $155,000—and a tax on lump sum distributions in excess of five times that amount or $775,000 in 1996. (These figures are indexed annually for inflation.)

Death trap: Additionally, there is a 15% estate surtax on any of your excess retirement plan accumulations.

Meaning: There's an excess accumulation if the value of all your pensions exceeds the present value of a single life annuity of $155,000. Choosing beneficiaries:

Annual minimum distributions must be calculated based on your life expectancy or the joint life expectancy of you and your designated beneficiary.

Loophole: By using a joint life expectancy, the annual distribution will be smaller.

Loophole: You can select a beneficiary who is much younger than you. You don't have to name your spouse as beneficiary. You can name a child or grandchild or friend.

Loophole: Any gains on the amounts in the plan are not taxed annually or separately. They are only taxed as part of an overall distribution.

Trap: Capital gains in the plan do not receive preferential tax treatment. Gains distributed from the plan are taxed as ordinary income.

Loophole: Certain distributions incidental to a divorce are tax-free if they are directly rolled over into an IRA. Miscellaneous:

Companies are required to withhold 20% in tax on distributions from company plans that are not directly rolled over into an IRA.

Loophole: Be sure to ask your company to transfer your pension money directly from the company to an IRA.

Loophole: By taking the money into your own hands and forcing the company to withhold 20% in tax, you can cover any underpayments you have in estimated tax. You can even ask the company to withhold more. Withheld tax is considered to have been paid in equally over the year, so any estimated tax underpayments you have will be entirely wiped out.

Designate a charitable remainder trust as the beneficiary of your pension plans. Name your spouse as the income beneficiary of the trust so your pension will escape estate tax on your death and your spouse's death.

Trap: You can't avoid the 15% excise tax on excess pension plan accumulations by setting up a charitable remainder trust.

Loophole: There is a $5,000 exclusion of money paid from a company retirement plan to an employee's beneficiary.

Source: Edward Mendlowitz, partner, Mendlowitz Weitsen, CPAs, 646 Highway 18, E. Brunswick, NJ 08816.

Retirement Tax-Planning Loopholes

Retirement brings its own set of tax rules and benefits. *Here are some loopholes you can take advantage of...*
Pension plans:

•**Distribution loopholes:** The amounts you receive in payouts from your company pension or profit-sharing plan are generally fully taxable.

Loophole: If you contributed to the pension plan with some of your own after-tax dollars, that contribution is not taxable when you take it out. Obligatory before-tax contributions to your employer's pension plan and 401(k) contributions, which are made with pretax dollars, are taxable when you take them out. Voluntary nondeductible contributions to an IRA are not taxable when withdrawn.

Special loophole: Pensions from certain state governmental agencies are not subject to state income tax.

•**Loopholes for lump-sum distributions:** Lump-sum distributions from pension and profit-sharing plans qualify for special tax breaks.

Rollover loophole: You can roll over the money into an IRA and postpone paying taxes until you take the money out of the IRA.

59½ loophole: As long as you're at least 59½ years old, your lump-sum distribution may qualify for special five-year or 10 year averaging. You may end up paying a very low tax rate on the distribution.

•**Withdrawal loopholes:** You must begin making annual withdrawals from your IRA and pension or profit sharing plan when you reach the age of 70½.

Loophole: You can postpone your first withdrawal until April 1 of the year following the year you reach 70½.

Trap: If you elect to defer your first withdrawal until April 1, you must make a second withdrawal for the second year by December 31.

Trap: If you miss the deadline for making withdrawals, you'll be charged a 50% penalty tax on the amount you should have withdrawn, but didn't.

•***Excess distribution loophole:*** Avoid penalties on excess distributions from your pension plans.

The penalty: You'll be charged a 15% penalty tax to the extent your annual distributions from all your plans exceed $155,000—or to the extent that you get a lump-sum distribution that exceeds $775,000.

Grandfather election loophole: If you made what is known as a grandfather election on your 1987 or 1988 tax return, you might be exempt from the 15% penalty tax on part of your excess distribution. See your tax adviser for more detailed information.

Social security:

Up to 85% of your Social Security benefits are taxable, depending on your total income. The calculation for taxing Social Security benefits includes tax-exempt interest you've earned from municipal bonds.

•***Taxable bonds loophole:*** You may be better off owning taxable bonds rather than tax-exempt ones since taxable bonds pay higher interest rates.

Social Security benefits are based on your income. It's important to check periodically on your earnings record with the Social Security Administration. Errors more than three years old are hard to correct. If you catch a mistake early on, you'll be able to fix it.

To check: Fill out and mail to the Social Security Administration Form SSA-7004, *Request for Earnings and Benefits Estimate Statement.*

•***Part-time-income loophole:*** If you receive earned income, even though you're on Social Security, you still have to pay FICA and Medicare taxes on that income.

Your Social Security benefits will be reduced if your income exceeds certain limits.

Loophole: You can earn up to $8,280 if you are between 62 and 64 years old before there is any reduction in your Social Security benefits. For persons aged 65 to 69, the limit is $11,520. If you are 70 or older, there is no limit on the amount you can earn.

Note: There is no reduction in benefits for unearned income, such as dividends and interest.

Also, be sure to squeeze the maximum tax benefit from your home.

•***Home loophole:*** If you're 55 or older, you don't have to pay tax on the first $125,000 of profit on the sale of your home. This is a once-in-a-lifetime exclusion. Married individuals are entitled to only one exclusion per couple.

•***Inheritance loophole:*** It's not a good idea from a tax standpoint to give the family home to your intended beneficiaries before you die. *Reason:* The recipients take over your tax basis in the property, which is generally its cost. When the recipients sell the property they will pay income tax on the full appreciation in value since you bought the property.

Let your beneficiaries inherit the family home. They will receive it at its stepped-up, date-of-death value and income tax will be forgiven on the appreciation. This same loophole applies to other appreciated property. For instance, instead of selling stock and giving your children the proceeds, give them cash and let them inherit the stock.

•***Education/gift loophole:*** A way to reduce your taxable estate is to make annual gifts to family members. You can give up to $10,000 a year to each of any number of recipients ($20,000 a year if your spouse joins in the gift) without having to pay federal gift tax.

In addition to $10,000 or $20,000 amounts, you can also make gift-tax-free gifts for education expenses. To qualify a payment as a tax–free gift, however, you must make it directly to the college or other institution.

There are two ways to make gifts to children and still control the use of the money. Set up a trust for the children or open a custodial account under the Uniform Gifts to Minors Act.

Trap: Don't make yourself the trustee or custodian of these accounts. If you do that, the assets will be taxed in your estate when you die.

•**Life insurance loophole:** Premium payments on life insurance are not tax deductible, and any proceeds that are eventually paid out are not considered taxable income. Many senior citizens have fully paid-up life insurance policies from which they receive dividends. They get 1099s from the insurance company for these dividends. The dividends are not taxable until the cumulative amount of dividends received exceeds the total amount of premiums paid by the policyholder.

•**State of residency loophole:** Many states have income taxes. Some do not. If you anticipate substantial retirement income, you might consider relocating to a state without income tax.

Source: Edward Mendlowitz, partner, Mendlowitz Weitsen, LLP CPAs, 646 Highway 18, E. Brunswick, NJ 08816.

How to Convert Taxable Income into Tax-Free Income for Your Retirement Years

Structuring savings to avoid future taxes is an overlooked aspect of retirement planning.

Opportunity: By taking advantage of the tax-favored treatment provided by the Tax Code for insurance products, it may be possible to increase your future after-tax income while reducing estate taxes and other expenses that deplete amounts you can leave to heirs. A comparison between a *conventional investment* and an *insurance-product investment* can demonstrate the opportunities offered by the latter.

Conventional investment: At current market rates* you can spend $50,000 to buy a 12-year certificate of deposit (CD) earning 6% that will mature with a value of $100,000. The CD interest is taxable every year. So, if you are in a 40% tax bracket (combined federal and local), you'll have to pay $1,200 in taxes on the $3,000 in interest that the CD earns annually. That's more than $14,000 in taxes over the 12 years.

*All figures are based on market rates and available insurance products at the time of writing.

At the end of the 12 years, you will get $100,000 from the CD and be able to reinvest it to earn $6,000 annually (again at today's rates) or $3,600 after taxes.

Pitfalls: This income will be counted in the calculations that can cause your Social Security benefits to be subject to income tax. Additionally, the CD will be taxable as part of your estate should you die during its term.

Insurance investment: Also at current rates you can invest $50,000 in an immediate annuity that pays $10,578 annually for five years. Because part of this is return of principal, only $578 is taxed annually. So the immediate tax bill is cut by more than half.

The annuity proceeds can then be used to buy an investment-grade life-insurance policy that accumulates cash value on a tax-deferred basis.

At the end of 12 years, it's possible to begin withdrawing $7,500 annually from the life-insurance policy tax-free for the rest of your life. Future after-tax income more than doubles. Moreover, money taken out of the policy does not count in calculations that can result in the taxation of Social Security benefits.

When you die, the insurance benefit provided by the policy is not taxable income to the policy beneficiaries, and probate is avoided on the assets.

With careful estate planning, it may also be possible to remove the policy proceeds from your taxable estate.

Result: After-tax retirement income is increased, Social Security taxes, probate expenses and estate taxes are reduced.

The deal is even better if the insurance investment is made through a joint policy that pays on the death of the survivor of a husband and wife. That's because the cost of the death benefit is much lower, which increases the amount that can be withdrawn tax-free each year.

Review your investment portfolio well in advance of retirement to see if you own assets that could advantageously be shifted into insurance investments to obtain the benefits described above. Even funds withdrawn from retirement accounts may be profitably invested in this manner. *Requirements...*

•**An investment horizon of more than 10 years.** You must be confident that you won't have to cash in your investment within that time. The time is needed to take advantage of tax deferrals that let investment earnings compound at an accelerated rate.

•**Insurability.** You must be in good health to obtain an attractive insurance policy. However, if you are not in good health but your spouse is, you may insure your spouse for investment gain.

•**Expert advice** in selecting insurance products that meet your financial and tax-planning needs.

Source: Alan Nadolna, president, Associates in Financial Planning, Suite 308A, 633 Skokie Blvd., Northbrook, IL 60062.

Retirement and State Tax Traps

Before selecting a place to live in retirement, check how local tax laws will affect you.

Key: Many different taxes can have a big impact on you and your lifestyle in retirement ...so don't look at just a few of the main taxes —such as income, inheritance or property taxes...

•**Income taxes.** What's the tax rate? Is there a tax exemption for pension income? Is Social Security taxed? Is there an increased exemption for senior citizens?

•**Inheritance taxes.** Sixteen states impose inheritance taxes owed by beneficiaries in addition to estate taxes owed to the IRS.

•**Investment income.** Is investment income taxed at a higher rate than regular income, as in New Hampshire, Massachusetts and Tennessee?

•**Local taxes.** Are there county or city taxes you may be overlooking, that could add substantially to the tax bill?

•**Pension taxes.** A dozen states tax pensions that were earned by working in the state, even if you move to another state. The state you move to will probably give you credit for the tax—but if you move to a low-tax state, the credit will not cover the full tax, so you may lose some of the tax benefit of the move.

•**Property taxes.** Does the state offer lower property tax rates to senior citizens? What tax exemptions are available? Is personal property —such as automobiles—taxed as well as real estate?

•**Sales taxes.** Many states with attractively low income tax rates make up for it with steep sales taxes. Examine how sales tax will affect you.

Source: Edward Mendlowitz, LLP, CPA and partner, Mendlowitz Weitsen, LLP 646 Highway 18, E. Brunswick, NJ 08816.

Uncle Sam Will Pay You To Job Hunt

Time to look for a better job? The government may let job hunters deduct expenses, even if the search is unsuccessful.

For those expenses to be deductible the job seeker must be looking for a job in the same trade or business in which he/she is currently active.

Example: If a bookkeeper and is looking for a job as a comptroller, her expenses are deductible. But if she were hunting for a job as a real estate broker or a magazine circulation manager, she would get no deduction.

If a person is unemployed temporarily, his occupation is considered the kind of work he did at his last job. His expenses are deductible if he is looking for the same kind of work.

Problem: No job-hunting expenses can be deducted for searches for one's first job or after a long period of unemployment. The IRS gives no guidance as to what a *long period* is. Check with a tax adviser.

Limits: Job-hunting expenses are claimed as miscellaneous itemized deductions on Schedule A of Form 1040. Miscellaneous deductions, including job-hunting costs, are deductible only to the extent that, in total, they exceed 2% of Adjusted Gross Income (AGI).

There is a further deduction limit for high-income taxpayers. If AGI exceeds $114,700 (or $57,350 if married filing separately) in 1995, itemized deductions must be reduced by 3% of AGI in excess of this threshold.

A person who is reimbursed for job-hunting expenses by his employer will need to file IRS Form 2106, *Employee Business Expenses*, to report the income and take the deductions.

The benefit of job-hunting deductions depends on what tax bracket a person is in. If he is out of work for most of the year and has little income, he won't get much of a tax benefit for job-hunting expenses. Documentation is critical especially for unsuccessful job hunts and out-of-town interviews. Keep records of everything spent and all correspondence, including proof of the job opening and the names of the interviewers.

These expenses are deductible even if a job seeker doesn't end up with a new job...

• **Cost of preparing résumés** and letters for prospective employers, including typing, printing, envelopes and postage.

• **Photographs to send with résumés.**

• **Fees to employment agencies**, résumé consultants, recruiters, and career consultants.

• **Newspaper and trade magazines** with employment ads.

• **Cost of advertising for employment.**

• **Cost of assembling portfolios.**

• **Transportation costs**, such as taxi fares to and from employment interviews.

• **Telephone calls.**

• **Cost of bringing a spouse to an interview**, if the prospective employer requests it.

• **Fifty percent of meals and entertainment** expenses related to a job search. *Example:* Breakfast or lunch with someone who can introduce a prospective employer.

• **Out-of-town travel expenses**, including transportation, lodging and 50% of meals and entertainment—provided job-hunting was the primary purpose of the trip. If the primary purpose of the trip was personal, a job seeker can still deduct job-hunting costs such as local transportation to call on prospective employers.

• **Fees for legal and accounting services** or tax advice relating to employment contracts.

Education: Advancing one's education to become a better job candidate is deductible when the course work maintains or improves skills required in the business or meets the minimum requirements of a new employer.

What's deductible: Tuition, books, laboratory fees, dues paid to professional societies, fees for journals.

Child care: If a job seeker hires a baby-sitter to enable him to go on job interviews or attend classes, he can take a child-care credit for the amounts paid for the service. The baby-sitting expenses are not, however, directly deductible as job-hunting expenses.

Source: Laurence I. Foster, partner, personal financial planning practice, KPMG Peat Marwick, LLP, 345 Park Ave., New York 10154.

Strategies for Writing Off Family Debt

Family loans can be written off if they are not repaid—even if they are not fully documented. The IRS had regarded the loans as gifts unless they were formalized and accompanied by standard loan paperwork. But the Tax Court now says all that is required is minimal evidence that loans have been made to family members in the past...and that some have been repaid. Canceled checks, deposit slips or bank records will be considered adequate evidence. Bad loans cannot be deducted until proven uncollectible. It is not necessary to start a lawsuit if you have reasonable grounds for believing the debtor doesn't have assets or the ability to repay your loan.

Source: Randy Bruce Blaustein, tax attorney with the accounting firm of Blaustein, Greenberg & Co., New York.

Residence Trusts

A qualified residence trust lets you move your home out of your estate, transferring its current worth at a discounted gift tax value to designated family members at some predetermined future date. Once the property is in the trust, its value is frozen for tax purposes. This allows the designated recipients—typically your children—to take over the real estate tax-free, despite years of appreciation.

Caution: Like other trusts, this one can be complex. See a tax adviser and an estate planner.

Source: David Gerson, tax partner, Ernst & Young, LLP, accountants, New York.

Protecting Financial Privacy

Accountants' documents are not protected from the IRS. Accountants do not usually have a counterpart to attorney-client privilege, which protects communications with lawyers. But accountants' documents are protected when the work is the result of being hired by an attorney to assist with legal advice. Under those circumstances, the attorney's privilege can apply.

Source: Pete Medina, tax consultant, Ernst & Young, LLP, New York.

How the IRS Finds Your Assets After You Die

When an estate, tax return is required to be filed for a taxpayer who is not survived by a spouse, it is likely that the IRS will be interested in examining that tax return. Each additional dollar that can be added to the taxable estate by the IRS means extra tax at relatively high estate-tax rates. Don't be surprised if the IRS agent insists on reviewing savings, and checking, account records dating back five or more years for the purpose of ascertaining whether annual gifts in excess of $10,000 were made and not properly reported. Searches of local property records are helpful to the IRS to determine if gifts were made of real estate and not properly reported.

New Traps in Dealing With the IRS

The IRS recently announced that it was going to eliminate the full-scale Taxpayer Compliance Measurement Program audits (TCMP), where information used as guidelines for ordinary audits is gathered.

Now the agency will probably elicit the same information piecemeal in its ongoing audit programs.

Result: Taxpayers should be more careful about how they conduct themselves during audits. Becoming familiar with the various types of IRS agents and learning how to deal with them is crucial.

Revenue agents:

To qualify as a revenue agent, IRS employees must have an undergraduate degree in accounting. They typically work in the field auditing corporations, other businesses and wealthy individuals.

Contrast: While correspondence audits (initiated by mail) are limited to the issues described in the letter, revenue agents are responsible for auditing a taxpayer's entire return.

Caution: Taxpayers can represent themselves before revenue agents if the issue is *factual,* but not when the issue is *technical.*

Example: Providing documentation related to your interest expense is factual. Calculating the interest deduction arising from residential mortgage interest as well as interest on taxable and nontaxable investments is technical.

New development: Most revenue agents use the Market Segment Specialization Program (MSSP) to guide their audits. The MSSP offers detailed guidelines for auditing various types of businesses, focusing mostly on discovering unreported income.

Example: The MSSP instructs agents auditing self-service laundries to check the business's water bill to determine the volume of business being done.

So far, 30 types of businesses have been completed and another 60 to 75 are in various stages of completion.

Important: Always understand what a revenue agent is requesting. This should be written down on Form IDR *(Information Document Request),* which outlines what the agent wants to see...and when. Too often, communication problems spring up between agents and taxpayers…and agents will never turn down any information that they are offered.

Strategy: Revenue agents work on many audits simultaneously and tend to manage them by moving from one to another. Monitor how current the agent is on your case. He/she could be tending to other higher priority audits. The result is that you are asked to extend the statute of limitations.

Doing so is never good. *Reasons:* Corroborating witnesses could disappear, records could get lost, and the interest you owe continues to build up until you pay the disputed tax.

At the end of the audit, you will receive a revenue agent's report that states the issues, the amount of the deduction or income in question, and the tax due.

Options: You can sign Form 870 and be billed for the taxes. If you want to appeal the agent's decision, you can take the case to the appellate division.

Source: Pete J. Medina, a principal and tax consultant on practice and procedure before the IRS, Ernst & Young, LLP, 787 Seventh Ave., New York 10019.

$63,000 IRS Mistake

The IRS sent a mistaken $63,000 refund to the Purcellas, then realized its mistake and put a lien on their property to get the money back. The Purcellas protested that the lien should be lifted because they'd done nothing wrong. *Court:* The lien is lifted and the Purcellas can keep the $63,000. *Why:* To recover a mistaken refund the IRS must either file an erroneous refund suit within two years or add the amount of the refund to an outstanding tax assessment. The IRS had done neither.

Source: *Debbie Purcella*, D. Colo., No. 89-K-847.

Summer Camp Has Tax Benefits

If you send your child to day camp during his/her summer vacation, camp costs can qual-

ify for the child-care credit. *More information:* Consult your tax adviser.

Source: James Glass, Esq., 402 W. 20 St., New York 10011.

Bad Debt Deducted

A father advanced $35,000 to his daughter to help her open a business. When the business failed and she couldn't repay the loan, the father claimed a bad debt deduction. The IRS noticed that the loan's terms had never been written out or documented. Therefore, it concluded that the money really was a gift, not a loan and, therefore, denied the deduction.

Tax Court: Deduction allowed. Both parties involved had intended the arrangement to be treated as a loan. The father had made several similar loans to other family members, all of which had been repaid on time. This clearly indicated that family members recognized their undocumented loans as being genuine.

Source: *Loy E. Bowman*, TC Memo 1995-259.

When Music Lessons Are Deductible

Clarinet and music lessons bought on a doctor's advice to correct teeth defects are deductible to the extent that the total exceeds 7.5% of your AGI.

Revenue Ruling 62-210.

Source: Robert S. Holzman, PhD, professor emeritus of taxation, New York University.

Disclaimer Beats Taxes

A father died and left his estate to his son. The son disclaimed all but $600,000 of the inheritance so the rest could pass to his stepmother tax-free under the unlimited estate tax marital deduction. But the IRS denied the marital deduction, taxed the full estate and imposed gift tax on the property passed back to the wife, saying she received it not from her husband but from the son.

Court: The disclaimer was "nothing more than a blatant attempt to avoid estate taxes." There was nothing illegal about it. After the son disclaimed, the property passed to the wife. The disclaimer worked.

Source: *Quinto Depaoli, Jr.*, CA-10, No. 94-9015.

When the IRS Becomes Aggressive

Revenue officers can become very aggressive if they think that a taxpayer does not have the ability to pay his/her tax liability in full in a reasonably short period of time. The revenue officer wants to be able to get his hands on the taxpayer's assets before the taxpayer spends the money or otherwise makes it difficult for the revenue officer to levy or seize.

Strategy: When the revenue officer gives you advance warning that he is likely to levy the money in your bank account, you do not have an obligation to leave the money in the account. You can withdraw the money before the levy is served on the bank and use the funds as you deem appropriate. That may or may not include using part of the money to pay down your IRS debt.

Source: Randy Bruce Blaustien, tax attorney with the accounting firm Blaustein, Greenberg & Co., New York.

When Do You Need Someone to Represent You Before the IRS?

If the items the IRS is questioning are of insignificant dollar amounts or are fully documented, there is little reason to engage the services of an experienced tax professional. However, if your tax return contains deductions for items such as casualty losses or a bad

debt for a loan you made to a relative or friend, it is probably advisable not to meet with the IRS yourself. A tax professional will know how to prepare you for the audit and present the documentation to support these deductions in the most favorable light possible.

Source: Randy Bruce Blaustien, tax attorney with the accounting firm Blaustein, Greenberg & Co., New York.

Tax Filing Must Be Done Through the Post Office

Tax filing must be done using the US Postal Service, not a private overnight delivery service. If you want proof of mailing, you should send the tax return by certified mail. You must have the post office clerk rubber-stamp the date mailed on the certified mail receipt. You do not need to request a return receipt signed by the recipient.

Source: Edward Mendlowitz, partner, Mendlowitz Weitsen, LLP, CPAs, East Brunswick, NJ.

Schedule C Tax Alert

Audits are cumbersome and time-consuming. But there are ways to minimize your chances of being audited. *Loopholes...*

•***Loophole:*** Report all your income on your return. If you leave some income out, and the income is reported to the IRS, you can be sure you will get a notice telling you what you left off the return and refiguring your tax.

If the amount omitted is large enough, or if the IRS finds out about an omission in a non-routine manner (such as auditing someone who paid you money), and indications are that you have not reported that income, your return could be referred to a revenue agent for a full-scale audit.

•***Loophole:*** Get extensions and file in October. Returns are normally due on April 15, but the due date is extended to October 15 if you get two extensions. Getting extensions and filing at the absolute last day (October 15) might reduce your chance of an audit.

Reason: The requisition of returns that are going to be audited is done in September or early October. Returns filed on October 15 might miss this selection process.

The IRS denies that this is the case, but my experience in practice shows that it is true.

Trap: If you file after the extended due date, that will definitely increase your chances of audit. Filing after the extended due date for a number of years in a row will greatly increase the odds you'll be audited.

•**Loophole:** Don't file an amended return. My experience is that filing an amended return on Form 1040X increases your chances of audit.

Avoidance strategy: Make sure you report all your income and take all your deductions the first time. If you do file an amended return, include copies of all substantiation for the item you're amending with Form 1040X. You may avoid a full-scale audit by giving the IRS the backup it needs for the amended item.

•**Loophole:** Be very careful in filing Schedule C. Schedule C, *Profit or Loss from Business*, is the most audited form you can file. But you can reduce your chances of being audited by following these simple rules…

Enter a principal business code (line B on Schedule C). Every type of business has a code number. You will find them listed on page C-6 of the instructions to Schedule C. If you don't enter a code number or enter an incorrect one, you will increase your chance of being audited. Using the code number, the IRS will do percentage analysis of the items on your return based on the averages of other taxpayers in the same business.

Example: The IRS will compare your gross profit percent—your percentage of gross profit to sales—with everybody else who has the same code number. If your percentage deviates too much from the average, the IRS will audit your return.

The IRS is changing its emphasis on auditing from a random basis to an industry basis. It is targeting industries for audits, different ones each year. It uses the code number to target the industries it is looking at this year.

Try not to show a gross loss on line seven—where your cost of goods sold is greater than your income. A gross loss will increase your chance of audit. *Reason:* When a person shows a gross loss the IRS makes a presumption that he does not have the required profit motive for being in business, and it will deny any losses.

Put the right numbers on the right line.

Example: Payroll taxes do not go on the line that says taxes and licenses but on the line that says other expenses.

•**Loophole:** Settle your divorce without going to court. The IRS reads court-ordered divorce decrees to see if there is income that should have been reported.

•**Loophole:** Hesitate before claiming a non-business bad debt deduction. This is a frequently audited deduction. If you have to claim one (a loan to a friend's business, for example) attach a copy of a properly drawn note that bears interest and states the due date. In addition, attach copies of any efforts you have made to collect the debt.

•**Loophole:** Answer all questions and include all necessary forms with your return. An omission of this kind can lead to an audit.

Example: If you don't answer the question at the bottom of Form 1040, Schedule B, regarding foreign bank accounts, you could be audited. And if you don't answer all the questions on Schedule C regarding your accounting and inventory methods you could be audited.

Dangerous oversight: Failing to file Form 6251 when you owe the Alternative Minimum Tax could lead to an audit…as could failure to file Form 5329, *Additional Taxes Adjustable to Qualified Retirement Plans (including IRAs), Annuities and Modified Endowment Contracts* when you've taken a pension-plan distribution before age-59½.

Source: Edward Mendlowitz, partner, Mendlowitz Weitsen, LLP, CPAs, 646 Highway 18, E. Brunswick, NJ 08816.

Tax Audit Alert

The risk of an IRS audit is going up in spite of IRS budget cutbacks. Over 4,000 revenue agents have been freed to do regular audits as a result of the cancellation of the IRS's *Taxpayer Compliance Program* of super audits. The IRS will be able to conduct many more audits probably including the returns that already were selected for the super audits. Regular audits also are targeted at returns with *questionable* items on them…super audits are randomly selected.

Source: Don Rocen, a partner, Coopers & Lybrand, LLP, 800 M St. NW, Washington, DC 20036.

IRS Seizure Tactic

Before the IRS can seize a person's house or business it must ask for permission to enter the premises. The revenue officer will ask the taxpayer to sign a consent form. If the taxpayer fails to give his/her consent, the IRS must seek a court order (which is generally granted). *Action:* Refuse to grant consent when the revenue officer asks for it. It takes a few weeks for the IRS to get a court order. In the meantime the taxpayer should consider filing for the protection afforded by the bankruptcy laws. Filing a bankruptcy petition stops the IRS in its tracks…the planned seizure cannot be carried out.

Tip-Off that Something Is Wrong With Your Tax Return

Revenue agents are trained to identify unusual items. For instance, the use of round numbers indicates that a taxpayer has estimated a particular deduction rather than relying on actual records. No deduction being claimed for home mortgage interest could pique an agent's interest as to how you were able to purchase a residence without taking a loan. Also, high real estate tax expense, but a modest amount of income reported on a tax return, is indicative that some income may not have been reported.

Source: Randy Bruce Blaustein, tax attorney with the accounting firm of Blaustein, Greenberg & Co., New York.

Stock Gains Can Trigger High Taxes

If your stocks or mutual funds have done well this year, but you believe a downturn is likely—so you take profits, then reinvest—you will owe tax on all gains from your sales.

And if you hold shares of a company that is being taken over for cash—as in the $81-a-share offer for CBS from Westinghouse—you must accept the buyout and pay tax on the gains. *Self-defense:* If 1996 gains will produce a large tax liability, increase withholding for the rest of the year to avoid a huge tax bill in April.

Source: Robert Willens, tax specialist, Lehman Brothers, New York.

Think Before You Sell

Think twice before selling highly appreciated securities if you're seriously ill or getting on in years.

Reason: You'll pay a capital gains tax unnecessarily.

Better: Let your heirs inherit the securities. That way you'll beat the capital gains tax.

Another way to avoid capital gains tax: Set up a charitable remainder trust. Give the securities to the trust. Let the trust sell them (with no capital gains tax). You'll get income for life from the trust without the capital being diminished by the taxes.

Bonus: An income tax charitable deduction.

Source: Laurence I. Foster, a tax partner in the personal financial planning practice of KPMG Peat Marwick LLP, 345 Park Ave., New York 10154.

When to Wait Before Calling the IRS

Taxpayers who owe the IRS money are generally well advised to keep in close touch with the IRS to prevent it from taking adverse collection action. This includes levying on bank accounts and salary. Before the IRS will agree to enter into a payment agreement it requires that a personal financial statement be submitted. If your financial statement reflects a savings account or other liquid investment, the IRS expects you to use this money to pay your tax liability before it will consider a payment plan for the unpaid portion of your debt. *Strategy:* Use the cash and other liquid assets to pay necessary living costs before calling the IRS to work out a payment plan. Life, auto and medical insurance premiums can be prepaid to use up cash or liquid assets.

Proving that You Are Not A Responsible Person

The term *responsible person* is used by the IRS to identify a taxpayer who is personally liable for unpaid payroll taxes incurred by a business. These unpaid payroll taxes are called trust fund taxes and they represent the employee's share of FICA and withholding tax. Generally, anyone who has the ability to direct how a company's money is to be spent is a *responsible person.* Even a nonowner could be held to be personally liable for unpaid trust fund taxes if he/she directs that other debts or expenses of a company are paid instead of paying the payroll taxes. To prove that you are not a responsible person…document that you did not sign checks. If you did sign checks, try to establish that more senior people in the company directed you as to the expenses which should be paid—and which should go unpaid.

Asking the IRS to Remove A Late Filing Penalty

The IRS will assess a late filing penalty of 5% per month (up to a maximum of 25%) of the unpaid tax if your income tax return is filed late and no extension has been granted. Many times the IRS will be willing to abate the pen-

alty if you can establish *reasonable cause* for the late filing. Being physically or emotionally incapacitated at the time your tax return was due is generally considered reasonable cause. *Another approach:* Take the position that your late filing was an isolated event in an otherwise perfect record of compliance—you always file on time. And…appeal to the IRS that the imposition of a late filing penalty will cause you to suffer an unnecessary financial hardship.

Unpaid Liability Problem

Many businesses do not remit payroll taxes when required—because the money is needed for working capital—and eventually find that the unpaid liability can never be paid. *Strategy:* Work out a solution to the problem before the IRS seizes the business. In cases such as this, the solution may be to file for bankruptcy protection, reorganize by selling assets to a new corporation (with the formal approval of the IRS), or discontinue the business because it is unprofitable and cannot be turned around.

Source: Randy Bruce Blaustein, tax attorney with the accounting firm of Blaustein, Greenberg & Co., New York.

When You Don't Report All Your Income…

When the IRS finds out that someone hasn't reported a significant amount of income…

Significant is a relative term but a good rule of thumb is an understatement exceeding 25% of the gross income reported on the tax return for a period of two or more years. It does a taxpayer no good to file an amended return to correct income after being targeted by the IRS as a tax cheat. In fact, the filing of an amended tax return, after being contacted by the IRS, can be used by the government in court as an admission of criminal intent. The person shouldn't make any statements to the IRS special agents investigating the case. Contact an experienced criminal tax attorney for guidance.

Source: Ms. X, a former IRS agent still well-connected.

Installment Sale Payment Taxation Rules

Installment sale payments are taxed under the rules in effect when they are received, not the rules at the close of the sale. When the favorable tax rate for capital gains was repealed by the 1986 Tax Reform Act, an investor lost the benefit of the lower capital gains tax rate on payments received after the Act's effective date.

Source: *Chapman L. Sanford*, CA-5, No. 93-5240.

Easily Overlooked Deductions

Use this list as a reminder of some of the deductions you can easily overlook when you prepare your tax return...

Medical:
- **Alcoholism** and drug abuse treatment.
- **Contact lenses.**
- **Contraceptives**, if you purchased them with a prescription.
- **Hearing devices.**
- **Hospital services fees** (laboratory work, therapy, nursing services, and surgery).
- **Impairment-related work expense**s for a disabled individual.
- **Lead paint removal.**
- **Medical transportation**, including the standard mileage deduction of nine cents per mile.
- **Orthopedic shoes.**
- **Seeing-eye dog.**
- **Special equipment for the disabled.**
- **Special diet foods** prescribed by a physician and taken in addition to your normal diet.
- **Special schools** for a handicapped child.
- **Tuition fees** charged by a school for medical care.

- **Wigs** essential to mental health.

Taxes:
- **Real estate taxes** associated with the purchase or sale of property.
- **Foreign taxes** (if not otherwise taken as a credit).
- **Self-employment tax.** If you work for yourself, you can deduct half of the self-employment tax you paid.
- **State personal-property taxes** on automobiles.

Charity:
- **Appreciation on property donated** to charity. Generally, when you give appreciated long-term capital gain property to charity, you get a deduction for the full fair market value of the property and avoid paying tax on the appreciation.
- **Contributions** to public parks.
- **Cost of a qualified nondependent student** who is living with you.
- **Out-of-pocket expenses** relating to charitable activities, including the standard mileage deduction of 12 cents per mile.

Investments:
- **Amortization of premiums** on taxable bonds.
- **Fees for a safe-deposit** box to hold investments such as stock certificates.
- **IRA trustee's administrative fees** billed separately.
- **Worthless stock** or securities.

Employment:
- **Dues to labor unions.**
- **Education** that either maintains or improves skills required in your present line of work.
- **Employment agency fees.**
- **Résumé preparation costs** associated with looking for a new job in your present occupation.
- **Trade or business tools** with a life of one year or less.
- **Uniforms and work clothes** not suitable as ordinary wear.

Business:
- **Business gifts** of $25 or less per recipient.
- **Business use of cellular telephones.**
- **Cleaning and laundering services** when traveling.

•**Depreciation on home computers** to the extent they are used for business or for investments.

•**Passport fee** for a business trip.

Miscellaneous:

•**Accounting fees** for tax-preparation services and IRS audits.

•**Appraisal fees** for charitable donations or casualty losses.

•**Breach-of-employment contract** damages you have paid.

•**Casualty losses.**

•**Employee contributions** to state disability funds.

•**Gambling losses** to the extent of gambling gains.

•**Penalties** on early withdrawal of savings.

Source: Nadine Gordon Lee, tax partner, Ernst & Young, LLP, 787 Seventh Ave., New York 10019.

Early Distributions

If you take money out of your IRA before the date you turn 59½ you might be subject to a 10% early withdrawal penalty.

Loophole: You can avoid the penalty either by taking the money out as an annuity in annual installments based on your life expectancy or by using the money for medical expenses.

Source: Edward Mendlowitz, partner, Mendlowitz Weitsen, LLP, CPAs, Two Pennsylvania Plaza, New York 10121.

Sure IRS Audit Red Flag

Cash accounting method is increasingly being attacked by the Internal Revenue Service. By law, it is available only to service businesses with gross receipts of less than $5 million. But the IRS often refuses requests from those that fit that definition to switch from accrual to cash accounting, and now is challenging, during audit, companies that have always used the cash method, claiming that it does not provide a "clear reflection of income."

Source: *Washington Perspective*, Coopers & Lybrand, LLP, National Tax Policy Group, 1800 M St. NW, Washington, DC 20036.

Tax-Preparer Loopholes

Just because you've hired a professional to prepare your tax return doesn't mean that you can sit back and relax. There are steps you can take to help your preparer do a better job… and that means more tax savings for you.

•**Ask the right questions.** The only way to know what to ask your tax preparer is to educate yourself about the tax law.

Purchase a tax-preparation guide, and familiarize yourself with the basic concepts. Review the tax forms so you'll have an idea of what your preparer will need to know about your tax situation.

Loophole: By being knowledgeable, you'll be able to ask intelligent questions. You won't waste valuable time and money questioning your accountant about basic or irrelevant matters.

•**Give your accountant/tax preparer the right information.**

Loophole: It could open up a whole string of related expense write-offs you may not have known existed.

Example: If you tell your accountant your child has a serious learning disability, you might open the door for deducting the cost of special education or training. If these expenses aren't deductible this year, your preparer can advise you about how to turn them into a deduction next year.

•**Organize your records.** Don't just walk into your accountant's office with a bag of receipts.

Loophole: Your accountant can spend only so much time with you during the busy tax-preparation season. If he/she gets stuck shuffling through a lot of messy paperwork, he will have less quality time to spend figuring out the best tax strategy for you. Organizing your papers will enable your accountant to consult with you on broader tax-planning issues…and make the meeting much more valuable.

•**Never make a decision about the deductibility** of an item without first discussing it with your preparer.

Loophole: A taxpayer may think an item is not deductible when it really is a legitimate deduction. Don't take the chance of missing out on a tax-saver. Your accountant will know the IRS's current treatment of all types of deductions.

•**Bring your expense diary.**

Loophole: Your accountant can give you the best advice as to whether your diary is up to IRS standards and able to withstand an audit. And if it's not in good enough shape for your 1996 return, he'll be able to show you how to make it foolproof for your 1997 return.

•**Bring all your canceled checks for the year.** Organize them by category to make them easier for your accountant to sift through. Group together all your rent checks, all credit card checks, all checks written out to cash, etc.

Loophole: Your accountant is certain to find some deductions you didn't know about.

Example: If your accountant sees a check for a deposit on a house, he will ask you a whole battery of questions that may lead to deductions. Although the deposit itself is not deductible, the cost of the move may be if you are relocating for business-related purposes. Or you may not have known that the "points" you paid to a bank to get the mortgage on the new house are deductible.

By seeing the deposit check on the house, your accountant will be clued in to ask the right questions about related deductible items.

•**Tell your accountant about any patterns of expenditure.** These include bills that you pay with certain regularity, such as monthly or quarterly.

Loophole: Part of those payments may turn out to be deductible.

Examples: The business phone calls appearing on your phone bill or the home-office portion of your utility bills.

•**Have your accountant give you a projection of your 1996 taxes.**

Loophole: You'll see early in the year where you stand. Ask your accountant what you can do now to help cut taxes for the present year.

•**Get some financial-planning advice.** Your accountant will have all your financial records in front of him. So get more out of your tax preparation by asking about investment alternatives.

Example: If you have $50,000 in a bank certificate of deposit, ask your accountant if he recommends leaving it there or doing something else with that money.

It's important to remember that not all advice that saves taxes makes good investment sense. When in doubt, get a second opinion.

Source: Edward Mendlowitz, partner, Mendlowitz Weitsen, CPAs, 646 Highway 18, E. Brunswick, NJ 08816

Independent Contractors

An issue of intense scrutiny for the IRS is the status of independent contractors employed by business. *Two IRS concerns:*

•**That companies are avoiding** employment taxes by categorizing employees as contractors.

•That 1099s are issued to all contractors so payments of income do not go unreported by recipients—especially when payments are made to the members of a family that controls a private business.

When the IRS finds that contract workers really are employees, heavy liabilities for back employment taxes may result. And there may be other costly complications as well…

•**The company's qualified benefit** and retirement plans may be threatened with *disqualification* because employees who should have been covered under them were excluded.

•**Liabilities may arise** under workers' compensation rules and other local labor laws.

Self-defense: If the company makes extensive use of independent contractors, be prepared to defend their status as contractors rather than employees.

Audit red flag: The company's payroll has decreased while 1099 amounts paid to contractors have increased—especially if workers who formerly were employees have switched to contractor status. Be able to demonstrate a real change in work duties that justifies the change in tax treatment.

Source: Marvin Michelman, director, IRS practice and procedure, Deloitte & Touche LLP, Two World Financial Center, New York 10281.

New Rights for Taxpayers

Parts of the proposed Taxpayer Bill of Rights 2 have been adopted by the IRS. *Here are the most useful...*

•**Taxpayer Assistance Orders/TAOs.** Emergency help in fending off an IRS collection action—or expediting an urgently needed refund—can be requested by Filing IRS Form 911, *Taxpayer Assistance Order*, with the IRS's Problems Resolution Office (PRO). But until now, relatively few TAO requests have been granted.

The new rules increase the authority of the PRO to grant TAOs, and reduce the levels of review they are subject to within the IRS—potentially making them easier to obtain.

•**Collection appeals.** As of April 1, 1996, taxpayers may appeal IRS collection actions such as liens, levies and property seizures.

Therefore, taxpayers now have two rounds of appeals—first, of the audit findings that result in a tax liability...second, of collection steps taken by the IRS to collect the tax liability.

•**Separated spouses.** The IRS will take steps to assure that when it moves to collect tax from one spouse who signed a joint tax return, the other spouse who shares joint liability for the return will be notified of the action when the spouses are separated or divorced and are living apart.

Source: Marvin Michelman, director, IRS practice and procedure, Deloitte & Touche LLP, Two World Financial Center, New York 10281.

IRS Loses Too...

These taxpayer victories over the IRS may help you save on your tax bill...

•**Raymond E. O'Bryant made a large tax payment to the IRS**—and the IRS sent back the entire amount to him in a mistaken refund. When the IRS later realized its error, it simply acted as if the original tax bill remained unpaid and put a lien on O'Bryant's property to collect it.

Court of Appeals: When O'Bryant paid his tax bill, it was extinguished...so the IRS could not continue collection actions on the tax debt. If the IRS wanted to get the refund back, it had to bring a separate legal action to do so. But it hadn't done that before the statute of limitations ran out—so O'Bryant could keep the refund.

Source: *Raymond E. O'Bryant*, CA-7, No. 94-2230.

•**The US Supreme Court** has ruled that a person who is compelled by practical necessity to pay someone else's tax bill can sue the IRS for a refund of the taxes later. This decision overrules the IRS's position that only the person who legally owes a tax can sue for its refund.

Facts: Lori Williams's divorce settlement gave her sole ownership of the family home—but before the divorce was final, the IRS put a lien on the home to collect taxes owed by her husband. Lori couldn't sell the home with the lien on it, so she paid her husband's tax bill. Then she sold the home and sued for the refund.

Supreme Court: Lori had no alternative but to pay the tax she didn't owe, so her refund suit is allowed.

Source: *US v. Williams*, US Supreme Court.

•**Before making a bid at an IRS auction**, you can obtain the IRS's appraisal of the property that is being auctioned.

Case: A potential bidder on jewelry at an IRS auction made a Freedom of Information Act request for appraisals of any jewelry the IRS had in its possession. The IRS answered that such appraisals were confidential.

Court of Appeals: When the IRS obtains an appraisal of a property after seizing it from a taxpayer, the appraisal has nothing to do with any tax dispute so no confidentiality applies. The information must be released.

Source: *Robert Kamman*, CA-9, No. 93-16600.

•**A couple fighting a tax dispute** filed a Freedom of Information Act request with the IRS demanding that it produce voluminous data on all similar tax cases dating back to 1978. The IRS refused, saying that the request was too broad and meeting it would be "prohibitively expensive." The couple then modified the request by asking the IRS to start with only the "most current" materials. The IRS still refused.

Court of Appeals: The IRS cannot refuse to comply with a Freedom of Information Act request simply because it is burdensome. Instead, the IRS must cooperate with the couple to draw up a manageable request that it can meet.

Source: *Michael Ruotolo,* CA-2, No. 94-6236.

•**Carol Davis defeated the IRS in court**, and the IRS was ordered to pay the legal fees she had incurred during the dispute. But the IRS appealed the fee award.

Decision: The award was upheld—and the IRS had to pay the legal fees Carol incurred during the appeal as well.

Source: *Carol Davis,* D. Colo., No. 93-C-1173.

•**The IRS added penalties to Robert Fisher's tax bill for taking improper deductions.** He claimed the penalties should be waived because he had taken the deductions on the advice of competent tax counsel. But both the IRS and Tax Court sustained the penalties without explanation.

Court of Appeals: The IRS "cannot make a taxpayer haul it into court to discover the rationale for its decision"—rather, it must explain itself. The Tax Court was at fault, too, because it couldn't have reviewed an explanation the IRS had never given.

Source: *Robert D. Fisher,* CA-10, No. 93-9029.

•**Before leaving on a trip**, a couple informed the IRS that they wouldn't be reachable and then hired a lawyer to deal with the IRS for them. But they failed to give the lawyer a power of attorney for tax matters.

The IRS then sent a tax deficiency notice to the couple's home. They didn't receive it until after the deadline for responding had passed, but the IRS said the notice was valid because the couple hadn't properly authorized the lawyer to represent them and had left no other forwarding address.

Court of Appeals: The IRS knew the couple had left home and had hired the lawyer. It should simply have asked the lawyer to get the power of attorney. The notice was invalid.

Source: *Anthony Teong-Chan Gaw,* DC Cir., No. 93-1619.

•**Sallyanne Cook had a graduate degree** and worked a full-time job. The IRS tried to hold her liable for taxes and penalties on a fraudulent joint return that her husband had prepared and she had signed—arguing she was too sophisticated in financial affairs to escape liability as an "innocent spouse."

Sallyanne's defense: Her husband had their return prepared by a CPA without consulting her and had handed it to her to sign on the morning of the day it was due as she was leaving the house for work. She had asked some questions about it in the few moments she had and had been assured that everything was proper before she signed it.

Tax Court: Sallyanne had met her obligation to make "reasonable inquiries" in the little time she had, so she was an innocent spouse and wasn't liable for the taxes.

Source: *Cecil H. Cook III,* TC Memo 1995-247.

Valuable Tax-Saving Compensation Ideas For 1997

This is the time of year to find the best tax-favored compensation strategies for 1996.

Aim: To provide executives with the most valuable benefit packages possible at the least after-tax cost. *Some of the best strategies to take now...*

Deferred compensation:

Voluntary programs under which executives defer receiving part of their pay until a later year can be used to reduce their personal tax bills...

•**By electing not to receive a portion of pay until a later year**, executives avoid current taxation of the deferred pay.

•**If deferred pay ultimately is received when recipients are in a lower tax bracket than they are now**—such as after retirement, or after a lowering of tax rates—they will owe less total tax.

•**Interest that is credited to deferrals compounds on a pre-tax basis**—providing employees with the same benefit of tax-deferral for investment returns that is provided in a qual-

123

ified plan. Savings grow faster than they would in a taxable account earning the same return.

Timing: An election to defer pay must be made before the pay is earned, and the IRS interprets this to mean before the year in which pay is earned. So companies with deferred compensation programs should have their executives making appropriate elections now.

SERPS:

• **Supplemental executive retirement plans** (SERPs) are increasingly being provided to highly paid executives whose qualified-plan benefits are restricted by recently enacted tax law changes. *Key:* Qualified-plan benefits cannot be based on more than $150,000 of compensation (down from $235,840 under old law).

But a SERP can be designed to provide highly paid employees with benefits based on compensation in excess of the $150,000 limit.

Advantages: Deferred compensation programs are not governed by qualified plan rules. Thus, they can be provided to selected employees, and arrangements with individual employees can be custom-designed to meet particular needs.

Deferred pay generally is not taxable to the employee until it is actually paid out—and at that time the company may deduct the payment.

Caution: The company's obligation to pay deferred compensation is merely contractual, so payments may be at risk if the company is unable or unwilling to pay them when they become due.

However, trust arrangements can be used to increase the security of deferred-pay programs:

• **A rabbi trust** can be currently funded with amounts needed to finance deferred compensation. Money in the rabbi trust can be used only to pay deferred compensation—and may be placed under the control of a third-party trustee—to assure that management won't spend it on something else, and that the money won't disappear during a corporate reorganization or hostile takeover.

But a rabbi trust does not offer 100% security. That's because trust assets remain the property of the company—so if the company becomes insolvent, they will be within the reach of creditors.

• **A secular trust** can be used to provide full security for deferred pay by placing the funds used to finance it beyond the reach of the company's management or creditors.

Catch: Because receipt of the future benefit becomes a certainty, the tax treatment changes. The executive is taxed immediately on the benefit, even though it won't be received until a later year. And trust earnings are currently taxed as well.

But when the benefit is paid out in the later year it is tax-free (since it has already been taxed).

Plus side: The company gets an immediate deduction for its contribution to a secular trust. This is a major economic benefit, since otherwise the company can't claim its deduction until years later when it actually pays the benefit. And this tax saving can be shared with executives in a way that helps them pay their SERP-related tax bills.

Example: A company plans to make a $10,000 payment to a SERP funded by a secular trust for an executive in the 40% tax bracket. It will pay $4,000 cash to the executive for him to use to pay his tax bill, and deposit $6,000 in the secular trust. The company can deduct the full $10,000 right away.

Key considerations:

• **Rabbi trusts are best** used with voluntary deferral programs since they preserve the desired tax deferral for employees.

• **Secular trusts are best** for SERPs that provide benefits on pay in excess of the $150,000 limit, because payment of the benefit is certain.

Other methods of securing benefits generally haven't been approved by the IRS.

Insurance:

• **Split-dollar insurance.** This is a flexible form of insurance the cost of which the company and executive share in a mutually advantageous manner—and which can be provided to employees on a selected basis.

How it works: The company acquires a cash-value insurance policy on an executive's life and pays most of the premium—with the executive paying a portion equal to the cost of a term insurance policy with the same benefit.

Or the company can pay the whole premium and include the "term equivalent" cost in the executive's taxable compensation.

Key: The company recovers its entire investment in the policy...

•**From policy proceeds** if the executive dies.

•**From the policy's cash value** if the policy later is distributed to the executive.

So if the company pays one $10,000 premium on a $1 million policy and the executive then dies, the company recovers its $10,000 and the employee's beneficiary collects $990,000.

Example: Say the company buys a $1 million policy on a 35-year-old executive, paying a $10,000 annual premium. After 10 years the arrangement is terminated—perhaps the executive is leaving the business. At that point the company has paid $100,000 into the policy which has a cash value of $140,000.

The company then gets back its $100,000, and the policy with its $40,000 cash value is transferred to the executive. *Advantages...*

•**The company has provided 10 years** of insurance benefits to the executive at no cost other than the time-value of money.

•**The executive emerges** with the $40,000 value of the policy, the policy remains in force with premiums and benefits based on his age and health 10 years earlier and commissions and expenses on the policy have already been paid. The executive would be unable to buy a new policy on such favorable terms.

Key: The accumulating cash value of a split-dollar policy grows on a tax-deferred basis, and can be used creatively to fund many other kinds of benefits, such as a SERP. If an employee stays with the company for the long term and the arrangement is kept in place, borrowing against cash value can be used to pay policy premiums—eliminating any future cost of the arrangement to the company.

Disability:

•**Disability insurance.** During their working years, employees are much more likely to become disabled than to die—yet people who have adequate life insurance often lack disability insurance.

Trap: Corporate group disability policies often do not provide sufficient benefits to meet the needs of top executives—so extra coverage may be a valuable benefit.

Tax angle: Alternative tax treatments exist for disability premiums and benefits.

•**Premiums can be paid for employees** as a tax-free benefit—but then any benefits received by an employee under the policy will be taxable income.

•**Premiums can be included** in employee income and taxed—after which any benefits received under the policy will be tax-free.

Planning: People naturally are reluctant to incur a tax bill they can avoid, but it can be advantageous to pay a tax on disability premiums in order to collect tax-free benefits later.

Reason: Most disability policies provide a benefit equal to about 70% of income. For individuals in a 30% tax bracket or higher (federal and local combined), a 70% disability benefit taken tax-free provides as much or more after-tax cash as 100% of regular salary when needed the most, during a family financial crisis.

Health:

•**Health insurance.** To control rising health care costs, most companies are increasing the share of costs paid by employees—through limitations on coverage and increases in co-payments and deductibles.

Opportunity: Generally, medical benefits must be provided to employees on a nondiscriminatory basis. But a quirk in the tax law lets special medical benefits be offered to selected employees, provided the benefits are funded through insurance, rather than direct payment.

Example: A company's major medical plan excludes benefits for psychiatric treatment. The company can provide coverage for such treatment to certain employees on a selective basis if it funds the coverage by buying an insurance policy covering psychiatric illness, instead of having the plan pay out such benefits directly.

Riders to the company's insurance coverage may provide other such valuable medical benefits to key employees, perhaps even covering copayments and deductibles. Consult with the firm's insurance adviser.

Source: Alan A. Nadel, partner, Arthur Andersen, LLP, 1345 Avenue of the Americas, New York 10105.

A Very Helpful Tax Quiz

Tax season is approaching, and what you don't know about taxes can cost you money—a lot of money…

1. Which is more valuable, a $500 tax deduction or a $500 tax credit?

2. Child-support payments are tax deductible. True or false?

3. What's the lowest federal income-tax bracket?

4. Profits from the sale of tax-free municipal bonds are free of all federal taxes. True or false?

5. Social Security benefits are not subject to income tax. True or false?

6. Married couples generally pay more in income taxes than the combined total they would pay if they were single. True or false?

7. How many hours does the IRS estimate it will take you to prepare your Form 1040, including record keeping? 6.4…9.5…11.5…or 15?

8. Death benefits paid from a life insurance policy are free of income tax. True or false?

9. The bigger your federal tax refund, the better. True or false?

10. All state tax refunds are taxable by the federal government. True or false?

Answers: 1. The tax credit, which reduces your taxes dollar for dollar. A tax deduction saves you only the percentage of your tax bracket. For example, if you're in the 28% tax bracket, a $500 tax deduction would save you $140 in taxes if you itemize your deductions. 2. False. Alimony payments are deductible, but not child support. 3. 15% 4. False. The interest earned is generally free of federal taxes, but any profit from the sale of a muni bond is taxable. 5. False. As much as 85% of benefits may be taxed if the recipient earns above a certain level of "provisional" income during the year ($44,000 for a married couple in 1995). 6. True. This is known as the "marriage penalty." 7. 11.5. If you also include Schedules A, B, D, E and SE, it should take 27.5 hours. 8. True. They are not necessarily free of estate tax, however. 9. False. The larger it is, the more money you've lent the government interest free. 10. False. If you didn't itemize on your 1994 tax return, any state refunds received in 1995 are not taxable. Part of the refund may not be taxable even for itemizers.

Source: Institute of Certified Financial Planners, a national association representing the top financial planners in the country. For a free list of CFPs in your area, call 800-282-7526.

How to Establish Legal Residency

To establish legal residency in the state of your choice—if you spend part of the year in different states: Open local bank accounts… join instate organizations…execute a will referring to your chosen domicile… spend more time in the chosen state than anywhere else… register investments at the chosen address… notify the Social Security administration of the chosen address…declare the chosen state as your legal residence on all forms requesting such information.

Source: Robert Coplan, tax partner and national director of estate business planning, Ernst & Young, LLP, 1225 Connecticut Ave. NW, Washington, DC 20006.

7

Smart Business Moves

The Limited Liability Company

The hot new form of business organization is the *limited liability company*—an entity that combines the best traits of a corporation and a partnership. It has been approved by the IRS—and almost all of the 50 states have now authorized its use.

Tens of thousands of companies have adopted limited liability status. Your company —regardless of size or current legal status—should be examining how to use it as well.

The essentials:

When organizing a business—be it an entirely new business, subsidiary or a joint venture—the key issues for the owners are management control, taxes and legal liability.

Traditionally, a partnership (or proprietorship) has been the best form of organization for attaining flexible management control and minimizing taxes. *Reasons:*

•**Partnerships have great leeway** in allocating responsibilities and corresponding gains and losses among partners.

•**A partnership's income is taxed** to its partners personally—so the extra layer of corporate taxation is avoided, and active partners can benefit from deducting business losses (such as from start-up expenses) on their personal returns.

Trap: Partners are *personally liable* for the obligations of the partnership. So if the business fails or is sued, their personal assets may be at risk.

In contrast, a corporation shields its owners from liability for the business's obligations. But it also is taxed as a separate taxable entity—and is therefore subject to a whole *extra level of taxation.*

Intermediate form:

For many years, businesses that desired to combine selected traits of the partnership and corporate forms of organization have used *S corporations* or *limited partnerships*. But each of these has *disadvantages...*

•**S corporations.** These generally provide "pass through" tax treatment much like a partnership, while providing their owners with corporate protection against personal liability.

However, S corporations are subject to many restrictions. *Key disadvantages...*

•**They can have no more than** 35 shareholders.

•**Corporations**, most kinds of trusts and foreigners cannot be shareholders of an S corporation—thus limiting its usefulness to a corporate group.

•**An S corporation** can have only one class of stock—so owners must share returns in proportion to their stock holdings. Gains and losses cannot be allocated flexibly as with a partnership.

•**Limited partnership.** This type of partnership has at least one general partner who exercises management control over the business, and may have many limited partners as passive investors.

The partnership avoids corporate taxes, may flexibly allocate gains and losses between the general partner and limited partners and provides its limited partners with corporate-like protection against liability.

But the general partner remains personally liable for the business's obligations.

New, improved options:

The new *limited liability* form of organization that is surging in popularity is an entity treated for most legal purposes as a corporation—but for tax purposes as a partnership.

Result: It provides the tax advantages of a partnership and legal protection of a corporation without the disadvantages of an S corporation and a limited partnership. Numerous benefits result in comparison to other forms of organization...

•**A limited liability company** (LLC) may have any number of owners instead of only 35 as with an S corporation. So LLC status can fit any size business—big or small.

•**An LLC may have any kind of shareholder**, so it can fit into a tiered parent-subsidiary arrangement as part of a corporate group.

•**An LLC provides "pass through"** of gains and losses and flexibility in assigning man-

agement control without a general partner remaining personally liable for its obligations.

•**The accumulated earnings** penalty tax that the IRS can apply to regular corporations with more than $250,000 in retained earnings does not apply to LLCs.

Personal tax break:

Another major advantage of the limited liability status is that it provides valuable tax advantages, including...

•**Breaks on distributions.** When a corporation or S corporation distributes an asset to a shareholder, the corporation is treated as if it has made a taxable sale of the asset at fair market value.

But when an LLC distributes property to an owner, no tax generally results.

But—as an LLC, no tax will be due. No gain will generally be recognized until the owner sells the real estate—and then it will be taxed to him.

•**Stepped-up basis.** An LLC can be a valuable estate planning tool for the owner of a private business.

When the owner of a property dies, the property passes to heirs with stepped-up basis—their basis in it becomes the property's current market value, so they can sell it for that amount without incurring gains tax.

Catch: If the property received is in the form of stock, stepped-up basis applies to the shares but not to the company's assets.

Opportunity: There may be no liquid market for a private company's stock—and if it sells assets to raise cash (such as to pay estate taxes), corporate gains will be taxed as a result of the sale. However, when the owner of an LLC dies, stepped-up basis applies to the *assets* of the business. Heirs can sell business assets *tax-free.*

•**Pass through losses.** Shareholders of S corporations can personally deduct business losses that amount to no more than their basis in the company's stock—the amount that was paid for it—plus loans made to the business and adjustments for pass through income from the S corporation.

But under more generous rules, an LLC owner can deduct losses that he/she is liable for even if no money was paid into the business.

Example: A business owner personally guarantees a loan for the business. The business then incurs large losses (but the guarantee is *not* called in). If the business is...

•**An S corporation**, the owner cannot use the guarantee to support his deduction of businesses losses, because he did not actually advance any cash to the business.

•**An LLC**, the owner can deduct the losses since he is liable on the guarantee.

•**Income shifting opportunities.** An LLC can serve as an efficient vehicle to transfer wealth for a family that owns a business. Interests in the business can be given to children and grandchildren, therefore...

•**Income earned on their shares** is generally taxed to them at their own tax rates.

•**Assets corresponding to their ownership shares** are removed from a parent's taxable estate.

Key: The parent who creates the LLC can retain management control over it even after giving away a majority of the ownership interests.

Planning strategies:

The advantages of limited liability status are so great that it should usually be the *first choice* of any new business. Use it unless there is some reason not to.

But...there are potential problems with LLC status...

•**State law restrictions.** State laws authorizing LLCs are new and vary in detail. This can be a problem for businesses operating in more than one state. So consult with an attorney on state laws before acting.

•**Higher tax rates.** Because top personal tax rates now are higher than top corporate rates (39.6% versus 35%), LLC status may add a few percentage points to the business's tax bracket.

But this short-term cost usually will be more than offset in comparison to the corporate level of tax and the taxes on distributions to shareholders.

Businesses now operating through regular or S corporations may find it costly to convert to LLC status, because they would first have to liquidate and pay a large resulting tax bill. But in the long run, the expense for many companies may prove worthwhile.

Existing corporations can:

•**Expand through new LLCs** run as subsidiaries or brother/sister entities, placing new lines of business in their LLCs.

•**Create a new LLC** and transfer selected assets or lines of business to it. *Caution:* Transferring too much may cause the original corporation to undergo a "deemed liquidation," so consult with an expert before acting.

Businesses now run through partnerships—such as law and accounting firms, medical practices and other professional firms—won't have to liquidate to elect limited liability status, so they often *can* convert directly into limited liability partnerships (LLPs) as the Big Six accounting firms have done.

Source: John N. Evans, tax partner in charge of the Enterprise Group, Arthur Andersen, LLP, 1345 Avenue of the Americas, New York 10105.

When Failure Breeds Success...

Don't let a failure end a manager's career. Some of today's top business leaders with big failures in their pasts include Jack Welch, CEO of General Electric, who managed a plastics plant that blew up...Ed Artzt, CEO of Procter and Gamble, who had a warehouse full of a new detergent crystallize just before he was to bring it to market...and Bernard Marcus, who founded Home Depot after being fired from a regional hardware chain.

Other famous failures: Sam Walton, whose first store failed...Henry Ford, who suffered an early bankruptcy...and Walt Disney, who was fired from an ad agency because he couldn't draw.

Source: John Kotter, PhD, Harvard Business School, quoted in *Fortune*, Rockefeller Center, New York 10020.

Growth Leaders

The following are industries that are expected to have the best growth potential over the next decade...along with their projected annual rates of gain...

Computers and office machines	9.0%
Communications equipment	7.1%
Electronic components	6.4%
Medical services	5.5%
Refrigeration, heating and service industry equipment	4.2%
Business services	4.1%
Special industry machinery	4.1%
Air transportation services	4.0%
Medical instruments & supplies	3.9%

Source: The WEFA Group, economics consultants, 401 City Ave., Suite 300, Bala Cynwyd, PA 19004.

Home Businesses That You Can Start For Under $1,000

Whether you're looking for additional income or have recently left your job, it may be time to start your own business.

Despite what many entrepreneur magazines say, you don't need a king's ransom to get started—only around $1,000 for many home businesses.

Bonus: If your home business earns money three years out of five, it will qualify as a business in the eyes of the IRS, and you can take all expenses connected with it as tax deductions.

If possible, keep your full-time job until you're sure that the income from the venture will at least equal your current income. Here are six businesses to consider...

Easy businesses:

•**Business-loan broker.** Every business must occasionally borrow money. Your job is to find lenders to provide them with that money. You then charge a fee of 5% or more of the amount loaned.

No specialized equipment is needed, but it's best if you have some business experience—preferably in finance or bookkeeping.

How it works: Seek sources of loan money through "capital available" ads in publications ranging from *The Wall Street Journal* to your local newspaper. Check out local banks and commercial finance companies. If they're not interested in your services, they may know of others that might be.

Important: Most of the loans being sought are as small as $10,000. That's too small for banks and other professional lenders to pursue, but they will welcome the business if it is brought to them.

Strategy: Find borrowers through small classified ads in the "business services" section of your local paper. Call borrowers and say, *I have money available...$10,000 and up.* Would-be borrowers will break down your door once word spreads.

•**Import-export agent.** US-made products are hot all around the world. But foreign buyers don't know how to reach US sellers...and US sellers don't know how to reach foreign buyers.

You act as facilitator—called an EMA (export management agent)—bringing buyer and seller together and taking a 10% commission on everything you sell. You don't actually buy or sell, so you don't need capital...or much business experience.

How it works: Get names and addresses of foreign companies seeking US products from US Department of Commerce publications, such as *Trade Opportunities,* and from state and local chambers of commerce and business-development groups. If you know a foreign language, concentrate on companies where that language is spoken.

Locate US companies selling what foreign buyers want by consulting the *Thomas Register of American Manufacturers,* found in most public libraries. Also check out trade publications and associations for the appropriate industry. *Example:* If you were exporting textiles, a good source would be *Textile World.*

Tell the US source you have an overseas buyer for a specific number of items at such-and-such a price...and negotiate from there.

•**Mail order.** You just need a telephone, typewriter, a fax machine or fax modem, and a product you believe in to start your own mail-order business.

Best: A product you can develop based on your own experience or passions. For example, something for bowlers if you bowl.

How it works: Find a manufacturer or distributor that makes what you want to sell. Find them by checking business directories…phone books…trade publications…industry associations. If possible, attend a trade show of the industry in which you're interested.

Arrange a drop-ship deal with the supplier. You take orders from customers. Then the supplier warehouses the items and ships to customers. You pay wholesale to the supplier and charge what the market will bear.

To get customers, place ads in publications serving your target audience—bowling publications to sell to bowlers…plumbing journals to reach plumbers. Later, you can expand by renting mailing lists from publications and organizations in your field.

Important: Pick products that appeal to a specific market. Products that are supposed to appeal to everyone seldom appeal to anyone.

•**Newsletter publishing.** Newsletters are publications that provide information about a particular area of interest. Find a subject that interests you, and write about what you know —a sport or hobby, unusual vacation spots or exotic foods. I know of one newsletter about shipwrecks and sunken treasure…another written for church secretaries.

How it works: Anyone reading a specialized magazine is a potential customer for a newsletter serving that field. Rent mailing lists of readers of publications serving your niche …for about $100 per 1,000 names. Refer to the Yellow Pages under *Mailing List Brokers* for companies that supply this service. Subscription prices on newsletters start at $12 a year and run into hundreds of dollars.

•**Wake-up/shopping services.** People will pay $25 to $50 a month to be awakened at the right time each morning or to be reminded of anniversaries, birthdays and other events. They'll pay even more if you can perform special services such as running errands or buying special gifts.

Find customers by placing a small classified ad in local publications…and with notices posted on local bulletin boards. No special skills or equipment are needed. You will be placing—not receiving—calls, so you don't even need an extra telephone.

•**Writing nonfiction articles.** Write about your own experiences—your job…your hobby …your vacation. If you knit or crochet, write about that. If you buy birdhouses, write about that. There are thousands of publications in the US. Most rely on outsiders to fill their pages.

To find your market, check out the periodical section at your library. Look through *Standard Rate & Data Service,* available in most libraries. It lists data on thousands of publications.

Study back issues of any chosen publication to determine the length of articles and writing styles. Construct your article to imitate the kinds of articles the publication has been running. Then contact the editor, executive editor or senior editor to briefly discuss your article. If you make your introduction brief, the editor will likely give it a look.

You can get by with just a typewriter…but you may find it easier writing—and rewriting —on a computer.

Payoff: Smaller publications may pay only $100 for an article. But the more articles you publish…the easier new articles will be to sell. Many magazines will pay $1,000 to $3,000 for articles.

Source: Tyler Hicks, publisher of the *International Wealth Success Newsletter,* 24 Canterbury Rd., Rockville Centre, NY 11570. He is author of *199 Great Home Businesses You Can Start (And Succeed In) for Under $1,000.* Prime Publishing.

How to Ace Any Job Interview

Whether you're looking for a better job or helping a friend find one, there's nothing more important than *being prepared* for the job interview.

Here are the most common questions interviewers ask candidates today—and answers that will improve your chances of landing the job...

Tell me about yourself and where you've been. This is almost always the first question you will be asked.

Believe it or not, it's a loaded question. While the interviewer is truly interested in hearing about your experiences, he/she is also listening to see how organized your thoughts are and how well you can get a large amount of information across quickly.

Don't start from the beginning of your career and give a blow-by-blow description. Candidates who do this are nervous because they are not prepared with a more condensed answer. They use the long-winded approach to relax.

Better: Before your interview, identify your top five accomplishments and summarize your work experience so that you can efficiently relate the information in less than one minute.

Important: You must demonstrate past productivity. If you suffered some setbacks along the way, leave them out—or mention them in a positive light by saying what you learned in the process.

Why do you want to work here? Even if you are not asked this question directly, you must somehow communicate to the interviewer that you would love to work for the company.

Solution: To leave the best impression, make two points—the company has a terrific reputation among your colleagues in the industry and you're passionate about its products or services.

Tell me how you handled a recent crisis. Most interviewers consider any situation in which you had to accomplish more with fewer resources—or overcome great odds—to be a crisis.

Strategy: A week before the interview, list several crises you handled well in your current job. Create three to five bulleted points outlining how you solved each problem. Be specific and give clear details.

Important: Be concise. Don't spend the entire interview relating one story, no matter how powerful the anecdote.

What are some of your biggest accomplishments? Use what I call the *60-second sell.* Quickly describe your top five selling points. Limit your accomplishments to experience during the past five years.

Examples: Accomplishments can include heading up a major project...saving your current company money...or situations in which you worked hard to pull off the unexpected.

Important: If possible, use accomplishments that showcase talents that will be an asset in your new job.

Why do you want to leave your current job? Interviewers want to see how you refer to your boss or company. *Acceptable responses...*

•**I'm interested in growing professionally and expanding my responsibilities**—both of which aren't being offered where I am now.

•**My company underwent a restructuring**, and my position was eliminated.

Important: Never say a bad word about your previous supervisor, regardless of what you think of him.

Source: Robin Ryan, president of Ryan Consulting & Training, a firm that specializes in helping people do well in job interviews, 11834 SE 78 St., Renton, WA 98056. She is author of *60 Seconds & You're Hired.* Impact Publications.

When to Say 'No' To a Job Offer

Say no when: Starting pay is low but you're promised a big raise "soon." Will the company put the date and amount of the raise in writing? Will it guarantee in writing a performance review in so many months? You have every reason to doubt the good intentions of a company that will do neither.

Say no when: You don't meet the person you'll be working for. The personnel department or a committee does the hiring, so you aren't able to measure your compatibility with the boss-to-be. If the company won't arrange a face-to-face meeting, it could mean the boss and your job are about to go out the window.

Say no when: The specifics of your job are not made clear. If all you get are vague answers when you ask about details, you may be headed toward a "broken job." The company may only want you for a short-term project or —even worse—to fill a head count.

Source: Nick Corcodilos, president, North Bridge Group, management consultants and executive recruiters, 73 Old Mountain Rd., Lebanon, NJ 08833. He is author of *The New Interview Instruction Book: A Guide to Winning Job Offers.* North Bridge Press.

Who's a Better Boss— A Man or a Woman?

Women often advance faster under male bosses than female bosses. Women can advance their careers by getting to work with a male boss who thinks that the woman's advancement will help his own career. Surprisingly, capable women who are on the rise are more likely to be "shot down" by female superiors who see them as threatening.

Source: Laurie Rudman, psychologist, University of Minnesota at Minneapolis, reporting research findings in *Executive Edge*, Box 37, Corte Madera, CA 94976.

What Good Managers Have

The best managers share one skill—knowing what their most important responsibilities are. Review the list of *your* business activities and decide which ones only you can be responsible for, and keep a sharp focus on them. Consider delegating other tasks, even if you think you can do them better than others. And avoid being distracted by "interesting" work problems that can devour time, but which are of only marginal importance.

Source: Ted Pollock, management columnist, *Production*, 6600 Clough Pike, Cincinnati 45224.

How to Be an Effective Boss in The New Workplace

In today's increasingly informal work environment, being a boss means working harder to form productive and appropriate relationships with employees.

Bosses must learn new ways of judging the proper degree of informality and intimacy in different workplace relationships.

How much distance?

In most companies—especially smaller ones —healthy boss/subordinate relationships are based on mutual respect, consideration and even warmth—expressed through informal conversation and an occasional touch on the arm or back.

However, the line between acceptable professional interaction and unacceptable intimacy is a fine one. It is most often crossed when a manager's misjudgment leads him/her to…

•**Exaggerated and/or wholesale expressions of affection and concern.** Others quickly read this as insincere or as a weakness —a person who has no skill at making close bonds outside the workplace.

•**Limiting expressions of praise or concern** or pats of encouragement to one or a few people in the group. This is quickly perceived as favoritism.

Problem: Once you are seen as unfair in your treatment of people who report to you, your ability to lead the group is undermined. The employees you supervise will not trust you to give them fair opportunities for growth. Some may resort to office politics and in-house rivalry.

Key: Focus on learning to move closer to and farther away from subordinates—as appropriate for getting the work done. A hands-on manager does not have to lose the authority he needs to keep the work focused on setting and meeting the right goals, meeting deadlines, making sure people get to work on time, complete their tasks and don't fight with one another or harass coworkers.

Challenge workplaces without walls:

Distance is forced on managers as more employees spend large portions of their workdays in the field or at home, communicating by phones and computers. Managers must vigorously hone their skills at maintaining authority and direction as subordinates gain more control of their jobs. In these circumstances, independence affords employees increased self-confidence and autonomy. But they also become more resistant to authority. The new styles of working make it more difficult for managers to assess performance, quality and professional growth.

A manager's most valuable tool is communication. To deal with the changing structure of the workplace, it is vital to press for more frequent and concise communication than was necessary when everyone saw each other every day.

Effective: Set up a communication web that helps all employees in the company or the department to share experiences, mistakes, accomplishments, etc.

Encourage them to communicate often—openly sharing their ideas, problems and solutions. Make the communication web useful—not merely a reporting device for management control. Play your role in the web as a trusted counselor and guide.

Source: Harry Levinson, PhD, The Levinson Institute, Inc., 404 Wyman St., Suite 400, Waltham, MA 02154.

How to Make It In the Singles Market

In today's dogfight for market share, many companies ignore a big opportunity—single adults. Not long ago, single people were thought of as either freewheeling swingers or impoverished seniors. Today, major segments of the single population are found in all age groups and include those who have never married…divorced individuals…and even singles living together.

And today's singles are not waiting until they get married to make important buying decisions. As singles, they're purchasing home appliances, furniture and nearly any other product or service that couples might purchase, including baby clothes.

But while singles and couples buy many of the same products and services, singles must be reached through a different mix of media and messages.

How to reach your singles market:

•**Broaden market research.** As a rule, singles have more leisure time and more disposable income than family people. Across the age groups, many are interested in romance, personal appearance, leisure activities, upscale clothing, sports, travel and entertainment.

Nonetheless, most companies miss opportunities to reach singles because they are ignored in research and test marketing. In fact, businesses will never know if their products or services are missing this market segment unless singles—as a demographic group—are specifically the target in the research.

Example: Conduct research focus groups for singles to get valuable insights on how they react to products and marketing messages.

•**Tailor the message.** As a group, singles respond to marketing messages that include them, and many are turned off by advertisements that show only traditional families.

Example: A picture of a product or service being enjoyed by a mother, father and children. Simply putting a few unattached adults in the ad can subtly broaden its appeal to include singles. McDonald's ads picture such a wide variety of diners at its fast-food restaurants that virtually no one would feel excluded. By contrast, a single person might hesitate to eat in a restaurant whose ads pictured only families or couples.

Similarly, don't alienate singles in special offers. Often, companies make these offers to consumers' family members, as some airlines have done with frequent fliers.

That type of offer can be profitable if it is advertised in family-oriented media. But if singles see it, they might feel so alienated that they switch brands. With some products, the number might not be great, but in today's fight for market share, no loss is acceptable.

Many marketers have included the singles segment by extending offers not just to family members but also to a friend or companion of the customer's choosing.

•**Consider new types of media.** To reach a high concentration of singles, consider magazines and radio and TV programs that deal with personal appearance, travel and other activities popular with singles. Then use market research to develop the message and to select the best geographical areas.

The majority of media, however, reaches both singles and married couples raising families. For that reason, examine carefully the demographic breakdown of readers, viewers or listeners. If there are a significant number of singles, there is no point in placing an ad that turns them off.

•**Develop new products or modify existing ones.** If market research shows that your product or service isn't reaching its potential in the singles market, consider changes.

Example: Many resorts have special offers for singles, especially at times of the year when families traditionally stay at home.

Caution: Since many singles are sensitive about their status, the market message for special products must be tuned just right.

Several years ago, Campbell's failed in an attempt to market smaller soup cans to singles. The image came across as too lonely.

To avoid such mistakes, test products and concepts thoroughly before putting them on the market.

Source: Judith Langer, Langer Associates, Inc., market research and market strategy consultants, 19 W. 44 St., New York 10036.

Nerd Power

Bill Gates of Microsoft typifies the newly powerful nerd—as do Hillary Clinton and Ross Perot. Businesspeople, by and large, do not understand how influential these smart, but socially "uncool" people, are—or how to appeal to them.

Nerds know more than the average consumer about products and services...and how they are delivered. And they are skilled at using "word-of-keyboard"—communicating rapidly via electronic media to large numbers of people when they find something wrong or right about a product or service.

To be prepared: Shed the notion that nerds never leave their computers. They do shop in person. But they communicate electronically.

Important: Make sure managers learn how to use the Internet and other systems to support more conventional company marketing. And view nerds within the company as a potential source of talented new managers. The myth that nerds are not capable of rising to the top is now shattered.

Source: Edith Weiner, president, Weiner, Edrich, Brown, Inc., trend analysts and consultants, 200 E. 33 St., New York 10016.

Reading Body Language

Watch the body language of a sales prospect.

•**A turned-away head** indicates an unspoken objection. Try to get the prospect to verbalize it.

•**A turned-away shoulder** may mean the customer is distancing himself. Ask a personal question to regain rapport.

•**Open hands with palms up** indicate the customer wants more information.

•**Handling an object** is a sign of thinking. Be quiet and let the customer continue this action.

•**A pointed finger** suggests the customer is saying something important. Listen carefully.

•**Folded arms** suggest "show me." Skip to a presentation of benefits.

•**Wandering eyes** can indicate you have lost the customer's attention. Change the subject to get eye contact back.

Source: Rhonda L. Wickham, editorial director, *Cellular Business*, 9800 Metcalf, Overland Park, KS 66212.

What Phone Companies *Really* Charge for a Call

How to make the calculation: Pick a frequently dialed long-distance phone or fax number. Before dialing it, dial the long-distance carrier access code for a particular phone company to route the call through that carrier.

Then *change* the access code in order to dial the same number through *different* carriers. At the end of the month, look at your phone bill to see your real cost-per-minute charged by each carrier.

Codes of leading carriers:

MCI	10-222
NYNEX	10-288
Sprint	10-777

Example: To call 1-212-555-1212 through NYNEX dial 10-288-1-212-555-1212. Since there are hundreds of smaller carriers nationwide, check your local carriers for their codes.

Every phone carrier has its own access code and it's perfectly legal to use them. You incur no penalty from your regular designated carrier when you make a call using the code of another carrier.

Access codes work from all phones and with credit cards. They also work on operator-assisted codes by dialing "0" after the code and before the regular phone number.

To find the code of a carrier that's not listed here, call the carrier's business office and ask for it.

To simplify dialing, program the code into the auto-dialer on a phone or fax machine.

Source: Richard E. Hetherington, consulting engineer, 3 Worrall Rd., Plymouth, MA 02360.

How to Cut Costs Without Cutting The Company's Throat

It is news to no one that effective cost cutting is as important to a company's long-term health as is increasing sales.

Challenge: Cutting costs without sacrificing quality, customer service or the ability to adapt quickly to change. This is not at all easy to do —but it is far from impossible.

Cutting costs while building value:

Never jeopardize quality, customer loyalty or brand value in any expense reduction program.

That means identifying the 20% of customers who are most likely contributing 80% of the company's profits—and making sure everyone in the company understands what is key to keeping those customers loyal.

Rule of thumb: A 1% to 2% increase in the number of customers who become repeat customers adds as much to the bottom line as an 8% to 10% reduction in costs.

Essential steps to take:

• **Structure information-gathering systems** that provide up-to-date data on the trends in customer satisfaction, perceptions of quality and value and propensity to purchase company products and services in the future.

• **Make employees aware** of the importance of this continuing flow of information. Encourage them to alert management when they feel strongly that a cost-cutting move will adversely affect one of these strengths.

• **Make sure that cost cutting proceeds** only after a "customer-impact" assessment has been made for each proposed cut. Then, as cuts are made, track changes in customer satisfaction and perceptions of value and loyalty— and use the information accordingly to adjust decision-making.

Valuable input:

For any cost-cutting program to work— especially when there is a high risk of eroding competitiveness—intensive employee input is essential. Line employees generally know where the first—and usually the easiest—10% of cuts can be made, and these employees are key to keeping the effort effective over time.

Getting employees' suggestions and cooperation requires…

• **Developing a first-class communications system**—both upward to management and downward to the front lines.

•**Willingness to put headquarters and management perks**, prerogatives and overhead under scrutiny—as well as line operations.

Further steps:

•**Eliminate services** that are no longer of any value to customers. *Clue to getting the most out of this exercise:* Start looking for waste at the top—not out in the field.

•**Drop entire businesses**, product lines and/or options which no longer fit the company's strategy for improving value and quality.

•**Improve the company's information resources**—even while reducing costs. Sophisticated information technology is now essential for companies of all kinds to keep on top of their markets...their competitors...their customers...their processes.

Equally important: Computers and software are increasingly essential for gathering and analyzing the information required to make prudent cost-cutting decisions for your company.

Source: Barry Sheehy, principal, The Atlanta Consulting Group, management consultants in business transformation and quality improvement, 1600 Parkwood Circle, Suite 200, Atlanta 30339. Sheehy is currently working on his latest book, *Be Quick or Die—Winners, Losers and the Race for Value in the New Economy.*

How to Cut the Company's Utility Bills

Most companies surely know by now that they can't count on their utility company representative to look for all of the ways money can be saved on utility expenses. Today, utility companies are more concerned with energy conservation measures than they are in finding the best billing structure for individual customers.

Traps: Many companies continue for years under their original billing formula, when they should have switched to another...smaller companies often pay a residential rate instead of the lower commercial or industrial rates for which they qualify.

Where to start:

Do research. If you can't get a copy of the official tariffs for the service options from your utility, try the state's department of public utilities, where they will be on file. Studying these may reveal a lower rate.

Important: Understand that utilities charge both on the basis of how much electricity the company uses during a month and the peak demand necessary for your particular operation over the course of a year or an 18-month period.

Example: If your company has a plant superintendent who comes in at 6 am and turns on the lights, the heat and all of the machinery, there will be a spike in voltage during that period which doesn't represent the company's true usage. But it will be recorded by the utility, and it goes into the equation used to come up with a total usage rate.

Solution: Arrange for a staggered start-up that avoids such unrealistic peaks. Many companies also avoid peaks by running an extra shift to stretch out the use of equipment so that it isn't too intensive at one time.

Possible power problems:

Review fluctuations in utility bills and search carefully for causes as to why one month is so much higher than previous months or the same month a year ago.

There are, of course, seasonal variations and if the weather is unusually hot or cold, it can drive up utility costs. But just as the company wouldn't tolerate fluctuations of 40% to 60% in its raw materials or office supply costs, it should question major swings in utilities bills.

There are specific steps the company can take to reduce utility costs...

•**Check meters.** Be sure that meters are recording only your company's usage. This can be a big problem in multiple unit buildings.

Example: We once helped a client discover that his company had been paying for the operation of another tenant's printing press. *How we found out:* We turned off the circuit breaker and waited to see who complained about the loss of power.

•**Combine bills to control costs.** If your company has expanded into new space which is covered by several meters, it may be getting a half dozen bills every month. Ideally, electricity should be billed in a single invoice for the entire company—at a lower rate.

Solution: Hook up all the meters so that they feed into one from which the monthly bill is then calculated. Unlike water and sewer charges where there's a financial incentive to use less, in most utility districts, the best rates go to the biggest users.

•**Run an audit of utility expenses.** Even if utilities are included in the company's rent, this is worthwhile every few years to make sure the landlord isn't overpaying—which is, of course, reflected in rent increases.

Audits are generally paid for on a contingency basis, with the independent auditors receiving a percentage of the annual savings of the company's or the landlord's utility charges. To find an auditor, contact the local economic development agency...chamber of commerce ...trade association...or local businesses that have experience with utility audits.

Source: Tom Bray, president, PROAudit, a consulting firm that provides utility bill auditing services for companies, Box 514, Lincoln, MA 01773.

How to Sell When You're Out of Stock

If the company is out of stock on an item, always tell customers who call in to order the exact day on which you can ship to them.

Never overpromise. If you are not absolutely certain when you can ship, tell the customer you will call back with the exact information—and do it, prepared to write an order.

And—of course never ask customers to call back in a few days to see if the items are available. That's a sure invitation to have them shop the competition.

Source: Linda Fracassi, president, Learning Essentials, Inc., telephone sales training and consulting firm, Box 5141, Toms River, NJ 08754.

There Are Ways to Cut Legal Costs— They're Not Difficult

In today's complicated business climate, there will always be areas beyond the control of most companies. But, contrary to popular opinion, there are measures that can be taken to control one essential and expensive expenditure—legal fees.

The first step is to recognize that litigation cost-management requires active involvement. Never entrust control to legal experts without going over the case...getting a handle on costs, fees and possible settlement value...and options as to what legal work needs to be done immediately and what can wait.

While very few law firms would deliberately overbill a client, their services must be closely monitored by a responsible in-house manager to ensure that all of the hours billed are for cost-effective work on the company's case.

How to do it: Exercise the company's right to be furnished with a legal work "menu" showing the fees on the right-hand side. Also request a list of future legal work—with hours and cost estimates—for approval before work is performed.

Example: When you find out that six hours of work on a follow-up motion that your attorney admits is more tactical than vital will cost $1,200 plus up to $900 for a court appearance, you may decide not to finance such war games between attorneys.

Basic damage-prevention options:

In addition to the all-important cost-reporting system, there are several vital steps clients should take to protect themselves from legal overbilling...

•**Request preliminary estimates.** Your lawyer should supply cost estimates for basic discovery, filing fees, motions and depositions.

Based on your version of the facts, he/she should be able to provide a good indication of how strong the company's case is and whether it is worthwhile pursuing.

•**Set the ground rules.** Make it clear that no work will proceed unless it is submitted in writing, together with an itemization of hours needed and estimated costs. Any work done without approval will not be paid for, and only cost-effective moves will be authorized—such as using court form interrogatories before taking detailed depositions or preparing special interrogatories.

• **Know who your lawyer is.** This may sound obvious, but it's not uncommon to have many associates in a law firm billing on your company's case. You have a right to know who will be working for you and what their fee schedule is. Also, find out what your option would be if the partner in charge of your account should decide to leave the firm.

• **Aggressively negotiate fees.** Law firms operate under different fee structures. There are flat fees, contingency fee arrangements, annual retainer agreements and combination fees. If you don't ask, you will never know what your choices are. It's not unusual for companies to save up to or more than 25% on legal fees by negotiating charges up front.

• **Keep track of the overall budget.** With each billing, your company has a right to request a statement of total fees and costs-to-date, including whether the case is running over, under or within budget projections. In a major litigation case, get budget projections at least once every two months so that you will be on top of the company's exposure to liability, costs, fees and damages.

• **Dictate the billing periods.** Many companies favor longer billing periods, such as every six months or when expenses reach $25,000.

However, monthly billing generally gives the client much tighter control on costs than less frequent billing. Request a complete breakdown of hours, hourly rate and the initials of each individual performing the work.

Ask for explanations of questionable items, such as when billing costs always come out to even hours. Also question why a paralegal might take 2.5 hours to digest a three-hour deposition.

Important: Request that some person at the law firm review and approve your company's bills before forwarding them for payment. While partners are usually immune from such review, just the knowledge that time sheets and disbursements are being monitored helps eliminate unreasonable costs.

• **Keep track of the paper trail.** Many clients don't want to be bothered with too much paper. But that paper keeps you on top of work being done on your case.

You have a right to request copies of all correspondence, motions, responses to motions, etc. This should not increase your fee costs.

Make sure that any interrogatories that you will have to answer are sent to you by the law firm immediately. This will avoid last-minute overtime charges and courier service charges.

• **Avoid attorney warfare.** Exercise the option to request that frivolous objections—often designed for nothing more than venting the spleens of young lawyers jockeying for position—be stopped. Such tactics are expensive and usually don't make or break the lawsuit. Also—watch out for hotshot lawyers who only know how to play hardball. In my experience, the top 10% of lawyers got there because they practice the art of civility, diplomacy and courtesy.

• **Consider alternate dispute resolution.** Litigation in a court case can cost $1,500 to $5,000 per day—often totaling into six figures depending on the length of a trial. Arbitration can frequently be completed in a half day and mediation in a few hours. The advantage of mediation is that you have the choice of a retired judge or a specially trained and certified attorney. Get names from the American Arbitration Association (212-484-4000)...or the American Academy of Attorney Mediators (214-361-5121).

• **Forge a cooperative relationship with attorneys.** Litigation cost-management is only effective when you work with lawyers—not against them. Question, but don't second-guess. In the last analysis, you should follow the attorney's advice. While you are paying the bills, you don't want to jeopardize the success of your case by cutting costs too deeply.

Source: Marshall T. Hunt, senior partner, Cummins & White, one of the leading insurance and litigation law firms in Southern California, 2424 SE Bristol St., Newport Beach, CA 92660.

Smarter Pricing Strategy

Many businesses don't price to reflect a product's superiority, believing customers won't pay more than competitors charge. Why not? Because customers don't see the superior value until after they have bought the product.

Better idea: Use advertising and sales techniques to quantify the value of benefits—thus justifying higher prices.

Examples: Our brand will save your business $10,000 a year in maintenance costs. Or in a consumer market, an advertisement can say that the additional price amounts to less than the cost of a cup of coffee.

Companies can also frame the buying decision in such a way that customers feel obligated to make the purchase. *Examples:*

•**International Paper's** ads show how a $5,000 copying machine can be jammed by a cheaper paper product.

•**Michelin Tire's ads say**, in effect, "Other tires are for people who care about traction but ours are for people who care about their families."

Source: Thomas T. Nagle, PhD, a managing director of Strategic Pricing Group, Inc., price and competitive strategy consultants, 10 Speen St., Framingham, MA 01701. He is coauthor with Reed K. Holden of *The Strategy and Tactics of Pricing.* Prentice-Hall, Inc.

Smarter Bill Paying

Pay toward the end of whatever time period you choose for handling payables. *Example:* Suppose you regularly hold invoices until more than 30 days have passed. Many creditors divide incoming payments into "current," "30-to-60 days" and "more than 60 days." If payment in more than 30 days causes you no problems, then you might as well wait until approximately 55 days to pay—your payments will stay in the same category where creditors are concerned, and you will gain several extra weeks to pay.

Source: Robert Jaffe, contributing editor, *Horizons,* 1185 Avenue of the Americas, New York 10036.

How to Set up Better Retirement Plans For Company Executives

To attract and retain great managers, companies of all sizes should consider an innovative improvement of their 401(k) plans.

Traditional plans allow employees to shelter income from taxes until they retire—when their tax bracket will presumably be lower. And...companies often match employee contributions dollar for dollar and can deduct total contributions from their own taxes.

Basic 401(k) disadvantages:

•**A maximum of $150,000** of an executive's annual income can be counted toward his 401(k) contribution. If a manager makes $325,000 and the plan allows a contribution of up to 6%, the manager can contribute only $9,000. That is below the $9,240 limit that the IRS allows employees to contribute each year on a pre-tax basis.

•**Highly compensated employees**—those now making around $66,000 a year or more—can shelter only 2% more than the total amount that lower-paid employees contribute.

Example: If the lower-paid employees as a group contribute 2% to a 401(k) plan—people earning $66,000 a year and up can shelter only 4%. That means that the same manager who could have contributed $9,000 can now shelter only $6,000.

•**Plans can easily become very costly.** *Reason:* Companies whose 401(k)s include all compensation, including bonuses and overtime, can incur higher costs than anticipated, because contributions must be calculated for higher-paid as well as lower-paid employees. This is especially true for a company that offers big incentive pay to its sales force and also high overtime pay to its hourly workers.

Better ways:

By setting up what's known as a 401(k) Mirror Plan, companies can let managers and highly paid employees shelter more income.

The IRS has no rule on the minimum salary needed to qualify for such plans, but to protect themselves against an IRS challenge, companies should usually set the minimum pay somewhere above $66,000. And as a rule, plan participants should not exceed 20% of the workforce.

Mirror Plans allow them to contribute up to 100% of their compensation—whether salary or incentive pay. Many companies, however, let highly compensated employees contribute up to 25% of their pay and match the first 10% with an equal company contribution.

That means that the same $325,000-a-year executive who could contribute only $9,000 to his traditional 401(k) can now also shelter up to $81,250 in a Mirror Plan.

Comparing the plans:

The IRS considers a 401(k) to be a "qualified plan." The term means that the plan meets IRS standards and therefore contributions are generally tax-sheltered as long as the plan is properly administered. To maintain this tax benefit, however, 401(k)s must be nondiscriminatory against lower-paid workers.

Mirror Plans are one way to enhance executive benefits. *Others include:*

• **Supplemental executive retirement plans**, for which the company pays the entire cost of additional retirement benefits.

• **A large variety of stock options** which the company can give to its executives.

• **Phantom stock plans**, which link retirement income to the company's worth at the time an executive leaves the company, although no actual stock is issued.

Mirror plans differ from all these because they require employee contributions. In most cases, that makes them less expensive for the company.

Since Mirror Plans are designed for highly paid employees, they aren't "qualified" in this sense of the word.

That doesn't mean, however, that they are more likely to be challenged. In fact, Mirror Plans have enough history for financial experts to know how to design them so that they are as challenge-proof as traditional plans.

For that reason, companies that want to set up a Mirror Plan should choose benefits and legal consultants with a solid track record in these plans.

Note: Traditional plans may permit early withdrawals for loans and for hardships. Mirror Plans allow withdrawals under all of the same conditions but don't permit loans.

Potential disadvantages of mirror plans:

• **Unlike traditional plans**, contributions made by employees and the employer aren't deductible for the company until the benefits are actually paid.

Example: In a traditional plan, if an employee contributes $1,000 and the employer matches it, the contribution is tax-deferred for the worker, and the total of $2,000 is immediately deductible for the company.

In a Mirror Plan, the $2,000 can't be deducted until the contributions are dispersed at retirement—or for one of the other special reasons. At that time, however, the entire amount is deductible—plus whatever it has earned in the meantime.

• **Contributions to Mirror Plans** are subject to claims of the company's creditors. *Impact:* If the company owes money, creditors can go after Mirror Plan contributions.

Companies can protect contributors to a large extent by putting the contributions into what is known as a rabbi trust. This shields their contributions from virtually every attack unless the company goes bankrupt.

The name was coined several years ago when a congregation set up the first trust to protect its rabbi's benefits plan.

Source: Kelly O. Finnell, president, Executive Financial Services, Inc., retirement planning and administration specialists, and member of M Financial Group, 530 Oak Court Dr., Memphis 38117.

Travel Costs Will Rise

Business travel costs are expected to rise much faster than the overall rate of inflation. This year, travel costs are projected to rise an average of 5.2%. That compares with a projected rise of only 2% last year. Overall inflation is running at around 3%. The biggest increase is expected in hotel rates—7%. Air travel and car rental rates will be up 5%, while business meal costs will be up more moderately—by 3%.

Bonus to New Owner Is Deductible

A small business was bought out by a long-time employee, who promptly paid himself a $400,000 bonus for "past services." The IRS disallowed the company's deduction for the payment, saying the new owner was simply taking cash out of the business. It noted that the corporate minutes did not authorize the payment. *Tax Court:* The new owner had worked 12-hour days and six-day weeks for modest pay during many years as an employee, so the compensation for past services was justified. Also, small-business owners routinely ignore paperwork, so the lack of authorization was not important. Deduction allowed.

Source: *Acme Construction Co.,* TC Memo 1995-6.

Telemarketer's Obligation

Telemarketers are now legally obligated to remove from prospect lists—and never to call again—any person who tells a solicitor that he/she does not want a repeat sales call by that company.

Source: Federal Trade Commission rule, 12/31/95.

Create Your Company's Own World Wide Web Site

Companies large and small are creating sites on the World Wide Web to display products and services, streamline interaction with customers and transact business.

Giants such as Ford Motor Co. and Time-Warner have spent hundreds of thousands of dollars to create lavish Web sites with sophisticated graphics.

But creating a Web site isn't rocket science. You could create a respectable site at your kitchen table for literally nothing by designing it yourself and keeping it simple. Or a computer professional could design a no-frills site for $500.

The cost of maintaining a Web site runs as low as $40 a month.

Bottom line: The World Wide Web is still in its early stages as a business tool. There are no reliable statistics on Web usage and thus there is no way to determine which businesses—if any—are making money on the Web.

But it is no secret that the Internet in general—and the World Wide Web in particular—holds enormous potential for commercial applications. Business owners and managers should have a grasp of the costs, opportunities and pitfalls of doing business on the Web. Waiting too long to explore the Web could give rivals a competitive edge.

Where to start:

First decide exactly what you want a company Web site to accomplish. That will determine complexity, cost and skill needed to design the site, as well as the possible payoff, if any, from a Web site. *Breakdown of potential uses of a business Web site:*

• **Enhanced visibility.** If the company simply wants to display products or services, it can use a site to show graphic descriptions as well as textual details of the product or service. It can also add an address or 800 number so users can get more information. This is the easiest, cheapest site to create.

Problem: Prospective customers will skip past your site if all you offer is a few lines of promotional copy and an 800 number.

Important: Even a simple product-display Web site must be well-designed to get a user's attention.

Example: Ragu Spaghetti Sauce uses warmth and humor to promote its products (http://www.eat.com).

• **Customer service.** If the company wants to reach customers easily, on-line interactivity is a great way to do it. *Examples:*

• **Dell Computer's Web site** provides lots of production information, as well as an E-mail access to customer service (http://www.dell.com).

•**Federal Express** lets customers trace a package through its Web site (http://www.fedex.com).

•**Marketing.** For companies seeking to sell products or services over the Internet, interactivity is necessary—so that customers can use their computers to place orders. Some companies are doing this in a user-friendly way, with just as much security as is available to customers who place conventional phone orders.

Example I: L.L. Bean sells through its catalog on-line. You then can order merchandise or a catalog by direct entry on the computer screen or by calling an 800 number (http://www.llbean.com).

Example II: Virtual Vineyards sells wine through their Web site and uses direct entry to collect names for their mailing list by having users enter their name and address on the screen (http://www.virtualvin.com).

Example III: "software.net" appropriately uses its Web site to sell computer software (http://www.software.net).

Beyond the basics:

Once the company decides what it wants to accomplish on its Web site, it must design several additional components of the site. *Here are the guidelines:*

•**The Web site must be simple** and quick to access, so users don't run up high connect charges waiting for your material to appear on the screen.

•**The site must be kept fresh** with frequent updates. Users won't return to your Web address if it is left unchanged for months.

Helpful: Strictly speaking, you don't have a Web address. You have a URL, which stands for *uniform resource locator.* That's the string of characters that begins with http://www.

Where to start:

A good first step is to sign up with a commercial on-line service such as America Online (800-827-6364), CompuServe (800-487-0453) or Prodigy (800-776-3449).

All of these services offer free sign-up and low trial rates. All three offer easy-to-use Internet access. All let you get your feet wet by creating your own Web site in a user-friendly set-up procedure using on-screen prompts—and requires minimal technical knowledge. While this service is intended primarily for personal Web sites, very small businesses, especially home-based ones, are making use of it with positive results.

For larger companies, which can generate higher volumes of electronic traffic on their Web site, it is advisable to have an expert do it for you.

Where to search: The company's ad agency may have someone on staff who can help. Business contacts may have referrals. Computer magazines feature ads for Web-site creators.

Helpful: Go on-line and study sites similar to what you are looking for and then contact the company whose site it is. Ask who created the site.

Many Web-site providers have sprung up to help businesses get on the Internet. Such providers can take you from basic design to actually getting your site on the Web.

While few have meaningful track records in this very formative business, some have been involved from the beginning and do have a long list of business clients that will vouch for the high quality of their service. These Web-site providers include....

•**Tenagra Corporation** (http://www.tenagra.com).

•**TriNet** (http://www.trinet.com).

•**BBN Planet** (http://www.bbnplanet.com).

•**Open Market** (http://www.openmarket.com).

Strategy: Choose a Web-site provider the same way you would the supplier of any business service. Ask for samples of the provider's work. Ask for references and check them out. If possible, check with customers who weren't offered as references to see how satisfied they were.

Key considerations: Decide exactly what the provider will actually do...whether he/she will only design a site or go a step further and help you get the site on-line. Having one provider do it all will keep details from falling through the cracks.

The cost factor:

Expect to pay $500-plus to create a professional, but bare-bones, site. Fifty dollars a month and up will keep it running.

A well-designed site with a few bells and whistles will cost about $2,000. Such features as interactivity might raise the cost up to $20,000 and the monthly cost to about $400.

Payoff: You can make money from a Web site if you use it for direct selling, because sales generated can be tracked easily.

Or, the site might not bring in revenue for the company, but could help the bottom line by reducing spending.

Example: FedEx saves money each time a customer uses its Web site instead of calling its 800 number.

Reality check: Even for successful on-line sellers, big profits from a Web site are probably several years in the future. Most sites probably won't ever earn money, but will be seen as an adjunct to advertising, public relations and customer relations spending.

Becoming visible:

You could create the best Web site in the world, but if no one sees it, all the money you spent is wasted.

Solution: Explore the various on-line catalogs and search engines that will guide viewers to your site. Users connect to such a service and are directed to hundreds or even thousands of different Web sites.

Opportunity: You don't pay to sign up with these services. You can list with as many as you want.

Best bet: Go on-line and actually explore catalogs and search engines. Many can be accessed directly from America Online and other commercial services. *Some of the biggest services, along with their Web addresses:*

- **AltaVista** (http://www.altavista.digital.com).
- **Excite** (http://www.excite.com).
- **Galaxy** (http://www/tradewave. com).
- **InfoSeek** (http://www.infoseek. com).
- **Inktomi** (http://inktomi.berkeley.edu).
- **Lycos** (http://www.lycos.com).
- **Magellan** (http://www.mckinley.com).
- **Open Text** (http://www.opentext.com).
- **WebCrawler** (http://www.webcrawler.com).
- **Yahoo** (http://www.yahoo.com).

Source: Jill H. Ellsworth, PhD, senior partner at Oak Ridge Research, Internet marketing consultants, 101 High Rd., San Marcos, TX 78666. *E-mail:* je@world.std.com. She is also coauthor with Matthew V. Ellsworth of *Marketing on the Internet.* John Wiley & Sons.

Weekend Entrepreneuring

End of the month and short of cash? Again? The easiest way to come up with an additional source of income is by becoming a weekend entrepreneur.

You're in control:

The advantage of being a weekend entrepreneur—rather than committing to a second job or putting in extra hours at your regular job —is that you control your time. You can work a little or a lot.

Most part-time, weekend jobs require very little initial investment, experience or overhead. All they take is a good idea, dedication and courage.

To generate extra income, you must be able to spot a trend and recognize what needs are unfulfilled. *Key:* Find services or goods that you can provide that will make other people's lives easier.

Example: Two brothers in Oregon set up the adult equivalent of a weekend lemonade stand in the parking lot of a supermarket. Instead of lemonade, the brothers served fashionable gourmet coffee to weekend shoppers.

Think it through:

Four questions to help you get your idea organized and launched...

- **How much time** can you devote to a source of additional money (SAM)? A SAM is not supposed to require a 40-hour workweek. But you should devote a consistent number of hours each week, whether it's for promoting your business, sending out bills or rolling up your sleeves and sewing quilts.

- **Will family members support** and help you? Get a commitment from them to help you in specific ways at specific times…and hold them to it.

• **What are the insurance needs**, licensing requirements and tax laws regarding your SAM? You don't want surprises from your insurance agent, the town or the IRS six months down the road.

• **Are you willing** and able to take on the responsibility of customer satisfaction? You will engender a great deal of goodwill among your customers if you act responsibly, but they will never forget it if you let them down.

SAMs that work:

SAM opportunities are everywhere. The key to determining the one for you is to establish a weekend business that takes advantage of your interests, abilities, knowledge or skills.

SAM ideas that have paid off for other weekend entrepreneurs…

• **Car detailer.** Clean and polish cars from top to bottom. Since their cars have to be immaculate, start with real estate brokers first. Go into an office, introduce yourself, drop off flyers and offer to do the first car free. Charge a minimum of $40 per car.

• **Pet meals on wheels.** Deliver cumbersome 20-pound bags of dry pet food and heavy cases of canned goods to pet owners' doors. Blanket a neighborhood with flyers and contact veterinarians and dog groomers to let them know you're in business. Don't charge a delivery fee, just mark up the pet food after negotiating a close-to-wholesale price from local distribution centers or retailers.

• **Recycling pickup service.** Save your neighbors the trouble of hand-feeding cans and bottles into recycling machines at the supermarket or loading their cars with recyclable material that must go to the dump. In exchange for keeping any cash refund, volunteer to recycle items that don't have a cash value, like newspapers in some states.

• **Special-occasion sign rentals.** If you're handy with a jigsaw and have an artistic flair, create ready-to-rent "yard cards" for high-profile celebrations. Signs in the shape of bunny rabbits, teddy bears and carousel horses are great for kids' parties, while a humorous sign planted on a front lawn for a 40th birthday party will bring you $25 a day, $35 for three

days or $50 for a week. You make the signs, install them and pick them up.

• **House portraits and custom stationery.** People love to use portraits of their homes to create distinctive stationery…to send as holiday greeting cards…or simply to frame beautifully and hang in the house. If you're good with a camera or a sketch pad, show your portfolio to homeowners in an upscale neighborhood and offer to photograph, sketch or paint their homes. Try charging from $85 for a pen-and-ink sketch to $150 for a color photograph. Adjust your prices depending upon the response.

Source: Jennifer Basye, author of *How to Become a Successful Weekend Entrepreneur*. Prima Publishing. Her latest book, *The Air Courier's Handbook: Travel the World on a Shoestring* (Big City Books) provides strategies for traveling cheaply by air.

Don't Be Fooled by People Who Always Appear Busy

Key: Make sure they are busy in productive ways. But do not equate daydreaming with lack of productivity—employees in creative fields need time to develop insights and ideas.

Source: Sharon Johnson, editor, *Motivation Strategies for Managers*, 70 Hilltop Rd., Ramsey, NJ 07446.

Computers for Sales Forces… The Time Has Come

For companies that still are not convinced that equipping sales reps with computers pays, here is a rundown of the increasingly powerful and affordable advantages that such a move creates…

• **Increased credibility.** Salespeople aren't eager to admit it, but they often have trouble convincing a prospect that they are experts in the technology of their product or service.

Computers can help them cross the credibility barrier.

Example: When clients ask for technical information and a sales rep doesn't have the information at hand, he usually promises to get them what they need as soon as possible. That's usually by fax, phone or overnight mail. But the information isn't always what the client wants, and the whole overblown process makes follow-up questions hard to field.

With a laptop computer, a well-trained salesperson can call up technical data immediately to answer a prospect's questions during the presentation, not hours or days later. He/she can also give prospects the data on a disk or in a printout.

•**Greater consistency.** It's tempting—especially for newer salespeople midway through an important presentation—to exaggerate product descriptions or to modify purchasing terms.

Or, when product specifications change, it's often hard for sales managers to get memos out to everyone in the field.

Solution: With information on-screen, managers can be assured that every rep is "reading from the same page."

•**Enhanced sales rep expertise.** With so much to remember about products, clients and terms, computers help salespeople keep it all at their fingertips.

•**Dramatized presentations.** Apart from data that computers enable salespeople to provide to clients, newly available software allows them to display it in impressive formats.

Laptop computers can also run video presentations that show clients actual scenes of how a product or service will help solve their problems. Still other software and equipment can turn a laptop computer into a slide projector.

•**Better forecasting.** Since computers let sales information flow quickly from people in the field to the home office, managers have up-to-date figures on which to base forecasts. Making the decision:

To determine whether it pays to equip your own sales force, consider these typical costs for laptops:

•**Hardware.** $3,400 to $9,000 for a laptop with 16 to 24 MB of RAM, 500 to 800 mega-bytes of space on the hard disk, an internal modem and CD-ROM capability. *Leasing:* $350 to $400 a month.

•**Software.** Most laptops come with communications, word-processing and database software. Graphics, presentation and networking software are also available at an additional cost.

•**Training.** Budget an initial $500 to $1,000 per person per day.

Since it is costly to give laptops to every sales rep in the field—and time-consuming to train those reps—start slowly. First give them to top sellers, preferably to reps whom others see as leaders. Then broaden their use to more salespeople.

In that way, expenditures are held to a minimum while the company has time to fix problems that come up.

More important: By giving computers to sales leaders, a company can allay the fears of other reps who may be reluctant to carry laptops computers.

Source: James J. Rafferty, director of business development, Price Waterhouse, LLP, management consultant services, 6500 Rock Spring Dr., Bethesda, MD 20817.

Workplace Violence Is Still Growing— Avoidance Strategies

A detailed study by a major insurance company revealed a frightening statistic: As many as 2.2 million American employees are the victims of physical attacks at the workplace every year.

And...another 6.3 million are threatened.

When violence occurs in the workplace, the consequences can be very costly—easily running into millions of dollars. In addition to the costs of damage to property, higher insurance premiums and lost business, the legal costs are almost always the biggest bill resulting from an attack on the company.

Reason: In addition to employees—who can sue the company if they are victims of violence—customers, salespeople, suppliers and others who happen to be on the premises can have similar exposure.

This makes it urgent to take serious steps to reduce the company's vulnerability to the growing threat of violence.

Key: Important in heading off problems related to workplace violence is screening out employees with a history of workplace violence. Even if it is impossible to completely deter violence, the effort to protect the company from violent individuals is in itself a critical legal issue. *How to do it...*

• **Better reference checking.** Checking references can have legal ramifications, although many businesses have grown lax. In most courts, however, the important point isn't whether the company succeeds in checking references but whether it makes a reasonable effort.

Example: A business that hires an employee who hid a history of violence could be held liable in many states if it doesn't make an attempt to check his/her references, if such a check might have revealed the employee's violent background.

By contrast, a company that does make an effort—even though it turns up nothing—could escape liability if the employee becomes violent on the job.

Effective: Ask job applicants to sign an attorney-drafted release that authorizes a prior employer to provide information regarding an applicant's employment and releases that employer from any liability in so doing.

Occasionally, asking for a release will shake loose a reference you otherwise couldn't get. But even if it doesn't, the release further documents the company's effort to check the employee's background.

For the same reason, always keep a written record of the company's efforts at checking references.

• **Check criminal records.** As an added safeguard, especially in sensitive jobs, it often pays to check applicants' criminal records. But don't proceed before having an attorney review the procedure. *Reason:* Laws that govern the interviewing and hiring of people with criminal records are tricky and vary from state to state.

Example: It is risky to deny an applicant employment on the basis of a record of arrests. The Federal Equal Employment Opportunity Commission (EEOC) says that because minorities have a disproportionate number of arrests, denying employment on that basis can constitute discrimination.

For candidates with conviction records, the EEOC and the laws of many states require companies to consider the nature of the crime, the age at which it was committed, the status of the applicant's rehabilitation and the type of job for which he is applying when weighing the hiring decision.

Example: A 35-year-old applicant for the position of comptroller was convicted at age 18 of taking a neighbor's car without permission. He had no further brushes with the law. In this case, the company probably can't use the conviction as a reason to reject him.

Reasons: The crime was nonviolent and has nothing to do with the job he is applying for. And he's had a clean slate for 17 years.

On the other hand, a recent conviction for embezzlement would surely be adequate grounds for rejection in this particular case.

Safest: Depending on the laws of the state involved, job applications should ask applicants about prior convictions as well as details of the conviction. The scope of what may be asked also depends on the laws of the particular state involved. Check with counsel, also, about whether to add a statement on the job application that "conviction does not automatically disqualify applicants for employment" and that the company will consider other factors, such as age, nature of the crime, etc.

Advantages: In court, the questions are still further evidence that the company made a reasonable effort to weed out violence-prone workers.

Action plan:

Take all threats of violence seriously, and act on them immediately. *How to do it...*

• **Set up a violence response team**, composed of people from human resources, security, operations, as well as legal and medical, if the company has these departments.

Mission: To intervene in case of violence or a threat, according to the disciplinary procedure of the company. If violence does occur, intervention may consist of medical attention, notifying the local law-enforcement agency and discipline or dismissal of the violent worker.

• **Establish strong relationships** with local law-enforcement officials. *Aim:* To be able to rely on prompt response when a violent incident is reported.

• **Train supervisors**, especially response team members, in handling violence. Many human resources consultants, as well as large law firms, offer this type of training. *Typical cost:* $5,000 for a day's training for up to two dozen managers.

• **Communicate a violence prevention policy.** The key requirement of such a policy should be that all employees report violence or threats of violence to the response team.

• **Keep an eye on potentially troubled employees.** These include individuals who seem overly bound up in their work...have a romantic obsession...lack support of family or friends...act withdrawn or disgruntled...are going through a period of stress...show a strong fascination with weaponry or military equipment...display paranoid behavior...have trouble taking criticism about their work.

Be especially alert to incidents when these employees let their troubles or obsessions influence their conduct.

Example: It is perfectly normal to have an interest in firearms or military equipment, but it is not normal for a worker to talk about the damage that a gun could do to employees in the reception area.

His supervisor or a member of the response team should immediately explain that such comments are not appropriate.

He should be told that, if they continue, his comments could be grounds for starting the company's system of progressive discipline.

• **Rethink termination procedures.** Before firing an employee for threatening violence, make sure the discharge doesn't violate the Americans with Disabilities Act...or any other federal or state antidiscrimination laws. In some cases, the employee might claim mental illness, which is covered by the statute.

In addition, to minimize the chance of litigation, be sure that terminations never come before proper disciplinary procedures have occurred. If, during any stage of the disciplinary process, an employee begins to exhibit irrational, excessive or aggressive behavior, be prepared to bring in a business psychologist trained in handling difficult employees.

Source: Mark L. Sussman, managing partner at the law firm of Jackson Lewis Schnitzler & Krupman, 1000 Woodbury Rd., Woodbury, NY 11797.

Job-Finding Secrets... Demand Is There

If you are over 50 and want to find a job, there are more opportunities than you imagine. In fact, to land some jobs, it's actually easier if you're over 50.

Skills:

While job markets vary considerably around the country, the best fields for people over 50 include...

• **Computers.** That may be surprising, since many older people are unfamiliar with computers, and a few are terrified of them.

The facts: Computer skills are easy to learn, and demand is likely to continue for many years. Moreover, many skills you learned earlier in life can be wedded today to computers.

• **Sales.** Companies know that many types of customers feel more confident with older salespeople. So they're eager to recruit seniors. If you lack sales experience you may have to take a sales course or go through the company's training program.

• **Jobs that require trust**, such as banking, other financial services and personnel work. When it comes to trusting someone with money or confidential information, many companies prefer older employees.

Whether you're entering a new field or pursuing an earlier career, it pays to consider the following steps...

• **Take an aptitude and/or personality test.** Local colleges can usually recommend a variety of commercially available tests. Ask for the vocational counselor or someone in the psychology department. But don't rely completely on test results in choosing a new occupation. Instead, use them as a guide to steer you toward jobs for which you have a natural aptitude.

•**Consider a career counselor.** Counselors watch the job market and can often help you see opportunities that otherwise might be missed. *Typical cost:* $500 to $2,000, depending on how long the counselor works with you and how many tests he/she administers.

To find an effective career counselor, ask for recommendations from your network of business colleagues, or call the American Society for Training and Development, 703-683-8100.

The right company:

Once you have a good idea about your career direction, it's time to research companies that can offer job prospects.

How to do it: Contact trade associations, talk with vocational counselors at colleges, tap members of your network, read industry magazines (usually available at local libraries) and seek out current and former employers, often with the help of the Chamber of Commerce.

From local senior organizations, find out which companies in your area have a good track record for hiring older employees. For names of local senior groups call Forty-Plus, 202-387-1582, or the American Association of Retired Persons (AARP), 202-434-2277.

Many companies, including Disney, Manpower temporary agency, Builders Emporium and Travelers Corp., specifically recruit older workers. AARP has a list of more than 200 others nationwide.

Image:

John Malloy, author of *Live for Success*, sent several actors out to find jobs in businesses they knew next to nothing about. They did, however, know how to cultivate the image of successful applicants. Nearly all got second interviews or job offers—which they turned down, of course.

Conclusion: By looking successful, appearance often becomes reality.

•**Do your best to appear healthy.** Even companies eager to hire older employees often hesitate when applicants appear to be in poor health. So unless you're in top physical condition, spend a month or two getting into shape before you go on job interviews.

•**Lose a little weight, and do some light exercising** as your doctor recommends. It improves your confidence as much as your image.

•**Cultivate the appearance of someone who belongs on the job.** That means wearing the clothes that a top professional would favor in the industry you've targeted. Don't dress like a 22-year-old graduate. It won't make you look young, just a little foolish. If your hair is gray, it may make sense to dye it, but only if the job is done by a professional. Don't worry about repercussions when your natural hair color grows in. Companies don't fire employees for having prepared creatively for an interview.

Polish your presentation. If you're afraid of appearing awkward in interview situations, consider taking a course in public speaking, such as those offered by Toastmasters and Dale Carnegie. They also help boost your confidence level.

Résumés and interviews:

Trap: Paring down your résumé in hopes that a shorter work history will make you seem younger.

Reality: What you have going for you is your experience. If a company wants a younger employee, a short résumé won't fool them. But it might cost you a job offer from a company that's looking for someone with broad experience.

•**Think of it from the employer's point of view.** By hiring a highly experienced employee, it won't have to spend the time and money needed to train a younger person.

•**To prepare for an interview**, ask a friend, preferably one who's currently in a managerial position, to help you rehearse. During the interview, make eye contact, and don't be afraid to use physical gestures.

Source: Terry Harty, project manager for the Computer Learning Center of San Francisco and coauthor of *Finding a Job After 50*. Career Press.

Good News About 401(k) Plans

401(k) plans for small businesses, including one-employee firms, now are being offered by growing numbers of financial institutions. Insurance companies such as Principal Financial Group, Metropolitan Life and Nationwide, and mutual fund groups such as Scudder and T. Rowe Price, now manage 401(k) plans for firms with fewer than 25 employees. These firms "bundle" management services and investment options for client employers. *Typical cost:* About $1,000 to set up a plan, plus an annual fixed fee of $500 to $1,500, and an annual per-participant fee of $6 to $35.

Source: Robert C. Carlson, editor, *Tax-Wise Money*, 824 E. Baltimore St., Baltimore 21202.

Where the Jobs Are

The portion of the US population aged 45 to 54 will grow by over 40% in the next six years. This surge in sheer numbers will create huge consumer demand for businesses that provide services to this age group, and profit opportunities for investors in such businesses. Now is the time to look for winning long-term investments in companies that are poised to take advantage of this population surge. *Attractive:* Medical and drug companies…life insurers… and the travel and recreation industries—especially restaurants and gambling firms.

Source: Michael Metz, chief investment strategist, Oppenheimer & Company, Inc., research department, One World Financial Center, New York 10281.

Smarter Job Hunting

Always ask for an information interview when a potential employer says there are no jobs available. Say you are interested in the organization and would like to meet for a half-hour to see if you and the company might be a good fit in the future. Request a specific date—do not leave it up to the company to call you back with a time.

Source: *The Smart Woman's Guide to Résumés and Job Hunting* by Julie Adair King, marketing consultant in the Indianapolis area. Career Press.

Career Change: Planning Strategies

If you want to change your career, now's the time to do it. Employers today are more accepting of the idea of career change, new professions are emerging and retraining opportunities abound.

But careful planning is essential. *Steps to take:*

• **Determine if your career is the real problem.** If you are less than satisfied with your current work, your career itself may not necessarily be the cause of your anxiety. Instead, the problem could actually be with the job you're doing. *Questions to ask yourself…*

• *If I changed jobs—not my career— would I find the fulfillment I'm seeking?* An accountant I know was fed up with the restraints of corporate life. She couldn't get excited about the company's goals…and didn't even like wearing corporate business clothes.

Instead of changing careers, however, she found a similar job at a nonprofit organization whose goals she shares…and where she can dress casually. Today, she is—very happily— the organization's controller.

• *If I kept my job but changed my lifestyle, would I be happier?* Many people who sit behind a desk and perform routine tasks all day have fantasies about having a more exciting career. One solution might be to find a job at a smaller company where you can do your same job but play a greater role. Another solution is to keep your job, but take up a hobby …or work weekends on other income-producing projects.

• **If you need a career change**, research the day-to-day routine of the new career. *Reason:* Many careers aren't exactly what they seem.

Examples: Nursing isn't just caregiving—it's dealing with stress…professional writing isn't nearly as solitary as it sounds…opening a business requires as much sales skill as financial acumen.

Helpful: Before rushing into a new career, subscribe to a professional journal…attend conferences or seminars where you can meet others in the profession…join a professional organization.

Those people who are successful in a new career do well because it matches their personality and values, regardless of how drastic the change may be.

•**Get great advice.** Large corporations don't change directions without getting the best advice they can find. Neither should you.

Helpful: Create your own "board of advisers"—a group of people whose judgment and experience can help steer you in the right direction. Advisers can include people who know you from work in your community…have extensive knowledge of the new field you're entering…appreciate your talents… have changed careers themselves.

Spell out your plans to members of this informal group and ask for honest feedback. They're likely to suggest ways that you can improve or fine-tune your plans.

Also ask for support and advice from your extended family. After all, they may have to bear the brunt of a temporary reduction in your income. Because family members know you better than most other people, they can often make useful recommendations.

Important: Don't take their advice as gospel. You're the one who has to make the ultimate decision.

•**To make the transition smooth**, move slowly. A slow transition makes sense when your finances are unstable or you're facing a personal crisis such as a divorce.

Example: Take a part-time job in your new profession to build up experience before you completely cut ties with your present source of income. Or, take a transition job in or outside of your targeted profession that gives you

more time to study or prepare for the new career.

Source: Joyce Schwarz, a career consultant whose corporate clients include AT&T, Walt Disney and IBM, 1714 Sanborn Ave., Los Angeles 90027. Schwarz is author of *Successful Recareering.* Career Press.

Customer Credit Problems— Early Warning Signs

•**A low ratio of assets to liabilities**, especially when accompanied by a limited availability of liquid assets to cover short-term obligations—including your company's.

•**A large amount of debt compared with equity**. Troubled customers—ones with more than three times as much debt as equity—will always pay the interest on their bank loans before they will pay vendors for goods already in-house, especially when the bank has a lien.

•**An inventory turnover rate** that is lower than the industry average. Get information about averages from trade associations, Robert Morris Associates (a Philadelphia-based association of bank lending officers) or many other sources.

Example: If the average turnover for a particular industry is six times, and your customer turns over its inventory only five times a year, that could indicate trouble.

If it turns out, however, that last year's turnover rate was 4.5 times and the year before that was 4.0, things are looking up for your customer. That customer would actually be a better risk than a company whose current inventory turnover is also five times, if that figure is lower than in previous years. What is important is the direction of the numbers. In this regard, credit managers need to act like stock market analysts.

•**A company's average receivables** as a percentage of sales that is higher than industry norms. This could be a sign of overly generous credit terms or ineffective billing and collections. In either case, it suggests that the company may have a hard time paying its bills.

Operating indicator:

These tend to show up before problems appear in a company's financial statements or its balance sheet. Credit managers should be alert to the following indicators when they visit a company, or they can question salespeople who visit more regularly…

• **Physical neglect of manufacturing facilities**, offices and equipment, including such visible symbols as a company's fleet of trucks.

• **Unusual, seemingly nonstrategic, disposal of assets** or auctions of equipment.

Example: When construction and engineering consultants Morrison Knudsen's financial problems became public, it turned out that the company's last few profitable years had been due to selling assets to mask a lack of real operating profits.

• **Returning merchandise without authorization** and then reducing payments accordingly. Returned goods are not the same as cash, and the credit department should be notified immediately so that they can pursue the matter with the customer.

• **Purchases above and beyond normal needs.** This could indicate that a company is having trouble purchasing from other sources. Worse, it could be a sign that the customer is stocking up in order to cover itself in case your company refuses to ship more goods in the future. This, of course, implies that the customer knows he's not going to pay the bill in a timely manner. Be especially wary of requests for *additional credit* if there are any other warning signs.

Source: Stanley Tulchin, chairman, Stanley Tulchin Associates, an international collection agency, 400 Post Ave., Westbury, NY 11590.

Injury and the Pregnant Worker

There is new risk of legal action against the business because of injury to pregnant workers and/or their unborn children. Not only can the mother sue for problems caused by exposure to environmental or safety risks, but children—up to age 19—can sue the mother's employer for injury in the womb. *Defense:* Accommodate workers whenever their doctors recommend a change in working conditions. If the worker refuses a job shift, have an attorney draft a waiver for her to sign, releasing the company from liability.

Source: Jesse Graham, at the law firm of Parker Chapin Flattau & Klimpl.

New Horizons

Secretarial and receptionist jobs are good stepping-stones to higher positions—*including management*. Secretarial jobs often require word-processing, spreadsheet, database and on-line skills. Receptionists need excellent communication, organizational and customer service skills. These are important skills for higher positions in most companies as well. *Bottom line:* Jobs that have been thought of as dead-end positions in the past can be real career opportunities today—if taken seriously.

Source: Kathryn Marion, editor, *The Reality Check Gazette*, 8667 Sudley Rd., Manassas, VA 22110.

8

The Winning Edge

The New Age of People Skills and
The Service Revolution

Edith Weiner, Weiner Edrich, Brown, Inc.

The mantra of "quality customer service"—enunciated and underscored through countless books and embraced by corporate executives from coast to coast produced little in the way of real quality. On the contrary, while corporate America was embracing the concept of excellence in customer service, the customer was experiencing more and more of what is best described as "schlock service."

Examples abound: Restaurant servers who don't serve...toll-free service numbers that put customers through touch-tone hell...retail store salespeople who have no answers...etc., etc., etc.

In coming years, there will be a backlash against schlock service. Companies will increasingly treat their customers with personalized attention and will deliver products and service in an increasingly timely and proficient manner.

Reason: As competition intensifies in all sectors of the economy, companies are gradually accepting the tough reality that customers are tough to win...and losing them is increasingly painful.

The demand for an end to schlock service will combine with the growing population of professionals laid off through the downsizing era. Many of the individuals in the huge group will become part of the new age of entrepreneurialism in America. And a sizable percentage of these new entrepreneurs will end up in service-providing enterprises.

As the backlash against schlock service gains momentum, there will be a notable surge in the growth of small businesses that provide customized service. *There will be:*

• **A proliferation of businesses serving the "time deprived."** Capitalizing on the opportunities created by two-income households, shrewd entrepreneurs will increasingly offer shoe repair at the customers' place of work...hot meals at commuter train stations... errand services for the return of video movies, library books...drop off and pick-up of dry cleaning...food shopping, etc.

• **A new class of private chefs** who go to the time-deprived customer's home to prepare affordable meals.

• **Faster growth in the area of personal training**—where professionals help their clients master the techniques of fitness training that cannot be found at the local health club.

• **New types of service providers** who help harried clients sort through the vast and ever-expanding array of choices in everything from vacation options to appliance selection to restaurants.

This "option shock" that combines with time-stress of two-earner families creates great opportunities for service-oriented entrepreneurs who have the people skills to know their clients quickly and intimately and who can stay abreast of the mushrooming of choices to match individual clients' preferences with just the right choice of vacation package, new-car features, computer software, etc.

Better Thinking

Choose TV shows carefully, focusing on news and information programs...play bridge instead of bingo, blackjack instead of slot machines...do jigsaw and crossword puzzles, and play word games like Scrabble or anagrams...start something new—take an art class.

Source: K. Warner Schaie, PhD, is director of the Gerontology Center, Pennsylvania State University, University Park, PA.

No More Blues

Cure the blues by doing something for someone else...for yourself...or for your home.

Examples: Invite some friends over to dinner—and use the good china...take three upbeat friends to lunch...plan a vacation...volunteer at a local soup kitchen...talk about your feelings to a good friend—or a good therapist...take a class...sing—even if you think you don't have a good voice.

Source: Liz Carpenter, former White House press secretary, quoted in *On the Edge of Darkness: Conversations about Conquering Depression* by Kathy Cronkite. Delta Books.

Cure Negative Self-Talk

Cure negative self-talk by becoming more aware of it. Put a rubber band around your wrist for at least 24 hours—under your wristwatch, if you are concerned people will see it. Listen very closely to your thoughts about yourself. Every time you put yourself down, snap the rubber band to condition yourself to be aware of the negative thoughts. Use the rubber band periodically to check on your progress in eliminating negative self-talk.

Caution: Do not lie to yourself about shortcomings. Learn to handle them in a positive way, without putting yourself down.

Source: *Don't Let Jerks Get the Best of You* by Paul Meier, MD, cofounder, Minerth Meier New Life Clinics, Richardson, TX. Thomas Nelson Publishers.

Create Your Own Learning Plan

Do not rely on traditional education to take you closer to your personal vision. Your learning depends more on activities and experiences in daily life than on time spent with professional educators. Create a learning plan to help you develop skills and use learning tools, from books to computers. Join professional associations, and contribute to your community. Experiment at home and at work with new things to learn and new ways to apply your knowledge.

Source: *Design Your Future: Live Your Vision in the Ever-Changing Learning Society* by Paul Siegel, who runs seminars based in Long Beach, CA, on future design and vision. Learning Society Publications.

Eight Ways to Master Stress and Improve Your Health

Stress is the body's natural, primitive alarm system. It is a series of a dozen or more reflexes that alert you to impending danger and prepare you to fight off or flee an attacker.

When this "fight or flight" alarm goes off, your blood pressure shoots up to deliver oxygen to muscles…excess adrenaline is released, providing super energy…and your adrenal glands pump out more cortisone to protect you from an allergic reaction like asthma.

The stress response was the perfect protective device for our Stone Age ancestors who were constantly under threat of attack by wild animals.

Problem: The human body is not able to distinguish between the life-and-death stress of being attacked by a charging animal and the modern-day hassle of having to wait in a long line for 30 minutes.

When you're stuck in a traffic jam and worried that you'll miss an important meeting at work, your body reacts in exactly the same way it would if you saw a bloodthirsty tiger smashing through the car's rear window.
Danger signs:

When you're feeling edgy or overwhelmed, it's easy to diagnose your problem as "stress." But stress comes in many varieties. Sometimes people get so used to living with constant pressure they don't realize they are "stressed out."

Common warning signs of stress include an inability to focus or concentrate, irritability, restlessness, fatigue, neck or shoulder pain,

insomnia, indecisiveness, sweaty palms, racing heart, compulsive eating, smoking or drinking and stomachaches and headaches.
Reality check:

• **Each evening**, do a mental/ physical stress check. Ask yourself, "How did I feel today?" Identify any physical symptoms you may have experienced, like aches and pains, as well as psychological reactions to stress, such as snapping at a colleague or family member.

• **Rely on others to alert you** to the possibility that you're experiencing stress. You may think you feel and look fine. But if co-workers comment, "You look tired " or, "You usually don't make mistakes," stop and try to identify the stress you may be facing.

• **Don't ignore the silent signals of stress**, those only a doctor can identify. You may feel you're handling life well, but your blood pressure could be sky-high or your thyroid out of whack. Get a regular physical checkup every three to five years. If you're over 65 or have a serious medical condition, such as diabetes or cardiovascular disease, get checked more often.
Simple solutions:

• **Cultivate your sense of humor.** Studies show that laughter elevates the body's natural painkillers, and a good belly laugh will instantly relieve stress. Make it a point to watch a funny movie or your favorite television sitcom several times a week, particularly when you are feeling overwhelmed by life.

Keep audiotapes of your favorite comedians in the car and listen to them on your way to work. They are especially useful when you find yourself stuck in a traffic jam.

Don't dwell on the reports of disasters that headline the morning newspaper every day.

Learn to laugh at yourself when you make mistakes. If you can find the humor in stressful situations, you'll take some of the pressure off yourself to be perfect.

• **Eat smart.** A healthy diet will provide you with all of the nutrients and energy you need to withstand stress. Cut back on saturated fats. These are found in certain cuts of red meats, poultry skin, whole milk, cream, butter and commercially prepared baked goods.

Increase your intake of fresh fruits and vegetables and whole grains. Eat five or six vegetarian meals each week…and limit red meats to two servings a week. Enjoy lean skinless poultry and fish three or four times a week.

Don't overdose on caffeine—it will leave you feeling edgy and less able to handle pressure. If you're a coffee drinker, opt for high-quality espresso. It has about half the caffeine per serving that regular American coffee has.

Limit alcohol intake to one drink each day.

Cut back on refined sugar. Cookies may give you an instant "high," but 90 minutes later your blood sugar will crash, and you'll feel tired and shaky. If you crave sweets, have a teaspoon of honey or jam on a piece of whole-grain bread. Carbohydrates stimulate a brain chemical that helps keep you calm.

Always eat a nutritious breakfast that includes a grain, such as low-fat dry cereal or oatmeal… some protein, such as skim milk…and a piece of fruit. Breakfast eaters are more alert and aren't as likely as nonbreakfast eaters to get the jitters or get drowsy around 10 am or 11 am.

•**Get out and exercise.** Physical activity —especially the aerobic type that gets your heart pumping—triggers the release of two natural feel-good chemicals, serotonin and endorphins.

Get at least 30 minutes of exercise a day. You needn't cram your activity into one session …10 minutes here and there can be beneficial.

•**Refocus negative stress.** When you're under pressure at work or at home, look for other things to concentrate on—things that are enjoyable but require full concentration and involve different "circuits" in your brain and body. See the scariest horror movie around… take a roller coaster ride…play a game of tennis.

Even activities that seem nonstressful can offer "alternative stress." During World War II, Winston Churchill was able to defuse his concerns about the war by painting. He would lose himself in his oil painting for hours, and because his name was going on each picture he felt "challenged" to do his best work.

•**Set realistic goals.** If you aim to lose 30 pounds in one month, you'll probably label yourself a failure and feel more stressed when you lose only eight. But if you set out to lose a pound a week, you'll feel a sense of accomplishment when you meet your goals.

•**Learn to relax.** Use relaxation techniques to maintain your calm. Four or five times a day —or whenever you begin to feel stress—practice deep breathing for 60 seconds. Breathe in through your nose, filling your abdomen with air. Hold for several seconds, then breathe out through your mouth. If you are under a great deal of pressure, consider taking a yoga or progressive relaxation course. Listen to relaxation tapes during your lunch hour or just before bedtime.

Learning to relax will also help you sleep better. When you are sleep deprived, you can't effectively manage stress. Prepare for a sound sleep by taking a comfortably warm bath a few hours before bedtime. Warm water relaxes the muscles.

Schedule exercise five or six hours prior to going to bed. If you work out late in the evening, you'll be too revved up to nod off.

Don't drink alcohol within a few hours of bedtime. While alcohol may make you feel sleepy, it will also give you a wakeup call two hours after you nod off. Instead, have a warm glass of milk. It contains tryptophan, a sleep-inducing chemical. Or have a piece of whole-grain toast with honey. And—go to bed and get up at the same time every day, even on weekends.

•**Prepare well for work.** To withstand stress at work, you will need to prepare yourself thoroughly—whether you're making a presentation to 20 people or writing a report for your boss.

Every morning, sort out the day's tasks, then tackle the most important ones first. Use "positive imaging" to improve your skills.

Example: If you must give a speech, visualize yourself walking up to the podium, making a clear presentation and effectively fielding tough questions.

•**Maintain a strong family/social network.** If you invest enough time and energy in maintaining an adequate network of friends and support within your family, the stresses of your day will be greatly reduced.

Communicate with those in your network. Share your burdens with them—and encourage them to share their concerns with you. Studies show that people who have strong family and social support systems are better equipped to weather life's stresses…and may be physically healthier as well.

Source: Peter G. Hanson, MD, director of the Hanson Peak Performance Clinic at Porter Hospital in Denver and consultant for medical acupuncture to the Denver Broncos football team. He is author of *The Joy of Stress: How to Make Stress Work for You.* Andrews and McMeel.

How to Keep Worry, Fear and Anxiety Under Control

Remember the last time a friend urged you to "relax" when you were feeling upset?

That counsel probably wasn't too helpful. When you're truly worried or anxious, it's simply *impossible* to make yourself feel relaxed.

Nervousness arises from the "fight or flight" response built into the body's autonomic nervous system (ANS). The ANS cannot be turned on or off by an act of will.

It turns on automatically when it senses danger—a sudden noise, an angry voice or even a troubling thought. It floods the bloodstream with adrenaline, causing your palms to sweat, your heart to race and your muscles to tense. Try to "calm" this adrenaline, and you'll only become frustrated and upset.

Relaxation techniques like deep breathing, meditation and yoga can help *prevent* anxiety. But these techniques are of little use if you're *already* anxious. In fact, they tend to produce the opposite effect—much like a friend who urges you to relax.

Many therapists persist in using relaxation techniques as a primary treatment for anxiety. In my work as a stress-management counselor, however, I've had better success with a different approach.

Instead of having my clients try to "relax" their worries away, I teach them to turn anxiety into excitement—in other words, to turn "bad" anxiety into "good."

Making worry work for you:

A worry is a negative thought about something over which you have no control. You're releasing adrenaline not over a real threat, but over an imagined one.

There's nothing you can do with this adrenaline. You can fight an attacking dog, but you can't fight or resolve a fear. As a result, you feel stuck, tense and unhappy.

A few years ago, I discovered a simple technique for turning worry into excitement. My inspiration came from an unlikely place—skydivers.

The moment before leaping from the plane, first-time skydivers are terrified. Once the parachute opens, however, this intense fear turns instantly into exhilaration. What happens? Their terror is channeled into a feeling of incredible "aliveness."

You can apply this scenario to your own fears. Replace your fearful, out-of-control fantasy (worry) with an exciting fantasy that gives you a feeling of personal control.

The Mardus maneuver:

With a little practice, a technique that I call the Mardus maneuver can provide relief from worry in just one second.

What to do: Whenever a worry arises, think instead of something exciting—a sexual encounter, winning the lottery, acing a tennis serve at the US Open, etc.

I call these positive fantasies "the new R & R." That's because they tend to be *risqué* or physically risky.

To test the physiological benefits of the Mardus maneuver, I've tried monitoring my clients with biofeedback equipment.

What I've found: Each client registers a rise in adrenaline when I ask him/her to worry. When he/she switches to an exciting fantasy, there's an even higher surge of adrenaline. But the client has a smile…and reports feeling not anxious, but good. Like the opening parachute, the exciting fantasy turns bad stress into good stress.

The best part of this technique is that the "good" stress is closely followed by a natural and automatic feeling of relaxation.

This technique can be used whenever a worrisome thought pops up. It can also be applied to specific problem areas of your life.

Overcoming insomnia:

What makes insomnia so unbearable is not only the loss of sleep, but also the constant worrying associated with sleeplessness.

If you're suffering from insomnia, try to convert the worry of "bad" insomnia into "good" insomnia. *What to do:* As you lie in bed, conjure up a "risqué or risky" fantasy.

Apply that same feeling to your present situation. From good insomnia, you'll pass into a state of relaxation. You may even drift off to sleep. If a phantom fear pops back up, just dive back into your "R & R," and repeat the process.

Burning out a worry:

Another way to gain control over your ANS is to worry *on purpose*. My work with biofeedback has shown that a worry always precedes a rush of adrenaline—which makes you feel more worried. In other words, although worries may seem to just happen to us, we actually *make* them happen.

Here's how to break this cycle. Imagine you are at an old-fashioned drive-in movie theater. Project your worry on the big screen for 20 seconds or so. Show the worry in full color, in all its fearsomeness.

Next, imagine one of those refreshment-stand commercials, with talking hot dogs and dancing soda cups. Enjoy this ad for 20 seconds, then go back to your worry movie for another 20 seconds. Continue this for a few cycles, and you'll notice that you're no longer taking your worry movie very seriously.

Procrastination:

Any unpleasant or difficult task is made many times worse by the self-imposed anxiety of procrastination.

The logic of procrastination is, *I can't do this now, because I don't have the time* (or the resources, or the energy, etc.).

Like fear, procrastination causes the release of adrenaline, which makes you enervated and anxious. *Instead:* Move from the "thinking" stage to the "doing" stage.

Example: Procrastinating about cleaning your house? Instead of fretting, take control of your situation by entering the doing stage. Pick up one piece of clothing *right now.*

Follow the five-minute rule. For the next five minutes, vow to automatically do whatever you've been worrying about. Do not stop to think. After five minutes, take a break. Ask yourself, *Do I want to continue the task?* If so, continue working. Even if the answer is "no," you've managed to assert control.

This new-found control will make you feel better and in charge…and it will move you a step closer to completing your task.

Dealing with anger:

Some people deal with anger by bottling it up inside. I call these people "stuffers." Others let anger out by yelling at someone or something. I call them "yellers."

Problem: Neither approach can meet your four basic needs when you're angry. These needs are…

•**To feel better.**

•**To remain "connected"** to the person who upset you.

•**To get an apology for**, or an explanation of what hurt you.

•**To avoid feeling guilty** when expressing your anger.

Stuffing your anger makes you feel worse because it involves withdrawing from the source of your anger. By not speaking up, stuffers ensure that they will not get an apology or acknowledgment.

Yellers suffer, too. They pretend to be in control but really aren't. And by pushing others away, they cut off communication. Of course, once they cool off, they feel guilty for having blown up.

There's another option. By expressing your anger in a clear, first-person statement, you gain control over your angry feelings…and meet these four goals. You're not fighting your upset feelings but learning to channel them instead.

Imagine stubbing your toe on a box on your way to an important meeting. If you tend to stuff your anger, you'll probably hold your breath, wince and pretend it didn't hurt. If you're a yeller, you might curse, or rant against whoever put the box there in the first place.

Better: Say something like, *Ow, I just banged my toe, and I'm really hurting.*

By following this third approach, you…

…feel better physically, because you're asserting control over your situation.

…deal directly with the source of your anger.

…avoid feeling guilty.

…are more likely to get help and understanding from others—perhaps even an apology from whoever left the box there.

The world is full of stresses, and you'll never eliminate them all. But you'll be happier and more relaxed if you realize that instead of fighting your own negative feelings, you can learn to control them.

The ANS works automatically, but the system has two buttons—one marked "worry," the other marked "excitement." By learning to press the excitement button when you're stressed, you begin to control your phantom fears.

Source: Craig B. Mardus, PhD, a stress-management consultant based in Williamstown, MA, and a consultant to the Canyon Ranch Spa in Lenox, MA. He is the author of *How to Make Worry Work for You: Simple and Practical Lessons on How to Be Happy.* Warner Books.

Verbal Abuse… Self-Defense

Verbal abuse takes place all the time—in our schools, on our streets and in our homes and businesses. Sometimes it assaults us as obscenities, insults, ethnic or sexist epithets or vicious taunts. Often it takes the form of sarcasm, ridicule and even subtle putdowns under the guise of being helpful.

Since verbal abuse is dangerous to our health and well-being, it's important to establish an environment in which verbal abuse almost never occurs.

Why verbal abuse occurs:

Someone who is a verbal abuser is not necessarily a sadistic person who takes pleasure in the suffering of others. Many verbal abusers are not even consciously aware of their actions.

If asked to explain their abusive behavior, they often say, *It's for his own good…she's stubborn and refuses to cooperate…*or *somebody has to be in charge.*

People who use verbal abuse often grew up in homes where verbal abuse was the norm. Some are verbally abusive because of psychological problems, physical disorders and unresolved traumatic experiences in their pasts.

Verbal abusers are often unaware that there are other methods for dealing with tension and conflict.

Identifying verbal abuse:

There is always a nonabusive way to transmit a message with painful content. Verbal abuse occurs when you are hurt by other people's words. How else could you feel when your boss yells, *Will you please explain why you can't do anything right?…*or when your spouse screams, *Your behavior is disgusting… and I am not going to put up with it any longer* …or when your friend says, *That outfit almost makes you look thin.* The reasons verbal abusers say things are quite different from the reasons of people engaged in normal conversations. They are not interested in the answers to their questions or statements as would be expected by others in similar circumstances. They are not really even interested in the issues they raise. People who consistently use verbal abuse are interested in only two things:

•**Demonstrating their power to get—** and keep—the attention of the people to whom they're speaking.

•**Provoking an emotional reaction** in the people to whom they're speaking, which is additional evidence of their power.

Verbal abusers are aware of these two desires, but they are usually skilled at rationalizing and suppressing them.

How to stop verbal abuse:

•**Be aware.** Determine in what situations you experience verbal abuse.

Examples: When you talk to your teenage daughter…when your neighbor comes over for coffee.

What are the situations outside your personal life during which you encounter verbal abuse? Who is the most verbally abusive person you deal with?

•**Improve your verbal skills.** Remember the source of a communication problem usually is not a person but a sequence of language.

Pay attention to language and the way words are said.

•**Respond differently.** Instead of answering an abusive comment with a counterattack, debate or pleading—try to clarify and investigate the language that seems to be deliberately hurtful. Use neutral intonation and impersonal language. Examples to avoid misunderstanding and hostility…

• *I think I must have misunderstood you. Could you repeat that for me, please?*

• *I know you wouldn't have said that unless you had a good reason. Could you tell me what it was?*

•**Defuse hostility.** If an intimate relationship (with your spouse, parent or child) exists in a verbally abusive environment, don't bait or fuel the pattern.

Strategies: Write an angry letter to the person with whom you can't communicate, then throw it away…or if you are in the mood to perpetuate the bad feelings, warn the other person.

Example: Instead of starting an argument the minute you arrive home from work, you could tell your spouse, *I want to warn you— I've had a horrible day, and I'm so mad I don't trust myself to talk straight. I'm going upstairs for a few minutes. I'll be down as soon as I stop feeling like Attila the Hun.*

•**Diverting response to an attack.** Instead of being swept up in the personal attack when someone says, *Why can't you ever do anything right?*, try to lighten the situation.

Response: I think it's because of something that happened to me when I was just a little kid. We were living in Indianapolis at the time …no, wait! It couldn't have been Indianapolis because that was the year my Aunt Evelyn came to visit us and brought her dog. So it must have been while we were living in Atlanta. Anyway, we were…

This responds directly to the presupposition that the verbal abuser actually wants the question answered.

•**Resist the temptation to be right.** If your goal is to persuade the person to stop using disrespectful language toward you—and move to a win-win situation—you'll have to stop the linguistic combat.

Example: A husband screams at his wife, *What's the matter with you, anyway? You're supposed to know something about kids and nutrition?* She might scream back, *I do not intend to put up with this kind of theatrics! Don't ever talk to me like that again!*

Better: The more productive response is, *I know you too well to believe you would be this angry over a few potato chips. You must have spent the whole day in a pressure cooker…do you want to tell me about it?*

This answer allows her to defuse the verbal attack and bring it to an end with no loss of face on either side.

Source: Suzette Haden Elgin, PhD, founder of the Ozark Center for Language Studies, Box 1137, Huntsville, AR 72740. She is the author of 24 books on verbal self-defense. Her latest book is *You Can't Say That to Me! Stopping the Pain of Verbal Abuse.* John Wiley & Sons.

Learn to Say No

Take charge of your life by saying "no" more often. You cannot do everything that everyone wants you to do. Unwanted socializing, interruptions, crisis management and attempting too much at one time can all be solved by saying "no." *Important:* Learn to say "no" tactfully: *I would love to, but I have a rush project that must come first…*or *I am afraid I would do a very poor job for you, because…*

Source: Richard Leider, management consultant who specializes in executive career development, Minneapolis, and author of *Life Skills.* Pfeiffer & Co.

A New Form of Intelligence More Powerful than IQ

It has always been thought that IQ is the best indicator of how well you will do in life. But a more critical factor influencing success at work and in personal relationships can be how emotionally smart you are.

Emotional intelligence reflects the functioning of your emotional brain—the part that generates and regulates feeling and fear, mood and anger—just as IQ shows how well the thinking part of your brain is working.

Emotional intelligence is a key tool for getting along with others, taking control of your life, thinking clearly and making decisions.
The power of feelings:

Emotional intelligence is made up of five closely related factors…

•**Self-awareness.** Feelings have a major influence on all our decisions.

When making a decision, your brain doesn't unemotionally tally up the pros and cons to produce a neat printout.

Instead, it processes all the relevant data, which in turn help you produce a feeling about what you should do.

When your emotional brain is working well, this feeling is shaped by your entire life's wisdom and experience. If you're not in touch with your feelings, you won't hear the emotional message.

•**Mood management.** Depression, anxiety and anger interfere with working memory—your brain's ability to integrate facts and ideas. This prevents you from thinking straight or working smart.

Emotional intelligence allows you to manage your moods by cheering yourself up when you're down…calming yourself when you're anxious…and helping you to express anger effectively when you are upset.

•**Motivation.** The ability to maintain hope and optimism—even when you encounter setbacks—is crucial in working effectively toward your goals.

•**Empathy.** Sensitivity to other people's feelings is key to understanding their needs and modifying your behavior. In marriage, empathy means fewer fights and less stress. At work, it's a key management skill.

•**Social skill.** The ability to deal with the emotions of others—to harmonize, persuade and lead—draws on all aspects of emotional intelligence.

Example: A study conducted at Bell Laboratory found that the most trusted, valued employees don't stand out because of their IQs or academic backgrounds, but because of their ability to get along with others.

Emotional intelligence is the key to being a team player, and it is perhaps the most critical tool available in the workplace today.
Being more sensitive:

Like IQ, emotional intelligence is partially predetermined by the brain with which you were born. But emotional intelligence can be shaped constantly—much more so than IQ—by learning from the repeated experiences of life. *Here's how to boost your emotional intelligence…*

•**Make a habit of self-awareness.** You can dramatically improve your emotional intelligence by listening to yourself and observing your own behavior.

Helpful: Remind yourself to think about your feelings as you're talking to co-workers, spending time with friends or pondering decisions.

•**Learn skills to calm anxious feelings.** When you're nervous or worried, activities such as exercise, listening to music or a hobby will distract you. Such activities are also effective at banishing anxious thoughts.

Another strategy: Practice a relaxation exercise for 15 to 20 minutes a day, and you will be able to call on it when you feel anxiety building. Sit quietly and focus on your breathing, saying to yourself the words *in* and *out.* When your mind wanders, simply refocus on your breathing.

•**Find ways to lift your mood when you're down.** Intense feelings of anxiety are important, provided they are not prolonged. When they are, however, such feelings can distract you and cloud your judgment and perspective.

Strategy: A brisk walk works for many people…or completing a long-postponed household chore.

•**Fine-tune your empathy** by discussing your spouse's or close friend's feelings. Trying to understand the feelings of others helps heighten your emotional sensitivity. One way to do this is to compare your reading of someone's emotional state with what he/she is actually feeling.

•**Increase motivation by nurturing hope.** When your confidence dips, set a new goal immediately, determine what it will take to reach it and resolve to have the energy and persistence to pursue those steps.

Every time you evaluate what appears to be a hopeless situation, form a plan and turn the situation around, you move toward a more optimistic mind-set.

•**Improve specific social skills.** Heighten harmony at home by listening and speaking to others nondefensively. Resist the urge to defend yourself against any and all criticism. Try to separate the criticism or the anger from the emotional message that is behind it.

Example: Someone who says, *You're always so selfish* may actually mean *I feel so hurt.*

•**Tune in to your feelings that complicate relationships.** Feelings of self-righteousness or that you're an "innocent victim" can become a toxic habit. They're really excuses.

When you find yourself thinking this way, stop and challenge these thoughts.

Example: In an argument, recognize when strong emotions threaten to overwhelm reason. Agree to call a 20-minute time-out so you can cool down with your self-management skills.

Be frugal with your criticism—and generous with praise—at work. When you must criticize an employee or co-worker, try to do it artfully …and do it in private.

Empathy for the feelings of the person who is receiving the comments gets results, while an insensitive put-down creates resentment and bitterness between you.

Source: Daniel Goleman, PhD, author of the best-seller *Emotional Intelligence.* Bantam Books. He is a psychologist and writes about behavioral and brain sciences for *The New York Times.*

Time for a Change? How to Change

Events at work move so quickly today that your success depends largely on how well you are able to adapt to change—and how fast you spot and seize the opportunities that change presents.

But before you adjust to change and profit from it, you must first identify parts of your own personality that need to be fine-tuned. By listening carefully to your critics and dropping negative behavior and emotions, you will be more likely to excel in environments that embrace new ways of doing things.

Here's how I help patients recognize that it's time to change parts of their personalities—and how I help them do it.

Signs that you need to change:

•**You find life is consistently dissatisfying and uncomfortable**—and you are restless for no obvious reason. Consider the possibility that something in your personality needs to change. Whenever you experience negative emotions for an extended period of time—weeks on end, for example—you must look inward to find the reasons why. Negative emotions are messages from your spirit or inner self and are worth listening to.

•**You find yourself complaining a lot**—especially if it's about a person, or a number of people, in your day-to-day life. This is true if you complain to them about others. Complaining is an emotional release and a way to get attention without taking responsibility for making needed changes. It offers little practical reward and, long term, leaves others with a negative impression of you.

•**Significant people with whom you have daily contact express unhappiness with you.** This is really a sign that you need to consider making some changes in your behavior —and perhaps in your personality as well.

Even when the other person's feelings have a great deal to do with his/her own general unhappiness, you are better off dealing with that person's complaints rather than fighting them, in order to reduce your overall level of stress.

•**You find yourself consistently postponing things you would really like to do**—or passing up opportunities you really would like to take advantage of.

If you're constantly making personal sacrifices, there is something about your personality that is causing you to put your needs second.

One way to recognize this trend is to imagine yourself 30 years from now. What would you regret not having done? Saying, *Someday I'm going to…*is an excuse to keep doing what you're doing now.

• **You sense other people think more highly of you than you think of yourself.** During your life, have teachers, colleagues, supervisors and friends thought more of you than you think of yourself? In that case, you need to change. You're wrong…they're right. You're reacting to how you feel while they are reacting to how you are. How you feel is distorted by a lifetime of painful feelings and of not feeling good enough.

How to change yourself:

Dissatisfaction with life or yourself can provide the motivation for change, but it cannot organize and direct the process. *Steps to pursue any kind of change within yourself…*

Step 1: **Consider adopting novel and temporarily artificial attitudes and ways of being.** Many people obstruct their own self-change because they identify so strongly with their behavior. They can't imagine acting or thinking in a significantly different way than what they are used to—even though temporarily and enthusiastically adopting different behavior may lead to tremendous personal growth.

Step 2: **Consider becoming someone you respect more**…someone who deserves more of your compassion and care. Respect, understanding, caring and fairness are not qualities that are just used toward others. They also can be used creatively toward yourself.

Strategy: I recommend that many of my clients do a mirror exercise every day. It's done by simply standing in front of a mirror and looking into your own eyes for a minute or two.

If you can manage a long, quiet look and feel a sense of support and caring for yourself, then you are already doing well in terms of self-acceptance.

Step 3: **Identify attitudes and actions that might make you feel more caring** toward others and yourself. This step carries the process to specific ideas for new ways of thinking and behaving.

Use your imagination as freely as possible to come up with as many strategies as you can,

covering the whole spectrum from most conservative to most radical.

Important: Rehearse your experiments in your mind, in a journal, on tape or with supportive friends. The exercise will help make your strategies a permanent part of your personality rather than temporary solutions.

Step 4: **Implement your strategies and commit yourself** to practicing new attitudes and actions. A single experiment is usually insufficient to establish momentum in the process of self-change. We need to make repeated attempts to establish value-driven behaviors and attitudes.

Step 5: **Reward yourself each time you have completed a self-change experiment** —regardless of its success or failure. Celebrating inner growth nourishes us during the sometimes lengthy process of self-change and establishes a positive context for further achievement.

Strategy: Keep a journal to record your self-change. Without it, you are likely to forget how far you have come—and how much you have accomplished. A journal allows you to have insightful conversations with yourself and to look back frequently and validate accomplishments from the very different perspective of growth and change.

The difference between coping with your own life and creating it is a big one. To progress is a courageous and magnificent achievement.

Source: Tom Rusk, MD, associate professor of clinical psychiatry at the University of San Diego and medical director of the Carondelet Psychiatric Care Center, Richland, WA. He is author of *Instead of Therapy: Help Yourself Change, Change the Help You're Getting*, and *Get Out of Your Own Way: Escape from Mind Traps.* Hay House.

Six Ways to Winning Friends and Influencing People

When Dale Carnegie arrived in New York in 1912, his first job was at the YMCA teaching public speaking.

Soon after, he broadened his course to include better strategies for getting along with people in everyday business and social situations. Carnegie didn't have textbooks or case studies to follow. The subject had not been explored before. He merely worked from notes he had scribbled on index cards.

After 15 years, he put his ideas and lessons in a book, *How to Win Friends and Influence People*, which was published in 1936. The book was an immediate success. Carnegie soon started a company to spread his message and wrote two more best-selling books.

Though Carnegie died in 1955, his proven principles in human relations can still widen your circle of friends and help you succeed at work...

• **Express genuine interest in and appreciation of others.** An expression of interest can be as simple as using a pleasant voice on the telephone. When someone calls, say hello in a tone that implies, *I'm happy to hear from you.* As simple as it sounds, the impact is extraordinary.

Smile at people. Learn their names and how to pronounce them. Get the spellings and the titles right. Remember their birthdays. Ask about their spouses and children. Don't limit those expressions of interest to the so-called important people in your life.

Don't forget the assistants, the receptionists, the messengers and all the under-recognized people who keep your life on track.

Ask about their days. People will respond immediately to a genuine expression of warmth, honest admiration and heartfelt interest.

• **See things from the other person's point of view.** Always try to see the other person's perspective. Here is a series of questions to ask yourself to better appreciate other people's motives and to teach yourself to respect their viewpoints...

• **What life experiences does the other person bring to our discussion?**

• **What is the other person trying to achieve here?**

• **What subjects or issues is the other person trying to avoid?**

• **What other constituencies does the other person serve?**

• **What will it take for the other person to consider our encounter a success?**

Make a genuine effort to figure out what the other person wants to achieve—and then provide assistance...or even exceed the person's expectations. In the end, you'll benefit directly or indirectly.

• **Respect the dignity and inherent worth of others.** Everyone wants to be heard, and nearly everyone responds well to people who listen to them. Listening is one of the best ways to show respect. It's a way of saying, *What you think... and do...and believe is important to me.*

Treat employees like colleagues—and don't dictate, berate or talk to them in a condescending manner.

Engage people. Challenge them. Invite their input. Encourage their cooperation. Respecting others is the bedrock of motivation.

• **Recognize and reward people for honest effort and real accomplishment.** Everyone wants to be told that they're doing a first-rate job—from the president of the most successful corporation to the clerk at the supermarket checkout. People want to be recognized for being smart and capable.

When rewarding employees, money may work—but it's not the only effective reward. Encouragement is often far more valuable and, in some cases, more rewarding to the spirit.

A little bit of recognition—a dash of praise at precisely the right moment—is often all it will take to transform a good employee into a great one.

• **Handle mistakes**, complaints and criticism with care. Until recently, contradicting and demeaning other people were widely accepted forms of interaction, even in the best companies. "Barking rights" were thought to be an executive prerogative. Loudness was equated with toughness...stubbornness with superior knowledge...and argumentativeness with honesty. Those days are over.

Solution: Create an environment in which people are open to receiving advice or constructive criticism. Spread the word that mistakes are a natural part of life, and be willing to admit your own mistakes.

Criticism or spreading blame almost always causes people to cover up mistakes. People who have received harsh criticism are far less likely to take risks, to be creative, to go out on a limb.

Any criticism should begin with praise and appreciation. Avoid arguments as you would rattlesnakes and let the person save face at all costs. Gentle persuasion always works best.

•**Show enthusiasm in all that you say and do.** True enthusiasm is made up of two parts —eagerness and assurance. Be excited about something and express confidence in your ability to handle it.

You can't fake enthusiasm. But you can create it, nurture it and put it to work for you. The way to acquire enthusiasm is to believe in what you are doing and in yourself, and have a burning desire to get things done. Enthusiasm is easier to attain when you have real goals in your life, things you are genuinely looking forward to accomplishing. Let that happen, and enthusiasm will grow inside you.

Source: Stuart Levine, CEO of Dale Carnegie & Associates Inc., 1475 Franklin Ave., Garden City, NY 11530. He is coauthor of *The Leader in You: How to Win Friends, Influence People and Succeed in a Changing World.* Pocket Books.

 # How to Make New Friends

As we progress through life, some unforeseen developments—like leaving a long-term job or losing a long-time partner—may make us want to expand our social horizons. Making new friends may seem difficult. People who act to build new, mutually supportive relationships reap rich rewards.

Loneliness:

Researchers have discovered that a sense of belonging and attachment to others causes the brain to produce endorphins and other chemicals that induce a feeling of well-being.

Conversely, loneliness produces discomfort, so lonely people often seek substitutes for meaningful friendships. Many of these forms of temporary relief for loneliness are actually harmful.

Examples: Alcohol, tobacco and drug abuse …overeating…workaholism.

Overindulgence in these habits is one reason lonely people die younger than those who enjoy healthy personal relationships.

Fear of reaching out:

Inability to make friends often originates in childhood. When mothers or fathers fail to provide emotional support, their children may grow into adults who are wary and fearful of reaching out to others. People who want to put childhood disappointments behind them and make new friends can succeed.

They must first be willing to think through *who they really are.*..and decide how they want to relate to others.

Then they must take positive steps to encourage others to reciprocate their desire for building new friendships.

The friends you want:

Every relationship between two individuals is different, with many types of friendship at different levels of intimacy.

Most people generally want friends who enjoy sharing experiences…are open and honest…accept them for themselves…keep in touch…can be counted on for support.

It is up to you to decide what kind of friends you want. Each of us has a different balance between our desire for companionship and our need for emotional support, and so forms a unique image of an ideal friend.

Exercise: Compose an imaginary personal ad describing yourself and/or the friend you are seeking.

First take some time to think about your own personality and how you like to spend your time. *Ask yourself:*

• *What activities do I enjoy doing alone …and could I share some of them with other people?*

• *What childish behavior patterns have spoiled previous relationships…where did they come from and can I stop them?*

• *Am I afraid of rejection because of earlier painful experiences…and did I overcome the pain?*

Example: *Friendship Wanted—I want to meet people who share my enjoyment of activities—both outdoors (camping, cycling) and indoors (movies, Scrabble), and who like to discuss their diverse outlooks on life.*

How to make new friends:

To create opportunities to strike up new friendships:

• **Carry an interesting book** or pamphlet with you.

• **Wear an unusual T-shirt.**

• **Walk a dog.**

• **Go window shopping.**

• **Have a party** and invite each guest to bring a friend, too.

Take active steps to meet new people…and to become closer to people you already know.

Suggestion: Get more involved with people who share some of your interests…

• **Always attend large family gatherings.** You will find that your relatives are more interesting than you thought when you were a kid.

• **Find out more about the people at work.** Take every opportunity to attend trade shows and conventions where you will have the chance to meet new people.

• **Join service,** sports or volunteer organizations. The other people there all share at least one of your interests. When you get to know them better, you will find some who have even more in common with you.

• **Join specialty clubs** such as chess and card clubs.

• **Enroll in continuing education classes** in subjects you want to learn more about.

• **Visit libraries and bookstores**, especially for author readings and literary discussion groups.

Getting started:

Make a list of specific things you might do to make a friend. If you have trouble thinking of any, begin with some of the suggestions above. Then choose one from your list—*and do it.*

Example: Recall someone you used to talk to at work a few years ago but have not seen lately. Call him/her up and suggest that you get together and catch up on each other's recent activities.

Two weeks later, go back to your list and choose another reaching-out activity.

Take the initiative:

When you reach out to others, most respond. If, like most people, you feel uneasy initiating a conversation with a stranger, remind yourself he is usually just as anxious as you are.

Secret of conversational success: Relax and just start to talk. Most people will soon respond.

If you are afraid you will be tongue-tied, think of some neutral subject that is interesting to most people, and decide what you would like to say about it. Mentally rehearse a few introductory remarks until you are so familiar with them they will trip off your tongue.

Don't be discouraged when you meet the occasional cold fish. Persist and you will soon find plenty of other people who are more receptive.

Conversation starters: *Where do you live? …What are your hobbies and interests?… Where did you go on your last vacation?*

Source: Perry Treadwell, PhD, a consultant on relationships. He is the author of *Making Friends, Leaving Loneliness Behind.* Health Communications.

How to Read Faces Yes…Faces

A lot of very important information about what people are thinking and feeling is conveyed through facial expressions. But most of us pay so much attention to what's being said —or what we want to say—that we don't notice the hidden messages in expressions.

Faces are easy to read if the person with whom you're speaking is frank, cooperative and wants you to know how he/she feels. Face reading is much more difficult if he is embarrassed, reluctant, ambivalent or deceptive… unless you know the clues to watch for.

Conversational signals:

Conversational signals are facial movements made either when we're speaking or listening to punctuate the conversation. A speaker makes facial movements in order to emphasize a phrase, usually by raising his eyebrows or pulling them down and together.

The raising or lowering of the brow also can signify a question at the end of a statement. We've found that people who already know the answer to the questions they're asking usually raise their eyebrows. A person lowers his brow only if he really doesn't know the answer to the question he is asking.

A lowering or joining together of the brow indicates that the listener is thinking or perhaps perplexed about something. When you see that expression on someone's face, it usually means you should rephrase what you were saying.

Hiding emotions:

Although all people show their emotions with the same expressions, there are differences among people that are due, in part, to our culture. As we grow up, we all learn when to show what emotions to whom. I call these *display rules.*

Example: It's the contest winner who cries, not the losers, because we're taught that you don't show your disappointment in public.

When we manage our expressions, it may be for strategic rather than cultural reasons— to hide our interest, intentions or emotional reactions.

Example: The boss criticizes you, and you don't want him to know how annoyed or upset you are.

Status is also signified by facial clues. The person who is higher in status has more right to look directly at the other person. If you're in the subordinate position, you're more likely to look away, while the person who dominates will look directly at you.

Our expressions are easy to recognize when we're not trying to manage them. But when people try to hide their feelings, it takes some skill to know what to look for. Certain expressions are harder to suppress than others.

Examples: When you're angry, it's difficult to prevent your lips from narrowing. That's the best way to detect anger in someone else because it happens to people even before they know they're angry.

With fear, it's hard to prevent a slight lifting and pulling together of the eyebrows and a momentary widening of the eyes. With sadness, the inner corners of the eyebrows go up.

Microexpression: When people attempt to censor their own feelings, they try to interrupt their involuntary expressions. Instead of an emotion lasting on the face for two to three seconds, as it would normally, it flashes on the face briefly, for only a quarter of a second.

The smile:

Much of our most recent research concerns the smile. We have identified 18 different kinds. *The most revealing among them:*

• **Smile of enjoyment involves not just the lips**, but the muscles around the eyes as well. Crinkling the muscles all around the eye is the sign of genuine enjoyment.

• **Polite**, social smile, the one you give when your boss makes a joke, involves only the lips. Usually it is slightly more tilted up on one side of the face than the other. The eye muscles will not be involved.

• **Miserable**, grin-and-bear-it smile is the one you make when the dentist says you need a root canal. You smile, not because you're a masochist, but because you want him to know you'll go along with it although your misery shines through. Here the lips are pressed together with the lower lip pushed up.

• **Qualifier smile** is one you put on when you are criticizing someone. You end the criticism with a smile that takes a little of the edge off your criticism and makes it much more difficult for the person being criticized to respond aggressively.

Learning to read faces:

The only way to gain expertise in reading faces is to pay attention to them. Start looking at people when they talk, and try to figure out what they're feeling from their expressions rather than just their words.

What to look for in encounters: Changes in a person's expressions from one meeting to another. A normally happy person who looks annoyed one day (even if he says he's not) is probably upset about something.

Another helpful exercise is to videotape a television program, preferably a drama or soap opera. Watch the replay with the sound off, and concentrate on the facial expressions of the performers. Then rewind the tape, and play it with the sound on to see if you were correct in what you picked up.

Though you are watching actors, the exercise will train you to look carefully for subtle facial expressions.

Source: Paul Ekman, PhD, professor of psychology, University of California Medical School, San Francisco. He is author of *Telling Lies* and *Why Kids Lie*. W.W. Norton.

What Your Body Is Saying When You Are Silent

Body language that exudes enthusiasm, confidence and approval: Leaning forward, feet flat on the floor—legs and arms uncrossed …a vertical, firm handshake…an appropriate smile—not a continuous one, which is a sign of powerlessness…direct eye contact—but not in some other cultures, where it is disrespectful …mirroring the other person's body language.

Source: Patricia Bell, founder, Corporate Communications, communications consultants, St. Louis.

How to Ask for What You Want

Would you like to have more satisfaction at work? And—more harmony at home? More of the information and resources you need for success? Full control over your life, along with the love and support of those around you? Just ask. Barriers:

It's truly amazing how much in life is there for the asking. From a better table at a restaurant to a raise at work to a hug from your spouse, the world is full of good things that you won't have unless you request them. Learn how to ask…and a whole new wonderful world will open up for you.

Why is it so many of us have such trouble asking for things that would make our lives much better? One common barrier is ignorance. We just don't know what's available and possible…what we truly want and need or how to ask.

Another barrier—the limiting beliefs we were taught by our parents, our teachers and the world. *If you really loved me, I wouldn't have to ask. The world is not a responsive place. My success would deprive someone else.*

Pride makes it hard to ask—for directions, explanations, a helping hand. We don't want to appear needy. Low self-esteem makes us feel unworthy of having our wishes fulfilled. Our needs aren't truly important. We don't deserve to have them satisfied.

But the biggest barrier is fear. First and foremost, fear of rejection. And fear of humiliation and fear of looking stupid…and fear of punishment.

Conquering fear:

Realize that you create your own fear… every bit of it—and 90% of the fears that prevent you from asking are based on nothing but fantasy.

Just what are you afraid of? As an exercise, fill in the blanks: *I would really like to…and I scare myself by imagining…*

Example: I would really like to ask my wife to spend more time with me, and I scare myself by imagining that she will become angry or withdraw.

Now, check out your fantasy: Ask the person involved if he/she would react the way you fear. If that's not an option, it's up to you —imagine asking for what you want, and substitute a positive, encouraging result in place of the feared outcome. How would it feel to get what you want?

•**Analyze your fear**—and make it disappear. Ask yourself: *What's the worst thing that can happen? Is it all that bad? Would I survive it? Would I even remember it next week?*

Key point: Rejection is an illusion. If you ask for something—a raise, a better table, more time from your spouse—and are turned down, you haven't truly lost anything. You're no worse off than before. What is the best thing that can happen if you start asking for what you want? The sky is the limit.

•**Feel the fear and do it anyway.** Fear is a great ogre that, more often than not, simply disappears when you stand up to it. You can only grow stronger (whether you're lifting weights or overcoming your fear of asking for a special favor) by pushing against resistance. Your fear shrinks and your courage expands.

•**Build up slowly.** You start lifting weights with five pounds, not 50. The asking muscle develops the same way.

Begin by asking safe people for minor things. Celebrate each one as a victory.

Then ask someone who seems more risky for something a little bigger.

Give yourself permission to be a learner. The first time you ask for a big bank loan, you'll probably do it awkwardly. Big deal! The awkward stage is a step on the journey toward mastery.

Learning how to ask:

Asking is a skill that can be acquired. Most of us never had positive role models to watch and learn from. *Helpful:* It's never too late to grasp the basic principles and put them to use.

•**Ask as if you expect to get it.** Put yourself in this frame of mind and it affects everything —your tone of voice, expression, posture, choice of words—to create a self-fulfilling prophecy.

Questions to ask yourself: *How would I be if I knew I'd get what I wanted? What would I be saying? How would my body feel, stand and move? How would my voice sound?*

•**Ask with conviction.** Imagine the librarian you're asking for help in finding an obscure research report desperately wants to give you what you want. She loves to help people and passionately wants to do her job well.

•**Ask the right person.** Someone who has the power—or the emotional maturity—to grant your request.

Examples: It makes no sense to ask a needy, frightened friend to listen at length to your troubles.

Find the appropriate helper. If you're 55 years old and want to learn how to roller-blade, you'll do better to ask the middle-aged instructor of a class at the Y, than a 20-something hotshot giving lessons in the park.

•**Be clear and specific.** Do you want help from a friend in getting ready for a party? Exactly what kind of help (cleaning up, ordering food, preparing) do you want? And when do you want it? Specific requests are more convincing.

•**Be positive.** Focus on what you want, not what you don't want.

Example: *Please close the door softly when you leave, not Don't slam the door when you leave.*

•**Ask from the heart.** People respond to the desire in your voice. At the same time, ask politely, kindly and with respect.

Eye contact is key. People are more likely to trust you, and you'll pick up on their nonverbal responses.

Strategy: Focus your attention on the other person's left eye. It creates direct contact with the right side of the brain—for a heart-to-heart connection.

•**Ask with humor and creativity.** Humor captures attention, breaks down resistance and creates a positive atmosphere in which requests are readily granted. Is it any coincidence that advertisers—people who ask for a living—often inject humor into commercials?

From *no* to *next:*

Once you start asking for what you want, you're bound to hear the word *no.* You'll hear no quite often. Turndowns come with the territory…can you handle them?

Reframe the meaning of rejection. When your request (for money, attention, a bigger suite at a resort…) is turned down, what does it mean? Invariably, you're the one who decides—you give meaning to the simple fact of rejection. It's all too easy to decide that it means you're inadequate, unlovable or a failure. Why give rejection a meaning that will make you miserable and unlikely to try again? A *no* doesn't really say anything about you… don't take it personally.

Instead, regard every *no* as a step on the road to *yes.*

Before we sold *Chicken Soup for the Soul,* which was on *The New York Times* best-seller list for a full year, we were turned down by 33 publishers. 33! With each rejection we came closer to success.

An insurance salesman we know suffered with each rejection—and in that business, there are many. Then he figured out that since he had to see about 20 prospects to make one sale for a $500 commission, each *no* was worth $25. Before long, the 20 calls became 10 and the $500 commission became $1,000.

Source: Mark Victor Hansen, an inspirational speaker, located in Newport Beach, CA, who has addressed more than one million people. He is coauthor of *Chicken Soup for the Soul*, Health Communications, Inc.

Improve Your Mood

Exercising is the best way to improve your mood. *Other ways to cheer yourself up:* Listen to music, read, talk to friends or do chores.

Source: Robert Thayer, PhD, professor of psychology, California State University, Long Beach.

Mini-Meditation

A five minute session lowers blood pressure, reduces levels of stress hormones and boosts feelings of well-being. *What to do:* Sit comfortably, straight and tall…become aware of your breathing…visualize a mountain scene, noticing all the details…imagine changes taking place, the sun arcing across the sky, violent storms whipping up…focus on the mountain's stillness and calm throughout these events and carry this calm with you all day.

Source: Jon Kabat-Zinn, PhD, director, Stress Reduction Clinic, University of Massachusetts Medical Center, Worcester, MA.

Stress Is Normal

Failing to accept stress leads to constant frustration at unchangeable things like rush-hour traffic and sudden rainstorms. But do not accept stressful things that can be changed. Whether it is an un-rewarding job or smearing windshield wipers, some sources of stress can be changed—and should be.

Helpful: Instead of wishing that something would change to make you happy, identify

changeable problems and work on them to improve your own happiness. But graciously and maturely accept things that cannot be changed.

Source: *Minding Your Body: 100 Ways to Live and Be Well* by Joseph S. Rechtschaffen, MD, internist, New York. Kodansha International.

How Your Emotions Affect Your Health—Proven Ways to Stay Well

The flood of news about health and fitness these days can be more confusing than helpful. If you've been exercising or eating "right" for years but still feel frustrated and unfulfilled, you are not alone.

There are ways to take charge of your health such as tapping your inner resources in more effective ways. The kinds of changes that we support are simple and are designed to increase self-awareness, since all aspects of life are interdependent.

Example: When you're worried about something, you're also likely to have an upset stomach.

What may appear to be individual events are really interconnected aspects of a larger, more complex system.

When you master small changes, you build a fortified base from which to take further steps on your healing journey toward wellness.

Although many people associate wellness only with fitness, nutrition or stress reduction, wellness is really much more. Wellness brings people into a domain of self-responsibility and self-empowerment.

Set goals for wellness:

Goals keep you on course. And more than that, goals are like magnets—they tend to attract people and resources that help get them accomplished. It's almost magical how this happens.

Often people set their sights too high and then quit completely when they don't make the grade. Approach these "impossible" goals by breaking them down into manageable parts.

Breathing reduces stress:

Stress is inevitable—you need it to warn you about the negative forces of life. But there are many forms of stress that wear you down and cause a variety of health problems.

You may not be aware of it, but every tense situation—or even memories of tense situations—causes a change in breathing. The more stressed you feel, the more shallow your breathing becomes. Consciously breathing deeply can relieve tension, quiet fear and relieve pain. So before you reach for aspirin or antacid tablets, do some breathing.

Emotions and health:

There is a heavy price to be paid when feelings are denied or repressed. Lethargy, boredom and a lack of enthusiasm toward life may be the consequences. Those who are unaccustomed to dealing with feelings in healthy ways often seek out other means to cover up those feelings or distract themselves, such as alcohol, food, drugs, TV, unhealthy relationships or compulsive work.

Befriend your emotional self. Accept emotions as valuable signals that tell you something is in need of attention. *How to acknowledge emotions…*

- **Write an angry letter** and then tear it up.
- **Compose a poem** about your grief.
- **Draw**, paint or even dance to express your feelings.
- **Exercise vigorously.**
- **Talk about your feelings.**
- **Let fear be there.**
- **Let discouragement be there.**

Don't try to chase these emotions away. Look at them. Express them when it is appropriate to do so. Then move on.

Simplify your life:

Becoming well in body, mind and spirit is not nearly as difficult as it may seem. Wellness is not a matter of accumulating something, like more research or experience.

Rather, wellness is realized by unburdening yourself of all those things that prevent the natural state of healthiness from being present. To become well is to appreciate simplicity. *Examples:*

- **Simplify your life.**
- **Simplify your diet.**

- **Take time to rest your mind.**
- **See your loved ones** as brand-new every day.
- **One breath is precious**…one smile… one day of seeing the sun.

Honor your body's wisdom:

Inhabit your body. Learn to start listening to what it is saying to you and trust what you hear.

Listening to others instead of yourself…or saying yes when you mean no are just two examples of the many ways you shortchange yourself. Wellness is about "coming home"— taking up residence inside your own body once again.

Reprogram yourself:

Current research in the field of psycho-neuroimmunology verifies what folk healers have known for centuries—that thinking and emotions have a direct impact on the strength of the immune system.

The immune system is the first line of defense against disease. Strengthening your immune system consciously, through the use of imagery or nurturing self-talk, gives you a much better chance of maintaining whole-body health.

Connect to the earth for healing:

When was the last time you sat on the ground or touched the earth in some way? This may seem silly, but physical contact with soil, natural waters, sunlight and fresh air is healing.

When stress has built up, very often a walk around the block is all that is needed to restore perspective.

Beyond that, you connect with forces stronger than the individual self in nature, and this puts everything in perspective.

A partnership in healing:

There will be times in your life when you need the care and attention of a helping professional—a doctor, psychologist, social worker, etc.*

When you're looking for such professionals, it's important to find people willing to take the

---

*Helping professionals interested in learning more about developing partnership relationships with their patients or clients can contact Wellness Associates, 707-937-2331. A book, *Wellness for Helping Professionals: Creating Compassionate Cultures*, is available from Wellness Associates.

time to answer questions and listen to your concerns. If you find someone who is unwilling to do this, switch to someone who will.

Bottom line:

Getting started on these small changes will help you make a difference in your life. We hope that you will experience increased self-awareness and self-appreciation…have a sense of greater inner strength…and, above all, live a healthier life

Source: John Travis, MD, and Regina Sara Ryan, coauthors of *Wellness: Small Changes You Can Use to Make a Big Difference.* Ten Speed Press. Dr. Travis is director of Wellness Associates, 21489 Orr Springs Rd., Ukiah, CA 95482.

The Smart Way to Handle Negative Emotions

Most people try to fix negative emotions like anxiety, anger or sadness. Instead of solving our problems, however, this approach inevitably leaves us frustrated and confused. It doesn't work because feelings are uncontrollable.

But we can control what we do. This simple fact is the basis of a way of life called Constructive Living. By helping us focus on what we can control (our behavior) rather than what we can't (our feelings, other people, the past), Constructive Living makes life more satisfying and meaningful.

Roots of constructive living:

Constructive Living is based on two schools of Japanese psychotherapy…

•**Morita therapy** represents the action side of Constructive Living. Developed in the early 1900s by psychiatrist Morita Shoma, it has its roots in Zen Buddhism.

•**Naikan therapy** is the reflective side. It was developed in the 1930s by Yoshimoto Ishin, a businessman-turned-priest.

Despite its origins, Constructive Living is *not* a therapy. It's a way of living learned through daily practice and observation.

The importance of action:

Like the weather, feelings are unpredictable. Sadness and anger come and go. So do joy and excitement. The most sensible approach to handling such feelings is to accept them… and *continue doing what you need to do.*

Example: If you're nervous about starting a new job, do not fixate on your anxiety or try to eliminate it. Let it encourage you to learn as much as possible about your duties beforehand. Your performance will be enhanced… and you will probably find yourself feeling less anxious.

Bottom line: Trying to *change* the way you feel makes no more sense than trying to will a storm to stop. Just wait.

While you wait, take action toward your goals. Doing so prevents you from dwelling on things you cannot control and brings a sense of accomplishment—which should lead to greater happiness and satisfaction. Even if it doesn't, focusing on your *purpose* and *behavior* rather than your feelings will give you a sense of calm and contentment.

The problem with western psychotherapy:

Conventional psychotherapists have things backward. They try to help their clients feel better so that they can take steps to improve their lives.

You don't have to feel good about yourself to make changes in your life. In fact, things usually work the other way—we feel better as a result of having made constructive changes.

Feelings that are labeled "negative" in psychotherapy often have very useful roles.

Morita exercise:

Exercise I: Next time you find yourself brooding about someone who treated you badly, do something useful and vigorous. Wash your car, for instance, or vacuum the house.

By the time you're done, the troubling thoughts will probably have passed…and you'll have accomplished something.

Exercise II: List all the chores you have to do, then tackle them in alphabetical order. The point is to do—not agonize about what to do.

Exercise III: Over the next 24 hours, try several activities that you haven't tried before—knitting, cooking a new recipe, painting, etc. This teaches you not to let fear or other feelings keep you from trying something new.

The role of reflection:

Balancing the *Morita* side of Constructive Living is *Naikan*, the reflective side.

Naikan teaches us to revere all the gifts we have been given. It shifts our focus from ourselves to other people.

When we fail to get what we want, it's very easy to feel unhappy. We feel that we haven't gotten our fair share. But nothing we have is exclusively ours.

Our bodies are a gift from our parents, who got their bodies from *their* parents. We are sustained by food grown and processed by people we've never met. Even our ideas are based upon the wisdom of others. Conventional therapy encourages people to review the bad things that happened to them in the past—all the ways others hurt or disappointed them.

How much time do you spend thinking about the ways *you* hurt other people?

Even if your parents were neglectful, you owe them a debt for giving you life. The fact that you reached adulthood means that *someone* in your past took care of you. The proper response to recognizing all that we have been given is gratitude. Rather than focusing on how much the world owes us, focus on how much we have received from so many sources. Naikan exercise:

Exercise I: At the end of the day, spend 20 minutes recalling what people did for you that day...what you did for others... and any trouble you caused others. Don't devote time to reviewing troubles others caused you. Most of us are already skilled at that.

Exercise II: Once a week, find something broken and fix it. *Examples:* A leaky faucet, a jammed copier, etc. This is a way of expressing gratitude to the things that support you every day.

Exercise III: Think of someone you haven't been getting along with—a co-worker, for example. Say "thank you" to that person 10 times a day.

Exercise IV: Every day, secretly perform a favor for a family member. If anyone detects your "secret service," find another secret service to do. We tend to do things for others with the idea that we'll get something in return.

This exercise reminds us that the world doesn't owe us anything.

Source: David K. Reynolds, PhD, a leading expert on Eastern psychotherapies in Coos Bay, Oregon. He is the author of more than 30 books, including *A Handbook for Constructive Living*. William Morrow.

Best Way to Control Anger

Slowly inhale through your nose for three seconds. Pause and think "relax," then exhale for three seconds. Repeat until you're calm.

To avoid anger: Express your feelings assertively, not aggressively. Instead of telling a friend, "You are provoking me," say, "I feel provoked."

Source: Guylaine Côté, PhD, associate professor of psychiatry, University of Sherbrooke, Quebec.

Best Ways of Handling Lies

If you sense someone may not be telling the truth, don't challenge him/her directly. It would likely produce more lies. *Instead:* Explain that you want to build a bridge and encourage frankness.

Be aware, too, that when people lie, they tend to think they have a good reason. Statements that help in uncovering the truth...

• **"Are you worried about how I might react to what you are telling me?"**

• **"I know that this may be uncomfortable**, but it appears that there is more to this story. Let's put the cards on the table so we can put this issue to rest."

• **"I have a sense that there is really more to this story than what you have told me.** Is there anything else you would like to add?"

• **"Perhaps there is some reason why you can't share with me what really happened."**

Source: Paul Ekman, PhD, author of *Telling Lies*, quoted in *Personal Selling Power*, Box 5467, Fredericksburg, VA 22403.

Smarter Marital Argument Resolution

To win marital arguments, give up control. In warfare and business, control is essential to victory. But at home, the opposite is true. The exercise of power is not a suitable way to win an argument. No adult in a loving relationship should try to control another. Instead, recognize that your spouse is a partner, entitled to different views and opinions, and accept his/her right to disagree. Then move toward a mutually satisfactory solution. *Example:* Instead of arguing about wallpaper patterns, go through wallpaper books together until you find one you both like.

Source: Gerry Spence, attorney, Jackson, WY, and author of *How to Argue and Win Every Time.* St. Martin's Press.

Some People Can Make Us Sick

We all have to deal with difficult people, but some are positively toxic. They tear you down, mix you up, get you mad, give you competition when you need support. They genuinely don't wish you well.

Not only do these poisonous personalities upset you emotionally, the stress they create can lead to serious illness, including cancer and heart disease.

Protect yourself: Instead of stewing and suffering, take the danger seriously enough to fight back with proven techniques that let you walk away unscathed, if not always smiling. Who are toxic people?:

Most toxic behavior is easy to spot—the boss from hell who loudly ridicules your work …the snarling checkout clerk…the friend who always rains on your parade…

But it's just as deadly when it's silent—the spouse who sulks endlessly instead of saying what's on his/her mind.

Or when the put-down is covered over with a joke or an "only kidding" veneer of friendliness: *I love your dress…I saw one just like it at the thrift shop.* The key to recognizing toxic people is how they make you feel. Being with them can make you feel physically queasy or nervous. You may have trouble sleeping or smolder with anger for hours, even days.

One thing all toxic people have in common —they make you feel *small, insecure, not good about yourself.*
Antidote:

Learning to deal with difficult relatives and friends may make them more reasonable. It may get your boss to treat you more sensitively. But the point isn't to change them. The point is to change you…to gain control over your reactions, and spare your mind and body endless wear and tear…

• **You *don't* have to take it out on yourself** with self-destructive stress outlets like smoking or overeating.

• **You *don't* have to waste energy** trying to win the approval of someone who has none to give.

• **You *don't* have to develop a disease** or seek therapy to repair the damage toxic people cause. Instead, you can handle it by yourself.

You won't have to keep things inside anymore…if you firmly decide, like the character in the movie, "Network," I'm mad as hell and I'm not going to take it anymore.

My clients who have mastered these techniques have found them invaluable in coping with the terrors who infest their lives. Most say that their health, their attitudes, their business ventures and their personal relationships have improved dramatically.

• **Tension blowout.** One of my favorite techniques to get rid of the tension caused by toxic people is to literally blow it away. This gives you physical control over your emotions. I do it constantly.

• **Breathe in through your mouth** for two seconds.

• **Hold the breath for three seconds**, as you think of the toxic person.

• **Blow him out of your system** as you expel the breath with all your might.

• **Stop for two seconds.** Repeat the process until you've completely ejected the toxic person.

•**Stop the thought.** If you get very angry or tense each time you think of the toxic person, put an end to the instant replay. Whenever he, or his behavior crosses your mind, say—with firm determination, silently or out loud—*stop the thought!*

•**Humor.** Take a lesson from stand-up comics who turn the tables on hecklers with a devastating comeback—*I'm not going to engage in a battle of wits with you…I never attack someone who's unarmed.* Memorize a small repertoire of one-liners. It doesn't matter if it's funny to anyone else, as long as it's funny to you.

Or use humor to lighten up the moment for yourself. If you have a boss who screams and rants, *picture* him in a diaper, waving his pacifier.

•**Vicarious fantasy.** Someone makes you so mad you feel like pushing him off a bridge? Imagine it! This is especially valuable where you can't do anything. One of my clients remembers a superior officer in the Army who abused the whole squad relentlessly. The client couldn't yell back, so he imagined the sergeant's head exploding…and felt much better. Remember, this is only a fantasy! Never use violence.

•**Calm questioning.** Questions like *Why did you say that?* or *What did you mean by that?* force toxic people to see how mean or ridiculous their behavior is. As long as you're calm and reasonable, you'll be in control. It can humanize the situation…on your terms.

Example: A business associate is rude and abrupt. Ask calmly, Are you in a bad mood?

•**Direct confronting.** Talk about your feelings…*When you ignored my questions, it made me feel that I didn't matter. When you criticize everything I do, it makes me feel shaky and sick inside. If we talk in a direct way, we can solve this problem more effectively.* You won't feel like a victim, and others will respect you for speaking your mind.

•**Mirroring.** If someone talks to you abusively, use exactly the same tone right back. This forces him to see his own behavior…and experience how it feels to be on the other end.

Example: An attorney I know was involved in negotiation with an orally hostile colleague, who screamed over the phone and wouldn't let her reply. She held the telephone receiver away and started barking like a dog.

That stopped him cold. *Why did you do that? Because that's how you sound, like a barking dog,* she said. *Now if we talk like the civilized professionals we are, maybe we can get something done.* It worked wonders.

•**Give them love.** Deep down, everyone—even the angriest man or woman—wants the same thing…love and acceptance. People are toxic because they feel especially insecure and low in self-esteem. If you can imagine the pain a nasty person must be in, you may be able to smile, and give back friendly words.

•**Give them hell and yell.** Sometimes you have no choice but to vent the anger and frustration. Instead of keeping it in, let it out.

•**Unplug.** Ask yourself if this relationship, marriage, job is worth the toll on your mental and physical well-being. It isn't easy, but sometimes you must simply unplug yourself from the person.

Source: Lillian Glass, PhD, a communications specialist based in Beverly Hills. She is author of *Toxic People: 10 Ways of Dealing with People Who Make Your Life Miserable.* Simon & Schuster.

Think Your Way Out of Boredom and Sleepiness

Hyperventilate by breathing deeply and rapidly for a few moments. Think about something exciting and stimulating while keeping your eyes open. As soon as you feel the state of your consciousness shift, refocus on where you are and what you should be paying attention to. To avoid becoming bored again, listen with close attention and alertness to detail.

Source: *The High-Performance Mind: Mastering Brainwaves for Insight Healing and Creativity* by Anna Wise, a San Francisco–area researcher and trainer on the use of brainwaves to improve personal performance and health. J.P. Tarcher.

Etiquette Mistakes that Even Polite People Make

Being busy is never an excuse for being rude. Here are some big mistakes that people who are usually polite make when they are pressed for time...

Mistake: Leaving your phone number too quickly on someone's voice mail or answering machine. Busy people talk quickly because they're hoping to accomplish a great deal in just a short time.

Most busy people are unaware, however, that in their haste, they are making it difficult or even impossible for the person receiving the recorded message to write down the information.

Strategy: Before you leave your phone number, say, *Here's my number,* followed by a one- or two-second pause. This pause gives the other person a chance to get a pen. Then pause after every few digits, and repeat the entire number at the end so the person can double-check what he/she has written.

Mistake: Finishing someone else's sentence ...idea...or story. Many busy people are eager to show that they're on top of details and familiar with procedures and information. Unfortunately, this eagerness often causes them to interrupt people who are talking.

Strategies: Force yourself to listen to the person who is speaking. Whenever you have the urge to interrupt, stop and remind yourself that it will only do you more harm than good.

Mistake: Artlessly ending a business lunch or dinner. Signaling for the check is never easy to do at a business lunch, especially when one of your lunch companions is talking.

Strategies: Instead of looking at your watch or cutting the person off by saying abruptly, *I've got to get back to the office,* gently touch the other person's arm and mention that you need to use the rest room. On your way, ask the waiter to bring you the check after you return to the table—or leave your credit card with the waiter.

If you are someone's lunch guest, be alert to subtle signals from your host that it's time to wind up the lunch meeting.

If you are the host, be alert to long pauses or long glances around the room, which usually indicate that your guest is ready to leave.

Mistake: Rushing through office doors or around corridors. Even though you're in a hurry, it is bad form to show it.

You run the risk of bumping into people and then not being able to apologize properly. In addition, you convey the image that you are in the middle of a crisis or are disorganized.

Strategy: Take a deep breath, slow down, and let other people go first, motioning them to do so with a wave and a smile. Never run at the office, no matter how busy you are. Your ease and patience will help others take it easy as well.

Mistake: Not writing a thank-you note. A quick letter may seem silly and inconsequential when you have a million things on your mind—but *not* writing one can be costly.

A personal note of thanks always brightens someone's day. And in most cases, your host or the gift-giver expects a note and won't forget if you neglect to send one.

Helpful: Carry your business stationery or correspondence cards in your briefcase or tote bag. Handwritten notes are especially appreciated in today's high-tech world.

Important: Your letter should arrive no later than one week after the event...gift...or favor.

Source: Nancy Tuckerman, who worked in the White House as staff coordinator to Jacqueline Kennedy, and Nancy Dunnan, author of numerous books on business management. They are authors of *The Amy Vanderbilt Complete Book of Etiquette.* Doubleday.

9

Investment Savvy

Economists Look Ahead, One Year, Five Years, 10 Years

With the stock market setting records recently and debt-strapped consumers nervous about spending, three top economists tell how to make sense of the present and share their visions of the future…

The coming year:

Joseph Carson
Dean Witter Reynolds

I think economic growth this year will be uneven and slow—probably in the low 2% area at best. Though the economy jumped in the third quarter of 1995, growing at a rate of 4.2%, it was accompanied by a drop in the prices producers paid for goods. This decline means that what was bought during the third quarter was heavily discounted—a sign of a weakening economy.

•**Interest rates.** For the economy to grow, interest rates must remain low. But I don't think rates will decline as much in this year as they did last year. For example, I doubt that a 5% rate on the 30-year bond is possible.

•**Presidential election effect.** Both the stock and bond markets could remain in narrow trading ranges this election year. As interest rates decline, the stock market will react to corporate earnings reports rather than stock-price multiples. Even with a budget deal in place, investors may worry about the next course of policy after the election.

•**Exports and capital spending will be among the strongest growth areas in the coming year**, but they will be constrained by the continued financial problems in Japan, the depression in Mexico and very weak growth in Europe. Capital spending will continue to be stronger in the productivity-enhancement area instead of expansion of capacity or infrastructure.

•**Investment implications.** If we agree to bring down the deficit and then move to a flatter tax structure, which will be a major issue in coming months, those two policy changes would be very positive for financial assets.

The move by millions of investors to assets such as stocks and bonds will probably continue for another 10 years. That's great for the financial markets.

Further powering the markets will be low inflation, aging demographics and tax law changes. When inflation is low, housing goes back to being simply shelter instead of an inflation hedge. Our aging population will save more, and any reduction in marginal tax rates will favor assets that create wealth.

•**Stock market.** I expect the Dow Jones Industrial Average to rise to 5,800 this year, and the Standard & Poor's 500 to rise to 680. But the challenges to this scenario are greater than existed in 1995.

•**What could go wrong?** If the Federal Reserve misreads the economy's performance and doesn't ease short-term interest rates enough, it could result in a more serious economic slowdown. The chance of a recession this year is low right now, but that could change if monetary-policy mistakes are made.

The next five years:
Irwin Kellner, PhD
Chemical Banking

The five-year outlook is quite bright. Looking back five years, we've seen the economy recover from its ninth postwar recession.

Inflation has slowed to 2½% or less—rates not seen since the 1960s. And inflation should come down even further due to economic changes brought on by technology…a shift in power from labor to management…and a changed attitude on the part of consumers, who are simply refusing to pay higher prices.

This long-term decline in the rate of inflation has brought with it declines in interest rates. Yields have the potential to go lower over the next five years because inflation will remain subdued, and we will have a deficit-reduction package in place. For the first time in 25 years, we have a real opportunity to reduce and eventually eliminate the budget deficit—thereby slowing the growth of debt.

As that becomes more believable to the market, rates will decline further, which will help reduce the deficit by cutting Washington's interest expense.

•**More jobs.** Lower interest rates lower the hurdle rate for business investment returns, so there will be greater investment in new technology. That will make US business—already back to a position of world leadership—even more competitive globally. The more competitive companies are, the more they will produce goods and services here instead of importing them.

That means more jobs for Americans, who will then be able to pay more taxes, helping the government reduce its deficit.

•**Hot industries.** Over the next five years, I see the number of jobs in industries such as technology, communications and manufacturing growing faster than in the past five years. These will be permanent, full-time jobs rather than the recent trend toward temporary and part-time positions.

Reason: A major portion of recent corporate earnings growth has been due to cutting costs—largely people. But there comes a time when phones don't get answered and service to customers slips. I think we've reached the point where the pendulum has to start swinging the other way on hiring.

•**Growth rate.** I don't see sparkling economic growth—as we enjoyed in the 1960s, 1970s and 1980s. I think we'll probably average 2½% to 3% growth during the next five years along with modest rates of inflation in the 2% zone. The unemployment rate should get close to 5%.

•**The stock market will probably go up an average of 10% per year**, but there will be bumps along the way. I don't envision a recession occurring before the year 2000 because recessions usually are spawned by an overheated economy, which I don't expect to happen.

The next 10 years:
Stephen Roach, PhD
Morgan Stanley

Ten years ago, America had its back against the wall, competitively speaking. We have since fought out of that predicament, thanks to massive corporate restructuring, downsizing, rightsizing and productivity enhancement.

Ten years down the road, we may be addressing an entirely different set of issues—

namely, how to deal with a system that did not reward the agents of change, *the workers,* for their contributions to America's turnaround.

This could result in a more inflationary period and some destabilization of the financial markets.

Reasoning: The strategies of corporate restructuring and competitive revival have taken a disproportionate toll on American workers, who are also consumers and voters.

So far, the fashionable way to get productivity gains has been to make more with less— through deep cost cutting and by pushing workers harder. But workers want their slice of the pie. Gain sharing via profit sharing and stock options has reached only a relatively small portion of a company's work force.

More and more, employees want to get a piece of the benefits that they feel they have been delivering to the companies' bottom lines. These tensions are setting the stage for a potential round of worker backlash that could lead to a major change in the US economic environment if it is not addressed quickly and adequately.

As a result, over the next 10 years, we risk undoing much of the progress that has been made.

•**Avoiding the problem.** This is actually a global problem, but because America was on the leading edge of restructuring, we will face the fallout before other industrialized nations —those nations that are only now getting around to following our lead.

In the next decade, we must strive to balance the burden of productivity enhancement. Efficiencies must be uncovered not just by "slash and burn" cost cutting but also by rebuilding—giving workers new tools, new technologies and investing in human capital with training and education.

•**Another decade of federal debt.** Despite what we're hearing from the new-wave Republicans and contrary to the current conventional wisdom on Wall Street, I don't expect a balanced budget by the year 2002—or any time in the foreseeable future.

There just isn't a broad enough political will for balancing the budget in America. This country believes that we must provide a safety net for the disadvantaged, and that view is not going to change. But we can—and must— learn to use resources and deliver services more effectively.

•**New consumers.** Consumers of the 1990s are scared and overworked as well as underrewarded. Work force reductions are now affecting white-collar workers who were previously insulated from economic distress. These fearful new consumers are no longer able to deliver spontaneous bursts of spending.

In the next 10 years, I expect consumer spending to remain under pressure. This should produce some new trade-offs in discretionary-spending choices.

People seem more willing to drive older cars, wear last year's clothes and forgo sleek new appliances and furnishings in order to spend money on the latest in electronics.

In this income-constrained environment, we expect more of the same as America moves headlong into the information age.

Sources: Joseph Carson, chief economist, Dean Witter Reynolds Inc., Two World Trade Center, New York 10048; Irwin Kellner, PhD, chief economist, Chemical Banking Corp., 270 Park Ave., New York 10017; Stephen Roach, PhD, chief economist, Morgan Stanley & Co. Inc., 1585 Broadway, New York 10036.

How Anne Scheiber Turned Just $5,000 Into $22,000,000!!

When Anne Scheiber died recently at age 101, her passing was front-page news. In an act of stunning generosity, Miss Scheiber left her entire estate—$22 million—to a private religious school in New York.

Equally astonishing to many people was the revelation that this humble woman made her fortune in the stock market by starting with a $5,000 investment more than 50 years ago.

I was Miss Scheiber's stockbroker for 20 years. Though she worked as an auditor for the IRS and knew something about money, her millions were the result of simple investment strategies that can be used by anyone.

•**Stocks outperform all other investments over time.** As an IRS auditor from 1920 to 1944, Miss Scheiber could see firsthand from the returns she examined over the years that the surest way to wealth in America was by investing in common stocks.

Her first investment was in the mid-1930s, when the economy and the stock market were at their lowest points. She had a secure government job, so she had money to invest. She continued to invest through World War II, cutting back on nonessential expenses to do so.

Through the boom of the 1950s and 1960s, the recession of the 1970s and the bull market of the 1980s, she continued to make three or four stock investments each year.

Her early views of the stock market were right on target…

•**Don't invest before doing your homework.** Though Miss Scheiber was well aware of the risks of investing in the stock market, she reduced the odds of failure by researching companies before investing in them.

She never listened to tips or rumors. Instead, she questioned me and my predecessors, sometimes showing up unannounced to ask about things she didn't understand and to consult the firm's research.

She also kept herself well-informed by reading newspapers, magazines and anything else that might help her pick a winning stock in a particular industry.

Example: Back in the 1940s, Miss Scheiber thought that the stocks of the big movie studios might be worthwhile investments. Before she bought any shares, however, she kept meticulous records of the movie box-office results found in *Variety*. This exercise helped her determine which studios had the best films. Then she looked at the financials of the studios she favored.

•**Invest in well-known companies** that make high-quality products. When Miss Scheiber died, she owned about 100 different stocks, and I don't think any of these were bad investments.

Miss Scheiber only bought industry leaders she thought would stand the test of time. Her portfolio included Coca-Cola, PepsiCo, Loews, Bristol-Myers Squibb, Monsanto, Phillips Petroleum, Homestake Mining and Schering-Plough. All were established companies when she bought them.

Miss Scheiber bought a few stocks solely for their high dividends, which she used for income. But mostly she bought companies that research told her would keep growing over the years.

•**Diversify your portfolio.** No one could accuse Miss Scheiber of putting all her eggs in one basket. Even most mutual funds today aren't as well diversified as her portfolio was when she died. The stocks she owned were in a variety of industries, from consumer products and drugs to energy and mining.

Her strategy was to focus on a different industry at a time. She knew that even if a few of her investments went bad, they wouldn't hurt her total portfolio too much.

She was so widely diversified that she was bound to have enough winning stocks to make up for an occasional loss. She didn't care if a stock declined temporarily—she always believed that a good company's stock would go back up.

•**Invest for the long term.** Miss Scheiber started out planning to never sell. She was certainly prepared to sell if she had to, but it wasn't her intention to make money fast. She only bought 100 or 200 shares at a time, and most of the dividends from her stocks were used to buy other stocks. Her buy-and-hold strategy insulated her from short-term market swings and put long-term economic growth on her side.

Example: Miss Scheiber originally bought 500 shares of Schering-Plough in 1953 for $6,000. At the time of her death, the investment had grown to be worth about $4 million.

•**Be a tax-wise investor.** The more you make in the stock market, the more important it is to seek relief from taxation. The only time Miss Scheiber broke her own investment rules was to limit her taxes on the income generated by her investments.

In her later years, the cash flow from all her investments reached $750,000 a year—most of it tax-free. That is because she reinvested her cash flow in tax-exempt securities.

In addition, all of the corporate mergers and takeovers of 1994 produced for Miss Scheiber about $300,000 in realized capital gains—all of it taxable.

But 1994 also produced big losses in the few bond funds she held because of rising interest rates. So she sold shares in her bond funds at a loss to offset the taxable gains from her stocks. Selling investments to offset taxes is not for everyone. You must be fully aware of what you are doing.

•**Money isn't everything.** Making lots of money in the stock market is part of the American dream. Riches provide the ability to buy and do what you want.

Miss Scheiber wasn't interested in any of that. She could have lived lavishly over the years, but she chose not to. Instead she lived frugally in a small apartment. She watched her money, took care of herself and lived a long life.

In the end, she knew that despite amassing great wealth, she couldn't take it with her. Rather than squandering her millions before she died, she used her wealth to help society.

Source: William Fay, who was Anne Scheiber's stockbroker and friend for the past 20 years. He is now retired and lives in Pennsylvania.

Sheldon Jacobs Reveals His Secrets of Winning Personal Investing

My experience is that businesspeople often make one of the following three mistakes...

•**Being too busy.** The business takes up so much time and energy that personal investing gets shunted aside. You'll get around to it tomorrow—but tomorrow never comes.

•**Being too daring.** With little time to think through a prudent investment strategy, many busy businesspeople invest on hunches or on tips heard at the office.

•**Being too cautious.** Some successful people are so afraid of losing their hard-earned wealth that they cheat themselves out of investment earnings by sticking to the safety of insured bank accounts and government securities, despite their minuscule returns.

Problem: Each of the mistakes above is potentially very damaging over time. *Reasons:*

•**If you're always too busy or preoccupied**, you'll never get to first base with your investing.

•**If you only play for the big win**—responding to every tip and rumor that comes along—you probably won't have any wins at all.

•**If you are overly cautious**, seeking safety in bank accounts, you risk losing everything. The low return that bank accounts pay will be more than consumed by inflation and taxes. You'll end up with far less than you started with.

Shifting gears:

Getting your personal finances into healthy shape isn't that difficult these days—thanks to the availability of more than 5,000 mutual funds, investing in everything from growth stocks to foreign securities to US Treasury bonds.

By picking the right mix of mutual funds, you can match the return you want to get with the degree of risk you are willing to take. Mutual funds are managed by investment professionals.

Important: The right mix of mutual funds can be used for your own personal investment portfolio. It also can be used to fund the business's pension plan or 401(k) defined contribution employee retirement plan.

Key: Concentrate on two areas in building a mutual fund portfolio or in analyzing and improving the investment portfolio you have now.

•**Asset allocation.** Having the right mix of stocks, bonds and cash in your portfolio is the greatest single determinant of investment success.

As a starting point, I suggest a mix of 75% stock funds and 25% bond funds for the average person.

Specifics: If you're younger—say under 45—then you have longer time horizons and can take more risks with your money. In this case I would raise the stock portion and cut the bond portion of your portfolio to 90:10 or even 100% equities.

If you are older, increase the bond portion to maybe 35:65.

Important: If your business or profession is cyclical and a bad season could put you in a financial bind, consider opting for conservative short-term bond funds, especially ones that invest in US Treasury securities. These funds produce returns that outrun inflation, and offer a considerable degree of safety as well.

If your personal income is more predictable, opt for stock funds that offer significant growth prospects.

Helpful: The investment mix you offer employees through the 401(k) plan should have a broad enough mix of both stock and bond funds to satisfy the asset allocation needs of both younger and older workers.

Index funds:

Managers of most funds actively buy and sell securities in search of a high return. Managers of index funds only try to replicate a broad market average such as the Standard & Poor's 500-stock index. Over the long run you'll do no worse than the average fund—and may do better.

Index funds offer a passive, hands-off way to fund investing. You can buy them and merely hold on, assuming that rising markets over time will increase your wealth.

Source: Sheldon Jacobs, editor in chief and publisher of *The No-Load Fund Investor*, One Bridge St., Irvington-on-Hudson, NY 10533.

Frugal Investing Made Easy

Investing isn't as scary or as hard as it seems. It also does not have to be very expensive. Here are my five rules for becoming a successful investor…

•**Reduce your risk** by putting your investment dollars into at least four different asset categories that are likely to react in different ways to economic events.

•**Reduce your investment cost** by dollar-cost-averaging—investing the same amount of money regularly, no matter what the financial markets and the economy are doing.

•**Hold on to those investments** for as long as you can.

•**Plan well in advance** when to draw cash out of your investments to meet expected needs such as college tuition, a down payment on a house or supplemental retirement income. Otherwise you'll hurt the long-term return on your portfolio.

•**Pay little or nothing to acquire**, hold or liquidate your holdings by buying no-load investments. They don't charge fees when you invest or sell.

Four assets to own:

•**Cash.** Put an amount equal to three months' living expenses into some form of interest-bearing cash-equivalent account.

Smart place to put the cash: Put it in a no-load, low-cost Treasuries-oriented money market fund.

Keep only enough money to pay your bills in an interest-bearing checking account.

•**Stock mutual funds.** Most frugal investors in their 30s and 40s should aim to have 70% to 80% of their total investments in stock funds. Reasons…

•**History shows that over time**, stock investments outperform all types of fixed-income investments.

•**Your investment is professionally managed.**

•**You can invest as little as** $50 to $100 per month.

•**Your investment is a portfolio of stocks** rather than individual shares in a single company.

Stock fund strategy: Put 55% to 65% of your money devoted to stocks in a good-quality US stock fund. Use either an index fund or a fund whose manager buys and sells securities more frequently.

An index fund replicates the Dow Jones Industrial Average or the S&P 500, both of which include big, powerhouse growth stocks.

Important: Don't listen to those people who say that index fund investing is a stodgy strategy. More than half of the other types of mutual funds generally do worse than index funds over time.

•**International stocks.** Put the remainder of your equity allocation into funds that invest internationally. Foreign stocks complement your core investment holdings because markets around the world rarely go up and down together in identical cycles. You can buy a diversified group of foreign stocks through a no-load international mutual fund.

• **Fixed-income securities.** You don't have to be a rocket scientist to find a great group of solid fixed-income investments. These are investments that provide you with predictable cash flow.

One example is a certificate of deposit. The longer the bank holds your money, the higher your return will be. An even better fixed-income investment is a bond mutual fund.

Reason: A bond fund is professionally managed and provides diversity.

Strategy: People in their 30s and 40s should put about 10% to 15% of their portfolios into an investment-grade corporate or short-term government-bond fund. That eliminates the need for worrying about the return of your principal.

Dollar-cost averaging:

Dollar-cost averaging uses the volatility of the securities markets to your advantage. The simple technique...

• **Select a regular time period**—monthly, every other month, every quarter, etc.—to contribute a fixed amount of new cash to your investment portfolio.

• **Stick to this plan for 10 years or longer.** You will buy more shares as the market falls—and fewer shares as the market rises.

Source: Scott Spiering, president of Spiering & Co., a fee-based investment advisory firm, Four Embarcadero Center, Suite 730, San Francisco 94111. He is author of *The Frugal Investor.*

The Stock Market Can Do Great Things for You On Only $50/Month

Americans do not save enough. They also do not invest enough. Even people who put away money for long-term goals, such as college, a home down payment or retirement, do

so in the least risky ways—in certificates of deposit and accounts paying fixed rates of interest, or in government bonds.

Problem: Investments like these produce returns roughly equal to the combined rate of taxes and inflation.

The only way to beat taxes and inflation—to actually increase your wealth, rather than preserve it—over the long haul is to invest in common stocks.

The problem, of course, is that stocks are risky. So, for small investors, I believe mutual funds are the perfect way to invest in stocks. I invest in them because I don't have the time or the inclination to do the research necessary for individual stock investing.

Funds offer the following advantages to the small, modest investor who wants common stocks...

• **Convenience.** Scores of excellent mutual fund companies offer a broad range of funds. You can open an account with a single fund family that offers funds that invest internationally as well as domestically, in big companies and small ones and in various styles—such as growth or value. If you choose to invest in them in the future, all your paperwork will arrive on a single statement in one envelope.

• **Professional management.** The fund industry tends to attract some of the best professional stock pickers in the business.

It is no coincidence that three of the most successful money managers of our time—John Templeton, Peter Lynch and John Neff—each made his mark in funds, rather than private money management.

Mutual funds provide the best-lit playing field in the investment industry today.

• **Instant diversification.** The typical equity mutual fund today has positions in literally hundreds of individual stocks.

This significantly reduces your risk of stock investing. You are less vulnerable to the kind of unforeseen event that can batter an individual company's shares.

A well-diversified portfolio is less volatile—less prone to wild price swings—than one made up of only a few stocks.

• **Affordability.** It is possible to begin an investment program with any of more than two dozen no-load mutual fund families that require an initial investment of $50 and a minimum monthly contribution of just $50. That entire sum goes to work at once. The only fees you pay are the annual expenses the fund incurs, which average less than $1.50 for every $100 invested.

By contrast, if you were to buy $50 worth of common stock every month, you might pay commissions equal to, or even greater than, that amount.

• **Discipline.** Although investing $50 a month doesn't sound like a lot of money, over time it can grow into a sizable nest egg—more than $3,500 in just five years. Given the stock market's historic rate of return, it can grow enough to pay for a few years of college 18 years down the road. And—based on a 10% compounded return—it adds up to more than $280,000 in the 40 years it would take a 25-year-old to reach retirement age.

• **Risk reduction.** Stock prices and the value of shares of mutual funds that invest in them fluctuate from day to day and month to month. If you invest systematically, putting in $50 a month, you tend to even out these price swings over time. This approach, called dollar-cost averaging, smooths out price swings and automatically reduces risk.

• **Lessons in investing.** As you invest regularly and follow the progress of your investments, you will learn more and more about the financial markets.

The most basic lesson you'll learn is that it's easy to say, "Buy low, sell high"…but it's hard to do. The natural inclination of people whose investments go up in value is to put in more money…and when they go down, to sell them. By investing the same amount every month, regardless of whether the market is up or down, you take advantage of the fact that stock prices have risen an average of two out of every three years since the 1920s.

If you begin a regimen of investing $50 a month in a stock mutual fund, you need to choose one fund. If I could only pick one fund in which to invest, my choice would be an all-weather fund from a long-established company that has a consistently strong, five-year record of excellent returns in good years and a history of not losing too much in bad years. Your second fund:

After you have been investing for at least one year, and you have more money available, begin putting an additional $50 a month into a second fund with the same fund family. I favor international diversification for this second fund. Foreign markets tend to zig when the US zags.

Your third fund:

When the time comes to add a third mutual fund, I favor a small-company fund. Most mainstream funds—as well as international funds—are heavily weighted with big companies. A small-company fund can add the most distinctive voice to the choir. But by then, you'll have the real-life market experience to make your own choices, based on your interests and tolerance for risk.

Winning investment strategy:

By investing systematically and not trying to "time the market," you will also likely have made a lot more money than you would have investing at a fixed rate of interest…and will not have taken on undue risk.

The rules for investing this way are the same for each of the two dozen fund companies that offer the service…

• **You send a voided check** so the company can verify your checking account number. From then on, $50 is deducted automatically from your checking account once a month.

• **If for some reason you have to stop making contributions** before the company's minimum is reached—usually $2,500 to $3,000—your account will probably be closed and all moneys in it returned to you.

Caution: Don't send any money until you've received prospectuses and enrollment materials from the fund family. You can get these by calling its 800 number.

And then, jump in. The only investment alternative is to tread water.

Source: Don Phillips, president of Morningstar Inc., an independent research company that tracks and rates mutual funds. The company publishes a newsletter, *Morningstar Mutual Funds*, 225 W. Wacker Dr., Chicago 60606.

Top Stock-Portfolio Newsletters

Over the years, I have found that only about 20% of the 170 newsletters that offer sophisticated portfolio advice outperform the market indexes over the long term. Adjusted for risk, here are my three top newsletters over the past 10 years.

•*MPT Review.* Edited by Louis Navellier, this has been a successful newsletter since 1980. Up 955%. Monthly. $225/yr. 800-454-1395.

•*Systems and Forecasts.* Edited by Gerald Appel. Up 219.7%. 24 issues. $225/yr. 800-829-6229.

•*Zweig Performance Ratings Report.* Edited by Michael Schaus, codirector of research at Zweig Securities. Up 298.4%. 24 issues. $205/yr. 516-223-3800.

Source: Mark Hulbert, editor of *The Hulbert Financial Digest*, which tracks and rates the performances of investment newsletters.

Bear-Proofing Your Portfolio

With the major stock market indexes up more than 20% since the start of the year, your investment portfolio has probably produced amazing returns.

If you're like most investors, you're probably nervous about where the stock market is headed.

Here are strategies to consider for preserving the value of your portfolio—no matter what happens to the market during the coming months. By taking action now, you will be able to relax, no matter what happens.

•**Sell half your position in stocks** that have had big gains this year. This is one way to have your cake and eat it.

Example: Last year, you bought 1,000 shares of a company at $10 a share. Now the stock's price is $50. Even if you believe, for sound reasons, that the stock could go higher, you could protect your profits by selling 500 shares. That way, you would pocket $20,000 in gains (before commission and taxes) and still profit from the company's future growth.

•**Set stop-loss orders** to protect yourself in case a stock fails to perform as you had hoped. Stop-loss orders authorize your stockbroker to automatically sell a stock once it reaches a price determined by you. This does not mean it will be sold at your price but at the available market price.

Example: Let's say you buy 1,000 shares of a company at $10 a share on the expectation that its earnings will grow at 20% a year. But the company suddenly encounters supply problems and those expectations are dashed. Subsequently, the stock drops to $7 a share while you're away on a fishing trip.

Had you placed a stop-loss order to sell your stake at $9 a share, your position might have been liquidated before the stock lost another two points.

A good rule of thumb is to sell automatically when a stock drops 20% below its highest price since you've owned it.

•**When buying stocks now**, only invest if there is little downside risk. Don't be dazzled by the prospect of big gains—without considering the possibility of big losses.

I hold onto a stock if it has the potential to increase its value by at least one third over the next 12 months. But I won't buy a promising stock unless I also think its downside potential—its negative risk for investors—is half that amount. To put it another way, I look for a risk/reward ratio of at least two to one.

Example: If we think a stock is likely to go up by 40% over the next year, it might be a potential purchase as long as we also think that it is unlikely to lose more than 20% of its value over the same period.

•**When in doubt**, hold onto the stock. The best approach to investing in stocks is to take a long-term view and to measure the success of your portfolio's performance over the next five to 10 years, not the next quarter.

This strategy allows you to filter out the temporary surges and dips in stock prices and focus instead on what hopefully will be the steady increase in their market value.

For this reason, there's something to be said for the advice of some successful older investors who say their secret was to buy stocks decades ago and stick them in a box. This strategy prevented the investors from selling when things got shaky or overheated. And because their stocks were generating dividends for them year after year, these investors got maximum mileage out of the enormous power of compounding—or the phenomenon of earnings producing more earnings.

•**Diversify by buying bonds.** Bonds generate a flow of income, which can be reinvested in stocks when a buying opportunity arises. There's no magic number for allocating a percentage of your portfolio to bonds or bond funds. Buy as much as you need to feel comfortable.

Good news: I don't think bond yields will rise much the next several months, making bonds an ideal investment.

Source: Douglas Raborn, chairman of Raborn & Co., a portfolio-management firm for individuals and retirement plans, 777 E. Atlantic Ave., Suite 301, Delray Beach, FL. For the five-year period ending September 29, the average annual return was 17.35%, compared with 17.38% for the S&P 500.

Beware of Hidden Risk

Unusually high yields from a "safe" money-market or short-term bond fund may indicate hidden risk. If your fund pays a yield that is considerably higher than its competitors, ask the fund manager how it does so.

Danger: Fund managers often are paid according to how their funds perform, so they usually have an incentive to seek extra yield from investments that carry more risk than investors might deem appropriate.

Key: You don't get something for nothing in a competitive market. If the fund manager can't clearly explain how the higher earnings are obtained—such as through a temporary waiver of fees—be wary and consider moving

out of the fund and into one that may have a lower yield but an established performance record.

Source: Roger Merritt, director of managed funds ratings, Fitch Investors Service, One State St. Plaza, 32nd Floor, New York 10004.

Costly Investment Mistake

Buying a stock immediately after its price falls with the assumption it will bounce back. *Reality:* Many stocks that decline now drop even further. Before investing in a cheap stock, evaluate why its price has dipped.

Source: Marc Perkins is chairman of Perkins Capital Management in Delray Beach, FL. He is a frequent participant in *Barron's* prestigious roundtable interviews.

Diversification Is a Good Thing

Too much diversification in your mutual-fund portfolio is better than too little. However, that doesn't mean you need to own dozens of funds. *Rule of thumb:* For most investors, three to four different funds should suffice—assuming that each has different goals and investment philosophies.

Source: Norman G. Fosback, president, Institute for Econometric Research, 2200 SW 10 St., Deerfield, Florida 33442.

Do Not Ride a Stock Down

If disappointing earnings or other bad news drives a stock's price down, check the stock's fundamentals. If they remain sound, consider holding it for the long term. But if growth is slowing unexpectedly and estimates of future earnings are being revised downward, take your losses and invest elsewhere.

Source: Gary Pilgrim, manager, PBHG Growth Fund, Wayne, PA.

Hot...Hot...High Tech

Technology is a mystery to many investors —and to many Wall Street experts, too. Although it affects our lives in many, many ways, technology is difficult for most people to visualize. It is also a very tricky sector in which to invest.

Despite the general lack of knowledge about technology, nearly everyone is investing big money in companies that make technology.

While we believe that investing in technology stocks provides investors with enormous upside potential, we caution that the inherent volatility requires investors to have longer investment time horizons—and stronger stomachs—in order to weather the dramatic ups and downs that are typical for stocks in this group.

Why technology is hot:

Investors are drawn to high-tech stocks because few other industries provide the same kind of growth. Further feeding investors' appetites for technology stocks is the belief that technology will continue to play an ever-expanding role in our lives and in business. We do not believe that technology is just a fad.

Approximately 85% of our portfolio is now invested in technology stocks. While we expect normal corrections to occur along the way, we do not believe that an extended pullback in technology stocks is imminent. However, there have been some examples of wild speculation by growth-hungry investors, causing big money to rush in and out of individual technology issues for reasons that are not justified.

Example: The hysteria from the initial public offering of Netscape Communications, which makes software that provides easy access to the Internet. People who bought Netscape shares in the aftermarket on the first day of trading lost a bundle when reality set in, and the price plunged by more than 20% before the day was done.

The rise of technology:

Back in the 1980s, business spent big to develop consumer products. During the 1990s, the focus of spending has shifted to technology that enhances productivity. Most of the companies in which we now invest make equipment or provide services that help corporate customers improve productivity levels and remain competitive. We think this trend in technology-based capital spending will continue well into the next decade.

Investment strategies:

To spot trends in the technology sector, investors must always do their homework. It is important to stay abreast of the latest technology developments and industry news. This is a challenge for the average investor, but reading related articles in *Barron's, Business Week, Forbes* and *The Wall Street Journal* as well as in industry trade publications provides a good starting point.

Keep these points in mind as you read and search for investment ideas...

•**Look at the little companies** that feed the broad technology trends. Technology includes a wide range of industries—electronics, telecommunications, semiconductors—and companies that provide equipment and services for both related and unrelated industries.

Example: Information-services companies that help the health care industry track their managed-care programs.

•**Look for companies that provide the infrastructure** for better-known products and services. Examples of these include companies that manufacture or test integrated circuits for the wireless telecommunications industry.

•**Look for companies with strong management.** Qualities include vision and leadership ability and a track record of success— factors that make companies profitable.

•**Look for companies with low price/ earnings ratios** (P/Es). Historically, emerging-growth companies have sold at P/Es ranging from 0.6 to 1.5 times their estimated earnings growth rates. We look for companies whose ratios are at the low end of this range, selling at a discount to their growth rates.

•**Think long term**...and don't panic. Anyone who invests in technology stocks should have an investment horizon of at least five years. Ten years is even better. He/she also should be firmly committed to the stocks being purchased.

If we are confident about a company's long-term potential, a 20% pullback in the stock's price will not deter our enthusiasm. And—we tend to let our winners run rather than rushing in too quickly to take profits.

Source: Lee Kopp, president and chief investment officer...Sally Anderson, senior vice president and senior portfolio manager...and Steve Crowley, vice president and senior portfolio manager, Kopp Investment Advisors, an investment-management firm in Edina, Minnesota. 800-333-9128. The firm manages $2.6 billion (*minimum account size:* $1 million).

If the Stock Market Makes You Nervous...There Are Attractive Alternatives For You

In recent years, the stock market has rewarded the optimists and penalized the pessimists.

But the pessimists may be rewarded yet. There hasn't been a major market correction in five years. What should you do with your money now if you feel strongly that the bull market may be cooling? Here are our strategies for stock investors who are uneasy...

•**Don't change your strategy.** If you're a long-term investor with a time horizon of 10 years or more—and you're happy with the stocks and mutual funds you own—leave them alone. Presumably you have an investment strategy that is designed to work for you over the long haul, so stick with it.

Responding to every anticipated move in the stock market makes you a market timer. Even the great professionals have trouble timing the market consistently.

Better: A long-term strategy that ignores temporary ups and downs in the stock market should give you a higher return over time.

Exception: If you own stocks that have large profits and you're not comfortable with the market's future, sell some of your stocks. Remember the Wall Street adage that no one ever lost money taking profits. You'll pay long-term capital gains taxes of no more than 28%...and about 72% or more of the profit will wind up in your pocket.

Important: If you're five years away from retirement—or will need the money soon to buy a home or pay tuition—you shouldn't be too heavily invested in the stock market. You're better off in more conservative investments.

•**Put the money** you were going to invest in stocks into safer places instead. If the stock market frightens you, shift cash to money market accounts where it will be safe and readily available when the market quiets down.

Another alternative: US Treasury bills. They pay higher returns than bank accounts or money markets...and they have the absolute backing of the government, making them completely safe. They are also free of state income taxes. You can buy them from a bank or broker, paying a commission to do so.

You can also buy Treasury securities at the nearest branch of the Federal Reserve through the Treasury Direct program and pay no commission at all.

Anyone above the 28% tax bracket should investigate tax-exempt money market and short-term bond funds. In most cases, they will offer higher after-tax returns with no additional risk.

•**Rethink your asset allocation.** The key to successful investing is having the right mix of stocks, bonds and cash. The right mix depends on your own personal financial situation and current economic conditions.

Strategy: Depending on your goals, you might want to examine your allocation annually—or at least every time there is a shift in the investment markets—to see if the mix still makes sense for you.

If the market makes you nervous, change the allocation by adding new money to bonds and cash.

Pay particular attention to your allocation after a long rally in the stock market. Maybe you started with 50% of your assets in stocks. Now, after a long market run-up, rising prices have pushed that stock allocation to 65% of assets. Take profits to restore your allocation to the way you want it to be.

•**Invest in foreign markets now.** Economies around the world move at different paces...and so do international stock markets.

Example: The Japanese economy and the Japanese stock market stayed weak when the

US economy and the US stock market were booming.

Strategy: If you believe the US stock market is turning sluggish, shift money to foreign stock markets that are doing better. Most investors will be better off buying shares in a foreign stock mutual fund.

Important: Pick foreign mutual funds that only invest overseas. Global funds invest internationally and in the US—the market you want to avoid.

If you are a more sophisticated investor, you can invest directly in foreign stocks through American Depositary Receipts (ADRs). They represent shares of foreign companies but trade on US stock exchanges. Any stockbroker can sell them to you.

• **Use investment money to pay off debts.** This offers a better return on your money than investing in a stagnant stock market. It is also better than putting the money in a low-return bank account. The higher the interest rate on the debt, the better the payoff to you.

• **Invest the money in your home.** Studies show that money spent on a new kitchen, master bathroom or extra room can add to the value of your house on a dollar-for-dollar basis.

• **Invest in yourself.** Use money that might have gone into stocks to take courses that will improve your skills and learning potential. Adding to your education could help you find a new, better job. You could also use the money to launch a part-time or sideline business, which could grow into a full-time venture someday.

• **Give away the money.** Anyone can give $10,000 to anyone else each year and not incur a federal gift tax. Once the money is given away, it is out of your estate and your income taxes forever.

Strategy: Use the money to create custodial accounts for college-bound youngsters age 14 and older. At age 14 and beyond, income from the custodial account is taxed at the child's lower tax rate. If you hold appreciated stock and sell it, you'll be hit with a capital gains tax at a rate as high as 28%. If you give it to a child in a low tax bracket, the child can sell it and pay taxes at a 15% tax rate.

Warning: Never give away money you might need for your own security. Examine your finances—with the help of a financial adviser—before giving any money away to make certain you can spare it.

Source: Laurence I. Foster and Thomas J. Hakala, partners in the personal financial planning practice of KPMG Peat Marwick LLP, the accounting and consulting firm, 345 Park Ave., New York 10154.

Is it Time for Smaller Stocks?

This year's big bull market has been led by larger companies, with smaller stocks not doing as well. But as the economy slows, smaller stocks should do better. *Reason:* They are less directly tied to economic cycles and less dependent on exports, which can fall steeply in a recession or slowing economy.

Source: David J. Corcoran, president, York Securities, discount brokerage in New York.

Protective Options Versus Stop-Loss Orders

Better than stop-loss orders for knowledgeable investors—*protective options. Example:* If a stock's share price has moved from $30 to $50, buy a put option exercisable at $45. This gives you the right to sell the stock at $45 anytime until the option expires. If the stock keeps going up, you still own it and are still making profits—minus the price you paid for the put. If it drops, no matter how far, your price of $45 is protected. *Alternative:* Sell the stock at $50 and buy a long-term call option (one-year) exercisable at $50. This guarantees you can buy the stock for $50 plus the price paid for the call option. If the price drops, you need not exercise the option.

Source: Gary Lahey, professional securities trader, Chicago Board Options Exchange.

Mutual Fund Investing's Seven Deadly Sins

Mutual fund investing is so simple that many people convince themselves they can outsmart the markets.

Bad move. The only way to build wealth with mutual funds is to avoid the urge to be recklessly aggressive or to second-guess major moves in the economy.

These are the biggest mistakes being made now by mutual fund investors...

Error: Avoiding stock funds because you think they're too risky for you. By now, most people realize that stocks are an important part of every portfolio. The big mistake they make is not putting enough into stocks.

Most investors in their 40s and 50s should have at least 60% of their portfolio in equities. For younger people with a longer investment horizon, the portion in equities can approach 100%.

Error: Avoiding the stock market when it's high. The simple fact is that the market is always too high. If you invest the same amount consistently—once a month or once a quarter—you'll do well over the long term, regardless of how the market is doing at any given time.

The lesson: Don't base fund investments on emotion or guesswork. Invest according to your schedule. If now is the time of month or the quarter when you typically buy shares, just do it, even if the market is high. In the long run, stock prices will be even higher.

Error: Following the leader. Financial magazines pour praise on whichever mutual funds and fund managers are hot. Lately the hot sector has been technology funds. Before that it was emerging markets. Before that—gold.

Before you buy specific funds, select the types of funds you must own to achieve your long-term goals. The younger you are, the more risk you can take. Such funds include those that invest internationally or in small, little-known companies. Invest in those funds regularly.

Error: Worrying about asset selection, rather than asset allocation. In a study of the performance of large pension funds, researchers found that decisions about how people divided their money among stock funds, bond funds and cash accounted for 85% of results.

Meanwhile, asset selection—picking individual securities—only contributed to 20% of performance. This adds up to more than 100% because market timing accounted for a negative 5% of results.

Result: Asset allocation—how you divide your assets among different types of funds—is much more important than picking the next hot fund.

Error: Failing to rebalance when markets surge. Suppose the perfect portfolio mix of stocks and bonds for you is 50% stocks and 50% bonds. This means half of your portfolio should be made up of stocks, and half bonds. If the value of your bond fund declines, and bonds now make up only 40% of your portfolio's worth, you must realign the assets.

Strategy: Put your monthly or quarterly investment into bonds—and even trim profits from stocks—to bring your holdings into balance. When bonds bounce back, trim them in favor of stocks.

This is not a guarantee that you will buy low and sell high—but it is a strategy to help you sell when things go up and buy when they go down.

Error: Rebalancing too often. Adjust your mix no more than twice a year, as you review your overall portfolio. Don't act until one asset class is around 10% out of whack, or else the market's volatility will whipsaw you.

Error: Taking excessive risk. This is always tempting in a bull market. The rising tide lifts nearly all stocks, but some inevitably rise higher than others. Hold the risk of your overall portfolio to your personal comfort level.

Source: Gerald Perritt, portfolio manager of Perritt Capital Growth Fund, which has returned 14.5% compounded annually over the past five years. He is author of several books on mutual fund investing, including *Mutual Funds Made Easy!* Dearborn Financial Publishing.

How to Put Together The Right Mutual Fund Portfolio for You

You can be a great mutual fund investor. To me, that means two things.

First, focus on the proven winners, funds with relatively low risk and relatively high reward potential.

Second, allocate assets aggressively toward equity funds.

Let's lay the foundation for successful mutual fund investing.

You're younger than you think. If you're under 85, you're a long-term investor. If you need income, sell portions of your holdings to meet living expenses.

Important: You don't have to dramatically change your investment strategy because you've reached a certain age.

•**Avoid bond funds.** Bond funds are sold hard by brokers—but these funds are never going to deliver what you really want...*a high total return over time.* They're not a good long-term investment because rates fluctuate.

Strategy: If you want to have money in cash, use either money market funds or five-year Treasury notes.

Strategy: There are better ways to invest for income. They include great utility funds and real estate funds.

•**Own the right number of funds.** If you have $20,000 or more to invest, own at least six funds. Diversification is a powerful tool. But no matter how much you're investing, never own more than 12 funds. With too many—your odds of beating the market almost certainly disappear. You're becoming an index-fund investor. *Note:* If you owned all the growth-stock mutual funds, your performance would be almost identical to the S&P 500.

Better: Own an S&P 500 Index Fund instead. Its expenses are much lower.

•**Ignore your broker.** Brokers like to sell the high-commission funds and heavy-load funds that eat into your profits. Often, these funds are not sold based on merit. And—brokers are encouraged to sell bond funds.

•**Avoid growth**—and aggressive growth—funds for now, at least. I'm worried by these funds' emphasis on technology. *Better:* At this stage of the US bull market, value funds and small-cap funds are more attractive.

•**Be a global investor.** Even though some international funds—particularly those with big holdings in Latin America—got crushed last year, I still think a smart mutual fund investor should have up to 50% of his/her money abroad.

That's where strong long-term growth will be for decades.

•**Consider using sector funds.** Do this only if you use some market timing discipline. You can use sector funds without swinging for the fences.

Examples: Utilities, health care, telecommunications and real estate look good right now.

Source: William E. Donoghue, president of *Donoghue On-Line.* Mr. Donoghue is the author of many investment books, including *William E. Donoghue's Mutual Fund SuperStars: Invest in the Best, Forget About the Rest.* Elliott & James.

Peter Lynch's Powerful Rules for Mutual Fund Investors

Making money investing in mutual funds isn't at all complicated. *Here are my simple rules...*

•**Forget about bond funds and hybrid funds.** If you're investing for 10 years or longer, stick with stock funds. Stocks have outperformed every other investment over time.

•**Pick funds with consistent annual returns.** Go with funds that have performed well over each of the past five—or 10—years. *Be sure that each fund's current manager is responsible for the record.*

•**Avoid funds with high annual expenses.** Over time, these expenses erode returns—and cause managers to take big risks to perform as well as peer funds with lower expenses.

•**Small-company funds beat big-company funds.** Small-cap funds have greater volatility, but over time they produce larger returns than large-cap funds. Look for a good small-cap fund whose portfolio matches the Russell 2000 small-cap index.

•**Don't play "musical funds."** Once you've chosen a good fund, stick with it.

Source: *Peter Lynch is one of the country's shrewdest stock-pickers. He is the former manager of the Fidelity Magellan Fund and coauthor of the new book* Learn to Earn: A Beginner's Guide to the Basics of Investing and Business. *Fireside.*

Answers to Your Big Questions about Mutual Funds

Investors are pouring big money into mutual funds. Yet I'm always surprised at how little most people know about the funds in which they invest.

Here are answers to the most common questions I'm asked by average fund investors.

Do I really have to read a fund's prospectus before investing? Yes. Though a common prospectus can be complex, the good news is that you don't have to read all of it.

There are only two sections that are vital to making investment decisions. The rest is often information the fund has to mention in order to fulfill its legal obligations. What to read...

•**Statement of objectives.** This outlines the types of investments the fund makes, such as in large- or small-capitalization companies, bonds or international stocks. It also discusses the strategy the fund's manager uses, such as investing for capital appreciation or for income. The statement is usually found in the first few pages of the document.

While this section of the prospectus is usually in plain English, some fund families group all or many of their funds in the same document. Be sure to look for the statements that relate to the specific funds in which you are interested.

Warning: Funds have been known to stray from their stated objectives and invest in secu-

rities other than the ones described in their prospectuses.

Solution: Make sure the fund is buying the types of securities you expected. You can do this either by monitoring its annual, semiannual or quarterly reports...or by calling the fund company and asking for the most recent top 10 holdings. You can be misled easily by the name of the fund or its advertising.

A fund's stated objectives will at least give you an idea of what you could be getting into.

•**Fee table.** This discloses all the costs you'll pay to buy and own mutual-fund shares. If it's a load fund, the table will tell you what the charges are when you first buy into and/or sell off shares.

It will also tell you if there are any management and 12b-1 fees, which are deducted from your account annually and are used to pay for marketing, distributing and advertising. The fee table is on page two or three of the prospectus.

Important: Avoid funds that have total operating expenses of 2% or more for a domestic equity fund—slightly higher for an international fund...or 1% or more for a bond fund. This information can be found in the fee table or by calling the fund company.

How many funds should I own? That depends on how much money you have to invest.

If you only have a few thousand dollars to invest, buy one or two asset-allocation funds. They invest in a combination of stocks, fixed-income securities and cash—depending on the state of the markets.

If *you have* a much larger sum and you want to be well diversified, investing in 10 funds is not out of line—provided there is little or no duplication in the investment style and portfolios of the funds.

What red flags should I look for when considering a fund? To me, the most important reason to avoid a fund is poor performance. However, one year doesn't tell you enough about a fund's performance. Three to five years is a much better indicator.

We've all heard the adage that past performance is no guarantee of future results...and that's certainly true. But, for the most part, it's the only thing investors really have to go on.

Strategy: Always compare a fund's performance with its peer-group average. You can check rankings in an independent fund research service such as *The No-Load Fund Investor*...or in newspapers and magazines. Avoid a fund if it has underperformed or performed wildly throughout its history.

Do bond funds make sense? And if so, when? Bond funds make the most sense for conservative investors who want to diversify their bond holdings—in other words, when you want to own a lot more types of bonds than Treasuries.

The argument can also be made that riskier types of bonds, such as corporate bonds or high-yield bonds, are best purchased through a mutual fund. That's because the fund can buy far more types of issues than you can hold as an individual.

In addition, it is often difficult for individuals to buy small amounts of these types of bonds through their brokers.

Beware: Bond funds aren't actually bonds. And bond-fund managers don't necessarily buy and hold each issue the way individuals would hang onto them—collecting interest and getting back the principal. Instead, bond-fund managers are constantly trading and, therefore, are subject to the daily price fluctuations that typically occur in the bond market.

Though bond funds provide more stability than stock funds, there are many different types of bond funds with different types of risk.

Example: A Treasury bond fund has no credit risk—but it has high interest rate risk. Other funds, such as high-yield bond funds, have less interest rate risk but high default risk.

Municipal bonds are best for those people looking for tax-advantaged investments. Funds are often a great way to invest in municipal bonds because you can diversify your credit risk and because municipal bonds are often hard for individuals to obtain.

Source: Sheldon Jacobs, editor and publisher of *The No-Load Fund Investor,* Box 318, Irvington, NY 10533. He is author of *Sheldon Jacobs' Guide to Successful No-Load Fund Investing* and *The Handbook for No-Load Fund Investors.*

Mutual Fund Trap

While banks may pressure you to buy their mutual funds, that's not the best place to buy them.

Reasons: Banks collect fees from the mutual fund companies to sell their products. The bank may be more influenced by the prospect of this fee than the fund's performance. That cost (load) comes out of your pocket in the form of higher fees, lower returns—or both. You will do better buying no-load funds.

Note: Mutual funds purchased from banks are not federally insured like other bank deposits. So you are not buying safety when you purchase mutual funds from a bank.

Source: Martin Weiss, president of Weiss Research, Inc., and editor of *Safe Money Report,* 4176 Burns Rd., Palm Beach Gardens, FL 33410.

No-Load Stocks Can Be Bargains

They are sold by companies to investors—bypassing brokerage commissions. Among the top firms offering no-load shares are Exxon, McDonald's, Mobil and Procter & Gamble. Many smaller, riskier firms also sell stocks directly to investors. *Helpful:* Buy directly if you want to accumulate the stock over a long period. No-load stocks are usually tied to dividend-reinvestment plans—dividends are used to buy additional shares. Initial investment may be only $100 or $250. *Information:* Contact the company directly or write to DRIP Investor for a free list of no-load stocks.

Source: Charles Carlson, editor, *DRIP Investor,* 7412 Calumet Ave., Hammond, IN 46324.

Best Performance Figures

Morningstar's Don Phillips advises investors to look at six-year annualized returns when sizing up a fund's performance—not five-year returns. *Reason:* Five-year returns no longer include the third quarter of 1990—the last time the S&P had a double-digit quarterly decline, dropping by 13.7%. By asking the fund for six-year data, you will have a much more realistic picture of its long-term record.

Source: Don Phillips, publisher of *Morningstar Mutual Funds,* an independent newsletter that evaluates mutual funds.

What's in a Name?

Mutual fund names can mask a fund's true investment strategy.

Example: Kemper's Small Capitalization Equity Fund sounds like it invests in small-company stocks. Yet the median market capitalization of the stocks it owns is close to $1 billion. Most true small-cap stocks have median capitalizations of around $250 million.

Self-defense: Read the fund's financial statement carefully...use Morningstar reports to compare the fund with others in its cate-gory. If there are big differences, the fund may not be right for you.

Source: Alan Lavine, author of *Getting Started in Mutual Funds.* John Wiley & Sons.

A Family Investment Club

A family investment club is a great way to teach children about money—and it can be quite profitable. *How it works:* Each family member contributes a specific amount of money—as little as $5—each month, regardless of how the market is doing. Family members help research stocks by reading financial publications and keeping abreast of the news. They also vote on which stocks to buy. *Additional benefit:* Open the club up to relatives, such as cousins and grandparents, and you'll bring your entire family together.

Source: For free information on how to start a family investment club: National Association of Investors Corp. (NAIC), 711 W. Thirteen Mile Rd., Madison Heights, MI 48071.

10

Retirement Planning

New Definitions of Retirement
Edith Weiner, Weiner Edrich, Brown, Inc.

A dramatic revolution in how Americans spend their "mature" years is well under way. In contrast to the traditional image of the avuncular, graying grandparent who spends endless hours crocheting or playing golf, today's seniors are aging energetically and productively.

Reason: While people who reached retirement age at the usual 65 in the 1950s and 1960s expected no more than 10 or 15 years of retirement, and expected little more from those years than quiet time, people today live longer, so they expect up to 25 years of retirement. This is often the case despite the fact that more and more people are forced to work beyond the age of 65 due to the financial pressures of increasingly uncertain Social Security benefits…reduced pension benefits…and the high cost of maintaining a lifestyle of abundant amenities.

Adding fuel to the revolution is the growing complexity of senior demographics. The older population is less and less characterized by graying married couples spending their mature years in blissful serenity. Instead, we see a growing number of single seniors who keep working well into their 70s…as well as a large population of divorced retirees…and more and more people in their 60s and 70s whose children have moved back in with them.

Result: There is increased diversity in the lifestyles of older Americans. With less pressure to conform to society's conventional expectations that retirees make themselves "scarce," seniors can now more comfortably pursue activities that were largely unheard of as recently as a decade ago. These activities include starting second careers…taking academic courses…starting businesses… entering politics…spearheading new volunteer projects and community programs.

The economy will benefit from the emergence of a new highly experienced entrepreneurial class. And the nonprofit community will benefit from the growing contribution of hardworking and energetic mature volunteers.

Bottom line: As the new millennium approaches, retirement will less and less be defined in traditional terms. Instead, people in their 60s, 70s and beyond will be considered to be living the third phase of their lives, following youth and middle age. These years will be exceptionally productive and will transform society's perception of oldness to one of vibrancy, mental clarity and creativity.

How to Make the Most of IRAs

The 401(k) plan has gotten so much attention lately that many people have overlooked or neglected their Individual Retirement Accounts (IRAs).

Both are valuable investment tools for a wealthy retirement, so you may need to reassess your IRA investment strategy.

The rules:

If you or your spouse are not covered by a qualified plan at work you can make a tax-deductible contribution of $2,000 a year—regardless of how much is earned. The earnings in IRA investments accumulate tax-free until they are withdrawn starting at age 59½.

You can still contribute to an IRA if you are covered by a qualified plan, but you begin to lose the deduction if your income exceeds $25,000 (single) or $50,000 (married).

Determining how to invest your IRA money is very important. Here is a step-by-step guide on how to do it right...

•**View your IRA as just one part of your overall financial picture.** Some people think you should manage your regular taxable investments one way, your 401(k) another way and your IRA yet another way. I disagree. You need to look at all your investments as a single portfolio and formulate an investment plan for the entire pot.

The biggest decision you need to make is how much money to put in stocks and how much money to put in bonds.

Our idea of a super-conservative portfolio: 60% stocks and 40% bonds. Younger people in their 30s and 40s can put even more in stocks.

•**Map out an investment strategy for your 401(k) plan**—before your IRA. The investment choices in your 401(k) plan are determined by your employer, and the menu is much more restricted than for an IRA, where you are able to invest in just about anything you wish.

Since many 401(k) plans today offer a wide range of stock-fund choices, spread your stock investment among several funds, with an emphasis on aggressive growth and international funds.

•**Map out a strategy for your IRA. We suggest growth-stock funds.** In this category, we are especially partial to index funds, which match the securities in a given index, such as the Standard & Poor's 500...and don't try to outperform the market by constantly shuffling their holdings.

•**Set up an automatic investment plan with a mutual fund**, and have the fund debit your bank account by $166.66 a month, which is equivalent to $2,000 a year.

•**View your IRA as an insurance policy.** If you're a young family just starting out, and only have enough money either to make an IRA contribution or begin saving for college in a taxable fund, contribute to the IRA. Even though you'll have to pay a penalty if you withdraw funds early from an IRA to pay for college, you'll also have the benefit of generating tax-free earnings for 18 years.

Source: Harold Evensky, principal of Evensky, Brown & Katz, a fee-only financial planning firm in Coral Gables, FL.

401(k) Double Check

The 401(k) plan is the fastest-growing employee benefit in the US. About 25 million workers participate in 210,000 plans. That's more than a six-fold increase over the level of participation just 10 years ago.

While by now most people understand the big benefits of 401(k) investing, few are aware of the hidden traps. *Here's what to do...*

•**Make sure your employer is actually forwarding your contributions to the 401(k) plan.** Just because you have authorized your company to reduce your salary by a set amount each pay period does not mean it is happening.

Reason: Sloppy bookkeeping or administrative work is usually the culprit. Both problems occur more frequently at smaller companies rather than larger ones.

It is not uncommon to discover that even though your salary is being reduced for 401(k) contributions, none have been made...or that the contributions are less than you authorized.

Self-defense: Pull out your last quarterly or semiannual 401(k) statement. Match up the employee contributions shown on the statement with the 401(k) deductions shown on your payroll stub. The amounts should agree. If they don't, contact the plan administrator. In many cases, the administrator is in the human resources department at your company.

Important: If your plan administrator or employer is unwilling to correct the problem, you have certain rights that are described in the plan document, including complaining to the US Department of Labor and the Internal Revenue Service, which jointly oversee 401(k) plans.

•**Make sure that you have not contributed more than the legal maximum allowed.** This year, the most you can contribute is $9,240. But if, for example, you instructed your employer to reduce your salary by $200 a week, you would exceed the limit before the end of December.

Self-defense: Review your payroll stubs as soon as they arrive. Keep an eye on the total contribution to be sure you don't exceed $9,240. If you have already exceeded it, ask your company to reverse some of your contributions. There is a grace period during which your employer can "back out" your excess contributions without penalty.

•**Make sure your company is forwarding your contributions to the plan in a timely manner.** Even though your company reduces your salary every week or month by the amount you authorized, it may not immediately turn over that money to the plan. Some employers can hold employee contributions for up to 90 days after they receive the funds. I believe that holding employee contributions for even one month is too long.

Self-defense: Complain to the plan administrator, and share your concerns about the lag in investing employee contributions with your coworkers.

If your company knows that employees are scrutinizing the administration of its 401(k) plan and that delays in investing employee contributions are affecting morale, the situation may improve.

•**Make sure the matching contributions your employer promised are actually being made**—if, of course, your company has a matching contribution plan. The most common company matching contribution is 50 cents for each dollar an employee contributes—up to 6% of your salary.

Problem: Sometimes the employer contributions are not made—or if they are, they are not made in accordance with how the company said they would be made.

Self-defense: Pull out your 401(k) statement, and check the employer contributions box. If nothing is listed—or if the amounts seem small—ask the plan administrator for an explanation.

Source: Avery Neumark, an attorney and accountant who is director of employee benefits and executive compensation for Rosen, Seymour, Shapss, Martin & Co., 757 Third Ave., New York 10017. He is also a commissioner of the New York State Insurance Fund, which writes workers' compensation policies for business.

Secrets of a Secure Retirement From Ted Benna— Inventor of the 401(K)

It is easy to ignore the need to save for retirement. Current demands on your income are probably high, while retirement money won't be needed for years.

But—unless you begin to take seriously the need to save aggressively for retirement, you can expect a dramatically different lifestyle in your later years.

My strategies for changing the way you think about saving for retirement...

•**Assume you are going to retire tomorrow—even if you're only 35.** Think about this every time you pay your bills. It will force you to address the issue regularly rather than blocking it out of your mind. It will also encourage you to make retirement savings a priority—not an afterthought.

Formula: If you began saving 10% of your annual income in your 30s, continue saving at least this much each year.

But if you're in your 40s or older and haven't yet set anything aside for retirement, you must save 15% to 20% of your gross income.

People in their 50s who haven't saved a significant amount should save 30%.

How to tell if you are on track: By the time you reach age 50, you should have accumulated at least two times your annual earnings. Include your regular investment accounts and the balances in any contributor retirement program such as a 401(k), 403(b), SEP or IRA.

•**Don't expect to receive much in benefits from Social Security.** The Social Security system is deteriorating. And it is under attack from Congressional budget cutters. Whatever happens, the system will almost certainly be unrecognizable within 25 years.

Don't count on Social Security at all if you are younger than age 50...and expect a significant reduction in benefits if you are between ages 50 and 62.

•**Expect to live much longer than you think you will.** A big argument among people who avoid saving aggressively for retirement is that they probably won't live beyond age 75.

Reality: The average person who retires today at age 65 should count on spending about 25 years in retirement, since we're all more conscious of our health than ever before and medical technology improves each year.

While life expectancy tables insist that most people will live until age 79, this is determined by statistical projections rather than by what actually happens to any one individual. Personally, I would like to be surprised by living 10 or 15 years longer than anyone expected. But I wouldn't want to be surprised by not having enough money to live comfortably during those extra years.

•**Expect that inflation will continue to be modest**—but that it will continue. Recently, the annual inflation rate has hovered between 3% and 4%. From 1936 through 1993, it averaged 4.2%.

Inflation doesn't stop when you stop working. While a 3.5% inflation rate may not have a big impact during your first years of retirement, it can have a devastating effect 10 to 15 years later.

Example: Someone who retires with $75,000 in income this year would need about $127,000 in income 15 years from now to enjoy the same standard of living at a 3.5% inflation rate. If that person lived to age 90, he/she would need around $300,000 per year.

The combined impact of increasing longevity and continuing inflation means you'll probably need more than you think to support your retirement.

•**Formulate a realistic investment strategy.** The rate of return you get on your investments is the single most important factor that will influence the size of your retirement nest egg.

Solution: Aim to earn at least 9% on your investments over the long haul to make your savings last when you retire.

While 9% may seem high if you're used to sticking with bank CDs, historical analysis has shown that most prudent investors who are willing to put at least 60% of their money into solid growth stocks or stock funds can achieve a 9% return over most periods of 10 years or longer.

Risk-free investments should be kept to a minimum in retirement. In the past, retirees have favored such a conservative approach because they didn't want to run the risk of losing any principal.

Problem: Such a strategy may have been reasonable when people could expect to live for only 10 or 12 years after retiring. But this approach is dangerous these days, when many live much longer. Such conservative investments have low rates of return that don't keep up with inflation and taxes over the long term.

Better strategy: The only way to keep ahead of these twin threats is to have an investment strategy that calls for putting a significant part of your portfolio into common stocks or into mutual funds that invest in stocks.

Over the last 69 years, the average annual return on stocks was 10.2%, compared with 3.7% for short-term investments such as bank CDs...4.8% for long-term bonds...and 8.5% for balanced portfolios consisting of 60% stocks and 40% bonds. While the differences between these rates of return may seem modest, a few percentage points of difference can work out to hundreds of thousands of dollars more in your retirement nest egg over several decades.

• **Try to resist early retirement.** During the last decade, there has been a push by corporations to cut costs by reducing the size of their workforce.

About 25% of all employers with pension plans offered some sort of early retirement deal between 1991 and 1993...and most convinced their eligible workers to accept the offers.

Problem: While generous severance packages may make the first few years of early retirement fairly easy financially, the long-term financial stability of retirees is in jeopardy.

Because of the combined threat of lower Social Security benefits and reduced private pensions, there just won't be enough retirement money available to provide comfortable incomes for most people who want to retire before age 65.

If you start working at age 21, retire at 55 and live until age 85, you'll spend almost half of your adult life in retirement. You should be sure that you can count on having enough income to spend it right.

• **Think long and hard before starting your own postretirement business.** Unless you spent a lot of time developing your sideline business before you retired, you may discover that starting up your own company late in life is the quickest way to exhaust your retirement nest egg. Succeeding as an entrepreneur requires different skills than it takes to be an employee of a large company. It is estimated that one of every five new businesses fails during the first five years of operation. Yet it is estimated that 20% of retirement-age people plan to start their own businesses or to work for themselves.

To safeguard your financial future, do not use your retirement savings to start a new enterprise or to cover your living expenses while you're attempting to do so. Remember, the new business is supposed to be a substitute employment, not a money drain. If it does not generate the level of income you expected, lower your standard of living to fit your new situation rather than drawing down retirement resources that you will need when you are no longer working.

Source: R. Theodore Benna, who in 1980 discovered a little-noticed tax-law provision that led to the creation of the 401(k). He is president of The 401(k) Association, which helps members maximize their plans, 1 Summit Sq., Doublewoods Rd. and Rte. 413, Langhorne, PA 19047. He is author of *Escaping the Coming Retirement Crisis.* Piñon Press.

Lump Sum or Monthly Annuity Distribution... Which One is Better?

Should I take my retirement money as a lump sum? Annuity? Many pensions offer retirees two forms of payment—a little at a time through an annuity or as a lump sum. This decision could be the most important financial decision of your life—but it is very hard to get an objective opinion.

Reason: The annuity is an insurance- industry product, so people in the insurance business are likely to tell you to take your pension as an annuity. People in the investment management business will tell you to take it as a lump sum and roll the money over into an investment account.

The answer to this question draws attention to an important lesson. There are few all-or-nothing decisions in personal finance. People who are willing to sacrifice some potential income for the assurance that they will receive steady payments are best served by taking part of the money as a lump sum and part as an annuity.

Strategy: If you retire at or before the normal retirement age, you generally should take the lump sum. Then when you are older, there is nothing to prevent you from investing in an annuity.

There are some very innovative annuity products being developed, such as immediate payment variable annuities. Your money is invested in mutual funds, and you begin receiving investment payments immediately.

In a few years, you probably will have a better choice of annuity products than what is available now. If you can't wait, shop around now. Don't just take the annuity your employer or broker offers. This is a competitive business, and once you buy, it's difficult to change your mind.

Important: If you or your spouse go into a nursing home, your lump sum distribution would have to be used to help pay nursing home costs. A lot of people in that situation wish they had chosen an annuity for part of their savings because nursing-home care has wiped out their long-term savings. An annuity at least assures a continuing income—for your spouse and for you if you leave the nursing home.

Source: Jonathan Pond, president of Financial Planning Information Inc., 9 Galen St., Watertown, MA 02172, and author of *The New Century Family Money Book.* Dell. He appears regularly as a commentator on PBS-TV's *Nightly Business Report.*

Retirement Investment Strategy Formula

Ignore the common advice to keep a portion of your investment portfolio in stocks equal to 100 minus your age. *Example:* A 65-year-old using that formula has 35% of his/her investments in stocks (100 – 65 = 35).

Problem: As people live longer, this strategy has become too conservative. Retirees need to continue increasing—not just preserving—their capital until at least their mid-70s.

New rule of thumb: Multiply your age by 80% (0.80), and put at most that percentage in bonds or bond funds and the rest into stocks. *Example:* A 65-year-old should have at most 52% of his investments in bonds (65 x 0.80 = 52), and at most 48% (100 – 52 = 48) in stocks.

Source: Jonathan Pond, president, Financial Planning Information Inc., 9 Galen St., Watertown, MA 02172.

Your IRA May Be Your Biggest Asset... Here's How to Make The Most of It

The first step towards getting the most from an IRA is to fund it fully. When you leave an employer, you may have the option of leaving your money in the employer's retirement plan or taking a lump sum distribution of your benefits and rolling it over into an IRA. If so, you're almost always better with the IRA. *Why:*

•**Security.** Many corporate pension plans are underfunded. Even if your employer's plan is fully funded, you can't be sure what its status will be years from now. With an IRA, you know your money is there. It's in cash, under your control and won't be put at risk by bad investments.

•**Investment control.** You can invest your IRA funds in almost any way you wish—aggressively, cautiously or taking advantage of special opportunities available to you. But funds left in an employer plan are controlled by the plan trustee. If you have any say at all about how the funds are invested, it's very, very limited.

•**Control over distributions.** A company pension plan typically will provide you with fixed annuity payments on a set schedule. But an IRA gives you many more choices about how to receive your money. *You can take...*

•The same type of annuity payout, or

•Minimum distributions to keep as much money as possible in the IRA for as long as possible to get larger, tax-deferred investment returns, or

•Early distributions in any amount you wish to meet personal needs.

Example: Your spouse is legally required to be your beneficiary of a company retirement account unless he/she signs a waiver of spousal rights. This can be a complicating factor when trying to leave funds to children—especially from a prior marriage.

•**Bequest planning.** If you have substantial savings and wish to leave some of them to children or grandchildren, an IRA offers great advantages over a company plan.

No such rule applies to IRAs. In fact, you can divide your funds among several IRAs, each with a different beneficiary. This is a clean way to distribute funds among heirs. It may provide children with tax-favored investment accounts from which they will reap benefits for their entire lives, as explained below. This isn't possible with funds left in a company plan.

Key: When you make a rollover to an IRA from an employer plan, set up a new IRA to hold the rollover funds. Don't mix the rollover money with funds in other IRAs.

It is possible that the state may have a law making IRA funds immune from creditor claims when the funds were received in a distribution from a qualified retirement plan. A segregated IRA is needed to be able to trace all funds back to a plan distribution.

Beneficiary planning:

After you've funded an IRA, to make the most of it—leave funds in it for as long as possible, to reap the greatest benefit from compounding tax-deferred growth.

Because mandatory IRA withdrawals are determined by life expectancy, you can use an IRA to build family wealth by naming the youngest beneficiaries to take the IRA—children or even grandchildren. *Payout rules:*

•**Child beneficiaries.** If you die before reaching your required beginning date (RBD) for taking mandatory withdrawals from the IRA—at age 70½—a child beneficiary can elect to take annual distributions from an inherited IRA over his own life expectancy. That is so even if this is 30 or 40 years or more. All the while, the account will reap tax-deferred investment earnings. It's easy to see that even a small bequest can build up to a huge amount when invested on a tax-deferred basis over such a period. If you do reach your RBD, having a child beneficiary reduces the minimum you must withdraw from the IRA each year because required distributions are computed on the basis of joint life expectancy. A nonspouse beneficiary is treated as being up to 10 years younger than the IRA owner for this purpose. The slower payout leaves more for the child to inherit—and again, once the child does inherit, further distributions are made over the child's own life expectancy, so funds can remain in the account for decades.

•**Spouse beneficiary.** Of course, you must provide for your spouse's financial security first. Here too, planning ahead is key to making the most of the IRA.

Typical: A surviving spouse takes an IRA as a beneficiary and simply receives payouts over his/her life expectancy. On the spouse's death, any amount remaining in the IRA is taxed and distributed to heirs. That's the end of the IRA benefit.

Better way: The spouse can elect to take an IRA as his own, rolling over the inherited funds into a new IRA opened in the spouse's name. The spouse can then name a child as a beneficiary to the account.

This creates the same benefits described above. Thereby the minimum required annual distribution is reduced. In addition—the child beneficiary eventually will inherit the IRA intact, take minimum payouts determined by his own life expectancy and receive many years—perhaps decades—of tax-deferred IRA earnings.

Critical: The election to treat an IRA that's inherited from a spouse as one's own is often overlooked, at great potential cost to the family.

Plan now so your spouse will know to make the election should the time come.

•**Joint beneficiaries.** If you wish a child to inherit IRA funds, do not name your spouse and the child as joint beneficiaries of one IRA which holds all your retirement money.

Trap: The spouse's much shorter life expectancy (shorter than the child's) is applicable to the child and will increase the child's mandatory payouts and leave less for the child.

Better: Open a separate IRA for each of your beneficiaries—spouse and children.

You can have as many IRAs as you wish. Fund them with different amounts, and transfer funds among them to reflect changing family circumstances until you reach your RBD for mandatory distributions.

You remain able to withdraw funds from any of the IRAs to meet your needs at any time.

An IRA may be the largest part of your estate, so it's important that IRA planning be combined with sound estate planning advice.

Trap: Many estate planning experts are not experts on the complicated rules governing IRAs. As a result costly mistakes take place.

Both these kinds of trusts are currently being used with increasing frequency by estate planners.

Revocable trusts keep assets out of probate and under professional management to protect them from financially inexperienced or "spend-thrift" heirs.

Q-tip trusts are used to provide for the financial security of a spouse while retaining control over the ultimate disposition of trust assets to children or other heirs.

Indeed, many estate planning advisers today almost automatically recommend that these trusts be used to hold family assets.

Problem: They can cause the loss of all future benefits from an inherited IRA.

Why: When an IRA owner dies, the life expectancy of a revocable trust or Q-tip trust generally becomes zero—so all the money in the IRA must be paid to the trust by no later than the end of the calendar year following the IRA owner's year of death. All is then subject to tax.

Also, a Q-Tip trust in a will is a revocable trust and the problems described above apply.

Q-tip trusts also face a second set of difficulties. They are required by the Tax Code to pay out all their income to the spouse beneficiary annually. When a trust fails to do so, its assets become ineligible for the marital deduction and are subject to estate tax.

But few if any IRAs have governing documents that require the distribution of all current income to a Q-tip trust. Thus, leaving such an IRA to a Q-tip trust will disqualify the trust and incur a big surprise tax bill.

Note: Voluntary distribution of all IRA income to the trust does not meet the requirements of the Tax Code. The IRA must be legally required to make such distributions. And even if an IRA should be required to pay out all current income to a Q-tip trust, the goal of leaving as much money as possible in the IRA for as long as possible would be defeated.

Source: Seymour Goldberg, professor of law and taxation, Long Island University and senior partner in the law firm of Goldberg & Ingber, 666 Old Country Rd., Garden City, NY 11530. Mr. Goldberg is the author of *A Professional's Guide to the IRA Distribution Rules*, Second Edition. New York State Society of Certified Public Accountants.

Don't Have Too Much Money in Your IRA

When IRA withdrawals exceed $150,000 per year, a 15% penalty tax applies.

Trap: If you roll over a large amount of money from a corporate retirement plan into an IRA and follow the standard strategy of keeping money in the IRA for as long as possible to reap tax-deferred investment gains, minimum distribution rules may force you to take withdrawals that exceed the penalty limit beginning at age 70½.

Planning: Examine your IRA account well before you reach age 70½—in your 50s is best. If there's a risk of having too much money in the IRA, plan earlier withdrawals to stay under the penalty limit and refrain from making further rollovers into an IRA.

Source: John Beatty, vice president and manager, private resources division, The Northern Trust Company, Chicago.

Review Your 401(k)

Review your 401(k) plan investments periodically. Change them as you grow older, recognizing that high-risk, high-return investments are more appropriate when you are young... when personal tolerance for risk changes—as when you inherit money or take on a new long-term obligation...when the current prices of stocks and bonds change so much that one becomes cheap relative to the other. But do not change investments to try to time the market... or follow the current "hot" trend or market adviser...or try to profit from what you think the market will do in the future. Your 401(k) account is for long-term investing—so manage it with a solid, stable long-term strategy.

Source: *Standard & Poor's 401(k) Planning Guide* by Alan J. Miller, CFA, New York financial adviser. McGraw-Hill.

Better Investments For Retirees

Many retirees forsake all possibility of financial growth by investing too much in CDs, bonds and bond funds.

Better: Invest in income-oriented funds that hedge inflation by emphasizing both growth and rising dividend income. Typically they invest in utilities, large-cap stocks and real estate investment trusts—quite safe but with some risk of principal.

Source: Jonathan Pond, CPA, president of Financial Planning Information Inc., Nine Galen St., Watertown, MA 02172.

To Retire Comfortably By the Age of 65...

To have at least $1 million by the time you retire at age 65, you'll need to save only $5,200 a year—if you start at age 30 and your money earns an average annual rate of 8.5%. If you're just getting started saving at age 40, you'll have

to sock away $12,700 a year...and at age 50, your annual savings would have to be $35,400.

Other benefit of early saving: You can earn an even higher return by putting more into the stock market—since over time your nest egg will most likely weather volatility.

Strategy: First set aside as much as possible in your 401(k)—up to $9,500 this year. Next, concentrate on your IRA—up to $2,000. Then, save for retirement outside of tax-deferred accounts. Pond's three favorite no-load growth funds now: Janus (800-525-6125)...T. Rowe Price Capital Appreciation (800-6385-660)... and Neuberger & Berman Focus Fund (800-877-9700).

Source: Jonathan Pond, president of Financial Planning Information Inc., Watertown, MA, and author of the *New Century Family Money Book.*

Preretirement Social Security Double Check

Verify your earnings record with the Social Security Administration every three years to be sure it doesn't contain errors. Call the Social Security Administration (800-772-1213) and ask for a free *Request for Earnings and Benefit Estimate.* Compare your listed earnings with your W-2s from the same years—you should have them attached to old tax forms. If you find errors, report them immediately and find out how to have them fixed. If you wait too long, they may not be correctable.

Source: Joel Lerner, author of *Financial Planning for the Utterly Confused.* McGraw-Hill.

Smarter 401(k) Investing

Working couples unable to fully fund both retirement plans should concentrate on maximizing contributions to the better one. Focus on plans at companies that make contributions ...that allow employees to control those contributions…where you intend to stay long enough to keep its contributions when you leave…that offer a wide range of investment options.

Source: Ted Benna, one of the foremost experts on retirement savings plans and president of The 401(k) Association, Langhorne, PA.

Examine Your 401(k) Plan

If the investment options it offers aren't sufficient, speak up and ask for others…if the plan provides projections of future earnings from investments, be sure they reflect what will be left after fees and management costs are subtracted and are expressed in today's dollars…compute what you'll keep from investments after paying tax on withdrawals, and see if it will be enough to live on.

Source: *Pensions in Crisis: Why the System Is Failing America and How You Can Protect Your Future* by Karen Ferguson, director, Pension Rights Center, Washington, DC. Arcade Publishing.

Planning Ahead— You and Your 401(k)

Don't withdraw money from your 401(k)—borrow it instead. Most companies allow plan participants to borrow up to half the amount in their 401(k)s—up to a maximum of $50,000.

Benefits: The loan interest rate is low—usually only one or two percentage points above the prime rate…you are required to pay back the loan within five years, so your nest egg is protected…and you are paying yourself back —not a bank—so you get to keep the loan principal plus interest.

Have the loan payments automatically deducted from your paychecks. You won't miss the money.

Dangers: If you leave your job, you'll probably have to pay the remainder of the loan in full—usually within six months. If you can't, the amount due will be deducted from your

plan benefit and, if you are under age 59½, you'll have to pay income tax on the loan plus a 10% penalty.

Source: Nancy Dunnan, author of *Dun & Bradstreet Guide to Your Investments 1995.* She also hosts a personal-finance talk show on public radio station WNYC in NY.

Retirement Savings Mistake

Many employees over age 40 who leave their companies use their lump-sum 401(k) distribution checks to pay bills.

Problems: If you're under age 59½, the lump sum will be taxed as much as 50%…and you will have spent your retirement savings.

Better: Always move the lump sum into a rollover IRA or a new 401(k) plan. If you need money, take out a home-equity loan or a 401(k) loan, or explore taking monthly distributions from your IRA—without tax penalty.

Source: Anthony Gallea, a senior portfolio manager at Smith Barney in Pittsford, NY, and author of *The Lump Sum Handbook.* Prentice Hall.

Best Places to Retire Overseas

Don't believe everything you hear about foreign retirement havens. Some spots that have long attracted American retirees have lost their appeal. On the other hand, some countries you probably never thought about have some terrific advantages.

When you consider overseas retirement, you'll obviously pay attention to features such as climate and cost of living. *But don't overlook…*

•**Acceptance by local residents.**

•**Easy travel access.** Some countries are nearly 24 hours away by plane.

•**High-quality medical services.**

•**Availability of inexpensive domestic help.**

•**Political stability.**

•**The presence of an American or nearly American lifestyle.** That usually requires democracy and a large middle-class population.

My favorite places for retirement, based on these criteria…

Portugal:

Portugal's best retirement spot is the Algarve —the southern part of the country. *The advantages:*

•**Climate.** The climate is typically Mediterranean, with long dry summers and showery winters.

•**Language.** Long a mecca for the British, the Algarve is a place where you can get along in English.

•**Cost of living.** You can get along on as little as one-third of what you'd spend at home. A three-bedroom house would cost $80,000–$150,000, and a couple can live comfortably for $1,800–$2,000 a month. That includes domestic help. Recreation opportunities include lots of tennis courts and golf courses.

Medical care isn't yet as good as it is in the US or even Uruguay (see below), but it's quickly improving. In an effort to attract retirees, the Portuguese government is building two hospitals in the area.

In the case of serious illness, however, excellent hospitals in several European capitals are only a short plane trip away.

Another big plus for the Algarve—its proximity to other European cities and to Gibraltar, where there are tax and investment opportunities for those who establish residency outside the US.

Potential drawback: Although the Portuguese are noted for their honesty, the same isn't true of a small fringe group that preys on the increasingly large influx of tourists.

Uruguay:

Yes, Uruguay. It is over 12 hours by plane from most US cities, but the country is a wonderful retirement haven.

Much of Uruguay has a climate similar to that of southern California's—dry and mild. Winters are slightly cooler, but since seasons are reversed, that gives retirees the opportunity to return to the US to enjoy its summer.

The country has an excellent medical system. One option is health-maintenance coverage for the equivalent of about $25 a month. The other option is to use private doctors, who charge only a small fraction of what you'd pay in the US. Most Americans would find the culture typically European. Music, theater and antique shopping abound.

•**Cost of living.** One-half to one-third of what it is in the US, and there's no income tax. There is, however, a small national sales tax and minimal property levies.

Potential drawback: Since not much English is spoken, a good knowledge of Spanish is virtually essential.

Venezuela:

While there is crime and poverty in Caracas …other parts of the country can be ideal retirement spots for Americans.

In many areas, the cost of living can be even lower than in Uruguay or Portugal.

•**Ciudad Bolivar**, a town with an ideal climate and beautiful setting near the mountains.

•**Merida**, a mile-high city with a spring-like climate year-round.

•**Tovar**, a town near Merida with German-Swiss influence.

With a sufficiency of English-speaking residents, these towns don't require an immediate knowledge of Spanish, although it's certainly useful for any longtime stay.

These and other towns have also been insulated from any of the disruptions that have resulted from the last two political coups in this country. And despite the political upheavals, there was no confiscation of property.

•**Venezuela's exotic terrain** provides nearby access to mountains, beaches and jungles.

•**Health care is excellent** in major cities, though perhaps not as good as in Europe, Uruguay or the US.

•**A cost of living** that's less than half of what it is at home.

Worth considering:

•**British Columbia.** Vancouver is a beautiful, cosmopolitan Canadian city in a country with excellent health care. Americans, however, may not like the rainy climate or the relatively high cost of living, at least when compared with alternatives in Latin America or Portugal.

•**Costa Rica.** Long a favorite of American retirees, the country rates high in nearly all criteria, especially the presence of an American lifestyle. *Drawback:* Crime is on the rise in some areas.

•**Ireland.** Most Americans wouldn't enjoy the cold, damp winters, and the cost of living is as high as in the US. But the country can be an especially exciting place to retire if you want to explore Irish history.

Source: Jane Parker, relocation consultant and coauthor of, *Adventures Abroad, Enjoying the Travel/ Retirement Option*, Gateway Books, 2023 Clemons Rd., Oakland, CA 94602.

The Common Mistakes Retirees Make When They Relocate

Mistake: Moving to a state or community because you have a good time there on vacation. This is one of the most common mistakes made by relocating retirees. They expect their permanent experiences to be extensions of their vacations.

Problem: When you're on vacation, you're typically seeing everything through rose-colored glasses and are not likely to see or admit drawbacks.

Solutions: Before you decide to move to a new area, spend a week or two there during the off-season. See if the weather is tolerable and if all the conveniences and services are available to you during those months.

Subscribe to the local newspaper, and follow events for six months. Are taxes rising? Has the local infrastructure kept up with growth? How's the crime rate? Is there enough to do in the off-season?

Mistake: Not fully understanding the impact of a new climate. Extremely warm or cold weather may seem manageable, but often it's more oppressive than most people realize.

Example: One of every three people who moves to Florida ends up leaving the state. Their biggest disappointments are the hot climate and the inability to generate a comparable income.

Solution: Once you've determined the year-round climate, ask yourself a series of questions:

•Do I want this weather all year?

•Will I miss the change of seasons?

•Can I handle months of high humid-ity or severe cold?

•Is this climate good for my health?

Mistake: Buying a house/condo that is too small.

Solution: Even if it is just you and your spouse, move to a house or apartment that has at least three bedrooms.

You'll want space for visiting children, grandchildren and friends. You may need extra closet space and even an office if you decide to continue working or if you want to generate some extra income.

Mistake: Letting friends influence where you decide to move. In an effort to be comfortable and happy, many retirees move to communities where their friends have already relocated. But you should not ignore important issues, such as cost of living and employment. While having a network of friends is important, it's not as critical as making sure you're happy where you'll be living.

Reason: Friendships come and go, but your surroundings will remain the same. Your friends can always visit you, or you can visit them.

Mistake: Underestimating the cost of the move. A relocation can easily cost $40,000 today, if you factor in the costs of buying and selling a home, changing health care policies, shipping a car or two, new appliances and improvements on the new place.

Taxes are also an important consideration. Before you settle on a place to relocate, find out how state income and property taxes compare with those you pay now and whether your pension will be exempt from state taxes.

Solution: Call your accountant or the state's Department of Taxation to see what rules apply in your case.

Source: Lee Rosenberg, CFP, retirement expert and author of *50 Fabulous Places to Retire in America* and *Retirement Ready or Not.* Career Press.

11

Enjoying Your Leisure

Secrets of Flea Marketing

Flea market shopping has its own set of rules. If you know them, you can increase your chance of finding a treasured item and avoid the risk of being overcharged or stuck with a fake.

Shrewd flea market shoppers have found items such as historic glassware, rare comic books, one-of-a-kind movie promotions, an original newspaper covering President Kennedy's assassination and jewelry that turned out to be set with diamonds.

Other savvy flea market shoppers routinely find valuable Hummel statuettes, historical firearms, and pet-oriented collectibles, dolls, vintage toys, musical instruments, patriotic items and even parking meters. Here is some guidance for newcomers to the world of flea markets from Harry L. Rinker, Jr., author of *The Price Guide to Flea Market Treasures*.

Look for flea markets with:

•**A high percentage of booths that are protected from the weather**…or a section of indoor booths. Their presence means the operator is attracting dealers who value their merchandise and who can afford to protect it.

•**Easy-to-see price tags on every item.** Their absence means that dealers charge a variety of prices, depending on what they think a given customer will pay.

•**Dealers who have neat, clean display cases.** It's an indication that the sellers themselves value the merchandise.

•**Lots of old furniture that is at least in fairly good condition**—not pieces quickly repaired just to put on display.

•**Several booths with jewelry dating from the turn of the century to the near present.** They're usually a signal that other high-value collectibles can also be found in the market.

Avoid markets with:

•**Booths that sell cheap, new items** such as gym socks and T-shirts. They're signs that the operator isn't interested in dealers who sell antiques or collectibles.

•**Reproductions and fakes**, such as copies of old door stops or cast-iron banks. They're more signs that dealers are unlikely to stock items of special interest.

The best:

•**Ann Arbor Antiques Market**, 5055 Ann Arbor-Saline Rd., Ann Arbor, Michigan 48103. About 350 dealers on third Sundays of the month—April through October, Box 1512, Ann Arbor, Michigan 48106.

•**Birmingham Fairgrounds Flea Market**, Alabama State Fairgrounds off Highway I-20. More than 600 dealers on the first weekend of the month, year-round. 800-362-7538.

•**Brimfield Market**, near Brimfield, Massachusetts. From 3,000 to 5,000 dealers for six days each month in May, July and September. 413-245-3591.

•**Cow Palace**, off Highway 101 near San Francisco. More than 350 dealers on weekends in February, May and August. 503-282-0877.

•**First Monday Trade Days**, downtown Canton, Texas. More than 4,000 booths Friday through Monday, year-round. 903-567-6556.

•**Portland Expo Center** near Portland, Oregon. About 1,250 dealers on weekends in March, July and October. 503-282-0877.

•**Renninger's Extravaganza** in Kutztown, Pennsylvania. More than 1,200 dealers, Thursdays through Saturdays in April, June and September. 717-385-0104.

Resources:

When you shop at a conventional store, you usually know something about it and have probably read a couple of advertisements that describe its merchandise. Ironically, few shoppers bother to get similar information before they go to a flea market.

Caution: Don't judge a flea market by the size of the ad it puts in trade publications. The best markets often do only modest advertising. There are also many regional flea market periodicals and guides. Ask local dealers for their names.

Negotiating:

•**Don't examine an item and then tell the dealer you're a collector.** That signals a great interest in the piece. Instead, tell the dealer you're considering buying it for, say, a relative.

•**If you can't agree on a price, come back at the end of the day** when the dealer is ready to close. No dealer likes to haul merchandise back home.

•**Ask for a receipt that fully describes the purchase.** Some dealers will refund your money if you later discover the merchandise is flawed (though not if you're merely dissatisfied with it). Without a receipt, you have little chance.

•**If the flea market is indoors**, ask to take the merchandise into the daylight. Artificial light often makes it hard to spot flaws, such as hairline cracks in glassware.

•**Befriend the dealers who sell you good merchandise.** If you give them a list of items you want, they'll often find them for you. Reciprocate by sending the dealers new customers.

Items to avoid:

•**Autographs.** Collecting them is a skilled art, best done through reputable autograph dealers.

•**Cheap infant's toys** that may have nostalgic value but which are also easy to fake.

•**Unlicensed sports paraphernalia.** A lot of it is poorly made.

•**Limited editions.** If you like the item, of course, buy it. But don't expect it to appreciate in value because of the supposedly small quantity that was made.

Caution: There's usually no way to tell an original from a fake unless you're knowledgeable about the type of merchandise. That means educating yourself.

Helpful: Collectors' clubs listed in trade publications that cover flea markets. These organizations can usually recommend books, courses and other materials that can help you learn more about a wide range of collectible items.

Source: Harry L. Rinker, Jr., author of *The Price Guide to Flea Market Treasures*. Wallace-Homestead Book Co.

What Casinos Don't Want You to Know

Even if you have never been to a casino, the odds are good you'll go some day. More than 90 million people visit US casinos each year.

And casinos are proliferating so fast that by the year 2000, 95% of all Americans will live within a three-hour drive of one.

If you do visit a casino—and you aren't an experienced gambler—keep these rules in mind...

• **Limit your games.** Only a few casino games are suitable for novice players. I list them below...and you should stick to them.

• **Learn the rules in advance.** Before you go, study the rules and learn the odds for any game you might want to play.

• **Limit your expectations.** If you're going simply because you like playing games, stay home and play a board game with friends. If you visit a casino, consider it a form of expensive entertainment in which the odds of winning are against you. Casinos aren't run for your benefit. They are run to make lots of money for the people who own them.

• **Leave when you're ahead.** With the odds always in the casino's favor, the longer you play, the more likely you will lose. If you win a reasonable amount, quit even if you only played for 10 minutes. If you don't, you will lose your winnings...and more.

Warning: Some people should never gamble. Don't do it if you can't afford any losses... and certainly don't do it if you've had problems with compulsive gambling before—losing more than you could afford or not knowing when to stop.

Games to avoid:

Every casino offers a variety of different games. *Some of the games—in particular, the following ones—should be avoided at all costs...*

• **Keno.** Casinos love it, and they provide players with comfortable chairs with arm rests, so that they'll stay and play a long time. That's because the house edge in Keno is high—25%. Over time, the casino will pay out 75 cents for each $1 bet. The payoff for picking a winning number is three-to-one...the odds of picking a winning number are four-to-one.

• **Roulette.** It's the slowest game in a casino, and the odds are 5.26% against you when the wheel has both a "0" and a "00." I always tell friends that instead of playing roulette, they should just mail the casino a check for the money they were bound to lose playing.

• **Big Wheel.** This is not found in every casino, which is just as well. The casino edge is around 15%.

• **New-fangled, exotic games.** The list is long and varies by casino.

General rule: If you've never heard of a game and don't know the rules or the odds, stay away from it no matter how enticing it looks.

Games to play:

An unsophisticated player should really only touch four games in the casino...

• **Slot machines.** They are mindless and demand no skill, so anyone can walk in the casino door and play. *Downside:* The casino usually has a 10% edge in slots.

Don't assume that if you almost won on one spin, you might then win on the next. Most slots contain a random number-generating chip, which determines by pure chance where the wheels will stop on each spin—even before you pull the handle.

Important: Play the maximum number of coins the machine will take. If the slot has four lines and it takes four quarters to activate all of the lines, put in four quarters. If you hit the jackpot and didn't put in all the coins you could have, you will be grossly disappointed.

• **Blackjack.** The advantage of blackjack is simplicity. All you have to know how to do is count to 21. The disadvantage is that the casino's edge is around 5%.

Strategy: The seats at blackjack tables are there because that hefty casino edge guarantees the longer you sit and play, the surer the casino will take your money. Play as long as you are winning. As soon as you stop winning, quit.

• **Craps.** This can be a very complicated game, and few people really know how to play it. But the casino edge is only 1.5%...and a very simple strategy can cut that edge to less than 0.05%.

From experience: Bet on the pass line if you think the shooter (the person throwing the dice) is going to win—and bet on the don't pass line if you think the shooter is going to lose. That reduces all the complexities of craps to a simple win-lose bet.

Helpful: People tend to get a big kick from throwing the dice. If you want to try it, go ahead. The dice don't know who is throwing them, and you won't change the odds on whether your bet wins or loses.

•**Baccarat.** Play is fast, and it can be intimidating for the unsophisticated player. Some casinos let you play for as little as $5.

Baccarat is a card game, but the rules don't matter much. All betting is either on bank or player. All you must do is pick one or the other. Put down $20, and say, *I'll bet bank.* That's all there is to it.

Important: Not only is baccarat simple to learn, but the house edge is small—about the same as craps.

Rules to play by:

To tip the odds in your favor, here are my commandments for making you a wiser casino gambler…

•**Never gamble when you're tired or unhappy…or feeling negative.** The danger is you'll try to boost your mood by making ever-bigger bets. That is suicidal. Don't count on gambling to change your attitude or your luck. See a movie until your mood improves.

•**Never gamble more than you can comfortably afford to lose.** Know your financial limits before you start, and stick to them. If losing anything more than $200 would hurt, take only $200 into the casino.

•**Never start gambling without setting a target** on the winnings—or losses—for you to quit. Set a target for how much in winnings it would take you to walk away satisfied…and a limit for the losses you will tolerate before quitting.

•**The longer you stay at a casino table,** the greater the risk you will walk away a loser. Never forget that you may have a lucky streak, but eventually the laws of probability will catch up with you. Quit while you're ahead. If you stay around, you will give back your winnings.

•**Stash your winnings.** Always place at least three-quarters of your winnings in a safe-deposit box at your hotel, where they'll be out of reach until you go home. If you win $1,000, put $750 beyond reach so you can take it home. If you lose the remaining $250, stop gambling.

•**Never play if you're angry.** You should stop immediately if something upsets you. If the dealer annoys you, walk away from the table. Angry people do dumb things.

•**Don't try to make up losses by doubling your bets.** Increase your bets when you are winning. Over time, the law of probability works. But in the short-run, weird things happen. You could lose on 20 straight bets. Let your winnings run…but limit your losses.

•**The real struggle in gambling isn't between you and the casino**—it is between you and yourself. The casino will always be there. But it's up to you to decide when you want to play. You should gamble only when you feel like it…and only when you can afford it.

Source: Lyle Stuart, veteran casino gambler, president of Barricade Books and author of *Winning at Casino Gambling.* Barricade Books. He has won as much as $200,000 in one day of casino gambling…but has lost as much as $100,000 another day.

Las Vegas Winner

To win in Las Vegas, play bingo. Since 1989, casinos have lost an average of 2.44% per year on bingo. *However:* Visitors rarely play bingo —it is the locals who are winning.

Source: Donald Currier, editor, *Las Vegas Insider*, Box 29274, Las Vegas 89126.

How to Become a Game Show Contestant— How to Win…too

Some people think that all they have to do to become a game show contestant is write to the address they see on TV.

When I was the contestant coordinator for *Jeopardy!*, we used to test 200 people a day who hoped to be on the show—and maybe we accepted two.

The odds were just as daunting when I worked on *Wheel of Fortune.* The other 99% of applicants never got a chance to be on the program, but many of them could have avoided rejection.

Here are six ways to improve your odds of becoming a game show contestant during the interview process...

•**Be realistic about your talents.** Choose your game show according to your skills. At every game show I've worked, people would come to auditions even though it was obvious this was not their show.

At *Jeopardy!* we had people come in and score a zero on the written test. They couldn't answer a single question.

Sitting on the couch at home, all game shows seem easy. That's the illusion. If people couldn't play along at home, they wouldn't watch.

But with five cameras, a studio audience and other competitors, it's not quite as simple. You need to be very good to hold up under that pressure. So on *Jeopardy!*, we made the written test to qualify as a contestant a bit harder than the actual questions in order to select only the best contestants.

If you're only competitive and not superior to the players you see on TV, you might not pass the test.

Strategy: Don't pick your show because it offers the most valuable prizes or even because it's the most fun to watch. There are word games such as *Wheel of Fortune*...trivia games such as *Jeopardy!* and *The Price Is Right*...and a wide variety of puzzle word games. Spend some time determining which category—and which game—caters to your strengths.

Note: The best-known shows are going to be the hardest to get on as a contestant.

•**Know your show.** Once you've selected a game show that's appropriate for your skills, watch it on TV for a while. Don't just try to answer the questions. Look for details, such as the jargon the contestants use.

Examples: If your show is *Jeopardy!*, practice putting your answers in question form and pay attention to the betting strategies. For *Wheel of Fortune*, the jargon is *I'd like to buy a vowel*—and *Come on, $5,000.*

These are the details to which the people playing at home tend to pay less attention than

the games themselves. But if you don't know them, they can hurt how you do at the audition.

•**Be personable.** Once you're in the audition, few things matter as much as your personality. A *Jeopardy!* contestant is very different from a *Price Is Right* contestant, but the basic element of pleasantness is always there.

•**Be as upbeat as possible.** The game show executives look for contestants who will make their programs seem exciting. Again, you need to know the show. If you're auditioning for *Jeopardy!*, you don't have to jump up and down ...but if you're aiming for *The Price Is Right*, you should jump.

•**Don't take anything for granted.** Even if you've already passed the written test and the audition and have been called to the studio, you can still be cut from the show—for just about any reason.

Example: On one program, a contestant's contact lens was causing him to blink too much during the rehearsal. The producer insisted we cut him to avoid the possibility it would happen during the show.

The studio is really the final interview. And even if you're simply phoning the show to confirm your rehearsal, be upbeat and energetic. Game shows have more than enough qualified potential contestants. Don't give them a reason to reject you.

While you can be rejected for any number of problems, game shows try to find a diverse group of contestants. You are not likely to be turned down on the basis of race, gender, age or occupation.

•**Take the process seriously.** Game shows seem lighthearted on television. That's the idea —they're supposed to be fun to watch. But game show producers take these shows very seriously.

Treat the show's application process as you would an interview for a job. Dress nicely for tests and the interview...be ready to display a knowledge of the show...and consider your responses to potential questions before you arrive.

Example: On many shows, the host asks the contestants about their occupations or families…or to relate an amusing anecdote. Those questions come from interviews the contestant coordinators conducted earlier in the process.

Have an interesting story or two prepared, but try to tell them with a degree of spontaneity, just as you would answer questions about yourself during a job interview. If you manage to survive the show's selection process, you earn the right to join the real competition—the game itself.

How to win at least something:

The skills and knowledge you'll need vary from show to show, but there are some strategies that will improve your odds of bringing home a prize.

•**Study the system of prize distribution** for the show in which you are interested. These distribution systems can be as different as the games themselves.

Examples: On *Jeopardy!*, only the winner keeps his/her cash. The other contestants receive parting gifts. But on *Wheel of Fortune*, all the contestants keep what they've won.

Consider the prize system when you're planning your strategy. If coming away with something is more important to you than actually winning the grand prize, you can improve your odds by selecting a game show that has more than one winner.

•**Consider your prize goals.** Are you happy with any award…or are you in it for cash only?

Many shows offer only merchandise—not cash—while nearly all shows give the losing contestants parting gifts. On some game shows, those gifts can be significant. So if you see victory slipping away, it might be worth angling for the second-place prizes.

All prizes, whether they are cash or merchandise, are considered earned income by the IRS—so they are taxed at the fair market value (the lowest price you may find in an ad or a store). If you win a $30,000 boat, your tax bill could reach five figures. Of course, you can choose to turn down a prize after the game, but that's probably not what you had in mind.

•**Be better prepared than your competitors.** If possible, familiarize yourself with the mechanical aspects of the game.

Example: One of our first $100,000 winners on *Jeopardy!* practiced at home with an impro-

vised buzzer to improve his timing. When he was on the game show, he was able to buzz in before the other contestants and that was a big part of his success.

Also, if there's a home version of the show available—either a board game or a computer game—buy it and play it often.

Source: Greg Muntean, a former game show contestant coordinator. He is coauthor of *How to Be a Game Show Contestant.* Ballantine Books.

Shrewder Lottery Playing

Most people who play the lottery either choose their numbers at random or plug in dates that have significance to them—anniversary dates or family birthdays.

Their assumption: Since winning numbers are chosen at random, there is no way to improve a player's chances.

In fact, mathematical strategies can make a huge difference in playing the lottery.

Key: Choose unpopular numbers that are not likely to be selected by other lottery players.

Result: While your chance of winning the jackpot remains the same, the amount you stand to win is much larger…since you will be splitting your prize with fewer other players.

In a "6/49" lottery (where the players choose six numbers between 1 and 49), there are about 14 million different combinations available. In a typical game, 20% of those combinations—2.8 million different plays—are selected by no one.

A shrewd lottery strategy will consistently land you within that 20% window, giving you a strong chance of pocketing the entire jackpot …should you win.

The larger the jackpot, the better your return on every dollar you wager.

Reason: A disproportionate number of the other bettors will be playing combinations that you will be avoiding. These are the unpopular numbers that you should be targeting when you play the lottery…

•**All numbers over 31,** for the simple reason that they will not be chosen by anyone playing birthdays or anniversary dates. At least four of your six choices on a ticket should be 32 or higher.

•**Numbers ending in 1, 2, 8, 9...and 0.** Most people tend to select numbers ending in 3 through 7. *Especially unpopular:* 10, 20, 30 and 40.

On the other hand, avoid playing the more popular numbers or combinations, including...

•**Multiples of 7,** which are favored by the superstitious who think seven is a particularly lucky number.

•**Single-digit numbers** (1 through 9). Use no more than one of these among your six choices. That's because large numbers of people choose them. If you win with these numbers, you will likely be sharing a jackpot.

•**Numbers that form vertical, horizontal or diagonal patterns** on your bet slip card. These are also quite popular, since random selection is governed by the eye, which moves in these directions.

•**The combination 1-2-3-4-5-6,** which may be the most popular combination of all.

Bottom line: By playing the least popular numbers, you can increase the amount of money you bring home by more than 600%.

Source: Alan Reiss, president of US Mathematical Labs, Box 76, Wayland, MA 01778. His company sells two mathematical tools for lottery players—a computer software program available for both the IBM and Mac and a mechanical "Win-Wheel"—to help people generate "original" sets of numbers unlikely to be selected by other players.

How to Bluff Like a Poker Pro

During the past 20 years, I've been associated with many of the best poker players in the world. All are outstanding bluffers.

That doesn't mean they bluff more than the average weekly player—just that they bluff more strategically. Experience teaches them when a bluff is likely to succeed and what psychological value it can have even if it fails. Best bluffing strategies:

•**Don't change your style when you bluff.** You can look your opponent in the eye or not

...chatter like crazy or keep silent—as long as you are consistent.

•**In most cases, don't bluff a weak player.** Chronic losers stay in the hand when they shouldn't and call another player's hand when they shouldn't. Even with a weak pair, they will call a bet. They tend to fall in love with their cards. If several weak players are left in the hand, don't even think of bluffing.

Important: Don't bluff the night's big winner. The pile of money in front of him/her and his belief that he's on a roll will make it more likely that he will stay in the game and call your hand. Conversely, if a player is losing heavily and is playing his money instead of his cards, he will be easy to bluff.

•**Play the other person's hand—not your own.** That's what great players do. This means figuring out what an opponent probably has. This is done through observation and experience.

Mentally track how your opponents play. Good players can figure out the parameters of an opponent's hand—what he will call with, what hands he will raise with and what hands he will fold against a raise.

If it comes down to two players in a seven-card game and you think your opponent has one pair of middling-value cards—a below-average hand—you can probably bluff him into folding, no matter what you hold. Your bluff will be more convincing if the face-up cards in your hand are strong. In particular, scare cards—an open pair or a possibility for a flush or a straight—will scare a weaker opponent.

•**Exploit your position when you are the dealer in a game like draw poker.** After you deal the cards, one player bets and the rest fold. This can be a great time for you to raise, as the last player to act.

If the remaining player takes three cards, you know he has a high pair. A classic bluff would be for you to raise and then draw two cards, creating the impression that you have three of a kind. Even if two players are in the same hand and each takes three cards, you are still in a good position to bluff. If both players pass the betting on to you after the draw, bet. They will probably fold.

•**Show your losing bluff hands occasionally.** Do this if your opponents are mumbling that you only bet on great hands. This is a pure reverse-psychology play. It convinces your opponents that it is not necessarily meaningful when you raise the stakes. Once they believe that you don't always have great cards when you raise, you'll win big pots when you actually have great cards because they'll all think you're bluffing.

Source: Edwin Silberstang, one of America's leading authorities on card games, based in Studio City, CA. He has written more than 30 books about games and gaming, including *Winning Poker for the Serious Player: The Ultimate Money-Making Guide!* Cardoza Publishing.

Recording Your Family's Life Story

Each family has its own history. By interviewing family members—and recording their reminiscences on audiocassette or videotape—you'll preserve your own family's history and pass on this treasure to future generations. Here's how you can do it…

•**Prepare questions in advance.** Choose questions that will elicit as much information as possible. *Helpful:* Avoid questions that can be answered with a simple yes or no. *Better:* Questions that elicit feelings, emotions, anecdotes, reminiscences.

Examples:

• *Do you know what your first name means?*

• *Where did you first arrive in the United States?*

• *What possessions did you have with you?*

• *Do you remember any stories your own grandparents might have passed along to you?*

• *What were you like as a young person?*

Write them down in a logical order—but be willing to veer off in other directions if necessary.

•**Don't try to accomplish too much.** No one can tell his/her entire life story in one sitting. Concentrate on one or two specific periods in your subject's life.

Examples: Coming to America as an immigrant…surviving the Great Depression.

•**Be prepared.** *For you:* Have a notebook with your questions listed…a tape recorder…a supply of good-quality tapes…batteries…video recorder (if you're going to video the interview). *For your subject:* A few days before the interview, ask the subject to collect any materials that might help him tell his stories or prompt memories.

•**Choose the right place.** Find a room that's quiet, where you won't be disturbed and where you'll both feel comfortable. *Best:* The subject's home.

Consider having a child present so that child can have the memory of hearing these stories. *Helpful:* Limit the session to one hour.

•**Interviewing techniques.** Don't expect answers to all your questions. There may be things your subject doesn't want to talk about. *Helpful:* Borrow a trick professional journalists use and try asking the same question in various ways. Phrased differently, the question may elicit the type of response you're looking for. Don't interrupt the silences. When your subject stops speaking, wait a few moments before moving on. Often, if you don't say anything, he will continue revealing information you would have lost had you gone on to the next question.

Remember: Everyone has a story to tell—if only someone would listen, if only someone would ask.

Source: Bill Zimmerman, author of *How to Tape Instant Oral Biographies.* Guarionex Press.

Funtastic Children's Museums in the US

Many cities in the US have museums designed specifically for young children, with exhibits that are *meant to be touched.* Here are my favorites…*

•**Arizona Museum for Youth** (Mesa, Arizona) is one of the country's only art museums for children. The museum's main exhibit changes three times a year. Visitors are invited

*All admission prices are subject to change without prior notice.

to take part in creating art to take home. *Admission:* $2/person (children under age two are free). *Information:* 602-644-2468.

•**Bay Area Discovery Museum** (Sausalito, California) has, among many other exhibits, an "Underwater Adventure Tunnel" that simulates the environment under San Francisco Bay. *Admission:* $7/adults, $6/children ages one through 18, under one are free. *Information:* 415-487-4398.

•**Chicago Children's Museum.** *Highlight:* "WaterWays" exhibit. Donned in raincoats provided by the museum, children learn the many uses of water. Activities include creating fountains and geiser-like exhibits that climb to 50 feet. *Admission:* $5/adults, children under one are free. *Information:* 312-527-1000.

•**The Children's Museum/Boston** is renowned for its preschool learning area (which features a kid-sized neighborhood market and a variety of play equipment), but is also a pioneer in teen exhibits and programs. *Admission:* $7/adults, $6/senior citizens and children ages two through 15, $2/one-year-olds. *Information:* 617-426-6500.

•**The Children's Museum/Houston** enables visitors to step into the daily lives of other cultures via a number of unique exhibits. *Admission:* $5/person (children under age two are free). *Information:* 713-522-1138.

•**The Children's Museum/Indianapolis** is the largest of its kind in the country. Kids can explore history, science and other cultures. The preschool area has "playground physics" experiments. *Admission:* $6/adults, $3/children ages two through 17. *Information:* 317-924-5431.

•**The Magic House** (St. Louis) features a two-story indoor slide, a high-tech art exhibit for older children and a "Little Bit of Magic" exhibit that entertains young and old with everything from a ball pit to musical stepping stones. *Admission:* $3.50/person (children under age two are free). *Information:* 314-822-8900.

•**Museum of Discovery and Science** (Ft. Lauderdale, Florida) teaches visitors about the Everglade ecosystem. And—children can also try out a variety of musical instruments at the sound exhibit. *Admission:* $6/adults ages 13 through 65, $5/senior citizens and children ages three through 12. *Information:* 305-467-6637.

•**Please Touch Museum** (Philadelphia) is one of the country's first museums specifically designed for children age seven and under. Visitors learn about "growing up" all around the world. *Admission:* $6.95/person. *Information:* 215-963-0667.

•**Seattle Children's Museum** has a child-sized town where a child can play the role of fireman, doctor, restaurant worker, others. *Admission:* $3.50/person. *Information:* 206-298-2521.

Source: Joanne Cleaver, author of *Doing Children's Museums: A Guide to 265 Hands-On Museums.* Williamson Publishing.

A Wonderful Zoo

Fort Worth Zoological Association features a World of Primates exhibit that houses all the families of the great apes on 2.5 acres. This indoor, climate-controlled tropical rain forest is the only one of its kind in the US and houses endangered lowland gorillas and more.

Fort Worth Zoological Park, 1989 Colonial Pkwy., Fort Worth, TX 76110. 817-871-7051.

Source: Conservationist Anthony Marshall, author of *Zoo: Profiles of 102 Zoos, Aquariums, and Wildlife Parks in the United States.* Random House.

You and Your Ancestors

A thorough physical exam today includes questions about your health...and the health of your siblings, parents and grandparents.

Doctors now realize the more they know about your medical history, the better they can predict your medical future.

Whether your parents or grandparents had high blood pressure or diabetes may be crucial in managing your health.

Where to begin:

The US offers more avenues for genealogical research than most countries...with new sources of historical information opening all the time.

Here's how to track down elusive ancestors...

• **Start with the family.** Work your way back in time by first talking to the oldest members of your family. Even if you hire a professional genealogist to assist your efforts, he/she will expect you to provide as much preliminary information as you possibly can.

Older relatives can tell you the family history as they remember it. They also can help fill in the family medical history.

Important: Time tends to cloud memories and telescope events, so don't expect precision from everyone you talk to. Recollections about past events, such as births, marriages or when the family moved from one town to another, can be a few years off the mark. Double-check important details with more than one person.

Helpful: Older family members can help with the oral history...also with vital written records such as diaries, journals, letters and other personal documents.

There's usually one person in each family who collects such documents. The documents may be in a bottom dresser drawer or in an attic. Give yourself time to find them. Once found, they may provide a detailed history of your family.

• **Civil records.** These records can confirm birth, marriage and death dates.

They can tell you where your family lived when—and which ancestor was in military service at what time.

Strategy: Plan a vacation to the area where the family used to live. That will give you time to search for those old civil records.

New England towns began compiling such records as early as the 17th century. Most places along the eastern seaboard will have records dating back to the early 18th century.

Check out the records in the cities and towns where ancestors once lived. Every state has an office where vital statistics or vital records are kept. Check with directory assistance in the appropriate state capital to locate the repository. Each state also has official archives and a state historical society where historical records are permanently kept. If actual records are not kept, you may be directed to where these records are housed.

Check local libraries for histories of the town or region. Town historical societies can be sources of information, too.

• **Federal sources.** The first national census was in 1790, but it was a simple count. The first census showing names and individual statistics was in 1850.

The basic source for historical information is the National Archives and Records Administration in Washington, or one of the 12 regional National Archive centers around the US.

The Department of Defense in Washington, DC, can tell you exactly where military records are stored.

Important: Naturalization records will help trace your family's foreign origins. To find such records you must know when and where the ancestor reached the US.

Search those family records for details on the ancestor's port of entry and date of entry into the US.

• **Church and synagogue records.** Churches and synagogues that your ancestors attended may have detailed records on births, marriages, family addresses and more. The church cemetery may have death records on many generations of the family.

Helpful: Long before governments began compiling records on citizens, such records often were compiled by local churches. The church may still have some civil records or such records may have been passed along to the state's archives.

Important: Most denominations have centralized record centers where documents from local churches were sent.

Mormon family history library:

The Family History Library in Salt Lake City is the most extraordinary resource on earth for anyone—Mormon or not—researching family history.

It holds records of every kind—from census documents to military records—on hundreds of millions of people in the US and overseas. The staff is courteous and helpful.

For anyone seriously interested in tracing his/her ancestors, this is the place to begin. If you can't get to Salt Lake City, there are some 1,500 Mormon Family History Centers around the world. These centers do not have the original material that is found in Salt Lake City, but they have important information available on CD-ROM.

Abroad:

We all have ancestors that came from overseas, so it can be helpful checking foreign sources for those elusive ancestors.

Start with the national archives or national library in each country. That country's embassy in the US—or the nearest consulate—can tell you how to reach the national archive or library.

Warning: Don't expect records in most countries to be as complete and accessible as they are in the US. Church and military records tend to be available where they weren't destroyed by war. But even industrialized countries such as England only began conducting censuses in the comparatively recent past.

Important: Records from Eastern Europe (including Russia), long inaccessible to outsiders, are rapidly becoming available. In the past five years, the Mormon Church tracked down and reproduced many civil and church records in Eastern Europe and continues the job.

Hiring a professional:

A professional genealogist can move faster through the basic source material (civil, church and military) than the amateur.

Professional genealogists don't widely advertise their services. You will have to track one down yourself. The Mormon Family History Library lists researchers familiar with every region of the US and the world.

Check out the bimonthly publication, *Genealogical Helper.* It is published in Nibley, Utah near Logan, Utah, and is available in most public libraries. It lists researchers by region.

Source: James B. Bell, former director of the New York Historical Society and the New England Historic Genealogical Society. He is author of the most recent edition of *Searching for Your Ancestors: The How and Why of Genealogy.* University of Minnesota Press.

Tip Guidelines

Tipping at expensive restaurants can be confusing. *Solution:* If you were happy with the service, tip 20% of the bill, excluding the tax. If there was a captain—the person who took your order and managed the waiter—give him/her 25% to 30% of the total tip. If there was a sommelier, someone who recommended and served the wine, give 10% of the cost of the wine and tip in cash—$5 minimum.

Source: Letitia Baldrige, one of the country's top etiquette experts and author of *Letitia Baldrige's New Complete Guide to Executive Manners.* Rawson Associates.

How to Get Better Service In Any Restaurant

Here's what you can do to make sure that your waiter and table at any restaurant are excellent…

Faster service:

Strategy I: To make the waiter aware that you are looking for efficient, fast service, tell him/her that you are facing a time crunch and would like to eat as soon as possible. That not only draws your waiter's attention to your priorities, but also lets him alert the kitchen. Your food will probably arrive quickly. How fast you and your guests eat is then up to you.

Strategy II: Call in advance to let the manager know that you would like prompt service. To meet your request, you will likely be seated at a table being served by the restaurant's most efficient waiter.

Avoiding two big problems:

•**Struggling to get the waiter's attention.** To be sure this won't happen, excuse yourself from the table after you arrive. Find your waiter and explain your needs. Ask him to keep a careful eye on your table throughout the meal, especially when you and your guests are ready for the check.

•**Rotten service or waiter rudeness.** You can make a scene and get up to talk to the manager. But this approach almost always involves agitation that is difficult to hide from your guests. Your stress will likely ruin the meal for others.

Better: Realize that there is no elegant way to solve the problem while you're at the restaurant, unless you excuse yourself and talk firmly but politely to the manager or owner. Once you leave, however, there's plenty you can do. Contact the restaurant's manager or owner by mail or phone and politely outline your grievances. In many cases, the owner or manager will be so dismayed that you may be invited back for a drink, hors d'oeuvres or dessert—compliments of the restaurant.

Source: Eric Weiss, president of Service Arts, a company that runs service workshops for the restaurant and hospitality industries, Box 6973, FDR Station, New York 10150.

How to Relax on Vacation

If you can't completely cut the lines of communication to your office, set aside "windows" of time each day to make contact (via phone, fax, pager or modem). Devote the rest of your day to full enjoyment of your vacation.

Source: David Williams, MD, medical director, Executive Health Program, Scripps Clinic, La Jolla, CA.

Main Source of Boredom

Main source of boredom: Ourselves. Most boredom comes from unchallenging jobs, unfulfilled expectations, lack of physical activity and being too much of a spectator and too little of a participant in activities. All these things are under our own control, at least to some degree. Eliminating boredom requires willingness to take responsibility for it and to do something about it. Simply taking antiboredom steps—like searching for ways to make a job more interesting or trying to get promoted to a more interesting one—will relieve the boredom.

Source: *The Joy of Not Working: How to Enjoy Your Leisure Time Like Never Before* by Ernie J. Zelinski, innovation consultant, Chicago. VIP Books.

Better Pumpkin Carving

Select a smooth-skinned pumpkin. If you plan to put a candle inside, remove the top…if you plan to set the pumpkin on an electric light, remove the bottom. Scoop out the pumpkin until the shell is about one inch thick. Draw a design on paper—markers or pencils do not work well on pumpkin skin. Put the paper design against the pumpkin and use push pins to perforate it. Then poke the holes all the way through with an ice pick. If you have trouble seeing the holes, dust the design with flour.

Source: *Better Living: Tips for Saving Time and Money* by Sherri Brennen, Norfolk, VA, TV broadcaster specializing in home issues. WVEC-TV.

Finding Hard-to-Find Videotapes

Can't find an obscure video you'd really like to add to your film library? A video detective agency can search traditional video distribution channels and a network of 5,000 collectors to find new or used videos. It even looks overseas for videos never released in the US. *Cost:* $10 to $300 for the search and the video, depending on the difficulty of the job. If the video is not located, there is no charge. Each customer must agree to a maximum price that he/she will pay for a video before the company will start a search. *Success rate:* 95%. *More information:* A Million and One World-Wide Videos, 800-849-7309.

Smarter Video Renting

Rent early Friday morning, before the inventory of the most popular films is depleted… consider renting from a smaller store that will reserve a video days in advance…"rent" for free or for a modest fee at the local library.

Source: John Ewold, editor, *Consumer's Best,* 4033 44 Ave. S., Minneapolis 55406.

12

Estate Planning

Biggest Estate-Planning Mistakes...and How to Do Everything Right

This is the time of year when most people review their estate-planning documents.

To the rescue: Here are the biggest mistakes people make with their estate plans—and the best ways to provide for your family and shield your assets...

Mistake: Thinking that estate planning involves only a will. Estate planning involves not only determining who will get your assets after you die—which is what a will does—but also planning for your disability, old age and illness. Basic steps to take...

•**Draw up a durable power of attorney**, which designates a relative or trusted friend to handle your financial affairs if you become incapacitated.

Strategy: To make things easier for the person you designate, try to simplify your finances. Consolidate all of your assets into one or two brokerage accounts. Choose firms in which mutual funds, CDs, stocks and bonds can all be held. That way your assets are in one place and someone unfamiliar with your finances can quickly and easily take control in an emergency.

•**If you don't have a close relative or friend**, consider setting up a revocable living trust and naming a bank as the trustee. This allows you to be in complete and total control of your finances during your lifetime, but also permits the bank—a good neutral party—to step in as trustee should you become ill.

Many people avoid these arrangements because they mistakenly think that banks will do a poor job managing their money. But your assets are often safer with bank trust departments—which are subject to audit and staffed by professional trust officers—than with private individuals who are not subject to scrutiny.

•**If you have significant assets**, be sure you have a good umbrella insurance policy that protects against big liability claims that can wipe out your family's resources. For a few hundred dollars a year, you can purchase up to $2 million in liability coverage. It will pay out after the limits on your homeowners' and auto insurance policies have been exceeded.

Talk with your financial adviser to determine if you need this coverage.

Mistake: Not setting up a "credit shelter" (or "bypass") trust. The IRS only taxes estates that are larger than $600,000 and allows spouses to leave each other unlimited amounts of property free from estate tax.

Many couples think they can avoid federal estate taxes altogether by leaving everything to each other. That's not a problem when the first spouse dies because the survivor can make use of the unlimited marital deduction. But when the second spouse dies, the amount of the estate that exceeds $600,000 is subject to tax.

Solution: Establish a credit shelter trust to shield estate assets that exceed the unified credit in the combined estate. The surviving spouse gets the income from the trust during his/her lifetime. After the surviving spouse's death, the assets pass to designated heirs.

Establishing such a trust allows a couple to pass on as much as $1.2 million estate tax free —and can save well over $200,000 in estate taxes.

Mistake: Thinking that life insurance is all you need to protect your family. If you are in your 30s or 40s, you have a much greater chance of becoming disabled before you reach age 65 than you have of dying by that age. Unfortunately, most people have either no disability coverage or inadequate policies.

Solution: Even if you have a policy at work, buy as much disability protection as you can get—or as much as you can afford. To lower the cost, consider extending the waiting period from 30–to–90 days to 180 days before you can collect benefits.

Mistake: Making no plans to shelter taxable life insurance proceeds. Even if you do not have significant assets, a big life insurance policy payout can magnify the size of your estate and make it subject to a big tax bill.

People don't realize that life insurance proceeds are subject to estate taxes.

Solution: To make sure that your family has enough money to live on, you could transfer ownership of the insurance policy from yourself to an *irrevocable life insurance trust.*

The trust can provide your spouse with income for life, and the trust's proceeds can pass to your children—free of estate tax—after your spouse dies. If your spouse already has sufficient assets, you can give the trustee the power to sprinkle income between your spouse and your children. Consider such a trust if insurance plus all other marital assets push your combined estate over $1.2 million.

Mistake: Thinking that asset-protection planning is only for the rich. In our litigious society, *everyone* needs to protect his/her assets. If you own a business or have rental property, make sure all the legal documents for these enterprises are in tip-top order. Most are not.

Also consider setting up a *limited liability company,* a new entity approved by 47 states that combines the advantages of a corporation and partnership and shields your personal assets from lawsuits.

Mistake: Failing to maximize the annual $10,000 gift tax exclusion. Most people are familiar with the IRS rule that allows you to give away up to $10,000 per recipient per year —$20,000 if the gift is jointly made by a couple—free of gift tax.

This is the easiest and most cost-effective way to reduce the size of your estate, since you don't need a lawyer to set up such a gift-giving program. The trouble is, most people typically limit their generosity to their children.

If your estate is large and you don't need the income produced by all of your assets, consider making additional gifts to your grandchildren and the wives and husbands of your adult children.

Mistake: Making gifts to someone who uses the money for educational or medical bills. Say, for example, you want to help your adult children pay for their children's college tuition bills. If you give them the money to pay these bills, you can easily exceed the annual $10,000 limit on tax-free gifts. In fact, college costs alone can exceed $20,000 a year.

Solution: If you pay such medical or educational costs yourself, they are not counted against the annual $10,000 exemption. So by paying such bills directly, you can wind up making tax-free gifts that far exceed the $10,000 limit.

Mistake: Not asking yourself "what if?" when planning your estate. Posing hypothetical questions can help you make estate plans that will deal with even the most unlikely scenarios.

Example: Let's say you have set up a trust for your grandchildren's benefit, naming their father (your son-in-law) as a trustee. In case his marriage to your daughter later dissolves, the trust documents should state that he can no longer serve as trustee if they are legally separated or divorced. Also be sure to name a successor trustee.

Source: Martin Shenkman, CPA, an attorney specializing in estate planning who practices in New York and Teaneck, NJ. He is author of several books on personal finance, including *The Complete Book of Trusts*. John Wiley & Sons.

How the Rich Keep Their Assets

By filing annual income tax returns, most individuals are familiar with the need for income tax savings and are comfortable with implementing tax-saving strategies.

In contrast, though, many do not give similar attention to estate tax savings. Indeed, there may be psychological obstacles in dealing with death-related matters.

Still, this aspect of tax savings is the key to how the rich keep their assets for their families. Who should plan:

You may think that using estate planning strategies are only for those on the *Forbes* 400 list of the richest Americans.

It is by using these strategies that wealthy families have been able to preserve estates for future generations. Today, with the value of homes and size of retirement plan benefits, many Americans have assets of more than the $600,000 that can pass tax free for federal estate tax purposes ($1.2 million for married couples). Such individuals may not consider themselves wealthy but should take lessons from the rich on how to protect assets from being dissipated by death taxes.

Lifetime gifts:

Lifetime giving is an important way to save estate taxes. Every American can give each year up to $10,000 each to as many people as desired. Married couples can "gift" up to $20,000 per recipient.

Example: A couple with three children can remove from their estates $300,000 in five years ($20,000 per year times three children, times five years) without any tax—more if they make gifts to grandchildren.

Caution: Do not give away property needed to produce income to live on.

Additional tax-free gifts: Besides the annual exclusion, a person can pay for another's college or medical costs without gift tax.

Example: A grandparent can give a grandchild $10,000 per year and pay college tuition.

Note: The payment of college or medical costs must be made directly to the provider of the benefits…the university, the doctor….

Lifetime exemption:

In addition to the $10,000 annual gift tax exclusion (and extra gifts of education and medical expenses), each individual has a $600,000 lifetime exemption for estate and gift tax purposes. Typically, people think to use this exemption at death but there are compelling reasons to use it during one's lifetime.

Lifetime gifts up to $600,000 will remove from one's estate not only the property but also all future appreciation on the property.

Example: Stock worth $600,000 today may be worth $1 million at the time of death. A gift of this stock today would have passed the stock tax free. Holding the stock until death would create a taxable transfer of $400,000.

However, there is always the possibility that Congress may eliminate or at least reduce the exemption (as was attempted during the Bush administration).

Middle-class solution: Middle-class families may be reluctant to part with control over such a large sum during their lives. Married couples can get the benefit of their exemptions

221

while alive without losing the use of the funds with complementary spousal trusts.

Each spouse sets up a trust with $600,000 to provide income to the other spouse for life. A spouse can be cotrustee of the trust. The trust can provide that principal is available for the spouse-beneficiary if needed and that appreciation on the property stays in the trust. When each spouse dies, the principal remaining in the trust passes to the couple's children or other family members without estate tax.

Dynasty trusts:

Wealthy families...DuPonts, Rockefellers and Kennedys...have kept the family fortunes by keeping property within a trust and out of the hands of the tax collector.

Congress made it more difficult, but not impossible, to do this by imposing a generation-skipping tax.

Example: If a grandparent puts money in a trust for the benefit of a child for life, with the property passing to the grandchild at the parent's death, no estate tax is due on the parent's death (the estate tax "skips" this generation). However, generation-skipping tax comes into play if transfers exceed $1 million per grantor (the person setting up the trust). Careful use of this exemption ($2 million for married couples) can result in sizable accumulations for future generations (without generation-skipping tax). Assuming a 7% return (after income taxes), a $2 million trust would double in value every 10 years, resulting in a trust of $32 million after 40 years!

Other advantages: By keeping property within a trust, assets can be protected from the claims of a child's or grandchild's creditors or dissipated in the case of divorce. Also, expert management by professional trustees can optimize trust assets over time.

Caution: States (other than Idaho, South Dakota and Wisconsin) have a Rule Against Perpetuities that limits the period of time that a trust can run.

Life insurance trusts:

Most individuals own life insurance to provide their families with income after his/her death and/or to supply the estate with funds to pay death taxes and other expenses.

By shifting ownership of a policy to a life insurance trust, the proceeds are removed from the insured's estate (assuming he/she lives three years beyond the date of the transfer). The proceeds are still available for their intended purposes.

Note: If a trust is set up to buy a policy, there is no three-year waiting period for tax-free treatment.

Family limited partnerships:

Those who own businesses or large portfolios may want to use a slightly more complicated arrangement to reduce transfer taxes. A family limited partnership allows older family members to transfer property to the younger generation at substantially discounted values without loss of control over the property.

This arrangement has been used successfully by many individuals, including Marshall Cogan, (the owner of New York's famed "21 Club"), Sam Walton and by other leading American entrepreneurs.

Intentional grantor trusts:

Aristotle Onassis was able to provide income for Jackie Kennedy Onassis with gift tax savings by intentionally making a trust subject to the grantor trust rules.

This is called a "defective grantor trust."

More specifically, this type of trust is designed to ensure that the grantor will be liable for income taxes on income earned by the trust.

But the payment of income tax will not be treated as a gift to the recipient of the income. This arrangement can work not only for the wealthy but also for those of moderate means.

Terms:

An irrevocable trust provides that income will be paid to a beneficiary for life.

The terms of the trust ensure that the property will not be included in the grantor's estate upon his death.

However, income will be subject to the grantor trust rules for income tax purposes.

Example: A grantor is treated as the owner of a trust (and subject to income tax) if the trust gives the trustee discretion to "sprinkle income" among a group of beneficiaries and the trustee is related or subordinate to the grantor (under the grantor's control).

Caution: This type of trust has not yet received definitive approval from the IRS…and it has not received definitive approval from the courts.

Source: William D. Zabel, a partner in the law firm of Schulte Roth & Zabel, New York, and author of *The Rich Die Richer and You Can Too.* William Morrow and Co.

Write a Last Love Letter To File with Your Will

Write a last love letter and file it with your will. In it, say and re-say all the things you have felt for your spouse over the years. Update the letter whenever you wish.

Objective: To overcome the guilt that a spouse often feels over things left unsaid when the other spouse dies.

Source: *222 Terrific Tips for Two* by Caryl Krueger, author and lecturer on family resources, Escondido, CA. Abingdon Press.

Ten Most Frequently Asked Questions About Living Trusts

With living trusts, you avoid probate and legal fees, while keeping control of your property during your lifetime and after death.

A living trust may also help you reduce estate taxes. Here's how they work…

What are living trusts?

A trust is a legal form of ownership in which property is held for the benefit of another person or persons. Simply stated, a living trust is a type of trust created by individuals or couples during their lifetimes to benefit themselves and their families.

You can name yourself trustee, and, as trustee, you have complete control over the property placed in trust.

Advantages:

•**It avoids costly and time-consuming probate for assets held in the trust's name.** This is especially valuable when you own property that would otherwise go through probate in more than one state.

•**It helps to ensure continuity of your business.**

•**It lets you keep your affairs private**—whereas probate documents are public.

•**It provides for you and your spouse in the event of disability**, or for minor children if you have them.

Disadvantages:

•**Trust assets are subject to creditors' claims.**

•**Property must be transferred** from your name to the trust's.

•**Because you avoid probate**, you forfeit court supervision of your estate upon your death.

Cost: Living trusts are more expensive to create than wills. They cost $500 to $2,000, depending on the attorney and the work involved. There are no ongoing fees if you act as your own trustee.

Why can't I just use a will?

Wills do not accomplish as much as living trusts. For example, when you die, property held in joint tenancy, retirement benefits and insurance proceeds are paid to named beneficiaries regardless of what your will says. With a living trust, you are able to control how all these assets are distributed.

Bonus: Wills can easily be contested by unhappy heirs…but living trusts are just not as easy to contest.

How do I put my property into a living trust?

Simply list the property in the trust documents. *Better:* Put title to bank accounts, real estate, cars, stocks, bonds and other assets in the trust's name. You can instruct that jewelry, art or other personal items pass through the trust and go to specific individuals.

Trap: Any property omitted from the trust must pass through probate. Some states have minimums—$500 or so—others do not.

How do I choose a trustee?

Initial trustees are usually you and/or your spouse. To avoid having to amend the trust when a trustee dies, list "successor" trustees to take over when the initial trustees cannot serve.

Best candidates: Your adult children, relatives, friends…or financial institutions. You can name individual or joint trustees.

How do living trusts save estate taxes?

In general, they don't. But you save significant probate and legal fees.

Living trusts, like wills, can help a married couple save estate taxes by permitting them to take full advantage of the $600,000 estate-tax exemption in the estate of the first spouse to die.

Tax alert: Legislation is pending in Congress that would gradually increase the exemption for estate taxes from $600,000 to $750,000. If passed, the bypass trust will save you even more in estate taxes.

How it works: Instead of leaving everything to your spouse on your death, you leave $600,000 worth of assets for the benefit of your spouse, ultimately passing to your children or other beneficiaries. By using this technique, called a bypass trust, in the living trust, you can save as much as $235,000 in estate taxes. You can, however, accomplish the same tax-saving result by including a bypass trust in your will.

How can I make changes to my living trust?

Because living trusts are "revocable," you can change any terms of the trust at any time. It's best to use a lawyer, though you can do it yourself with forms that you can buy.

Most common: Changing trustees or how trust assets are distributed at death. *Exception:* People who set up joint trusts with their spouses cannot change provisions that have become irrevocable at the first death, such as bypass provisions. Any change must be made before the first spouse's death.

Do I have to file additional income-tax forms for the living trust?

No. As long as you and your spouse are still alive, you file taxes on Form 1040, using your Social Security number for all accounts, even though they are held in the name of the trust. However, when the first spouse dies, trusts that have bypass provisions must file a fiduciary tax return (Form 1041).

Will my living trust be valid if I move to a different state?

Yes, a living trust typically is valid anywhere in the US. *Caution:* Louisiana has unusual laws …so consult a financial adviser if you move there.

Community property state trap: If you move to or from California or another "community property" state, consult an adviser to make sure your trust includes the proper language for a community property state. You will also need a new will that conforms to the laws of your new state of residence.

If I create a living trust, do I still need a will?

Yes, you need a *pourover will.* This puts into the living trust any property that is not already there at your death.

Example: If you die in an airplane crash and your estate receives $1 million of insurance, the proceeds are paid to your estate, not the living trust.

The pourover provision in the will shifts the money into trust, although it must pass through probate initially.

And, you would need a will to name a guardian for minor or disabled children.

Will a living trust protect my assets in the event of lawsuits?

No. Because you have total control over the property in trust, its assets are not shielded from lawsuits or creditors.

Nor are assets protected should you consider an extended stay in a nursing home.

In this last situation, only getting the assets out of your name will provide protection.

Source: Stephen M. Rosenberg, CFP, president, Rosenberg Financial Group, Inc., a firm specializing in retirement planning, 2517 Moody Rd., Warner Robins, GA 31088. He is author of *Keep Uncle Sam from Devouring Your Life Savings.* Career Press.

Estate Planning And Second Marriages

Second marriages can pose unique estate planning problems when there are children from first marriages.

The spouse with children from a prior marriage wants to protect the interests of those children. The spouse also wants to accomplish traditional estate planning objectives—saving estate taxes, ensuring liquidity for tax and administration costs and providing for the surviving spouse.

Making all these objectives mesh is where planning is crucial.

Prenuptial and postnuptial agreements:

The laws in most states give a surviving spouse certain rights in the estate of a deceased spouse. These are called *elective rights*.

They allow the surviving spouse to request a portion of the estate (called the elective share) regardless of the terms of the deceased spouse's will.

Example: In New York state, a surviving spouse's elective share is one-third of the deceased spouse's estate (the children from the prior marriage would then receive two-thirds of the estate). In an increasing number of states, the elective share must be received outright, instead of being placed in trust.

To prevent a surviving spouse from taking an elective share—and to provide the greatest flexibility in estate planning—*prenuptial agreements* and *postnuptial agreements* are used to waive elective rights and settle other questions as well.

Caution: Make sure these agreements comply with state law. For example, in New York, the agreement to waive an elective share must be notarized for such a waiver to be effective.

Tax clauses:

Who should bear the tax burden? Estate plans should address this issue.

Assume there is estate tax on the estate of a deceased spouse.

A typical tax clause in a will imposes the estate tax obligation on the "remainder," the portion of the estate after paying all specific bequests, funeral expenses and other costs. The remainder is the interest that is usually left to the children.

Thus, the typical tax clause puts the tax burden on the children.

The surviving spouse's estate can be taxed… if the deceased spouse's estate leaves an interest to the surviving spouse that is taxable when he/she dies—but ultimately passes to the children of the surviving spouse (the deceased spouse's stepchildren).

Who should bear the tax burden in this instance…the second estate or the children from the first marriage? Without careful pre-planning the children of the first marriage automatically are liable for the tax.

Better way: The couple should buy *second-to-die life insurance* to meet this tax burden. Then, neither the second estate nor the children's interest is reduced by taxes. Second-to-die insurance pays off only when the second spouse dies.

Using trusts:

Assuming that valid waivers of elective rights have been made, spouses can then use trusts to craft estate plans that satisfy a number of objectives.

Example: The decedent's will sets up a special trust (called a qualified terminable interest property [Q-TIP] trust). Under this trust the surviving spouse receives all of the income from the trust. When the surviving spouse dies, the property remaining in the trust passes automatically to the beneficiaries named by the decedent—the children from a prior marriage.

Thus the interests of the children have been protected while the surviving spouse has been provided for.

What is more, a Q-TIP trust also defers estate tax until the second estate, another objective.

Problems of younger spouses:

Sometimes with second marriages, the spouse may be about the same age as the children from the prior marriage. In this case, trusts may not be the best way to provide for the children since they may not live long enough to enjoy the property placed in trust for them.

Better: Use life insurance to give the children property of equivalent value.

Make sure ownership of the policy will not incur any estate tax on the proceeds. The policy can be owned outright by the children or held in trust. A trust provides more flexibility and may be the better alternative.

Caution: If the insured owns the policy and then transfers it to the children or into a trust,

225

there is a three-year waiting period before the proceeds become tax-free.

Retirement plans:

Retirement plan benefits may be a significant asset in an estate.

But they can be subject to three taxes—income...estate...and excise taxes.

Generally, benefits pass to someone named in the plan. They do not pass according to the terms of a will unless there is no named beneficiary in the plan.

Two special considerations in planning for retirement benefits...

•**IRA benefits.** A trust can be used to provide for both the IRA owner's surviving spouse and children from a prior marriage. Benefits held in the IRA are paid to the trust in installments over the life of the surviving spouse, thereby deferring income tax.

Estate taxes can also be deferred if the following conditions are met...

•**The trust must be irrevocable and valid under state law.**

•**The surviving spouse must be clearly identified as beneficiary.**

•**A copy of the trust instrument must be given to the custodian of the IRA.**

•**All of the income from the IRA** (or the minimum distribution amount required for beneficiaries age 70½ and older if this is higher) and the trust must be distributed to the surviving spouse. When the surviving spouse dies, funds remaining in the trust pass to the children of the prior marriage.

•**Qualified retirement benefits.** Federal law protects the rights of a spouse in the pension of the other spouse. Pension benefits must be paid in the form of a joint and survivor annuity unless the nonparticipant spouse waives survivorship rights.

Caution: A statement in a prenuptial agreement giving up survivorship rights is not a valid waiver since a waiver can only be made by a spouse—and a fiancé is not yet a spouse. The prenuptial agreement can, however, provide that the fiancé will sign a waiver following the marriage.

Source: Harvey J. Platt, Esq., partner in the law firm of Platt & Platt, New York City, and author of *Your Living Trust and Estate Plan.* Allworth Press.

Will Signing Smarts

Have extra witnesses observe the signing of your will—even more than the law requires. *Reason:* If your will is ever probated, one or more of your witnesses may have died or moved away. Also, use witnesses you know personally so you'll be able to locate them quickly and easily.

Source: Larry Burkett, author, *Women Leaving the Workplace.* Moody Press.

Estate Planning Strategy

Consolidate as much of your finances—including checking, mutual funds, stocks, bonds, credit cards, loans, etc.—at one brokerage or bank. *Reasons:* By merging your finances, you will make it easier for those who must manage your affairs if you are disabled...probate will be simplified since heirs will be able to request information from a single source...and you will be better able to manage and invest your money since it will all appear in one monthly statement.

Source: Martin Shenkman, New York attorney specializing in estate, tax and financial planning.

13

Very, Very Personal

Answers to the Most Common Questions About Sex

As a sex therapist, I often see couples who are so caught up in their work that they have no time—or appetite—for sensual pleasure. They lose sight of the pleasures of intimacy and sexuality.

Couples frequently come to me because they want to reverse this pattern of all work and no play. They know just how important sexuality is to a strong relationship...and are looking for strategies that will help them become physically attracted to each other again.

Here are the answers to the most common questions my patients ask...

How can my spouse and I keep work-related stress from harming our sexual relationship?

When partners return home after work each day, they should simply listen to one another let off steam...and try to be supportive.

Unfortunately, couples often try to solve each other's problems. That creates rather than relieves psychological tension. The partner whose problems are being discussed often feels controlled and/or inferior—and those feelings soon give way to anger. Anger quickly leads to fighting...and nothing kills off sexual desire faster than an argument. When patterns like this emerge, sexual activity dies down.

Solution: Become a sympathetic listener. Practice letting your partner speak without interruption, even if his/her difficulties make you feel anxious. Convey the message that he/she is competent and able to solve his/her own problems.

Offer advice only if you're asked to do so. When it's your turn to talk, encourage your partner to listen carefully to you.

A relationship is about companionship, not about meeting unfulfilled needs from childhood. Discuss ways you and your partner can make the relationship more responsive to your needs—how you can become more sympathetic and tender toward one another.

How can we put each other in a sexual mood?

Women want to feel loved before they have sex. They crave touching and affection for their own sake.

Many men express love through their sexuality. For them, foreplay is often used as a means to an end—intercourse.

Solution: Take the fore out of foreplay. Rediscover touching for its own sake. Reawaken your sensuality, as opposed to your sexuality.

Exercise: Lie in bed with your eyes closed. Let your partner's hands roam over your body for up to 45 minutes. Don't touch back. Don't think about how your partner feels. Focus only on your own sensations. Trade places, and repeat the exercise. This exercise should not be used as foreplay. Just experience the arousal itself.

Helpful question: *What can I do to turn myself on?*

Does the frequency or duration of lovemaking matter?

Every couple is different. Some couples make love five times a week. Others make love only once a month. For some, sex lasts hours. Others take minutes.

There's no such thing as sexual normalcy. The important issue is whether you both agree on frequency. Stop trying to measure up to ideals presented in magazines or on TV. Find the pattern that suits both your needs. Remember, the best sex is an expression of yourself. Learn to accept your sexual desires and appetites—and those of your partner—just the way they are.

What are the most common sexual problems today?

Couples complain that they've lost their sex drive...or the man complains of impotence or premature ejaculation...or the woman says she doesn't have orgasms.

Most couples blame each other for whatever isn't working in their relationship. *Better:* Take responsibility for your own actions, good and bad. It's important to let go of the anger and get back in touch with each other. Laugh. Have fun together.

Exercise: Express your anger—gently. Write letters to each other, stating everything you're angry about. End the letter by closing the door on past hurt and opening it to a more positive present and future. Take turns listening as you read each other's letters aloud. Don't defend yourself or interrupt. Just empathize.

My body isn't quite as firm or as shapely as it once was. What can I do to feel sexier?

Exercise and proper eating will make you look and feel better—but even with hard work, few middle-aged people are able to regain the bodies of their youth.

Strategy: Learn to appreciate your body and your partner's. Try not to be overly concerned with your partner's appearance. After all, few people are married to models.

People who dislike their appearance rarely, if ever, actually look at their bodies. They're more concerned with their face or hair.

Exercise I: For five minutes each day, get undressed and examine your body in a full-length mirror. Look at the lines and curves that please you most. This will help boost your self-esteem.

Exercise II: Take turns washing each other's hair, making it a real head massage. As you do, look at your partner's body. Focus on what you find attractive about it and how you feel touching it. If you feel like it, share your thoughts with your partner.

What's the best way to spice up my sex life? Sex need not be limited to the bedroom. In fact, that can be the worst place to make love. *Reason:* That's where our loudest arguments occur.

Better: Break out of your normal routine. Try initiating sex with your clothes on...or in the backseat of your car, as you did when you were a teenager...or check into a hotel.

Source: Dagmar O'Connor, PhD, a sex therapist in private practice in New York City. She is the author of the book/video set *How to Make Love to the Same Person for the Rest of Your Life and Still Love It.* DagMedia Corp.

How to Have Great Sex Every Time

Of all the concerns voiced by women undergoing sex therapy, none is more common—or emotionally distressing—than an inability to achieve orgasm during intercourse.

Only about 30% of women achieve orgasm regularly during intercourse (coitus).

Some women endure years of sex without a single coital orgasm. Typically, a woman relies upon a partner who "jumps through hoops" to bring her there, but never achieves the ideal.

Result: Sexuality, robbed of its playfulness and spontaneity, becomes more a chore than a pleasure.

To the rescue:

A variant of the standard missionary position—known as the *coital alignment technique* (CAT)—not only helps the woman have an orgasm during coitus, but also boosts the odds that she and her partner will climax simultaneously.

Men who have long considered themselves sexually inadequate, as well as women who have worried they were frigid, can begin to experience sex with all its physical pleasure and emotional intimacy.

Bonus: Because good sex is usually synonymous with good communication, this improvement in a couple's sex life often carries over into other aspects of their relationship, bringing new levels of intimacy, contentment, and—important in this age of AIDS—commitment.

Unlike some other alternative lovemaking techniques, CAT is relatively straightforward. Couples have differed in the time necessary to master the technique, but with persistence, most have succeeded. Once mastered, it is remarkably effective—and quite reliable.

Recent study: Sexual response was measured in couples involved in committed relationships—before and after receiving CAT training. Prior to learning CAT, only 23% of the women reported achieving orgasm during intercourse on a regular basis. After CAT, that figure jumped to 77%. Before CAT, no women reported having regular simultaneous orgasms with their partners. Afterward, one-third of the women reported doing so.

Almost all participants reported at least some improvement in their sex lives following CAT training. In fact, the only participants who failed to benefit were those whose relationships were already jeopardized by nonsexual factors.

CAT basics:

CAT encompasses five distinct elements, each designed to maximize contact between the penis and the clitoris, thus maximizing sexual response in both partners...

1. Positioning. The woman lies on her back. The man lies atop her, facing her much as in the conventional missionary position, but with his pelvis overriding hers in a "riding high" orientation.

His penis should be inserted into her vagina, with its shaft pressed firmly against her mons veneris—the soft fleshy mound covering the pubic bone above the vagina. She wraps her legs around his thighs, with her legs bent at an angle not exceeding 45 degrees and her ankles resting on his calves.

Important: He must let his full weight fall on her and must avoid using his hands or elbows to support his weight. While she may find this weight uncomfortable initially, it is essential to keep his pelvis from sliding back down off of hers.

2. Limited movement. Conventional intercourse involves a great deal of pushing, pulling and bracing of the arms and legs. CAT coitus focuses narrowly on the couple's pelvic movement. In fact, little additional movement is possible during CAT, given the partners' positioning. If additional movement is possible, the positioning is faulty.

3. Pressure-counterpressure. During ordinary intercourse, the man sets the rhythm while the woman moves little, if at all. In contrast, CAT calls for a rhythmic movement that is virtually identical for both partners.

Procedure: She performs an upward stroke, forcing his pelvis backward. He allows his pelvis to move, yet maintains a continuous counterpressure against her pelvis (and her clitoris).

In the downward movement, the pattern of movement is reversed, with the man pushing downward and the woman maintaining the counterpressure against his penis. As her pelvis moves backward and downward, the penis shaft rocks forward against her mons veneris, sliding to a shallow position in the vagina.

Note: Although the force of pressure and counterpressure is quite intense during CAT, the partners' actual movement is surprisingly slight.

4. Full genital contact. Repeated thrusting of the penis into and out of the vaginal "barrel," typical of conventional missionary intercourse, affords little direct stimulation of either the clitoris or the penis.

Typical result: His orgasm, even if perceived as pleasurable, is far less powerful than it might be…and she, having gotten little if any clitoral stimulation, fails to climax at all. In CAT, the penis and clitoris are held tightly together by pressure and counterpressure …and the penile-clitoral "connection" is rocked up and down in an evenly paced, lever-like fashion. This vibratory motion all but guarantees orgasms for both partners.

Bonus: Orgasms produced by CAT differ significantly from those produced by conventional in-and-out sex. Whereas a conventional orgasm is limited to a pulsating sensation, a CAT orgasm combines this with a "melting" sensation.

Among participants of the recent study, 90% of all subjects said that CAT intensified their orgasms…and 60% said that it increased their desire for more frequent sex.

5. "Passive" orgasm. In ordinary coitus, the man thrusts faster and more deeply as he becomes increasingly aroused, while the woman typically slows down or even stops moving altogether. At the moment of climax, the partners' movements often become disconnected and may fall completely out of sync.

Result: The orgasm is incomplete, almost "spoiled."

Better: CAT prescribes complete coordination of movement by the partners, up to and beyond the moment of climax. In other words, both partners make no effort to "grab" for orgasm, instead letting it "overtake" them.

The transition from voluntary motion preceding orgasm to the reflexive, involuntary movements typical of orgasm itself is thus fully coordinated. The possibility of incomplete orgasm is drastically limited.

Crucial: A conscious effort by both partners not to hold their breath or suppress natural sounds. Breathing freely and giving full rein to grunts, moans, spoken words and other vocalizations greatly facilitate orgasm—for the

noisemaker and the listener alike. Some couples report that the "reversed" CAT is an effective variation of CAT—if the man is much heavier than his partner.

Source: Edward W. Eichel, MA, a psychotherapist in private practice in New York City and the originator of the coital alignment technique. CAT is described in greater detail—and, yes, illustrated—in his book *The Perfect Fit.* Signet. Eichel is now developing a CAT self-help videotape. For more information, call 212-989-1826.

Never Criticize In Bed

Do not critique your partner's sexuality or sexual behavior. To improve your sex life, say what you want in a positive way. *Example:* Instead of *You've got to make it last longer,* say, *I would love it if sex could last longer.* Do not expect rapid improvement—like other habits, sexual performance does not change quickly. *Helpful:* Share how you feel about changes being made or attempted, and continue to try to improve.

Source: Jane Greer, PhD, marriage and sex therapist, New York.

Fragrance That Heightens Male Sexual Response

Jasmine oil heightens male sexual response by stimulating the region of the brain that controls erections. And it's not the only mood-altering oil. Coriander fights stress and fatigue. *Relaxing:* Chamomile, cypress, juniper, marjoram and myrrh. *Stimulating:* Eucalyptus, ginger, pine and rosemary. These "essential oils" can be inhaled from a handkerchief or added to vegetable oils and used in massage.

Source: Jeanne Rose, chairman, National Association of Holistic Aromatherapy, Box 17622, Boulder, CO.

Unnecessary Surgery

Surgery to widen the vaginal opening during childbirth is rarely helpful. Called *episiotomy,* this common surgical procedure does *not* reduce the risk of vaginal or rectal tears. In fact, episiotomy increases the risk of tears. Yet in

1979 (the most recent year for which statistics are available), 63% of all vaginal deliveries involved episiotomy. Women should discuss episiotomy with their doctor or midwife. Many doctors who perform episiotomy routinely are unaware of the problems associated with the procedure. Episiotomy may be necessary in cases involving fetal distress or breech delivery.

Source: John M. Thorpe, Jr., MD, associate professor of obstetrics and gynecology, University of North Carolina at Chapel Hill School of Medicine.

Hysterectomy Alternative

Alternative to hysterectomies for women with excessive menstrual bleeding: A new procedure called *endometrial ablation.* Excessive menstrual bleeding is usually treated by scraping the lining of the uterus. But if the lining grows back and the bleeding resumes, a hysterectomy is often done. The new procedure burns the lining instead of scraping it.

Result: The lining does not grow back— and no hysterectomy is needed.

Added benefit: Hysterectomy patients usually spend one week in the hospital and six weeks recovering. With the new procedure, 95% go home the same day. Endometrial ablation is available in most metropolitan areas.

Source: James Daniell, MD, PC, clinical professor of obstetrics and gynecology, Vanderbilt University Medical School, Nashville.

Missed Pap Smear Tests

Missed Pap smear tests—not misread ones — deserve the blame for most cases of advanced cervical cancer. Labs have long been blamed for misreading the tests. But in a recent study, it turned out that 29% of women with advanced cervical cancer never had a Pap test—and 24% hadn't had one for at least five years. Only 7% of cases involved misread Pap smears. All women who are or who have been sexually active or who have reached age 18 should have an annual Pap test.

Source: Dwight T. Janerich, PhD, professor of epidemiology, University of Utah, Salt Lake City.

Kegel Exercises Beat Incontinence in Women

The exercises strengthen pelvic-floor muscles surrounding the openings of the urethra, vagina and anus. *What to do:* Contract pelvic muscles for five seconds, relax for five seconds. Repeat 12 times—eight times a day. *To identify pelvic muscles:* Practice interrupting urine flow during urination.

Source: *Consumer Reports on Health,* 101 Truman Ave., Yonkers, NY 10703.

Control Premenstrual Depression

Premenstrual depression can be controlled with sertraline (Zoloft). *Recent study:* More than 200 women with a history of premenstrual depression were given sertraline. Six out of 10 reported feeling less depressed. They were better able to function both at work and at home.

Source: Kimberly A. Yonkers, MD, assistant professor of psychiatry, University of Texas Southwestern Medical Center, Dallas.

Natural Strategies for Avoiding Troublesome Breast Cysts

Breast cancer gets lots of media attention— and rightly so. But far more common is *fibrocystic breast disease.* At some point during their lives, 70% of women develop the fluid-filled, tender or painful breast lumps that characterize this condition.

University of Vermont gynecologist Christiane Northrup, MD, answers the most common questions about breast cysts...

•**What causes breast cysts?** During ovulation and just prior to menstruation, fluctuating hormone levels can cause breast cells to retain fluid—resulting in cysts.

An estrogen/progesterone imbalance also appears to promote cyst development, but doctors don't know exactly how—or why. In some cases, cysts are linked to abnormally high levels of estrogen. This is usually caused by eating too much fat.

Other women develop breast cysts despite having normal estrogen levels. *Good news:* The lumps usually disappear following menopause.

•**How can I tell a tumor from a cyst?** Cysts typically feel like a bunch of peas or grapes just under the skin. A painful lump is nearly always a cyst. Cancerous lumps are generally not tender.

•**Is breast cancer more common among women who get breast cysts?** In the 1970s, a few studies indicated that this might be the case. But subsequent research at the National Cancer Institute found that the vast majority of fibrocystic breast disease diagnoses did not involve an increased risk of cancer.

Exception: About 1% of women with fibrocystic breasts have *ductal atypia*. These abnormal breast cells sometimes turn cancerous.

•**If I discover a lump in my breast, what should I do?** Have your doctor examine it at once. He/she may want to obtain additional tests, such as a mammogram, sonogram or needle aspiration/biopsy.

If the lump contains fluid, odds are it's a cyst. It should disappear once the fluid is removed.

Important: Perform monthly breast self-examinations to spot lumps as early as possible.

•**Are certain women more likely to get breast cysts?** Fibrocystic breasts are more common among women who are sensitive to caffeine…and those who have heavy periods, severe menstrual cramps and/or premenstrual syndrome.

•**The lumps in my breasts are very painful. What can I do for relief?** First, avoid all sources of caffeine. That goes for chocolate and caffeinated soft drinks, as well as coffee and tea. And don't overlook over-the-counter painkillers and diet aids. Many contain caffeine.

To keep your estrogen levels in check, adopt a low-fat, high-fiber diet. This diet should contain no dairy products…and should be high in whole grains, fruits, vegetables and beans. After three months, add dairy foods back into your diet to see if they make a difference.

•**Are nutritional supplements helpful?** Many women get at least partial relief by taking a daily multivitamin or a daily pill containing 400 to 600 international units (IU) of vitamin E.

Also helpful: Selenium (24 to 32 micrograms a day)…vitamin A (1,000 to 5,000 IU a day)…capsules of evening primrose oil, flaxseed oil or black currant seed oil (500 mg four times a day).

•**A friend of mine suggests that I try massage. Is that helpful?** Yes. Massage relieves discomfort by dispersing excess fluid to the lymph glands, where it's channeled out of the body.

What to do: Rub your hands together until they are warm, then massage each breast in concentric circles about 30 times. Use both hands, with your fingertips meeting in the middle. Move clockwise on the right breast, counterclockwise on the left breast.

For persistently painful breast cysts, I often recommend self-treatment with topical iodine. Iodine seems to affect estrogen's ability to bind to breast cells. Apply iodine tincture in a three-inch-square patch to your upper thigh or lower abdomen. If the stain fades within a few hours, apply it to another area of the upper thigh or lower abdomen.

Repeat these applications as long as they continue to fade within a few hours. When you can see a slight stain that persists for 24 hours, stop the treatment.

Source: Christiane Northrup, MD, assistant clinical professor of obstetrics and gynecology, University of Vermont College of Medicine, at Maine Medical Center, Portland. She is the author of *Women's Bodies, Women's Wisdom.* Bantam Books.

Infertility and Women

One in three cases of infertility involves a problem with the male alone. In another 20% of infertile couples, abnormalities are detected in both partners. In about half of all cases, the problem lies solely with the woman.

Source: Stuart S. Howards, MD, professor of urology, University of Virginia, Charlottesville.

All Men Can Be Dads

Almost all men can become fathers through a new procedure to extract sperm from the testicles. Men who have no viable sperm in their semen almost always have some unmoving sperm in their testicles. Those sperm can fertilize an egg if they are injected into it. This used to require expensive, painful surgery to obtain the sperm.

New method: The sperm are aspirated through a thin needle in a procedure that is simple enough to be done in a doctor's office.

Source: Richard J. Sherins, MD, director, male infertility program, Genetic & IVF Institute, Fairfax, VA.

Unexplained Infertility

Unexplained infertility is often the result of leukocytospermia, a condition in which the man's white blood cells adversely affect his sperm cells. *Good news:* In a recent study, fertility rates increased *eightfold* when the man and the woman began taking the antibiotic *doxycycline*. Antibiotic therapy costs as little as $100, *in vitro* fertilization about $10,000.

Source: Emmett F. Branigan, MD, assistant professor of obstetrics and gynecology, University of Washington School of Medicine, Seattle. His one-year study of 95 couples with unexplained infertility was published in *The Journal of Reproductive Medicine*, 8342 Olive Blvd., St. Louis 63132.

Women and Conception

Ovulation is the only time when an egg is receptive to fertilization. But because a woman's time of ovulation varies and a man's sperm can live for three to five days inside the woman, there are actually only about 18 days per month when a woman can be sure *not* to conceive. *To track ovulation:* Watch for vaginal mucus that turns slippery, like raw egg white, and becomes plentiful. Record daily body temperature—it drops slightly before ovulation, then rises for about three days afterward.

Source: Jonathan Scher, MD, obstetrician and gynecologist in private practice in New York and coauthor of *Preventing Miscarriage: The Good News.* HarperPerennial.

Stress and Low-Birth Weight Babies

Too much stress during pregnancy increases the risk of premature delivery and low birth weight. *Danger:* Low birth weight and prematurity increase risk of mental retardation, cerebral palsy, blindness and life-threatening infections. In a recent study, pregnant women rated their own stress levels. Each unit increase on one scale was associated with a 55-gram decrease in infant birth weight...and each unit on a second scale was associated with a three-day decrease in developmental age at birth. Availability of prenatal care had no effect on a woman's stress levels.

Source: Curt A. Sandman, PhD, professor and vice chairman, department of psychiatry, University of California, Irvine. He led a study of 90 married, upper-middle-class women.

Half of the Weight Women Gain During Pregnancy Is Due to Bodily Changes

About half of the 25 to 35 pounds doctors recommend a pregnant woman gain are the result of bodily changes—growth of the uterus and breasts, and increases in blood volume and body fluids. Seven pounds come from extra fat, protein and other nutrients the body stores to prepare for breast-feeding. Typically, only six to eight pounds are from the baby.

Source: *The Pregnancy Cookbook: Easy Recipes for Nine Months of Healthy Eating* by Marsha Hudnall, MS, RD, nutrition director for Green Mountain at Fox Run, a women's health management center in Ludlow, VT. Berkley Books.

A Woman's Role In Impotence

A woman's role in impotence is real and significant. Impotence is based in fear or anger stemming from childhood. These feelings can be present in either partner.

Examples: A man may lose his erection if his partner is ambivalent about sex. Impotence can develop situationally—surrounding conception, childbirth and surgery.

Important: In cases when the woman is not the cause of impotence, her reaction to a lost erection may maintain the problem.

To overcome impotence: Start by focusing on sexual pleasures other than intercourse.

Source: Dagmar O'Connor, PhD, a sex therapist in private practice in New York. She is the author of *How to Make Love to the Same Person for the Rest of Your Life and Still Love It,* a book and video set from DagMedia Corporation.

Treat Impotence Promptly

Treat impotence promptly to increase the likelihood of a cure. Erections bring oxygen-rich blood to penile blood vessels and nerves. The longer a man goes without an erection, the greater the damage to the lining of the blood vessels. Sufficient damage can eventually make erections impossible. *Good news:* Most cases of impotence are highly treatable when attended to early.

Source: Irwin Goldstein, MD, professor of urology, Boston University School of Medicine.

Size of Average Penis

When erect, the average penis is 5.1 inches in length and 4.9 inches in circumference. When flaccid, the average penis is 3.5 inches in length and 3.9 inches in circumference. Researchers concluded that an erect penis should be considered "subnormal" only when it is 2.8 inches or less in length and/or 3.5 inches or less in girth. In this study, about 2% of men fell into that category.

Source: Study of 80 men by Jack McAninch, MD, chief of urology, San Francisco General Hospital.

Half of the People Under 40 Have Cohabitated

The number of couples choosing cohabitation instead of marriage rose 80% between 1980 and 1991. Cohabiting couples are often less sexually faithful than married ones. Twenty percent of cohabiting women have cheated on their partners, compared with 4% of married women.

Sources: Studies by Larry Bumpass, PhD, professor of sociology, University of Wisconsin in Madison, and Renata Forste, PhD, former assistant professor of sociology, Western Washington University, Bellingham.

Baldness Remedy Alert

Rogaine is not a cure-all—*nor is it risk-free. Important:* See a dermatologist before trying minoxidil to determine if it is appropriate for you…or if there is an underlying condition, such as a hormone imbalance or anemia, causing your hair loss. If you have heart disease, talk with your cardiologist—minoxidil can affect blood pressure. Appropriate candidates—*men or women*—have a one in three chance of significant hair growth. Minoxidil can only help those with *hereditary* hair loss within the past two to five years. It works best for overall thinning…less well for a receding hair line. Discontinue use if you see no improvement after nine months.

Source: Neal Schultz, MD, a dermatologist in private practice, 1040 Park Ave., New York 10028.

Baldness Cure Coming?

Most men who suffer from hair loss dream of someday, somehow, regaining a full head of hair.

Good news: Researchers from Baylor College of Medicine in Houston announced recently that they may have located the gene responsible for *congenital generalized hypertrichosis* (CGH), a rare disorder that makes sufferers excessively hairy.

Studying the DNA of a Mexican family with CGH, Dr. Pragna I. Patel and her colleagues have narrowed the search to a region of the X chromosome. Once it is fully identified and cloned, this "atavistic" gene may aid in the treatment of hair loss.

Source: David W. Freeman, editor, *Health Confidential*, 55 Railroad Ave., Greenwich, CT 06830.

Better Personal Ads

To be most effective, personal ads should tell more about you than about the kind of person you are seeking. Tell about your values, interests and a desire for friendship. Avoid negative statements. Be honest about your looks. Be as specific about your requirements as possible. A few quality responses are better than dozens of answers that don't interest you. Do not be too serious—saying in an ad that you are looking for a long-term commitment can be a turnoff. If a short-term relationship is right, it can become a long-term one.

Source: Basha Blumenthal-Kaplan, PhD, psychologist who runs groups for singles in Westchester County, NY, quoted in *Cosmopolitan*, 224 W. 57 St., New York 10019.

Sexual Fantasies And Gender

Men's fantasies tend to be more sexually explicit, containing lots of visual imagery and anatomic detail. Women's sexual fantasies focus more on affection, feelings and romance.

Men are likely to fantasize *doing something* sexual to a partner—whereas women are likely to fantasize having something sexual *done to them.*

Source: Harold Leitenberg, PhD, professor of psychology, University of Vermont, Burlington.

Burnout... How to Prevent It

Burnout is the term used to describe the condition of emotional and physical collapse brought on by virtually unchecked escalation of pressure. Although burnout is not rampant in the business world, it is a problem that we all have to be aware of in order to protect ourselves, our families, our business associates—and our friends.

Most emotionally well-adjusted people protect themselves against burnout intuitively by setting up defense mechanisms when the pressure gets rough—time off from work, closed doors, reduction in overall activity, etc.

Others get caught up in a self-destructive whirlpool.

Most vulnerable: People with a driving ambition for which they're willing to sacrifice a large part of their lives. Burnout victims invest their time, energy and money in tasks that are difficult, if not impossible. And they often commit themselves to a great deal of work without relief or support.

The terrible thing about burnout is that it often affects people who set out to do something wonderful or worthwhile. Little by little, they find themselves getting more stretched and desperate. The harder they try, the worse the situation becomes until they just can't try anymore.

The burnout process:

Burnout usually follows a predictable sequence that can be interrupted at almost any stage. If you're aware of what the sequence is, you can take steps to prevent burnout from running its course.

Stage I: The first sign of burnout is overenthusiasm. Stage I burnout candidates tell long and nervous tales about how wonderful everything is. People who hear these monologues often wonder why this person is so intent on explaining everything.

Stage II: Physical symptoms—ulcers, rashes, back pain, neck pain, colds, flu, etc.—emerge. Stage II cases become antagonistic. They start wondering whether the people who are close to them are part of the solution or part of the problem.

As others become less enthusiastic about the project and start to withdraw support, the Stage II burnout candidate drops friends, relatives and colleagues who aren't supportive.

Stage III: Deprivation symptoms set in. The individual starts to feel hollow because he/she is not being emotionally nourished, but this feeling is kept secret. Although the person still thinks he's doing great things, he doesn't enjoy them as much as he used to—he doesn't feel as important.

The person starts to think that he's not working hard enough, lacks commitment or needs a more challenging assignment. He may take a workshop on stress reduction and a few tranquilizers to numb the discomfort. Or he may start drinking to relax.

During Stage III, some people figure out that something is wrong and take a vacation. Though they feel better for a while, it doesn't last because burnout is insidious and progressive.

Stage IV: The sense of emptiness and of impending defeat increases. In Stage IV, desperate moves are made—scientists fake results, businesspeople borrow from the mob. They still function, but they take big risks with their careers, their finances, their relationships and their lives. They're desperate to avoid failure, even at the expense of other important aspects of their lives.

Stage V: The lies and deceptions grow. The Stage V burnout sufferer becomes cut off from people because he can't tell them what's really going on. The circle of people who are willing to help gets smaller and smaller.

At this point, burnout is hard to distinguish from depression. The person finds it almost impossible to do even ordinary things, like getting out of bed in the morning. Problems that were once seen as challenges become overwhelming. *Other symptoms:* Insomnia, oversleeping, nervousness, forgetfulness, distraction.

Stage VI: This is the terminal phase where the person either gets fired, goes bankrupt, collapses, has a breakdown, becomes suicidal or ends up with a serious physical illness.

How to avoid burnout:

Each of the above stages represents a warning from nature that you're traveling on too fast a track. This doesn't mean that you're a bad or weak person, just that there's a large, immovable object in front of you and you're heading for a collision.

If you think you're in danger, the best way to avoid it is to open yourself to support, love and nurturing. Look for people to help you. And you've got to take care of yourself.

Recommended: Make a list of all the things you once found relaxing and rejuvenating—lying on the beach, reading mysteries from cover to cover, hiking, spending time with friends. Then figure out why you stopped doing these things and how you can get them back into your life.

Many people advise burnout victims to cut their workload immediately. *Trap:* Unless you've decided what to do with your free time, that won't help. Burnout victims are success-oriented people who need plans before they can feel good about cutting their workload.

Warning: The earlier the burnout is caught, the easier it is to treat. By Stage VI, the victim is psychologically, emotionally and financially exhausted. It will take an extensive period of nurturance and recuperation, and possibly even a career change, to recover.

Important: In an abusive environment—where self-serving or sadistic bosses rule—a hardworking, ambitious employee may go through the six stages in a matter of weeks or months if no action is taken. To avoid burnout, such an employee may have no choice other than to leave the company—or at least transfer to a different department.

Source: Martin G. Groder, MD, a psychiatrist and business consultant in Chapel Hill, North Carolina. His book, *Business Games: How to Recognize the Players and Deal With Them,* is available from Boardroom Classics, Box 11014, Des Moines 50336-1014.

14

Nutrition, Fitness and Exercise

Why Diets Fail

One out of three Americans is overweight, ranging from a few pounds to obese. Most of these people have been on numerous types of diets—many of which have failed.

Here's why dieting no longer makes sense —and new thinking about effective weight loss…

Why dieting fails:

When you diet, your brain—in an act of self-defense against perceived starvation—signals your body that you need more food…and lowers your metabolism so you store more fat. Both actions make it harder to reach your dieting goals.

With each repeated cycle of dieting, it takes longer for a person to lose weight and the weight comes back quicker. What's more, you are likely to accumulate extra pounds each time.

Important: Taking off weight isn't the main problem—keeping it off is. Despite the best nutrition, exercise regimens and diet plans in the world, 90% of dieters regain one-to two-thirds of lost weight within one year and almost all of it within five years.

Breaking the diet mentality:

Getting out of the self defeating diet mode requires that you accept that obesity is a complex medical problem that requires a multi-pronged solution—including possible drug intervention.

Being very overweight is not a result of a lack of will-power or discipline, so stop blaming yourself for your size and deluding yourself that you won't wake up hungry tomorrow. You will, because your brain sabotages your best efforts at psychological control and makes it impossible to resist cravings.

Also recognize that constant dieting can perpetuate your weight problem by adversely affecting your metabolism.

Important: A chronic overweight problem can only be managed, never cured. To keep your weight in "remission," you must be constantly vigilant, eating healthfully and exercising regularly.

A healthy eating plan:

Here's how to start on a healthy eating plan for life...

•**Stop obsessing over your weight** and your appetite. *Trap:* Rather than keeping you "in control," mental preoccupation with dieting is practically guaranteed to keep you overweight because you're constantly thinking of food.

•**Adhere to the following eating guidelines** developed by the Department of Agriculture...

•**Eat 20% of your calories from protein sources**, 20% from fat and 60% from carbohydrates. People with a weight problem should reduce their carbohydrate intake to about 40% and increase protein intake to 40%.

•**Cut back on foods that are high in saturated fats**, including potato chips, ice cream and red meat. They aren't good for you and seem to spark primitive hunger urges.

•**Decrease your intake of simple carbohydrates**—sugars. Instead, concentrate on eating more complex carbohydrates—breads, rice, pasta, potatoes, fruits and vegetables—which will give you energy and make you feel full.

•**Don't skip meals.** Not eating at regular intervals is a foolproof way to get fat—it convinces your body you're starving and need to conserve fat.

•**Don't eat less than 1,200 calories a day.** When you go on such a low-calorie diet, your body starts to break down muscle tissue to use for energy so it doesn't have to dip into its fat stores. You lose weight, but you lose muscle as well as fat, which means that after your diet you'll end up with a higher percentage of body fat to muscle mass. That will make your metabolism work even slower.

•**Start or continue an exercise program.** *Ideal:* Engage in aerobic activity—walking, running, swimming or bicycling—for an hour three times a week. *Second best:* Exercise moderately for 30 minutes five times a week.

To build muscle and offset muscle loss brought on by dieting, also engage in resistance training—using free weights or weight machines—twice a week. Weight training can speed your loss of fat, help you ward off osteoporosis as you age and enhance you endurance.

Important: Unless you are willing to exercise regularly, you will not succeed in keeping weight off.

Role of medications:

If you've been consistently 20 or more pounds overweight from year to year despite real efforts to lose, you may be a candidate for appetite suppressant therapy. See a physician about two drugs that we've recently learned to use to great advantage...

•***Fenfluramine* reduces hunger substantially** by sending satiety messages to the stomach and downsizing cravings for protein and carbohydrates.

•***Phentermine* causes you to eat more rapidly** and to eat less.

Although the drugs can be used separately, they have been found to work even better in combination, allowing you to lose up to 15% of your body weight. However, because these drugs can only correct—and not cure—the permanent physiological imbalances that have altered your body's weight-control mechanism, you may have to take them long-term to maintain your weight loss.

Finding a physician:

It can be difficult to find a physician who will prescribe fenfluramine and phentermine because many people in the medical community still do not believe obesity is a physiological problem.

Discuss drug treatment for obesity with your primary care doctor. If your doctor won't prescribe drugs for you, ask for a referral to an obesity specialist. Or contact the American Society of Bariatric Physicians (303-779-4833) for the name of a doctor who prescribes medication as part of a comprehensive weight-control program. Approximately 60% of physicians today offer such a program.

Source: Steven A. Lamm, MD, clinical assistant professor of medicine at New York University School of Medicine in New York. He is author of *Thinner at Last.* Simon & Schuster.

Strategies for Lifelong Health

Eating low-calorie, nutrient-dense foods—those containing as many nutrients as possible per calorie—may increase your life span.

Over time, you'll become substantially younger in...
- **Form** (body shape).
- **Feature** (appearance).
- **Function** (how well your body works, including your brain).

You'll improve your eyesight and hearing, sharpen your intelligence, reduce your need for sleep, have more pep and enhance your sense of well-being.

A nutrient-dense diet diminishes hunger—since it works continuously to provide energy and a sense of fullness.

Perhaps most important, you'll increase your resistance to colds and flu as well as more serious diseases, including...
- **Clogged arteries and heart disease.**
- **Breast, lung and liver cancer.** At least 70% of overall cancer risk is related to diet.
- **Leukemia.**
- **Inflammation of the large bowel** (diverticulitis). More than half of Americans older than 50 have diverticula, balloon-like outpouchings of tissue that can become swollen and painful.

People who start the antiaging diet at age 20 could theoretically live to age 140. But you'll extend your age whenever you start if you follow the program consistently. Even if you never become thin, simply dropping below your usual weight—and staying there—will extend your life.

How we know this: When I began our two-year stint in a sealed environment in the Arizona desert in September 1991, we (the eight-member Biosphere team) had less land than we needed to grow food. Under the regimen I devised on a computer program I created, we lost weight, felt great and substantially reduced our total cholesterol levels, blood pressure and fasting blood sugar. These were the identical changes that animals (including primates) showed on a similar diet.

Seven simple steps:

1. On the same day each week, weigh yourself before breakfast. Decide if you want to aim for weight loss and health promotion only, or add the life-extending element of the antiaging plan. To extend your life, you'll have to reduce your weight at least 10% and preferably 20% below your set point (usual weight). After four weeks of rapid weight loss, you will work towards slow, steady weight reduction.

2. Have a complete physical. Discuss your plan with a trusted and receptive doctor.

Ask whether there's any medical reason you shouldn't strictly limit your calorie intake indefinitely. If you go on the plan, have basic tests done (blood pressure, pulse, total cholesterol, High-Density Lipoprotein [HDL] cholesterol, fasting blood sugar, tests for autoantibodies and white blood cell count) after four to six months...and then annually. Test results should show improvement quickly.

3. Choose between rapid orientation and gradual orientation. For the gradual route, eat one low-calorie, high-nutrient meal during the first week, two such meals during the second week and so on until you're participating fully.

For other meals, eat wholesomely and sensibly. Meanwhile, cook and freeze meals you'll need later. Seek out local restaurants that serve dishes consistent with your goals. Prepare your friends and family for the big change you're making in your life.

4. Avoid caffeine, sugar and dairy products other than nonfat ones. Base all your meals on foods derived from plants—grains, beans, rice, pasta, breads, vegetables and fruits. Eat red meat and poultry in small amounts only, if at all. Start with 1,800 calories a day. If you're losing weight too fast, slowly increase your intake to a maximum of 2,200 calories a day.

5. Begin and maintain a program of moderate exercise with your doctor's approval. A good way to start is to take a brisk 30-minute walk three times a week.

6. Take one multivitamin/mineral pill a day. It should provide about 50% of the Recommended Daily Allowance (of the major vitamins and minerals). *Also take…*

• **500 milligrams** of vitamin C.

• **300 to 400 International Units** (IU) of vitamin E.

• **100 micrograms** of selenium.

• **25,000 IU** of beta carotene (toxicity levels for beta carotene are not yet known).

Optional: 0.5 to 1 gram of magnesium…0.1 milligram of chromium in organic form…and 20 milligrams of coenzyme Q10 (CoQ10), an essential part of the membranes of the energy factories of the cell that may help prevent cancer.

Note: It is important to check with your doctor before taking these or any supplements.

7. Plan how you want to spend your longer, healthier, more vigorous life.

Antiaging eating:

• **Sprinkle two tablespoons of wheat germ** (flakes) on salads, soups, hot and cold cereals or casseroles daily.

What to buy: Refrigerated, unprocessed wheat germ found in health food stores tends to be fresher than the processed kind sold in supermarkets.

• **Add a heaping tablespoon of oat bran or wheat bran flakes**, which provide 10% of daily fiber requirements, to salads, soups, cereals or casseroles.

• **Sprinkle brewer's yeast** (a powder), one of the healthiest of all foods, over grains or salads…stir it into stews…toss it with unbuttered air-popped popcorn with a little low-sodium soy sauce to make it stick.

• **Substitute fresh lemon juice** for salt, salad dressing and sauces on steamed vegetables.

• **Discover the world of healthful whole grains**…amaranth, barley, bulgur, millet and wheat berries.

• **Choose dishes that are steamed, broiled or roasted** (without butter) in restaurants…avoid those that are sautéed, fried, braised, creamed or escalloped.

Lessons from the East:

These foods, commonly used in Japanese cooking, are nutritional wonders with almost no calories…

• **Shiitake mushrooms.** These large, meaty fungi are filling and loaded with healthful minerals as well as fiber and vitamin D. Fresh ones are great in vegetarian stews and stir-fries. Dried ones must be soaked in hot water for 15 minutes before cooking.

• **Seaweeds** contain vitamin B6…calcium… iron…possibly vitamin B12 (usually sparse in vegetarian diets) and vitamin D. *These two seaweeds are popular:*

• **Kombu.** Cut into strips with kitchen shears. Add in first stages of cooking soup. Before adding to stir-fries or casseroles, cover strips with water and soak for 10 to 15 minutes or until soft. Add, minced, to recipes for leafy green vegetables.

• **Nori.** The thin, dark-green sheet wrapped around sushi rolls. Cut or tear pieces and add to stir-fries and casseroles. Toast a sheet and crumble it over salad, rice, vegetables or baked potatoes.

Anyone who requires a low-salt diet should avoid nori, which has a high-sodium content.

Resources:

If you can't find specialty items in your local stores or markets, you may be able to get them by mail from Walnut Acres, Penn Creek, PA 17863. 800-433-3998. Williams Sonoma, Box 7456, San Francisco 94120. 800-541-2233.

The antiaging kitchen:

Organizing your pantry simplifies planning and cooking. *For example:*

• **Alphabetize spices** for easy access.

• **Store grains, legumes and dried pastas** in one-quart glass jars labeled with large letters.

• **Spend half a day each week** preparing and freezing enough nutrient-rich dishes for the following week.

Source: Roy L. Walford, MD, who spent two years sealed in Biosphere 2 in the Arizona desert as team physician. A leading gerontologist, Dr. Walford is a professor of pathology at the University of California, Los Angeles, School of Medicine. Building on his previous book, *The 120-Year Diet*, is his latest book, *The Anti-Aging Plan: Strategies and Recipes for Extending Your Healthy Years.* Four Walls Eight Windows.

Foods that Can Change Your Mood

Sweet and starchy carbohydrates boost the level of a "stress-relief" chemical in your brain, serotonin, making you feel relaxed and in emotional control. *Examples:* Bagel, pasta, baked potato.

Foods high in protein can help increase mental alertness when you are running low on mental energy. *Examples:* Fish, poultry and dairy products.

Source: Judith Wurtman, PhD, nutrition researcher, Massachusetts Institute of Technology in Cambridge.

How Food Allergies Affect Behavior

The behavior of some children with allergies improves significantly when allergies are addressed.

Watch for a child's behavior after eating chocolate—the caffeine and sugar can give some children more energy than they can handle. Caffeine in any form is a powerful stimulant that children should not have without a doctor's approval.

If you suspect your child has a food allergy, have him/her tested. Changing eating habits could make a big difference.

Source: Mitch Golant, PhD, clinical psychologist, Bel Air, CA, and author of *The Challenging Child.* Berkley Books.

Soybeans Are Very, Very Good for Your Health… How to Make Them A Wonderful Part of Your Diet

If you are not eating soy foods already, now may be a good time to start. *Reason:* A recent University of Kentucky study links soy con-sumption with lower cholesterol levels and reduced risk of cancer.

For generations, soybeans have been a staple in Japan and other countries in the Far East. But here in the US, soybeans are often associated with bland "cafeteria food." (Soy was widely used as a meat extender in the 1960s and 1970s, but the products available then were vastly inferior to those now on the market.)

Also: Americans are often unfamiliar with soy-based foods…or they're dubious about the taste of soy…or they're uncertain how soy dishes are prepared.

In fact, soy dishes are very tasty when they're prepared properly. And soy is surprisingly easy to work into your daily diet. It's also an extremely inexpensive source of protein, calcium and many other valuable nutrients. Health benefits:

The Kentucky study, led by James W. Anderson, MD, reviewed 38 prior studies spanning 25 years and involving more than 700 participants. The evidence shows quite convincingly that consumption of soy brings…

•**Reduced risk of heart disease.** When people with moderately or even highly elevated cholesterol add soy protein to their diets, cholesterol levels drop an average of 13%.

Unlike many dietary approaches to cholesterol reduction, eating soy reduces the level of "bad" (LDL) cholesterol without lowering "good" (HDL) cholesterol levels.

Surprising: Adding soy to the diet helps reduce cholesterol levels even in individuals who continue to eat a high-fat diet. Of course, this is not to suggest that soy consumption can be used as an excuse to continue poor eating habits.

Soy is one element of a heart-healthy lifestyle. Other elements include lowering fat intake, eating more fruits and vegetables, exercising regularly and reducing psychological stress.

Soy reduces heart attack risk by lowering cholesterol levels and inhibiting oxidation of cholesterol in the bloodstream—by about 50%.

Benefit: LDL cholesterol is harmful only once it has been oxidized (that's when it adheres to artery walls, forming fatty plaques that interfere with blood circulation). So, preventing oxidation of LDL may be just as important as lowering total cholesterol levels.

Preliminary evidence suggests that a soy component called genistein helps block formation of fatty plaques—and makes platelets less likely to clump together. This lowers risk of stroke as well as heart attack—one more reason why even individuals with normal cholesterol would do well to eat soy.

•**Reduced cancer risk.** Scientists compared cancer rates in Japan and other "soy-friendly" countries with rates in the US and in other countries with low soy consumption.

What they found: Soy consumption is linked to reduced incidence of cancer of the breast, colon, prostate and lung.

To separate the effects of soy from other aspects of diet or environment, scientists also compared soy consumption and cancer risk within the same culture. The results were similar.

Example: Japanese who eat one serving of soy-based food a day are less likely to develop cancer than Japanese who eat soy infrequently.

Several additional studies found that cancer rates in animals fed soy foods are far lower than rates in animals not fed soy. There's also evidence that soy inhibits the growth and spread of existing tumors.

•**Reduced discomfort during menopause.** Women in Japan are far less likely than American women to be plagued by hot flashes, night sweats, mood swings and other symptoms of menopause. One Australian study found that menopausal women who ate soy foods had 40% fewer symptoms than women who didn't eat soy.

How do soy foods ease menopause discomfort? The answer seems to involve isoflavones, a class of compounds found only in soybeans.

•**Reduced risk of osteoporosis.** Soy foods may prevent bone loss via three mechanisms…

Mechanism #1: Most types of protein cause calcium to be excreted in the urine. Soy's calcium-excretion effect is comparatively weak.

Mechanism #2: Many—but not all—soy foods are good sources of calcium, and it is in a form that is easily absorbed by the body. Look for calcium-fortified soy products.

Mechanism #3: Isoflavones help keep bones from breaking down. No one really knows why.

Adding soy to your diet:

The more soy you eat, the greater the benefit. Evidence suggests that eating three or four servings of soy foods a week reduces your cancer risk by about 20%. Eating one serving every day cuts your risk by as much as 45%. There are many ways to add soy to your daily diet…

•**Soymilk.** Pour it on your breakfast cereal—instead of milk. Made from ground soybeans and water, soymilk comes in a variety of flavors, many of them quite delicious. Soy milk is a good alternative to milk for individuals suffering from lactose intolerance.

Soymilk is sold in unrefrigerated cartons. You can buy low-fat, no-fat and whole-milk varieties. Sweetened soymilk is easier to take if you aren't used to the flavor.

•**Tofu.** Though it strikes many people as an unappetizing white blob, tofu is very versatile. Bland and porous, it takes on the flavors of the foods and spices with which it's cooked. Use soft tofu instead of cheese to stuff into pasta shells or to make a spicy dip. Firm tofu is delicious marinated and stir-fried with vegetables and garlic sauce.

Caution: Tofu sold without packaging (floating in tubs of water) is sometimes contaminated with harmful bacteria. Buy commercially packaged tofu only.

•**Textured soy protein.** More commonly known as textured vegetable protein (TVP), this product is made from soybeans that have been dehydrated, defatted and formed into granules. Add water, and you've got a great base for sloppy joes or taco filling. If you like, mix it half-and-half with ground beef.

•**Soy flour.** When a recipe for bread, muffins, etc., calls for wheat flour, try substituting soy flour for 25% or so of the total. That will give the bread a pleasing texture and enhanced flavor. Don't use all soy flour or you will get a leaden effect.

•**Second-generation soy products.** You can buy soyburgers, tofu hot dogs, tofu lasagna, soymilk ice cream and a host of other convenience foods that substitute soy for more familiar ingredients.

Obviously, these don't taste exactly like the originals, but many of these imitations are excellent.

Cooking with soy:

Here are my favorite soy-based recipes, reprinted from my book *The Simple Soybean and Your Health*...

Creamy chocolate pie:

Although this dessert is too fatty for everyday eating, it's a great way to overcome "tofu-phobia."

10-ounce package semisweet chocolate chips

3 tablespoons corn sweetener

20 ounces tofu

9-inch graham cracker pie crust

1. In a double boiler, heat the chocolate chips until completely melted. Stir in the corn sweetener.

2. In a blender or food processor, blend the tofu until smooth. Add the chocolate mixture and blend until creamy. Pour the filling into the pie crust.

3. Chill the pie overnight.

Makes 8 servings. *Per serving:* 321 calories, 6 g protein, 17 g fat, 43 g carbohydrate. 44% fat.

Onion Dip:

Another good choice for the uninitiated.

1 pound low-fat tofu

2 tablespoons fresh lemon juice

2 teaspoons sugar

1 package dry onion soup mix

1. In a blender, combine the tofu, lemon juice and sugar. Blend until smooth.

2. In a small bowl, combine the tofu mixture and soup mix. Stir by hand.

3. Refrigerate the dip for at least two hours to let the flavors develop. Serve with raw vegetables or crackers.

Makes 2⅛ cups. *Per two-tablespoon serving:* 20 calories, 1.8 g protein, 0.4 g fat, 2 g carbohydrate. 18% fat.

Sloppy Joes:

Perfect for a quick family dinner. (If you prefer, make your sloppy joe sauce from scratch.)

1 cup textured vegetable protein

1 cup boiling water

16-ounce can sloppy joe sauce

4 whole-wheat hamburger rolls

1. To rehydrate the TVP, place it in a medium saucepan and pour the boiling water over it.

2. Add the sloppy joe sauce to the TVP. Cook over low heat until heated.

3. To serve, pour the TVP mixture over the hamburger rolls.

Makes 4 servings. *Per serving:* 196 calories, 15 g protein, 2 g fat, 32 g carbohydrate. 10% fat.

Source: Mark Messina, PhD, a leading authority on the health benefits of soy foods and founder of the National Cancer Institute's research program on soy's anti-cancer properties. He is coauthor of *The Simple Soybean and Your Health.* Avery Publishing Group.

Thin Women Live Longer

The most recent US weight guidelines recommend weights up to 20 pounds heavier than those listed in the 1959 Metropolitan Life Insurance Company tables. *Trap:* These more liberal allowances have lulled women into believing that weight gain isn't harmful. *It is.*

Source: JoAnn E. Manson, MD, codirector of women's health, Harvard Medical School, Boston.

Reduce Risk of Stroke

Stroke risk might be cut by eating more fruit and vegetables and using healthy oils. One study found that for every increase in the intake of fruits and vegetables to three servings a day, the risk of stroke in men dropped by 22%. One serving consists of a piece of fruit ...or a cup of leafy vegetables...or half of a cup of cooked vegetables...or six ounces of fruit juice. Another study found that men with high levels of alpha-linolic acid, found in canola oil, soybean oil and walnuts, had 28% less risk of stroke than those with low levels.

Source: Matthew Gillman, MD, assistant professor of ambulatory care and prevention, Harvard Community Health Plan, Harvard Medical School.

Proven New Nutritional Plan for Beating Arthritis

As a cardiologist, I've long used a natural, nutritional approach for prevention and treatment of heart disease.

To my surprise, many of my heart patients have found that my nutritional therapy also helps reduce pain and swelling in their arthritic hands, knees and other joints. This observation led me to review the literature on nutrition and arthritis.

Ultimately, I developed a program of eating guidelines and nutritional supplementation designed specifically to ease the pain and inflammation of arthritic joints. (Of course, these same strategies help reduce the risk of heart disease.)

Follow these guidelines for at least eight weeks, and you'll see a significant reduction in pain and stiffness...

•**Raise your blood pH.** Each day, have a glass of carrot, apple or cherry juice. These juices have an "alkalyzing" effect on the blood.

Avoid orange juice, grapefruit juice and other citrus juices...as well as tomatoes, potatoes, eggplant and other foods from the nightshade family.

These "acidifying" foods *lower* blood pH. A lower pH promotes formation of crystals in your joints, which leads to arthritis.

•**Eat chlorophyll.** Be sure to drink a glass of green barley, chlorella or frozen wheat grass every day. Each of these is rich in this green pigment.

Chlorophyll helps remove excess heavy metals from the joints. Heavy metal atoms cause accumulation of free radicals, highly reactive compounds that damage the joints.

•**Eat cayenne and garlic.** Both herbs have an anti-inflammatory effect, helping to reduce swelling and pain.

I urge my patients to take a daily cayenne capsule. If it upsets your stomach, have it with bread or crackers. If stomach upset is severe, stop taking cayenne.

Garlic stimulates the immune system, which supports healing. Garlic also contains the antioxidant mineral selenium. It helps control free radical buildup.

•**Eat omega-3 oils.** Found primarily in flaxseed and fish oil, omega-3 oils stimulate the production of *leukotrienes*, natural compounds that inhibit inflammation.

I recommend taking one 1,000-mg flaxseed oil capsule after each meal. The capsules can be found in any health-food store.

Another way to boost your omega-3 intake is to eat at least one—and preferably two—helpings of fresh fish per week.

•**Drink ginger tea.** In addition to being soothing to the stomach, ginger is a potent anti-inflammatory agent. I recommend one cup a day.

•**Eat Certo.** This pectin-containing gelatin powder, available in any supermarket, is very effective at reducing swelling in the joints.

Each day, consume one tablespoon (mixed with apple juice or another alkalyzing fruit juice to form a soupy gelatin).

It's unclear why Certo relieves arthritis.

•**Take multivitamin supplements.** A combination of antioxidant nutrients is the best way to fight free radicals.

Although fresh fruit and vegetables are rich in antioxidants, the best way to be sure that you get enough is to supplement your diet with multivitamins.

Be sure to select an iron-free supplement. Too much iron has been linked to an elevated risk of heart disease.

The supplement you select should contain no more than 1 mg copper (half the government's recommended daily allowance).

It should also contain folic acid, vitamin B-6, vitamin D, zinc and calcium—deficiencies in any of these nutrients can cause arthritis.

The supplement should also contain selenium and vitamin E. Both nutrients are especially good for morning stiffness.

• **Take *coenzyme Q-10* and *quercetin*.** I recommend 30 mg of coenzyme Q-10 after each meal…and 100 mg to 500 mg of quercetin once a day.

A remarkable substance, coenzyme Q-10 works to stabilize the membrane of every cell in your body. That prevents cell breakdown in your joints.

Quercetin blocks the release of *histamines* (inflammation-producing chemicals) into the bloodstream.

Both supplements are available in health-food stores.

• **Avoid caffeinated beverages**—coffee, tea and soda—as well as chocolate. A diuretic, caffeine washes nutrients out of your body, thereby undermining your efforts to eat a healthful, nutrient-rich diet.

Source: Stephen Sinatra, MD, director of education at Manchester Hospital and a cardiologist in private practice in Manchester, CT. He is the author of *Optimum Health.* Lincoln Bradley.

Fasting Can Be Very Good For Your Health… How to Do It Right

Fasting is a potent tool for achieving optimum health. Studies from Scandinavia, Russia and Japan suggest that a medically supervised fast boosts immune function and helps control arthritis, asthma, anxiety and depression.

I myself have seen fasting bring amazing—and lasting—benefits to patients with high blood pressure, angina, psoriasis, colitis, fibroids and lupus.

Fasting boosts longevity, too. Animals fed nutritious but very low-calorie diets live two times longer than well-fed animals.

Implication: Americans eat too much fat, sugar and protein…and consume too many calories. The long-term effects of our national overindulgence are reflected in the high incidence of high blood pressure and other chronic, degenerative diseases.

What is fasting:

Fasting means abstaining from all food and drink (except water) for a specified period of time. It does not mean starvation.

Soon after a fast begins (48 hours for women, 72 hours for men), the body goes into protein-sparing mode. It conserves essential tissues (heart, lungs, etc.) while sacrificing fat, tumors, fatty deposits in blood vessels and other nonessential tissues for fuel.

If you have broth, fruit juice or another beverage during a fast, you won't go into this protein-sparing state. *Result:* Many of the benefits of fasting will be lost.

Starvation doesn't begin until about five weeks—and that's far longer than anyone should fast. My patients' fasts usually last from one to four weeks.

Caution: For a fast of three days or longer, your doctor must monitor your blood electrolytes (sodium and potassium) to ensure that you have sufficient nutritional reserves.

For a list of health-care professionals in your area who have completed a six-month program in medical fasting, contact the International Association of Hygienic Physicians, c/o Mark Huberman, 204 Stambaugh Building, Youngstown, Ohio 44503.

Why fasting works:

Recent experiments suggest that free radicals and other harmful waste products of cellular metabolism build up inside cells. In addition, we're continually exposed to harmful compounds generated outside the body, such as food additives and natural food toxins.

Result: A gradual decline in cellular function.

Fasting affords a "quiet" interlude during which the body does a kind of "internal house-cleaning." Rather than take in food—and create more waste—it eliminates existing waste. And since no energy is expended toward digestion, the body can devote more energy to healing.

Fasting is not a magic bullet:

Whatever health benefits you get from a fast, you won't maintain them if you go right back to the same unhealthful habits you had before the fast.

Fasting should not be used for weight control. People who fast as a quick, easy way to lose pounds usually gain the weight back once the fast is over. A long-term commitment to sound dietary practices and regular exercise is needed for lasting weight loss.

Fasting can give you a head start on making long-term lifestyle changes. It cleans the palate, raising its sensitivity to simple flavors. Lettuce, for example, tastes sweet after a fast. Less-healthful foods like peanut butter seem heavy and salty.

Heightened sensitivity to tastes, along with the enhanced physical and mental well-being that most people feel during a fast, helps motivate you to sustain healthful habits.

Who should not fast:

Fasting can be dangerous for women who are pregnant or nursing, and for anyone with…

- **Kidney failure.**
- **Hepatitis or other liver trouble.**
- **AIDS or advanced cancer.**
- **A personal history of life-threatening heart arrhythmia.**

Fasting interferes with certain medications, too. During a fast, taking acetaminophen can damage the liver, for example, while taking an antihypertensive drug can cause a dangerous fall in blood volume.

What to expect on a fast:

Many people believe that fasting makes one feel sick, uncomfortable or continuously hungry. Not true. Headache, fatigue, weakness, confusion and other symptoms can occur, but they usually pass after the first day or two. Hunger ends completely after the second day. After that, most people feel great.

How long should a fast last:

For a reasonably healthy person who wants to "cleanse" his body, a one-week fast is probably appropriate.

If you're coming down with a cold or sore throat, a day or two without food—combined with bed rest and lots of water—will help rid your body of the virus.

People with hypertension, heart disease, lupus, asthma, arthritis or another chronic ailment may need to fast for three to four weeks. A doctor's care is essential.

Preparing for a fast:

Eat mostly raw fruits and vegetables for a day or two before starting your fast. Such a diet acts as an intestinal "broom."

Too much refined or starchy food before a fast dries out the stool. (Most people have one bowel movement at the start of the fast, then no more until the fast is over.)

Other important strategies…

- **Rest.** If you plan to fast for just a few days, and your job isn't stressful, it's fine to go to work. But you'll derive greater benefit if you stay quiet and relaxed—napping, reading, listening to music, etc.

- **Drink lots of water.** Have one to three quarts (four to 12 eight-ounce glasses) a day. Water helps your body flush out wastes.

- **Avoid tea and other herbs.** During a fast, they can cause liver and kidney problems.

- **Avoid extremes of heat and cold.** Steam baths, saunas, etc. can make you dehydrated. And since you'll become cold easily while fasting, you may need to dress more warmly than usual.

- **Break your fast gradually.** Eating a big meal too soon after a fast can cause indigestion and painful elimination. *Better:* Reintroduce solid food gradually over three to four days.

Source: Joel Fuhrman, MD, a family physician and fasting specialist in Belle Mead, NJ, and a staff member of Hunterdon Medical Center in Flemington, NJ. He is the author of *Fasting and Eating for Health: A Medical Doctor's Program for Conquering Disease.* St. Martin's Press.

People Often Mistake Thirst for Hunger

To tell the difference: Think back to the last time you ate. If it was less than one hour ago, you're not likely to be hungry. Try drinking some water or juice to stop "hunger pangs."

Source: Audrey Cross, PhD, professor of nutrition, Columbia University School of Public Health, New York.

Underactive Thyroid And Obesity

Contrary to a common myth, hypothyroidism does not make a person fat. Obesity is caused by eating more food than the body requires—usually because of dietary habits and psychological factors. Hypothyroidism simply slows down the body's metabolism—lowering the body's need for food. The appropriate response is to reduce the amount of food eaten. Someone who does not reduce it will gain weight—but the gain will come from overeating, not the underactive thyroid.

Source: *The Thyroid Sourcebook: Everything You Need to Know* by M. Sara Rosenthal, a health writer who was treated for thyroid cancer, Etobicoke, Canada. Lowell House.

Weight Gain Causes Foot Problems

As weight increases, feet grow larger and a person is more likely to have foot and ankle trouble. *Example:* Overweight women were three times as likely to have ankle pain as women of normal weight.

Source: Carol Frey, MD, orthopedic surgeon, University of Southern California Foot & Ankle Clinic, Los Angeles, and author of a five-year study of 580 women.

No More Overeating During the Holidays

Successfully keeping your weight down around the holidays can be done without great sacrifice or stress. *Steps to take before you go visiting...*

•**Spoil your appetite.** You will be better able to control your eating at a party if you have a small, healthful snack before you leave your house. Fasting before a feast will only lead to binging.

•**Politely request low-fat foods.** Call your hosts in advance and explain that you're trying very hard to lose weight. Ask if it's possible for you to have no-fat foods, such as a salad for dinner and cold fresh fruit for dessert. Volunteer to pick up whatever your hosts do not already have.

•**Eat with awareness.** Pay attention to what you are eating and recognize the moment when you're no longer hungry. Stop when you've had enough.

•**Remember the event's true purpose.** On your way to the event, remind yourself that companionship—not food—is the real reason why everyone is getting together. This will take your focus off your desire to eat. When you nourish your soul, your appetite decreases.

•**How you eat is important.** Instead of eating an entire dessert, have just a spoonful. Close your eyes and let it melt in your mouth, and enjoy the full flavor. Follow this advice and you are likely to eat less.

Source: Dean Ornish, MD, president and director of the Preventive Medicine Research Institute in Sausalito, CA. His most recent book is *Eat More, Weigh Less.* Harper-Collins.

Beauty Queen Tells How She Took Off 185 Pounds... And Kept Them Off

When I became Rose Festival Princess of Portland, Oregon, in 1970, I was 5'8" tall and weighed 140 pounds.

Within two years, I was pregnant with our first child—and eating my way to 210 pounds. During the next 14 years, I had four more children and binged regularly—especially during each pregnancy. By 1986, I weighed more than 300 pounds.

In 1990, while reading my diary detailing the misery of my obesity, I finally decided that enough was enough. I became smarter about losing weight and lost a total of 185 pounds by 1994. Today I weigh 135 pounds—and have maintained that weight for the last year.

247

But while losing weight is a long and difficult process, keeping it off also takes great effort. *Here's what has worked for me...*

•**Consider weight maintenance a daily activity.** Once I dropped down to my ideal weight, I focused on maintaining it. It's all a matter of self-defense against those high-calorie, unhealthful foods.

My weight is my first thought in the morning and my last thought at night. The idea is to keep your food intake always in the forefront of your mind.

Strategy: Every morning, I tell myself, *I'm going to be in control of my eating today.* If I ate too much the day before, I tell myself, *It's OK that I overate yesterday. I'll eat fewer calories today or exercise for an extra half-hour.*

At night, I analyze anything I might have done wrong that day and try to determine how to do it right the next day.

•**Don't fall into the trap of overeating low-fat foods.** Though some diet experts say you need to reduce only your fat intake in order to lose weight, the truth is that many low-fat foods cause you to gain weight because of all the sugar they contain.

As a result, calories are ultimately what count to maintain your weight.

Strategy: Here is a simple caloric formula to use as a guide for your weight maintenance...

•**Women** can determine how many calories a day to eat by multiplying their weight by 11 calories.

•**Men** can multiply their weight by 12 calories.

Example: By multiplying my current weight of 135 pounds by 11 calories, I have determined that I can eat 1,485 calories a day without gaining weight or exercising like a maniac. If I exercise, I can eat more—depending on how rigorous my fitness regimen is.

•**Develop a personalized maintenance plan.** Though you can follow an established diet plan if it works for you, you might prefer to devise your own plan. *Strategies...*

•**Count calories carefully.** I use a customized three-ring notebook. In the Daily Menu section, I plan ahead by listing exactly what I am going to eat that day. I determine if there will be any special meals or party foods to which I might be exposed, so I can keep the day's calorie count under control. Then each night, I review my Daily Menu, making note of any additions or deletions, and add up the total calories. *Important:* If you overeat one day, don't let it set you back. Instead, compensate the next day by eating less or exercising more.

•**Take time to improve your self-image.** I have learned that how I feel about myself has a great deal to do with whether I stick to my weight-loss plan. I regularly use a list in my notebook to remind me to keep my nails polished and my makeup applied.

•**Analyze every food mistake you make.** Whenever I find myself eating something that's not in my Daily Menu, I retrace my steps to see how I got to the point of no return. Then I try not to make the same mistake a second time.

Example: Let's say I have eaten a cookie. I'll think, *What was the weak link in the chain of events that allowed this cookie to end up in my hand? Was it when I got into the car...or perhaps when I went into the bakery?*

Once I've identified the actions that took place to produce the moment of craving, I try to stay on alert the next time those actions occur. Then, whenever I do resist a cookie, candy bar, between-meal taco or other high-calorie food I don't need, I place the money I would have spent in a jar that says, *Lose a Pound...Gain a Life.* Once a month, I count up that money and send a check to World Relief. For every five cents I contribute, I not only maintain my weight, I also help keep a baby alive and healthy for one day. It's a very satisfying feeling.

•**Give up your biggest craving.** It may be cheese, chips or peanut butter. Mine was chocolate. When I allowed myself to eat it, the snack triggered a stronger impulse to eat and I gorged on anything I could get my hands on. But since I gave up chocolate—cold turkey—four years ago, I have maintained better control of my weight than ever before.

Reason: Giving up the food that has the most control over you will enable you to control your urge to eat other foods. Thinking about giving up chocolate forever was at first incomprehensible for me. But actually doing it has been surprisingly easy.

While you're at it, empty your cabinets and refrigerator of any high-calorie and low-nutrition foods, such as potato chips, cookies, candy and nuts. What you don't see, you won't be able to eat. Instead, buy more fruits and vegetables.

•Ask someone to help support and motivate you. When you have support, anything is easier. My husband helps me plan what to eat and reviews my charts regularly. He does the food shopping, so that I won't be tempted to toss junk food into the cart. And he helps me to review my Daily Menu each night.

Example: I'll show my husband my daily checklist, and he'll say, *You did well today with planning your food, honey, but you didn't exercise, and I notice you haven't for a few days—so tomorrow I'll exercise with you.*

I know I'll have to watch my weight for the rest of my life because every day I am faced with choices about how much and what to eat. I can't escape it.

Maintenance is a lifelong challenge—though it gets easier and more automatic the longer you keep at it.

Source: Rosemary Green, a homemaker in Beaverton, OR. She is the author of *Diary of a Fat Housewife: A True Story of Humor, Heartbreak and Hope.* Warner Books.

How to Reduce Food Intake and Lose Weight Without Feeling Deprived

By age 50, we often find that the rules of eating have changed but nobody warned us about it.

Researchers estimate that we lose the capacity to burn an additional 500 to 750 calories a week for every decade we live. "Creep syndrome"—gaining a pound or two a year—adds up. Anyone who does not adjust is in for a fat awakening.

Each year, Americans spend $33 billion on diet programs and products. They have the right idea, since one-third of US adults over age 20 are overweight. Yet 95% of the millions of people who lose weight gain it back.

The secret of the fortunate five percent is gaining control.

Food control training—not willpower, but control power—is your ticket out of the revolving door of weight loss and weight gain.

About half my clients are over 50. They're finally letting go of long-cherished myths: *I'll start my diet tomorrow…this meal doesn't count…I can't be rude to my host…*and the Big Lie—*I'll just have a little.*

They've reached the dangerous decade, when overweight takes its toll in high blood pressure, diabetes and heart disease. As they face mortality, they're more honest about their role in preserving their own health. To get started, define your "personal thin." That's the weight that will improve your health, appearance and quality of life. It's the weight that allows you to walk briskly up a flight of stairs but doesn't require starvation.

Look at yourself naked in the mirror. Imagine yourself looking as you want to look. Keep that image—not the image of a *Cosmo* or *GQ* model—in your mind. You can achieve it. Twin threats:

•Deprivation. Whether constantly eating, incessantly exercising or anorexic, Americans are enslaved by food. To let yourself feel deprived is to surrender to the control of food —to deny yourself freedom and self-determination. Deliberately avoiding fattening foods is not deprivation. It is liberation.

•Craving. Even a strong food craving usually dissipates within four to 12 minutes. Ride your craving like a wave. Rehearse a response and remember, cravings are just feelings, not commands.

Trigger foods:

Your trigger foods are the ones that make you want more. Most people crave foods made with sugar, flour and/or fat. But personal preferences vary a great deal. *In general…*

Men love salty, crunchy foods—chips, pretzels, salted nuts.

Women and younger people of both sexes love sweets, especially chocolate.

Everyone loves finger foods. They're so easy to buy…and eat.

Creamy foods evoke childhood. They're often high in fat, which has a slightly sedating effect. *Examples:* Puddings, mashed potatoes, ice cream—even sticks of butter and mayonnaise.

If after eating a small amount of any food (or even while eating it) you feel intense cravings for more, you can't trust yourself to have that food.

Consider your trigger foods your enemies, not your friends. Post a list of these foods on your refrigerator.

Other solutions...

Have it on your birthday or on the last day of your annual vacation—never at any other time. If, like most people, you can't eat a couple of chocolate morsels without finishing the package, strike chocolates from your personal menu.

My clients express more relief, not regret, when they recognize each enemy and refuse to let it destroy them.

They admit they can't love something that keeps making them feel bad about themselves. Home:

- **Ban trigger foods from the house.** Availability creates craving.

- **If your housemate must have your trigger food**, literally lock it up—and give him/her the only key. Ask him to keep it out of your sight. We are "visual eaters." If we see it, we want it. Let him hide it or even put it in a locked box if nothing else works.

- **Do not eat so-called snack foods**...which I believe are responsible for the fattening of America.

- **Start dinner** with a glass of chilled tomato juice.

- **Pay attention to what, where and when you eat.** Don't eat while standing up, working, cooking, talking on the phone or watching TV—it's too easy to overindulge without enjoyment.

- **Feel obligated to clean your plate?** Don't load it up—and don't have seconds.

- **Buy only small amounts or packages of food at a time.** You can't eat what isn't there.

- **Frequency can destroy control far more than quantity.** The ad writer who first wrote, "Bet you can't eat just one," pinpointed the downfall of millions. Don't have just a little...every day.

- **Do whatever works for you.** During a recent book tour, when people fed me endlessly for weeks, I kept my bathroom scale in the middle of the living room as a reminder not to overdo.

Restaurants:

- **Remember the hidden calories in salad dressings**, and vegetables and foods that are sautéed in butter or oil. Ask for balsamic vinegar or use a light dressing. Ask for vegetables and foods to be steamed or poached or sautéed in wine or broth.

- **Ignore the breadbasket.** Can you really flake some crust off a roll and ignore the rest? (I've seen a few women do it, but never a man.) Ask the server to remove the basket or not to bring it in the first place. If that would miff your fellow diners, move the basket to the opposite side of the table and turn over your bread plate. Or, give back the bread plate.

- **Remember, white is light and green is lean.** Order fish, seafood, white poultry, egg white omelets, vegetables, fat-free yogurt. And exercise, exercise, exercise.

Source: Psychologist Stephen Gullo, PhD, president of the Institute for Health and Weight Sciences in New York City. He is the author of *Thin Tastes Better: Control Your Food Triggers and Lose Weight without Feeling Deprived.* Random House.

How to Resist The Foods You Love

Here are a few ways to resist the irresistible foods that show up at social gatherings...

- **Just say that you're allergic to the food that's being offered**—or that you have a medical problem. (You do...you're allergic to fat.)

- **Mention to at least one fellow party-goer that you can't have specific foods.** You'll then be too self-conscious to eat it.

- **Do what Scarlett O'Hara refused to do**—eat before you go.

- **Remember**, thin people say, *No, thank you.*

All About Olestra

Olestra (Olean), the newly approved dietary fat substitute, has already been linked to diarrhea and cramping. *New fear:* That it depletes the body of disease-preventing nutrients like carotenoids and vitamins A, D, E and K. Eating as few as three olestra-containing snacks a week reduces the body's store of carotenoids by 10%. *Impact:* Olestra snacking could cause up to 9,800 more cases of prostate cancer a year—as well as many additional cases of heart disease, stroke, blindness and other types of cancer.

Source: Meir J. Stampfer, MD, DrPH, professor of epidemiology and nutrition, Harvard School of Public Health, Boston.

Cholesterol, Nutrition, Weight and More

Our fascination with nutrition and how the foods we eat help or harm us continues to grow. Unfortunately, conventional nutritional science is quite primitive, resulting in considerable confusion even within the medical community.

This confusion exists because the general public and many physicians don't know how to interpret accurately the flood of new research on nutrition.

To help clear up some of the uncertainty, here are the answers to the big questions I'm frequently asked...

What is cholesterol—and what is the difference between "good" and "bad" cholesterol?

Cholesterol is a waxlike substance that is needed for the body's normal metabolism. It travels through the blood system in little protein "packages" called lipoproteins.

One type of cholesterol is *low-density lipoprotein*—or *LDL*. It is commonly referred to as "bad" cholesterol because it damages the arterial walls. *High-density lipoprotein*—or *HDL*—is called "good" cholesterol because it appears to protect the arteries from damage.

Your body naturally produces all the cholesterol it needs. This is why you don't need any dietary cholesterol and should avoid foods that raise the cholesterol levels in your blood. If your cholesterol is too high, you are at greater risk of developing coronary artery disease.

What to do: Ask your doctor for your total cholesterol count and how it breaks down into LDL and HDL. Total cholesterol should be less than 180 milligrams per deciliter of blood—but a higher level may be fine if the ratio of HDL to LDL is high. If your total cholesterol level gets low enough—under 140, for example—you may not need to worry at all about the HDL/LDL level.

Exercise has been shown to boost HDL. Alcohol may also raise HDL, but since it has many adverse effects, I don't recommend you start drinking in order to boost your HDL level. If you do drink, opt for red wine and stick with one or two glasses per day.

How can I lower my level of bad cholesterol?

Controlling cholesterol has more to do with what you *don't* eat than with what you *do* eat. While some foods help lower cholesterol, no one food will dramatically reduce cholesterol.

What to do: Cut back on saturated fats, which are found in meats, eggs, butter, whole milk and whole-milk products. They are also found in processed foods made with animal fats and in palm and coconut oils. The amount of saturated fat you consume has the most direct dietary influence on how much cholesterol circulates in your blood. Foods that contain cholesterol can boost your blood cholesterol level.

Don't assume that products labeled *cholesterol free* are harmless. They may contain saturated fats, so read package labels carefully.

Oat bran can lower cholesterol slightly. Other foods and beverages that may be helpful if consumed each day include fruits and vegetables, onions, raw garlic, chili peppers, shiitake mushrooms and Japanese green tea.

How important is fiber...and how much do I need to eat?

Fiber is a term for the *indigestible* components of the plant foods we eat. The intestines of people who eat a lot of fiber function better, since fiber increases the bulk and frequency of bowel movements. Constipation is often caused by a lack of fiber.

Studies have shown that adequate fiber intake may also lower the risk of colon cancer and prevent the incidence of irritable bowel syndrome and diverticulitis (inflammation of the intestines).

What to do: The average adult should eat 40 grams of fiber each day—about twice as much as most people consume. You can increase your fiber intake by eating cereals that contain bran. Read labels carefully to make sure the product contains between four and five grams of bran per one-ounce serving. You can also increase your fiber intake by including hearty amounts of fruits, vegetables and whole grains in your diet.

Should I be concerned about the pesticide residues on fruits and vegetables?

Yes. Most produce carries traces of pesticides. And the waxes that coat fruits and vegetables (apples, cucumbers, peppers) often contain fungicides, which are toxic and cannot be removed, except by peeling.

What to do: Look for foods labeled *organic* or *pesticide free.*

Be aware, though, that the term *organic produce* may or may not have any meaning, depending on local laws. In California, Oregon and some other states, produce cannot be labeled organic unless it meets strict criteria. But not all states have stringent guidelines. Ask your store's produce manager if you're unsure. Since pesticide-free produce is more costly, you should know which fruits and vegetables are most likely to be contaminated.

Produce that worry me most: Apples, carrots, celery, grapes (and raisins), green beans, lettuce, oranges, white mushrooms, peaches, peanuts, potatoes, strawberries and wheat flour.

What's the best way to cook vegetables?

I prefer steaming or microwaving, which does the least damage to nutrients. Steaming can be used for many foods, including breads, vegetables and fish. Microwave ovens are convenient for thawing and heating as well as for making simple, individual servings. But there's some evidence that microwaving proteins for 10 minutes or more creates new, unnatural forms of proteins that may be harmful.

How can I better control my weight?

My advice can be summed up in two words —*eat less.* Since fat is the densest source of calories—nine calories per gram compared with five calories per gram of carbohydrate or protein—the easiest way to consume fewer calories is to cut down on fat and eat more fruits, vegetables and grains.

At the same time, increase your aerobic activity to help burn off calories. As long as you stay on a low-fat diet and exercise for 30 minutes, five days a week, you should not regain the weight you lose.

Source: Andrew Weil, MD, director of the Program of Integrative Medicine at the University of Arizona College of Medicine in Tucson and a leading expert on alternative medicine, mind/body interactions and medical botany. Dr. Weil is the author of six books, including the best-sellers *Spontaneous Healing* (Knopf) and *Natural Health, Natural Medicine* (Houghton Mifflin).

---

10 Secrets of Successful Weight Loss

If you're trying to lose weight, it's easy to be discouraged by the experts. Doctors and dietitians routinely cite pessimistic figures like the notorious "95% failure rate." According to this statistic, 95% of all dieters gain their weight back—and then some.

The truth about weight loss may not be nearly so dire. A 1993 survey by *Consumer Reports* found that one in four readers who used commercial diet programs had kept off at least two-thirds of the weight they had lost.

Twenty-five percent is still a lower success rate than most of us would like. But instead of focusing on dieting failures, I decided to look at what's different about people who *don't* gain weight back.

I consulted the experts who *really* matter— 160 people, each of whom had lost at least 20 pounds (average weight loss for this group turned out to be 63 pounds) and who had kept the weight off for at least three years.

It turned out that there were 10 common threads among these "successful losers"...

1. They believed they could do it. Most of the people I surveyed had lost and regained their weight at least five times before success-fully keeping it off. But they didn't give up.

The turning point for many of them came when they realized they were sick and tired of the weight-loss battle. Instead of using this feeling as an excuse to stop trying to lose weight, however, the successful dieters some-how felt empowered by it. The feeling made them resolve to take control.

2. They lost weight for themselves—not someone else. All her life, one young woman I interviewed had been told by her mother (and everyone else), "You have such a pretty face—if only you'd lose some weight!"

She lost and gained weight repeatedly. Inside, she was angry that people didn't accept her the way she was. By the time she entered college, she weighed more than 200 pounds. But it was there that she met a man who loved her that way.

Ironically, because she finally felt accepted, she was able to lose weight once and for all—for her own sake.

3. They found out what worked for them. About half the people I talked to lost weight on their own. Others used a commercial diet center or a self-help group...or consulted pri-vately with a dietitian.

In addition, successful people learned to accept a target weight that was realistic *for them*. This goal might be slightly above their ideal weight, but they knew they could go no lower without starving themselves.

4. They were willing to learn a new way of eating—for life. Many dieters go back to their old eating habits once they lose weight. That's why most dieters regain weight.

The weight-control masters accepted low-fat eating as a *way of life*. They learned to enjoy fruits, vegetables and grains. They found ways to add low-calorie flavor by using spices, lemon or lime juice and low-fat products. Gradually, they noticed that they didn't feel good when they ate high-fat foods.

5. They deal with slipups immediately. While they aren't obsessed with the scale, most weigh themselves once a week to once every few days. They have a narrow window of acceptable weight regain (typically five to 10 pounds). When their weight exceeds this

"buffer zone," they do what's necessary to lose it.

Some people exercise more. Others cut back on sweets...pay closer attention to portion sizes...or keep a food diary to increase their awareness of what they eat. But each person I talked to had a plan of action—and used it before the weight gain could get out of hand.

6. They say nice things to themselves. Negative self-talk can be self-fulfilling. An exam-ple is the "now-I've-blown-it" phenomenon that's familiar to many of us: *I ate one cookie. I'm a pig. I might as well eat the whole bag.*

The weight-loss masters give themselves positive and encouraging messages even when they make mistakes: *I resolved not to eat two helpings, but I slipped. I'll be more careful the rest of the day.*

7. They exercise. Nine out of 10 of the suc-cessful people I interviewed exercise regularly. They aren't fanatics, and few of them work out every day. But they've managed to find simple activities—like walking—that they can work into their daily routine.

8. They face their feelings. Back when they were overweight, many of the people I spoke to automatically turned to food when-ever they felt upset, bored, lonely or anxious.

What they learned to do instead was get to the *source* of the negative emotion—by notic-ing the feeling, identifying the cause and figur-ing out a way to solve the problem.

Many of their solutions are quite simple. When bored, they leave the house and do something fun. When lonely, they call a friend. When angry, they confront the person who's mistreating them.

9. They enjoy life. A number of the now-successful people used to spend so much energy taking care of others that they neg-lected their own needs. Eating was their only reward.

Some people who kept weight off have developed what I call a "healthy selfishness." They're still considerate of others, but they take care of themselves, too.

As one woman put it, *I found that when my own needs were met, I was better at meeting the needs of others.*

They've also found ways to reward themselves without food—from pursuing a hobby to seeking more satisfying relationships.

10. They get support. They ask their families not to leave junk food lying around…call a buddy when they're tempted to overeat…and request encouragement and pep talks from friends and family.

Source: Anne M. Fletcher, MS, RD, a registered dietitian who has counseled hundreds of overweight people. A leading writer on nutrition, she is the former executive editor of the *Tufts University Diet & Nutrition Letter* and the author of *Thin for Life*. Chapters Publishing Ltd.

Ten More Ways to Lose 10 Pounds

Ten pounds is the difference between slipping easily into our clothes or struggling to zip zippers and buckle belts. Here are 10 painless changes you can make in your eating habits and lifestyle that virtually guarantee you'll take it off—and keep it off.

1. Have your meals on small plates. As long as your plate is full, psychologically you won't feel deprived, even though you are eating less.

2. Don't be coupon driven. You don't want fattening food, no matter how tempting the coupon.

3. Use evaporated skim milk. Nondairy creamers are loaded with calorie-packed fat.

4. Make a commitment to walk—or bike —all distances under a mile. Burn your calories, as well as reduce them, and you'll lose weight with a left-right punch.

5. Go vegetarian several times a week. Calories from meat, no matter how lean, pile onto your hips a lot faster than calories in vegetables.

6. Switch proportions. Double the size of vegetable servings, while cutting in half chicken, fish or meat portions.

7. Squeeze fat from your diet. Use non-stick vegetable sprays.

8. Rinse canned vegetables for a full minute. You'll cut the salt by 40%—and reduce your water retention.

9. Skim fat from soups before heating. Drop ice cubes into the soup—or refrigerate—and then lift the fat off the top.

10. Bank calories. If you're going out to dinner, eat lighter meals during the rest of the day.

What makes this approach to weight loss so different from traditional dieting is that you don't have to plunge headlong into a radical lifestyle change and implement all 10 weight loss techniques simultaneously. It's best not to "go on" a diet at all—but to tinker gradually with your old habits, until you've developed new ones with which you are comfortable.

Trap: Eighty-five percent of all who go on diets regain the lost weight. Incorporate one or two changes over several weeks until you find your comfort zone. Then add another change or two. You'll find not only your eating habits have changed dramatically, but your waistline as well.

Source: Joan Horbiak, president of Health and Nutrition Network in Philadelphia and author of *50 Ways to Lose Ten Pounds*.

Dieter's Diary

To stick to your diet: Have a motivation diary in a room far from the kitchen. When you crave sweets, pick up the diary and write, *Don't give up* or *Thin tastes better*…be wary of well-meaning friends and relatives who want you to celebrate occasions with food…instead of telling yourself you are fat, try saying, *I feel squishy*—then head for the gym to firm up.

Source: Psychologist Stephen Gullo, PhD, president of the Institute for Health and Weight Sciences in New York City. He is the author of *Thin Tastes Better: Control Your Food Triggers and Lose Weight without Feeling Deprived*. Random House.

Watch What You Eat

If you're going to indulge, pay attention. Instead of cramming down mounds of junk food, savor smaller amounts of such treats as gourmet chocolate, caviar or champagne.

Helpful: Practice eating in front of a mirror, so you'll become more aware of your relationship with food and appreciate what you're eating—even if you're eating less.

Source: *That Special You: Feeling Good About Yourself* by Rita Freedman, PhD, psychologist in private practice in Scarsdale, NY. Peter Pauper Press.

Low-Fat Cooking Basics

Use nonstick cookware to reduce the amount of fat needed to prepare foods…sauté foods by adding a bit of water or broth to the pan instead of fat…remove all visible fat and skin from meats, chicken and fish prior to cooking …skim off all fat from meat juices and stocks before making soups and sauces…cut back on fat from cheese by using fat-free and low-fat varieties—and by using only half as much of such strongly flavored cheeses as sharp cheddar and Romano.

Source: *The Low-Fat Epicure* by Sallie Twentyman, RD, editor of *The Low-Fat Epicure* newsletter, Washington, DC. Berkley Books.

What Tomatoes Can Do for You

Eating tomatoes cuts prostate cancer risk in half. Approximately 10% of all men develop prostate cancer. A new study found that men who ate 10 or more servings of tomatoes each week benefited from the high content of *lycopene,* an antioxidant. Other antioxidants, such as beta-carotene and vitamin A, had no effect on the risk of prostate cancer. Cooked tomato products seemed to bring out more lycopene than raw ones. While tomatoes are the best food source of lycopene, there is a variety of other cancer-fighting foods to include in your diet, such as broccoli, cabbage, soybeans and carrots.

Source: Edward Giovannucci, MD, assistant professor of medicine, department of nutrition, Harvard Medical School, Boston. The nine-year study of 47,000 men between the ages of 40 and 75 was recently published in *The Journal of the National Cancer Institute.*

Healthier Ways to Cook Hamburgers

Partially precook them in a microwave oven for one to two minutes, pour off the juices, then fry, broil or grill. This method removes most of the potentially carcinogenic compounds that form when meat is cooked at high temperatures.

More help for hamburger lovers: Pick a very lean cut of beef—top round is best. Keep servings small. If using ground beef for spaghetti sauce or chili, brown it in a skillet, blot it with paper towels, rinse with hot water and drain completely before mixing in other ingredients. Consider mixing beans or grains with chopped meat to enhance flavor and boost fiber content.

Source: *University of California, Berkeley Wellness Letter,* Box 412, New York 10012.

Creamy Dishes Without Cream

Replace the cream called for in the recipe with an equal amount of evaporated skim milk. *Alternative:* Replace one cup of heavy cream with one cup of regular skim milk plus one-third cup of instant nonfat dry milk powder. These substitutions work in quiches, sauces, casseroles, custards, puddings and other traditionally high-fat dishes.

Source: *Brand Name Fat-Fighter's Cookbook* by Sandra Woodruff, RD, nutrition consultant, Tallahassee, FL. Avery Publishing Group.

Nonfat Pancakes

For nonfat pancakes: Replace each tablespoon of oil in the batter with three-fourths as much nonfat buttermilk, nonfat yogurt, applesauce or mashed banana. *Example:* If a recipe calls for two tablespoons of oil, use one-and-a-half tablespoons of your chosen fat substitute.

Also: Replace each whole egg with three table-spoons of egg white or fat-free egg substitute.

Source: *Brand Name Fat-Fighter's Cookbook* by Sandra Woodruff, RD, nutrition consultant, Tallahassee, FL. Avery Publishing Group.

Less Gas from Gassy Foods

Gas produced by eating cabbage and related vegetables increases the longer the vegetable is cooked. To reduce gas, cook cabbage briefly. Stir-frying works better than boiling or steaming. *Other gas-causing vegetables:* Broccoli, brussels sprouts, cauliflower, turnips. All will produce less gas if cooked for less time.

Source: *Wind Breaks: Coming to Terms with Flatulence* by Terry Bolin, MD, gastroenterologist and associate professor, University of South Wales. Bantam Books.

Red Meat/Breast Cancer Connection

Meat raises breast-cancer risk. Women who ate red meat about once a day had nearly twice the risk of developing breast cancer as women who ate it about once a week. Researchers did not try to pinpoint reasons for the relationship —but said that lifetime dietary habits may influence a woman's hormonal systems.

Source: Study of more than 14,000 women, led by Paolo Toniolo, MD, MSPH, professor of environmental medicine, New York University School of Medicine, 560 First Ave., NY 10016.

Drink Your Milk

Drink the leftover milk in your cereal bowl. *Reason:* Some of the vitamins and minerals in fortified cereals are dissolved into the milk while you eat.

Source: Richard Wood, PhD, associate professor of nutrition, Tufts University Human Research Center, Boston.

Drinking Milk Puts Out Chili Pepper Fires

If milk is not available when you experience that uncomfortable burning sensation in your throat, put some sugar on your tongue and swallow it…or eat a piece of bread. Drinking water is not very effective.

Source: Paul Bosland, PhD, director, Chile Institute, Las Cruces, New Mexico.

Milk: Another View

Milk has been connected to breast cancer through a growth hormone given to cows. Whether or not that research stands up, drinking milk can be risky.

Problems in children: Diabetes, anemia and colic.

Problems in adults: Arthritis, cataracts, anemia, infertility in women and ovarian cancer. The more milk you drink, the greater the risk.

Best sources of calcium: Dark green, leafy vegetables like broccoli, kale and collards (not spinach)…beans…calcium-fortified foods.

Avoid calcium wasters: Animal protein—including beef, poultry and fish…caffeine…salt…tobacco…a sedentary lifestyle.

Source: Neal Barnard, MD, president of Physicians Committee for Responsible Medicine, 5100 Wisconsin Ave., Washington, DC 20016. His most recent book is *Eat Right, Live Longer.* Harmony Books.

Vitamin D Is Important

Add vitamin D to your diet if you live north of the imaginary line that connects Baltimore, Cincinnati, Topeka, Denver and Sacramento.

Reason: Sunlight—the basic source of vitamin D—is weak during January and February, so people living in that region may not be able to synthesize the vitamin through their skin.

Worse: For those who reside north of the line connecting Boston, Milwaukee, Minneapolis and Boise, sunlight is too weak for four months out of the year.

Self-defense: Eat more vitamin D–rich foods —including milk and fatty fish...consider vitamin D supplements containing up to 400 International Units of the vitamin a day.

Source: Bess Dawson-Hughes, MD, chief, Calcium and Bone Metabolism Laboratory, Tufts University, Boston, who led a study of 250 Boston-area women.

Vitamin C and Your Teeth

Do not chew vitamin C tablets. Vitamin C is another name for ascorbic acid. Pieces of chewed tablets can lodge between teeth, where the acid can eat away tooth enamel— especially in older people with receding gums. *Self-defense:* Simply swallow the pills.

Source: Alan Winter, DDS, associate clinical professor of dentistry, New York University School of Dentistry, and partner, Park Avenue Periodontal Associates, 30 E. 60 St., Suite 302, New York 10022.

Don't Discount Beta-Carotene

Don't discount beta-carotene—despite reports released a few months back indicating the contrary. *Reason:* Two of the three medical studies reported were flawed.

Problem: They used only high-risk people ...and the higher death rate was not statistically significant. In nonsmokers and nondrinkers, other studies have shown beta-carotene helps prevent stroke and heart disease.

Best: Get 15 mg of beta-carotene daily from vegetables and fruits—particularly sweet potatoes, carrots, spinach, cantaloupe and mangoes.

Source: Bruce Yaffe, MD, internist in private practice, 121 E. 84 St., New York 10028.

Sparkling Waters May Be Sugary

Some clear beverages are really sugary soft drinks—but are placed on supermarket shelves near plain bottled waters and fruit-flavored waters. *Self-defense:* Read the label to see the calorie content. Water has no calories. Soft drinks can contain 50 or more calories per six- to eight-ounce serving.

Source: *Environmental Nutrition,* 52 Riverside Dr., New York 10024.

Does Caffeine Really Boost Thinking Ability?

Yes. In a study, individuals drank either caffeinated coffee or decaf. *Result:* Those who drank the caffeinated coffee reported feeling more clearheaded, happier and—surprising— less anxious. *Plus:* They scored higher on tests measuring attention, problem-solving and recall. The decaf group experienced no improvement in these skills. *Lesson:* A cup of coffee before a test, presentation, etc., might improve your performance.

Source: David Warburton, PhD, professor of psychology, University of Reading, England. His study of 18 coffee drinkers was published in *Psychopharmacology,* Springer Verlag, KG, D-141 91 Berlin.

Kids and Fiber

The right amount of fiber for kids—in grams—is the child's age plus five. So a seven-year-old, for example, needs 12 grams of fiber per day.

Easy ways to get fiber: Fruit, three or four grams...one-half cup serving of vegetables, two to three grams...fiber-rich cereal, one to five grams.

This formula is for children up to age 20. By age 20, they reach the minimum adult fiber level of 25 grams per day. For adults, daily fiber intake should be 25 to 35 grams.

Source: Christine Williams, MD, director, Child Health Center, American Health Foundation, New York.

Food's Fiber Content

Crunchiness is not an indicator of a food's fiber content. *Example:* Cooked spinach has more fiber than cooked cauliflower, one-half cup of beans or an apple.

Source: Beatrice Trum Hunter, author of *The Great Nutrition Robbery*, writing in *Consumer's Research*, 800 Maryland Ave. NE, Washington, DC 20002.

Cereals Listing Whole Grains First Are Best

The healthiest breakfast cereals have whole grain listed as the first—and therefore main—ingredient. Also check the nutrition label for sugar content. A prudent daily sugar limit is 50 grams (four grams equals one teaspoon). Look for *low-fat* cereals—not necessarily *no-fat* ones. *Reason:* Whole grains contain essential fatty acids, vitamin E and other important nutrients.

Source: *Brand Name Fat-Fighter's Cookbook* by Sandra Woodruff, RD, nutrition consultant, Tallahassee, FL. Avery Publishing Group.

Beware of Trendy Fish Preparations

Trendy fish preparations can increase the risk of illness. Some chefs claim the lime-juice marinade in *seviche* effectively cooks fish and kills parasites—but this is not so. Pan-seared fish, with the outside cooked and the inside virtually raw, is also risky. And there is no evi-

dence to support the idea that dipping shellfish in hot sauce protects against disease.

Self-defense: Only eat fish that is cooked until well done.

Source: Lawrence Ash, PhD, parasitologist, University of California at Los Angeles.

E. Coli Strikes Vegetarians

E. coli strikes vegetarians, too. Vegetables grown in soil fertilized with only partially composted animal manure can be contaminated with the potentially deadly E. coli bacteria, which is most often found in meat. *Self-defense:* Before eating, thoroughly wash all fruits and vegetables.

Source: Dean O. Cliver, PhD, professor of food microbiology, University of California School of Veterinary Medicine, Davis, and author of *Eating Safely: Avoiding Foodborne Illness*. American Council on Science and Health.

Food and Flatulence

Fiber and starch create more gas in the colon than other foods do. But the gas usually has little aroma. Odorous gases depend on foods and spices. Some spices are especially likely to produce smelly gases. In general, gas production increases about one hour after meals—with a large meal producing more than a small one.

Self-defense: If troubled by gas, eat smaller, more frequent meals—of the safer foods.

Source: *Wind Breaks: Coming to Terms with Flatulence* by Terry Bolin, MD, gastroenterologist and associate professor, University of South Wales. Bantam Books.

Large Fish Danger

Large fish such as swordfish, shark and muskellunge should be eaten no more than once a month. *Reason:* They may contain potentially dangerous levels of chemical contaminants. *At greatest risk:* Sport fishermen who catch and eat large amounts of fish from questionable inland waters.

Source: American Institute for Cancer Research, 1759 R St. NW, Washington, DC 20009.

How to Shrink a Potbelly: Seven Strategies That Work... Two that Don't

Last winter, a doctor wrote to *The Journal of the American Medical Association* seeking advice on how to treat one of his patients—a 66-year-old man who was neither sedentary nor overweight, but who nonetheless had a prominent potbelly.

The *Journal*'s brief response was penned by exercise physiologists J. Anthony Spataro, PhD, and Linda Van Horn, PhD. We asked him to explain more fully what causes potbellies—and how they can be eliminated...

The first rule is you can't diet a potbelly off. Of course, being overweight will make a potbelly worse, and it's sensible for many health reasons to cut down on dietary fat. But dieting is no potbelly panacea, as many thin people with bulging bellies have learned.

Likewise, you can't sweat it off. Running, swimming, bicycling and other aerobic exercises are good for your heart, but they do not guarantee you a flat stomach.

In fact, jogging can actually exacerbate a potbelly.

Reason: It's hard to hold your stomach in as you run. The stomach muscles jiggle as you go, causing them to weaken and allowing your belly to distend.

What can you do?

I've found seven strategies for getting rid of a potbelly...

1. Drink less beer. The term "beer belly" is no joke. People who consume large quantities of alcohol—beer in particular—tend to have more visceral fat. That is the kind that collects in and around the liver and other internal organs.

Beer drinking is especially likely to cause a "hard" potbelly. It may feel like "all-muscle," but it's really fat—fat that raises your risk of heart disease and intestinal problems. So forget about those six-pack evenings. Have no more than two beers a day.

2. Avoid late-night meals. I'm not talking about having a snack—some chips or a small bowl of ice cream while watching the late show. I'm talking about stuffing yourself, then going to bed with a full stomach.

Going to bed with a full stomach keeps your stomach muscles relaxed and stretched all night. Over a period of years, this leads inevitably to a potbelly.

Instead, eat as early in the evening as possible. Keep meals small, and make breakfast your biggest meal of the day.

3. Improve your posture. Slouching only makes a potbelly worse. You need to start walking—and standing—tall.

Posture test: Stand with your back and shoulders against a wall. Pull everything up—butt, shoulders and stomach—and stand as erect as possible. If you just can't seem to straighten up, you may have *lordosis*, an inward bending of the lower spine. Ask your doctor to refer you to an orthopedist. He/she can fit you with a posture-improving elastic back brace worn under your clothes.

4. Exercise your stomach muscles. Make a conscious effort to hold in your stomach as you walk around. Doing so will strengthen your stomach muscles—the obliques and rectus abdominis—and prevent them from sagging.

Helpful exercise: The crunch. It's a lot like a bent-knee sit-up. Lie on your back with your knees bent and your feet flat on the floor. Do not sit up far enough to touch your toes. That can cause lower-back pain. Instead, raise your head and shoulders only a few inches—until you feel a slight burning sensation in your stomach muscles.

Hold for 10 seconds, then ease back gently. Repeat as many times as you can—and do it every day.

5. Exercise your lower back. Weak muscles in your lower back can leave you prone to lordosis, which in turn causes the stomach to protrude.

Strength-boosting exercise: Lie face-down on a strong table with your legs dangling down. Grip the table and raise your legs up horizontally behind you. You'll feel it right in the small of your back. Bring your legs back down slowly and gently. Do three sets of 10 repetitions, three times a week.

6. Stretch your hamstrings. If you sit at a desk all day or exercise without stretching, your hamstrings, the muscles in the backs of your thighs, are probably very tight. That makes it harder for them to support your body and keep you standing straight.

The best way to loosen your hamstrings is with regular toe-touching exercise.

What to do: Gently, without bouncing, and keeping your knees slightly bent, reach as far down as you can. Hold for 10 seconds. Straighten up, take a breath and repeat twice. Or sit on the floor with your feet in front of you and lean over as far as you can to touch your toes. You should be able to reach farther with each passing day.

Also important: Stretching your hip flexors. Do this by performing the hurdler stretch. Sit on the floor with one leg in front of you and the other bent back beside you. Reach forward toward your outstretched foot. Hold this position for 10 seconds. Repeat twice and then switch legs.

7. Perform strength-training exercises. By age 65, the average person's muscle strength drops 20%. Circuit training in a gym can forestall this loss—and prevent the gradual weakening that leads to a potbelly.

Source: J. Anthony Spataro, PhD, an exercise physiologist and epidemiologist with the New Mexico Department of Health in Santa Fe.

Physical Fitness Does Keep Us Alive Longer

A study of almost 10,000 men showed that after five years, those in a fitness-building exercise program had nearly half the risk of dying early as their physically unfit contemporaries.

Source: Larry W. Gibbons, MD, MPH, president and medical director of the Cooper Clinic, Dallas.

Health Clubs Can Be Unhealthy

Even the cleanest-looking health club can be full of germs.

Self-defense: Grab a towel when you walk in and keep it between your body and the equipment…instead of wearing skin-baring tank tops and short shorts, exercise in T-shirts and thigh-length shorts…wear flip-flops in the shower. Pooled water on shower floors and damp carpeting can lead to athlete's foot… before using a hot tub, make sure the water is clear—cloudy water and deposits along the sides of the tub are signs of bacterial growth.

Source: Rodney Basler, MD, dermatologist and past chairman of the American Academy of Dermatology's task force on sports medicine, Lincoln, NE.

Not All Motorized Exercise Machines Work

Passive-motion exercise machines claim they do the work and that you build muscle and lose weight. *Reality:* They do not provide effective workouts. To benefit from exercise, you have to sweat for yourself.

Source: Mary Ellen Franklin, EdD, associate professor of physical therapy, East Carolina University, Greenville, NC.

The Path to Excellent Health

How would you like to shed those pounds that you've been trying to lose, without running a single mile, without learning anything about step aerobics and without ever having to hear some muscle-bound trainer advise you to "feel the burn"?

Well…the next time you get up from watching TV and head for the refrigerator, keep on walking—out the door, around the block, to the newsstand, to a neighbor's house—anywhere. Just walk. Doctors will tell you that walking is the safest way to burn fat (and keep it off). And unlike running, walking is a low-impact activity…that means much lower risk of injuries to joints, bones and muscles.

You can burn as many calories walking as you can jogging—it just takes a little longer. Walking briskly (at about four miles per hour) you burn 100 calories per mile. At that rate, a three-mile walk every day will amount to a loss of 35 pounds over the course of a year! And you get both short- and long-term cardiovascular benefits.

Important extra benefit: As those pounds drop off and you improve the overall health and functional ability of your heart, you'll find that your outlook on life improves, too—for exercise not only burns calories, it also works off stress.

Starting at square one:

Before you start your fitness walking program—or any new exercise program—it's important to check with your doctor. If you have an existing or chronic medical condition—diabetes, arthritis, high blood pressure or heart disease—you should make sure that your new exercise plan will not make it worse.

Minimum: Have a resting electrocardiogram. And if you're over 45, a smoker or have known cardiovascular problems, a cardiac stress test is strongly advised. After you pass these tests—and there's every likelihood that you will—you'll know that you're up to the demands of an introductory program in fitness walking.

Initial goal: Three to five 15- to 60-minute exercise periods per week.

During these exercise periods, you should be able to increase your heart rate to more than 70% of maximum capacity.

To find out and monitor how fast you should walk: Subtract your age from 220…this is your maximum heart rate. Take your pulse, at rest, for 60 seconds. Subtract your pulse rate from your maximum heart rate. Multiply the answer by 0.6. This number is your target zone. Add your pulse rate to your target zone. The answer is your target heart rate.

As you walk, take your pulse for 10 seconds and multiply that number by six. If your pulse is less than your target heart rate, step up your pace. If you're exceeding your target, slow down.

Before you begin your walk: Do five minutes of stretching exercises. Stretch your calf muscles by placing both hands against a wall and leaning into the wall with your left leg straight and your right knee slightly bent. Both feet should be flat on the floor. Hold this position for about 30 seconds. Repeat with your right leg straight and your left knee bent.

Stretch the muscle in the front of your thigh (the quadriceps) next. From a standing position, reach behind your back and grab your right foot with your left hand. Pull the foot toward your buttocks while keeping your right knee pointed toward the floor. (Steady yourself by holding onto a chair or railing.) Hold the position for about 30 seconds and repeat with the opposite hand and foot.

Finally, stretch the muscle in the back of your thigh (the hamstring). Again, from a standing position, place your right heel on an elevated surface (such as a stair). Keep your right knee slightly bent, and lean forward from the hips, extending your hands toward your right ankle. Hold the position, repeat with your left leg.

Do these exercises gently. Don't bounce and don't force your muscles if they don't do what you want them to do immediately.

The walk:

Start out at a slow to moderate pace for the first five minutes, then walk briskly for about

25 minutes. After 10 minutes at your faster pace, check your pulse. Are you at or near your target heart rate? Adjust your pace to stay within your target range.

As you walk, relax your shoulders and swing your arms to match your stride. End your walk with a five-minute "cool-down" in which you slow your pace and finish off with another five minutes of stretching exercises to prevent stiffness.

Fitness walking basics:

- **Drink eight to 10 glasses** of water a day.
- **Wear light-colored or reflective clothing** at night or in the early morning.
- **Battle boredom** by listening to music or a recorded book on a portable tape player.
- **If you have a blister or sprain** that can be made worse by walking, don't walk.
- **If you become dizzy or develop pains in your chest or your arms**, stop walking immediately and go to the nearest emergency room.

If the shoe fits:

Part of the fun of starting any new sport is "suiting up." Selecting a new pair of shoes for your fitness walking program can help to reinforce your commitment to exercise. But how do you know which shoe is right for you?

Faced with the array of athletic shoes currently on the market, let common sense be your guide. Don't buy a pair of shoes designed for running, sprinting, basketball, high-impact aerobics, etc. Buy walking shoes. Take your exercise socks to the store with you, and put them on before trying on the new shoes. *Important:* Always shop for shoes in the afternoon. Feet swell as the day wears on, and shoes bought in the morning can pinch in the afternoon.

What to look for: Comfort, cushioning and an appropriate degree of ruggedness. Select a lace-up shoe with good heel and arch support, a flexible sole and a good overall fit. Look inside the shoe—and feel with your hand—for any irregularities (seams, lumps, etc.) that could trouble your foot.

Too busy to exercise?

Stressed-out executives with a crammed schedule and a sedentary lifestyle are among the people who could benefit most from exercise—but there are only 24 hours in a day, no matter how big the numbers are on your paycheck. No time for an exercise program? Make exercise a part of the workday.

If you're stuck at the office day and night—use the stairs. When you need to go over some numbers with someone whose office is a few floors above you, skip the elevator and get there the old-fashioned way.

If you're a commuter, park the car a 15-minute walk from the train or bus station. You'll get your half-hour walk in every day.

And if you find that you've arrived early for an appointment, don't sit in the lobby looking at old magazines. Walk around the block, explore the neighborhood. You have everything—fitness, health and well-being—to gain, and nothing to lose but a few extra pounds.

Source: Daniel M. McGann, DPM, 10490 Garvey Ave., El Monte, CA 91733.

Relieving Cramps While Exercising

Relieve a side cramp while exercising by lowering the intensity of your workout...raising your arms over your head...breathing deeply.

Reason: Cramps—or stitches—are caused by lack of oxygen. Raising your arms expands your diaphragm and allows you to take in more oxygen faster. Once the stitch subsides, resume your pace.

Source: Beth Martin, exercise physiologist and operations manager, Cardio Fitness Center, New York.

Exercise Cuts Risk Of Diverticulitis

The risk of developing diverticulitis may be cut dramatically when you exercise and eat a high-fiber diet. A study of almost 50,000 men showed that those who did not exercise and ate little fiber were 2½ times more likely than their physically active, fiber-munching contemporaries to suffer from the painful bowel disease, which is marked by cramps, a bloated feeling or bleeding. Researchers found that all types of vigorous exercise were helpful.

Best: Jogging and running.

Source: Walid H. Aldoori, MD, assistant professor of epidemiology at Memorial University of Newfoundland in St. John's, Newfoundland.

Exercise and Arthritis

Exercise eases arthritis pain. Many people with arthritis stop exercising because they fear movement will make the disease worse.

Reality: Sensible exercise can ease pain and avert disability. Walking, swimming, stretching and aerobics can reduce joint pain and stiffness, build stronger muscles and bones, and improve overall health. *Particularly comfortable:* Exercising in water.

Source: John Perkins, MD, medical adviser, Arthritis Foundation, national office, 1314 Sprint St. NW, Atlanta 30309.

Exercise Helps to Cure Insomnia

Exercise cures insomnia. When previously sedentary people followed a four-times-a-week exercise regimen consisting of two 60-minute sessions of aerobics, plus two brisk 30-minute walks, they fell asleep faster and slept longer than they could previously. *Theory:* Exercise boosts feelings of well-being, counteracting negative emotions that interfere with sleep.

Source: Abby C. King, PhD, assistant professor of health research & policy and medicine, Center for Research in Disease Prevention, Stanford University, Stanford, CA.

Teens Don't Exercise Enough

Only 37% of teenagers get regular exercise. That compares with about 55% as recently as six years ago.

Source: Survey of 11,631 students by the Centers for Disease Control and Prevention, 1600 Clifton Rd. NE, Atlanta 30333.

Exercise Improves Hearing

Subjects were able to hear faint sounds twice as well after they had worked out for one-half hour two or three times weekly for two months.

Possible explanation: Improved circulation to the inner ear may improve hearing ability.

Source: Study of 26 people by Helaine Alessio, PhD, associate professor of exercise physiology, Miami University, Oxford, OH.

Exercise vs. Breast Cancer

Women who averaged four or more hours of exercise a week had a 58% lower risk of breast cancer than nonexercisers. Exercising one to three hours a week cut the risk by 20% to 30%.

Theory: Exercise alters levels of hormones that play major roles in the development of breast cancer.

Source: Leslie Bernstein, MD, professor of preventive medicine, University of Southern California, Los Angeles.

Microwave Cooking Is Declining

In 1990, 10% of new food products were intended for microwave cooking. By 1993, the figure had dropped to less than 3%. *Reasons:* Lack of flavor…inconsistent performance of microwaves…a comeback in real cooking for meals that do not require significant advance preparation time.

Source: Christopher Wolf, publisher, *Food Channel*, 515 State St., Chicago 60610.

Beware...The "Healthy" Diet Can Actually Be Bad For You

Poor eating habits have led to an epidemic of obesity in the US. One in three adult Americans is now obese, as compared with one in four just 10 years ago.

Even people who follow the conventional wisdom for healthful eating—lots of carbohydrates, little fat and protein—often fail to lose weight. Why? Because, hormonally speaking, those guidelines are dead wrong.

When it comes to obesity, eating carbohydrates is a bigger problem than eating fat.

The trouble with carbohydrates:

Modern humans are genetically identical to our Stone Age ancestors. Our digestive system, like theirs, evolved to handle a diet based on protein, fiber-rich vegetables and fruit.

Grains—the chief source of carbohydrates in modern diets—were unknown until the advent of agriculture, 10,000 years ago. That's only yesterday in evolutionary terms.

Problem: Carbohydrates cause a sharp rise in blood sugar levels. In response, the body makes more insulin, the hormone that lowers blood sugar levels and "tells" the body to store excess calories as fat.

Insulin also affects the body's synthesis of eicosanoids. These potent "superhormones" control virtually all physiological functions in the body—from the circulation of blood to digestion.

For optimum health, eicosanoids must be in balance. But high insulin levels cause the body to make more "bad" than "good" eicosanoids.

This can lead to platelet clumping, high blood pressure, reduced immunity and other potentially dangerous conditions.

A better way to eat:

Over the past 14 years, I have developed a simple yet precise eating plan that allows you to regulate levels of insulin and other hormones...and reach an ideal metabolic state.

Athletes call this state the "Zone," but in reality it is simply optimal control of hormonal function. You needn't be an athlete to realize the benefits. My program has been tested on heart patients, "ordinary" people and elite athletes, including professional football and basketball players.

All have reported greater mental focus and energy, better physical endurance, painless weight loss and improved cardiovascular function.

How do you reach the Zone? Treat food with the same respect you accord to prescription medications.

Specifically, you must regulate the amount, proportion and rate of entry into the bloodstream of all the nutrients you eat. And I mean each time you eat. Counting calories isn't necessary.

Eating in the zone:

My eating plan has five major components...

•**Protein.** Besides serving as building blocks for every cell, dietary protein causes release of glucagon. This hormone works in opposition to insulin and works to maintain blood sugar levels.

To maintain proper glucagon levels, it's important to eat the right amount of protein. *Easy formula:* At each meal, eat about as much protein as would fit in the palm of your hand. For most people, this translates into three to four ounces of low-fat protein.

Animal foods contain arachidonic acid, a fatty acid that the body uses to make "bad" eicosanoids. The fattier the meat, the higher the arachidonic acid content. That's why it's best to stick to chicken, fish, wild game (or range-fed meats), tofu and other low-fat protein sources...and to avoid organ meats entirely.

•**Carbohydrates.** For optimal hormonal balance, each meal should contain the proper ratio of carbohydrate to protein—4 g of carbohydrate for every 3 g of protein.

Emphasize "favorable" carbohydrates like fiber-rich fruits, vegetables and legumes. Since these are absorbed into the bloodstream slowly, blood sugar rises slowly...and insulin production is moderate.

Avoid "unfavorable" carbohydrates such as bread, rice, pasta, tropical fruits, dried fruits and fruit juices...and starchy or sweet vegetables, such as corn, potatoes, squash, carrots, peas and beets. These foods enter the bloodstream quickly, initiating a drastic insulin response.

If you do eat grains, stick with whole grains whenever possible. Their higher fiber content means slower absorption into the bloodstream.

What about dessert? An occasional treat is okay, as long as you balance your carbohydrate and fat intake by taking a "dose" of protein just beforehand—a few ounces of cottage cheese or sliced turkey, for instance.

• **Fat.** Though often treated as a dietary villain, fat in moderate amounts slows the rate of carbohydrate absorption, thus helping to moderate insulin response.

Fat also sends a satiety (satisfaction) signal to the brain, making you feel so full you'll want to stop eating.

Your ratio of grams of dietary fat to grams of dietary protein should be 1 to 3. Zone-favorable fats are largely monounsaturated—olive oil, canola oil, almonds, macadamia nuts, natural peanut butter and avocados.

Avoid butter, red meat and other sources of saturated fat.

• **Caloric restriction.** Have no more than 500 calories per meal. Too many calories from any source raises insulin levels.

• **Timing.** Except for the time you spend asleep, let no more than five hours pass between Zone-favorable meals or snacks.

This works out to three small meals and two snacks a day. If you eat breakfast at 7 a.m., have lunch no later than noon. If dinner isn't until 6:30 p.m., grab a mid-afternoon snack. Have a small snack at bedtime, too.

Vital: Snacks should respect the same four-to-three-to-one ratio of carbohydrate to protein to fat.

Examples: One ounce of hard cheese (or two ounces cottage cheese) and half an apple...or one small muffin baked from a mix to which you added protein powder and substituted olive oil for butter.

Source: Barry Sears, PhD, former staff scientist at the Massachusetts Institute of Technology, and president of Surfactant Technologies, a biotechnology firm in Marblehead, MA. He holds 12 patents for cancer treatments and dietary control of hormonal responses and is the author of *The Zone*. HarperCollins.

The Japanese Secrets Of Diet...Longevity And Good Health

People are starting to realize that the traditional Japanese diet may be the healthiest in the world, both for achieving longevity and for maintaining slim and fit bodies. *Facts:*

• **On average**, each Japanese citizen lives 2,628 more days than we do. In fact, the Japanese live longer on average than any other people. In 1989, the average life span was 81.39 years for women and 75.61 years for men. In the U.S. (in 1987) it was 78.3 years for women and 71.5 years for men.

• **Low cancer death rates.** The death rates for prostate, breast and colon cancers are the lowest in the world. The prostate cancer rate in Japan is 4.6 per 100,000 people compared with 22.1 per 100,000 in the U.S. and 29.9 per 100,000 in France. The Japanese breast-cancer rate is 8.3 per 100,000 people compared with 32.5 per 100,000 in the U.S. and the staggering 52.8 per 100,000 in England. Finally, the Japanese colon-cancer rate is 9.8 per 100,000 people compared with 20.3 per 100,000 in the U.S. and 26.5 per 100,000 in West Germany.

• **Low heart disease rate.** The death rate for heart disease in Japan, 117.9 per 100,000 people, is the lowest in the world, almost one-third the U.S. rate of 308.8 per 100,000. In the remote island fishing village of Okinawa, which has not yet been infiltrated by Western-style diets, heart disease averages 79.5 people per 100,000.

How to eat like the Japanese...

• **Consume fewer calories.** The Japanese have an average daily intake of 2,600 calories, the lowest of any industrialized nation. People in West Germany, France, the Netherlands and the U.S. have the highest caloric intake, about 3,400 calories. The number of calories a person should eat every day depends on such factors as body size, physical activity, age and sex.

• **Eat more fish.** In certain parts of Japan, people eat about six ounces a day on average. Fish contains a much higher percent of protein than fat, and in the traditional Japanese diet, protein accounts for 15% of total calories eaten each day.

Soybeans, in products such as tofu (soybean curd) and miso (fermented soybean paste) are another important source of protein. Miso is usually served in soup. Tofu is a key ingredient in either the main dish, the side dish or the soup. Although the Japanese do eat beef, the amounts are nowhere near those consumed by Americans.

•**Reduce fat intake to 15%–20%** of total calories. That's significantly less than the 30% recommended by the American Heart Association.

The fat consumed in the traditional Japanese diet comes from fish and the oils in soybean products, all of which have significant amounts of omega-3 fatty acids, which are believed to protect against heart disease and cancer.

This is in contrast to the fats eaten most by Americans—saturated fats (from animal products) and partially hydrogenated polyunsaturated fats (such as salad oils).

•**Consume adequate amounts of carbohydrates**, fiber, minerals and vitamins. When it comes to carbohydrates, rice is the ideal staple food, superior to bread in almost every way. It has fewer calories and is more filling than bread. Because rice comes in kernels that must be carefully chewed, it takes longer to digest than bread. *Note:* Brown rice provides the vitamins that white rice loses in the milling process.

The Japanese diet is not only high in fiber, but in precisely the kinds of fiber that aid in weight loss. Seaweed, for instance, contains certain gums that slow fat absorption. Soybean fiber reduces fat levels in the blood.

•**Eat more vegetables.** In Japan, vegetables are in the soup, the main course and are featured exclusively in the side dishes. Boiling, called ohitashi in Japanese, is the most common method of preparing vegetables, resulting in fewer calories. Some vitamin C may be lost—but the Japanese eat a lot of raw fruit to compensate.

Four main types of seaweed (kombu, nori, wakame and hijiki) are a key source of vitamins and minerals. They provide all the cal-

cium a person needs, making it unnecessary to consume dairy products that are high in fat and difficult for many people to digest. Hijiki, for instance, contains an incredible 1,400 milligrams of calcium per 100 grams. *Bonus:* Seaweed has no calories.

•**Give up rich foods.** For snacks, the Japanese opt for vegetables and fruits that are high in pectin. *Favorites:* Apples, oranges and carrots. Eating raw fruit that contains pectin helps reduce hunger.

•**Drink green tea.** In Japan, green tea (ocha) is served with every meal and drunk throughout the day. This provides the high water intake needed to fight hunger and control weight. Green tea is a nutritious alternative to pure water, because it's high in antioxidants, including vitamins C and E, which are believed to slow the aging process.

•**Avoid salted**, pickled and smoked foods. These have been linked to high stomach cancer rates in Japan, particularly in its northern areas, which lack fresh fruit and vegetables in the winter.

About salt: Although the average American salt intake is 12.2 grams per day, salt consumption should not exceed eight grams per day. You'll never see a salt shaker on a Japanese table.

Source: Hirotomo Ochi, PhD, founder of the Japan Institute for the Control of Aging, Fukuroi City. He is the author of *East Meets West: Supernutrition from Japan* and *Dieting Can Ruin Your Health*, Ishi Press International, 1400 N. Shoreline Blvd., Mountain View, CA 94043.

Better Eating on the Road

Heart Smart Restaurants International (HSRI) gives seals of approval to restaurants offering foods lower in fat, sodium and cholesterol. HSRI-certified restaurants also agree upon request to serve skim or 1% milk...cook with vegetable oil, not butter or margarine...trim visible fat from meat...skin poultry...serve salad dressing on the side...accommodate special dietary requests made in advance. HSRI has recruited more than 800 restaurants in 44 states.

For a list or more information: 800-762-7819.

Safe, Lasting Weight Loss...Breakthrough Drug Regimen Makes It Possible

If you've been trying unsuccessfully to lose weight, you should know about the prescription medications *fenfluramine* (Pondimin) and *phentermine* (Ionamin, Fastin). Taken in combination, these drugs make it *easy* to lose excess pounds...and keep them off.

Unlike over-the-counter appetite suppressants (which can cause elevated blood pressure) and prescription amphetamines (which are habit-forming) fenfluramine and phentermine are safe *and* nonaddicting.

Who should consider fenfluramine/phentermine therapy? Anyone 20% or more above his/her ideal weight...who has more than 25% body fat...or who has failed repeatedly when trying to lose weight via a restricted- calorie diet and exercise.

These drugs should not be taken by anyone who...

...is pregnant or planning to become pregnant.

...is taking MAO inhibitor antidepressants like Marplan, Nardil and Parnate.

...has an unstable heart condition or uncontrolled high blood pressure.

...has a history of alcohol or drug abuse.

People with glaucoma must be monitored by an ophthalmologist while taking the drugs. What to expect:

Expect to take the drugs for three to six months. During this period, you'll lose 15% to 20% of your weight. To speed weight-loss...

• **Keep fats to less than 30%** of your diet. Fortunately, the drugs reduce your desire for food—especially calorie- and fat-laden carbohydrates. That makes it much easier to eat a wholesome diet.

• **Get plenty of exercise.** It's *possible* to lose weight without exercising. However, things go faster if you do regular weight-lifting (bigger muscles burn calories faster than small muscles)...and walk, run or do another form of aerobic exercise for 30 minutes a day.

In most cases, it's best to stop taking the medications once your weight loss levels off (typically after three to six months).

You may be able to keep the weight off by sticking to your exercise schedule and diet. If not, simply go back on the drugs. You may have to take fenfluramine and phentermine intermittently for the rest of your life.

Side effects—including dry mouth, mild insomnia, headache, drowsiness, diarrhea and nausea—are rare, and usually minor. Still, it's a good idea to be cautious when driving.

A month's supply of fenfluramine and phentermine costs about $50. You'll also have to pay for monthly doctor visits (usually $35 to $100 each).

How the drugs work:

Fenfluramine works by blocking the absorption of the neurotransmitter serotonin by brain cells (neurons).

The resulting elevation in serotonin levels boosts your mood, helps curb the agitation and deprivation associated with hunger and dampens hunger pangs.

Phentermine boosts energy levels by raising levels of two other neurotransmitters—*norepinephrine* and *dopamine. Result:* You eat more rapidly but consume less.

A good doctor is essential:

Make sure the doctor you pick to supervise your weight-loss regimen is experienced in helping people lose weight with medication.

If your own doctor is unfamiliar with these drugs, ask to be referred to a bariatric physician (obesity specialist). For a list of bariatric physicians in your area, contact the American Society of Bariatric Physicians, 5600 S. Quebec, Ste. 109A, Englewood, Colorado 80111. 303-779-4833.

You might consider giving your doctor a copy of this article and asking him to review the medical literature on fenfluramine and phentermine.

Problem: Some doctors are reluctant to prescribe these drugs—because no long-term studies yet exist. (Six years is the longest people have taken them regularly.)

I've found patients can abruptly *stop* taking fenfluramine and phentermine even after taking the drugs for years—with no ill effects.

Other doctors were scared off these drugs by a highly publicized 1994 study.

But this study—which found brain damage in monkeys given high doses of a related but far more potent drug called *dexfenfluamine*—has since been refuted.

Source: Steven Lamm, MD, clinical assistant professor of medicine at New York University School of Medicine in New York City. He is the author of *Thinner At Last.* Simon & Schuster.

Inexpensive Ways To Shape Up

Rent—or buy—workout videos from your local video store…contact an area high school about evening exercise classes for adults…create your own home gym by buying a single well-made exercise machine—the cost will be less than joining a health club…exercise with friends to make it more difficult to put off working out.

Source: Patrick Netter, home fitness expert and consultant, J.P. Netter Marketing, 11693 San Vincente Blvd., Los Angeles 90049.

Cook with Wine

Cook with wine to prepare tasty meals without fat and salt. Most of the alcohol and calories in wine burn off during cooking, but its enriching flavor remains. Use inexpensive but reliable table wines. Avoid expensive wines—cooking with them is wasteful. Also avoid wines labeled as cooking wines—they contain a lot of salt.

Source: *Minding Your Body: 100 Ways to Live and Be Well* by Joseph S. Rechtschaffen, MD, internist, New York. Kodansha International.

Safer Exercising For Beginners

The more health risk factors you have—smoking, high blood pressure, high cholesterol, etc.—the slower you should start.

Warning sign: If, while exercising, you find yourself huffing and puffing and your pulse is too high, slow down. In time, you'll be able to increase the intensity of your workouts.

Source: *Hold It! You're Exercising Wrong* by Edward J. Jackowski, founder of Exude, a one-on-one motivational and fitness company based in New York. Fireside.

15

Very, Very Smart Education

Educational TV

Educational TV helps preschoolers after they start school. Preschoolers in low-income areas who watched educational programs were not only better prepared for school, they were also better performers on verbal and math tests as late as age seven. Preschoolers who mainly watched adult programs and cartoons performed worse than expected on the same tests.

Source: Study of 250 children from low-income areas around Kansas City, led by Aletha Huston, PhD, and John Wright, PhD, professors of human development, Center for Research on the Influences of Television on Children, University of Kansas, Lawrence.

How to Handle a Child's Bad Report Card

When a child gets bad grades, it's natural for parents to be upset, frustrated and even angry. But overly emotional reactions to poor scholastic achievement don't address the causes or improve future grades. *The big mistakes...*

Mistake: Becoming more upset than your child about the grades. Strong negative reactions send a signal that the grades are your responsibility, not the child's, leading him/her to believe that you'll solve the problem.

Better: When the next report card arrives, don't open it. Just leave it on your child's pillow. Your child will be surprised. When he asks why you didn't open it, say, *Because it's your report card.* This strategy will send a clear message to your child that grades are his responsibility. Suggest that you discuss the report card together after the child has looked it over.

Mistake: Yelling and threatening your child over the grades. Just as the wise parent does not fight with a child over how much he eats at the dinner table, so a grade-savvy parent backs away from arguments about grades.

Children don't need threats or punishment to motivate them. They want to do well. After all, good grades feel much, much better than bad ones.

269

Trap: If you get angry about report cards, children will recognize that they can use school issues to upset you...that low grades get your attention. For many, negative attention is better than no attention.

Better: While it isn't productive to yell or punish your child, you must let him know you're disappointed.

Example: Say, *I am really disappointed in these grades—and I know you can do better.*

Mistake: Incorrectly punishing your child. The knee-jerk reaction that most parents have is to randomly deny children things that they like —or even to ground them for several weeks. Punishment rarely motivates children—or anyone else, for that matter.

Better: Take away only the privileges that are specifically interfering with good study habits.

Example: Tell the child who spends too much time in front of the TV or on the telephone that these privileges must be earned. After the child has improved his grades, TV or telephone time will no longer have to be cut back.

Mistake: Being timid or apologetic when discussing the matter with the teacher. Meeting with your child's teacher is a great opportunity to enlist the teacher's help. Schedule time to meet with the teacher, focusing on your child's specific areas of strength and weakness...discussing recommendations for improvement. A teacher who says the child is not working up to his potential is being too vague.

Better: Ask the teacher to be more specific. A teacher could say that the child does not have a strong sense of the reading material and needs to spend more time concentrating on it. Ideally, the teacher will suggest specific strategies to help your child retain the necessary information.

Mistake: Not coming up with a study plan. The only way your child will be able to achieve better grades is if he develops better study habits.

Strategy: Help your child create a homework plan. *A good plan includes...*

- **List of all course subjects.**
- **Schedule of outside activities**—piano lessons, basketball, etc.—and how much time each takes each day.

- **Amount of time each night** that must be devoted to studying.
- **Amount of homework time** each subject requires.
- **Books that need to be brought home** on different nights.
- **Where and at what time** homework will be done.

Once this list is complete, suggest the child sign it, like a contract. Everything your child needs to work on is now spelled out in black and white.

Mistake: Not recognizing that the problem may be health-related or out of your child's control. Sometimes parents sense there is something wrong with their children even before school specialists do. Don't minimize or ignore your intuition. Have your child tested, or make appropriate allowances if you suspect any of the following...

...a hearing problem.

...a vision problem.

...a learning disability.

...a physical illness.

...serious social problems, such as school bullies or negative friends.

...an uncaring—or unsympathetic—teacher.

Once you identify the problem and have it treated, your child will have a much better chance to work hard and improve his grades.

Source: Nancy Samalin, director of Parent Guidance Workshops, 180 Riverside Dr., New York 10024. She is author of *Love and Anger: The Parental Dilemma.* Penguin Books. Ms. Samalin's parenting strategies are also available in an audiotape series, *Good Parents, Great Kids.*

How to Do Well on Standardized Tests

Every year, about one million high school juniors and seniors take the Scholastic Assessment Test (SAT), the all-important college entrance exam.

While the SAT is the best-known, it is by no means the only standardized test. Most graduate schools and professions use them as qualifying tests.

Here's how anyone can do well...

Preparing for the test:

•Allow at least six to eight weeks of active preparation. Excellent preparation can raise a student's percentile ranking by 10 or more percentage points. On the SAT, such an increase can mean the difference between going to a state school or an Ivy League college.

Preparation courses offer advantages over private tutors and are less expensive. They drill you on the types of questions you'll see and create the same type of pressure-filled environment.

The quality of review courses varies. Sit in on a class and see the materials—too much can be just as bad as too little. Ask what is the documented average improvement...the nature of the guarantee...whether free tutoring is available.

•The best materials are those prepared by the same people who publish the actual test. Avoid computer software. Purchase books containing the actual exams given in previous years.

•Just looking over practice questions is not enough. Practicing 10 hours a day using the wrong technique makes you good at doing the wrong thing. Learn techniques for answering the different questions you'll face.

Examples: On standardized math tests, figures are drawn "to scale" and answers can often be estimated visually. Questions based on complex reading passages can often be answered using common sense.

Taking the test:

•Show up early. Position yourself for a good seat when the doors to the room open. When you enter the room, look for a wall seat near the back of the room—for more elbow room and fewer distractions.

•When the test begins, don't leap into the first question. Survey the exam for a minute or two to get a sense of the difficulty of questions.

•Don't rush through the easy questions. You'll make careless errors. And don't labor over difficult questions at the end—most test-takers are going to get those wrong anyway. Instead, spend most of your time on the medium ones, which tend to occur in the middle of any question type or any section.

•Don't rush to finish. Most standardized tests are designed to prevent all but the very best test-takers from finishing. Be willing to leave some blanks if you can't finish. Unless you're aiming for a near-perfect score, you really shouldn't push yourself to finish.

•Trust your hunches on easy questions— but not on hard ones. Answers to hard questions are never obvious. They usually appear in order of difficulty—easiest ones first and hard questions toward the end of a section.

•Guessing rarely hurts—and can help significantly. No standardized tests penalize guessing, including those that deduct a fraction for an error. Errors cost only a fraction more than "blanks"—which also count against test-takers.

Strategy: If errors are not penalized, guess. If errors are penalized, guess if you can certainly eliminate at least one choice.

•Use process of elimination. It is almost always easier to show why a choice is incorrect than to show why it's correct—especially for difficult questions.

Reviewing your performance:

•If you're sure you bombed, cancel your score. If you guessed at most of the answers or couldn't answer many of them, your fear is probably justified.

To cancel, notify the test administrators at the conclusion of the exam or up to five days later. The cost of the test is nonrefundable, but the schools to which you apply will never see the result.

•If you are unhappy with your score and plan to retake a test, see whether you can request your original answer sheet. Reviewing your answers and mistakes is highly valuable. A number of test publishers will make it available to you for a nominal fee.

Source: Adam Robinson, education consultant and co-founder of the Princeton Review, a national program that helps students do well on standardized tests. He is author of seven books on education, including *What Smart Students Know: Maximum Grades, Optimum Learning, Minimum Time*. Crown Publishers.

Investing for Education

When saving for college, invest in a growth-stock mutual fund. On average, this type of fund pays a much higher rate of return than fixed-income investments—so long as college is at least seven years away.

Strategy: When your child reaches college age, do not sell the shares yourself and use the proceeds to pay tuition, or you'll pay a 28% capital gains tax rate. Instead, give the shares to the child and have the child sell them. The child will probably pay a 15% tax rate. You can also give $10,000 to each child free of gift tax each year—$20,000 if you make the gift jointly with your spouse.

Source: William G. Brennan, a CPA in private practice in Washington, DC.

College Financial Aid

Most parents need financial help when they are paying for their children's college educations. Unfortunately, many parents are not familiar with the best ways to apply for and receive financial aid.

Here are the most common mistakes people make when applying for financial assistance from a college...

Mistake: Assuming that you're not eligible for financial aid.

Reality: There is no real income cutoff. Sometimes families with incomes in excess of $150,000 receive financial aid.

Mistake: Failing to do any advance planning for the application process. Eligibility is determined by taking a snapshot of your family's financial situation. If you are applying for aid for your child's freshman year of college, the year that will be scrutinized is from January 1 of your child's junior year in high school to December 31 of his/her senior year. Any financial or investment transactions you make during that year could help—or hurt—your child's chances of getting aid.

Mistake: Missing the deadlines. It's crucial to apply for aid at the same time your child is applying to colleges. The best sources of information about aid-application deadlines are the schools themselves. *Important:* Find out if the material must be postmarked, received or processed by the deadline.

Mistake: Being unaware of other attractive borrowing options.

Reality: Even if they don't qualify for need-based student loans, virtually all students qualify for unsubsidized Stafford Loans. The colleges' financial aid offices can tell you how to apply for these loans.

How they work: Although the child is charged interest while in school, it is at an attractive rate based on the 90-day Treasury bill plus 3.1%. The rate is set each year at the end of May.

Some colleges have their own loan programs, which may have very attractive terms. There is also the federal Parent Loans for Undergraduate Students (PLUS) program, which allows you to borrow the total cost of education less any aid offered.

Mistake: Assuming that outside scholarships are where the real money is. These awards represent less than 1% of all financial aid.

Strategy: If your child wins an outside award, try to convince the school to reduce the loan and work-study portions of its aid package rather than the grant money dollar for dollar.

Mistake: Assuming financial aid packages are set in stone.

Reality: It's frequently possible to negotiate a better package than the one you are initially offered by the college. The first offer a college makes is often not its best offer. The college wants to see if you will blink—and it is leaving room for bargaining. Your strongest bargaining chip could be a better financial aid package from another school. But be honest, since you may have to provide a copy of that package.

Source: Kalman Chany, president of Campus Consultants Inc., a fee-based firm that counsels families and conducts corporate seminars on maximizing financial aid eligibility, 968 Lexington Ave., New York 10021. He is author of *The Princeton Review Student Access Guide to Paying for College.* Random House.

Better Buys in College Education

•**Arizona State University** (*Tempe*) has more than 45,000 students and is strong in engineering, geology and physics.

Tuition: $1,950* per year for state residents/ $7,960 for out-of-state students.

602-965-9011.

•**Auburn University** (*Auburn, Alabama*) has more than 22,000 students and offers more than 100 majors. Its strengths are business, architecture and engineering.

Tuition: $2,250/$6,750.

334-844-4080.

•**California State University** (*Chico*) has 13,000 students. It is strong in social sciences and business.

Tuition: $2,006/$9,386.

916-898-6321.

•**Framingham State College** (*Framingham, Massachusetts*) has only 3,000 students but offers cultural opportunities. *Example:* The New England Philharmonic rehearses on the campus.

Tuition: $3,394/$7,528.

508-626-4500.

•**Kansas State University** (*Manhattan, Kansas)* has 15,000 undergraduate students and is known for its biology and engineering programs.

Tuition: $2,085/$7,429.

913-532-6250.

•**Purdue University** (*West Lafayette, Indiana*) has 34,685 students and offers more than 300 programs. It has strong programs in engineering, communications and management.

Tuition: $3,056/$10,128.

317-494-1776.

•**US armed forces academies** pay you to attend—$570/month (out of which students pay for books, computers, uniforms, haircuts, etc.). A congressional nomination is required, and you must agree to five years of active duty upon graduation.

*All tuition amounts quoted are subject to change without prior notice.

More information: US Military Academy (West Point, New York, 914-938-4041)...US Naval Academy (Annapolis, Maryland, 800-638-9156)...US Airforce Academy (Colorado Springs, Colorado, 719-472-2520).

Source: Nicholas Roes, an economics and government instructor at Marist College in Poughkeepsie, NY. He is author of *America's Lowest Cost Colleges*, a directory of more than 1,000 fully accredited colleges and universities with low or no tuitions. NAR Publications.

 # Great Games for Smart Kids

When toddlers can do their simple four- or five-piece wooden puzzles so quickly that they are bored, take all the pieces of two or three puzzles and dump them out together. This will restore the challenge and extend the puzzles' useful life.

Source: Peter Baylies, publisher, *At-Home Dad*, a quarterly newsletter, 61 Brightwood Ave., North Andover, MA 01845.

What to Do When Your Child Hates School

Parents can make the school year easier by knowing what to say when kids complain...

•**Don't deny your children's feelings.** It's natural to want to say, "No, you don't hate school." That may seem to be a supportive statement, but it's not. The key to understanding the situation is to talk to children's hearts, not their heads.

•**Ask indirect questions.** To understand the problem, be nonconfrontational. Don't ask, "Why do you hate school?"

Instead: Say, "Gee, something must have happened to make you feel that way."

Also ask if there's anything you can do to make the situation better.

•**Help children be specific.** Kids use the word "hate" a lot—they rarely give concrete answers. But you need to know the details.

Strategy: Ask if the teacher yelled or said something mean. *Is the work too difficult? Is it boring? Is a classmate a pest or a bully?* Ask the questions gently, so children know that any reply is acceptable.

•**Respond to the problem.** Whatever the issue, don't lecture. Kids hate that. Even if it turns out that your child was punished for doing something wrong, say, "What can you do in the future to make this situation better?"

The "you" in the question empowers children to improve matters on their own.

Strategy: Once you pinpoint the problem, talk to the teacher in a non-accusatory manner. Ask him/her what might help. Are there things you can do outside of class to help?

Example: If your child is bored because the material seems irrelevant, arrange a trip or a fun project that helps bring it to life. Or use videos, books or computer programs that focus on the subject. There is a lot of good information available to enhance nearly every topic.

If the work is too easy, do higher-level reading or problem solving outside of school with your child.

After handling the problem as best you can, acknowledge to your child that sometimes school is boring or that sometimes people are obnoxious. You want your child to learn that situations can be improved but also that few are ever ideal.

Important: When children have trouble keeping up with the rest of the class or concentrating over an extended period of time, ask the teacher if they should be tested for a learning disability. The sooner you catch a problem, the better.

But recognize, too, that many "learning problems" are often temporary. All kids develop differently. Not every six-year-old, for example, belongs in first grade.

Source: Nancy Samalin, director of Parent Guidance Workshops in New York and author of *Loving Each One Best: A Caring and Practical Approach to Raising Siblings.* Bantam Books.

16

Consumer Savvy

Return Mail Free

Return unwanted merchandise you receive in the mail by simply crossing out your address and writing *Return to sender—merchandise refused* on the box. This not only saves you from paying for the merchandise, but also saves return postage. *Caution:* This only works if you do not break the seal or open the box. If you break the seal, you need new postage to send the box back.

Source: Rochelle LaMotte McDonald, a mother of three in Anchorage, AK, and author of *How to Pinch a Penny Till It Screams.* Avery Publishing Group.

What to Buy... When

Big sales are held on different types of merchandise at different times of the year. *Here's how to time your major purchases...*

•**January.** Traditional after-Christmas and New Year's bargains include men's suits, linens (white sales), appliances and furniture.

•**February.** The season of love brings huge reductions on china, glass and silver, as well as mattresses and bedding.

•**March.** Watch for special pre-season promotions for spring clothing. Ski equipment is at an annual low as well.

•**April.** Big sales begin again after the Easter holiday, especially on clothing.

•**May.** Spring cleaning means specials on household cleaning products.

•**June.** Shop for furniture. Semiannual inventory is on its way in, and old items must go.

•**July.** Most stores liquidate their inventories to make room for fall goods during this month. Sportswear, sporting equipment and garden tools and supplies take noticeable dips.

•**August.** If you are in the market for a car, August is clearance time on current models. Look for deals on equipment linked to the summer season, too—patio furniture, lawn mowers, yard tools and camping gear.

• **September.** The best deals on school clothes are at the *end* of the month. Hold off until then and you'll save big.

• **October.** This is *the* month to do your Christmas shopping. Stores are postured to boost retail sales before the holiday season.

• **November.** Wool clothes, including women's coats and men's suits, come down significantly this month as store owners cut their inventories for their second shipment of the season.

• **December.** Next to August, this is the best time to buy a new car.

Source: Kenny Luck, director of business development and operations, Minirth Meier New Life Clinics, Laguna Hills, CA, and author of *52 Ways to Stretch a Buck*. Thomas Nelson.

Be Wary of Extended Warranties

Be wary of extended warranties for appliances or electronic products. They are big profit centers for the stores that sell them—and very few extended-warranty buyers ever use the warranties. In addition, most modern home appliances and electronic products that need repair will break down almost immediately. Such problems will likely still be covered by the manufacturer. If you do not have a problem within three to six months, chances are you will never have one.

Source: Barbara Berger Opotowsky, president, Better Business Bureau, New York.

Upgrading Your Computer

Best time to upgrade your computer: When the product has been around long enough for bugs to be worked out. Upgrade any product, hardware or software only when you have time to understand the changes involved. Beware of upgrading while you are in the midst of an important project.

Bottom line: If your current version of hardware or software does everything you need, think carefully about whether upgrading is necessary.

Source: Stephen Manes, computer journalist, writing in *The New York Times*.

Correct Credit Report Mistakes as Soon as Possible

Credit report mistakes and problems can do more than harm your chances of getting a loan. A growing number of auto and homeowner's insurers and employers rely on credit reports to determine whether to cover—or hire—individuals. Order reports and correct mistakes as soon as possible. Equifax (800-685-1111, nominal fee)...TRW (800-682-7654, one free report each year)...and Trans Union (316-636-6100, nominal fee).

Source: Gerri Detweiler, credit card and debt-control consultant and author of *The Ultimate Credit Handbook*. Good Advice Press.

How to Protect Yourself From Your Very Own Credit

The wave of new credit cards and offers are leaving many people confused about how to manage their wallets.

Cards are more convenient than cash and checks—and new promotions, perks and discounts are encouraging people to apply for more accounts than they need.

The result is widespread uncertainty over which cards best suit an individual's needs... and how to best use the ones the individual already owns.

Credit cards:

More than 6,000 financial institutions issue bank cards such as MasterCard and Visa. Discover, which is issued by Greenwood Trust Co., is also a bank card. Retail cards are issued by stores. American Express also offers a credit card in addition to its charge cards.

Problem: More than two-thirds of Americans use their credit cards as personal loans, carrying balances from month to month and making hefty interest payments. Many people who carry balances do not realize that they are almost always charged interest on all new purchases immediately. Therefore, they could be paying interest on purchases they intend to pay off completely at the end of the month, such as groceries, gasoline and meals.

Strategy: You only need two credit cards. Use one with a low interest rate—12% or less —for purchases you want to pay for over time. Use a second bank credit card—one that charges no annual fee and has a grace period during which time you are not charged interest on new purchases—for items that you plan to pay for in full each month.

Charge cards:

American Express, Diner's Club and most gas cards require you to pay the bill in full each month. These cards are useful if you want the convenience of plastic but don't want to run up large debts.

Charge cards, however, are not accepted in as many locations worldwide as credit cards. You may also need to carry a bank card for emergency purchases.

Debit cards:

With a debit card, the price of your purchase is deducted from your checking or savings account either immediately or within a few days, depending on the card.

Some ATM cards—also a type of debit card —now can be used to make purchases at gas stations and stores.

MasterCard and Visa both offer debit cards through banks, credit unions and other financial institutions. They look similar to credit cards and many of them can be used anywhere that credit cards like MasterCard or Visa are accepted.

Some people prefer to use debit cards because they don't want to carry cash or spend more than they have in their checking accounts.

Both MasterCard and Visa offer on-line debit cards that deduct money from checking accounts immediately. MasterCard's is called *Maestro*…Visa's is called *Interlink*. Both also offer off-line programs that take a few days to make the deductions. MasterCard's is *MasterMoney*…Visa's is *Visa check card*. These cards are available from most banks.

Drawback I: Fees for debit cards can be costly. Your bank may charge an annual fee of $12 or up to $1.50 every time you make a purchase with a debit card. In addition, merchants who accept the card may charge transaction fees—from 50 cents to $1.50.

Drawback II: Debit cards are not covered by the same consumer protection laws as credit cards. If you pay for something with a debit card and there's a problem with the merchandise, you can't refuse to pay the charge under the Fair Credit Billing Act. That law only covers credit and charge cards. And since the money has already been deducted from your account, it can be more difficult to get a refund.

Better: Unless you hate paying bills, use a credit or charge card instead of a debit card— and pay the bill in full.

Secured credit cards:

For people who can't qualify for a credit card because of bankruptcy or previous credit problems or because they haven't established credit, a secured credit card can be the answer.

How it works: You deposit between $250 and $400 in a savings account as a security deposit. In return, you get a MasterCard or Visa with a credit line that is equal to your deposit. The secured card looks and works just like a conventional credit card. No one will know it's different except you and the bank.

Strategy: Avoid banks that charge high upfront fees. Check out the program's reputation in advance with the Better Business Bureau to make sure there haven't been many complaints.

Also be sure that your payments will be reported on a regular basis to all three major credit bureaus since one of the purposes of the card is to help you rebuild your credit rating.

Potential pitfall: Some secured cards are reported to credit bureaus differently from regular, unsecured cards. If you are trying to build a new credit rating or rebuild a damaged one, you're probably better off with a card that is reported the same as an unsecured bank card. Most banks won't volunteer this information up front—you will have to ask.

Rebate cards:

These cards are offered by a variety of companies, from automakers to computer software firms. They provide cash rebates, discounts on goods and services and/or free merchandise. In most cases, the amount of the rebate is tied to how much you charge each year.

Drawbacks: If you're like most people and charge less than $200 a month, you won't earn much of a rebate. In addition, these cards charge higher interest rates than other bank cards—making them an expensive choice for cardholders who carry balances. They are only worthwhile if you charge several thousand dollars each month and pay the bill in full each month.

Affinity cards:

Many charities, professional organizations and membership organizations offer members credit cards stamped with their logos. The sponsoring organization usually receives a donation of part or all of the first year's annual fee, plus a percentage of purchases made on the card. One-half of 1% is common.

Strategy: Accept an affinity card only if the interest rate, annual fee and other terms are competitive with regular bank cards.

Frequent-flier cards:

Most airlines are tied into credit card programs that allow you to earn frequent-flier miles. In general, you earn one frequent-flier mile for every dollar charged on the card.

Those who charge at least $2,000 a month can usually earn a free round-trip domestic ticket in a year. If you're a big spender and can pay the bill in full each month, one of these cards could pay for next year's vacation.

Trap: Annual fees on these cards are usually expensive—$55 or more is common. If you carry a balance, any free ticket you earn could wind up costing you more in extra interest charges than the actual price of the ticket.

Example: United Airlines Mileage Plus Visa —issued by FCC National Bank in Chicago—

earns one frequent-flier mile for each dollar charged, with 20,000 miles required for a free round-trip domestic ticket. The annual fee is usually $60 for a standard card and $100 for a gold card. You would have to charge $1,667 each month to earn a free ticket in one year.

Strategy: If you are already earning frequent-flier miles from business travel or other tie-ins, you can use this type of card to earn enough miles to top off your other miles.

The most flexible programs are American Express's Membership Miles (800-297-6453), which allows you to earn miles on any of eight major airlines' frequent-flier programs...and Diner's Club Premier Rewards (800-234-6377), which allows you to earn miles on any US airline with a frequent-flier program.

These cards charge no interest because you must pay the bill in full. Both have steep annual fees, but if they help you get a free ticket, they may be worth it.

Source: Gerri Detweiler, a financial writer and credit card and debt-control consultant in Woodbridge, VA. She is author of *The Ultimate Credit Handbook: How to Double Your Credit, Cut Your Debt & Have a Lifetime of Financial Health.* Good Advice Press.

Best Ways to Slash Credit Card Costs

Issuers are flooding mailboxes with some of the best credit card offers ever. *To play this buyer's market...*

•**Find out what you are really paying.** If you took out a credit card with a low introductory rate during the past year or so, the rate you are paying now is most likely much higher.

"Teaser rates" usually go up after six months to a year, and the jump can be dramatic—from 6.9% to 18.9%, for example. Your current rate must be listed on your credit card statement.

Check to make sure the interest rate is not in the high double digits. If it is, switch to a card with a lower rate—or request a lower rate from that same issuer. You probably won't get the introductory rate again, but you should get one that's competitive.

•**Demand a better deal.** Five years ago, it was unheard-of for a credit card company to give a lower rate to a customer who asked for one. Now it's commonplace. If you pay your bills on time, an issuer may lower your rate by 2% to 5% at your insistence.

Here's how: Call the customer-service department and politely tell the representative you are going to close your account because of the high interest rate. Then say you would consider keeping it if the issuer were to give you a lower rate. If the first person you speak with is not helpful, ask to speak to a supervisor. Don't be intimidated. The credit card business is extremely competitive, and most issuers are struggling to keep customers.

•**Open your mail.** Save all the credit card offers you receive over several months. Then go through them carefully. While most aren't worth the paper on which they're printed, there are some gems—especially for short-term loans.

Problem: If you use an introductory rate to pay off balances on higher-rate credit cards, keep in mind that you'll have to either pay off the balance within six months...switch to another card at that time...or pay a hefty rate after the introductory period ends. If you're not willing to put the time into finding a new card, you're better off choosing a card that has a slightly higher, more stable rate.

•**Consolidate.** The average cardholder carries balances on five or six credit cards. Consolidating several high-rate balances into a low-rate card can save $200 or more in interest charges.

Here's how: Call the credit card company to which you want to transfer your balances (in this case, the Visa issuer) and ask for instructions. Some issuers will do it for you. You fill out an authorization form, and the issuer will pay off the balance you specify on another card.

Others will send you "convenience checks," which look just like personal checks. You simply write a check to pay off another credit card. The amount of the check or balance transfer will appear on your next statement, often as a cash advance.

Trap: Be sure the interest rate for transferred balances isn't higher than the advertised rate. Also watch for steep cash-advance fees for balance transfers—these can be as much as 2% of the amount you transfer. Many issuers will waive the fee if you insist.

•**Rack up the freebies.** The frequent-flier cards that are offered by almost all major airlines typically give cardholders one frequent-flier mile for every dollar charged on the card. Rebate cards offered by companies such as Blockbuster Entertainment and Shell Oil usually earn rebates toward products from the sponsoring company (free movie rentals and other entertainment in the case of Blockbuster ...free gasoline from Shell).

Caution: These cards are often expensive, with high annual fees and interest rates. In most cases, you'll have to charge thousands of dollars each month to earn anything significant, and you must pay your bill in full or you'll overpay in finance charges.

Strategy: If you do get a rebate or frequent-flier card, and you're disciplined enough to pay the bill in full each month, use the card everywhere it's accepted. This includes less traditional places, such as grocery stores, post offices, movie theaters—even when paying utility bills. Using the card for these small purchases will help you rack up miles or rebates very quickly.

•**Pay more to save.** While credit cards with no annual fees are common these days, don't completely rule out the idea of paying an annual fee if you carry a balance and the fee buys you a really low rate.

Source: Gerri Detweiler, a financial writer and credit card and debt-control consultant, Woodbridge, VA. She is author of *The Ultimate Credit Handbook: How to Double Your Credit, Cut Your Debt & Have a Lifetime of Financial Health.* Good Advice Press.

Frequent-Flier Programs More Enticing

Frequent-flier programs and tie-ins are expanding so fast that many people overlook ways to earn free miles. *Most-overlooked source:*

Long-distance phone calls made from your home. Each of the three major long-distance carriers credit customers with five miles for every $1 spent on calls. Miles are good on different airlines. *Catch:* You won't receive miles unless you sign up for the phone company's program.

Source: Randy Petersen, editor of *Inside Flyer*, 4715-C Town Center Dr., Colorado Springs 80916.

It Pays to Haggle

Discount stores, department stores, even fine specialty shops are often willing to negotiate a better price for customers who ask. *How:* Ask the sales clerk, out of hearing range of other shoppers, for the store's best price on a particular item. If the clerk can't help, ask to talk with the manager.

Source: *Penny Pinching: How to Lower Your Everyday Expenses Without Lowering Your Standard of Living* by Lee and Barbara Simmons, personal finance experts in New York. Bantam Books.

How to Hire the Best Home Contractor for You

Over the past 20 years, I have heard some horrible stories about unscrupulous contractors doing terrible things to home owners.

As the number of home-improvement projects in the US increases, some contractors find it easy to rip off people who have not had enough experience to know better.

A contractor is responsible for hiring others to install a new kitchen, add a new room or make major design changes. Here's how to hire the right one—and to make sure your interests are protected...

Sizing up the talent:

• **Ask friends for recommendations.** Then get two to three references from each contractor. *Best:* Visit at least one completed project as well as one project in progress.

Strategy: Ask each contractor's former clients specific questions about his/her work and work style. Points to discuss...

• *Was the job started on time?*
• *Did workers show up on time?*
• *Did they complete the job on time?*
• *Was the contractor always available?*
• *Did you get what you wanted?*
• *Were there any surprises?*
• *Was the contractor responsive to problems after the job was completed?*
• *What would you do differently if you were hiring a contractor again?*

Each of these questions is designed to yield critical information. Negative answers shouldn't necessarily rule out a contractor, but instead raise issues to discuss with him.

Example: You may discover that the contractor you like best isn't prompt about returning phone calls. By knowing this in advance, you can stress how important callbacks are to you and insist on a daily or weekly time to speak with him.

• **Interview the candidates you like in person.** Face-to-face meetings are always best, since you will be able to determine whether you are comfortable with the contractor. You don't want someone who looks impatient or seems reluctant to answer detailed questions.

Important: Before an interview with a contractor, put together a list of your general expected working rules. Give the list to the contractor, so that he knows up front what you expect.

Example: If you want to avoid having dirt tracked through your home, insist that the contractor bring his own portable bathroom.

• **Ask each of the contractors you like for a bid on the project.** They should provide free job estimates that are typed, easy to understand and specific. A good bid includes *start* and *completion* dates and pro-consumer clauses like daily working hours and promises to protect existing surfaces.

Important: Make sure there's no clause authorizing the substitution of materials without your written permission.

Making the choice:

If you find that all the contractors are great and all their bids are similarly priced, the answers to these questions may help you decide among them…

•*Does the contractor have a clean complaint record?* Call your local Better Business Bureau, which will provide a verbal or written report. Also, call your state's Attorney General's office…Building Department…and Licensing Bureau to find out about complaints. More than one recent complaint about a contractor is a red flag.

•*How many projects is the contractor working on right now?* If he is working on more than two or three projects at once, he may be hard to locate and is unlikely to spend much time at your job site.

•*Will he warranty the work for one year?* A written warranty should be part of the contract. All legitimate contractors will include one. A warranty is important because if something falls apart, it will usually happen within the first year. The warranty should state that the contractor will fix the problem within 10 days.

Before signing the contract:

•**Ask for copies of all professional licenses and insurance documents**—including the contractor's driver's license, which confirms his identity. Without it, you can't be sure that the other licenses you request actually belong to that contractor.

Important: Make sure the contractor purchases a performance bond. It is bought through a surety company for about $100. A surety company provides a bond to the contractor for one year and pays the home owner if the contractor skips out on the job. The performance bond covers the cost to complete the job if the contractor cannot for any reason.

Other important documents…

•**The contractor should have legible copies** of the occupational license from the city…a county license…and—in most states—a state license. Ask your state's Attorney General's office for a list of what is required.

•**A subcontractor needs to have** a county license and sometimes a city license.

•**The contractor should have workers' compensation and liability insurance.** Request a certificate of insurance. If the contractor is a sole proprietor with no employees, confirm that he has personal insurance or workers' compensation.

If your contractor or the people he hires aren't properly insured, you're liable for any mishaps. Request a copy of his insurance documents, and call the agent to confirm coverage.

•**Set up a payment schedule.** Like any businessperson, a contractor will want as much in the form of a down payment as possible.

Ideal: You provide 10% of the project's total cost on the day work starts, not when the contract is signed.

Strategy: Create a payment schedule pegged to specific work milestones. Be fair—but write the contract so that you withhold the final 10% to 15% until 20 days after the job is completed. That will give you time to see if everything was really done as you requested. In addition, it will give the contractor an incentive to finish promptly. It's a bad sign if the contractor balks at this.

•**Make sure you're getting what you pay for.** Have the contract state that you'll have an opportunity to inspect all materials before they are used.

Example: Consumers often get gouged on insulation jobs. Contractors frequently short-change people on the amount of insulation that is required.

Solution: Home-repair books or insulation packages can tell you how much you'll need based on the square footage involved.

Important: Count the bags before the insulation is installed. Some contractors bring empty bags to fool people who count this way. If in doubt, ask the company to provide a density test.

Source: Steve Gonzalez, a professional contractor in Fort Lauderdale, FL. He is author of *Before You Hire a Contractor: A Construction Guidebook for Consumers*. Consumer Press.

Shop Around For Medication

Discount pharmacies may have better prices on prescription drugs than mail-order companies. A recent survey found that a Wal-Mart store in northern New Jersey had lower prices on two of the most popular medications—*Procardia* and *Zantac*. Two mail-order firms had the lowest prices on three others—*Uniphyl, Psorcon* and *Premarin*.

Bottom line: Shop pharmacies and by mail order when looking for the best prices.

Source: *The New York Times.*

Credit Cards Are Being Revoked

Credit cards are being revoked from customers with good credit standing but who do not use the cards to the issuer's satisfaction. One bank cancelled 100,000 no-fee credit cards it considered unprofitable because holders did not use them often enough. Another bank threatened to close some accounts that paid no interest. It said people who want to keep the cards would have to charge $2,500 within six months…transfer a $1,000 balance and pay interest…or have their accounts closed.

Source: Ruth Susswein, executive director, Bankcard Holders of America, 524 Branch Dr., Salem, VA 24153.

Credit Card Warning

Beware of the new credit cards that have images of celebrities, celebrity artwork or stadiums. Cards are designed to attract fans who may overlook their drawbacks. *Strategy:* Before applying, call the issuer and ask about the interest rate after the introductory period expires… whether there are restrictions…and if there are fees for not using the card.

Source: Robert McKinley, president of RAM Research Corp., which tracks nationwide credit card rates, Box 1700, Frederick, MD 21702.

Better Auction Buying

During my nearly 30 years as an auctioneer at Sotheby's auction house, I've seen plenty of smart bidders make dreadful mistakes. Whether you are bidding for sculpture at a top auction house or an old wheelbarrow at a barn auction, the same strategies apply.

How to do well at any auction…

•**Always preview items before the bidding begins.** This may seem obvious, but you would be surprised by the number of people who don't bother to examine items before an auction.

In other cases, people just glance at an auction catalog and assume the items that interest them will look just as they appear in print.

But what you see in print or from afar on the auction stage may be quite different up close. Defects aren't always mentioned in the auction's catalog.

Example: An antique dresser may look great onstage, but once you've paid for it, you may find out it is missing a back leg.

When you notice a defect in an item you've acquired at an auction, it is no one's fault but your own…and there's usually no recourse. Every auction allows you to preview merchandise before it goes on the block. Use this time wisely to photograph or videotape items, if possible, and take notes.

•**Have a top bid in mind before the bidding starts.** Too often, people begin bidding on an item without determining a fixed, top-dollar amount. As a result, even a seasoned bidder gets carried away in the heat of competition and winds up overspending.

Solution: Write your top bid on a slip of paper, and hold it in your hand. This will remind you of your limit.

•**Correct your mistakes quickly.** Lots of bidders make honest mistakes at an auction. For instance, it's not unusual for an excited novice to bid—and get—an item that came up just before the desired one. Such a mistake can be fixed, but you have to act fast.

What to do: Stand up, and say in a loud voice that there has been a mistake…you bid on the wrong lot…and are terribly sorry. If you move too slowly and quietly up to the auctioneer, there's nothing that can be done to remedy the situation.

Reason: In all fairness to the auction house, it may be impossible to regroup the original bidders or re-create the charged atmosphere in the room, which is essential to any auction.

•**Stay right next to your partner.** I can't tell you how many times I've seen husbands and wives or other couples bidding against one another from opposite sides of the room—not realizing that their partners are also bidding.

•**Consider leaving your bid instead of participating in the auction.** Anyone who has exceeded his/her limit more than once should not actively bid.

Solution: Ask the auction officials if you can leave your top-dollar bid ahead of time. Many people are hesitant to do this because they are afraid the item will cost them the full amount they bid—even though the next-highest bidder may have offered hundreds less.

If you want to be sure this won't happen, put in your bid order and then attend the auction anyway.

Source: Robert Woolley, executive vice president and head of decorative arts at Sotheby's in New York, one of the country's oldest and most-established auction houses. He is author of *Going Once: A Memoir of Art, Society and Charity.* Simon & Schuster.

($69). Cost of all other equipment runs about $1,500 to $2,000. *Drawbacks:* Sound quality is unpredictable, with annoying delays between responses...transmissions are "half-duplex," so only one person can speak at a time (as on a CB radio...both parties must be logged on, so the timing of calls must be prearranged.

Source: John Edwards, computer industry analyst based in Mount Laurel, NJ.

Save Thousands of Dollars On Airfare

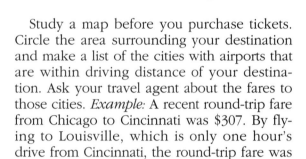

Study a map before you purchase tickets. Circle the area surrounding your destination and make a list of the cities with airports that are within driving distance of your destination. Ask your travel agent about the fares to those cities. *Example:* A recent round-trip fare from Chicago to Cincinnati was $307. By flying to Louisville, which is only one hour's drive from Cincinnati, the round-trip fare was $59—a savings of $248.

Source: Tom Parsons, editor of *Best Fares Discount Travel*, 1301 S. Bowen Rd., Suite 490, Arlington, TX 76013.

Cheap Long-Distance Telephone Calls via The Internet

Internet Phone is a software program that allows computer users to talk to one another over the Internet global computer network (201-768-9400). *Cost:* Usually $2 to $3 per hour —the normal rate for Internet service. *Needed:* 486 or Pentium processor computer...Windows 3.1 or newer operating system (software works only on PC-compatible computers)... soundcard...microphone...speakers...14.4 or faster modem...8 MB or more RAM...2 MB hard-drive space...WinSock compatible Internet connection...*Internet Phone software*

Buy the Right Toys

Buy toys that match a child's development and ability...

For nine-month-olds: Toys that respond dramatically. *Examples:* Activity centers with cranks to turn, balls to push, cars that roll and beep.

For three-to-four-year-olds: Toys that encourage the use of imagination, as well as motor ability. *Examples:* Props for make-believe, basic art supplies.

For five-to-seven-year-olds: Games that satisfy intellectual needs and demonstrate knowledge mastered. *Examples:* Learning games, construction toys, costumes, playhouses.

For eight-to-10-year-olds: Toys that make them feel grown-up. *Examples:* Crafts kits, chemistry sets.

Source: Jake Winebaum, editor, *Family Fun*, Box 929, Northampton, MA 01060.

How to Cut Your Family's Medical Bills...Fast

Health care for the average person is still expensive, despite the many moves by doctors, hospitals and insurers to cut costs. Here's what you can do to reduce your out-of-pocket expenses—even if you and your family are covered by health insurance...

Doctors:

•**Get your money's worth.** Be prepared. Bring notes about your medical history, symptoms and questions you want the doctor to answer. Bring articles that shed light on your medical condition and ask your doctor about their validity. Have your doctor explain what he/she is writing in your file.

Once you pay the bill, you're entitled to a copy of the lab report free. Ask your doctor to explain it to you.

The more you know, the better able you will be to gauge what treatments are appropriate for you—and which expenses are worth questioning.

•**Call your doctor first—it's free.** Take advantage of a doctor's phone hours. A recent Dartmouth Medical School study found that phoning saved each patient an average of $1,656 over a two-year period.

Warning: There's a difference between avoiding unnecessary visits to specialists and forgoing important preventive measures. People who save money by avoiding flu shots or treatment for high blood pressure are making serious mistakes.

•**Consider avoiding the annual physical.** Symptom-free adults under age 65 can save $200 to $500 a year by reconsidering whether they really need an annual physical. The American Medical Association's guidelines suggest that adults ages 21 to 40 have a complete checkup every five years...and every few years thereafter—depending on their health.

Drugs:

•**Ask your doctor to prescribe** generic drugs when appropriate. They are just as effective and much cheaper.

•**Request free samples** of prescribed medicines from your doctors. They often have a large supply.

•**Cut back on over-the-counter** (OTC) medicines. Most OTC remedies for colds, pains and minor problems don't really do any good—only 30% can fully prove their claims.

Hospitals:

•**Always get a second opinion.** An eight-year study by the Cornell Medical Center found that one out of four second opinions recommends against an operation. The long-term survival rate of people who take such advice is excellent. So even if your insurance company doesn't require a second opinion, get one.

Be sure to ask a lot of questions, since you make the final decision regarding your treatment.

Studies show that the operations most often considered unnecessary are tonsillectomies, coronary bypasses, gallbladder removals, cesarean sections, pacemaker surgeries and joint surgeries. Be particularly diligent about getting a second opinion in such cases.

•**Look for the least-expensive option.** Many procedures that traditionally required overnight hospital stays can now be done on an outpatient basis—up to 50% cheaper than regular hospital procedures.

When you discuss outpatient alternatives with your doctor, ask about new minimally invasive surgical techniques. They can be less expensive and less traumatic.

Trap: Never assume that your doctor or surgeon will automatically recommend the cheapest treatment. Be prepared to ask him/her about options you have researched.

•**Save on "incidentals."** Check to see what the hospital charges for various services before you check in. The most frequently hidden hospital costs are the $50-to-$100 fees for providing routine information when filling out forms. These charges are levied by 25% to 30% of hospitals. Ask to fill out the papers yourself—assuming, of course, you are well enough to do so.

•**Make sure your hospital stay is necessary.** Studies show that only one of every eight hospital admissions is medically necessary and only one of every five operations really makes sense. When you're told you should have a certain procedure or test, be appropriately skeptical.

Strategy: Ask your doctor the following questions about any recommended procedure…

•*What are the procedure's risks?*

•*Which hospital do you suggest—and why?* Some are safer than others…some are cheaper…some are both.

•*Are there any less-invasive alternatives to this type of surgery? Example:* Clot-dissolving drugs instead of heart bypass surgery.

•*Can I have this procedure done as an outpatient?*

•**Resist unnecessary tests.** Ask your doctor why a hospital test must be given. *Tests most frequently over-ordered:* Urinalyses, chest X rays and some blood tests. Insist on advance approval of tests and procedures.

•**Assume your bill is wrong.** A recent General Accounting Office study found overcharges in 99% of all hospital bills. Why does this matter to someone who has health insurance? Because more and more plans are now requiring patients to share hospital costs.

Strategy: Request a fully itemized bill. Then review it carefully. *Look for…*

•**Duplicate billing** (often for tests).

•**Shoddy testing** (don't pay for unreadable X rays).

•**Unauthorized tests** (if you previously specified that you wanted advance approval).

•**Phantom charges** (often for medications that may never have been given).

•**Bulk charges.** If you see a broad heading such as "radiology" or "pharmacy," ask for a detailed breakdown of the charges. Insurance:

•**Increase your deductible.** Talk with your insurance agent or with the benefits person at your company. The amount you save each year may be substantial, particularly if you are a healthy adult.

•**Avoid being overinsured.** Be prepared to absorb some occasional minor expenses rather than seeking a policy that covers every penny of your expenses all the time. This kind of insurance policy is never a bargain.

•**If your benefits are ever denied**, fight back. Some surveys show that policyholders who contest denials get partial or complete satisfaction 50% of the time.

Source: Frederick Ruof, chairperson, National Emergency Medicine Association (NEMA), an organization that specializes in providing consumers with information on ways to reduce medical costs. NEMA publishes a booklet called *How to Cut Your Family's Medical Bills by $1,000,* 524 Branch Dr., Salem, VA 24135.

Examine Hospital Bills Closely Before Paying

Watch out for phantom charges. *Examples:* Many hospitals have charged for tests that were not performed…drugs that were not administered…doctors' visits that didn't occur. Refuse to pay these charges, or notify your insurer if the bill will be sent to it directly. Also—ask your insurer about discounts it may have negotiated for hospital services. The amount shown on your bill may not be the true amount the insurance company pays—so your copayment should be lower as well.

Source: Joe Altman, health care consultant, Towers-Perrin, 695 E. Main St., Stamford, CT 06901.

Save on Towing Charges

Keep your battery terminals clean to avoid starting problems and costly towing bills. Clean the battery terminals occasionally with baking soda. Reduce the corrosion problem by smearing them with a thin coating of petroleum jelly.

Source: Andy Dappen, author of *Cheap Tricks: 100s of Ways You Can Save 1000s of Dollars* (Brier Books). He is a writer in Brier, WA, who specializes in ways to save money and live frugally. His work has appeared in many national publications.

Unshrink Wool Sweaters

Mix two tablespoons of baby shampoo in one gallon of lukewarm water. Soak the garment for 10 minutes. Do not rinse—blot excess water with a dry towel. Lay the garment flat on a fresh towel. Reshape it slowly back to its original size. Dry it away from heat and direct sunlight.

Source: Recommendation from the Wool Bureau, reported in *Cheapskate Monthly*, Box 2135, Paramount, CA 90723.

Less Expensive Ways to Enjoy Life Much More

Some people think that cutting costs leads to a life of deprivation...and little enjoyment. It doesn't. I'm living proof of that.

For more than a decade, I have been coming up with less expensive ways to have a great time. *What I've learned...*

Three keys to cost-cutting:

• **Hunt for bargains.** You can't take advantage of the good deals unless you know where to find them. When you read newspapers and magazines, look for entertainment bargains. Clip and save what you find in clearly marked files.

• **Plan ahead.** People often overspend because they feel they have no choice.

Example: You're "starving" and the only restaurant around is expensive. If you had planned ahead, you would have brought the two-for-one coupon you had for it at home.

• **Set a budget.** Decide how much you can spend on entertainment for the entire year. Then, how much you can spend on a family outing today.

Go have a good time...but save:

• **Eating out.** Families should always choose restaurants with children's menus.

Strategy: If a restaurant doesn't have one, negotiate. Ask for a smaller portion for your child at a lower price.

• **Movies.** Renting a video is cheaper than going to a theater to see a movie, and staying at home to watch a movie on TV is even cheaper.

Strategy: When you do go out to the movies, save money by attending matinees. Or catch a recent release at a second-run theater, which has much cheaper ticket prices.

• **Theater can get pretty pricey**, but that doesn't mean you have to eliminate it from your life.

Strategy: Buy discount theater tickets by using two-for-one coupons...go to a half-price ticket booth...join a discount theater club...or round up a group of friends and share a season seat.

• **Books, CDs, tapes, etc.** Many libraries have audio-and videotape and compact disc collections.

Strategy: "Rent" instead of buying. Or, rent before you buy. Be sure you like a new tape or CD before you buy it.

Used-book and CD stores also offer big bargains on merchandise.

• **Romantic evening.** A fancy dinner out followed by dancing is a great way to spend an evening. But there are cheaper ways to be romantic.

One of my favorites: A long walk with my husband. Along the way, we stop for an ice cream or a cappuccino.

• **Mini-vacations.** A vacation of any duration is special, even if it's just one day.

What my family does: We make a hotel reservation in a town an hour away, pick a place with a heated pool and a color TV with cable channels, and pack a cooler with fun food—elegant sandwiches or barbecued chicken.

• **Friends.** Get-togethers with friends don't have to be elaborate or expensive.

Strategy: I like the pot-luck approach to dinner parties of eight or more. Have everyone prepare a favorite dish. You save money and avoid an exhausting cleanup. Assign specific dishes—appetizer, main course, dessert—to different people.

Source: Rochelle LaMotte McDonald, a homemaker and mother of three. She is author of *How to Pinch a Penny Till It Screams: Stretching Your Dollars in the 90s.* Avery Publishing Group.

Cut Home Heating Bills By 10%

Cut heating bills 10% a month by keeping your furnace in top condition. Have it professionally inspected once a year. *Cost:* Approximately $50, which usually includes a filter change. Then change replaceable filters monthly—they cost about $1 each but can save $40 to $100 in heating bills each year. *Also:* Arrange furniture so heating vents are not blocked. Keep the door of the fan compartment tightly closed.

Source: Recommendations by the American Society of Home Inspectors, Arlington Heights, IL.

Wintertime Money Savers

Winter is the season of higher electric, gas, car maintenance and repair bills. But there are ways you can cut down on these typical winter costs without sacrificing great comfort.

Avoid costly car repairs:

•**Keep your gasoline free of water.** The most frequent problems mechanics see in winter are caused by water in the gas. To prevent problems, add a drier—such as Prestone Gas-Drier or Heet—to your gas tank every few fill-ups.

•**Check your radiator fluid and the condition of the radiator hoses.** If the fluid is low, add a 50/50 mixture of antifreeze and water.

In the coldest parts of the country or when an extreme cold snap strikes, you may want to alter this by using more antifreeze. Use a mixture of 70% antifreeze and 30% water.

Muddy-looking fluid should be changed.

Make sure that the rubber hoses leading from the radiator to the engine are not cracked, brittle, bulging or mushy when they are squeezed.

•**Keep your battery terminals clean** to avoid starting problems and costly towing bills. Clean the battery terminals occasionally with baking soda. Reduce the corrosion prob-

lem by smearing them with a thin coating of petroleum jelly.

•**Promptly repair any nicks in your windshield.** Stop those nicks that are smaller than a quarter from spawning "spider legs" and ruining the windshield. Cover them on both sides with transparent tape. Duct tape works, too.

Then get the car to a windshield-repair specialist. Cost of repairing a nick ranges from $30 to $50, compared with $300 to $600 to replace the entire windshield.

•**Check tire inflation** every few weeks with an accurate gauge. Changes in temperature alter tire pressure, and underinflation increases tire wear and gas consumption by as much as 5%.

Important: Check the pressure while tires are cold—before you start the car. Know how many pounds of pressure they require. Then check them again at the gas station after they've warmed from being driven on. Add the pounds of pressure that were needed when they were cold.

Save on heating:

•**Put on an extra sweater** and modify your heating habits. Keep the daytime thermostat at 65° (rather than 70°) and the nighttime temperature at 55° (rather than 60° or 65°). This can reduce your heating bill 15% or more. And turn down the heat when you leave to run errands.

•**Keep fireplace dampers closed when not in use.** Install glass fireplace doors. The glass doors will keep the heat that is generated by the furnace from escaping up through the chimney of your house. If you rarely use your fireplace, a piece of plywood blocking the fireplace is a great insulator. If painted black and covered by the facade of glass door, the plywood is barely noticeable.

•**Have your home's insulation checked by your utility company.** Many utilities will perform this inspection service free or for a nominal fee. Make sure your home's insulation meets the US Department of Energy's recommendations.

•**Wrap fiberglass insulation around the heating ducts** and the hot water pipes in basement, attic and crawl space. Putting two and a half inches of insulation around these ducts and pipes will pay for itself in one season. Save on lighting:

•**Replace incandescent lights with fluorescent lights** in areas that need light for hours each day.

Today's fluorescent tubes produce warmer hues that won't make your home feel like a factory, and they're three to four times more efficient. If you don't want to go to the trouble of installing the tubes, use compact fluorescent bulbs. They screw into standard sockets.

•**Use outdoor light fixtures** that turn on and off by means of built-in heat/motion detectors and timers. They're far more economical than those that burn nonstop.

•**Don't turn lights on and off frequently.** Turning the lights out every time you leave the room for a few minutes may seem like a good idea, but it shortens the life of the bulbs.

Source: Andy Dappen, author of *Cheap Tricks: 100s of Ways You Can Save 1000s of Dollars* (Brier Books). He is a writer in Brier, WA, who specializes in ways to save money and live frugally. His work has appeared in many national publications.

Before Buying Your First Computer

Computers are expensive, and buying the wrong one can be costly. *Questions to ask yourself before you buy…*

What software programs will I be using? To the uninitiated, this question may seem to be putting the cart before the horse. But smart consumers choose their software first, then buy a computer to run it.

Ask yourself what you hope to accomplish with your computer. Will you use it exclusively for writing? Will you need it to produce sophisticated graphics? Do you want it to print your checks or figure your taxes?

You must also decide whether to buy software that operates on a Macintosh computer …or on a PC system, which is used by IBMs and IBM-compatibles.

How to choose: Consider software you are already familiar with and the format—Macintosh or PC—that will be most useful by your family. What programs do you or your spouse use at the office? What do your kids have at school?

How much money do I have to spend? The good news is that computer prices continue to drop as technology advances. While any purchase hinges on your needs, you can find an adequate unit for less than $1,500. That price will buy you a package that likely includes a…

•**CD-ROM drive**, which operates CDs that are packed with information.

•**Built-in modem**, which allows you to access on-line services and communicate with other users.

•**Color monitor.**

•**Sound card**, which enables your computer to play music.

•**Basic software package.**

Important: A laptop computer can be a valuable second computer, but I don't recommend it as your first purchase. To get a unit with a color screen that is similar to your computer at work, you'll have to spend several thousands more.

How fast should the microprocessor be? The microprocessor is the postage stamp-sized chip that directs all of the computer's activities. The larger the megahertz (MHz) number, the faster the computer will process your work and your commands.

Buy the fastest microprocessor you can afford. The basic chip sold today is some version of Intel's 486 series, ranging in speed from 25 MHz to 100 MHz. A new chip called the 586 —or the Pentium—is much faster. Though it initially received bad publicity when it was released, Intel has since fixed the problem.

How much memory does my computer need? Computer memory comes in two forms…

•**Short-term, random-access memory**, commonly referred to as RAM. It is needed to run your software and handle the file on which you're currently working. To run today's software, home computer users will need at least four megabytes (MB), which is roughly equivalent to four million typed characters. Most programs run better with 8 MB or 10 MB.

•**Long-term, storage memory**, which enables the computer to store files and recall them, is contained in the hard disk drive. The size of your hard disk drive should be dictated by the demands of your software, which are listed on the packages. To determine how much long-term memory you'll need, add up all of your software requirements, add another 40 MB, then double the total.

Example: If your software requires a total of 100 MB, you'll need at least a 280-MB hard drive.

Source: Dan Gookin, one of the nation's most knowledgeable computer experts and author of more than 30 books on computers, including *Buy That Computer!* IDG Books Worldwide.

Tipping Tips

The rule against tipping owners of hair or nail salons is not absolute. *Solution:* If you're new to a place, ask the receptionist what the owner's policy is about "being given something extra." If you're a regular and the owner doesn't accept tips, remember him/her at the holidays.

Source: Letitia Baldrige, one of the country's top etiquette experts and author of *Letitia Baldrige's New Complete Guide to Executive Manners.* Rawson Associates.

Refunds on Late Mail Delivery

The US Postal Service's Express Mail delivery is often late, missing the next-day guarantee. To determine delivery date, call 800-222-1811. If it was delivered late, you can get a refund and free delivery. *One experience:* A refund rate of 25%.

Source: Ralph Ginzburg, New York–based photographer.

Laptop Computer Survival

Don't leave the laptop plugged into AC power all the time—it ruins the battery. *Helpful:* Completely discharge the battery once a month by leaving the machine on and unplugged overnight, being sure to turn off the "resume" command. To speed up the computer, delete unwanted files and run a cleanup utility. Tighten screws—they tend to loosen. Buy a spare power supply and battery—just in case.

Source: Harry Newton, editor, *Teleconnect,* 12 W. 21 St., New York 10010.

Easier Software Shopping

For easier software shopping, carry a card with the model of your computer and what sound and video cards it contains. Know how much room is available on your hard disk for programs. For IBM compatibles, run the CHKDSK utility at a C prompt. Read the small print on the software box to make sure the program's required chip speed, storage space, sound card and operating memory match your system's. Find out the retailer's return policy in case you cannot get the program to work properly.

Source: John Edwards, computer industry analyst and writer on high-tech subjects, Mount Laurel, NJ.

Winterize Air Conditioners

Winterize air conditioners that are left in windows all year by wrapping them in plastic and sealing with duct tape—or by buying air-conditioner covers. Remember to close the units' vents. For units removed for the winter…move them carefully. Be sure not to bend or damage the cooling fins on the back. Do not store air conditioners on a garage floor—

they could be damaged by de-icing salts from car tires.

Source: Robert Irwin, one of the country's foremost real estate and home care experts, Los Angeles.

Co-op Buying Savvy

Before buying a co-op apartment, examine the building's financial statements for the past two years…or ask a professional to do it. Calculate unpaid maintenance as a percentage of total maintenance. If it exceeds 5%, it indicates sloppy management and suggests the building will be short of money. It also may mean that the building is a slow payer and may have to buy second-class products because top merchants will not tolerate slow payment. *And:* Make sure the building has an adequate reserve fund—about four months of maintenance payments for the entire building.

Source: Herb Rose, co-op consultant, Mount Vernon, NY.

Better House Hunting With Kids

Schedule appointments for when kids are refreshed—such as after a nap or meals… bring along a stuffed animal, simple toys, a blanket and a change of clothes…ask kids for their help. *Example:* "Johnny, would you please see if the yard is big enough for your swing set?" Don't try to see too many houses in one day or spend more than half a day looking…and offer a reward for good behavior at the end of a long day.

Source: Lisa Linzer, real estate agent, L&S Realty, Stamford, CT.

Better Home Buying

Before buying a home in a new development, find out the developer's plans for later stages. *Traps:* Lower-priced housing built later may reduce the value of your home. Overbuilding may overload common facilities, such as parks, swimming pools and tennis courts. *What to do:* Closely examine the developer's plans…zoning laws…deed restrictions on matters such as housing density and minimum lot size…and the legal rights of the homeowners' association to enforce such restrictions.

Source: *The 106 Common Mistakes Homebuyers Make (and How to Avoid Them)* by Gary Eldred, PhD, former professor of real estate at the University of Virginia. John Wiley & Sons.

Better Lemon Buying

The best lemons are fully yellow. Ones with green rinds have less flavor and more acid. Look for rinds that are lightly pebbled and thin. A thick, rough or very pebbly rind means low juice content. If possible, buy organically grown lemons, which tend to have more flavor. Warm lemons are juicier than refrigerated ones. Take some out in the morning and let them warm up during the day…or microwave them for 20 to 30 seconds…or soak them in hot water for 10 minutes. If lemons are at room temperature, put them in hot water for a minute or two for even more juice.

Source: *Lemon Tree Very Healthy Cookbook: Zestful Recipes with Just the Right Twist of Lemon* by Michelle Sbraga, catering instructor, Phoenix. Avery Publishing.

17

Your Car

Airbag Self-Defense

Close to one million cars have been recalled for air-bag defects over the past two decades.

How to be sure your air bags will work when you need them: Watch the dashboard whenever you start the car. A light with the words air bag or passive restraint should flash a few times and then go out. If the light does not come on, or stays on when you drive, have your dealer run a computer check of the air-bag system. *Cost:* $20 to $60.

Source: National Highway Traffic Safety Administration, Rm. 5118, 400 Seventh St. SW, Washington, DC 20590.

Make Your Car Run Cheaper and Last Longer

The two cars in our family have lasted many years and many miles without giving us much trouble. That's partly because my wife and I take good care of my 1977 Honda Civic (62,000 miles) and her 1981 Honda Accord (120,000 miles).

Neither of us is a mechanical genius. We just like getting good value for our money. Here are our secrets…

• **Find a good, trustworthy mechanic.** Good mechanics increase a car's longevity and save owners money. Do they exist? Yes. Are they hard to find? Absolutely.

Strategy: Spend time and energy to find a mechanic who is local and honest. Ask knowledgeable car-owning friends for recomendations. If you are lucky enough to live in a state with an auto-fraud division, call it to check whether a repair shop has a lot of unresolved complaints.

• **Do simple work yourself.** I save money by avoiding our mechanic—whenever possible. *Easy tasks you can do yourself:*

• **Putting on new tires and windshield-wiper blades.**

• **Changing the oil and oil filters.**

• **Checking/replacing spark plugs.**
• **Changing air filters.**

If you don't know much about cars, pick up a book or two that illustrates how-to projects or take a car repair course at a local school or adult learning center.

The following three things will happen— you'll save money over time...you'll feel more confident behind the wheel...and you'll be more confident the next time you speak with an auto mechanic.

Important: If you intend to do repairs, such as replacing a coolant pump or wiper motor, get the car's shop manual. While the car's owner's manual is a good starting place, the shop manual is more detailed and easier to use —it's what mechanics use. Sears and other stores that sell auto parts carry them.

Don't take on difficult jobs if your mechanical skills aren't first-rate.

• **Cut gas consumption.** Dollars saved on gas add up. Conservative driving habits limit wear and tear. *Strategies...*

• **Turn off the car's air conditioner** when possible. With the air-conditioning on, gas mileage drops 15%.

• **Drive at lower speeds.**
• **Accelerate gently.**
• **Turn off the ignition** if your engine will be idling for more than a minute.
• **Get regular tune-ups** every 15,000 miles. This increases gas mileage by 10%.
• **Use the right motor oil.** "Multigrade" oil —marked 10-30W, etc.—reduces engine wear because it can accommodate a wide temperature range. Change oil exactly when the owner's manual says you should. Change the oil filter at least every *5,000 miles.*

Money-saver: Buy oil by the case in warehouse stores.

• **Buy the right tires.** I swear by steel-belted radials. They cost more but last twice as long. They also roll more easily on the road and give you several extra miles per gallon.

Warning: Don't mix radial and bias-ply tires. The car's handling will suffer.

Note: Rotating your tires is a waste of money —unless you do it yourself. It costs more to have someone rotate the tires than you'll save

in rubber wear. But keep an eye on your tires for smooth spots or greater wear on one side of the tread.

Source: Ernest Callenbach, an author and lecturer specializing in ecological and resource conservation issues. He is author of *Living Cheaply with Style: Ways to Live Better & Spend Less.* Ronin Books.

Beware of Cellular Phones in Your Car

Drivers with cellular phones in their cars have a 34% greater risk of being in an auto accident than drivers without car phones.

How some companies reduce risk: Equip salespersons and others who drive for business with phones that have special features— such as voice dialing—that allow the driver to keep eyes on the road and both hands on the wheel. Drivers should also be instructed to engage in safe phoning practices, such as recording incoming calls in voice mail and answering them from the car phone when the vehicle is stopped.

Source: Data from a preliminary study by Rochester Institute of Technology.

Safer Stopping On Icy Roads

Don't "pump" the brakes. *Better:* "Squeeze braking."

How: Shift into neutral (or, if you have a manual transmission, push the clutch in)... press steadily on the brake, to a point just short of lock up, then ease off—but not completely...slowly press down again on the brake pedal and hold it down.

Important: Unless your car is equipped with antilock brakes, don't slam down on the brakes. This may cause the wheels to lock and put you into an out-of-control skid.

Source: David Willis, AAA Foundation for Traffic Safety, 1440 New York Ave. NW, Suite 201, Washington, DC 20005.

What to Do Before Your Car Lease Ends...

When the end of a car lease approaches, many people are faced with critical choices but aren't sure what to do.

Here are your options and suggestions on how to make a decision that makes the most sense for you...

Option 1: Keep the car.

About 65% of Americans buy their leased cars. *When it pays to buy...*

•**You've incurred more than the maximum mileage** allowed on the car...and it has given you no problems.

•**You love the vehicle.**

•**You've exceeded your limit of free miles.** In this case, keeping the car may be the most cost-effective solution.

Beware: Before you buy the car, there's important math to consider. After a car has 30,000 miles on it, the average consumer spends $1,200 a year on routine maintenance—tune-ups, new brakes, tires, belts, hoses, etc. It may be cheaper to lease a new car than to finance and repair a used car.

Strategy: Compare the cost of financing a used car with leasing a new one.

Option 2: Sell the car.

This option makes sense if your leased car is of greater value than its purchase option at lease end. Why shouldn't you, rather than the dealer, take advantage of an equity situation?

If you have a lease-end inspection 30 to 60 days before your lease is over, you may discover that there are damages to your vehicle that you will have to pay for. By buying the vehicle and selling it outright, a lease's "normal depreciation" clause no longer applies.

Strategy: Invest about $50 to have someone clean the vehicle inside and out. This is also known as "detailing," and it can add $300 to $500 to its selling price. Then run a classified ad. Advertise the car for a little less than everyone else is asking for similar models and years.

Example: If the purchase-option price is $12,000 and the car retails used for $14,000 to $15,000, advertise it for $13,000 or so.

Begin this process about 60 days before the lease ends.

Option 3: Turn in the car.

This is a logical choice if you don't like the car...want to drive a newer model...or know that the car you're driving hasn't held its value as expected. *But first take these steps to avoid charges...*

•**Make sure the car is absolutely clean.** Detailing isn't necessary, but it might be a good idea and a time-saver.

•**If there are any scratches or dents**, get an independent estimate of the repair cost. Compare the estimate with what you'll have to pay the dealer for wear and tear. You'll almost always come out ahead by taking the car to a body shop yourself.

•**If the vehicle needs new brakes or tires**, find out the cost before turning it in. You'll profit by having the work done before the lease ends.

•**Take pictures or a video** of the vehicle in the event of a dispute.

Source: Kurt Allen Weiss, consumer advocate and former car salesman in New Jersey. He is author of *Have I Got a Deal for You! How to Buy or Lease Any Car Without Getting Run Over.* Career Press.

Car Shopping

Before you go car shopping, write out where most of your driving will be done...how many passengers will usually be in the car...how many miles a year you expect to drive...the extras you want, including comfort options as well as alarms and extended warranties...how much the new car will increase your insurance premiums.

Source: Kurt Allen Weiss, consumer advocate and former car salesman in New Jersey. He is author of *Have I Got a Deal for You! How to Buy or Lease Any Car Without Getting Run Over.* Career Press.

Keep Automatic Transmissions Cool

Remove leaves and debris from the cooling grid, located at the front of the car. *Also:* Replace transmission oil at regular intervals—every 25,000 to 35,000 miles, as recommended by your car's manufacturer.

Source: Brian Workman, manager of technical services, AAMCO Transmissions, Inc., transmission repair shops, Bala Cynwyd, PA.

For the Best Bargains On Cars

Buy models that are being replaced by new versions this year. *Examples:* Ford Escort, Mercury Tracer, Pontiac Grand Prix, Buick Century, Buick Regal and Oldsmobile Cutlass Supreme. Or—shop for out-of-favor types of cars, particularly sports coupes.

Alternative: Used cars coming off two-year leases—especially luxury models that have been well kept and have low mileage.

Poor deals now: Sport-utility vehicles, such as GMC Suburbans and four-door Chevy Tahoe Yukons. Their popularity makes their prices nonnegotiable.

Source: W. James Bragg, head of Fighting Chance, which sells car-pricing information to consumers, 5318 E. Second St., Long Beach, CA 90803.

New Car Savings

Save up to $1,000 on a new car by factory ordering the model you want—rather than buying one that is on the dealer's lot. Dealers often push vehicles that are on their showroom floors or in their car lots. They sweeten the deals by agreeing to cut prices and stressing that the on-site cars can be driven home immediately. *Problems:* Most models on the lot cost more to begin with because they are loaded with options—many of which you may not want or need. Purchasing a factory-ordered car guarantees you will get what you want—and nothing more.

Source: Ashly Knapp is CEO of Auto Advisor, Inc., a fee-based nationwide service in Seattle that haggles with car dealers on behalf of consumers.

How to Buy a Used Car

The quality of used cars is rising, making them more appealing and practical than ever before.

Reasons: The growth in popularity of leasing has brought a large supply of high-quality two- and three-year-old vehicles into dealers' showrooms. And—today's emphasis on frugality and value has improved the status of used cars, making them almost as appealing as new ones.

Steps to getting the best possible deal on a used car...

•**Determine your need.** How rugged does the vehicle have to be? How many passengers must it hold? How many miles are you likely to put on it each year?

•**Have a sense of what fits your budget.** The best way to gauge current prices is not by looking at industry guides. Those prices are always a bit out of date. *Better:* For several weeks, check the classified section of your local paper or your local *Auto Trader*, a magazine containing used-car ads, to get a sense of the market.

•**Call your insurance agent—before you go shopping.** You can get either a sport utility vehicle or a minivan for $10,000. But the sport utility vehicle will cost you 30% to 40% more in insurance every year.

•**Don't waste time buying a used car from an individual.** Here's where I differ in my thinking from many consumers. Most people believe they can always get a better deal from a private party. I don't.

Problem: Ads inevitably describe the car's condition as "excellent" or "very good." How can you tell without looking? You can't—

which means pursuing a private deal can be a big money-waster.

Better: Buy from a franchised dealer who also sells new cars...or from an independent used-car dealer. Many of these dealers place ads in the classifieds as well. *Reasons...*

•**A dealer will have a selection** right there on the premises, which makes comparison shopping easier.

•**A dealer will usually give you** at least a 30-day warranty. A private party probably won't.

•**A two-, three-or four-year-old vehicle** may still have some warranty protection, but this may be transferable only if you buy from a dealer. To find out, call the regional office of the manufacturer, or contact the manufacturer's financing arm.

•**You can complain about a dealer** to state authorities, but your only recourse against an individual is small-claims court. In a private deal, what goes wrong is usually your headache.

Rule of thumb: Buy privately only if you can get the car for 15% off the price being charged by a dealer. If you're good at fixing cars, you have more reason to seek a private deal.

•**Take the vehicle for a test drive** and have your mechanic look at it. How well the car runs is much more important than its appearance. You can always fix the outside...but that's not so with the engine or transmission.

If you're not allowed to take the car for a test drive or to your mechanic, walk away from the deal.

Make sure everything in the car works. Listen for odd noises. Check all lights, gauges and buttons, as well as sound systems. Bring along a tape and a CD to test the stereo. Nothing can cause you more grief—or lighten your wallet more effectively—than trouble with the electrical system.

If something is wrong, don't buy the car until the dealer's mechanic fixes the problem. Don't even put any money down until this is done.

•**Check the vehicle's exterior**, including the tires. Rub your hand on top of each tire. They should feel smooth in both directions. Slip a penny into the tire tread. If you can see

the top of Lincoln's head, the tires must be replaced.

Don't worry about rust underneath the vehicle. It's normal and is not a sign of internal damage.

•**Negotiate.** Unfortunately, you have less leverage when you are buying a used car than when you're buying a new car.

Reason: With a new vehicle, the dealer knows there's a guy across town peddling the exact same thing and is more likely to make concessions.

Strategy: Tell the dealer you're in love with another used car. Cite the model, year, mileage and price. It may get you a better price.

Get the discounts you deserve. The average vehicle logs 15,000 miles per year. If the mileage is greater, you should get a discount of 15 to 20 cents per mile. On the other hand, expect to pay more for a car that has seldom left the garage.

Avoid company cars because they take more of a pounding than other cars.

•**Be proactive.** If you know what you want, request it—even if you don't see it on a dealer's lot.

•**Don't waste time trying to line up financing** until you can specify the particular vehicle you have in mind. Most financial institutions won't give you a used-car loan until they know exactly what you're buying. Credit unions are an exception.

•**Don't baby your new used car.** After the purchase, use the 30-day warranty period to really test the car. Drive it 1,000 miles or more. Most problems will show up in the first 1,000 miles.

Source: Art Spinella, vice president of CNW Marketing/Research, an automotive market research firm in Bandon, OR. His company recently completed a two-and-a-half-year study of consumer attitudes about used cars.

Car-Rental Savvy

Reserve the smallest car available. Most rental agencies have more larger cars than compacts. If they run out of small cars by the time you arrive, they'll usually upgrade you at no extra charge.

Also helpful: Request a car with the lowest mileage.

Source: Herbert J. Teison, editor, *Travel Smart*, 40 Beechdale Rd., Dobbs Ferry, NY 10522.

How to Get the Best Car-Leasing Deal

At the dealership, act as if you're buying the car. Negotiate a price before you even mention leasing.

Reason: Most lease prices are based on a car's full sticker price. That makes monthly payments higher than they would be if based on a value below the sticker price.

Helpful: To find out dealer costs, check the *Pace Buyers' Guide—New-Car Prices*...then try to negotiate a price that is $250 to $600 above cost. Also, be sure the dealer is giving a fair residual value. Check the *Automotive Lease Guide's Residual Percentage Guide*.

Source: W. James Bragg, head of Fighting Chance, which sells car-pricing information to consumers, 5318 E. Second St., Long Beach, CA 90803.

Almost-New Cars At Used-Car Prices

More than a million two-year-old leased cars are expected to be turned in to car dealers this year.

Example: In 1992, Ford and Honda waged a fierce battle to see whether the Taurus or the Accord would be the best-selling car of the year. Ford won by offering a two-year lease program that put 40,000 cars on the road. Honda also heavily promoted its lease option. Many of these leases came to an end in 1994, and these cars were sold as used.

Important: While most of these cars are in good condition, check them out carefully before buying.

Source: Art Spinella, vice president, CNW Marketing/Research, a Bandon, OR, firm that tracks car leasing.

Odometer Tampering Is Rampant

Odometer tampering on used cars is still rampant. It is most common among cars previously owned by rental car companies and corporate fleets and those leased by individuals. These cars, while well maintained, are driven far more than average cars.

Self-defense: When looking to buy a used car—whether from a dealer or an individual—always look at the car's service records. See if the current mileage makes sense compared with the mileage when the car was serviced. If records are not available, contact the car's prior owner, whom you can find through the Department of Motor Vehicles. Otherwise—*don't buy that car.*

Source: David Solomon, certified master auto technician and editor of *Nutz & Boltz*®, Box 123, Butler, MD 21023.

 # Drivers Beware

The most dangerous driving day is Friday. *Most dangerous time of day:* Late afternoon to early evening. *Most dangerous month to drive:* November. The safest month is March...safest day, Sunday.

Caution: Medium and heavy trucks make up less than 4% of registered vehicles but are involved in nearly 10% of fatal accidents.

Source: National Safety Council statistics, Itasca, IL.

Car-Accident Smarts

Exchange information:
- License plate and driver's license numbers.
- Vehicle identification numbers.
- Insurers' names and policy numbers.
- Insurance agents and phone numbers.
- Names, addresses and phone numbers of others involved and witnesses.
- Names, badges and phone numbers of attending officers.

Documentation:
- Information on the accident site.
- Get the case number from the officer. Ask when and where you can get a copy of the report.
- Keep a camera in your car to photograph damage.
- Photograph everything around the accident—vehicles, traffic lights and property damaged by the event.
- Have two sets of prints made—one for yourself and an extra set.

And then...
- Meet with the insurance adjuster and repair shop.
- Have the vehicle inspected by a second repair shop to verify all the items on the estimate were done.

Source: Ron Alford, director of the Quality Information Institute, a consumer education organization specializing in the planning process of insurance and consumer issues in New York. He is author of *Auto Insurance Tricks & Repair Rip-Offs.* Plan Publishing.

The New Car-Leasing Traps Can Be Avoided

If you want to drive a new car or a luxury model but don't want to put up the cash to own it outright, leasing might make sense.

The best candidates for leasing are people who drive less than 15,000 miles a year and don't want to keep the same car for more than three years. But—be careful. It's easy to get trapped in a bad lease. The terms of many leases are confusing, and you could end up paying far more than you thought you were going to pay.

Here are the big lease traps—and how to avoid them...

Trap: Financing your lease with the wrong company. Financing companies have different ways of measuring wear and tear...and some offer benefits and extras. If you choose the wrong company, you could get a lousy deal.

Better: Choose a finance company such as Ford Motor Credit or GMAC. These companies are owned by the car makers and are less likely than banks to nickel and dime you with finance charges that run up your costs on the lease.

These companies also are more lenient about charges for wear and tear on cars—and they are more likely to offer free services such as roadside assistance.

Trap: Underestimating your mileage needs. Most leasing companies offer packages that include 10,000 to 12,000 miles per year. Many people don't pay attention to those limits and get charged for extra miles when they return the car.

In fact, our studies show that 85% of lessees exceed the mileage limits on their leases...and 40% of lessees pay for an extra 3,000 to 5,000 miles.

Solution: Buy more miles than you think you'll need. Your monthly payments will be higher, but you'll save money in the long run.

Before you decide how many extra miles to buy, ask about the price difference between buying extra miles at the beginning of the lease and paying for them when you return the car. If the gap is big, buy enough miles now.

Typically, one excess mile costs between eight and nine cents if you buy it up front—but one mile can cost as much as 15 cents if you pay for it later.

Trap: Not taking gap insurance. If your leased car is stolen or totally wrecked, you are responsible for replacing it.

Gap insurance protects you by covering the difference between the car's value and the amount you still owe on the lease.

Solution: Ask your dealer to add gap insurance to the package. Some leases include this, but most do not.

Trap: Taking a long-term lease. Many people assume that a long-term lease is cheapest. But a short-term lease—say two years, rather than four or five years—may be better.

An extra year or two of leasing can dramatically wear down a car, so your out-of-pocket expenses will be much smaller with a shorter lease.

With a longer lease, you'll start to pay sizable sums for maintenance, repairs and expenses like tires. Many of these costs are not covered in the warranty.

Solution: Consider leasing for two years. And if you want to hang onto the car for longer than 42 months, don't lease at all. Buying will be cheaper.

Trap: Not pushing for perks that come with many of the best leases. When you shop around for a lease, look for a dealer that offers…

• **Free maintenance.** Look for a dealer's policy that will cover all oil changes, new wiper blades, windshield washer fluid and at least some repairs.

• **Roadside assistance and beyond.** Some dealers offer free services if your car breaks down. Ask for a lease that covers flat tires and engine overheating and pays for hotel accommodations if you are stranded overnight.

• **Loaner car.** Your lease also should provide free use of another car when your leased vehicle is undergoing repairs.

If you are unable to win all three of these perks, settle for at least one or two of them.

Source: Art Spinella, vice president of CNW Marketing/Research, a fee-based company that provides auto-buying and leasing data to corporate clients, Box 744, Bandon, OR 97411.

Better Car Buying

Shop during the late fall or winter, when sales are slowest—and deals are easiest to come by. And try to shop during the last week of the month, when dealerships are competing in contests or pushing to meet sales quotas. If possible, shop late in the day—at dinnertime or afterward—when salespeople and managers tend to be tired and more flexible about closing deals.

Source: Kurt Allen Weiss, a former car salesman and author of *Have I Got a Deal for You!: How to Buy or Lease Any Car Without Getting Run Over.* Career Press.

How to Complain About The Car You Just Bought

After spending a lot of time shopping for and picking out a new vehicle, the last thing you want is a mechanical problem. But problems do occur. *Here's how to complain so you'll get satisfaction…*

Begin the dialogue on the phone or in person. Talk to the salesperson—as a courtesy—but don't assume this will resolve matters. If the salesperson cannot help you, speak to the general manager or the owner of the dealership. If you're referred to the service manager, talk to him/her in the late morning or early afternoon, when he's less likely to be busy.

If you still aren't pleased, call the car manufacturer's district representative. The dealer will give you the number. The representative has a stake in making you happy, and you'll almost always get justice.

Source: Kurt Allen Weiss, a former car salesman and author of *Have I Got a Deal for You!: How to Buy or Lease Any Car Without Getting Run Over.* Career Press.

Auto-Repair Rip-Off

Billing you separately for items that are really part of a single repair job.

Example: A dishonest mechanic quotes a price of $130 to recondition brake drums or rotors…then charges an extra $80 for repacking the wheel bearings—which must be done as part of the reconditioning.

Self-defense: Get a detailed written estimate of all parts and labor before agreeing to the job. And—always get a second opinion.

Source: Clarence Ditlow, executive director of the Center for Auto Safety, 2001 S St. NW, Washington, DC 20009.

18

Self-Defense

Choosing a PIN

Choose a Personal Identification Number (PIN) that means something to you—but not to others. Use digits that are secret or even embarrassing, such as your height and weight or your starting salary. Or pick a PIN that spells out a word on a lettered keyboard, like the ones on most telephones. *Examples:* 28257 spells bucks...2633 spells code. Pick an obscure word to spell out.

Source: Edward F. Mrkvicka, Jr., bank consultant in Marengo, IL, and author of *The Bank Book.* HarperCollins.

A Password that's Easy to Remember Is Easy to Break

Use of short, convenient passwords is a leading cause of phone and computer security breaches.

Bad passwords: Names of people or places, Social Security numbers, birth dates, account numbers, extension numbers and simple sequences such as "2468." *Frequent problem:* Passwords that are written on blotters or in phone books or diaries.

Good passwords: Long passwords of eight or more characters—each character increases the number of possible combinations geometrically—that are composed of a mix of letters and numbers that is as random as possible. Ideally, passwords should be changed every few months.

Source: Marc Leichtling, district manager, Fraud Initiatives Net-PROTECT, AT&T phone security service, quoted in *Business96*, 125 Auburn Ct., #100, Thousand Oaks, CA 91362.

ATM Trap

The charge for an automatic teller machine withdrawal is usually set by the bank that issues the card—not the bank that dispenses the cash. However at some ATMs in Alabama, Georgia, Idaho, Louisiana, Maine, Michigan, Nevada and Utah, the bank that owns the machine adds its own additional surcharge.

Source: *Consumer Reports Travel Letter*, 101 Truman Ave., Yonkers, NY 10703.

Beware of a New Bank Scam

Safe-deposit box rental bills now arriving in the mail are likely to be about 80% higher than last year.

Reason: Some banks are adding premiums for safe-deposit box insurance coverage.

Problem: Tricky invoices hide the fact that the insurance policy and fee are *optional*—not mandatory.

Self-defense: Pay only the rental fee and any tax. Include a note with your bill declining the insurance.

Important: Insure your safe-deposit box valuables with a rider on your homeowner's insurance policy.

Source: Edward F. Mrkvicka, Jr., a bank consultant in Marengo, IL, and author of *The Bank Book*. HarperCollins.

Credit Card Safety

Watch your charge or credit card after giving it to a store clerk, and take it back promptly—making sure the card returned to you is yours. *Also:* Never sign a blank receipt...do draw a line through blank spaces above the total when you sign...compare bills with your receipts... report questionable charges to the card issuer promptly...sign new cards as soon as they arrive...and cut up expired ones.

Source: Robert McKinley, president of RAM Research Corp., which tracks nationwide credit card rates, Box 1700, Frederick, MD 21702.

Hotel Safety

Ask about a hotel's security practices before booking a room. *Best:* Security cameras in elevators and public spaces...dead-bolt locks and peepholes on all room doors...entrances locked at night...24-hour security staff.

When checking in: Ask the desk clerk not to announce your room number so others can hear it...ask about the neighborhood and areas to avoid at night—and during the day...verify by phone any unexpected request by a staff person for admittance to your room...don't wear meeting tags that identify you as an out-of-towner on the street.

Source: Hank Stucken, director of security, Hotel Beverly, New York, quoted in *Travel Expense Management*, Brinley Professional Plaza, 3100 Hwy. 138, Wall Township, NJ 07719

Business Opportunity Scams

They are on the rise. Sophisticated criminals set up offices that look well-staffed and provide prospects with references who seem to be genuine—but who are really part of the scam. Investors are then tricked out of thousands of dollars to buy things like defective vending machines with supposedly guaranteed placements and territories. Scam artists cheat as many people as possible before complaints to state authorities mount. Then they move to a new location.

Source: Nicki Blum, former real estate broker who lost $30,000 in a scam and is now writing a book about the experience, quoted in *The New York Times*.

Garbage Can Fraud Ring

A garbage can fraud ring stole more than $10 million in dozens of states by recovering canceled checks, deposit slips and credit card receipts from trash receptacles...using the account information to create phony identification papers…then cashing counterfeit checks, filing false tax returns and even staging auto accidents to collect on fraudulent claims. *Self-defense:* Shred or burn personal financial records and receipts except for tax records—do not just throw them out.

Source: William Britt, chief, criminal investigation division, Internal Revenue Service, Atlanta.

Watch for Thieves In Ladies' Rooms

Thieves target ladies' rooms along some major highways by reaching over stalls and grabbing purses hanging on hooks. New Jersey officials removed all hooks in women's restrooms along the Garden State Parkway after an epidemic of these thefts. But some thieves put the hooks back themselves—and kept on stealing. *Self-defense:* Hold your purse, or watch it carefully at all times.

Source: David Solomon, editor, *Nutz & Boltz®,* Box 123, Butler, MD 21023.

Home Repair Frauds… Self-Defense

•**Never let a stranger talk you into** believing your home needs some repair. Even if it does, check out the repair person thoroughly and comparison shop.

•**Never sign any repair contract** without checking out the wording and the workers.

•**Unless you're dealing with a trusted worker**, ensure that the repair company is properly licensed.

•**If someone comes to your door**, never purchase his/her services without thoroughly checking him out.

•**Never pay all of a repair bill** if there are still a few things to finish up.

Source: Criminology expert J.L. Simmons, PhD, author of *67 Ways to Protect Seniors from Crime.* Henry Holt and Co.

Long-Distance Telephone Service Scam

Called "telephone slamming," this scam involves having your long-distance service switched from one carrier to another without your prior approval or realizing it. The new carrier is often a small, unknown outfit that charges exorbitantly high rates.

Other scams: Consumers unknowingly authorize a switch by signing contest entries or prize forms. Or, companies send checks for as little as $10 to prospective customers. By endorsing and cashing the check, the customer unwittingly authorizes the long-distance service switch.

Self-defense: Some local phone companies now allow consumers to put a freeze on their service—meaning it cannot be switched unless you authorize it directly, not even if a long-distance provider says you did.

Source: Neil S. Sachnoff, president, TeleCom Clinic, a telecommunications research, consulting and publishing company, 4402 Stonehedge Rd., Edison, NJ 08820.

Microwave Danger

Home microwave leakage detectors are not precise enough to give accurate readings. Microwave leakage is not typically a problem with an undamaged unit. If your unit was dropped or otherwise damaged, have it checked by a specialist in microwave repair—using professional equipment—before you continue to use it.

Source: Advice from Good Housekeeping Institute engineers, reported in *Good Housekeeping*, 959 Eighth Ave., New York 10019.

Be Wary Of Unsolicited Callers

When an investment offer comes to you unsolicited over the phone—*beware*. Check out if it's legitimate or a scam by asking, *How did you get my name?* If the caller doesn't have a good answer, it was probably from the phone book. *Do you have references?* Look for references from reputable sources that you can check. What are the risks involved? Every investment has some risk, so never believe a claim of a "sure thing." *Will you explain it in writing?* A scamster would rather push you into buying immediately. *Will you explain it to my professional adviser?* A scamster "won't have time" to do so.

Source: National Futures Association, 200 W. Madison St., Suite 1600, Dept. I, Chicago 60606.

Prescription Drug Self-Defense

Most of what many doctors know about prescription drugs they learn from the drug manufacturers themselves—but the information supplied by drug companies is often biased or incomplete.

Self-defense: Ask your doctor why he's prescribing a drug...if a generic equivalent is available...what its effectiveness, cost and potential side effects are. Read the patient inserts that come with prescription drugs. If you experience any unexpected side effects, call your doctor.

Source: Timothy McCall, MD, an internist practicing in the Boston area. He is the author of *Examining Your Doctor: A Patient's Guide to Avoiding Harmful Medical Care*. Birch Lane Press.

What the New Food Labels Really Mean

•*Light or lite:* One-third fewer calories or 50% less fat than comparable products.

•*Low calorie:* Forty calories or less per serving.

•*Calorie free:* Fewer than five calories per serving.

•*Fat free:* Less than 0.5 grams of fat per serving.

•*Cholesterol free:* Less than two milligrams cholesterol and two grams or less of saturated fat per serving.

•*Low sodium:* One hundred forty milligrams or less sodium per serving.

•*High fiber:* Five grams or more fiber per serving.

Source: Edwin Brown, MD, MPH, editor of *Medical Update*, 1100 Waterway Blvd., Indianapolis 46202.

Airplane Pillows Can Spread Disease

Airplane pillows are freshened at most once a day. Several other people may use a pillow before you get it. There is no way to know the scalp and hair conditions of previous users. *Self-defense:* Bring your own covering for the airline's pillow...or bring your own inflatable pillow.

Source: *Forbes FYI*, a supplement to *Forbes*, 60 Fifth Ave., New York 10011.

Car Seat Safety

Between 30% and 50% of all child car-safety seats are installed incorrectly, putting children at risk. *Problem:* Some car seats require extra pieces or dealer modifications before they can be connected securely. Other seat belt systems simply cannot be used with child-safety seats. Read the safety-seat instructions and the car owner's manual carefully to determine the best way to install the seat. *Guideline:* The seat should wiggle only slightly when rocked forward and back or from side to side.

Source: Jeff Michael, National Highway Traffic Safety Administration, Office of Occupant Protection, 400 Seventh St. SW, Washington, DC 20590.

Wraparound Sunglasses

Wraparound sunglasses offer the most protection from the sun. Any sunglasses that fit closely are also good. If sunglasses do not fit closely, almost three times as much UV radiation reaches your eyes. Make sure sunglasses fit comfortably and snugly.

Ideal: Frame distributes weight evenly on your nose...hinges are sturdy...and ear pieces don't have too much play.

Source: S*afe in the Sun* by Mary-Ellen Siegel, MSW, social worker and therapist, department of community medicine, Mount Sinai School of Medicine, New York. Walker & Co.

Nose Piercing Is Dangerous

Because the nose is designed to trap airborne bacteria, it is one of the dirtiest places in the body. Many virulent bacteria, such as *staphylococcus aureus,* are harmless as long as they stay in the nose. But should the piercing needle force them into the bloodstream, they can cause serious illness—even death.

Source: William Castelli, MD, medical director, Framingham Heart Study, Boston.

Gym Equipment May Be Dangerous

Gym-equipment-related injuries to children have dramatically increased since 1981. Never leave your child unattended around fitness equipment...don't leave stationary bikes, treadmills, free weights and other exercise equipment out in front of the TV or anywhere else children can get to them—keep all equipment locked away when not in use...shop for exercise machines with chains and gears that are covered with plastic or protective hoods.

Source: Mark Widome, MD, professor of pediatrics, Penn State University College of Medicine, Department of Pediatrics, Box 850, Hershey, PA 17033.

Common Hospital Billing Errors

Up to 95% of hospital bills contain errors, and most of these errors favor the hospital. *Watch out for...*

•**Incorrect billing codes.** There are more than 7,000 five-digit codes for diagnostic tests, surgical procedures, etc. Don't trust the number. Look for the *description* of each procedure listed.

•**Duplicate billings.** These occur frequently with urine tests and other common tests.

•**Redundant or shoddy testing.** You should not pay for unclear X rays, blood tests ruined because of inadequate samples or any test that has to be repeated because of a mistake by the hospital lab.

•**Unauthorized charges.** Hospitals sometimes charge your credit card without your approval. Always insist on advance approval. Don't pay for anything you didn't approve— even if you received the treatment.

•**Phantom charges.** Hospitals often charge for procedures that—while not performed in your case—are usually a routine part of patient care. Watch out for charges for tests that were ordered and then canceled.

•**Unrequested items.** Often, these carry confusing names so they'll slip by uncontested. A $15 "thermal therapy kit" may be a bag of ice cubes. A $5 "urinal" may be a plastic cup.

•**Unbundling.** Routine procedures are sometimes billed separately, and the sum of these parts is often greater than the whole.

•**Arithmetic errors.** They may be honest mistakes, but the hospital won't correct them unless you bring them to its attention. Don't pay the bill immediately upon your discharge from the hospital. Take it home and look it over carefully.

Source: John Connolly, EdD, former president, New York Medical College and the author of *How to Find the Best Doctors, Hospitals, HMOs for You and Your Family.* Castle Connolly Medical Ltd.

Self-Service Gasoline Danger

Gasoline contains benzene, which is a known carcinogen. So carelessness at the gas pump can harm your health.

Self-defense: If any gasoline gets on your hands or skin, wash the area immediately—so benzene will not be absorbed into the skin. If gasoline gets on your clothes, it will evaporate —but change your clothes if the spill touches your skin.

More pumping strategies: Keep a hand on the handle to be sure it stays in place and prevent spills…stand upwind while you pump, so you don't inhale the noxious fumes…don't top off the tank—filling to excess can cause gas fumes in the car.

Source: David Solomon, a certified master auto technician and editor of *Nutz & Boltz®*, Box 123, Butler, MD 21023.

Gas-Burning Appliance Danger

Some gas-burning appliances emit carbon monoxide and nitrogen dioxide. These emissions can cause headaches, fatigue, respiratory problems and nose, throat and eye irritation. *Self-defense:* Clean and vent appliances directly outdoors. Buy a carbon-monoxide detector to monitor levels of this colorless, odorless gas.

Source: Alfred Munzer, MD, Washington Adventist Hospital, pulmonary medicine department, Takoma Park, MD.

Lethal Gas Leaks

Gas furnaces may have deadly leaks of carbon monoxide. Any gas appliance can leak this colorless, odorless, tasteless gas if it is not properly maintained. The heat exchanger may be cracked or the exhaust vent leaking.

Self-defense: Have your furnace cleaned and tested annually. If you develop flu-like symptoms when the furnace is on, have it checked by a professional. The symptoms could be early signs of carbon monoxide exposure.

Source: Joe Nernberg, president, West Coast Plumbing, Heating & Cooling, Van Nuys, CA.

New ATM Scam

Beware: Crooks pose as bank guards to steal customers' ATM Personal Identification Numbers (PINs) and clean out their accounts. *How the new scam works:* The crook buys a jacket that looks like the ones worn by security guards…attaches a phony badge…and posts an out-of-order sign on the ATM. When a customer comes, the phony guard explains that the machine is temporarily out of order, but that the bank is giving customers a small amount of cash manually. He looks at the ATM card, gets the account number and PIN, gives the customer $100 in cash…then cleans out the account when the victim leaves. *Self-defense:* Never give your PIN to anyone.

Source: Jens Jurgen, *Travel Companions*, Box 833, Amityville, NY 11701.

Little-Known Allergen Exposed

Cockroach droppings are another common cause of congestion. If you've got roaches, call in an exterminator…and call him/her back at the first sign of the roaches' return. Even if the insecticides used by the exterminator prove irritating, they're unlikely to cause congestion.

Source: Nelson Lee Novick, MD, associate clinical professor of dermatology, Mount Sinai School of Medicine, New York City. Dr. Novick, who is board certified in both dermatology and internal medicine, is the author of 12 books, including *You Can Do Something about Your Allergies: A Leading Doctor's Guide to the Prevention and Treatment of Common Allergies.* Bantam Books.

Protect Your Garden

Discourage deer from destroying your garden. String together several bars of strongly scented deodorant soap and hang from low branches.

Other methods: Fill nylon stockings with human hair (from a local barber) to create balls about the size of oranges. Hang these balls from tree branches where the human scent will scare deer. Or make a spray-on repellent by mixing one teaspoon of red-hot pepper sauce and one teaspoon of unscented liquid soap (so it will stick) in a gallon of water. Apply to vulnerable tree trunks, branches and saplings.

Source: Bonnie Wodin, owner of Golden Yarrow Landscape Design, a garden consulting firm, Box 61, Heath, MA 01346.

Help for Acrophobia

Fear of heights can now be treated with virtual reality (VR), a computer technology that simulates real life. Patients wearing a special VR headset practice venturing into frightening scenarios—footbridges over water...outdoor balconies...a glass-enclosed elevator.

Once people with acrophobia become comfortable in the virtual world, they venture into similar situations in the real world.

Source: Barbara Olasov Rothbaum, PhD, assistant professor of psychiatry, Emory University School of Medicine, Atlanta. For more information, contact the Association for Advancement of Behavior Therapy, 305 Seventh Ave., New York 10001.

Know Exactly What Is in Your Wallet

At all times—so you can report if something is lost or stolen. *Strategy:* Arrange your credit cards so you can immediately see if one is missing. *Best:* Carry no more than two or three cards at a time, and keep a photocopy of all your credit cards at home—along with a list of whom to call in case of a problem.

Source: Christine Dugas, author of *Fiscal Fitness—A Guide to Shaping Up Your Finances for the Rest of Your Life.* Andrews and McMeel.

Is Your Tap Water Safe?

Most Americans take for granted that tap water is safe for drinking, cooking and bathing. Ask a resident of Milwaukee, though, and you might get a different opinion.

In 1993, 400,000 people in that city fell ill (and 100 died) when a gastrointestinal parasite called Cryptosporidium got into the municipal water supply.

Each year, thousands of Americans experience diarrhea and other gastrointestinal problems caused by exposure to tap water tainted with E. coli and other bacteria, viruses and parasites.

And, in roughly 17% of American households, tap water contains toxic levels of lead. A smaller percentage is exposed to unsafe levels of copper. Recent evidence suggests that copper can cause kidney problems and premature aging.

Chlorination has helped rid our water of disease-causing germs. Ironically, however, epidemiologists now suspect that many cases of bladder and colorectal cancer are caused by ingestion or absorption of trihalomethanes (THMs). That's a class of compounds formed when chlorine mixes with decaying leaves or other natural organic matter that inevitably finds its way into municipal water supplies. Lead is the biggest threat:

Ingestion of lead causes irreversible brain damage in children. In adults, lead can cause kidney damage, brittle bones and high blood pressure. In fact, lead in tap water may account for 100,000 cases of male hypertension a year, according to one recent estimate.

Where does the lead come from? Some older municipal water systems (including those in Boston, Chicago and New York) contain lead-jointed pipes. As water flows through these pipes, it picks up lead.

But most lead problems originate in the home. *Usual culprit:* Pipes made of lead or sealed with lead solder...or faucets made with lead.

Although lead solder was banned in 1988, federal law continues to permit faucets to contain up to 8% lead. New regulations specify, however, that any faucet that leaches more than a trace of lead must be sold with a warning label. If you're shopping for a new faucet, do not buy a faucet with one of these warning labels.

Having your water tested:

What about faucets already installed in your home? Replacing them with new faucets is unnecessary. Better to have a reputable lab test your water for lead...and then, if necessary, install a filter.

Some communities offer free lead-testing kits upon request. (Call your local water company to find out.) In most areas, however, you'll have to hire a lab.

Most labs charge $35 to $50. Here at the University of North Carolina, Asheville, we have set up a research program that charges $17 for lead testing ($20 for lead and copper).

To obtain a test kit: Send a check to Clean Water Lead Testing, 1 University Heights, Asheville, North Carolina 28804. 704-251-6441.

You'll be mailed two vials for collecting water, plus instructions and a mailing packet for returning the samples.

The test will show whether you have a lead problem...and, if so, whether it can be corrected by running the water for one minute.

Caution: Home lead tests are unreliable... and the chemicals used in the tests are highly corrosive to skin.

If your water contains little or no lead, there's no need to test your water again. *Exception:* If you have plumbing work done, recheck for lead afterward.

Flushing pipes:

What if tests reveal that your tap water contains lead? Some home owners try to protect themselves by running the water for a minute or two each morning.

Lead concentrations generally are lower in "purged" water than in water that has been sitting in pipes. Unfortunately, lead levels start rising immediately after the water is shut off. You'd have to purge the faucet every time you took a drink, filled a pot, etc.

Smarter: If your lead test shows that high initial lead levels can be reduced by running the faucet, then fill a gallon jug with cool water drawn after a 60-second purge of the tap. Keep it in your refrigerator.

Never fill the jug (or drink or cook) with water from the hot tap. It's capable of holding more dissolved lead than cool water, so it poses a greater threat to health.

Waterborne illness:

As our population grows, homes, farms, etc. are springing up near once-remote watersheds. Via seepage or spillage, germ-filled sewage from these developments can find its way into the water supply.

Self-defense: Call your water company, and find out the source of your tap water. If your water comes from surface water (lakes, ponds and streams) that has industrial wastewater discharges upstream, consider boiling your water for one minute. That's especially true if there has been one or more E. coli or chemical violations in recent years.

To reduce their risk of cryptosporidiosis, HIV-positive individuals and others with low immunity must boil their tap water—or drink bottled water.

Water-purification systems:

If your tap water contains high levels of lead or copper, and if purging doesn't solve the problem or it's too much of a hassle, install a water-purification unit. Four types are available...

•**Cation-exchange units** are 80% to 99% effective at removing lead and copper. *Cost:* Under $200.

•**Reverse osmosis** (RO) units are up to 99% effective at removing lead and microbes. *Cost:* $200 to $400.

•**Distillation units** remove virtually 100% of metals, plus cryptosporidium and other microbes. *Cost:* About $200.

•**Cation-exchange/granular** activated carbon (GAC) units get rid of metals, THMs and most microbes. *Cost:* About $200.

You need a cation-exchange or a cation-exchange/GAC filter only if your water test reveals a lead problem. A cation-exchange/

GAC, distillation or RO unit is appropriate if your town's water supply is subject to industrial wastewater discharges.

Each of these units is available in countertop and under-sink models. Make sure the unit you buy is certified by NSF International. (*Consumer Reports* rated water filters in September 1993.)

Should you be concerned about THMs? Check with your water company. THMs are a concern if levels have exceeded 50 parts per billion (ppb) in recent months. Consider a GAC filter for your entire water system, rather than for just one faucet. *Cost:* About $1,000.

What about bottled water:

Bottled water is another safe—and usually less costly—alternative. Over the past seven years, we've tested dozens of brands. All were lead-free.

Look for bottled spring water or distilled water, though, or you may just get bottled municipal water.

Source: Richard P. Maas, PhD, associate professor of environmental studies at the University of North Carolina, Asheville. He is director of the university's Environmental Quality Institute, a leading center for research on tap water purity.

How Burglars Think... And What You Can Do To Protect Your Home

About one in every 20 households is burglarized each year, and being victimized isn't a matter of chance.

My research into the thought processes of burglars has yielded some interesting patterns. Knowing about those patterns can help you change the way you secure your home.

What I've discovered about how burglars think—and what you can do to protect your family from them...

•**Burglars love recent home buyers.** You're most likely to be robbed during your first six months in a new residence. Why? New home buyers are not likely to have taken the immediate security steps appropriate for their new community. And—your neighbors are less likely to spot dangerous strangers if they don't yet know what you and your family look like. *Self-defense...*

•**Introduce yourself to your neighbors as soon as possible.**

•**Try not to advertise the fact you've just moved in.** Don't leave boxes or the realtor's sign on your front lawn longer than necessary.

•**Quickly bring your security system up to par with your neighbors'.** If other homes on your street have deadbolt locks, sensor lights and a burglar alarm, you should have them too—*as soon as possible.*

•**Burglars choose accessible locations.** Burglars first target a neighborhood, then a particular street. That means the location of your home is a crucial factor in whether it will be burglarized.

This is most apparent when you consider that the highest incidence of burglary occurs in poor neighborhoods, despite the fact that the payoff from these crimes likely will be low. Most burglars live in these areas, and their familiarity with the region will make their escape easier.

This accessibility factor also is important in wealthier suburban neighborhoods.

Homes within three blocks of a major road or highway exit are at significantly greater risk than other homes—particularly if those thoroughfares lead to a low-income area. But, paradoxically, homes directly on these major arteries are not at exceptional risk.

Reason: While burglars like to have a familiar escape route at hand, they prefer the relative seclusion of side streets.

Self-defense: If you're considering buying a new house, check with the local police department about the street's burglary rate before you buy.

If you already live in a house that is within three blocks of just such a heavily traveled area—such as near a highway exit or a major shopping area—then you would be well-served to invest in an alarm system that might seem excessive elsewhere in your town.

•**Most burglars prefer to work days.** There's a misconception that houses are at greatest risk of break-in when their owners are asleep in bed.

307

Reality: The rise of two-income households has created a daily eight-hour window of opportunity when no one is at home. So there's no longer any need for a thief to take the chance he/she will wake you up during the night.

In fact, the threat of encountering a home owner is the best deterrent to break-ins. Only about 18% of burglaries occur between midnight and 6 a.m. Most of them take place between 6 a.m. and 6 p.m. Almost three-quarters occur when no one is home.

Self-defense: If your family is out of the house during the day, take some precautions to disguise that fact. One of the most effective deterrents is to leave a car in the driveway or a rake on the lawn. Also, be sure your empty trash cans don't remain at the curb after the rest of the neighborhood has brought theirs in.

Exception: Don't expect burglars to be deterred by a television or radio left on in the house. By the time they are close enough to notice it, they're close enough to already know you are not home.

• **Burglars want your cash and jewelry**— not your appliances. There was a time when thieves headed straight for your TV set. But consumer electronics have come down in price in recent decades, and a stolen television now has little resale value. Moreover, these items are often bulky and difficult to carry and conceal. As a result, burglars are more interested in small and easily liquidated goods— particularly jewelry.

Self-defense: Choose a less obvious location for your jewelry and cash than the master bedroom. Items hidden in your bedroom will be discovered by a burglar—even if they're at the bottom of a drawer.

Best: Install a safe. Choose an out-of-the-way location, such as the basement, and have the safe bolted into place.

• **Make your home hard to hit.** Even a well-protected home can fall victim to a determined burglar. So, the best defense is to not be singled out in the first place.

Self-defense: Concentrate first on deterrence measures, such as motion-sensitive exterior lights and a car in the driveway. If you buy an alarm system, don't hide that fact—put a sign on your front lawn. A burglar alarm sign is one of the most effective deterrents available today.

• **Make it easy for neighbors to see your house**. Burglars search out homes that offer concealment from other houses and the road. Wooded areas, parks or side roads adjacent to your property provide thieves with an opportunity to watch and approach your home without being noticed.

Self-defense: Trim trees and shrubs that are around your doors. Make sure all entrance-ways are well lit, and visible from the windows of other houses on your street. Don't put up a high fence between your property and your neighbor's.

• **Make it look like you have a large family.** Our studies show that the larger the family, the less likely the home will be robbed. More family members make it more likely someone is in the house—or will be coming home soon. And—families with kids have less money to spend on the things thieves like, such as jewelry.

Self-defense: Even if you don't have children, it can be worth the effort to make it appear that you do. Leave a tricycle or other toys on the lawn.

Source: Simon Hakim, PhD, professor of economics at Temple University, Philadelphia, and author of several studies on burglary patterns and prevention. His upcoming book, *Securing Home and Business.* Butterworth Heinemann.

Smoke Detectors Last a Decade

If you have any smoke detectors that are more than 10 years old, consider replacing them. Install at least one smoke detector on *every level of your home*, especially *outside bedrooms*. Avoid putting them too near kitchens to prevent false alarms from cooking. Replace batteries annually or according to the manufacturer's instructions. Some detectors also have sensors that must be replaced every two years or so. Test all detectors monthly.

Source: Consumer Product Safety Commission, Washington, DC.

19

Technology 1997

What You Need to Know About the Internet

Access to the Internet and techniques for using it are changing so rapidly that companies that aren't in a high-tech business are holding it at an arm's length out of sheer intimidation.

It may be news to these companies that the Internet isn't as scary as it seems, and that there are wonderful ways to take advantage of all it has to offer.

The best opportunities on the Internet for businesses today…

Promoting products and services:

Best estimate: More than 30 million people around the world regularly tap into the Internet. Even a fraction of that number would constitute a sizable market. *How to reach them:*

•**Via World Wide Web sites.** These are computer-screen presentations in text, graphics and occasionally sound that companies can establish on the World Wide Web, a prominent and widely used section of the Internet. *Examples:*

•**Ford Motor Co.'s Web site contains detailed information about car and truck models**, including engine specifications, available colors and a list of dealers. A sophisticated graphics presentation lets Internet users view the cars inside and out.

•**Monti's**, a family-owned restaurant in Tempe, Arizona, uses a Web site to post menus and specials as well as coupons that Internet browsers can print out using their computers.

Cost: A bare-bones Web site can be set up for less than $100 by using software usually available from local Internet access providers. To keep your site active, these access providers typically charge $20 to $80 a month.

For $500 to $2,000, businesses can hire one of several companies (known as Web-site providers) to design a larger and professional-appearing site. To keep it posted, the provider typically charges $150 a month.

Both types of providers—access and Web-site—can be found by asking for recommendations from computer consultants—and through ads at the back of the many computing magazines available on newsstands.

Some businesses spend more than $150,000 on a Web site. *Example:* Macmillan, the publishing company, has one of the most sophisticated Web sites on the Net. It contains text and graphics on virtually every book Macmillan has published.

Web sites can also be used to post new-product notices and to hold events, such as contests, to promote a product or service.

Several companies are developing commercial Web sites where businesses can post information about their products and services. These include BizNet *(biznet@bev.net)* and BizWeb *(bob@bizweb.com).*

• **Newsgroups.** There are more than 10,000 groups of Internet users who regularly exchange information via their computers about an amazingly wide range of subjects.

Examples: Legal issues…office equipment …Star Trek memorabilia…exports to Poland …child-rearing…mental illness.

Internet directories, available in libraries and bookstores, list many of these so-called newsgroups. They can also be located on the Internet at *http://www.dejanews.com.*

Caution: Many newsgroups resent overt commercial intrusion, but most won't object to a notice that simply invites members to send for more information about a new product or new service—as long as it is relevant to the users of the newsgroup. *Cost:* Free.

Internet selling:

The simplest way to sell via the Internet is to invite orders from people who visit your Web site or read a newsgroup posting.

Example: A Web site can list phone and fax numbers where orders can be placed. Or it can give the company's E-mail address. To facilitate payment, businesses can set up customer accounts linked to their credit cards. Security has been a concern, but should be less of one as the technology improves.

Several software systems allow customers to send their credit card information directly over the Internet in a secure, encrypted form.

Examples:
• **First Virtual Payment**, a company that links banks with companies doing business on the Internet, *www.fv.com.*

• **NetCash, developed at the University of Southern California**, which uses coupons as a means of transaction, *http://www.teleport. com/~netcash/.*

• **Spry from Internet in a Box**, an access software developer, provides a coded way of exchanging credit card information, *www. spry.com.*

Though the potential for fraud does exist, one recent survey determined that it is no greater than that experienced on "800" number transactions.

Recommended: Before contracting with an Internet payment system, talk with other businesses that already use it. Payment systems will become even more secure in the future.

Another option: Selling through Prodigy, America Online or CompuServe. These commercial services have accepted advertising for several years. Other services, including Lycos and Yahoo, are now doing the same.

When a computer user accesses these services, he/she has the option of calling up commercial information on his screen if he is interested in a particular product or service.
Market research:

Computer users who see Internet postings can also be invited to respond to surveys in order to capture marketing information.

Examples: Monti's, the Arizona restaurant, uses a local newsgroup to invite comments from people who have eaten at the restaurant. Other companies have developed mailing lists from Web-site visitors who request information about products or services.

Moreover, new software now enables companies with Web sites to track people who sign on to it. The software is available from many Web-site providers and costs less than $500.

Though the programs generally don't capture names of people who visit a Web site, they will provide data on which organizations they are from, and which sections of the Web site they accessed.

Related opportunity: Through the Internet, businesses can access thousands of databases worldwide. These provide information on everything from the esoteric to the ordinary.

Examples: New patents, technological developments, incorporations in California, imports from Nigeria and changes in the curriculum at German universities.

With so much data now on-line, new Internet services have sprung up to help companies find what they need. One of the best is News Hound, a $9-a-month on-line service of the *San Jose Mercury-News*.

How it works: A subscriber who wants data about a company can ask News Hound to pull all the information it can find from newspapers, wire services and other sources. A printout is then sent via regular mail.

Recruiting employees:

The Internet has several sites where businesses can post employment ads. *Among the best:* Career Mosaic. *How it works:* Job hunters either fax or E-mail their résumés. *Cost:* Free to job hunters…an average of $10,000 to $18,000 to the business posting the ad.

Many Web sites and bulletin boards across the country also let job seekers post their résumés. These sites can be found through Internet directories and local Internet access providers.

Source: Jill H. Ellsworth, senior partner at Oak Ridge Research, Internet marketing consultants, 101 High Rd., San Marcos, TX 78666. *E-mail:* je@world.std.com. She's also coauthor with Matthew V. Ellsworth of *Marketing on the Internet.* John Wiley & Sons.

Internet Marketing

Internet marketing is revolutionary, but the best selling strategies are based on tried-and-true techniques. The main difference between Internet marketing and conventional marketing is that the Internet helps to level the playing field between large companies and small.

Large firms with huge ad budgets will have a hard time dominating the Internet, because Internet "real estate" is so inexpensive it is virtually unlimited.

Key: Write strong copy and use a headline that makes browsers want to spend time at your site when they reach it and keep on-line marketing information current and constantly test new approaches.

Foolproof PC Security Essentials

Internet invaders, computer viruses and snooping employees are all out to get the company's valuable data. *But PCs can be turned into digital fortresses by following these pain-free steps:*

•**Use antivirus software** on any computer that connects with or gets disks from another computer. *Windows* and *Windows 95* provide built-in antivirus programs. Run this software on a weekly basis to make sure PCs are safe and sound.

Important: To guard against new viruses, buy an antivirus product from a company that sends its customers regular updates. One such firm is McAfee Associates Inc. (800-866-6585). It sells *VirusScan*, a $105 Windows antivirus program with automatic updates.

•**Use backups.** Make frequent backups of vital data and store in a fireproof, theftproof location—preferably in another office or, better yet, in a separate building.

•**Encrypt data.** If someone *does* steal data, an encryption program will keep the thief from deciphering the information. One of the best programs is *PGP 2.7.1*, a product that's so powerful it is prohibited from foreign export under a federal munitions law. The software is available for $124.98 from ViaCrypt Inc. (800-536-2664).

Besides protecting hard and floppy disk data, encryption is a powerful tool for safeguarding information that's sent over in-house networks or public phone lines.

•**Install password systems.** Consider using a program like *Watchdog for Windows Personal Edition* from Fischer International Systems Corp. (800-237-4510). The $160 software prevents the unauthorized use of a PC and its resources by requiring its user to supply an ID and password.

Important: Avoid words that a hacker could successfully guess—such as the name of your company or a loved one.

Effective: Random letters make the best passwords, but can be difficult to remember. Instead, add extra protection by sticking a random number or punctuation mark in the middle of a password—such as "ICE6HOLIDAY" or "GROVER*JULY."

•**Terminate idle connections.** You would never leave your car running unattended. Likewise, you should never allow computers to be left unattended while they are connected to other PCs or to an on-line service or the Internet. An unguarded modem link is like an open door to a computer's data.

•**Beef up physical security.** To guard against "wandering disk syndrome," install a key-locked security device on all PC floppy disk drives. One such product is the $49.95 Sentinel from BookLock (800-451-7592).

A drive lock isn't foolproof, since the device can be pried open. The unit will, however, deter individuals who don't want to leave physical evidence of their crime.

Bottom line: Be determined and consistent in the company's security efforts. A halfhearted computer protection initiative makes about as much sense as closing a door halfway.

Source: John Edwards, a computer industry analyst and writer on high-tech subjects, based in Mount Laurel, NJ.

 # E-Mail Is Easy To Send Directly

E-mail is as easy to send directly through the Internet as through a commercial on-line service such as Compuserve. *But there's a catch:* If the message recipient's computer isn't turned on when the message is sent, the message will be "lost in cyberspace" and not be delivered. In contrast, commercial on-line services hold E-mail until the recipient's computer is turned on, then deliver it and send a confirmation of delivery to the message sender.

Source: Daria M. Hoffman, managing editor, *Update: The Executive's Purchasing Advisor*, 20 Railroad Ave., Hackensack, NJ 07601.

Computer Servicing Warning

Don't underestimate the need for repair or technical support when buying PCs. A new survey finds that 28% of companies require some help in the first 12 months after purchase. Best support rating (Grade A) is assigned to Compaq, IBM and Hewlett–Packard. The next best (Grade B) goes to Apple, AST and Dell. Packard Bell, ACER and Northgate get only a so-so Grade C—with a still lower Grade D given to Zenith, CompuAdd and Unisys.

Source: Survey by *PC Magazine*, One Park Ave., New York 10016.

Computers and Your Eyes

Injuries stemming from prolonged computer use can be minimized by keeping the screen squarely in front of the user and four to nine inches below eye level...directing light away from both user and screen...setting screen brightness the same as the brightness of other objects in the room...using an adjustable copy holder...opting for black characters on a white screen...attaching a glare filter to the screen.

Source: James Sheedy, chairman, Occupational Vision Committee, American Optometric Association, St. Louis.

New Computer Hazard

While wrist and hand injuries are common among heavy computer users, those who dictate to their computers, rather than type, are encountering throat problems. Cases of chronic hoarseness and sore throats are cropping up among users of speech-recognition software. The problem, it is believed, relates to the unusual speech pattern that such software demands—a halting style, leaving space between words. *Prevention:* Breathe out a bit between words that begin with vowels.

Source: Rebecca Shafir, a speech pathologist at the Lahey Clinic in Burlington, MA, quoted in *The Wall Street Journal*.

20

☼

Natural Healing Basics

The Relaxation Response

In 1975, when *The Relaxation Response* was first published, I explained how people could use a series of exercises to relax and improve their health. Since then, research on the relaxation exercises that my colleague Dr. Margaret Caudill of Harvard Medical School developed has yielded remarkable findings.

Big discoveries:

•**Chronic pain.** A recent study showed that relaxation techniques with cognitive restructuring and exercise can reduce the number of visits to HMOs by chronic pain sufferers by 36%.

•**Hypertension.** People with high blood pressure who participate in our clinic groups significantly lower their blood pressure. In one study, 80% of these people were able to decrease their blood pressure medications. Of that group, 20% gave up their medications completely.

•**Medical procedures.** People facing painful medical procedures, such as arteriography (a painful X-ray procedure), may cut their pain medication requirements by almost one-third if they use the relaxation response.

•**Postoperative complications.** Patients who have undergone cardiac surgery have fewer postoperative heart irregularities if they elicit the relaxation response before surgery.

•**Sleeping patterns.** About 75% of insomnia sufferers who follow our plan become normal sleepers. In fact, the average time for falling asleep decreased from 78 minutes to 19 minutes.

•**Spiritual awareness.** We have found that people who regularly elicit the relaxation response report an increased closeness to a power or energy that enhances their well-being.

Why stress hurts:

When we are under stress, our bodies release certain hormones and chemicals that increase our metabolisms, heart rates, blood pressure, breathing rates and muscle tension. If you are constantly under stress, the reaction could result in any number of physical and emotional symptoms, including headaches, stomachaches and anxiety. There is also evidence that chronic stress can lead to—or worsen—certain illnesses.

Good news: Everyone possesses an inborn bodily response that I call the *relaxation response*. This response decreases metabolism, heart rate, blood pressure, etc.

The basic strategy:

The relaxation response can help you unwind whenever you are feeling stressed—or prevent stressful feelings from occurring in the first place. *Steps to take...*

•**Sit comfortably, with your eyes closed.** Relax your muscles.

•**Breathe deeply**—into your abdominal area, not just into your chest. Place your hand on your abdomen, just below your rib cage. As you breathe in, you should feel your hand rise.

•**Silently repeat the word *one* as you slowly exhale.** Or simply focus just on your breathing.

•**If you have any intrusive thoughts, don't worry.** Just return to your deep breathing.

By performing this exercise for 10 to 20 minutes once or twice a day, you'll immediately begin to feel calmer and better equipped to deal with the hassles of everyday life.

New twists on the exercise:

Although my original guidelines for the relaxation response suggested that people repeat the word *one* as they exhaled, we have since found that the response can be elicited in many ways.

Some people prefer to say a prayer as they exhale or words such as *peace* or *serenity*. Still others who are simply too fidgety to sit still and meditate can use jogging to elicit the response.

Here's how: As you jog, focus on the cadence of your feet—left/right, left/right—rather than repeating a word. While most runners experience a high during their third or fourth mile, those who use the relaxation response often reach that high during their first or second mile.

You can enhance your experience by using imagery or visualization after you have elicited the relaxation response.

Strategy: Imagine a tranquil scene, such as a beach you once visited...a perfect sunset over a lake...or a crystal-clear stream. By doing so, you will feel the same peace and quiet you experienced when you actually were in such a setting.

Beyond the relaxation response:

At the Mind/Body Medical Institute, we have integrated the relaxation response with three other important self-help therapies—exercise, nutrition and cognitive work. Combined, they provide a potent tool to manage stress and improve health.

•**Exercise.** We know that regular exercise strengthens your body, helps you maintain a healthy weight, relieves both physical and mental tension and improves your mood.

Important: Check with your physician before starting any exercise program.

•**Nutrition.** Because of jam-packed lifestyles, many of us tend to eat on the run. We emphasize that in addition to exercising regularly, eating a healthy diet is fundamental for improving health and preventing the progression of certain chronic medical problems.

But eating habits are deeply ingrained and can be difficult to break.

Strategy: Start by asking yourself how you view food. Do you view eating as a way to alleviate stress? If your answer is yes, you probably need to learn how to deal more effectively with the stressors in your life. Do you eat because you're bored? If so, try to find other, more positive ways to fill your empty hours—such as exercise, reading or a hobby.

•**Cognitive work.** What you think and say to yourself over the course of the day has a profound effect on your emotions and physical well-being.

Many of us think endlessly about our problems and concerns and don't give ourselves the chance to take action or effectively work through our problems.

Some of our internal chatter focuses on ourselves. This can simmer over into our impressions of others or life in general.

Problem: When we send ourselves negative messages, we threaten our psychological and physical health.

You can improve your well-being by recognizing and changing your negative self-chatter. *Strategy if you're feeling tense, anxious or upset for any reason...*

•**Breathe deeply**—to interrupt your thought pattern.

•**Identify the negative thought and challenge it** with evidence to the contrary.

If you constantly criticize yourself, learn to dispute your negative reactions.

Rely on humor to defuse stressful situations. If you can find humor in even the most upsetting predicaments, you will feel better instantly.

Source: Herbert Benson, MD, founding president and associate professor of medicine at the Mind/Body Medical Institute of Harvard Medical School in Boston. He is also chief of the division of behavioral medicine at New England Deaconess Hospital. Dr. Benson is author of *The Relaxation Response*, Avon, and *The Wellness Book: The Comprehensive Guide to Maintaining Health* and *Treating Stress-Related Illness*. Fireside.

How to Enhance Your Body's Natural Ability to Heal

Telling a patient, *There's nothing more we can do for you* is an unconscionable medical hexing.

Trap: A negative attitude may depress the immune system and prejudice a patient's chances of recovery. Instead, doctors should encourage hope.

The body's natural ability to repair itself is remarkable, complex and very much underestimated. Especially for chronic or long-term conditions, I wish patients and doctors relied less on drugs or surgery than on the inborn potential for maintaining health and overcoming illness. *The body's amazing healing immune system:*

•**Operates continuously**, remaining on call as needed.

•**Can recognize its own physical damage.**

•**Can remove a damaged structure** and replace it with a normal one.

•**Constantly neutralizes the effects of serious injury** and directs ordinary moment-to-moment corrections as needed.

•**Works spontaneously** and automatically.

These processes function in individual cells, in bones, in organs and in entire body systems—circulatory, digestive, immune and more. The key is to help them do their job.

Example: Just as a polluted river will clean itself when people stop dumping sludge into it, clogged arteries will unblock themselves and blood will flow freely again if you exercise, reduce stress and stop eating saturated fats.

The greatest single philosophical defect of modern medicine is failing to teach medical students that healing is a natural power.

Doctors need to learn how to harness that power—and to accept that when treatments work, it's often because they've activated innate healing mechanisms.

Example: Antibiotics "cure" bacterial infections indirectly. The drugs simply kill off enough invading bacteria to allow the immune system to take over.

Obstacles:

•**Lack of energy.** Overwork, overexertion, poor diet, impaired digestion, inadequate rest and sleep, stimulating drugs, low thyroid levels and improper breathing may all contribute to this.

•**Poor circulation.** Conditions such as diabetes interfere with circulation. *Partial solutions:* Exercise, lose weight, stop smoking.

•**Weak immune system.** Influences include infections and, perhaps, an unhealthy mental state.

•**Poisons.** Toxic substances are all around us. *To escape their hazards:*

•**Move to a less polluted part of your city.** Or at least visit parks. Trees purify the air.

•**Minimize your exposure to chemical hazards in or near plastics**, rubber, leather, textiles, dye and paper manufacturers, dry cleaners and farmers that use agrichemicals.

•**Install filters in your home ventilation system**, especially if you have a respiratory ailment or live with a smoker.

•**Mental obstructions and spiritual problems.** Sadness and confusion may depress the immune system and create an imbalance in the autonomic nervous system.

When I completed my clinical training over 25 years ago, I vowed to avoid the drug-oriented

315

treatment patterns I'd been taught—except for treating short-term conditions.

Aspects of natural healing that I have integrated into my practice include:

•**Rest and sleep.** When deprived of rest, you're more susceptible to injury and illness. Many people know that a good night's sleep relieves a lot of common problems, such as migraine headaches. Sleep is free…has no side effects…and can't do any harm.

•**Breathing.** Simple techniques, practiced regularly, are very powerful for relaxation and improve many common medical conditions.

To deepen your respiration, think of breathing *out* (exhalation), which you can control better than breathing in (inhalation), as the first step of breathing.

Gently but completely squeezing air out of your lungs automatically invites more air into the next inhalation.

•**Tonics.** *Add these to your menu…*

•**Ginger**, a natural anti-inflammatory, such as for arthritis.

•**Garlic**, which powers up the cardiovascular system.

•**Siberian ginseng**, which reduces debilitation caused by aging and is said to promote sexual energy in men.

•**Green tea**, the most healthful caffeinated beverage.

•**Cordyceps**, an Asian mushroom that boosts vitality and may prolong life.

•**Exercise.** Walk at least two miles in 45 minutes every day. (Be sure to consult your doctor before undertaking any new exercise regimen.)

•**Nutrition.** This vital area of health is still almost completely ignored in medical school, and patients know it. Awareness of the role of nutrition is essential.

Eat more…

•**Vegetables.** Replacing animal foods with vegetables is one of the most healthful changes you can make. Wash fruits and vegetables well. Peel those that are not organically grown.

•**Fiber.** It's found in fruits, vegetables and whole grains, especially wheat and oat bran. *Advantages:* Various types of fiber promote bowel movements, prevent colon cancer and flush cholesterol from the blood.

•**Soy foods.** Available in almost endless variety at health food stores, soybean products may help protect against cancer, especially of the breast and prostate.

•**Omega-3 fatty acids.** *They are found in oily fish from cold northern waters:* Sardines, herring, mackerel, bluefish and salmon. These acids reduce inflammatory changes in the body …protect against abnormal blood clotting and possibly cancer.

•**Organic foods.** Seek out *unsprayed* apples, peaches, grapes (including raisins), oranges, strawberries, potatoes, carrots, lettuce, green beans, wheat and wheat flour.

•**Supplements.** The following supplement dosages are what I recommend for my patients. You may want to check with your own doctor before taking them. *Daily…*

•**800 international units** (IU) of vitamin E (400 IU for people under 40). Take vitamin E with a meal. It needs some fat to be absorbed.

•**1,000 milligrams of vitamin C** two or three times a day. (The body can't benefit from more than 1,000 milligrams at a time.) I take 4,000 milligrams a day in four installments.

•**200 to 300 micrograms of selenium.** Take more if you're at increased risk of developing cancer.

•**25,000 IU of natural beta-carotene** in tablet form or as a powder dissolved in water. beta-carotene is an antioxidant that is believed to help protect against cancer.

Drink more…

•**Water**…just until you're urinating more, unless your doctor advises otherwise.

Warning: Tap water often contains sediment, chlorine or other chemicals. You may want to use bottled water or install a home filtering system.

Eat less…

•**Protein.** One protein-based meal a day is plenty. Protein makes the digestive system work harder, possibly monopolizing the energy needed for healing.

•**Fat.** *Especially dangerous:* Deep-fried foods and animal fats including butter, and saturated or hydrogenated vegetable oils (such as palm kernal or coconut). These fats are bad for the heart…and may promote cancer and aging.

•**Processed food**—and foods containing chemical dyes, artificial sweeteners.

Source: Andrew Weil, MD, director of the Program in Integrative Medicine at the University of Arizona, Tucson, where he practices natural and preventive medicine. A practicing physician for more than 25 years, he is the author of six books, including the best-selling *Spontaneous Healing: How to Discover and Enhance Your Body's Natural Ability to Maintain and Heal Itself.* Alfred A. Knopf.

Beat Stress and Depression The Natural Way

The stress of modern life has given rise to a worldwide epidemic of depression. Mood disorders are more prevalent now than ever before, and they're occurring at younger ages.

What's causing this epidemic? Much of the blame may well rest with technology, and the sweeping lifestyle changes it has encouraged.

Our bodies and brains evolved for a Stone Age existence, when daily life was governed by the rising and setting of the sun and the changing of the seasons. Today, people seem to live at a breakneck pace, 24 hours a day, all year long.

Problem: Fast-paced living brings reduced levels of the neurotransmitter serotonin, a key buffer against depression.

On the advice of their doctors, many people have turned to antidepressants to relieve their malaise. For serious depression, that's prudent. However, it often makes more sense to find natural, nondrug ways to boost serotonin levels...

Get more light:

Exposure to bright light has been shown to raise serotonin levels. Unfortunately, indoor lighting averages only 200 to 500 lux. That's too weak to do the trick. Outdoors, sunlight can climb above 100,000 lux.

Being exposed to artificial light at *night* (when our ancestors would have been asleep) throws off the production cycle of *melatonin*. This key neurochemical affects a variety of bodily functions, including serotonin synthe-

sis, making it another important buffer against depression.

Antidote: Get outdoors as much as possible during the day. If you live in a "gray" climate, consider buying a light box (10,000 lux). This device (available for $200 and up) can be used while reading, exercising or watching TV.

Caution: Light boxes should not be used by people with retinal disease.

Best brands: Apollo Light Systems (800-545-9667), Hughes Lighting Technologies (800-544-4825) and The SunBox Company (800-548-3968).

Also helpful: Dawn simulators. These devices (such as those made by Pi Square, 800-786-3296) use light to awaken you naturally on dark winter mornings.

Seek out negative ions:

Air with high concentrations of negative ions—molecules with an extra electron—is clearly linked to positive moods. Unfortunately, city air contains 10 times fewer negative ions than air in the country or by the seashore. Ion concentrations are even lower inside air-conditioned offices.

Antidote: If you can't live in the country or near the ocean, buy a negative ion generator. These devices boost serotonin levels, improving mood and promoting sleep.

Be sure the machine you buy generates *small* negative ions. That's the kind shown to yield psychological benefits.

Best brands: Sphere One (201-942-9772) and Bionic Products of America (800-634-4667).

Get more sleep:

Adults today get 20% less sleep than before the invention of the electric light. Most of us need *at least* eight hours of sleep a night. Nearly 50% of Americans get less.

Sleep deprivation produces a sharp decrease in serotonin levels. It is strongly linked to depression.

Antidote: Make sleep a priority. If you feel sleepy during the day, or if you need an alarm clock to wake up, you probably need more shut-eye.

Strategies: Keep the bedroom cool and dark...avoid work or stimulating TV for at least one hour before bedtime…cut down on caffeine and alcohol…exercise late in the day (but at least five hours before bedtime)…rise at the same time each day. On days when you can't get the sleep you need, nap.

Get regular exercise:

Exercise—an excellent serotonin booster—is linked not only with better moods, but also with better overall health. Yet despite the so-called "fitness revolution," Americans get less exercise today than even 10 years ago. We get *far* less exercise than our hunter-gatherer ancestors.

Antidote: Find an exercise you enjoy, and do it regularly. Aerobic exercise several times a week is ideal, but any kind of exercise is better than none.

Rethink your diet:

Our ancestors survived mostly on green plants and small game animals, which were low in fat but *high* in cholesterol.

Lesson: While some middle-aged men and others at high risk for heart attack should take steps to lower high cholesterol levels, cholesterol levels below 160 confer a heightened risk of depression, accidents and suicide. Apparently, low cholesterol levels interfere with the regulation of serotonin.

That doesn't mean we should binge on saturated fat. It does suggest that we should be wary of cholesterol levels that are too high *or* too low.

What about carbohydrates? They do appear to improve serotonin function *temporarily*. Over the long term, however, a high-carbohydrate diet diminishes your sense of well-being.

Reason: Carbohydrates quickly raise blood sugar and insulin levels. Elevated insulin signals the body to store food as fat—making it less available for energy. Insulin also boosts production of certain prostaglandins linked to depression.

Antidote: Eat a diet that's more in line with that of our hunter-gatherer ancestors…

•**Emphasize fruits and vegetables while limiting consumption of grains and sweets.** When you do eat grain, stick to whole grains. They have a less drastic effect on blood sugar than white bread or processed cereal.

•**At every meal**, maintain a protein-fat-carbohydrate calorie ratio of 30%-30%-40%.

•**Keep meals under 500 calories.** Don't let more than five hours pass between meals (except when you're asleep). Frequent, small meals keep insulin levels lower than a few large meals.

•**Do not eat red meat or egg yolks more than once a week.** These foods contain a chemical precursor to a brain chemical that is associated with depression.

What about antidepressants?

Anyone who is so depressed that he/she has trouble functioning at work or at home should seek a medical diagnosis.

Fluoxetine (Prozac) is the best known of a group of antidepressants called *selective serotonin re-uptake inhibitors* (SSRIs). These drugs avoid many of the serious medical risks of older drugs.

But fluoxetine can cause decreased libido, delayed orgasm, insomnia and agitation…and may suppress melatonin levels.

Over the short term, this is probably not a concern. For patients who take the drug for a year or more, however, the effect on melatonin might have negative implications for long-term mood and health.

Sertraline (Zoloft) and *paroxetine* (Paxil) are similar to Prozac but may be better or worse in a given individual.

Fluvoxamine (Luvox) is another SSRI that appears to have fewer side effects than Prozac. Unlike Prozac, it raises melatonin levels.

Nefazodone (Serzone)—the newest antidepressant on the US market—affects serotonin more subtly and seems free of Prozac's most objectionable side effects. It may be particularly helpful in treating depression accompanied by anxiety or insomnia.

Venlafaxine (Effexor) acts on serotonin and boosts levels of *norepinephrine* (the neurochemical affected by earlier antidepressants called tricyclics). It has a good track record in treating cases that fail to respond to other medication.

Bupropion (Wellbutrin) does *not* act on serotonin. In fact, we're not quite sure *how* it works. In a tiny percentage of cases, it has been associated with seizures. This risk can be minimized by lowering the dosage and spreading doses out throughout the day.

Source: Michael J. Norden, MD, clinical associate professor of psychiatry at the University of Washington, Seattle. He was among the first to publish medical accounts of the varied uses of Prozac and has been a pioneer in the integration of psychopharmacology and alternative treatments. Dr. Norden is the author of *Beyond Prozac.* Regan Books/HarperCollins.

Melatonin... Miracle or Madness?

Miracle melatonin can be dangerous, despite popularity as a treatment for insomnia, cancer and more.

Risks: The most widely available dosage of 2 mg to 3 mg—up to 10 times the effective dosage—can cause insomnia...nightmares... headaches...mental impairment...and decrease certain hormones. Short-term melatonin use may be helpful, but first speak with your doctor.

Source: Victor Herbert, MD, JD, director of the nutrition program at Mount Sinai School of Medicine in New York City.

All About Melatonin

Is melatonin a miracle substance? Of course not. No compound holds all the answers to good health. But melatonin can improve health—in some cases dramatically. All you must do is learn how to boost your body's production of melatonin...and take supplemental melatonin when necessary.

I've used melatonin in my family practice for almost five years. In that time I've seen how effective it can be in helping people overcome everything from insomnia to cancer.

How melatonin works:

In humans, melatonin is produced primarily by the pineal gland—a pea-sized structure located deep in the brain. Melatonin is made only in darkness. When sunlight or artificial light hits your retinas, they signal the brain to shut down melatonin production.

When melatonin is present in the bloodstream, the body "assumes" that it's dark outside. Researchers have found that they can aid sleep—or quickly reset a person's internal clock—by giving a few well-timed milligrams of melatonin.

Melatonin and aging:

Early researchers felt that melatonin's most significant use would be as a sleeping pill—for insomniacs, victims of jet lag and shift workers.

Then melatonin's more fascinating properties began to emerge. *Most startling:* As we age, our natural melatonin production falls dramatically. By middle age, the average person secretes only half as much melatonin as he/she did during childhood. By age 80, it's only one-fifth as much.

The relationship between age and declining melatonin levels made some scientists wonder: Is melatonin a fountain of youth?

To find out, Italian immunologist Walter Pierpaoli, MD, PhD, took 10 young (four-month-old) mice and 10 old (17-month-old) mice. He transplanted the pineal glands from the old mice into the young mice, and vice versa. *Result:* The old mice gained muscle, exhibited more energy and developed thick, shiny coats.

Even more significant, they survived for 34 months—one full year longer than ordinary mice, whose life spans average 22 months. The young mice with the "old" pineal glands died at about 17 months.

Antioxidant properties:

Russel Reiter, PhD, a cellular biologist at the University of Texas, has shown that melatonin has remarkable antioxidant effects. In fact, his research suggests that it may be the most powerful antioxidant ever discovered.

Like other antioxidants, melatonin prevents heart disease, cancer, cataracts and other diseases by "mopping up" highly reactive compounds known as free radicals. Unlike other antioxidants—including vitamins C and E—melatonin is soluble in both fat and water. That means it can slip into every part of every cell in the body—including cell nuclei.

In Reiter's studies, rats given melatonin were less likely than other rats to...

...develop cancer when exposed to a powerful carcinogen.

...expire following exposure to ionizing radiation.

...develop lung cancer when exposed to a potent herbicide.

...develop cataracts.

Melatonin and immunity:

Melatonin has also proven to be a potent immunity-booster. Apparently, it stimulates the activity of killer T-cells, which seek out and destroy invading germs.

In studies of patients with cancers of the colon, kidney, liver, lung and pancreas, Dr. Paoli Lissoni of San Gerardo Hospital in Monza, Italy, found that melatonin aided the effects of interleukin-2, another T-cell booster.

Because melatonin is also an estrogen regulator, scientists theorize that it might be useful against breast cancer. High levels of melatonin reduce a woman's output of estrogen—and we know that most cases of breast cancer are stimulated by estrogen.

Melatonin and sex:

In many animals, it's well known that hormone levels control seasonal breeding patterns. Humans, too, tend to breed seasonally, conceiving more babies in September—when shorter days translate into more sleep and reduced irritability.

I'm not suggesting that melatonin is a natural aphrodisiac. However, a "melatonin-friendly" lifestyle, with plenty of sleep and a regular daily schedule, will make you feel more vital, less irritable...and more sexy.

Boosting melatonin levels:

Some doctors have begun urging their patients to take melatonin supplements. I prefer helping my patients adopt strategies designed to maximize the body's own production of melatonin.

It's a good idea to discuss these strategies with your doctor before trying them on your own, but here's what I recommend to my patients...

•**Go to bed on time.** Staying up late to talk or read hinders your body's production of melatonin. If you must get by on less sleep, get to bed at your usual time and wake up early.

In general, a lifestyle in sync with the sun makes it easier for your body to maintain its rhythm of melatonin production. It's just as important to lower melatonin production by getting outside for a brisk walk in the sunlight every morning as it is to raise it at night.

•**Eat fewer calories.** Although most melatonin is produced by the pineal gland, small amounts are made in the intestines. Eating fewer calories helps boosts intestinal melatonin production.

•**Avoid alcohol before bedtime.** Even a single drink in the three hours prior to sleep can disturb your melatonin production throughout the night.

•**Watch out for melatonin-blocking drugs.** Beta-blockers, taken for heart disease, can lower melatonin levels. These drugs should not be discontinued without a doctor's supervision. But if you take them, ask your doctor about taking a melatonin supplement.

Aspirin and other nonsteroidal anti-inflammatory drugs have also been shown to inhibit melatonin. If you frequently take over-the-counter painkillers, ask your doctor about taking acetaminophen instead of aspirin...or adding a melatonin supplement.

Taking supplements:

Are supplements safe? Yes. I've prescribed them to hundreds of patients, and not one of them has ever had a bad reaction.

I usually prescribe 2 mg to 3 mg a day. For patients battling cancer or another serious condition, I might up the daily dose to 10 mg or more. Supplemental melatonin should be taken only under a doctor's supervision.

The one side effect I know of—daytime drowsiness—occurs only with high doses. If you start feeling drowsy during the day, reduce your intake.

Take the supplement 30 minutes before bedtime—without food. If you have regular sleep patterns, but one night you're going to be out late, take melatonin at your usual time. That way, when you finally get to bed, you will have caused less disruption to your melatonin cycle.

Jet lag and shift work:

If you're flying cross-country on the "red-eye," take 5 mg of melatonin before or during the flight. On the night following your arrival in the new time zone, take another dose of 10 mg 30 minutes before your new bedtime. If you're taking a daytime flight, take melatonin only the night after your arrival.

For shift workers who must sleep during the day, I usually recommend taking supplemental melatonin just before bedtime. That provides the body with an artificial "nighttime signal" that makes sleep easier. Upon waking, seek immediate exposure to daylight or bright artificial light.

Source: Steven J. Bock, MD, director of the Rhinebeck Health Center in Rhinebeck, NY, and the author of *Stay Young the Melatonin Way: The Natural Plan for Better Sex, Better Sleep, Better Health and Longer Life.* Dutton.

Antioxidants and Fewer Health Problems

The foods we eat have a big impact on our health—both positively *and* negatively.

Study after study shows that antioxidants—disease-fighting chemicals that occur naturally in many foods—have certain properties that may boost the immune system. They also reduce the risk of health problems—particularly heart disease and cancer.

While the most powerful antioxidants—beta-carotene, vitamin C and vitamin E—are available in supplement form, researchers recommend we try to obtain them naturally through the foods we eat.

Antioxidant-rich foods:

It is most prudent to build a proper diet through a diverse combination of foods. There are several foods that contain all three antioxidants. *They include...*

•**Mangoes.** Mangoes contain 57 milligrams (mg) of vitamin C—almost the full Recommended Daily Allowance (RDA)—as well as ample amounts of beta-carotene and vitamin E. No other tropical fruit provides all three.

•**Sweet potatoes.** They are low in calories and loaded with beta-carotene and vitamins C and E. One to two sweet potatoes—with or without the skin—almost meets the RDA for all

three nutrients. Microwaving ensures that you don't lose these nutrients.

Other great sources:

•**Beta-carotene** is commonly found in leafy green plants. Most health organizations recommend eating five or six fruits or vegetables a day, which amounts to a diet containing 6 mg of beta-carotene.

Beta-carotene is "fat soluble"—meaning that you need to eat a small amount of fat with the beta-carotene in order to absorb it. Scientists have not yet determined the exact amount of fat needed, but it is not a lot. This is one example of how fat in moderation is important to maintain good health.

•**Vitamin C.** The RDA for vitamin C is 60 mg. But researchers say that you need between 100 mg and 500 mg daily to fight off cataracts and other diseases such as cancer and heart disease. *Rich sources...*

•**One papay**a (188 mg).

•**Half a raw red**, green or yellow pepper (170 mg).

•**One cup of broccoli**—steamed or microwaved (98 mg).

•**10 to 12 strawberries** (85 mg).

•**8 ounces of orange juice** (124 mg).

Vitamin C is highly sensitive to heat and cooking. So when cooking vegetables, use a pressure steamer...or lightly steam or microwave.

•**Vitamin E** is one of the most potent antioxidants when it comes to fighting off disease. Studies show that the current RDA for vitamin E—10 mg for men and 8 mg for women—is probably too low to be able to offer much protection against disease. Preliminary studies show that anywhere between 100 mg and 400 mg of vitamin E daily might offer better protection.

Vitamin E is most commonly found in high-fat foods, such as vegetable oils and nuts. But —you don't have to eat a lot of them to reach the RDA.

Examples: One ounce of sunflower seeds (14.2 mg)...or one-quarter cup of wheat germ (4.1 mg)...or two tablespoons of peanut butter (3 mg). Vitamin E can also be found in some leafy vegetables and in sweet potatoes.

Although some experts recommend complementing dietary "E" with supplements (contrary to advice regarding other antioxidants), be aware that the synthetic "E" in supplements is not as potent as the form naturally occurring in foods.

The Natural Supplement That Fights Heart Disease

A natural substance called *coenzyme Q* has been widely touted as a cure for everything from cancer to chronic fatigue. While these claims haven't been substantiated, the evidence does show that coenzyme Q is effective against heart disease. And it causes few side effects.

Also known as *ubiquinone,* coenzyme Q occurs naturally in mitochondria, the energy-producing "factories" of all cells in the body—especially those of the heart, which needs lots of energy for pumping blood.

Diseased hearts tend to be deficient in coenzyme Q, and coenzyme Q tablets seem to help several types of heart disease, especially the debilitating and potentially deadly condition *congestive heart failure.*

Ordinarily, oxygen-poor blood flows from the heart to the lungs, where it's oxygenated, re-turned to the heart and then pumped through-out the body. In those suffering from congestive heart failure—typically a result of a heart attack, high blood pressure or diseased heart valves—the heart loses its pumping efficiency. Inefficient pumping causes fatigue and shortness of breath, as well as an enlarged heart. If the right side of the heart fails, swelling occurs in the legs, abdomen and liver. If the left side fails, fluid builds up in the lungs.

In a rigorous double-blind study of 641 patients with heart failure, 322 "control" patients received a placebo while 319 received coenzyme Q (2 mg per kilogram of body weight per day). During the course of the one-year study, 73 in the treated group required hospitalization, as compared with 118 of the controls. Those taking coenzyme Q experienced an average of 20 episodes of fluid in the lungs, as compared with 51 episodes in the placebo group. All in all, the coenzyme Q group required less hospital care and experienced fewer serious complications.

Coenzyme Q also protects hearts from post-operative complications that often strike people who undergo coronary artery bypass surgery. In a controlled trial, 40 patients received either 150 mg of coenzyme Q or a placebo for one week prior to surgery. After surgery, blood tests revealed far less heart injury among the treated group than among the controls. The treated group also had a lower incidence of irregular heart rhythms.

Finally, a small controlled study of coenzyme Q in 12 patients with chest pain caused by lack of oxygen to the heart (angina) showed that 150 mg of coenzyme Q daily increased the amount of time patients could safely exercise.

I'm now convinced that anyone with heart failure will benefit from a daily dose of coenzyme Q (2 mg per kilogram of body weight). One kilogram equals 2.2 pounds, so this translates into 150 mg a day for a person who weighs 165 pounds. It's best to divide the total daily dose into three doses.

Coenzyme Q supplements are especially beneficial for individuals taking a class of cholesterol-lowering drugs called HMG-CoA *reductase inhibitors.* This class includes the popular drugs lovastatin (Mevacor) and simvastatin (Zocor). These drugs lower coenzyme Q levels in the body.

If you have angina or are scheduled for bypass surgery, take coenzyme Q both before *and* after surgery. Supplements are also appropriate for those with high blood pressure, high cholesterol, diabetes or a family history of heart disease. At this point I do *not* recommend coenzyme Q for individuals without cardiovascular risk factors or heart disease, although supplementation causes no harm.

Coenzyme Q—available without prescription in drugstores and health-food stores—costs about $30 and up for 100 tablets.

Source: Adriane Fugh-Berman, MD, a Washington, DC-based medical researcher who specializes in women's health and alternative medicine. She is the author of *Alternative Medicine: What Works.* Odonion Press.

Magnets: Stop Pain... Ease Arthritis...Help Heal Broken Bones and More

In China, France, Japan and especially in India, magnetic therapy has long been used to speed the healing of broken bones and soft-tissue injuries.

In the US, magnetic therapy is sometimes considered a form of quackery. But following the publication of several "pro-magnet" studies in the *Journal of Electro-* and *Magnetobiology* and other prestigious American medical journals, a few pioneering doctors in this country are starting to use magnets in their practices.

Already, magnetic therapy has proven effective at treating slow-healing fractures and arthritic knees and necks. Studies also suggest that regular use of magnets may reverse osteoporosis...prevent heart disease...slow tumor growth...and boost mental function in Alzheimer's patients.

I know from personal experience that people sleep better and wake up feeling more refreshed after a night on a magnetic mattress. I sleep on one myself!

Is magnetic therapy safe? Absolutely. Magnetic resonance imaging (MRI) machines routinely expose patients to magnetic fields as high as 15,000 gauss—with no negative effects. It stands to reason that a medical magnet rated at 200 to 800 gauss poses little threat.

How magnets work:

Recent studies have demonstrated quite clearly that when placed directly on the skin, a simple, handheld magnet did the following...

•**Increases blood flow.** It does so by stimulating cellular activity through the so-called "Hall effect." This is general heating of the magnetized area.

Some scientists think magnets improve the functioning of the autonomic nervous system, which could also stimulate blood flow to the affected area.

•**Diminishes pain.** This occurs via a combination of the Hall effect and possibly some stabilizing influence on the autonomic nervous system.

•**Speeds healing.** It does so by boosting the body's synthesis of adenosine triphosphate (ATP), the "fuel" that fires all cellular processes ...and by enhancing the blood's ability to carry oxygen.

Magnets versus arthritis:

Magnetic therapy helps relieve arthritis pain and slows the deterioration of cartilage inside arthritic joints.

For my patients with arthritis, I recommend sleeping on a magnetic mattress pad...or wrapping a flexible, magnetic bandage around the affected joint. If you do sleep on a magnetic pad, remove it for a day or two, every two to four weeks. This seems to prolong the beneficial effects.

Headaches and back pain:

Magnetic pillow liners appear to be an effective treatment for chronic headaches and jaw pain. People with chronic back pain have obtained significant relief from sleeping on magnetic mattresses, and/or using magnetic seat cushions.

Soft tissue inflamation:

Tennis elbow, carpal tunnel syndrome and other tendon or ligament problems heal faster when wrapped in magnetic bandages.

In most cases, the magnet is wrapped into place over the affected area—and left in place until the pain disappears.

Broken bones:

In some hospitals, powerful electromagnets are being used to speed healing of stubborn bone fractures. Magnetic therapy also seems to promote regeneration of spinal disk tissue.

Asthma:

Regular use of magnets helps prevent the violent allergic reaction in the lungs that is characteristic of bronchial asthma.

Helpful: Sleeping on a magnetic mattress... or wearing a magnetic bandage on your chest.

Putting magnets to work:

The benefits of magnetic therapy are often apparent within the first hour of treatment. In others, three or four days of steady treatment are required.

For maximum benefit: Place magnets as close to your body as possible. The strength of the magnetic field drops off sharply with distance.

A variety of magnetic devices are now available—including mattress pads, seat cushions, pillow liners, magnet-studded bandages and simple handheld magnets.

Good source of medical magnets: Norso Biomagnetics, 4105 Starboard Ct., Raleigh, North Carolina 27613. 800-480-8601.

Source: Ron Lawrence, MD, a neurologist in private practice in Agoura Hills, CA. He is president of the newly formed North American Academy of Magnetic Therapy, 17445 Oak Creek Ct., Encino, CA 91316.

Deepak Chopra's Secrets of Having Boundless Energy

Fatigue is one of the most common problems doctors are asked to treat. Complaints about exhaustion are likely to continue, given our busy schedules and many demands on our lives.

Yet despite the large number of people who feel tired day after day, fatigue is an unnatural state. Such fatigue does not occur in animals or children. When children and animals are tired, they rest and awaken renewed.

But adults have the ability to maneuver around their biological needs. They drive themselves...resist the natural, biological cycle of alternating rest and activity...and become depleted.

To banish common fatigue, we need to rediscover our basic harmony with nature. The secret of recovering our harmony can be found in a mind/body system of health, which is based on the understanding that your own mind/body system is inseparably connected to the systems of nature.

Watch what you eat:

You can increase your energy by eating fresh, pure foods. By contrast, foods that lack freshness and are highly processed deplete the body of energy. Foods especially rich in natural energy include...

• **Fresh fruits** and lightly cooked vegetables.

• **Wheat**, rice, barley and other whole grains.

• **Nonmeat sources of protein**, such as dried beans. For people who balk at a vegetarian diet, fish and poultry are acceptable substitutes.

• **Honey** as a substitute for refined sugar.

Foods that deplete energy and should be avoided include red meat, aged cheese, alcohol, coffee and smoked and canned foods. This does not mean you must completely avoid anything but energy-boosting foods.

Any system that is too rigid will create further imbalance. Instead, experiment with these suggestions and notice what proportion makes a significant difference in your own energy level.

Strengthen your digestion. Poor digestion can lead to fatigue in two ways:

• **Energy for the body is lost** when food is not adequately metabolized.

• **When food residue lingers undigested**, impurities and toxins may accumulate, placing stress on the body.

How to strengthen your digestion and boost your energy level:

• **Create a calm atmosphere for dining.** Instead of always working through lunch and watching TV during dinner, enjoy yourself and pay attention to your meal. Conversation is fine but avoid controversial subjects.

When the body is accustomed to a routine, digestion will be automatic. So stick to regular mealtimes.

• **Eat your biggest meal at lunch.** Research indicates that this is the time when metabolism is most efficient.

• **Sip warm water or herbal tea** throughout the day to normalize the metabolic rate and eliminate toxins.

Helpful: Fill a thermos with warm water, which enhances digestion. Keep it nearby and take a few sips every half-hour.

Reduce stress:

Tension drains the body of energy, causing it to function less effectively.

Better: Make it a priority to spend time on relaxing activities. Everyone has favorite pastimes, and some of these can even take place during the work day.

Classic stress-relievers: Meditation, a massage, sex, a warm shower or bath, playing or listening to music...and a change of scenery.

Exercise in moderation:

Americans' obsession with strenuous exercise is creating an epidemic of exhaustion. Pushing ourselves past what our bodies are naturally designed to handle results in long-lasting fatigue.

Solution: For maximum energy, exercise seven days a week for 15 to 20 minutes at a time. Some fitness experts recommend taking a day off between workouts—but that's be-cause our average workouts are too strenuous. Instead, exercise daily, but to only 50% of your capacity.

Example: If you are able to swim 20 laps, only swim 10. You'll feel energetic—and over time, your capacity will increase.

Keeping natural rhythms:

The body is most responsive to certain activities when they are performed at specific times of the day.

Before electric light was invented, our schedules were more in keeping with these natural rhythms under which our bodies evolved. Rediscovering them will help you feel energetic every day...

•**Awaken** between 6 am and 7 am.

•**Exercise in the morning**—or, if this is not possible, no later than three hours before bedtime.

•**Eat lunch** between 12 pm and 1 pm.

•**Eat dinner** between 6 pm and 7 pm...and wind down with restful activities afterward, such as going for a walk, reading, playing games with your family or listening to music.

•**Go to bed** between 10 pm and 11 pm each night.

Helpful: If you try going to bed at 10 pm but have trouble falling asleep, don't worry about it.

Just rest quietly with your eyes closed. Clear your mind, and avoid dwelling on anything that is troubling you. Your body will get the rest it needs. Over time, you'll notice an increase in energy in the morning, and you'll be able to fall asleep at the earlier hour.

Take pleasure in life:

Joy is a natural energizer. If you're having a good time, you'll never be fatigued. In fact, studies have found that 80% of people suffering from chronic fatigue score higher than normal on measures of depression and anxiety.

Solution: Practice shifting your awareness to the positive. We can't avoid negative events, but we don't have to dwell on them.

Treat others with kindness, tolerance and love...refuse to entertain negativity...and pay attention to the joy and playfulness that can be found all around you. Learn to meditate to help you get in touch with nature and enable you to see these simple joys.

Exception to the rule:

If you are bothered by persistent fatigue, have a thorough medical checkup to rule out a treatable physical cause—such as anemia, thyroid problems or mononucleosis.

Source: Deepak Chopra, MD, executive director of the Sharp Institute for Human Potential and Mind/Body Medicine, 1110 Camino Del Mar, Suite. G, Del Mar, CA 92014. He is the author of 16 best-selling books, including *Bound-less Energy,* Harmony Books, and *The Seven Spiritual Laws of Success.* New World Library.

Just Relaxing Aids Health

Relaxation is just as important as exercise—to stay healthy. Dozens of studies have shown that emotional stress impairs the immune system. Relaxation reduces this stress, helping boost immunity. In one study, men and women who were taught relaxation techniques had a significant increase in the activity of natural killer-cells—a key marker in immune-system health.

Source: Janice Kiecolt-Glaser, PhD, professor of psychology at Ohio State University in Columbus, OH, and a leading authority on mind–body medicine.

All About Herbal Remedies

Even if you eat right, exercise regularly and get plenty of sleep, herbal supplements can raise your health to a whole new level.

As explained here by one of the country's leading herbalists, Dr. Daniel B. Mowrey, so-called "tonic" herbs confer an impressive array of health benefits, including increased energy and stamina…heightened immunity…reduced risk of heart disease…improved liver function …reduced joint inflammation.

If you'd like to add herbal remedies to your medicine chest, start with the following eight tonic herbs.* All are available at health-food stores.

Unlike drugs, herbal preparations are not regulated by the FDA. Ask the store clerk to recommend a reputable brand.

You can take each of these herbs on a daily basis. Or you can rotate through the list, taking each herb for a few weeks at a time. The doses listed are based on capsules containing 850 mg to 900 mg of the herb.

Caution: Consult a doctor before starting any herbal regimen—especially if you have a heart ailment or another chronic illness and/or you are using prescription or over-the-counter medications. Herbal remedies can dangerously interact with certain drugs.

If you develop a rash, nausea, hives, headaches or hay fever-like symptoms while taking an herb, stop using it immediately.

•**Cayenne** is good for the cardiovascular system. A mild stimulant, the herb also helps maintain muscle tone in the stomach and intestinal walls and enhances digestion. Cayenne is also an excellent "activator herb," amplifying the benefits of other herbs you take.

Daily dose: Two capsules. Or use ground cayenne as a spice.

•**Echinacea** fights illness on two levels. First, it boosts levels of white blood cells, B- and T-lymphocytes and phagocytes—the key components of a healthy immune system. Second, it neutralizes invading microorganisms.

*Editor's note: Certain remedies are inherently unsafe. Comfrey, borage and coltsfoot can cause liver disease …chaparral can cause liver disease…mahuang can cause a rise in blood pressure that is particularly unsafe for those with heart or thyroid disease or diabetes… yohimbé can cause tremors, anxiety, high blood pressure and rapid heart rate.

German researchers have shown that echinacea stops staph, strep and fungal infections, along with a variety of viruses.

Daily dose: Two capsules. Be sure the capsules contain the *whole* root in powdered form, not extract.

Used intermittently, liquid extract of echinacea makes a soothing balm for sore throats. Using an eyedropper, let a few drops fall against the back of your throat.

•**Garlic.** This spice helps prevent heart disease by lowering cholesterol levels and blocking formation of fatty deposits in the coronary arteries. It also boosts levels of T-cells, a critical component of the immune system.

Animal and human studies have shown that garlic also relieves arthritis. It contains sulfur compounds, which are known to have significant anti-inflammatory properties.

Daily dose: Two pills. Or use a garlic clove or garlic powder in your cooking.

•**Gingerroot** is an excellent remedy for indigestion, constipation, diarrhea and nausea (including morning sickness). There's no good explanation for why it works. But my research suggests that ginger is even more effective than Dramamine at preventing motion sickness. It is also effective against the flu.

Be sure to buy capsules made from the *whole* gingerroot—not extract.

Daily dose: For mild motion sickness, two capsules 15 minutes before you depart (and two to four more every hour or whenever symptoms return). For serious gastrointestinal upset, take six to 12 capsules an hour.

•**Lapacho.** A South American herb, lapacho contains *napthoquinones* (N-factors), unique compounds that have antiviral and antibiotic properties. It's effective at preventing colds, flu and bacterial and fungal infections.

Taken in capsule or tea form, lapacho soothes painful joints…and boosts energy levels. Lapacho also stimulates activity of enzymes in the liver, enhancing its ability to remove toxins from the blood.

In Brazil, lapacho is used to treat leukemia and cervical cancer, and lapacho salve is used to treat skin cancer.

326

Studies suggest that the herb may also be effective against breast cancer.

Make tea by simmering the purplish paper-thin inner lining of the bark in hot water for 20 minutes, then strain and let cool. Leftover tea can be refrigerated.

Daily dose: To prevent illness, four capsules or two cups of tea. To treat an infection, six capsules or one to two quarts of tea.

•**Milk Thistle.** One of the world's most studied plants, milk thistle is very good for the liver. By stimulating protein synthesis, it boosts levels of key liver enzymes, speeding regeneration of damaged liver tissue. It also inhibits *lypoxygenase*, an enzyme that destroys liver cells.

Recent studies show that milk thistle can help reverse the effects of hepatitis and cirrhosis.

Daily dose: Two capsules.

•**Pygeum Extract.** Derived from the bark of an African tree, pygeum has been shown to prevent—and even cure—benign enlargement of the prostate. It contains *phytosterols*, potent anti-inflammatory compounds. Pygeum also contains *triterpenoids*, compounds that have an anti-swelling effect.

Daily dose: To prevent prostate enlargement, two capsules. To shrink an enlarged prostate, four capsules.

•**Yerba Mate.** This South American herb boosts energy and stamina without causing the jitters that caffeine can cause. Anecdotal reports suggest that yerba mate is also effective against asthma and allergies, though the mechanism is unknown.

Yerba mate is best taken as a daily tea. Pour boiling water over yerba mate leaves, let sit for 10 minutes, then strain and serve.

Daily dose: Two to four cups.

Source: Daniel B. Mowrey, PhD, president of the American Phytotherapy Research Laboratory, a nonprofit research facility in Lehi, Utah. He is the author of several books on herbal medicine, including *Herbal Tonic Therapies.* Keats Publishing.

This Chinese Herb Kills Germs Cold

Like most doctors, I am constantly exposed to cold germs and flu viruses. You might think I would always be getting sick. In fact, I almost never do.

What's my secret? I swallow a dose of the Chinese herbal remedy *ganmaoling* each time I even think I might be exposed to germs—whenever I'm near a friend, family member, patient, grocery bagger, etc., who has the sniffles or sneezes.

In the two years I've been taking this immunity booster I haven't caught a single cold.

I also take a dose before air travel. The recirculated air inside most planes is full of germs.

Ganmaoling is made from a combination of herbs, including Chrysanthemum indicum and Ilex asprello. It seems to halt viral and bacterial activity. There are no side effects.

I used to use the herb echinacea for colds and flu. But ganmaoling works better—for me. That's typical. Natural remedies work differently for different people.

To prevent illness, such as before air travel or after I've been around a sick person, I take a single dose of six to eight pills. Children should not take more than three or four pills.

If I feel a cold or flu coming on, I take eight pills three times a day for two days. Symptoms disappear within three days.

If my symptoms persist, I reduce the dose by half on the third day. By then, I usually feel better. Without ganmaoling, most colds last for a week—or longer.

Source: Carolyn Dean, MD, a New York City physician who is conducting clinical research in homeopathic acupuncture. She is the author of *Complementary Natural Prescriptions for Common Ailments.* Keats Publishing.

Green Tea Helps Prevent Cancer

Earlier studies found that green tea helped reduce the risk of several kinds of cancer.

New finding: Individuals who drank a daily cup of black, non-herbal tea (Tetley, Lipton, etc.) had a 75% reduction in risk for cancer of the upper digestive organs and a 60% reduction in kidney cancer risk. Both black and green tea contain *polyphenols*—strong antioxidants believed to have anti-tumor properties.

Source: Wei Zheng, MD, PhD, assistant professor of epidemiology, University of Minnesota School of Public Health, Minneapolis.

Herbal Remedies That Kill

Herbal remedies are rarely registered as over-the-counter drugs, even when sold for medicinal purposes. They are usually sold with foods and food supplements—and have undergone little or no quality testing. Proven health benefits of plant products like garlic have brought many sleeping drugs, sedatives and tonics to the market with little quality control. *Result:* A remedy may be ineffective—or even dangerous. In one case, 30 people died after taking an herbal slimming product prescribed by weight-loss clinics.

Source: Peter de Smet, clinical pharmacologist, Royal Dutch Association for the Advancement of Pharmacy, quoted in *New Scientist*, King's Reach Tower, Stamford St., London SE1 9LLS, England.

Which Mineral Supplements Should You Take?

Minerals—iron, calcium, chromium, zinc, etc.—are vital components of a healthful diet. But claims made about their health benefits extend far beyond the evidence.

As with vitamins, it's important to remember the distinction between taking mineral supplements to prevent or treat dietary deficiencies and taking them in higher doses in an effort to improve health in other ways.

Recently, there's been a great deal of controversy over chromium picolinate. This dietary supplement has become very popular with bodybuilders and with people involved in weight-loss programs. But despite all the hoopla, there is little evidence that chromium picolinate is effective for these uses.

Now a new study has raised questions about chromium picolinate's safety. When scientists exposed cells taken from the ovary of a hamster to high concentrations of chromium picolinate, they found that it caused severe chromosomal damage. This raised the possibility that the mineral supplement might be carcinogenic.

The industry that manufactures the supplements responded to this study within days, criticizing how the study was done and claiming that, when taken at the recommended dose, chromium supplements are completely safe. You have to wonder, though, if these critics might be more concerned with protecting their profit margins than your health.

There is less controversy about calcium, iron and zinc. Calcium supplements, especially when combined with vitamin D, exercise and/or hormone supplements, help prevent some of the normal bone loss that occurs as women enter menopause.

It's even more important, however, to build strong bones in the first place by getting enough calcium when you're younger.

Adolescents and young adults—particularly women—should get 1,200 mg of calcium a day. Most get less than half of that amount. Elderly women should consume 1,500 mg a day. There is about 300 mg of calcium in a glass of milk or a cup of yogurt.

Those who don't get enough calcium in their diet should take a supplement. It's usually less expensive to buy a separate supplement like calcium carbonate than to try to get the full amount of calcium in a multivitamin.

Women of childbearing age, especially those who donate blood or have heavy periods, often need supplemental iron. Your doctor can give you a simple blood test that determines whether you are iron-deficient.

It's best to have this test before you start taking iron. Too much iron in your system can pose a hazard to your health.

The average American gets only 80% of the recommended daily allowance of zinc, according to a recent study. If you suspect you're not getting enough zinc from your diet (good sources include shellfish, beef, beans and nuts), take a multivitamin that contains the recommended daily allowance.

Whenever you hear fantastic claims about the curative powers of mineral supplements, keep in mind that the multibillion dollar industry that manufactures them is behind a lot of the hype. As with vitamins, a balanced diet is the best way to ensure that you're getting the minerals you need.

A simple multivitamin containing the recommended daily allowances of vitamins and minerals is safe, however, and provides insurance against dietary deficiencies.

Beware of higher doses. Until further studies sort out questions of effectiveness—and safety —their risks and benefits simply aren't known yet. In the meantime, it's your choice whether you want to be a guinea pig. Personally, though, I think I'll stay in the control group.

Source: Timothy McCall, MD, an internist practicing in the Boston area. He is the author of *Examining Your Doctor: A Patient's Guide to Avoiding Harmful Medical Care.* Birch Lane Press. Dr. McCall may be reached c/o *Health Confidential*, 55 Railroad Ave., Greenwich, CT 06830…or via E-mail at Ask TM@aol.com.

Lessons from Our Prehistoric Past: Why We Get Sick… How Not to Get Sick

Why doesn't the human body work better? After all, it's efficient in so many ways. It digests all kinds of foods…it excretes toxins… and its immune system is capable of attacking millions of invading viruses and bacteria.

Yet all too often, the body falls prey to appendicitis, hemorrhoids, impacted wisdom teeth, colds, pneumonia, headaches, nausea, heart attacks and cancer.

How can the body be so effective in some ways—and so ineffective in others? Or to put it another way—why haven't these vulnerabilities been eliminated by natural selection?*

The old answer was that natural selection isn't powerful enough to eliminate these conditions. Scientists are now beginning to believe that's not the case.

When we look, we see that many ailments that at first seem destructive are actually products of natural selection. They represent a compromise between competing environmental pressures…or are themselves defenses against disease.

By focusing on the question, *What function might this aspect of the body serve?*, the emerging science of Darwinian medicine offers provocative explanations for many mysteries of human biology.

Darwinian medicine also suggests that many of the "cures" used to treat human illness may, in fact, work against the body's natural healing mechanisms.

This is not to say that you should ignore your doctor's advice or reject accepted methods of treating disease. However, I urge you to ask your doctor to explain the reasoning behind treatments that he/she recommends… and to present the evidence for their effectiveness. The medical profession can only benefit by expanding to include this evolutionary perspective—and by making sure that long-used treatments really do have a basis in science.

According to Darwinian medicine, the following medical "problems" may have benefits…

•**Fever.** When an adult patient has the flu or another infectious disease, doctors routinely recommend aspirin or a similar medication to reduce fever. Most of us are so familiar with this advice that we never stop to wonder if it really makes sense.

The benefit of using aspirin against fever has never been confirmed by scientific studies. In fact, there's good evidence to suggest that fever evolved specifically to protect us against infectious disease. Elevated body temperature

---

*Natural selection increases the frequency of genes that boost an organism's chances for survival and reproduction. Genes that cause an individual to die young or not to reproduce are gradually eliminated. As a result, individuals of the species are increasingly able to thrive in their environment.

makes bacteria and viruses more vulnerable to attack by the immune system.

Matt Kluger, PhD, a physiologist at The Lovelace Institutes in Albuquerque, New Mexico, demonstrated that infected laboratory animals that are prevented from developing fever tend to stay sick longer—and are more likely to die—than those whose fevers are allowed to develop.

Studies of children with chicken pox and adults with colds have found that suppressing fever may in some cases prolong illness. There is also evidence that treating fever can increase the risk of a potentially fatal blood infection known as septic shock.

Again, I do not advise never treating fever. Very high body temperatures occasionally cause seizures and brain damage. Also, many patients are willing to trade possibly slower recovery for relief from symptoms, and aspirin may speed recovery from some infections. But these findings illustrate the value of reexamining our long-held assumptions in light of evolutionary theory.

•**Iron deficiency.** Doctors often use iron supplements to treat patients whose blood iron levels are low. In some patients with tuberculosis or certain other chronic bacterial infections, however, a low level is one of the body's defenses.

Bacteria need iron to survive. When the body detects infection, it releases a chemical that lowers the amount of iron in the bloodstream.

Trap: Using iron supplements to counteract this natural defense only "feeds" the infection until it becomes more serious. Yet according to one recent study, only 11% of doctors are aware of this danger.

•**Morning sickness.** Independent scholar and biologist Margie Profet argues convincingly that a condition as common as pregnancy-related nausea surely could not be pathological—even though most doctors consider it as such.

Profet believes that morning sickness is beneficial—because it keeps mothers from eating foods that could be toxic to the developing fetus. Lending support to her theory is the recent finding that babies born to mothers who had morning sickness were less likely than other babies to have birth defects.

As recently as the 1980s, doctors prescribed the antinausea drug Bendectin to combat morning sickness. The drug itself was thought to be safe. Until recently, however, no one considered the possibility that the drug might interfere with the body's own mechanism for preventing the ingestion of toxins.

Doctors are now more cautious about recommending any drug during pregnancy.

•**Jaundice**—yellowish skin color caused by high levels of bilirubin, a by-product of hemoglobin breakdown—is quite common in newborn infants.

For years, doctors used exposure to bright lights to treat these babies. Now light therapy has fallen out of favor. *Reason:* Doctors realize that most cases of jaundice in newborns are harmless.

According to Darwinian medicine, jaundice may even be helpful.

John Brett of the University of California at San Francisco and Susan Niermeyer, MD, at The Children's Hospital in Denver, have noted that bilirubin has an antioxidant effect similar to that of beta-carotene. It "scavenges" free radicals, highly reactive molecules that can damage tissues.

When a newborn baby starts to breathe air, oxygen levels in his/her bloodstream increase suddenly. It's possible that high bilirubin levels protect the baby's tissues from oxygen-induced free-radical damage until other natural defenses are gradually put in place.

Again, I'm not recommending that doctors stop treating jaundice. In certain babies, high bilirubin levels can lead to brain damage. And Brett and Niermeyer's theory hasn't been proven. However, their work highlights the need for further research and for parents to discuss treatment options with a doctor.

•**Diarrhea.** We know that the function of diarrhea is to expel toxins and infectious agents from the lower intestinal tract. Research by Herbert L. DuPont, MD, and Richard Hornick, MD, at the University of Maryland School of Medicine in Baltimore, suggests that giving antidiarrhea medications for certain infections—such as Shigella—is likely to prolong the illness.

In some cases, antidiarrhea drugs can cause intestinal perforations or other complications.

What about traveler's diarrhea? Astonishingly, there has been little research on this subject. We just don't know.

Dietary dangers:

Darwinian medicine also sheds light on many lifestyle-related problems, such as obesity and heart disease.

Our bodies were not "designed" to sit in chairs for hours on end. They were designed to be continually active. Nor did we evolve to pluck our food from grocery shelves sagging under the weight of products laden with fat, sugar and salt. For millennia, intermittent food shortages were a normal part of human existence...and fat, sugar and salt—which are needed for good health—were in short supply.

This helps explain why we crave—indeed, why most of us would happily gorge ourselves on—foods that are bad for us. Our ancestors ate as much of these substances as they could.

The link between red meat in the diet and heart disease is well-established. However, some evidence suggests that the problem may not be red meat itself but farm-produced meat.

S. Boyd Eaton, MD, an Atlanta radiologist, has noted that meat from wild game has less than half the fat of meat raised on farms—and that the ratio of heart-protective Omega-3 fatty acids to saturated fat is higher in game than in farm animals. It may be that the breeding of animals to meet our taste for high fat has led to the connection between eating meat and heart disease.

• **Unsolved mysteries.** There is still a great deal we don't know about how the body has evolved to protect itself.

Take the common cold. The runny nose that causes so much discomfort may actually be the body's way of eliminating viruses and bacteria. It's conceivable that using nasal inhalers or oral decongestants could prolong a cold by interfering with this mechanism, though there's little evidence yet one way or the other.

Once we realize that many unpleasant symptoms serve a useful purpose, our approach to illness changes.

Instead of treating every symptom as an enemy that must be eliminated, Darwinian medicine encourages us to explore and study why the symptom might have evolved—so we can be sure that any treatment we devise fights the invader and not the body.

Source: Randolph M. Nesse, MD, professor and associate chair for education and academic affairs in the department of psychiatry at the University of Michigan Medical School, Ann Arbor. He is coauthor of *Why We Get Sick: The New Science of Darwinian Medicine*. Times Books.

Asthma Relief

A daily supplement containing at least 500 mg of vitamin C reduces the frequency of respiratory infections and asthma attacks...and helps control nasal congestion, watery eyes and other allergy symptoms.

Source: Leonard Bielory, MD, director, asthma and allergy research center, University of Medicine and Dentistry of New Jersey–New Jersey Medical School, Newark.

Amazing Flower Remedy Heals...and Heals... And Heals

Dried flowers of *calendula officinalis* are good for burns, cuts, scrapes, acne, tonsillitis and canker sores, vaginitis, rashes, athlete's foot and sunburn.

During the Civil War, these bright orange and yellow flowers provided the major line of defense against infection. Today you can buy dried calendula flowers, ointment, tincture or spray at most health-food stores—or grow your own.

Calendula flourishes in almost any climate, whether it's planted in a pot or in the ground.

Most nurseries sell bedding plants in the springtime. Be sure to ask for *calendula officinalis*—not marigolds.

Flowers harvested between June and September are most potent. Dry them out of direct sun on a mesh screen for one to two weeks. Store in an airtight container.

Hot calendula tea helps soothe ulcers. Gargle with cool tea for inflamed tonsils or canker sores.

To make tea: Pour 10 ounces of boiling water over ⅔ cup of the flowers. Let it steep for 15 minutes. Or add five to 10 drops of calendula tincture to a cup of hot water.

Apply tincture or spray to rashes, cuts, scrapes or acne with a cotton ball. Spraying is good for sunburn, vaginitis and pinworms. Use ointment on scabs, eczema and psoriasis.

To make ointment: Melt ½ cup of petroleum jelly over low heat in a double boiler. Add a handful of dried calendula flowers. Heat on low for an hour. Strain out the herb and pour into a glass jar.

Source: Jamison Starbuck, ND, a naturopathic physician in private practice in Missoula, MT. She is a visiting professor at the National College of Naturopathic Medicine in Portland, OR, and the Southwest College of Naturopathic Medicine in Scottsdale, AZ.

Using Aromatherapy To Stay Super-Healthy

We all know that certain odors can evoke powerful memories. The aroma of freshly baked bread might take us back to grandmother's kitchen…or a perfumed envelope might remind us of a special friend.

Now there's evidence that odors of certain "essential" plant oils foster key health benefits. The systematic use of these oils to promote health is known as *aromatherapy.*

In formal aromatherapy, essential oils are inhaled from a handkerchief…mixed with bath water…or added to skin products or massage oil. Or the oils may simply be spread through room air from a vaporizer or an aromatherapy *diffuser* (typically a ceramic ring around a light bulb).

Aromatherapists treat all sorts of illnesses, using a wide variety of essential oil preparations. While it's not yet clear whether all these preparations do what aromatherapists claim they do, there is now strong scientific evidence that the following oils, at least, are effective…

- **Chamomile** reduces anxiety.
- **Eucalyptus** helps clear stuffed nasal passages caused by cold or flu.
- **Lavender** seems to help people sleep.
- **Mint** promotes alertness.

Aromatherapy is often combined with massage. Massage itself is very relaxing, and most studies that have compared massage with and without aromatherapy have failed to find large differences in anxiety levels between the two. But a few good studies do show some additional anxiety relief with aromatherapy.

One recent study divided 51 cancer patients into two groups. One group received massage with unscented oil. The other received aromatherapy massage with 1% chamomile oil. The massage-plus-aromatherapy group showed dramatic reductions in anxiety and physical symptoms and a significant improvement in overall quality of life. The plain oil massage group experienced only slightly decreased anxiety.

While many people experiment with aromatherapy on their own, others hire a professional aromatherapist. Aromatherapists work with clients to choose an oil or a combination of oils that best suits the clients' personality and health status.

Except when used with a diffuser, essential oils should always be used in diluted form (a few drops in bath water or in eight ounces of massage oil). *Never* rub undiluted essential oil on the skin. With certain exceptions—peppermint oil capsules, for instance, are very helpful for irritable bowel syndrome—essential oils should not be taken internally.

If the application of any essential oil preparation causes redness or any other skin reaction, an asthma attack or other breathing difficulties, discontinue its use immediately. Any breathing problems should be promptly treated by a physician.

Even inhalation or vaporization of essential oils can cause problems in someone who is allergic to the oil being used. Anyone with asthma or another respiratory ailment should exercise great caution when inhaling essential oils.

Source: Adriane Fugh-Berman, MD, a Washington, DC-based medical researcher who specializes in women's health and alternative medicine. She is the author of *Alternative Medicine: What Works.* Odonion Press.

Warming the Heart

Warm baths may be good for patients with congestive heart failure (enlarged heart). But check with your doctor first.

Previously, hot baths were thought to stress the heart. But in a recent study, patients who spent 15 minutes in a 106°F bath or a 140°F sauna experienced increased cardiac output and improved pumping efficiency. *Theory:* Body warmth boosts blood flow to the heart and lungs.

Source: Chuwa Tei, MD, senior research scientist, Mayo Clinic, Rochester, MN.

The Cure-All Oil

Every first-aid kit should contain tea tree oil. It helps prevent bacterial and fungal infections *and* acts as a powerful pain-reliever. I use it on bug bites and stings, cuts, scrapes and scratches, ingrown toenails, acne, mouth ulcers and burns.

The oil also can be used on fungal infections, including athlete's foot and jock itch. I even prescribe it in my practice to prevent outbreaks of genital herpes.

Used by aboriginal people in Australia for thousands of years, tea tree oil has been commercially available in this country since the 1920s. It is expected to be approved by the FDA for use as an antiseptic and antifungal.

Use tea tree oil full-strength, right out of the bottle, once or twice daily until the problem clears up. Apply it sparingly with a cotton ball or your fingertip. Or purchase tea tree oil in an applicator bottle with a dropper tip.

Caution: Never drink tea tree oil or put it in your eyes.

To prevent mouth ulcers or genital herpes flare-ups, apply a few drops of the oil at the first sign of an outbreak. If sores are already present, tea tree oil can be used to alleviate discomfort and speed healing.

A good brand of tea tree oil is *Thursday Plantation.* It's available at most health-food stores, or from the manufacturer at 800-848-8966. *Cost:* About $10 and up for 25 milliliters (about 0.85 ounce). Because you use only a few drops at a time, this isn't costly.

Be sure the bottle specifically states it is oil of *Melaleuca alternifolia,* the botanical name of the tea tree.

Source: Christiane Northrup, MD, an obstetrician–gynecologist practicing in Yarmouth, ME, and assistant clinical professor of obstetrics and gynecology, University of Vermont College of Medicine at Maine Medical Center, Portland. She is the author of *Women's Bodies, Women's Wisdom.* Bantam Books.

Ginkgo Biloba: Memory Booster

Individuals who are fearful of losing their memory should know about *Ginkgo biloba.* This remarkable herb boosts circulation to the brain, strengthening memory and improving concentration.

Ginkgo cannot *restore* memory. Nor does it help memory impairment caused by antihistamines, blood pressure medication or alcohol. However, it may be able to help *preserve* the memory that remains in individuals suffering from Alzheimer's disease and other forms of dementia.

What explains ginkgo's remarkable properties? The answer seems to lie with unique chemical compounds called *ginkgolides* found in the herb. These compounds have been shown in rigorous experiments to boost blood circulation. Increased blood brings additional oxygen and nutrients to brain cells so they function more effectively.

European clinical research performed in the 1980s showed that an extract of ginkgo leaves was effective at increasing mental performance and improving short-term memory.

In Germany, doctors use ginkgo for a wide range of problems associated with poor blood circulation to the brain. That includes dizziness, headaches and ringing in the ears (tinnitus) as well as memory loss.

Ginkgo biloba extract is available at most health-food stores. *Cost:* $30 and up for 100 pills. Be sure to purchase preparations made by a reputable company like Solgar.

Research so far shows that as long as it's taken at the recommended dose, ginkgo causes no side effects—even with long-term use. Check with your doctor.

Source: Robert M. Giller, MD, a medical nutritionist in private practice in New York City. He is the author of *Natural Prescriptions*. Ballantine.

Fatty Acid Fights Strokes

Alpha-linolenic acid helps to lower stroke risk in middle-aged men who are at high risk for cardiovascular disease. The acid is one of the group of omega-3 fatty acids, which seem to reduce the chances of clots forming. This cuts the risk of stroke, since stroke occurs when clots form or become lodged in the arteries that feed blood to the brain.

Good sources of alpha-linolenic acid: Walnuts…soybean and canola oils. *Total recommended fat intake:* 30% of calories or less. Saturated fat should be less than 10%…polyunsaturated, 10%…and monopolyunsaturated, 10% (including walnut, soybean and canola oils).

Source: Joel Simon, MD, assistant professor of medicine and epidemiology, University of California, San Francisco, leader of a study of almost 200 middle-aged men.

Why Take Ginseng?

While I often recommend herbs for the treatment of specific maladies, I believe herbs can also be used to prevent illness. One herb that I find especially useful is ginseng.

I began taking ginseng more than 20 years ago. Back then, my goal was to increase my energy and enhance my overall wellness. In recent years, I've noticed that I never get sick. I don't even get colds. I suspect ginseng deserves at least some of the credit.

Recent studies in Europe and especially in Russia suggest that ginseng increases the body's resistance to stress and boosts immunity. The Chinese, who have been using the herb for more than 5,000 years, believe it increases energy levels.

Many convenience stores, grocery stores, drugstores and health food stores carry ginseng products. Ginseng is available in powdered, capsule or liquid form.

Good source of ginseng products: SDV Vitamins, Box 9215, Del Ray Beach, Florida 33482. 800-738-8482.

Be sure to follow label directions. Taking too much may be overstimulating—particularly when combined with high levels of caffeine.

Price varies according to the type and quality of root, how much ginseng the product contains—and how it was processed.

Ginsana, the leading product, costs $13 and up for 30 capsules. This preparation has been clinically tested more than any other ginseng product on the US market.

Source: Mark Blumenthal, director of the American Botanical Council, a nonprofit organization that publishes the quarterly journal *HerbalGram*, Box 201660, Austin, TX 78720. The Council is currently evaluating 500 ginseng products.

Calcium is Not Expensive

You can get the medically recommended dosages of calcium, multivitamins and vitamins C and E for as little as 12 to 21 cents a day. *Key:* Buy store brands—which are often made by the very same companies that manufacture the more expensive, best-selling supplement brands.

Source: Timothy McCall, MD, an internist practicing in the Boston area. He is the author of *Examining Your Doctor: A Patient's Guide to Avoiding Harmful Medical Care.* Birch Lane Press.

The Health/Success Connection

Health was once defined as the absence of disease. But optimal health requires an integration of physical, mental, spiritual and environmental well-being. It's a process of self-discovery that exerts a positive influence on us as individuals and on those around us.

Optimal health does not deal only with bio-medical science, nor is it naively based solely on the power of positive thinking.

In an effort to develop a model of optimal health, I interviewed 50 prominent people—actors, journalists, politicians and corporate executives. Each adhered to personal health practices and conveyed a personal conviction that he/she was acting out of a deep sense of higher purpose.

Among these individuals were James Burke, former chairman of the board of Johnson & Johnson...philanthropist Gordon Getty...producer Norman Lear...actress Lindsay Wagner ...and Senator Claiborne Pell of Rhode Island.

I wanted to be able to explain how these people achieved a healthy balance of mind, body and environment.

What I found: For these individuals, health is not an endpoint. It's a means to fulfill their personal missions in life.

These people didn't become fixated on overly restrictive diets, the right cholesterol level or the perfect body.

Their health practices were strikingly simple...

- **Restricted intake of red meat.**
- **Moderate alcohol intake.**
- **No smoking.**
- **Moderate exercise.** As Norman Lear told me, "I exercise every morning because I love the feeling, not because I know it's supposed to be good for me."

All the people I spoke to had ailments of one sort or another—including serious diseases such as cancer, heart disease and arthritis. They do not have charmed lives. However, they seem to cope better than most of us. *Here are the six strategies they used:*

1. *Overcome childhood trauma:*

Almost everyone I spoke to had had a major traumatic event before age 10—such as physical abuse, incest, a congenital condition or a life-threatening illness. Norman Cousins, the late author and founder of Saturday Review, was confined to a tuberculosis sanitarium from age 8 to age 10. Most of the other kids thought they would never leave the sanitarium alive. But Cousins refused to accept death as inevitable. He learned a lot about survival during his time in the sanitarium.

Cousins didn't deny the trauma of being institutionalized. But by envisioning a future beyond his immediate circumstances, he learned to detach himself from it. *Result:* He was strengthened, not debilitated, by the experience.

Lesson: Childhood trauma need not lead to a dysfunctional adulthood.

We can all learn to successfully cope with traumatic events from our past. And this is possible even without psychotherapy. *Key:* A perceptual shift from seeing the glass as half-empty to seeing it as half-full.

The crisis needs to be acknowledged and accepted as normal. It requires saying, This is horrible, but I'm going to take a step back and ask what the lesson is. This is a challenge.

2. *Develop a sense of empathy:*

Empathy is the ability to identify with the concerns and problems of another person. No one I interviewed believed that his/her ability to empathize had been inherited. Rather, empathy seemed to derive from their own feelings of being fortunate.

You needn't be wealthy to feel fortunate or appreciate the good things in your life. With few exceptions, all the people I interviewed were born into families of modest means. Six had not graduated from high school.

Lesson: These people didn't become empathic because they were wealthy and successful. They became wealthy and successful because they were empathic.

3. *Gain personal control:*

Control is the conviction that we as individuals can affect the course of our lives. It is a vital link between mind and body.

Control—or the lack of it—triggers powerful reactions in the body, including changes in blood chemistry, heart rate, digestion, immunity and more. *Strategies for developing control:*

- **Define your problem or challenge.** It can be anything from wanting to develop an athletic skill to making a major decision about your career, finances, health or personal relationships.

- **Reconstruct previous stressful situations.** Think about a distressing episode from your past. Jot down three ways it could have gone better and three ways it could have gone worse. Recognize that the event did not go as badly as it might have...that you influenced the outcome to a significant degree...and that your coping skills will improve.

Think about crises you successfully overcame or important decisions you made that had positive outcomes. All too often, our first response to a challenge is anxiety and the fear of failure.

Better way of thinking: The fact that you are facing a formidable challenge today confirms the fact that you were able to overcome similar challenges in the past.

Example: John Sculley left Pepsico to become chairman and CEO of Apple Computer in 1983. Two years later, Sculley found himself dealing with the worst crisis in Apple's history—the departure of founder Stephen Jobs. Sculley's success in handling past crises gave him the confidence he needed to direct Apple through that one.

•**Learn to recognize signals from your body** indicating that something is either right or wrong. This technique—called focusing—helps counteract our normal tendency to ignore stress signals such as rapid breathing, headaches, racing thoughts and rapid heartbeat.

•**Distinguish between what you can and cannot control.** If a crisis is beyond your control, deflect its impact by taking on new challenges. Doing so will reassure you that you remain the master of your own fate.

4. *Reduce psychological stress:*

Stress causes a state of overstimulation, in which heart rate and blood pressure are elevated. You're literally burning up your body to create energy to cope with the stress. Stress can be a risk factor for heart disease.

One of the best antidotes to stress is laughter. The instant you laugh, you shift from a destructive to a regenerative state. Meditation, self-hypnosis, biofeedback, progressive relaxation and visualization techniques are also effective against stress.

One of the world's best-kept secrets: Truly successful people are not overburdened by stress. Nor do they achieve success at the expense of their physical and emotional health.

In fact, many people in demanding situations thrive on stress.

Example: Lindsay Wagner views unpleasant situations as opportunities for growth. She refuses to let herself get stuck or feel victimized.

5. *Use friends as medicine:*

Social support is crucial in keeping us healthy. In one recent study, men with weak social ties had a death rate two to three times higher than those with strong ties. For socially isolated women, the death rate was one-and-a half to two times higher.

I had assumed that the people in my study would be lonely and isolated, in keeping with the cliché of "lonely at the top." They weren't. Although many of the participants are known to millions of people, their support comes from one or two friends or family members.

In developing social support, start with your immediate family. Follow family customs and traditions that have special meaning for everyone.

Nurture the bonds between you and your loved ones even when time and other demands separate you.

Pets and hobbies like gardening are also good for you. Studies show that caring for plants or pets lowers blood pressure. And when you elicit positive emotions in others—compassion, humor, love—your heart beats more slowly...your blood pressure drops...the electrical activity in your brain shifts to a slow harmonic pattern.

6. *Practice altruism:*

Altruism is willingness to help others, even if it means a sacrifice on your part. Pick anything you're concerned about and get involved.

It could be volunteering for a neighborhood project or tackling a social problem like homelessness.

All the participants in my study attributed their success and health in part to giving to others through service.

Source: Kenneth R. Pelletier, MD, PhD, clinical associate professor of medicine, Stanford University School of Medicine, Stanford, CA. He is the author of *Sound Mind, Sound Body.* Simon & Schuster.

Index

A

A.C.E. inhibitors in treating high blood pressure, 20
Acne, 34
Adjustable rate mortgages, mistakes in, 74
Adolescents. See Teenagers
Age spots, 35
Aging process, and caloric restriction, 1–2, 239–240, 245
AIDS, and blood transfusions, 39–40
Air transportation services industry, growth potential of, 130
Air travel
  empty seat strategy in, 47
  frequent-flier miles in, 45–46
  getting hard-to-get tickets, 46
  handling canceled flights, 47
  for people with heart conditions, 48
  reducing fear of flying, 47
  rights in overbooking, 48–49
  split ticketing for, 47
Alimony, tax treatment of, 102
Allergies
  and behavior of children, 241
  as cause of asthma, 3
  side effects from medications for, 9
  as source of tinnitus, 32
Alpha hydroxy acids (AHAs), 36
Aluminum as cause of Alzheimer's disease, 22
Alzheimer's disease, 22–24
  assessing risk of developing, 23
  best treatment for, 23–24
  causes of, 22–23

delaying onset of, 23, 24
Anger, learning to control, 173
Annuities. See also Investments
  grantor retained annuity trusts (GRATs), 103–105
  tax treatment of payments, 102
Antacids, side effect from, 9
Antibiotics
  and antihistamines, 9
  and blood thinners, 9
Antihistamines, and antibiotics, 9
Aphrodisiacs, fragrant essential oils, 230
Arguments, marital, 174
Arnold Securities (discount stockbrokers), 65
Arthritis
  and exercise, 263
  and milk, 256
  nutritional approach to treating, 244–245
  over-the-counter medications for, 7
Artzt, Ed, 129
Aspartame (NutraSweet), dangers of, 35
Assertiveness
  asking for what you want, 168–169
  learning to say no, 160
Assets
  advantages of consolidation, 226
  learning to keep, 221–222
Asthma. See also Allergies
  allergy as possible cause, 3
Athlete's foot, over-the-counter medications for, 7
ATM fees, 67–69
Automobile insurance
  disclosure of underwriting guidelines, 93

reducing cost for, 95
selecting deductible for, 95

B

Baby-sitters, questions to ask, 55
Backache, over-the-counter medications for, 7
Bacteria
  in health clubs, 260
  in kitchen, 31
Baldness
  encouraging genetic research on, 235
  treating with Rogaine (minoxidil), 234
Banking. See also Checking accounts
  and ATM fees, 67–69
  and balancing checkbook, 69
  and checking account fees, 64–65, 69, 85
  and checking account fraud, 83
  reducing fees for, 64–65, 67–68
Barter, 76
Bean, L. L., web site, 143
Bed-and-breakfasts, 45
Beer, and potbellies, 259
Benign prostatic hypertrophy (BPH), 21
Bentyl for irritable bowel syndrome, 27–28
Beta-blockers in treating high blood pressure, 20
Beta-carotene, flawed studies about, 257
Bill payment, timing of, 140
Bingo in Las Vegas, 210
Biofeedback for tinnitus, 32
Blood pressure. See Hypertension
Blood pressure reading, annual need for, 3
Blood sugar levels, effect of diet on, 264–265

Blood thinners
  and antibiotics, 9
  and green leafy vegetables, 8
Blood transfusions, protecting yourself in, 39
Body language, learning to read, 135, 166–168
Bond funds, hidden risk in, 186
Boredom
  counteracting, 175
  main source of, 218
Bras, problems from too-tight straps, 38
Breast cancer
  and breast cysts, 232
  diagnosis of, 26
  and exercise, 263
  and red meat, 256
Breast cysts, 231–232
Breast exams, annual need for, 4
Breathing disorders and elevation, 38
Burnout, learning to avoid, 235–236
Business. See also Finance; Job hunting;
  Managers; Retirement plans
  appealing to nerds, 135
  computers for sales force in, 145–146
  cutting costs in, 136–137
  cutting legal costs in, 138–139
  cutting utility bills in, 137–138
  evaluating credit risk of, 151–152
  growth leaders in, 130
  handling out-of-stock sales, 138
  male versus female boss in, 133
  paying bills in, 140
  and the pregnant worker, 152
  pricing strategies in, 140
  and productivity, 145
  reading body language in, 135
  reducing costs of, 136–137
  rising cost of travel in, 141–142
  secrets of finding jobs in, 148–149
  setting up retirement plans, 140–141
  and the singles market, 134–135
  starting home, 130–131
  strategies for changing careers, 150–151
  telephone charges for, 136
  and violence in workplace, 146–148
Business forms
  limited liability company,
    advantages of, 127–129
  limited partnerships,
    disadvantages of, 127–129
  S corporations, disadvantages of, 127–128
Business services industry, growth potential
  of, 130
Bypass trust, 224

C

Caffeine
  and hypertension, 20
  and thinking ability, 257
Calcium, best sources of, 256
Calcium-channel blockers in treating high
  blood pressure, 20, 26
Cancer
  breast, 26
  cervical, 26
  colorectal, 26
    annual need for testing for, 3–4
    diagnosis of, 26
  and Japanese diet, 265–266
  prostate
    cure rate for, 24

diagnosis of, 26
  and Olestra (Olean), 251
  reliability of test for, 22
  and tomatoes, 255
  reducing risk of, 24–26
  skin, 26
    diagnosis of, 26
    and tanning salons, 35
  testicular, 26
    diagnosis of, 26
Capital gains tax, methods of avoiding, 117
Cardiograms (EKGs), questionable need for, 4
Cardiopulmonary resuscitation (CPR),
  teaching to relatives of heart patients, 41
Career counselor, benefits of using, 149
Careers. See also Job hunting
  strategies for changing, 150–151
Carnegie, Dale, 163–165
Cash
  finding sources of ready, 67–68
  increasing cash flow with tax savings, 105–107
Casinos, rules for gambling in, 208–210
Cereals, whole-grain, 258
Certificates of deposit (CDs)
  laddering, 75
  as source of ready cash, 67
Cervical cancer, tests for, 26
Chagas, danger of, from blood transfusions, 40
Charles Schwab (stockbrokers), 65
Checking accounts. See also Banking
  balancing checkbook, 69
  protecting yourself from fraud, 83
  reducing fees for, 69, 85–86
  selecting spouse to control, 83
Chemical peels, 36
Chest X-rays, questionable need for, 4
Children. See also Infants; Parenting
  allergies and behavior of, 241
  calling pediatrician for sick, 54
  child-care credit for summer camp, 114
  communicating with, 53–54, 56–57
  and educational television, 269
  encouraging expression of opinions, 56
  handling poor report cards of, 269–270
  helping read better, 56
  and imaginary friends, 55
  museums for, 214–215
  need for fiber by, 257–258
  problems with milk, 256
  and puzzles, 274
  questions to ask of baby-sitters, 55
  tax-free income of, 102
  teaching about death, 55
  teaching values to, 55–56
  who hate school, 273–274
Child support, tax treatment of, 102
Chili peppers, stopping burning from, 256
Cholesterol
  economical use of drugs to lower, 17
  and nutrition, 251–252
  testing for level of, 5, 27
    annual need for, 3
    because of tinnitus, 32
Cleveland Clinic, 15
Clinton, Hillary, 135
Cogan, Marshall, 222
Cohabitation, by people under 40, 234
Coital alignment technique (CAT), 229–230
Cold medications
  over-the-counter, 7
  side effects from, 9

College education
  better buys in, 273
  financial aid for, 272
  saving for, 272
Colorectal cancer
  annual need for testing for, 3–4
  diagnosis of, 26
Communication
  asking for what you want in, 168–169
  with babies, 54
  body language in, 135, 166–168
  with children, 53–54
  encouraging expression of opinions by
    children, 56
  learning to say no in, 160
  and need for writing thank-you notes, 176
  with teenagers, 56–57
Communications equipment industry, growth
  potential of, 130
Compensation, tax-saving strategies for,
  123–126
Computer industry, growth potential of, 130
Computers
  and creating your own Web (WWW)
    sites, 142–144
  finding jobs with, 148
  sales reps' need for, 145–146
Conception, and ovulation, 233
Constipation, over-the-counter medications
  for, 7
Continuous positive airway pressure
  (CPAP), 30
Contractors
  doing business with, 60–61
  IRS concerns over independent, 121–122
Cooking. See also Diet; Foods; Nutrition
  basics of low-fat, 255
  creamy dishes without cream, 255
  decline of microwave, 263
  healthier hamburgers, 255
  nonfat pancakes, 255–256
  with wine, 268
Coronary artery disease. See Heart disease
Corporations, disadvantages of S, 127–128
Coughs, covering up, 28
Coumadin (warfarin)
  and antibiotics, 9
  and green leafy vegetables, 8
CPR (Cardiopulmonary resuscitation),
  teaching to relatives of heart patients, 41
Cramps, during exercise, 262
Credit cards
  with deductible interest, 74
  disputing errors on, 75–76
  grace periods on, 69
  and home equity lines of credit, 74
  reducing fees for, 65
Credit unions
  and ATM fees, 68
  and checking accounts, 85
  loans from, 69
Cruises, knowledge needed to plan, 43–44
Cytomegalovirus (CMV), danger of from blood
  transfusions, 40

D

Dandruff, 34–35
Death, telling children about, 55
Debt
  tax deductions for family debt, 112, 114

tips for management of, 78–79
Dell Computer, web site, 142–143
Depression, premenstrual, 231
Diet. See also Cooking; Foods; Nutrition
  antiaging, 1–2, 239–240, 245
  and arthritis, 244–245
  and blood sugar levels, 263–265
  and gassy foods, 256, 258
  and high blood pressure, 18–19, 20
  Japanese, 265–266
  and mood, 241
  need of children for fiber, 257–258
  overeating during holidays, 247
  and reducing cholesterol levels, 251–252
  reducing food intake, 249–250
  resisting foods you love, 250
  and risk of cancer, 25
  and risk of stroke, 243–244
  soybeans and tofu in, 241–243, 265–266
  and stress, 155–156
  and weight loss, 247–249
  whole-grain cereals in, 258
Disability insurance as employee benefit, 125
Disability payments, tax treatment of, 103
Discipline, effective, 51–54
Discount brokers, 65
Disney, Walt, 129
Diuretics in treating high blood pressure, 20, 26
Diverticulitis and exercise, 262
Divorce, tax treatment of property
  settlements, 102
Doctors. See also Health care
  calling your child's, 54–55
  protecting yourself from your, 4–6
  scheduling appointment with, 15

E

Economic cycles, and small stocks, 189
Economic predictions, 177–179
Economics, of health care, 15–16
Education. See also College education
  handling poor report cards of, 269–270
  and hating school, 273–274
  improving reading skills, 56
  television in, 269
Electric bills, reducing for business, 137–138
Electronic components industry, growth
  potential of, 130
Emergency funds, sources of, 79
Emotional intelligence, 160–162
Emotions
  anger as, 173
  handling negative, 172–173
  and wellness, 170–172
Employees, appearance of productivity in, 145
Employment. See Job hunting
Employment interview, preparing for,
  131–132, 149
Endometrial ablation, 231
Energy boosters, five minute, 24
Episiotomy, unnecessary, 230–231
Erythropoietin (EPO), 40–41
Escherichia coli, and vegetarians, 258
Escrow accounts, getting refunds on, 71, 83
Estate planning. See also Investments
  biggest mistakes in, 219–221
  and second marriages, 224–226
Estate taxes. See also Inheritance taxes
  disclaimers in avoiding, 114–115
  strategies to avoid, 219–223

Etiquette mistakes, 175–176
Exercise. See also Weight loss
  and arthritis, 263
  cautions for beginners, 268
  and chronic pain, 10–11
  and improved hearing, 263
  in improving mood, 31, 170
  inexpensive, 268
  and insomnia, 263
  lack of, among teenagers, 263
  and longevity, 260
  passive-motion, 260
  relieving cramps during, 262
  and risk of cancer, 25, 263
  and risk of diverticulitis, 262
  safe, 268
  and stress, 156

F

Facial expression, reading, 166–167
Family debt, tax strategies for writing off, 112
Family history
  medical reasons for, 215
  recording your, 214
  researching, 215–217
Fasting, and health, 245–246
Fastin (phentermine), and weight loss, 267–268
Fear
  controlling, 157–159
  of flying, 47
  of heights, 38
  of humiliation, 168–169
  of rejection, 168–169
Federal Express, web site for, 143
Fellowship grants, tax treatment of, 102
Fenfluramine (Pondimin), and weight loss,
  267–268
Fiber
  children's need for, 257–258
  and flatulence, 258
  in spinach, 258
Fibrocystic breast disease, 231–232
Fidelity (discount stockbrokers), 65
Finance (business)
  evaluating credit risk of customers, 151–152
  reducing business costs, 136–137
  reducing legal costs, 138–139
  reducing utility bills, 137–138
  and timing of bill payments, 140
Finance (personal)
  assets
    advantages of consolidation, 226
    keeping, 221–222
  and ATM fees, 68–69
  and balancing checkbook, 69
  and bank fees, 67–68
  and barter, 76
  and calculation of net worth, 78
  and checking account fraud, 83
  and choosing a financial adviser, 74
  common mistakes in, 76
  and controlling spending, 81–83, 84
  and credit cards, 69, 75–76
  and credit union loans, 69
  and debt management, 78–79
  economic predictions, 177–179
  and eliminating fees, 64–65, 85–86
  and escrow account refunds, 71, 83
  and financial planners, 86
  and flexible spending account for medical

expenses, 91
  and home equity loans, 74
  and home ownership, 69–74, 86–87
  increasing cash flow, 105–107
  increasing cash flow with tax savings,
    105–107
  investing, 181–183
  and laddering CDs, 75
  long distance calling plans in, 80
  mistakes in, 86
  and need for emergency funds, 79, 84–85
  protecting your, 63–64
  and recycling, 80–81
  and return on savings, 67–68
  and reverse mortgages, 72–73, 80
  and safe-deposit box rental, 83
  and sources of ready cash, 67
  tax-saving compensation strategies, 123–126
  tax treatment of foreign-earned income, 103
  and tax withholding, 76
  and tips for checking accounts, 85–86
  and tips for saving, 67, 77–78, 80
  and water conservation, 76
  women's need for knowledge of, 65–67
Financial aid for college, 272
Financial fees. See also Banking
  methods of eliminating, 64–65
Financial planners and advisers
  accountant as, 121
  choosing, 74
  fee-based versus fee-only, 86
Finasteride (Proscar), 21, 22
First aid
  for bee stings, 24
  improvising ice packs in, 39
  teaching CPR to relatives of heart patients, 41
Fish
  chemical contaminants in, 258–259
  health risks of raw or under-cooked, 258
Flatulence
  and cooked vegetables, 256
  and starchy foods, 258
Flea markets, rules of, 207–208
Flu shots, annual need for, 4
Food poisoning versus flu, 37
Foods. See also Cooking; Diet; Nutrition
  fiber content of, 258
  gas-creating, 258
  negative reactions with medications, 8–10
  pesticide residue on fruits and vegetables, 252
Food safety
  healthier ways to cook hamburgers, 255
  for vegetarians, 258
Foot problems, obesity as risk for, 247
Ford, Henry, 129
Fort Worth Zoological Park, 215
401(k) plans
  borrowing from, 106, 204
  examining investment options of, 204
  hidden traps in, 197
  reviewing investments in, 203
  for small businesses, 150
  smarter investing of, 203–204
Frequent-flier miles, strategies for, 45–46
Friends, making, 163–166
Fruits, pesticide residue on, 252

G

Gambling
  in casinos, 208–210

lottery, 212–213
poker, 213–214
Game shows, becoming contestant on, 210–212
Garbage, recycling, 80–81
Gassy foods, less gas from, 256
Gates, Bill, 135
Genealogy, tracing your family history, 215–217
Gift tax, strategies to avoid, 220–221
Glycolic acid peels, 36
Grantor retained annuity trust (GRATs), 103–105

H

Hair loss
  genetic research on, 235
  treating with Rogaine (minoxidil), 234
Halloween, carving jack-o-lanterns for, 218
Hamburgers, healthier ways to cook, 255
Hantavirus, avoiding, 28
Health care. See also Doctors; HMOs; Hospitals; specific conditions
  alternatives to hysterectomies, 231
  avoiding overpayment for, 15–16
  caloric restriction in, 1–2
  and chronic pain, 10–11
  for common winter ailments, 28
  covering up coughs in, 28
  economics of, 15–16
  and emotions, 170–172
  and food poisoning, 37
  HMO coverage of alternative forms of, 91
  for irritable bowel syndrome, 27–28
  laboratory mistakes in, 15
  mastering stress, 155–156
  problems with pop-up thermometers, 37
  scheduling doctor's appointments, 15
  sleep
    getting better night's, 31
    impact of snoring, 29–30
    strategies for lifelong, 239–240
  tax treatment of expenses, 103
  for tinnitus, 31
  unnecessary episiotomies in, 230–231
  by unqualified workers, 16–17
  women's issues in, 230–233
Health care workers, unqualified, 16–17
Health checkup, optimal use of annual, 2–4
Health clubs, germs in, 260
Health insurance
  determining amount needed, 90–91, 95
  as employee benefit, 125–126
  HMO as an alternative to, 89–94, 97
  and Medicare, 91, 95
  Point of Service (POS) plans in, 90
  state-approved policies, 94
  and taking advantage of discounts, 94
  and travel, 95
  and using spouse's plan, 94
Hearing
  improvement after exercise, 263
  and tinnitus, 31–32
  jet engine noise and impact on, 37
Heartburn, over-the-counter medications for, 7
Heart disease
  and shoveling snow, 38
  traveling with, 48
  in women, 17
Heights, fear of, 38
Hemorrhoids, over-the-counter medications for, 7

Hepatitis G, danger of from blood transfusions, 40
Heredity, and Alzheimer's disease, 22
High blood pressure. See Hypertension
History
  recording oral, 214
  researching family, 215–217
HIV, and blood transfusions, 39–40
HMOs (Health Maintenance Organizations), 89–91
  benefits of, 89
  challenging decisions of, 92–93, 97
  cost of, 89, 90
  coverage of alternate treatment by, 91–92
  coverage provided by, 89–90
  and Medicare patients, 91, 92
  worrisome trends in, 92–93
Holidays, overeating during, 247
Home businesses, starting, 130–131
Home equity loans and lines of credit, 72
  benefits of, 67
  and credit cards, 74
Home ownership. See also Houses
  and accelerating mortgage payments, 70, 74
  and capital gains on sale of home, 102, 109
  eliminating escrow/impound accounts, 71
  eliminating private mortgage insurance, 70–71
  and equity loans, 67, 72
  and escrow fund refunds, 83
  and homeowners' insurance, 64, 70
  and mistakes in adjustable rate mortgages, 74
  negotiating real estate fees, 73
  programs for first-time buyers, 74
  questions to ask before buying, 86–87
  reducing property taxes, 70
  and refinancing, 71–72
  and reverse mortgages, 72–73, 80
  shopping for mortgage, 73
Homeowner's insurance. See also Renter's insurance
Homeowners' insurance
  coverage of college housing under, 94
  gaps in coverage in, 64
  reducing cost of, 70
Hospitals
  finding best, 13–15
  getting best nursing care at, 12–13
  minimizing risks at, 11–12
Hotels
  getting best rates in, 47
  getting best rooms in, 48
  staying in a bed-and-breakfast, 45
House renovation and remodeling
  financial considerations, 61–62
  methods of, 58–59
Houses. See also Home ownership
  dealing with contractors, 60–61
  fixing up, 58–59
  inspections of, 59–60
  painting, 58, 60
  payback for renovation of, 61–62
Human T-lymphotropic virus (HTLV-1 and HTLV-2), danger of from blood transfusions, 40
Humor in making requests of others, 169
Hunger, distinguishing from thirst, 246
Hypertension, 17–20
  and alcohol, 18
  and caffeine, 20
  and calcium channel blockers, 20, 26
  and diet, 18–19, 20
  and exercise, 18

  medications for, 8, 20, 26
Hypothyroidism, 247
Hysterectomies, alternatives to, 231
Hytrin (terazosin), 21

I

Ice packs, improvised, 39
Imaginary friends, 55
Impotence
  need for prompt treatment of, 234
  women's role in, 234
Impound accounts, 71, 83
Income taxes. See also IRS (Internal Revenue Service)
  avoiding for capital gains, 117
  child-care credit for summer camp, 114
  common mistakes made on returns, 99–101
  converting taxable income into tax-free income for retirement, 110–111
  deductible and nondeductible expenses in, 103
  deducting cost of music lessons, 114
  deducting job-hunting expenses, 111–112, 119
  easily overlooked deductions, 119–120
  establishing legal residency, 126
  filing return through U.S. Postal Service, 115
  helping your tax-preparer find loopholes in, 120–121
  importance of reporting all income, 118–119
  on installment sale payments, 119
  and interest deductions, 103, 106
  loopholes in, 101–103, 108–110
    in pension plan distributions and IRAs, 108, 110
  minimizing odds of audit, 115–116
  quiz on savings, 126
  retirement loopholes, 108–110
  round numbers on return as indication of estimates on, 117
  on stock gains, 117
  strategies for saving on
    grantor retained annuity trusts (GRATs), 103–105
    increasing tax flow with, 105–107
    last minute, 101
  taxpayer victories over IRS, 122–123
  tax-saving strategies in, 101, 103–105, 123–126
  tax treatment of refunds, 102–103
  writing off family debt, 112, 114
Independent contractors, IRS concerns over, 121–122
Indigestion, over-the-counter medications for, 7
Infants. See also Children
  calling pediatrician, 54
  low birth weight, 233
  milk and colic in, 256
  refusal of, to eat, 55
  resemblance to fathers, 54
  talking to, 54
Infertility
  and milk, 256
  sperm aspiration for, 233
  unexplained, 233
  and women, 232–233
Inheritance taxes. See also Estate taxes
  on life insurance proceeds, 101
  strategies to avoid, 219–223
  use of disclaimer to avoid, 114–115

Insomnia. See also Sleep
and exercise, 263
over-the-counter medications for, 7
Installment sale payments, taxes on, 119
Insurance. See Automobile insurance; Health
insurance; Homeowners insurance; Life
insurance; Renter's insurance; Umbrella
insurance
Intelligence
emotional, 160–162
enhancement of mental abilities by
caffeine, 257
Interest payments, tax treatment of, 103
Interoperative autologous transfusion (IAT), 40
Investments. See also Annuities; Estate planning; 401(k) plans; IRAs; Money market
funds; Mutual funds
bear-proofing your portfolio, 185–186
for college education, 272
frugal mix in, 182–183
growth potential of industries, 130
long-term, 150
newsletters on, 185
for retirees, 203
saving on fees, 65
timing in selling stocks, 186
winning mix, 181–182
Ionamin (Phentermine), and weight loss,
267–268
IRAs (individual retirement accounts). See also
401(k) plans
avoiding early withdrawal penalty, 120
having too much money in, 202
making the most of your, 200–202
putting in trust for surviving spouse, 226
tax loopholes in, 107–108
Irrevocable life insurance trust, 220
Irritable bowl syndrome (IBS), 27–28
IRS (Internal Revenue Service). See also
Income taxes
adoption of Taxpayer Bill of Rights by, 122
aggressiveness of, 115
audit
red flag for, 120
reducing chances of, 115–116
and bonus to new owner, 142
concerns about independent contractors
121–122
definition of responsible person, 118
methods of locating assets of deceased
persons, 113
mistake made by, 114
need for tax professional as representative
before, 115
requesting removal of penalty for late
filing, 118
seizure tactics of, 117
strategies in communicating with, 117–118
taxpayer victories over, 122–123
traps in dealing with, 113

J

Jack-o-lanterns, carving, 218
Japanese diet
and cancer rates, 265
and longevity, 265–266
Jet engine noise, impact on hearing, 37
Job hunting
deducting expenses for, 111–112
expenses in, as tax deductions, 111–112
information interview, 150
over 50, 148–149
preparing for interviews in, 131–132, 149
refusing offer in, 132–133
secretarial and receptionist jobs in, 152
Johns Hopkins University, 15

K

Kegel exercises, and incontinence, 231
Keogh plans, borrowing from, 106

L

Lanoxin, side effects from, 9
Legal costs, reducing company's, 138–139
Licorice, side effects from, 9
Lies, handling, 173
Life, taking control of, 160
Life insurance
deciding on a policy, 96–97
estate taxes on, 101
second-to-die, 225
tax treatment of dividends, 102, 110
Limited liability company, advantages of, 127–129
Limited partnerships, disadvantages of,
127–129
Living trusts, frequently asked questions,
223–224
Loans
from credit unions, 69
income taxes on, 101–102
Lomotil, for irritable bowel syndrome, 27–28
Longevity, and physical fitness, 260
Lottery, strategies for winning, 212–213
Love letter to spouse, including with will, 223
Low-fat cooking, 255

M

Mammograms, annual need for, 4
Managers. See also Supervisors
becoming effective, 133–134
building on failures of, 129
prioritizing responsibilities by, 133
Marcus, Bernard, 129
Marital arguments, resolving, 173–174
Mayo Clinic, 14–15
Medical expenses, tax treatment of, 103
Medical instruments and supplies industry,
growth potential of, 130
Medical laboratories, mistakes made by, 15
Medical services industry, growth
potential of, 130
Medicare coverage, supplementing with
HMO, 91, 92
Medications
cholesterol-lowering, 17
eliminating, 3
and food, 8–9
for hypertension, 20
minimizing mishaps in hospitals, 12
negative reactions from combined use of, 8–10
over-the-counter, 6–8
possible drug interactions with, 4–5
for prostate disease, 21, 22
and risks of driving, 41
throwing away expired, 6
Meditation, and stress reduction, 170
Men
average size of penis, 234
impotence in, 234
melanoma in, 22
prostate cancer in
cure rate for, 24
diagnosis of, 26
and Olestra (Olean), 251
reliability of test for, 22
and tomatoes, 255
prostate disease in, 22
sexual fantasies in, 235
sexual response and fragrance in, 230
shrinking prostate in, 21
Mental abilities, enhancement of by caffeine, 257
Milk. See also Nutrition
and anemia, 256
and breast cancer, 256
and chili peppers, 256
vitamins from cereal in, 256
Minoxidil (Rogaine), 234
Money management. See also Finance
(business); Finance (personal)
Money market funds
as alternative to checking account, 85
hidden risk in, 186
Mood
effect of exercise on, 170
effect of foods on, 241
improving, 31
premenstrual depression, 231
Mortgages
accelerating payments on, 74
adjustable rate, 74
for first-time home buyers, 74
getting preapproval for, 73
mistakes in, 74
reverse, 72–73, 80
Municipal bonds, tax treatment of interest, 102
Museums, children's, 214–215
Music lessons, tax deduction for, 114
Mutual funds. See also Investments
diversification in portfolio, 186
investing in, 181–182, 183–184
as investment for education, 272
investment mistakes, 190–191
Peter Lynch's rules for investors, 191–192
reading prospectus, 192
reducing fees for, 65
selecting a portfolio, 191
Sheldon Jacobs answers big questions
about, 192–193
why not to purchase from banks, 193

N

Nasal congestion, over-the-counter
medications for, 7
National Tour Association, 48
Natural defenses of body, 2
Nausea, over-the-counter medications for, 7
Neighbors, dealing with annoying, 62
Nerds, appealing to, 135
Net worth, calculating, 78
Nightmares, 55
Nizoral (ketoconazole), 35
No, learning to say, 160
Nursing care, getting best while hospitalized,
12–13
Nutrition. See also Cooking; Diet; Foods; Milk
fiber in, 257–258
vitamin C in, 257
vitamin D in, 256–257

O

Obesity. See also Weight loss
  and underactive thyroid, 247
Office machine industry, growth potential
  of, 130
Olean (Olestra), 251
Olestra (Olean), 251
Onassis, Aristotle, 222
Onassis, Jacqueline Kennedy, 222
Oral history, recording, 214
Osteoporosis, and risk of stroke, 41
Outlook on life, changing, 162–163
Ovarian cancer, and milk, 256
Overeating, during holidays, 247
Ovulation, tracking, 233

P

Pain, chronic
  and exercise, 10–11
  origins of, 10
  reducing, 10–11
Pain relievers, side effect from, 9
Painting, avoiding color inconsistency, 58
Pap smears, annual need for, 4, 231
Parenting. See also Children
  authoritative versus authoritarian, 52–54
  communicating with children, 53–54, 56–57
  and discipline, 51–54
  fighting between siblings, 53
  helping teenagers solve problems, 56–57
  limiting television, 53
  spanking, 53
  teaching your child values, 55–56
Paris, best buys in, 49
Payroll taxes
  on income tax return, 116
  payment of, 118
Pediatricians, information to have when
  calling, 54
Penis, average size of, 234
Pensions. See also 401(k) plans; Investments;
  IRAs; Keogh plans; Retirement
    lump sum payout versus monthly annuity,
      199–200
    rolling over lump sum payout, 204
    state taxes on, 111
    tax loopholes in, 107–108
    tax treatment of rollovers, 102
Perot, Ross, 135
Personal ads, improving, 235
Personal cash flow, increasing with tax
  savings, 105–107
Pesticide residue on fruits and vegetables, 252
Phentermine (Ionamin, Fastin), and weight
  loss, 267–268
Physical fitness. See also Exercise
  and longevity, 260
PMS (premenstrual syndrome), over-the-
  counter medications for, 8
Pneumonia, vaccine for, 28
Poison ivy, over-the-counter medications for, 7–8
Poker, bluffing in, 213–214
Pondimin (fenfluramine), and weight loss,
  267–268
Potbellies, shrinking, 259–260
Preferred Provider Organizations (PPOs), 89–91
Pregnancy
  and need for episiotomies, 230–231
  potential liability from injury to employee, 152
  weight gain during, 233

Premenstrual depression, controlling, 231
Privacy, protecting financial, 113
Private mortgage insurance (PMI), 70–71
Productivity, versus daydreaming, 145
Property taxes, reducing, 70
Proscar (finasteride), 21, 22
Prostate, shrinking enlarged, 21
Prostate cancer
  cure rate for, 24
  diagnosis of, 26
  and Olestra (Olean), 251
  reliability of test for, 22
  and tomatoes, 255
Prostate-Specific Antigen (PSA) testing
  annual need for, 4
  reliability of, 22
Protective options for stocks, 189–190
Pumpkin carving, 218
Puppies, choosing, 57
Puzzles, extending useful life of, 274

R

Ragu Spaghetti Sauce, web site for, 142
Rainy-day money, need for, 84–85
Reading, helping children, 56
Real estate commissions, negotiating, 73
Receptionist positions, potential for
  advancement in, 152
Recycling, 80–81
Refinancing your home, 71–72
Refrigeration, heating and service industry
  equipment industry, growth potential of, 130
Renova (tretinoin), 36
Renter's insurance
  for college student living off campus, 94
  need for, 97
Report cards, handling children's poor,
  269–270
Restaurants
  getting better service in, 217–218
  tipping in, 217
Retin-A (tretinoin), 34, 36
Retirement. See also Pensions
  best places for, 204–206
  common relocation mistakes, 206
  converting taxable income into tax-free
    income for, 110–111
  investments for, 200, 203
  planning for comfortable, 203
  and state tax traps, 111
  tax-planning loopholes for, 108–110
  Ted Benna's secrets for a secure, 198–199
Retirement plans
  for executives, 140–141
  for small businesses, 150
Return-of-capital dividends, tax treatment of, 102
Reverse mortgages, 72–73
  disadvantages of, 73, 80
  types of, 73
Rodents, dangers from, 28
Rogaine (minoxidil), 234
Rosacea, 38

S

Safe-deposit boxes
  deducting rental from income tax, 119
  joint versus individual rental, 83
Sales
  and creating value, 140
  finding jobs in, 148

reps' need for computers, 145–146
  and selling out-of-stock items, 138
  and selling to singles, 134–135
Salt substitutes, side effects of, 8–9
SAT (Scholastic Assessment Test), 270–271
Saving
  common mistakes in, 78
  by conserving water, 76
  getting higher return on, 68
  by recycling, 80–81
  tips for, 67, 77–78, 80
Savings and loans, checking accounts at, 85
Savings bonds for education, tax treatment
  of, 102
Scholarships, tax treatment of, 102
S corporations, disadvantages of, 127–128
Secondhand smoke, danger to pets, 41
Secretarial positions, potential for
  advancement of, 152
Sex
  answers to common questions about, 227–228
  coital alignment technique (CAT), 229–230
  criticizing in a positive way, 230
  effect of fragrance on response, 230
  having great, 228–230
Sexual fantasies, gender differences in, 235
Sexually transmitted diseases, and risk of
  cancer, 25
Shaving, 37
Sibling rivalry, 53
Singles, selling to, 134–135
Skin
  and aging, 35–37
  care of, 33–35, 37
  chemical peels and dermabrasion, 36
  preventing wrinkles, 33–34, 37
  shaving, 37
Skin cancer
  diagnosis of, 26
  and tanning salons, 35
Sleep. See also Insomnia
  and exercise, 263
  getting a better night's, 31
  impact of snoring, 29–30
  nightmares, 55
Sleep apnea, 29
Snoring, 29–30
  reasons for, 29
  remedies for, 29–30
Snow, shoveling as stress on heart, 38
Social Security
  tax treatment of payments, 102
  verifying earnings record, 203
Sore throat pain, over-the-counter medications
  for, 8
Source of additional money (SAM), 144–145
Soybeans
  in creamy chocolate pie, 243
  in healthy diet, 241–243
  in Japanese diet, 265–266
Sparkling water, and clear sugary soft
  drinks, 257
Spastic colon, 27–28
Special industry machinery industry, growth
  potential of, 130
Spending. See also Finance (personal)
  learning to control, 81–83, 84
Sperm, aspiration of from testes, 233
Standardized tests, doing well on, 270–271
State taxes, and retirement, 111
Stockbrokers' cash management accounts, 85

Stock market
    alternatives to, 188–189
    bear-proofing your portfolio, 185–186
    Don Phillips' shrewd advise on, 194
    investing in, 179–181, 183–184, 186
    no-load bargains, 193–194
    potential of technology stocks, 187–188
    protective options, 189–190
    small stocks and economic cycles, 189
    stop-loss orders, 189–190
    taxes on gains, 117
Stop-loss orders for stocks, 189–190
Stress
    accepting, 170
    balancing of, by women, 39
    and diet, 155–156
    and exercise, 156
    and low-birth weight babies, 233
    mastering, 155–156
    questionable need for tests of, 4
    reducing with meditation, 170
    and risk of cancer, 25–26
Strokes
    occurrence of, 21
    and osteoporosis, 41
    reducing risk of, 243–244
Success after failure, 129
Sunburn, over-the-counter medications for, 8
Supervisors. See also Managers
    actions of effective, 133–134
    male versus female, 133
Supplemental executive retirement plans
    (SERPs), 124

T

Tacrine (Cognex) in treating Alzheimer's
    disease, 23–24
Tanning salons, dangers of, 35
Tax audits
    minimizing chances of, 115–116
    risk of, 116–117
Taxes. See Gift tax; Income taxes; Inheritance
    taxes; Property taxes; State taxes
Taxpayer Bill of Rights, 122
Technology stocks, potential of, 187–188
Teenagers
    doing well on standardized tests, 270–271
    increased maturity of, 57
    and lack of exercise, 263
Teeth
    brushing, 33
    preventing loss of, 33
Telemarketers, right to refuse future calls
    from, 142
Telephone, long distance charges for, 80, 136
Television, educational, 269
Tension. See also Stress
    triggers in, 38
Terazosin (Hytrin), 21, 22
Testicular cancer
    annual need for exam in, 4
    diagnosis of, 26
Thank-you notes, need for writing, 176
Thermometers, pop-up in poultry, 37
Thirst, distinguishing from hunger, 246

Thyroid, and obesity, 247
Thyroid function test, need for, 32
Tipping, in restaurants, 217
Tofu
    in creamy chocolate pie, 243
    in healthy diet, 241–243
    in Japanese diet, 265–266
Tomatoes, and prostate cancer, 255
Tour booking, 48
Transurethral resection of the prostate
    (TURP), 21
Travel. See also Air travel; Hotels
    by air, 45–47
    as air courier, 46
    best buys in Paris, 49
    booking tours, 48
    knowledge needed to plan cruises, 43–44
    planning a cruise, 43–44
    reading fine print in ads, 45
    relaxing during vacations, 218
    rising cost of business, 141–142
    services offered by U.S. embassy, 44–45
    staying in a bed-and-breakfast, 45
Travel advertisements, reading fine print in, 45
Travel and entertainment expenses, tax
    treatment of, 103
Tretinoin (Retin-A or Renova), 34, 36
Trusts
    bypass, 224
    charitable remainder, 117
    generation-skipping, 222
    grantor retained annuity (GRATs), 103–105
    living, 223–224
    qualified terminable interest (Q-TIP), 225
    residence, 112–113
    secular, 124

U

Umbrella insurance, 219
    adding to basic homeowners' policy, 64
    buying policy for, 95–96
United States embassies, services offered by,
    44–45
University of Pennsylvania Hospital, 15
U.S. savings bonds. See Savings bonds
US Tour Operators Association, 48
Uvulopalatopharyngoplasty (UPP), 30

V

Vacations. See also Travel
    relaxing during, 218
Vaccines
    annual need for flu shots, 4
    evaluating needs in, 4
    for pneumonia, 28
    for whooping cough, 29
Value(s)
    creating, 140
    teaching your child, 55–56
Vegetables
    flatulence and cooking of, 256
    pesticide residue on, 252
Vegetarians, and E. coli, 258

Verbal abuse, defending yourself against,
    159–160
Videos
    best time to rent, 218
    hard-to-find, 218
Violence in workplace, 146–148
Virtual reality, problems from, 41
Virtual Vineyards, web site for, 143
Vision testing, annual need for, 4
Vitamin C, effect of chewing on teeth, 257
Vitamin D, importance of, 256–257

W

Walking, benefits of, 260–262
Wall Street discount (stockbrokers), 65
Walton, Sam, 129, 222
Warts, 35
Water
    conservation of, in bathroom, 76
    sparkling, and clear sugary soft drinks, 257
Web (WWW) sites, creating your own,
    142–144
Weekend entrepreneuring, 144–145
Weight loss. See also Exercise
    dieter's diary in, 254
    without feeling deprived, 249–250
    prescription medications to aid, 267–268
    secrets of successful, 252–254
    strategies to help, 247–249, 254
    watching what you eat, 254–255
Welch, Jack, 129
Whooping cough, 29
Wills
    including last love letter with, 223
    need for, 66–67
    witnesses for, 226
Women
    alternatives to hysterectomies for, 231
    balancing of stress by, 39
    and danger of stroke, 41
    and episiotomies, 230–231
    foot problems and weight, 247
    heart disease in, 17
    incontinence in, 231
    and infertility, 232–233, 256
    need for financial knowledge, 65–67
    orgasms of, 228–230
    ovulation and conception, 233
    premenstrual depression, 231
    role in impotence, 234
    sexual fantasies, 235
    as supervisors, 133
    weight and life expectancy, 243
Workplace, violence in, 146–148
Wrinkles, avoiding, 33–34

Y

Yard sale, holding, 57–58

Z

Zinc
    and benign prostatic hypertrophy, 21
    as cause of Alzheimer's disease, 22
Zoos in Fort Worth, Texas, 215